January
1986

To my mom with
all my love,
You have been my
inspiration. It's been through
your love and support to make
this possible.
I love you,
Ruthie

The American Poetry Anthology

VOLUME IV, NUMBER 3
FALL 1985

Edited, with introduction, index
and biographical sketches

By

JOHN FROST

And the staff of the American Poetry Association

THE AMERICAN POETRY ASSOCIATION
Santa Cruz, California

INTRODUCTION

In setting out to edit this anthology, my thought was to put myself in the place of the reader and to remember my own emotions when I open any new book of poetry, hoping to find living ideas, understandable words, vivid imagery, human feelings expressed in verse. I learned much from poetry collections, and still remember the best of them with gratitude.

Poetry collections are a distinct type of literature. The editor's creative role seems at first glance limited, for he is obliged to collect poems not of his own making. That is not quite the case, however.

A large book of this nature is more than a mere collection of poems. The conglomerate represents a particular stage in the development of poetry. At the same time, it is large enough to reveal the breadth of creative effort in terms of treatment, poetic style and selection of themes. The poems do have an interconnection; they are imbued with the common ideas crystallizing and blossoming at a particular moment in history. They reveal the influences of contemporary science, art, politics, and written expression; they are animated and suffused by a common culture, whether each poet realizes it or not. One can think of the book as a literary moment frozen in time, a poetic time capsule. In this sense, this (or any) poetry collection is much more than the sum of its parts.

While working on the book I proceeded on the assumption that each poem was valuable, that it was a work of art produced by creative endeavor. The editors paid somewhat less concern to stylistic polish, more to frank thought and feeling, well-expressed. The editors decided not to burden each poem with comments, although many of the readers provided illuminating explanations. Each poem must stand on its own. I felt that explanations would detract from the reader's own distillation of the work, his osmotic perception of the poets' intuition, feeling, imagination, talent and wordsmithing.

Poetry is, of course, always at the leading edge of the evolution of our tongue; and we have generally acknowledged considerable poetic license in grammar, colloquialisms, capitalization, even spelling and the coinage of new words or combinations of old ones. In this volume, our editors have allowed flexibility in language and form, encouraging imagination and originality.

I submit this work to the judgment of the reader, and I shall consider its aims fulfilled if the content of the book as a whole broadens the reader's horizons, increases his skills as a poet, gives him an idea of modern poetic creativity, and helps him achieve a fuller appreciation and a greater love of the inexhaustible treasures of the English language.

John Frost

John Frost
Chief Editor
Santa Cruz, California
September 30, 1985

A Note on the Illustrations

In this edition of **American Poetry Anthology** we are featuring famous illustrations by noted American illustrators, including Harry Fenn, R. Swain Gifford, Homer Martin and Granville Perkins. The engravings, created during the nineteenth century, depict many regions of the country, and capture not only the grandeur of the American landscape, but also the spirit of America as a nation and culture.

We hope these illustrations will enhance the reader's enjoyment of this volume of poetry.

REFLECTIONS

Nocturnal shadows
    o'ercast a moonlit path
between lake and home.

Fog-shrouded waveless
    pond enraptures my soul with
timeless tranquility.

The haunting, stunning
    cry of a loon at dusk
resounds with sublimity.

Charles B. Rodning

RODNING, CHARLES BERNARD. Born: Pipestone, Minnesota, U.S.A. 8-4-43; Married: 6-15-68 to Mary Elizabeth Rodning; Education: Gustavus Adolphus College, B.S., magna cum laude, Biology, Chemistry, 1965; University of Rochester School of Medicine and Dentistry, M.D., 1970; University of Minnesota Health Sciences Center, Ph.D., Anatomy, 1979; Occupation: Associate Professor, Departments of Surgery and Anatomy, College of Medicine, University of South Alabama; Memberships: Fellow, International College of Surgeons; Fellow, American College of Surgeons; Member, Alabama State Poetry Society; Awards: Bacaner Research Award, 1979; Physician's Recognition Awards, American Medical Association, 1980, 1985; IOTA Delta Gamma Honor Scholastic Society; Phi Kappa Phi Honor Scholastic Society; Alpha Omega Alpha Honor Medical Society; Writings: *Furor Poeticus, Dramatis Fragare,* Comments: *The author's interest in the* Haiku *style of oriental poetry was rekindled while residing in Okinawa, Japan.*

Somewhere
in my fantasy
I am
a pretty girl
of face
and light.
A child
of some artist's
creation.
So near reality
I can
almost reach her.
But each time
she slips
into the shadows.
Waiting
for the time
we two
become
one.

Tamara J. Rogers

DAWN, AND NATURE AWAKES

O, this morning bright and clear,
When the night that has gone
Was so dark and drear.

The sun peeps o'er the mountains' crest
And shines upon
The world afresh.

The animals arise from sleep,
The blossoms unfold on flow'rs.
Nature awakes down deep,
A process which takes hours.

I was up with the shadows
At the crack of dawn,
Exploring the meadows
And watching the fawns,
For I am a lover of nature
And study God's every creature.

Nature is so wonderfully made,
That I'm afraid for the human race.
They've ruined God's perfect creation;
One day God'll make man humiliation.

Kristina Kilian

EASTER'S ETERNAL HOPE

If there had been no resurrection,
Where would that bright hope have been
That ever springs eternal
In the weary hearts of men?

If the grave had been victorious;
If in death there was a sting
Would tomorrow's promises
Be of better things to bring?

WOULD we all have the same incentive
To renew our faith each day;
To greet with smiles of gladness
Those we meet along the way?

WOULD chilly winter's profound silence,
Held suspended for so long,
Be broken some spring morning
By a red-bird's happy song?

BUT there's no need for speculation
For we know that hope was born
When Christ arose from the grave
That triumphant Easter morn.

Harry Withers

UNCERTAINTY

In the quiet of the day,
I hear music.

It is of a color of peacefulness;
Yet of a strain of tense impatience.
I sit quietly, and dwell
In the serenity of the harmony.

Where am I?
What has happened?

I feel, I have given into the quiet,
And have been swallowed up in the space.

All is "Not Well!"
There are intruders . . .
Trying to break down my walls,
Of already shattering glass!

Oh, be still my heart,
For your "beat" is not of the music.
Calm and loose yourself in the quiet,
And be at Peace!

For today is here;
And tomorrow, is yet to come?

Kathleen A. Boelter

LIFE

When Life is —
it's everywhere
and somewhere
and nowhere.

When Life is not —
it's nowhere
when everywhere
and somewhere.

Something.
Nothing.

Esti Cooper

MISTLETOE

It's with me like my — shadow
haunting,
not always thought about,
but there.

Someone sees and asks,
"What's there?"
I step between the question
and the — shadow.

"It's nothing," I reply, "but a
whimsy
of your imagination."
(How *quaint* you ask!)

But the truth
       falling

between
the asker and the — shadow
casts tender feelings

that have no place
to be
but hanging about like
mistletoe   after   Christmas.

Marilyn Gilbert Komechak

LANDS OF SUNSETS

From the darkening highway, I looked to the west.
And saw a sky inviting me to be her guest.
To her show of colors I've never before seen.
Above far away hills, she lined with trees so green.

A sunset so full of the promise of peace.
That it made life's problems and fears finally cease.
And changed clouds to appear as a new distant land.
That I could touch with my eye, but never my hand.

To the fantasy land journey, but never reach.
For it's like seeing the horizon from the beach;
You can see where the ocean is meeting the sky.
To my eyes it's true, but to my touch it's a lie.

But in its truth I feel, when this world gets me down.
I know that I'll find hope in this new land I found.
So my eyes will travel at the end of the day.
To touch distant lands of sunsets, far far away.

Michael P. Kohlbrenner

OUR LOVE

There are times when you have so much on your mind,
and the steady pace of life has quickened you on.
Those are the days when you have so much left to do;
there doesn't seem to be room for my presence.

And yet, I don't doubt your love for me.
I see it tucked away in your smile
or hiding in a quick glance that you send my way.
And I think of a time when you held me safely in your arms,
and I think of the next time I'll hold you again.

Our love is a lonely kind of love
because there's no other love like it in the world.
The closeness that we share has its good points,
and we both know it has its bad points;
but they always seem to fade away when we see each other again.

I know I'll never love quite like I've been loving you.
And that adds a kind of special ingredient to our relationship.
And so, as the years pass by,
when I seem quickened on by the steady pace of life,
believe in your heart that our love is real . . .
And watch for the signs I'll be showing you.

Karin L. Costa

THE FOREBODING WAVE

A smile received and given starts the amorous tidal wave,
An ominous murmur rises slowly from the depth,
Hands touch, and a slight curl lifts lightly in the
distance,
The brushing of lips heightens the sensations of the
torrent,
A yearning embrace, and the tips turn white commencing the
dull, threatening roar,
Bodies caress, and a violent surge erupts, building higher
and higher.

Oh vile beast that stalks innocent prey!
Cunningly luring them with sinful bait,
Encircling them, savoring its victory,
The white claws exhibited, then the quick kill,
The ignorant pitiful creatures only hear,
The loud roar like cynical laughter,
Relentlessly crushing them with a fatal blow.

The lethal wave, sated, transforms,
Becoming the innocuous ebb and flow,
As two more naive victims swim toward the treacherous,
currents of lust.

Sharon Lee

NUCLEAR NIGHTMARE

I feel the end of life is near
My eyes, that see what is not there.
I hear a ring, sent far in space . . . it calls an
end to the Master Race.

The midnight winds are clearly seen, as a reddish anger
swirls toward me.

Ten Million thoughts are standing near, as the Sun tears through
the atmosphere.
Ten Million Minds, thinking as one, as Twenty Million
tears fall to run, But,
at the middle, between head and feet,
Forty Million grains of salt fall to the streets.

One more second of time now gone, as 60 million Insects
run in fun; 360 Million marching feet
rapidly descending down melted streets.

The heart jolts and skips a beat, I put my sweat-soaked
bedcoat on a seat, and as I rise up on the floor, I
pray to God that I dream no more.

David J. Bacon

DEDICATION

I dedicate this darling especially to you
Just because for me the little things you do.

Whenever I am troubled
And things are hard to see
You talk to me with comfort
And turn my worries free.

You take my hand in yours
And gently lead the way
Down the path of happiness
To a new and brighter day.

And while we slowly walk
Into a brighter life
You caress me with the words
"I want you for my wife."

So what you are and what you think
The things you say and do
All took a part in building
My eternal love for you.

R. I. Crawley

FOR AFRICA — USA PRAY

Our Father in heaven, who created heaven
    and earth and all there within
Lord bless those people who are starving and
    dying, there, over in Africa's land
There is death by hunger, and death by
    man, the two deaths that thus exist
The ultimate cure is in your hands, we
    are aware of this
We know it is not man's place to question
    what your purposes are
We only ask and pray earnestly that you
    bless those people afar
And Lord we ask that you may bless the
    nations that are trying to help
For we are thankful that you taught us to
    think of more than ourselves
There's one more thing that we may ask
    Lord that you do today
To put it in our hearts and minds, for
    Africa, U.S.A., pray

                    Amen, Amen, Amen

Patricia A. Matthews

THOUGHTS ARE THINGS

For a thousand nights and a night
I have been telling myself stories.
Stories of who I really am,
Stories of who I am supposed to be.
Dreams and Plans and wishful thinking.
Indeed thoughts are things;
But I want them to be the seeds of action,
I don't want them to be sterile.
Those dreams that have nurtured my being,
And kept me alive wishing and hoping.
I don't want them to give just a flicker,
I want them to be a fire that is never extinguished.
I want to achieve, accomplish, arrive
Where I never dared to dream.

Chaya Reich

UNEXPLAIN

How can I tell you how much I love you
Darling I love you more than anything
I just wish I knew how I could tell you
It's a wordless love, a motionless thing
That fills my heart more each day and each night
It sweetly pours and covers over me
Making me feel more proud with you and right
To the pleasures of you loved, loving me
Without you near me I cannot survive
I need you to fill my life with pleasure
Because you are what makes me stay alive
I never felt this way in full measure
And I shall never again feel this way
Or lose this feeling I have now, today

Cindy L. Kukkola

TEARS OF WINTER TURN INTO FLOWERS OF SPRING

Watch the snow melt as the warmth of spring
    fills the air.
The winter is part of the past as the green grass
    gives the scenery a little flair.
Trees are starting to come alive, and their buds
    will soon appear.
As everything begins to bloom, it tells us that
    summer is near.
Nature's beauty and warm air can take away
    the winter's bitter storm and sting.
Now tears of winter can easily turn into
    flowers of spring.

Melissa Palinkas

MY ETERNAL HOME

Mighty hills of rock and earth, ancient mounds
Devoured by Time, echoes of age
Immemorial. Whispering sage
Speaks sweetly from my past — ancestral sounds
Of Life and Death, my blood quenches the soil. Grounds
I've walked in youthful innocence, a page
Written in the annals of my heritage.
Freedom unlocks my heart: no chains, no bounds
To trap my soul, my spirit's free in flight.
I've walked the trails of Taconic lands, soil
Whose bounty feeds her natives, makes them grow
Strong. Beauty is the fruit of Berkshire nights.
Splendid home of simple pride; sweat and toil,
Wind and rain carve the features of my home.

j. v. ruvolo

let me die for just a little while

    to sleep the dreams of angels
    to lift the spirit of time from my soul
    to kiss the sun at midnight
    to bleed the pain from my eternity

let me die for just a little while

    to see shadows in three dimensions
    to grow close to the nature of things
    to breathe valhalla into each lung
    to praise myself as never before

let me die for just a little while

    to no longer endure but live
    to smile without remorse
    to avail my mind of all its wonders
    to sing the rebirth of miracles

let me die for just a little while

    to sleep again the angels of dreams . . .

Robert E. Swan

SWAN, ROBERT ELSWORTH. Pen Names: Bobbie Van Wyck, Richard C. Wigre; Born: Grays Harbor County, Washington State, 1-28-51; Single; Education: Carlton University, Algonquin Tech., Canada; Olympia Vocational Tech., Washington State, B.A., in Music and Art, Multi-phasic Arts for Handicapped, Certified Dental Assistant; Occupations: Cellist, Multi-Phasic Arts Instructor, English Literature Tutor, Dental Assistant; Memberships: Honolulu Academy of Arts, N.A.P.A., (Network Against Psychiatric Assault), National Anti- Vivisection League, Greenpeace; Poetry: Untitled, free form poem, *Ambassador Press Anthology,* 1969; Untitled, avante-garde poem, *Ambassador Press Anthology,* 1969; Comments: *I translate silence into words to depict the suffering of people who by accident or design are different. I write because I must share the plight of the voiceless with society. My work is graphic and intense in its cry to humanity. My ideas come from observation and personal experiences. Equally I create montages of the wonders life exudes every day.*

VISION

Vision is not handicapped by the naked eye
For within our being lurks a crafty spy
Who can seek new horizons beyond compare
Search new vistas where others don't dare
Sight is not required for this special device
Which can conjure up fire as well as ice
One only has to seek that unusual place
That's in the general vicinity of the brain's base
In that seat of thought that is cognitive of all
Lies a beautiful instrument if one could just recall
It's called imagination and one should use it well
Casting others instrumentally with your spell

Stanley S. Reyburn

A NEW GENERATION

Feed me the knowledge of the universe
I will consume everything you set before me
I will digest it, and my bowels shall release their
droppings, and fertile shall their soils be.
Soils in which new minds can be planted
For the harvest shall be plentiful
Minds that will grow and establish new beginnings
For we are a new nation and a new beginning
New thoughts, new ideals
A new legacy, for a new generation
Yes feed me, let me consume it all
For the legacy I want to leave is Love, Peace, Dignity
and Pride
Let me leave something I can be proud of
Not destruction, but rebirth
A rebirth of new spirits, true spirits
One of giving and sharing
For it will only happen, when we as a nation collectively,
share what we have
Let this new generation begin.

Barbara Jean Green

EL RIFTO

At times a crazy rift descends
Upon my calm, routine existence.
I ever marvel at the havoc it sends
Blasting away my weak resistance!
An infinite column of events so bold
Invades my life, teases my head,
Leaves me breathless — sometimes cold;
Eases the boredom of the cloak I shed.
It signifies growth; it reflects a change
In thought, in heart, inside my soul.
It's a reaching out in ways so strange
To be myself — to be in control.
This rift is sporadic; it comes, then goes —
My other me, as one might say.
As years drift on its urge to impose
Comes slowly, like a deep snow on Christmas day.
In time will I leave my other me
Back there on the road I walk?
Like me, will it yearn for eternity?
Will it ever cease to prey, to stalk?

B. S. Dillard

tears for THEE

hear me o LORD
as i wander this present and this past
these i offer THEE
three tears i loose
the others are spent
TRINITY trio three tears for THEE
one for each day
each for this whatever
    "put my tears in THY bottle"
save them
    "are they not in THY book?"
know them
each is an ocean of catalog psalm
if only one survives the trapping skin
upon it rides a multitude of prayer
this is a tear with a 50/50 chance
it can wash a thousand tragedies out to sea
or bring ten thousand back to shore
but tragedy by mine be not always THINE
thus do THY will o LORD

Chris Miles

BEYOND THE FLESH

Time entwined with the mind
Space absorbed with the memory
Thought produced before all
Flesh feeling thoughts of time and space

This gestalt but a mere carnivalistic play
Let's choose a part for some scary fun
Involving the script of a sideshow drama
Déjà vu, haven't we done this before

Drink of the passionate flesh
Eat of the experiencing flesh
Breathe of the dreaming flesh
Flesh will come beyond the flesh

Dreams singing music of life
Flesh symphony of the unconscious
Senses notes of the whole

Life is death passing through the door of reality

Clifford B. Rawson

FEET OF CLAY

As I walk beneath the darkened sky,
That sparkles like a thousand fireflies,

My heart remembers days gone by;
Youth has passed and age is nigh.

I remember when I was quick and strong;
Days of glory seemed they would last so long.

Feats of strength they still remember;
I can recall just like they happened last December.

Young men coming up are told the story
Of days gone by and feats of glory.

They don't care for they must have their day;
When they are old and bent, they can see their feet of clay.

This is the way of life and death,
So from the cold ashes life springs with God's own breath.

John P. Hedrick

IF I WERE NEVER BORN!

I often wonder, if I were never born,
    What life would have been like.
And also what would happen?
    I would have not even a care!
And of the entire world, I would be totally unaware,
    If I had no life, and no breath,
Then I would never ever have to worry about death,
    My life would be totally complete,
Because I wouldn't have to worry about sleep,
    Nor would I have to worry about
What I am going to eat,
    I wouldn't have or know of any sort of feelings,
Nor with people,
    Would I have any kind of right, or wrong dealings,
But if I were never born,
    I would know nothing of the world!
I wouldn't know of the sun, or the moon,
    And I most surely wouldn't know morning from noon,
But that is all well and okay,
    Because if I were never born,
It really wouldn't matter anyway.

Arthur Mathews

MIXED-UP SEASONS

Warm Florida winter,
pregnant cool spring,
early labor pains
breech-birthing
hot summer prematurely.
Betty A. Harbison

PADDED WALLS

Well-padded walls
I see
Upon a mountaintop
in a cage made with
white bricks
I see
And white-tagged uniforms
All the day is medicine
they give me
So I will rest
And to insure my calmness
So that I won't go mad
But it has no matter
They think I'm mad already
The broken
dreamers' minds
they broke mine
With well-padded walls
I see.
Talya Goldman

MISSED

I miss you.
You were such a big part of my life
and now you're gone
You disappeared.
And I'm left with an empty ache
where once you were.
No! Don't leave!
Please stay.
Don't go, I can't bear it.
There are so many goodbyes.
Too many.
Missing someone hurts so much;
An eternal ache
The tears fall faster and faster.
I can't stop them.
I'll only remember the good times;
The laughter we've shared.
I'll disregard the bad times.
And I'll miss you.
Darlene Y. Pineda

A MOMENT IN TIME

We watched in awe, as the moon rose
While getting bigger and brighter
As it came closer,
While each of us in our own world
Was wishing for our favorite
Dreams to come true,
Bringing with them all the splendor,
Hope and happiness
That the full moon seems to be
Enticing and asking us to enjoy;
And for a full moment
We felt so carefree and happy
That we would have given anything
To prolong that special moment,
Because for once in our lives
We were defenseless human beings
With all our fears, hopes and dreams
Resting and depending
On the whim of the moon.
Pearlina Mills

TO BEAUTY

So tall and so slender,
I yearned that last time
I saw you, so tender.

I've burned for you, Miss J.
And since Christmas Night '78,
I've wanted you, to stay.

Few have lain beside me
Long enough to take back
What Thou hast given, so womanly.

Sleeping, you are divine.
Gently waking, your beauty
Surrounds me with sunshine.

Passion, Thou seest is me.
Yearn as I do, you should
Never have to. Utterly!

Michael J. Jelley

JELLEY, MICHAEL JOSEPH. Pen Name: Michael Ivanovitch Joli; Born: Boston, Massachusetts, 12-16-51; Education: University of Massachusetts, Boston, Fall, 1973 — Spring, 1975; Occupation: General Laborer; Awards: Special Guest Editorial Contest, *The Boston Herald:* "Propaganda, He Says; How Much Is Soviet Involvement in Afghanistan?" 1-83; Other Writings: *Venus Kallipyge* under pen name Michael Ivanovitch Joli; Themes: *I have explored numerous themes in poetry, focusing on nature, romance and political struggle.* Comments: *I think our people, as Americans, must realize that there are commonalities among all people, and that in being humans there is a common experience, in our needs and desires, and a struggle with living we all share.*

LIBERTY

Why do I feel so locked into this space?
when a splendid movie is showing
across the way.
The park is close by for some
healthy play,
And the peaceful lake is just
down the way.
Why do I feel so locked into this space?

A library is just a few blocks down,
And there's a big fair in town.
Thy symphony is nearby
playing like delicate lace,
And the local museum is
exhibiting a very famous face.
Why do I feel locked into this space?

When there's a well-known restaurant
nearby serving food excellent to the taste
Oh! it's such a waste
for me to remain locked into this space!

Deborah P. Cains

CAINS, DEBORAH PARKER. Born: New Orleans, Louisiana, 6-26; Married: to Roy Cains, Jr. (1 daughter: Latoyia); Education: University of New Orleans, BA; University of New Orleans, MA, 1982; Occupations: English/Reading Teacher, Orleans Parish School Board; Part Time Writing Instructor, Southern University of New Orleans; Memberships: National Council of Teachers of English; Themes: *Individualism, Love and Reality;* Comments: *Writing poetry gives me a sense of inward freedom and fulfillment.*

GHOSTS

These are ghosts.
Who walk the mind
And pound its blackened walls.
Whispers that beckon
And seep through the bars.
Rise, and fall, and then are gone.
Echoes, then silence
Then nothing at all.
Rattle the bars.
Cry and curse them,
But never wear them down.

Linda Chandler

TEENAGE LOVE

Her eyes fell
Her mouth grew tight
When she looked up,
She looked angry and hurt
She concentrated and tried to bend the
    can in her hand, but she couldn't
He started to laugh
She joined
The argument ended
Never again would the argument be
    remembered
And neither would the girl remember
    the boy
Nor the boy remember the girl

Teenage love lasts long to the lovers,
But to the older it is just a blink of the
    eye.

Ashley Newman

THE INVITATION

Sunlight on the wall —
What was left of it: cracked,
Broken bricks — leaving jagged
Gaps inviting you and me to
Pass through, beyond: but we
Were already tired of walking —
Tired of following fading paths to
The wall — that still marked the
End of the property, a line we
Often approached but never crossed —
Despite the invitation that was
Always there — pastureland — wide,
Rolling, restful — promising peace
If only we would enter there: but
How quickly we turned away —
Retracing our steps along crooked,
Darkening paths — where we soon
Forgot the wall: but — even now —
Have yet to forget the invitation.

Eugene E. Grollmes

WHALES

The sun is caught
In the arc of the tilting

Water. Small specks that
Might have been ships

Flash and disappear
Into the crests of waves —

There are whales here
Riding the certain currents

Shining hesitantly like mirrors
Toward the sky too far

Beyond them, forging signals
We happen to see.

Peter Weinstein

HAPPY

The clay
Wind chime tingles
In the peaceful flowing
Breeze of the day. It makes me feel
Happy.

Sheryl Winarick

DREAM ON

Life has its seasons,
without any reasons,
Light and darkness,
alternating view.
But dream on — the strength lies in you.

Though all your fine dreams
are shattered it seems,
and life feels pointless
in all that you do.
But dream on — the strength lies in you.

When in time the pain disappears,
You'll laugh again, and forget your tears.

Peggy Brooks Guthrie

GOD IS

God is someone who lives every day
And talks to us in many ways.
He makes the sun come out and the
moon go away, just as he watches
over us each day.
God is someone who lives every day
And will always be there to comfort
us any time, any day.
He is our constant companion and a
loyal friend, for which at any time,
upon Him we can depend.
God is all these things and much, much
more, all we have to do is just
knock at his door.

Lori McGee

THE PAINTER'S PALETTE

Oh, pale blue, yet truly blue,
My song's to you!
You colored skies — not yet,
But now you do!

Whence such a hue?
Not from oceans deep or mountains steep;
Nor gems that flash,
Nor storms that crash.

Thou bearest no gravity.
Thy dome hath ism.
Oh, faithful blue,
True blue, this song's to you!

Eleanore Lindsey

LOVE

Love is series of happiness
        Hopes full of dreams
        Feeling our senses in
        Adventurous schemes.

Love is eyes filled with laughter
        Minds full of wonder
        Hearts in pure chaos
        Beating like wild thunder.

Love is life filled with beauty
        Kissing on the lawn
        Taking proffered sweetness
        Making love until dawn.

Sandra Tenney Whitworth

SPRINGTIME

Spring is here; it is there,
Spring is everywhere!
With its bright shining leaves in their
coats of green
Lends a beauty to the forests the winter
cannot see.
The gentle rhythm of a springtime
rain
Gives power to the flowers to bloom once
again.
Oh! How striking — is the eagle when
in flight!
Oh! How lonely is the whippoorwill late
at night!

Donna Postell

THE GAME GOES ON

The opening moves advance the pawn.
A square, a breath; a child is born
The game begins again.
Advancing through the ranks
To in their turn be sacrificed
Or perhaps become queen.
How not unlike the little one
Dependent yet depended on for survival
By those far stronger.
And when they've gone (or if they've won)
The game, in fact, depends on them.
From pawn to queen.
Without them the mighty would reign
No longer.

Lesley D. Carsons

REQUIEM FOR A POET

How often I have set this pen to write;
a sonnet brimmed with beauty's flair,
as veils adorn her face and hair,
with flowing gowns of wedding white.
But each attempt was frightfully trite,
as I trowed, I could not share
the cryptic words owned by this mare,
that brushed the tomb of stagnant night.
And as I garden with steady feel,
earth sips with lust my muffled tear,
she knows the wave of punishment done,
for this goddess of mine became so real,
and I loved a poem with so much fear,
more fear than I for anyone.

Christine Melgar

GRANDMOTHER'S DREAM

When I sit down with make-up kit
I will admit I pray a bit
And look into the mirror bare
And see a face I wish weren't there.

Out come the things I know I'll need
To hide the lines no one should see,
The wrinkles deep, the sagging skin
Belie the face that used to be.

Cremes in bottles, stuff in tubes
Expensive things they say are "lubes,"
A patchwork job I must admit
But spare parts sure would make a hit.

Mrs. Tommie Phillips

A BEGINNING

I could write 'How Do I Love Thee.'
But is it love that expresses the story
Of two people's lives —
That are bound together by ties
only time will bring?
Is it how I love you that tells our story?
Oh, How I loved you — At least
I thought it was love, wasn't it?
It seems so long ago —
Yes, I'm sure it was love in the beginning —
But it was also I — who hated you —
And laughed with you —
And wept and sighed with you.
Could it be mere love to survive such wounds —
This test of you and I?
Years gone by — Only is it now
That I look back without longing to change our past.
But with the serenity of knowing
That we loved and hated — and laughed and cried.

Teri Lewis

#4

I'm so confused I wanna weep
or maybe it's better if I jus' gawn ta sleep.

'Tween rip-offs, unemployment, and high inflation
crime, starvation, and an incompetent administration.
None of this helps my situation.

My job played-out an' my new roof caved-in
Crime victims NEVER say forgive, but sweet revenge.
Acid rains and pollutants are killin' us all
seems a race 'tween mutha natcha an' the goof-balls.

Costs go up and wages go down, an'
quality gets shabbier and less is found.
But, don't fret brother, it's nuthin' down!

But on the bright side the notion is clever . . .
you sure as hell don't hafta go through it forever.

Richard Copeland

THE CHIEF

There sits the old one his hair a holy white.
His tired old black eyes still shining bright.
He is the last of his ancient tribe,
Who fought and struggled many a time to
Survive.

His were a people greatly misunderstood.
They only fought to keep their land and
Preserve a livelihood.
Yet, the white man ridiculed and shoved
Them in a corner.
Then suffered greatly for the Indian
Would take it no longer.

Now this old one says his last good-byes.
To the great one with quiet pleading eyes.
    "I lay down to an eternal sleep,
    Please bless those who eternally weep."

Jody Floyd Skinner

FOREVER

Forever, you said . . .
    you promised you'd love me forever . . .
Forever goes by so fast,
    and slips through my hands like grains of sand . . .

Marian Gormley

GOIN' BROKE FROM PUFFIN' SMOKE!

Just sending this short note to Earth
    From here inside the Pearly Gate
Hoping you'll heed my somber words
    Before you find it is too late.

I guess I died a bit too soon
    At the prime age of fifty-five
If I just had not smoked so much
    Perhaps I would still be alive.

I blew twenty thousand dollars
    In a long span of forty years
For those nicotine and tar sticks
    That caused me headaches, coughs, and tears.

I spent so much hard-earned money
    On that which just went up in smoke
I could not have lived much longer
    Without completely going broke.

Charles Hunnicutt

HUNNICUTT, CHARLES T. Born: Girard (Kent Co.) Texas; Married, with two children; Education: East Texas State University, Bachelor's Degree, Business Education, 1978; Occupations: Promoter, Writer, School Teacher, Founder of Y.E.S.: Youth Eliminate Smoking; Awards: Non-Smokers Inn, Smoke-Free Society Appreciation Award, 1985; Poetry: *Puffin' Poems,* book of poetry, Success Ideals, 1981; Other Writings: "Care Card," greeting cards, Hunnicard Creations, 1983; *Y.E.S. says NO to Smoking,* Eliminate Smoking Handbook, 1985; "Boomerang," word games, Success Ideals, 1980; "Ruff Riddles," game riddles, Success Ideals, 1979; Comments: *My poetry takes a satirical approach to the harmful effects of cigarette smoking. I try to express thought-provoking reading in* Youth Eliminate Smoking *so youngsters will turn thumbs down to smoking before it becomes habit-forming. I want to contribute to the "smoke-free-society-by-the- year-2000" movement.*

THE IGNORANT BYSTANDER

Once in life this Road I followed
The Road of everlasting love
Society's rules I swallowed
And lost my true love.

Rigid laws create phonies
People walk this earth in lust
Hypocrites kneel and pray
Yet, who makes a fuss?

Murders, Rapes and unruly acts
The news appears to say
Researchers say these are the facts
Yet, nothing stands in their way.

Be yourself the Good Book states
Let no one stand in your way
But! Society has a way to say
Do it my way — or lose your faith.

Stand tall — be proud of you
For no one is any better! Yet —
Remember the words of the Guru:
Ignorance includes people like you!

John F. Caramico

CARAMICO, JOHN F. Born: Johnstown, Pennsylvania; Education: St. Francis College, BA English); West Virginia University, MA English/Ed.; Indiana University, 30 credits, Rhetoric/Linguistics; Alter High School, Kettering, Ohio; Sinclair Community College, Dayton, Ohio; Memberships: NCTE: National Council of Teachers of English; Poetry: 'The Ignorant Bystander,' American Poetry Association, 3-13-85; Themes: *Common themes concern some aspect of life.* Comments: *Writing poetry is an opportunity to express my feelings about life.*

You touched
Something
In me
I'd forgotten
Was there.
I love you.

Jonnie Sullivan

AUTUMN

Orange moons and golden days,
autumn chill brings frosty glaze,
proud clouds race across the sky,
as summer bids her last goodbye.

Feathered friends plan swift migration
in excited animation,
cleaning, preening in the trees,
ruffled backs turned to the breeze.

Woodlands bow and genuflect
as autumn claims her season,
all nature tenders its respect,
to autumn's rhyme and reason.

Fir and oak cast down their treasure,
cone and acorn, autumn's measure,
Yule-tide waits around the corner,
mistletoe for Christmas garner.

Hearths glow brighter, children bundle,
sweet aromas fill the air
as autumn's charismatic signs are
clearly posted, everywhere.

Freda Helen Sullivan

THE FADING LIGHT

The fading light of evening
Like the rivers as they flow
Slowly melt the years away
Like springtime will the snow

The sun is slowly drifting
To the south side of the sky
As winter's icy fingers
Reach out surly through the night

That roll away the seasons
Like a wave upon the sea
To touch upon the land
With the softness of a breeze

As I feel another year
Slowly slip away from me
There comes a nagging emptiness
From deep inside of me

I lean against my windowpane
And stare out through the night
Adjusting to the darkness
Of my mind's fading light

Erik James Norder

TAKING AWAY THE MOMENTS

I'm left with just a picture
  a picture of how it was
You took my heart away
  left me with just a faded
                    picture.

You told me you cared
  you would hold me tight
Taking away the loneliness
  Instead I was left with just a
                    picture.

The memories of how it was
  were really special
but you walked away
  just left me standing alone
      with a faded picture.

Heather Tuff

THE CAROUSEL RIDE

The merry-go-round
sways up and down,
around and around —
the sounds of music
rising — falling.

We don't know which day
the melodies and carousel
will stop
and one of us
must dismount.

The lone rider then
will circle and circle
with cotton-candy memories,
reaching to children,
teaching grandchildren
to touch balloons
and mount
the carousel horses.

Agnes Nasmith Johnston

JUDGING OTHERS

You can't judge a book,
Simply by its cover.
So why do we judge character,
By the appearance of another?
Did we inherit,
This Sherlock style?
Or did we learn it from our elders,
Growing up as a child?
How does a person,
Get a dishonest face?
And why can someone not be trusted,
Simply because of their race?
Others should not be judged,
By the actions of a few.
But to trust,
Is not an easy thing to do.
We should be cautious and careful,
But most of all wise.
And try to view others,
Through unprejudiced eyes.

Tony M. Burnette

MAGIC MOMENTS

I catch your eye,
The magic begins
For a precious few moments
Our eyes are locked
In a soul-baring gaze
And without a word spoken,
Without a touch felt,
Our eyes say so much.
A current of love
Flows between us,
Casts a spell upon us,
And for an instant
Troubles seem so small,
Worries fade away,
No one else exists
As we are carried away
To a secret world
All our own
Where we are lost
In the sweet love we share.

Lisa Bratcher

FREE NOW

I see an eagle at the zoo.
I think of you,
and I want to set him free.
But the cage is locked.

I watch the lions pacing,
their eyes so dull
with a dream destroyed.
I think of you and wonder,
Are we really free?

You are there
but we are not.
I am here
but we are not.

Two zebras flee.
I think of you,
and you and me,
and I cry.

Kathleen Faith Lange

DARK, DARK, NIGHT

On a dark, dark night
They dare not walk alone
Common fright
Fear of broken bone
I see why, but don't really care
They're concerned over lightless streets
A fear of what might be there
Police walk no beat
Walking alone, shadows grow
Nervously strutting along
Jumping every time they don't know
Hiding their fears in a song
Most people care so little
Still no one ventures through
All living in a simple riddle
In this dark alley is who?
I too my fear
Common fright
Knowing what may be near
On a dark, dark night

Timothy Greiwe

ARMCHAIR TRAVEL

A longing to travel to a foreign strand
Fills many a heart in many a land.
A slice of life new and strange
Intrigues all who want a change.
I find fulfillment in magazines
That depict offbeat things and scenes.
By monorail or by airplane
Jaunty car or on the main
Above the earth or on the ground
My spirit wafts me outward bound.
In winter I may follow the sun
And go where scuba diving's done.
Or on a sultry summer's day,
Take a trip to Baffin's Bay.
Spring and autumn take their toll
As awesome beauty fills my soul.
In priceless ease I gird the earth,
There's no restrictions and no dearth
Of fun and knowledge as I roam
Around the world right here at home.

Edith Gulish

AND LIKE ME

All the love we've ever known,
Keeps dying and drifting away,
Seems like nothing can be done,
There isn't much to say.

Your soul must search further,
All hurt must be shoved aside.
You may sometimes have to pretend
That our love was never alive.

Look ahead and smile,
Someday your dreams will come true,
A special person will come again,
And like me,
They shall forever love you.

K.J. Thompson

VIVISECTION OF A SCALLION

Whose tears dissolve
this scalpel in my hand?
I weep in your sky,
you in my eyes.
Your tissue paper skin
binds my fingers
to the open wounds of river beds
scrubbed white;
the concentric layers of flesh unwind
a spiral wire;
as I peel them, minnows flash
in the gullies of our cells' common wall;
and inside one, a fiery wing
throbs in the belly of a turbine
still to be conceived.

Doris Anne Carbonaro

A LIFETIME

To share a lifetime such as ours
    Required from us a special gift.
We would not trade the golden hours
    Or merely let the moments drift.
Instead we listened, quiet talk,
    And breathed in rhythms quick or slow
To catch the wonder of the walk
    Of crazy thoughts and witless glow.
For like a stream that constant runs
    We've heard the music on,
And wished for neverending suns
    Of countless summers never gone.

A lifetime, then, with roots so deep,
We'll cherish, clasp, and ever keep.

Paul O. Ellis

unintended torture

if you could see   the terror
in my heart when I know
you're the one   at the end
of the wire   because

it's my job   to listen
to the first drafts   of love poems
written for others

it's easier   sometimes
to play the martyr
but all the best ones end up dead

and I never do anything halfway

Suzanne E. Litke

ARE YOU GOING MY WAY?

Hello sweet one,
    How are you today?

Can I walk with you?
    Are you going my way?

Your beautiful smile,
    Your wonderful expression;

Has lifted my heart,
    From sadness and depression.

If you're going my way,
    Can I tag along?

I will feel so good,
    I may burst into song!

Can I hold your hand,
    In my sweet one?

Can I hug you too,
    When our walk is through?

What did you say?
    You're going my way?

Thank you, dear,
    I will always stay near!

Jack Dixon

SIX WISHES

Of the many things
    Man aspires to be

I would recommend
    Prudence, primarily.

But this requires experience
    To gain

And often experience sings
    A woeful refrain.

Next after that, give me
    Sweet serenity.

Contentment is alone . . .
    Just myself and the sea.

Courage, though grand, can in-
    volve many choices.

Peace, is the absence
    Of dissenting voices.

If only some prophet would
    Appoint a commission

To teach one to talk and
    The other nine to listen!

Delores Hendricks

I came back here
to look for something
I had it in my head
but whatever it was
I was looking for
it's gone somewhere else instead.

Mark Kramer

IT WAS LOVE

Down by the seashore, sifting in the sand
    Out by the meadow, romping on the land
Away down the river, where the crystal waters fall
    I'd seen this pretty maiden, by memory did recall.

Her eyes were blue, her skin so fair
    She looked like an angel, awaiting me there.
Her poise was so perfect, so stately and tall
    My heart did a flip, when I heard her call.

Young maiden, pretty maiden, I answered her back
    I beckoned her come, her love I did lack
My voice was a whisper, her beauty I saw
    My heart stopped beating, and I stood there in awe.

Her eyes how they sparkled, her cheeks did glow
    I spoke to her softly, for I wanted her to know
I'd prayed for this maiden, God answered my call
    It was love at first sight, now and for all.

Ruth V. Kuehmichel

KUEHMICHEL, RUTH VERNITA. Pen Name: Ruth Mandel Kuehmichel; Born: Loyal, Wisconsin, 7-1-28, Clark County; Married: 1-11-47 to Harold C. Kuehmichel, Mother of 12 children, 9 sons, then 3 daughters, Born 1948-1969 at Marshfield, Wisconsin; Education: grades 1-8 at Sunnyside School, Loyal, Wisconsin, 1933-1941, High school at Midstate Technical School, Marshfield, Wisconsin, 1982-1983; Occupation: Domestic Engineer; Membership: P.T.A.; Poetry: 'Our Lord,' Religious, 1985; 'Character and Growth,' Spiritual, 1983; 'In the Garden,' Inspirational, 1984; 'By the Window,' Contemporary, 1984; 'Our Life,' love, 1983; Comments: *I like to write about nature and all the beauty I see around me, about God's great love and all creation itself. I write about love, trying to express my love for life itself and portraying the beauty of true love between man and woman. I try to portray life and love, as a great privilege and we have much to be thankful for.*

ON PHOTOGRAPHY

To paint the light, to paint the day in gray —
For truth's the beauty that we all desire —
The photograph speaks well to all and may
Delight and entertain, perhaps inspire.
The artist stands with camera held on high,
And must reflect the moment that endures,
With patience, wit and cultivated eye,
A glimpse of time the fragment he secures.
And further down the road he finds a clue,
The gift a pow'r that no one can rescind.
So if your task is art you must be true,
Or else you weave but nets to catch the wind.
'Tis said Columbus sailed without a chart,
The soul's surmise his science and his art.

James Weinstein

WHY?

Why must the foes always have bombs
While the allies are stuck in the rain?
Why must men go off and leave their moms,
At most, to return with half a brain?
Why must a man slay his brother unknown
When in another place he'd shake his hand?
Why must a man live a fox life — alone,
Gnawing stale rations in a mine-cratered land?
Are these young men but puppets on strings
Acting out orders as if in a play?
Where is it stated that true freedom rings?
Certainly not in the invasion planned for today.
How many bodies? Three-score or four?
No, there are too many — I can't take anymore . . .

Keith Thompson

TO TOUCH THE WOUND

"From age to age" a people are being gathered
to the Lord
"so that from east to west
a perfect offering may be made —"

Inheritants of the Spirit we eat the bread
and drink the wine,
believing in the actual gift,
— the body and the blood —

Even as we profess our faith we beseech,
"Lord give a sign!"
so that each of us are nothing more
than Thomases of our time.

Marie Viens

MORNING — A NEW BEGINNING

Like a drowsy child awakened from sleep
The morning mist is slow to rise
Stretching and yawning at the golden dawn
Then slipping into the mountain's deep lap.

With a warming touch the sleepless sun shakes
The nodding haze awakes
And the mist ascends to embrace all shapes
In a thin hushed gauzy glow.

This delicate and touching scene so soft and new
Like all young, innocent things, can't endure
Yet this is where beginnings begin
Forever, and ever, and ever again.

Debra Sue Heidt

TODAY

The more I think of the passing days,
    the more they slip away.

Memories are like flowers,
    while alive, they bloom in the summer sun.
    But as time passes, they fade
        to be pressed into our book of experiences,
        to be looked back upon, but never the same.

Today will be another memory,
    but only if it is significant.

So I live today with respect and joy,
    so the memory will be joyful and savored.

Each moment of today is important,
    for it forms the foundations of tomorrow.

If I do not give today, this moment,
    all I have, then tomorrow will have less
        in store for me.

I do not live for tomorrow, for I am too busy
    living and loving this moment.

For I am alive and I am happy with who I am.

Dianne M. Blake

PLEASE DADDY DON'T CRY

Please Daddy Don't Cry!
Ours is not to reason why.
After all these years of being
a strong and loving father.
And always being faithful
and standing by our mother.

Why you have to suffer so,
only god will ever know.
You suffered through raising your family,
helping us at any time no matter how costly.
You stood by us when we were young
your faith and love you always brung.
All the care and love we gave,
We suffered too, because a painless road
we could not pave.
We sat and watched you cry,
asking, Why God, Oh why?
We'll miss you Daddy, oh so very much.
And thank God for your loving touch.
Your passing will bring us great sorrow
but Thank God, for you a peaceful tomorrow.

So many beautiful memories you've left behind,
but Daddy, just keep this in mind.
Someday we'll all be together again.
Goodbye, Daddy, Goodbye.
Now Daddy, you don't have to cry.

Jacquelyn M. Williams

THE THISTLE'S PRICKY POD

Deny one not one's agonies . . . one's regrets . . .
One's misfortunes, the earth rebels against
Balance: Quakes, eruptions, floods,
Avalanches, tornadoes are fragments of being.
Enslave one not, teachers of cheap happiness.
One's shattered moments are unexplainably real.
One's tears, one's sorrows, change the sunshine.
Why! Is the monstrousness of suffering
A currency perhaps to be treasured?
Suffering often intensifies the spirit's beauty.
Life's storms magically birth the rainbow.

Don Blondeau

MY CHILD

What is a child?
Laughter and tears, sorrow and pain
No one but a child can say I'm sorry
And yet totally mean it from the bottom of their heart.

My heart can melt with a sleepy sigh
To say "I love you" is a small phrase for an adult
But to a child, it means I'm sorry or I'm glad you're my mom
My how a child can use you
But is it to their benefit or yours.

My child is what I have
No one can deny or would they
There's no changing the effect a child can make
On your life, so small and helpless

I mold her to what I think is perfection
And when my child disappoints me
Whom do I look to for comfort
But yes to my child and in the back
Of my mind, where did I go wrong?
Would I change my child?
No not I for she is me.

Jenny Pauley

PAULEY, VIRGINIA JOYCE. Pen Name: Jenny Pauley; Born: White Sulphur Springs, West Virginia, 1-14-50; Married: 11-14-67 to Allen Pauley, Jr.; Education: Charleston Beauty School, graduated 1968; Occupation: Hairstylist; Memberships: National Hairdressers Association; Comments: *I write poetry because it shows my inner feelings and because it relaxes me. I've always wanted to be a great poet since I was in elementary school and I had to memorize a poem, 'Trees' by Joyce Kilmer.*

WHO KNOWS

Don't laugh at a cripple until you have walked with his crutch.
Don't snob the less fortunate who haven't as much.
It's his cross he's carrying and it could be true,
He might be a bigger and richer person than you.

The fate of our life and what we do with them
Determine our final reward.
So if you have health and blessings are plenty,
Reach out to others and serve our Lord.

He was born a pauper and became the King,
Saviour and Father of all living things.
Think what a kind deed for others might do —
Who knows? The next one in need could be you.

Thelma V. Lowry

THE FLOWER AND THE WEED

Why must you be scolded; why must it be no;
Why can't you have this; and why can't you go?
You say look at the other kids, all of them free;
They're not kept at home, a prisoner, like me.

Please look at the flower, then look at the weed.
I'll give you the answer that I know you need.
To have pretty flowers think of the care you must give;
But the weed just needs dirt and some air to live.

Now, it takes so much to raise a child
To grow in beauty instead of wild.
Now and then a strong word from Father or Mother,
But always with love that you get from no other.

The beauty I speak of is hard to erase,
For it comes from the heart and not from the face.
I'll show you the way and hope you take heed,
That you grow as the flower and not as the weed.

David P. Wesp

NEW BEGINNINGS

Grasses peeping up along the road,
    Caressed by sun and rain,
Transform drab Winter's lifeless hue
    To vibrant green again.

Gay tulips tiptoeing down the path,
    Adorned in bright array,
Fold lovely petals close, at dusk,
    Then sleep, 'til break of day.

An acorn, bursting through the sod,
    Shed from its shell, and free,
Proclaims the miracle of new life —
    In happy birthing of a tree.

All life begins, and all life ends,
    In much the age-old way;
But for us who believe, and give glory to God,
    It begins, Resurrection Day!

Martha Mattox

NO MORE TEARS TO BE CRIED

Have you ever felt like crying,
But you couldn't shed a tear,
Because you had cried them all
Throughout so many long years?

It hurts when you've cried all the teardrops
With nothing but hurt left inside.
You can feel your heart breaking,
For there're no more tears to be cried

With you it was only make-believe,
When you'd tell me all those lies.
Only God knows how much I loved you,
But there're no more tears to be cried.

Someday, you'll find you're all alone,
And you'll feel so dissatisfied.
It's then that you'll remember
All the tears that I have cried.

Ruby Wallace Melford

MY POT OF GOLD

One day, I happened upon a rainbow;
On a spring day, after a May shower.
I found that this was a "special" rainbow,
Because with it came a special power.

This rainbow was different from all the rest —
Had all the colors; had all the pieces —
But it was rare: To this I can attest,
Because that's not where its power ceases.
It was sending out a message to me;
It seemed to say nothing at all tragic;
So, I went and followed the mystery,
And got caught up in all of its magic.
I went to find my treasure at the end,
And when its conclusion was within sight,
It flipped over to an inverted bend;
It turned upside-down to a smile so bright.

We all know: A handful of a rainbow
Is so hard to get and so hard to hold,
But when I reached the end of this rainbow,
I found out that you were my pot of gold.

Tami Gersbach

ATHENIAN REFRAIN

    Is there any music left?
In the sphere of my beloved city I listen
to the strains of a lonely, lost refrain.
Can I capture its melody and bring forth
the tunes of time trickling through eternity?

    Is there any music left?
Stand upon the Akropolis and listen to
the rhythm of a time when the muse was
just born floating o'er the world fancy
free, bringing her sweetness to a waiting
world!

    Is there any music left?
In the eons of time where music outstretches
her wings, I hear heavenly echoes of a time
past my life, and

    In the sphere of my beloved city I, at
long last hear the melodious strains of a
long, long, lost refrain.

Helen Melissas

THE GARDEN OF TREES THAT HAVE POWERS

I once lived long years ago
In a garden of trees that have powers.
I thrived on beauty and pleasures galore
Where crystal rivers flow.
I soaked up dew with grass and flowers
In a garden of trees that have powers.

But when I touched a tree one day
I found myself submerged in clay.
Oh clay! Oh clay! depart from me
You've covered my eyes and I can't see.
I miss that beauty and pleasures galore
Where crystal rivers flow.
In a garden of trees that have powers.

As the clay gripped harder and harder
I found myself cursed in hands of a Potter.
The shape of my soul his hands did bare
Because he had molded a clay body there.
"Hide my soul's nakedness," I said in prayers
Until this clay body falls away into tares.
Then I can live again among trees that have powers.

B. Elizabeth White

A MOMENT OF HAPPINESS

As I stood looking out the window at the winter
sky, I was alone and sad.

The clouds looked dark and distant. I just kept
staring at them, soon they became closer and
closer to me.

Then it seemed I heard someone say your loved
ones aren't so far away. For a moment I felt
happy in a strange sort of way. I held my head
erect to gaze once again at the gray winter sky.

Where are the clouds? Did they pass by, or
perhaps they ran away to cry.

Ludema Mills Garza

CHANCE

One Chance had gone and simply left in fear,
For what it saw and heard begat no care.
Vainly I sought to stop the quickened hare,
Yet nothing could I do to bring it near,
As chance had lent one bloom and would not hear.
To plead would give no fruit and just a stare.
So, poor I, threw myself to sweet despair,
Until somehow a soothing image should appear.

That is what thrashed my soul till I was found
Awash in grey of teary, moonless fright,
Waiting for the blow of enemy untold.
And even before I sought to find some ground
In which to sadly throw my tired psyche,
I saw the wingèd gleam of Death unfold.

Charles E. Klimicek Portales

THE END

The sky was spotted grey
on this cold sunny afternoon.
The howling wind was quietly
whispering through the trees.

The sun, leaving the day behind,
painted orange tails on some clouds.
A lonely bird sat on a cold shivering tree,
I wondered why he waited.

The bird fled darkness with some friends,
leaving the tree lonely once again.
I sat and pondered the blackness before me,
sipped the last of my sherry, pulled the
    drapes.

Frank Borsellino Jr.

MY DARLING . . .
Written 8-26-57

As every hour passes I think of you and all the nice
things that you do . . . Your love so honest and sincere
means more to me than anything else my dear . . . I
cannot help but wonder what the future will be like . . .
Will we both be happy while we face the trials and
tribulations of life . . . Making big problems seem
small and small ones nothing at all . . . Will our love
grow richer and deeper as we go along together . . .
Dreaming, planning, doing things for and understanding
for another . . . Promising to be faithful always and
forever . . . Loving you is what life means to me . . . I
hope you understand my feelings and my love for you . . .
Whom God has chosen to walk along with me into the
path of Eternity . . .

Mrs. Marion J. Monzo

JOHNNY IS DEAD TODAY

Tell the boys to lower the flag,
    because Johnny is dead today.

He died in battle — alone, but brave,
    and without his combat pay.

His wife in the states, sits and waits,
    for news that he's all right.

But as the telegram said — now he's dead —
    killed in the thick of the fight.

So tell the boys to lower the flag,
    because Johnny is dead today.

He's buried somewhere overseas on a beach,
    where the tide rushes in and away.

All the medals and speeches, probably won't reach,
    to where his soul's fighting now.

But at least he died proud, with his honor aloud,
    an it's over for him anyhow.

Yes tell the boys to lower the flag,
    because Johnny is dead today.

And although he's gone — life will go on —
    he's a hero on this special day.

Brad Thaxton

ARIZONA DETOURS

The memory of an unexpected smile,
The lizard sunning, or the uneventful mile.

The bluebird winging from swaying bush to bush,
the chipmunk as he darts under culvert with a rush.

The mother quail ushering her brood into the roadside weeds,
The hawk soaring down as the field mouse faster speeds.

The road runner waiting to play Russian roulette with your car
As it crosses in front of you always closer — never afar.

The jackrabbit running at full gait
Pursued by a hungry coyote who has spied the bait.

A wild horse marching ahead of a few
In an orderly line across the field fades from view.

An owl hoots high in the trees,
The swallows swoop for insects on the breeze.

A crow caws somewhere nearby,
A frog croaks from cattails where sits a butterfly.

The sun sets and a soft breeze bends the rushes,
The blue sky darkens, and the white cloud blushes.

The view when off the beaten track
Can be so good — one doesn't care to go back.

Elizabeth Borselli

READING

In deep introspection, each day without guile,
    I spend some time reading all that I can,
To share, and receive for myself awhile,
    The common needs of child, woman, and man.

Millie Hildebrandt

DID YOU KNOW MY GRANDMA?

Did you know my grandma?
The one with the sweet, sweet smile.
The one who was never too busy
To let me sit with her awhile.

Did you know my grandma?
The one with the twinkle in her eye.
The one who laughed at my silly stories
And dried my tears when I needed to cry.

Did you know my grandma?
The one with the tender heart.
The one who loved me just as I was
And always took my part.

Oh, how I miss her clear blue eyes.
Oh, how I miss that smile!
But, there's something she gave, I'll never lose . . .
It's the belief in myself, that I'm worthwhile.

Gayle M. Marks

CAROL MARIE

Carol Marie, so precious and dear
My only hope to keep you near
You will always be a part of me
When I look in your eyes it's love's reflection I see

Carol I wonder how you knew
I needed someone just like you
Come and be my guiding light
That came to my world late that May night

And though I try to hold back the years
Why can't I hold the dawn
And so I'll try to hold back the tears
When love is grown-up and gone

Carol I'll love you till I die
And when you read these words of mine
I'll be with you though we're far apart
And you'll be with me here inside my heart.

David Benjamin Leidy

MAKE MY HEART YOUR HOME

Oh come make my heart your home
You lift me at silent times
When leaves fall and clouds come
You bright up my sunless skies

Ah, wow you change winter into summer
Your love and life! Oh, come
Bring the air and streams its joyful tones
Oh come make my heart your home

You make melodies of birds and bees
With that loving look in your eyes
I can see blue heaven smiling over pale seas
When near you trembling time arises

Ah, wow you change winter into summer
Your love and life! Oh, come
Bring the air and streams its joyful tones
Oh come make my heart your home

Willie McMiller

JANCY LIMPERT DANCES

*This poem was inspired by a solo
performance of Jancy Limpert,
a modern dancer/choreographer
based out of San Francisco. Ms.
Limpert's solo dance was titled
"Incipient Stages."*

Weasely, mousy, Jancy bones jitter
Flinching from, pinching at, Limpert is leaping
Plumbing-pipe arms on hinges recoil
From things on the ground she imagines to foil
Grasshopper Jancy plunges into her crouch and,
Like scarfs in the wind, leaps gracefully out.
Then popping-out eyeballs, all bloodshot from fear,
Inside their sockets do blink, and to fright
They adhere.
Mistrustful mouth, clattering jagged with teeth,
Is let kissed all too often by ones of deceit.
So dances, so shatters this nervy red molecule,
Streaking the air with trails cochineal.
And by trial and error, in streaks of blood red,
She tries to escape all her fear, and the dread.

Nick Norden

CHILDREN

Children, children — what would we do without them?
The future of the world would be hopeless if they weren't here
There's a special place for them in my heart, which I hold dear

Children, children — don't grow too fast
You've got to make your childhood last
You're us grownups' dreams come true
So always remember that we love you

Children, children — all over the place
Look at that beautiful smile on that shining face
Look into their little glowing eyes
And tell me they didn't come from Paradise

Children, children — soon this messed-up world will all be yours
From the highest mountains to the sandiest shores
We will do our best to teach you well
And maybe, you can keep this world from going to Hell
Kids, we love ya!

James R. Cristofolini

DROUGHT

The nightmare unfolds without need of explanation
The queues of dark stick-figures
On the cauterized earth
Under the hopeless ochre sky
The seas of withered children
Starved even in the womb
They are the holocaust of our generation
And as in earlier times, the more fortunate shiver
And try to turn their faces away.

Would it be better if they had never lived?
Never known the sunlight
And their mothers' eyes
The taste of cool water
The sweet wind from the empty places?
The impoverished have this
If nothing else.

Do not ask me these shallow question
On the ethics of abortion
The policies of birth control
This is a matter beyond our small opinions
We cannot know.

E. M. Soloway

UNDER THE CATSKILL FALLS.

COME, BE MY FRIEND

Walk a space with me in this corner of the universe.
Take my hand and we will wander through my imaginings.
I will not take you to the dark valleys of my pain;
For those are my dungeons and I wish to show you light.

I will show you a laughing little girl running barefoot
Throughout fields of dew-kissed forget-me-nots,
And I will share with you a soul grown old too soon.
But the age is a mellowing more than a hardening.
I hope this journey will bring you joy.

I offer you this glimpse inside my mind
Not because I expect the gesture returned.
You are your own being and may not want the
intrusion. I, on the other hand, sometimes wish
To have the cobwebs brushed out of the attic where
I keep so much of myself hidden away from sight.

You may not even want to make the journey,
For fear of the price one must pay for such
Proximity of minds. As you wish, I will understand,
whatever you decide. But, if you venture to take
the plunge — Come, be my friend.

Judy Ann Hutcheson

KRISTI

Her hands were clutched around the covers of the book
As her blue eyes moved across the page.
It was a rainy day and she was passing the time
By reading.

She's only six, but she loves to read.

I don't know if I caught her in the middle of a sentence,
But I yelled into the living room,
"Kris, can you help me?"
She didn't say, "Oh, I'm too busy."
She just said, "OK."

She's only six, but she's a real friend.

From my conversations with her,
I found a new outlook on the world . . .
A wonderful kind of optimism,
An outlook that could only come
From that innocent, sincere person.

She's only six, but she's the kind of person
I'd like to be when I grow up.

Debra L. McCusker

NO TIME OF REMORSE

A modern day Cassandra,
cannot reach the modern mind,
to instill a word of warning
for a race, on the decline.

The world just laughed.
How dare this wrinkled hag,
intrude on life, their playground.
Go home, Old Witch of Woes.

Alone she stands, for all that once was good.
Sound education, family ties, samaritan deeds of old.
The rain, her tears, the wind, her hair.
Surround her like a cloak.

Slowly, she rises, her feet the raging tidal waves.
Thin arms outstretched towards the fiery mushroom globe.
Now, may you weep, my children.
There is no time left for remorse.

Victoria McMahon-Andrews

EVILS OF MONEY

Money is the root of evil so they say
Well I guess every word is true
It's proven every day
To everyone, Yes both to me and you.
Money can cause a lot of fights
Sometimes it can cause a divorce
But love is something to make it all right,
And that can only come from one source.
You can live without a lot of money
Money can never buy happiness, peace or love
You can only get them from your special Honey.
You have to find the kind of love that comes from above.
The old saying, money can't buy everything is very true
There are some things it could never buy
Money cannot bring peace of mind to you,
The more you have the more you want and that's why
When you have a whole lot of money
You have a lot of problems and a lot of cares
But if you have a SPECIAL person to call Honey
All your problems can be shared.

Judy Obuchowski

NECTAR IN A PLAIN BROWN WRAPPER

Poetry, he says,
is writing that
"forms a
concentrated
imaginative awareness
of experience,
in language chosen
and arranged
to create a specific
emotional response,
through its
meaning, sound, and rhythm;
a quality that
stirs the imagination
or gives a sense of
heightened
and more meaningful existence" —

— nectar in a plain brown wrapper!
— and to think I thought Webster was stodgy!

Daniel Moss

DUBLIN, MARCH 1981

There are no words in Dublin.
They've all been said before, and lie
plastered wet on darkened pavement
or hang unnoticed on cracked brick walls.
The people move swiftly in different directions,
splashing in stout-colored puddles
while the sun seems to balance on the crucifix
of the highest weatherworn steeple.
The poet's charm has vanished, slipping
down the city sewer in fragmented phrases,
until suddenly there is nothing;
nothing in the face of the ragged beggarchild
with deep blue eyes of no expression, nothing
in the baptismal rain that lingers
like an ancient veil of yellowed lace.
They walk quickly by,
grey and green,
hat and overcoat,
white untouched legs of uniformed schoolgirls —
all moving to some nowhere in particular.

Charlsie C. Anderson

A FRIEND

Who laughs when you laugh?
Who cries when you cry?
A friend.

Who celebrates your triumphs?
Who encourages you when you fail?
A friend.

Who accepts you as you are?
Who listens when you need to talk?
A friend.

Who offers an unbiased opinion of life?
Who doesn't demand you follow their advice?
A friend.

Who is neither black, white, brown, nor red?
Who is neither male nor female?
A friend.

A friend is just someone who cares.
My friend is God.
Who's yours?

Barbara J. Krebs

BEAUTIFUL CLINCH MOUNTAIN PINK DOGWOOD

Amidst the woodland so green and free,
A springtime beauty unfolds, the pink dogwood tree
Reminding me of little girls in organdy and bows,
As on their way to the church school they go.

Such an unfolding of beauties to behold,
For each has a blanket of pink softness that unfold
Here comes an array of blossoms new and free,
And smallness, aliveness, and pretty things to see.

Swaying to the rhythms that can please,
This quietness that puts my mind at ease
Yet, so alive these dancing branches and leaves,
A beauty that must be made from whistling wind breeze!

Oh, to look at you makes me glad it is true,
And as your petals soon will drop away
I know we shall again behold your blossoms and should,
Another day, pink dogwood, beautiful pink dogwood . . .

Carmen Frazier

A POEM FROM NO NAME BEACH

A poem for an hour
Soon the tide shall wash her clean,
Like the red hibiscus flower,
Never knowing, knowing what she means.
So if you chance to read her.
Remember the rain storm made her cower.
I'm afraid, she must go to sea.

I'm lyin' upon my Sandy towel
And see your happy teeth.
The memories not yet under trowel,
Not to have to bury them, that would be relief.
Here on Noname Cay I scratched my song.
The beach here carries memories,
Washed away, but strong.

The sun sets behind an awful cloud.
Sinking down anvil black.
How many poems will be allowed,
To flow to the shore from this grassy shack.
Before all the sand to the sea be lent,
Or the mountain fire remake the land,
Or simply lose interest and smolder dormant.

Tim S. Jackson

LET'S GET US MORE BARE LAND O.

England was a forest stand, but they axed down
    those forests n bared the land.
        Let's get that oak n walnut O.
        Let's have another farm O.

When westward moved the wagons, still, great redwoods
    covered the sea-mist hills.   Paul Bunyan
was there n saws m still.
        Let's get that pine n redwood O.
        Let's have another farm O.

Then southward moved the people's need,
    with saw n axe n spade O.
        Let's get that teak n mahogany — hee.
        Let's saw-m, chop-m down O.

Away, Away at rain forests play,
    with bulldozers, axes n saws — hay . . .
        with trucks n rivers n ships — hee . . .
        with a hah-ha-ha n a hee-hee-hee . . .
        n a very merry fiddle-dee-dee . . .

Let's get us more bare land O.

William Schilling von Canstatt Lutz

VON CANSTATT LUTZ, WILLIAM SCHILLING. Pen Name: William Schilling von Canstatt Lutz; Born: Berkeley, California, 1920; Comments: *The poet is moved by the instant flash of a passing moment, in a sudden ordinary word that vivifies a transient life in some forgotten time, in the common experience of man. He is deeply concerned with the Spanish poets San Juan de la Cruz, Machado, Jimenez and Lorca; with the Italians Ungaretti, Quasimodo, Palazzeschi, d'Annunzio and Eugenio Montale; with the Germans Rilke, Heine and Moericke; with the French Hugo, Jacques Prevert and Paul Valery; with the inescapable Shakespeare; with Blake, with Frost, Sandburg, Emily Dickinson, Edward Arlington Robinson, the Benets; with Lewis Carroll, Gilbert, Coward, Edward Lear and American ballads; with Greek Lyric Poetry and life-giving Cavafy; with Tu Fu and those Chinese poets who listened in the mist; and with Bassho and the Japanese Haiku masters who caught a lifetime in the fall of a leaf.*

SOJOURNER

Three o'clock is grieving time
Standard, eastern, or mountain.
Time to weep for children grown
Progeny unknown
And little dogs who tend to die.
Sojourn in the twynight recollecting
Renounce, deride, deny.
These are cherished lamentations.
Rise up
Rain your tears in cups of coffee
Dilute the instant
With some Liebsfraumilch.
Batter back perfidious pity
Ring down the curtain
On a mistral of gathering sighs.
Oscar Hammerstein where are you
Whiskered kittens make me cry.

Nancy J. Newman

MERRY GO ROUND

A merry go round is a magical thing
  So the children say
Its horses go up, and down and up and down,
  And 'round, and 'round and 'round.

Your horse can be the very first
  Or the last one if you choose.

Its music is a special kind
  The kind that makes you smile.

So come ride with me on the
  Merry go 'round
and we'll go up, and down,
  And up, and down
And 'round, and 'round, and 'round.

Joyce Gardner

REALITY

There are a thousand things that
  Reality is, or is a part of,
  But there also are,
  In life's brief lexicon,
  An endless list of things
Not real — in common language —
  Yet more close to truth
  Than touch-and-sight Reality.

The first of these comes first in life,
  When Time is longer than
  It later is,
  And boy and girl
  Are held, suspended, in the mists
Of childhood's magic, when innocence
  Engulfs the heart,
  And every dream is true.

Paul Ader

HOME AT EASTER

Easter to Easter, the visits meet.
Last night's train
Echoes in the last sense to sleep:
Another year,
Ties and rails of hopes and fears,
And whistles in the night —
The journey of the years;
But that train went by so fast,
In my dreams, in my sleep, in my past.

Kurt Herzberger

YESTERDAY'S NEWS

a light rain was falling . . .
someone was dying . . .
later on that day, a woman
  gave birth to her child

Donna Elizabeth

SHARED SO LITTLE

We did so much together
But shared so little.

Was our time together
Spent in vain?
Has it left with you
Memories of pain?
Do you recall the joy
Quicker than the sorrow?
Or does it matter to you at all?

Joan Marie Rooks

ROOKS, JOAN MARIE. Born: Cambridge, Massachusetts, 9-30-47; Single; Education: Attended American University, Washington D.C.; Columbia University, New York, New York; Georgetown University, Washington D.C.; Occupations: Lobbyist, Administrator, Actress, Model; Memberships: Massachusetts State Society of Washington D.C., Chevy Chase Citizens Associaton and other local civic groups; Poetry: *If In This Life,* Sonnets, 1966; *Be My Lady Bug,* collection of whimsical love poems, 1970; *Until Eternity,* prose and poetry concerning nature and love, 1975; Other writings: *Lady of Revere & the Man from Savannah,* collection of short stories, 1980; Comments: *I write as I have a need to clarify and share my experiences. My work deals — in both a serious and humorous manner — with the many forms of relationships, facets of love, and the diversity of nature that I encounter.*

LIFE'S ANXIETIES

Life's anxieties on the prey
Each one comes within its day
Knowing how to take each one
Will always be as though there's none
So take life as it were today
The day that brings tomorrow
Take of it from what you may
But leave some of its sorrow
For tomorrow is each day

Joyce Banks Piggue

LIKE A RAINBOW

Now,
  You can never
    Possess me, you
      Can only perceive
        Me to be what I am
      To you in your
    Thoughts, but
  Only for a
Moment

Betty Ryan

EMBER

When the flame burns fierce within me
And the yearning throbs without cease;
  The hunger rages unbridled,
  And the restlessness is king;
My soul cries out to the stars alight
  In the heat of the velvet night;
  Friends to he who wanders,
  To guide the one, the only one
Who can bring the ease and delight.

Joan Schernitz

REFLECTIONS

Indistinct reflections
Of a swift flowing stream
Rippling images
Are never what they seem.

The stream comes to rest
In a peaceful lake,
Only then do we see
The images it makes.

Cindy E. Tebo

LONELINESS

Darkness, Emptiness, Quiet.
Walking to someplace that isn't
reaching out to touch what's not there
and falling over things that aren't real.
Being not aware of who you are,
searching for the someone who is you
crying to yourself "people don't care"
you don't see them
nor they you

Deserine Fernandes

JUST BECAUSE

Just because I kill you with kindness
Doesn't mean I'm foolish.

Just because I gave you a part of my life —
Doesn't mean I gave you my all.

Just because you laugh behind my back —
And not in my presence
Doesn't mean I didn't hear.

Just because we share our feelings —
Doesn't mean that it is mutual.

Just because you thought you had my heart —
Doesn't mean you couldn't lose it.

Just because I listen —
Doesn't mean I believe.

Just because I don't scream out my feelings —
Doesn't mean I don't hurt.

Just because you walk in my life —
Doesn't mean you can't go.

Just because I gave you honesty —
Doesn't mean you had the right —
To take my kindness for weakness.

Just because you are gone —
Doesn't mean I'm not happy!

Odessa Motton

MEMORIES OF CHRISTMAS

Christmas is upon us, with all its hopes and fears

With the hustle and the bustle, we've grown used
to through the years

The shopping, wrapping and the trimming of the tree

Is all that seems important now, I am sure we all
agree

But let's all take a moment's pause, from our search
for worldly things

And think about the memories, that Christmas always
brings

Of the Little Baby Jesus and the manger where he lay

Sleeping in a stable in a land so far away

Of the Little Town of Bethlehem, and that brightly
shining star

Sending out its message, to the people near and far

Christ the King is born this day, you can hear the
Angel's singing

Peace on earth goodwill to all, is the hope that he
is bringing

Tom Sheppard

SHOOTING PRACTICE

I can feel something burning in my blood,
spawning bubbles that ripple to the surface,
I put on my army cap,
sling my B.S.A. airgun over my shoulder,
take the few pellets leftover from previous adventures,
and go to be outside and shoot a little,
the wind blows, but not as it should,
it's too hot and it doesn't slap across my face,
creating a stinging sensation,
I aim and miss the small can,
not really being much of a marksman,
a few shots later the light metal clang,
tells me I hit it, it doesn't matter.
My eyes glance at a baby cricket, cushioned in the grass,
I hate crickets, but he is more at home than I,
noisy children are playing football nearby,
it's time for me to leave,
airguns are illegal in residential areas.
Alone in my room, I think of the S.I. article,
on Idaho, Hemingway's hunting playground.

Rauan Klassnik

UNITY

Milk-white steed running 'cross an empty plain
    motorbike whizzing down the middle of a lane.
Princess on the charger, her hands interlaced
    girl on the cycle, hands 'round a muscled waist.
Knight on a horse, dressed in silvery mail
    boy in the drive offers a ride down the trail.

The same kind of wind blowing feminine hair
    the same kind of spirit prompting masculine dares.
The excitement of oneness, the thrill of the run,
    ties young girl to princess, merges one into one.
The two pairs are racing, moving side by side
    both are rejoicing in the love of the ride.

The cycle and charger blend and then fade,
    returning to the time from which they were made.
Joined in a moment by a ride with the dawn
    they're no longer one, by the spirit's not gone:
There's a little carelessness left with the knight
    and a bit of the stallion left in the bike.

Ann E. Simonsen

THE SPEAKER

Tall stands the man,
Aloof and looking down.
Expectant and hopeful
I, the listener, wait
Face uplifted to hear the truth proclaimed.
A word, a phrase — the message comes
Weak, lifeless and unsure,
And all men strain to hear.
Like a soul deranged,
The thoughts are broken and unclear,
And time is a burden.
Listen to you, I cannot.
Mutterings, vain and empty, clutter the air;
Annoy the ear of the sensitive soul.
Why murmur?
Speak up!
Declare the truth for all to hear;
Proclaim with faith; speak openly.
Truth is eternal —
All must hear.

J. C. Hicks

Tuffy,
         I love you so much and
         It hurts so bad
         To know you're gone
         Forever.
         That's such a long time.
         You were here for me when
                  I needed someone, some-
                           thing
         Anything.
         To hold on to, to cry to.
         To comfort me.
         You were a part of me.
                  as my hands, my feet, my
                           arms
         Permanent, or so I thought.
         I never thought to prepare
                  myself for what I knew,
                           deep down, would happen.
         I guess I thought you were
                  immortal;
         Eternal
         Forever.
         That's such a long time.
         Mellissa Frank

SOME CATS ARE NICE

Cats have various shapes and sizes,
But the kind that I most prize,
Is the one that's fat and lazy;
Maybe you will think I'm crazy.
One that likes to sit and doze,
Curling tail around his nose.
Not demanding much attention,
If his name you do not mention.

How I hate to call at places,
That have kittens with sweet faces.
But are devils, nothing less,
Fighting over my caress;
Digging claws into my knee,
Shedding hairs all over me,
Tumbling to the floor, and then,
Starting in to climb again.

If I had my way about it,
I'd arrange, Ah do not doubt it.
To invest in cat insurance,
And cat tonic for endurance.
         Barbara Allen

YESTERDAY AND TOMORROW

Yesterday and tomorrow are but dreams of
         what should have been and
                  what might be,

spun in the thin spider web of time that
         stretches in all directions and
                  traps isolated events

in my consciousness like flies trapped
         on shiny strands of
                  spider-silk.

All my hopes and fantasies are but winged
         creatures flying through the
                  ETERNAL NOW,

trying to become entangled in the time-web
         of yesterday and tomorrow and
                  be trapped forever

in the mainstream of my consciousness.
         Charles D. Booty

KEEP IT SIMPLE, SWEETHEART!

I am born,
you are born,
we all are born.

I feel,
you feel,
we all feel.

I need love,
you need love,
we all need love.

Life is so simple,
like this silly poem.
Honey, do not complicate it.

I want you deadly,
Do you want me?
Just think and decide:
you do want me?

If it is so,
give me a KISS
and,
Keep It Simple, Sweetheart.
         Ismail Ersevim, M.D.

THANATOPSIS
(View of Death)

Autumn ruffles a silken wind
         As the last rose of summer dies;
Evening whispers a low hello,
         And in my mind's eyes —
         I see Paradise.

I must go Home, I cannot stay,
         The urgency is greater
Than all the important things
         Of life — it cannot wait till later —
         For in my soul's eyes,
         I've seen Paradise.

O Blessed Jesus! Carry me Home!
         There are no chains to bind me!
My ears are filled with angel songs!
         Earth's treasures no longer blind me!

Send the bridge to carry me across
Though it stretch over all the skies!
         My heart is free! O rescue me!

         For in Thine eyes,
         I see Paradise!
         E. M. Scott

I LOVE YOU POP

I love you Pop please don't leave me.
I have to, son, it's time to die.
Can I go too and be with you?
You can't, my son, it's not your time.
Why must we die and leave the earth?
So we may live eternally.
When my time comes will I know how
To get to where you go to now?
You will, my son, if you have heard.
The meaning of the sacred word.
Living your life filled with His love
Will get you through the gates above
Goodbye my son I'll wait for you.
Because, my son, I love you too.

         E. Ray Bateman

HIS MAJESTY'S EVOCATION

Of all things around me
His Majesty's grace I see.

The magic of a blue sky,
Of a white cloud on high.

The miracle of a red rose,
Of everything that grows.

The shadow of a crimson leaf,
Of life's great love and grief.

The shape of all things to come,
Of which many remain undone.

Things to remember for years —
To remember with tears.

         Raymond Arthur Bush

BUSH, RAYMOND ARTHUR. Born: Buffalo, New York, 12-02-35; Education: University of Southern California; State University of New York at Buffalo; Occupations: Writer, Producer, Director for the stage, screen, and television; Comments: *The art of 'His Majesty's Evocation' (a search for truth and values in the landscape of life and death, emphasizing the theme of love) expresses the power of the imaginatin to transform life into something magical and colorful. The theme of love runs throughout my work. To advance the ideas of innocence, experience, time, hope, the past and present, I use irony or the doubleness of things: Life and death, the ideal and actual, human nature and human destiny. My symbolism conveys, gradually, the idea that Christian meanings can have a surprising ubiquity. And good poems are filled with ironies.*

NATURE'S WHISPER TO ME . . .

There is something that nature whispered to my heart today.
the intriguing and mystical feeling than I receive
from watching the dawn of a new day . . .

The stillness and beauty of the rising sun captures my
utmost attention, creating a new outlook on the approaching
day.

As an earthy type individual, the beauty and mystery of
life continually urges my soul to search and one day
discover all the answers my heart longs to know.

There is a beginning and an ending to life's long journey,
which continually reminds me that I must seek out
and experience life to the fullest in order to create the
writing I am compelled to produce.

To love unselfishly, to learn to give as well as take, to
reach beneath the surface of our plastic society and seek
out meaning, feeling and awareness, to express my
unique creative talents, and to seek out the answers
that Nature whispers to me daily.
For isn't this what life is really given to us for?

As the day begins fresh and new, ending in many colors
to create a beautiful sunset, so are our lives, beginning
new and fresh, ending in a beautiful array of colorful
experiences and knowledge to make our own sunset.
We must listen to Nature's call and respond with
thoughtfulness and sensitivity to the beautiful earth we
reside on, we shall become what we choose to be . . .

Judi M. Pemberton

JUST LIKE YOU

I am one lucky lad,
To have you for a dad.

You take me hiking and to fish,
But to be with you is all I wish.

I know you get mad when I break a rule,
'Cause I talk a lot, and get in trouble at school.

But I promise that I'll do better,
And do things right to the letter.

'Cause when I grow up, I want to be just like you,
And be strong and caring, and good-looking too!

I know I have bad manners at the supper table,
But I'm so fascinated when you talk about cable.

I really want to be a cable man,
Climb poles and ladders, and drive a van.

I know you get angry, 'cause I don't do what you want me to,
But be patient, 'cause I just want to be like you.

It's of you that I am so proud,
But you scare me, when you get loud.

I know that the things that you do are best for me,
But I'm only seven years old, you know, Daddy?

If you try to be more patient, and you know you should,
I promise I'll behave and listen, and try to be good.

So what do you say, is it a deal?
'Cause you know that I love you, and the way that I feel.

I know you love me for all that you do,
When I grow up, all I want is to be just like you!

Peach Renner

A MASTERPIECE OF LOVE

A masterpiece of creation
  became a revelation,
  when God planned the future generation.

From the dust of the land
  God in His image formed man,
  with His mighty hands.

Then one little breath of air
  of love He did share,
  just because He care.

And then He took from man a bone,
  so he would not be alone,
  Behold! He made woman to help man carry on.

Just as the symbol of the dove
  sent from above,
  a masterpiece of love.

Willie Mae Taulton

SOMETIMES

Sometimes she wonders, in the mirror she stares
She's gone under, no one really cares
It's hard to explain, it hurts to tell
She hides the pain, it feels like hell.
Sometimes she gazes, though nothing she sees
The hatred blazes, she prays on her knees
Layers of frustration, oceans of tears
So much hesitation, so much fear.
Sometimes she'll smile, unbeknown to her
Once in awhile, a memory will stir
The chance to live, to become alive
No more to give, she's broken the ties.
Sometimes she reaches, though nothing's in sight
Roaming on beaches, running in fight
She's all alone, on her own she must fend
Nowhere for a home, no one for a friend.
Sometimes she wonders why nobody cares
Sometimes she gazes a long, lost glare
Sometimes she'll smile though nothing is right
Sometimes she reaches with all her might.

Nancy Kell Hargett

CONFUSION

As I sit in my room,
Alone here I cry,
My tears are so silent,
They fall from my eyes.
  I cry not for happiness,
  I cry not for joy,
  I cry not for you,
  The awkward young boy.
My heart is so numb,
With feelings of pain,
I sit here alone with nothing to gain;
  I wish I could pull myself out from my shell,
  It's like living then dying,
  Then going to hell.
My song is forgotten,
My eyes are dismissed,
I think of the life that I sweetly kissed;
    I don't understand this feeling I sigh,
      As I sit in my room,
      Alone here I cry.

Unique Schreiber

FLAKES AND TEARS

As the snow falls
        slowly, softly,
The trees glisten sweetly, purely.
As the tears fall
        from my eyes,
It's not the sadness or the pain that cries.
The whiteness drops
        to the earth,
But is comforted by the piles of fluff.
My tears drop
        down my cheeks,
But you'll be there to dry them through the weeks.
The flakes descend
        as romping children,
Falling to bring happiness, joy, and fun.
The salty drops descend
        because things are perfect.
"I love you" is what brings the emotion to fact.
The flakes may melt but the memories,
Will be there — forever.

    Dena K. Barefoot

NORTHERN LIGHTS

In the midnight blue of a winter sky,
    No stars are showing this night;
Only luminous flames from a northern sky,
    In eruptions of marvelous light!
It transcends the brightest milky-way;
    And we're held by the wavering scene,
As gossamer curtains, in billowing display
    Their shades of red or green.
It transforms a world in weary sleep,
    In a panorama; like jewels —
In colors of emeralds, or garnets deep,
    Or delicate opal hues!
We view the performance as a heavenly trust,
    As it colors the sparkling snow;
That glitters and glows like diamond dust
    In a shimmering, mystical show!
How rarely we witness a like display,
    And we're awed, transfixed by the sight,
As the north sends Aurora Borealis our way;
    The gift of a northern night!

    Opal V. DeGrote

BLIND RAYMOND

I asked my friend Raymond what's it like
to be blind
And he answered I'm comfortable quite frankly
I really do not mind.
My sense of touch is finely tuned I can find my
way around in the dark
So I took a walk with Raymond and we ended up
in the park.
I shut my eyes and listened to the sounds of a
robin singing
behind me was the gentle peal of a distant church
bell ringing
Raymond whispered see with your heart not with your
eyes there is no ugliness here
I cannot distinguish between black or white I just
know beauty it's everywhere.
Don't pity me my inquisitive friend I'm more
fortunate than you'll ever be
I've taught you a lesson today what it's like
to be blind just like me.

    Rosetta M. Buchanan

VIEWPOINT AHEAD

"Viewpoint ahead" So I stopped for a look.
The view that I saw was one for the book:
Nothing but juniper, sagebrush and sand
Held in a hollow in this desert land.
Infinite skies were of azure blue.
And as I stood there I felt something new —
Silence! Who knows how it sounds
When the beat of living pulses and pounds?
I know that the next lovely sound that I hear
Will be sweeter by far since this silence so dear.

    LaVerne B. White

WHITE, LAVERNE BUSHAW. Born: Cripple Creek, Colorado, 1-10-10; Married: 6-3-31 to Wayne E. White; Education: Holy Names Normal School, two-year degree, Spokane, Washington, 1929; Occupation: Teacher of Piano; Memberships: Music Teachers' National Association; Poetry: 'Eyes That See,' 'Longing?' 'Choosing,' 'Prisoner Set Free,' 1960's and 1970's; Comments: *I write as a hobby — the rhythm of poetry — try to express the majesty of the universe and prayerful thoughts. I have never been published. I am happy to have my poem accepted.*

I wish to forget what I know
        Just to know what I do not know
But some wishes, rarely come true
        They just melt, and quicker than snow.

We are jailed in an hourglass
        Counting the year day after day
The future is running faster
        Than the present so far away
Some are already fifty-nine
        And they were nineteen yesterday
The aged wishing to stay young
        And they are still wishing today.

We are in a cell called earth
        Life is the sentence, birth the crime
We fought war after war, as if
        Loving one's neighbor is a shame
It is funny! Men crying peace
        And men making war are the same
Funnier still, you and I go die
        And the GENERALS get the fame.

Let us all wish, only one wish
        To never let, lovely earth blow
May that desire to fight die out
        And that PEACE that died out grow.

    Hacene Boulkhodra

A TEAR

A tear rolls down my face
Visions of sunny bright days
The picnics on the beach
Walks through the green forests

A tear rolls down my face
As I remember good times with friends
The parties that lasted all night
And laughing at jokes

A tear rolls down my face
With memories of quiet evenings
Roaring fire, candlelight, wine
And you by my side

A tear rolls down my face
I take your face in my hands
My lips touch yours lovingly
As my tear falls into your coffin

Goodbye

Sheryl Diane Ellis

WHY DO PEOPLE LAUGH?

Giggles from behind
drift
like steak aroma to my
nose/ears
and splatter.
I turn full circle
stop
then march onward
eyes low
chin on chest.
Why do people laugh?
What stimulation now?
Again the laughter
wails/haunts
down the hallway
hitting me like a cold flash.
I shiver, pressing on.
Through the door
in the distance
I see clouds forming faces
laughing/snickering —
I laughed back.

Deborah Bayley

ABSOLUTE ZERO

Pulls her down
the restless promise.
A lifetime spent
gazing through windows
perched on chairs
waiting

The waves live more vitally
swell and roar on beaches
through oceans, in dreams
resonates through dark
houses where such women
sit, stand, sleep, dream
wait

Always
another must set in motion
the clock with no hands
fire with no flame
only a distant memory
an echo, a steady tick, a burn
far back . . . back in the brain.

Susan Areizaga

TOGETHER ALONE

You didn't call tonight
like you said you would.
It's just me and the Platters
And I miss you desperately.

I miss your tenderness
wrapped around me.
I miss your lips,
your tongue, probing,
    searching —
Looking for answers
To the question "Why".

You had been hurt
And I was lonely.
But this only brought us
    Together alone.

You wanted her.
I wanted you.
Maybe it's better
    this way.
You gave all you had.
But I needed more!

Linda Glass

THE SEEDLING

I kept a promise I made him
    This time he would not have to stay
I took my son hunting
    For the first time today

I could see the joy in his eyes
    As he mocked my every move
And as I watched him sitting there
    My purpose in life came to view

Someone who is a part of me
    Who looks to me for direction
I owe him more than any other
    For without him I have no reflection

I must make the time to spend
    To teach him all that I know
Give a part of myself to him
    I can only reap what I sow

He will surely wither and die
    If I do not sustain him as he grows
My convictions are his water
    My son the seed I sow

Curtis L. Thompson

CALIFORNIA

California, O my pride
From all the mountainside
Until the cliffs above the ocean
You always arouse my emotion.
California, O land of beauty
State of dream and liberty,
Nobody can ever forget the feeling
Of happiness that you once bring.
I'll keep your freshness inside of me
While leaving far away from your magic.
You're so exciting, so wonderful,
For not coming back I would be a fool.
I'm fond of you, don't you see?
And here is where I want to be.
How long are we going to be separated;
I promise one day we'll be reunited.
California, land of God's blessing
Can't you hear my heart crying?

Bea Courouble

EASTER

White lilies in bloom,
Christ arose from the tomb.
I see His kind face,
And know of His grace.

The choir is singing,
"Worship The King."
The music is flowing,
And I know it is spring.

The Cross stands before me,
Its meaning I see.
Simplicity its beauty.
Christ died for me.

Tears misting my eyes,
Pure happiness inside.
Christ lives in my heart,
He was there from the start.

Maureen Margaret Bartlett

MY FRIEND

You came when I was lonely,
Feeling down and very blue,
You held me tight and whispered words
That made me feel like new.

I know that you're not mine to keep,
And I don't desire your heart,
I don't want you to be my love,
Just a friend who'll never part.

I know you'll never hurt me,
Like a love that I once knew,
You'll never reach that part of me
As only he could do.

But when I hear your special laugh,
And see that cheerful smile,
I can't help but feel good inside,
And love my friend awhile.

Tracey L. Eddings

MIRROR

Who is she —
Standing there in my place?
So lonely there beside herself —
With red tears running down her face.

Remaining there in her melancholy state —
living in her complete isolation.
Playing solitaire until the late —
waiting for her total deterioration.

The silence becomes so very loud —
the daylight much too dark.
Still she stays in my place,
does she still think she is so smart?

Why does she stare at me, —
her blue eyes so cold?
Is there a detection of familiarity,
can we possibly share the same soul?

Shelley L. Coombs

THE RED WINE

Whose lips were you kissing
before you kissed mine?
I smell the odor of dirty red wine
each time that I kiss you
oh, how could it be?
the red wine was flowing from lips that I see

You say that you love me but now, that's not so
it's the wine in the bottle you love I've been told
you say that you would always love me so true
and nothing could ever come between me and you

Now you are on the run and out every night
with her and your bottle and you think it's all right
all I do is think about how much I love you
how can I get you back
in these arms that love you

So give up the bottle and come on back home
come on to these arms that are needing you so
but darling I'll wait until my dying day
I'll wait just to be with you
in any old way

Lorraine C. Ivie

NEMESIS

Is this my nemesis for having tasted
the nectar of your lips?
Must I pay the exorbitant price
of eternal loneliness
for having loved you
in such an intense and unselfish way?
Was my love for you
such a nefarious crime?
Perhaps my settled love were not enough
for your nomadic soul;
but that was the only way
I knew how to love.
How can I forget what my soul feels for you,
when I myself ignore the forces
which foment my feelings towards you?
O, how I wish there was something I could do
to fructify the aridity of your soul;
but all my efforts will be in vain.
How can you force someone
to feel something
that one does not comprehend?
Well, nothing more can be said.
My empty cell awaits for me
to pay my debt.

Jose M. Salgado

LUCKY YOU!

I.

"This is to certify that you
Whom our computer has addressed by name
Already may have won a million (gold),
A six-week trip for two around the world,
Another house, or three new cars.
So order now, or give, within four weeks.
(You don't *have* to, but, frankly, failing
May cut you out of our next Big Sweeps mailing.)"

II.

This is to certify that you
Whose name this writer does not know
Already have received a prize that's worth
Much more, in lasting value, than the gold
Or any of those other long-odds lures:
Because you learned to read, you now reel in
The wit and wisdom of the world — pure bliss!
(As well as, sometimes, stuff like this.)

Henry L. Norton

THE WHITE DOVE

Spring is here, the fledglings said
and lifted their mouths for a morsel of bread
from the patient mother, who for weeks would fly
beyond the sight of the naked eye.
The storm could whirl 'round her fragile wing
and rain could pour when she tried to sing
but she knew the nest must be feathered and shared
with love, for the babies for whom she cared.

'Tis summer the mother whispered low,
spread out your wings for you must go.
Build now your nest and gather your bread,
Soon your own babies will have to be fed.
Gather soft grasses and pieces of straw,
your days of leisure will come no more.
Fear not the blast of autumn's rage,
freedom is more than a guilded cage.

Winter has come, the tired mother said,
snow now covers the stable shed.
Let the storm roar, on I must fly,
gathering food for my young, or they die.
So spreading her wings in flight of love,
she struggled on, the gentle white dove
'til the day was ended, her young were fed,
with a blessing once more of holy bread.

Mona Tate Friedman

FRIEDMAN, MONA TATE. Born: London, England; Married: 1-3-73 to Harold Friedman; Education: School for girls in France and England and also the Northfield Seminary in Massachusetts; Occupations: French Teacher and Actress; Memberships: L'Alliance Française; Poetry: 'The Sea,' 'My Mother,' 'Day After Christmas,' 'Good Day Good Day,' 'Paris,'; Comments: *My poems are inspirational and spontaneous. I started writing as a child. My two daughters: J. G. Anderson and Gwen Dole, are noted in the music and literary worlds.*

YOUR FRUSTRATION — MY ABUSE

Don't hang me up, to dry me out, like clothes you've washed.
I have feelings — when tied like a dog you plan to beat.
Trying to think — it's not real, until there is a repeat.
I have no place to run, but many wounds to heal.
My eyes nervously protrude, and my hands shake with fear,
    gritting my teeth, I can't think — knowing you're near.
I am overcome with heat, and try to snuffle tears my eyes
    must not show — to Mother of hatred love — who hates that
I live.

Elizabeth Bell

ALL THAT I AM

As the dawn of a new day unfolds, shadows of the night disappear as the melody of life rings out in perfect note. Sunlight bathes all nature's wonders in beautiful delight. Birds sing out in tune with each melodious note a song of thankfulness for their bountiful supply which Mother Nature has lovingly bestowed. In my life there is a flicker of enlightenment from within of better things to be. I know that today I can be anything I want to be. Life opens avenues for me, there are no restrictions unless I choose them so. The light of understanding awakens me to a higher state of mind, there I envision all that I am or ever hope to be. Reflections of small beginnings unravel in my mind as I finally realize that if I allow myself the freedom to build on solid structure of thought, the small beginnings will surely grow. Discipline and a right attitude become a determining factor in my life, allowing right choices to flow into a world of reality. Gone are the fears and the doubts I might have felt. Life's beautiful song has awakened me to the enlightenment of an abundant way of life with a better understanding of myself and all that I am or ever hope to be.

Alice P. Lawson

LAWSON, ALICE P. Pen Name: Danielle Lea; Born: Dallas, Texas; Married: Sammy Richard Lawson; widowed in 1974; mother of two sons, David and Don; Education: Attended Southern Methodist University earning a nursing degree in 1953; Occupations: Private Duty Nurse and Hospital Staff Nurse; Memberships: Member of the Research Council of Scripps Clinic and Research Foundation; Comments: *My affinity for the human race is the very center of my life. I write poetry because it is the only way of expressing my inner feelings that I like to convey to others. Every day is a beautiful symphony in the arena of my life.*

ADVICE

Ain't no use in your crying girl, 'cause he broke the golden rule,
You ain't the only woman that's been taken for a fool;

I know your pride's been shattered, like a broken looking glass,
But take a tip from one who knows, that feeling soon will pass;

What you think he was anyhow? He's just a mortal man,
And even the very best of them are finding it hard to stand;

Standing against all that temptation that's thrown at them day by day,
Why it's a mighty wonder it took him this long to stray;

Now you've got some serious thinking that really must be done,
If you're to keep your sanity so the battle can be won;

Now I ain't one to give advice about what others ought to do,
But I'd go right out and do like he done, I mean if I was you,

'Cause if by chance you did get caught he couldn't heap no blame,
'Specially when he knows you know he's already done the same.

Carol Ferguson

BEST OF ALL WORLDS

The best of all worlds,
    O Maker of Men,
Is the dream that is dreamed
    nor forsaken again;
Where ideals of Our Fathers
    remain upright and fair,
And the bullets of envy are
    deflected with care.
Where mythical grandeur
    isn't shaped by a bomb;
Doors of our councils
    not screened with alarms;
Satellite scanners not
    syncted with the fears
That have festered and grown
    through the waning years.
Forgive us the fetters
    now binding horizons;
May our bread on the waters
    be sufficiently guiding,
To show us which way we
    are hopefully biding.

Graydon E. Spalding

I've never touched
The autumn wind,
Or climbed a mountain peak.

I've never soared
With eagles, free,
Or felt the thrill of speed.

I've never found
A second wind,
Or pushed beyond my bonds.

I've never heard
A whippoorwill,
Or realized my dreams.

I've never done
So many things.
Perhaps I never will.

But once I knew
And loved a friend,
Whose loss I'll always grieve.

Jan Piccirillo

REVISIONS OF A DEATH

I tried
to know the things
that you are deep
            inside
But
all I found
is that we're bound by
            ourselves

To know you
to hold you
to keep you
            close
to be
            Friend
you defend you
Love you
            more than most

you love me
i   Love you
can we l(L)ove each other?

Giacchino Jack Urso

GOD KNOWS

ADAM

Unto thee I present this love of all loves.
You are the one in which God giveth for the purpose of life.
God created one man and one woman to create the population of the world.
As woman you are a true blessing to me, for man thinks the same.
Woman, they are that of a God-given gift in mind, body and soul.

EVE

I speak unto thee with the voice of a woman.
We give the respect though some do not deserve it!
As woman I must admit I need the love joys that only a man can give.
Let my man be a man for my inspirations.
Take thou soul and all the total body into his hands, present me
With heaven on earth.

CHILD

I am the child of Adam and Eve. My life here was predetermined.
Being the first is just what I am.
Be pleased with thou soul and be contented with my makings for I
Giveth riches of life to all.
(Pardon me not for I cannot condone sinners,) for I am not perfect myself.
Man as a first was Adam; woman as a first was Eve. Myself as a first was child.
So I ask of you dear God, the creator of heaven and that of earth: "Who Shall
My Mate Be?"

Eunice P. Ashlock, Jr.

A CASTLE IN THE SKY

It's A Castle in the Sky
It's high on high
If you can learn to fly
You'll reach it by and by (but only if you try)

It's floating on a cloud
It's a fair and brightly shining place
Where only goodness is allowed
It's there. A rightly divining place

It's floating in the sky
A place with golden gates
Where you'd better not be late
— You'd better always try —

It's A Castle in the Sky
It's floating high on high
It's there for you to reach if you try
And pass through those golden gates (but you'd better not be late)

It's A Castle in the Sky
It's high on high
If you can learn to fly
You'll reach it by and by (but, only if you try)

Roger B. Dahlberg

SHADES IN BLUE

I stood one day among the violets and blue bells,
Just gazing, just gazing at the light blue, the dark blue sky,
Sleek and beautiful She swiftly approached,
A shadow of glistening blue silver, silently She flew by,
        Silently She flew by.

Have you ever seen an aircraft, any airplane,
Ride a cloudless very blue horizon?
With the sun making Her an even darker blue silhouette,
The keen blue line of Her underside making a sharp knife tone,
        A sharp knife tone.

Cutting Her way across the field of blue,
She slips away into the blue Eastern yonder,
Then, as if the sky is sad to see Her go on Her way
There comes a fine sheet of rain like tears and a sigh of thunder,
        A sigh of thunder.

Mary V. Saunders

STANDING ON A HUMMOCK

*A Parody on James Wright's
"Lying in a Hammock, etc."*

Under my feet chaste snow
crunches a crisp, flinty sound.
Standing on a hummock, my
snow-burnt fingers shape
the snow with imagination.
Silence covers the street,
as snow drifts high
against the backyard fence.
I stare out the chilled pane,
as more snow falls steadily;
as hypnotizing as that other,
habit-forming, snow. Morning;
the sun floats over,
looking for someone to tan.
It has wasted my snowman.

Lynn Klajda

PRAYING MANTIS

I watched a praying Mantis
    Crawl upon a slippery pipe,
And wondered if he'd make it
    To climb another night.

He made the trip across the pipe
    With ease, no effort at all,
But when the pipe bent upward
    He began to slide and fall.

He caught himself just in time
    And raised up then to pray,
On his journey he began
    Again to climb and sway.

As I watched him on his way
    My Christian life I saw.
When troubles come and trials,
    I, too, begin to fall.

But with a strong abiding faith
    I look to God and pray,
And know that He will answer
    To guide each step I take.

Modena Abney

REBORN

I sit and watch the day die.
    There's nothing I can do
        But helplessly await the end.
            Its given time is through.

Spectacular the day's death,
    Dramatic its last throes,
        A strangely lovely moment
            As that final flicker goes.

It's done, it's gone, forever past.
No power can retrieve it.
    I saw the final spark go out
        And yet I do not grieve it

Because I know that like a soul
    It must pass through the dark
        To be gloriously reborn
            All fresh and new and stark

And brought forth into splendid light.
    Too fragile to defile
        It's blank, but ready to be made
            Into something worthwhile.

Carolyn L. Vaughn Asher

The shadows of the wood were deep — subdued
On that clouded Autumn morn
The wind shuffled its feet through the fallen leaves
Branches creaked — so forlorn

When, from the depths of the wood, a faraway cry
From a distant tangle of brush
As the mellifluous song arose
From the heart of a lonely thrush

I am that thrush — my song is for you
That is how much I love you.

Jim L. Barnes

UNDEFINED

The most important things in life
are unseen
For this reason
appreciation is limited
To the things more liquidable to the imagination
Creativity requires insight into areas not yet cultivated
Frustration appears with the capacity to see below the surface
Fear is the basis for solutions — Hate is inducement for strength
Wisdom serves as a buffer to prevent foolish mistakes
Love is still Undefined
To most it's merely a dream

LeRoy Wilson, Jr.

TRUE WOMAN

What is true woman?
She is all woman and proud of it.
She is all feminine, with character
and grace.
She is a standard of righteousness and purity,
And portrays a love the world does not understand.
She is a testimony to God in all that she does.
She stands up tall
And proclaims to the world,
"I Am True Woman,
I Am A Woman of God."

Sara Gross

AFTER BIRTH

They plucked the child from my belly.
Howled irritation, hurling
Accusations at my ill-begotten defense,
Echoed through to rest within celiac walls.
Flowing remains, still, undermine the pain
So politely ignored by those
Bearing witness to one miraculous sin.
Years of slow bleeding, of pressing fingers
That contact, fondle the interminable excess
Comforted by apparitions of my Truth
Disguised as godless will.

Tracey A. Thompson

IT'S A JOINT CELEBRATION

You say your birthday needs no celebration
And birth pain shouldn't note my declaration.
How little you know of this mother's bonds,
Starting before you knew the great beyonds.
No matter how you struggle to be separate, free,
The ties are there between you and from me.
Your heartbeat still softly mated to my memory.
As my thoughts and songs, I embroidery.
Each string a part of you for life long.
Remembering the day you gasped first air, your touch,
I welcomed your birth and life, then and now, very much.

Patricia A. Newgaard

THE GIFT OF LOVE

Some of us are touched with exceptional gifts bestowed
to us upon arrival. Some possess talent, beauty or
intelligence in some way or another. And then there
are the chosen few who possess the special inner glow
of life. They hold the secret to the greatest gift of
all, the key to the true meaning of life and the true
understanding of eternal happiness.

These are the ones who are here to teach his way, to
see life through his eyes and convey the spiritual
fulfillment of becoming one with the self and him with-
out fear. These will meet others who have fallen astray
and forgotten their primary purpose on earth. They will
touch minds and hearts and souls of many through words
of hope, words of truth and with the magic of love.

They excel a majestic aura, reuniting us back into his
never tiring, everlasting awaiting arms, where we once
came from. Even as their souls are extricated from their
earthly bodies and set free to pervade the heavenly skies,
they will still shine as immaculate stars, dancing silvery,
illustratively, through the nocturnal of the universe,
beautiful as he has created us.

Debbie Valero-Wright

GROWING UP

It's a crime to be knocked down
Or pinned against a wall
It's a crime to have your dreams shattered
Than to have had none at all.

It's the pain that fills your heart
That yearns to go away
And it's the youth who can't smile or sing
When they are lead astray.

Then it's time to make a choice in life
When the diverged road is reached
Whether to stay or go, and in which direction
Using the knowledge of all that's been preached.

And no matter which way you turn
Your days begin to count down
The present becomes past and the future to be
'Til the day comes to bare a smile or a frown.

Rose Yau

I'LL THINK OF MOTHER

When the snow melts away,
promising sunny days,
I'll think of mother, so giving in her ways.

When a cloud disappears,
leaving the blue sky clear,
I'll think of mother, so heartwarming and dear.

When leaves begin to fall,
and autumn's shadows so tall,
I'll think of mother, her love encompasses all.

When I fail no matter how hard I try,
and deep breaths are followed by an empty sigh,
I'll think of mother, forever she wiped the tears dry.

When I hit a low peak,
my mind burdened and weak,
I'll think of mother, her comfort I'll seek.

When of the world I am more knowing,
the changes of life all showing,
I'll think of mother, my love for her growing.

Kerry Lynne Barkley

THE CHOICE IS THERE

Life — it's only lived one day.
For our tomorrows; come what may.
  Yesterday's a memory —
  For it, we can't be sorry.

Here, this day, we own a prize.
It may cause sadness, it may bring sighs.
It may cause gladness, it may bring cries.
  It all begins at sunrise.

This gift I speak of is "today,"
To do with whatever we may.
  To pass each moment with a kiss,
  Embracing what we shouldn't miss.
  Or see moments as nothing more
  Than tools to make the day soar.

The choice is there for our taking
Every morning upon our waking:
To live today and know we've kissed her,
Or let it pass and learn we've missed her.

Judy L. Rehn

REHN, JUDY LYNN. Born: Milwaukee, Wisconsin, 2-27-61; Married: 2-11-84 to James D. Rehn; Education: Mount Mary College, University of Wisconsin, Parkside, B.A. 12-20-83; Occupation: Elementary Teacher; Comments: *The first time I wrote a poem, my boyfriend was my inspiration. He is now my husband, and continues to be my main source of inspiration. My family and loved ones have all been contributors to my poetry. Their love and closeness have inspired me to put my feelings into poetic words.*

THE GEESE

When the geese flock together
'Tis sure to be bad weather
and the Geese they used to go
over in flocks in the spring
and in the fall but they seem
to be over any type of
the year because of the change
in the season but they are
a wonderful migrating bird
to have fly over and have around.

Lawrence Peltzer

DRAGON OF DREAMS

Tread softly for the dragon sleeps
When moonlight comes, he crawls and creeps
Through village, town, and meadow keeps
Quiet as you pass him by
All havoc breaks on opened eye
Begins the tremble of Earth and Sky

I see the monster as he lay
And find it hard to creed thy say
Let me touch, then on my way

You blessed fool, you oaf, you cad!
Erase the thought that you just had

A touch, a pet, a gentle stroke, what dreaded temper could that evoke?

Have you not listened you mindless imp; can you be such a simple simp?

Your insults Sir, they phase me not, for I shall do just as I want

I see no good to persist; with mind of stone, you do insist

Be on your way, man of wise
Who covers truth in tainted lies

When blood boils and flesh screams
You'll know what is not as it seems
Reality cannot hide in dreams

Maria M. O'Sullivan

O'SULLIVAN, MARIA M. Born: New York City, 9-8-62; Education: Queens College, CUNY, B.A., English, 1984; Occupations: Teacher, Free Lance Writer; Memberships: PETA, People for the Ethical Treatment of Animals; Writings: *Tayder, Frogs, Mrs. Meanie and Me,* children's fiction, to be published in the near future; Comments: *Life is a conformity; writing is an anomaly. The author is creator and destroyer, entertainer and educator, bore and baffler. A writer doesn't have reality's boundaries. I commonly write about children, animals, and childish adults. And I always write for an audience, even if that audience is only me.*

ANGOTEE AT DAWN

i

The moments move like soft mists
On still waters
And I shall not forget this solitude
Or the cold dawn that tries in me
The patience of the fathers.

ii

Hoarfrost and the gelid seas:
I rest on these this frail life.
Like vast floes on still waters
The moments laze. Nothing here.
Ajornarmat.

iii

As I move through the night-sun's
                                    glow
I dream of certain distant lands
Where the springs are very often mild
And the summers hot as fire itself.

J. A. Zinsmeister

HIDDEN VALUES

Like a tarnished penny
    thrown away
"You're dull and useless
    now," you say
But what it is
    you fail to see
Is what is deep
    inside of me
A caring person
    with a heart of gold
An inner beauty
    so I'm told
Now when you stop
    and polish me
It's not really
    hard to see
Like the stars
    that shine above
There's someone here
    for you to love

Vicki Weichenthal

HOME

Home is made of such as these:
    A house set back among the trees;
A lovely house that breathes an air,
    Of happy people living there;
A leafy branch above the door,
    Paints lacy sunlight on the floor;
Geraniums nod upon the sill,
    Between crisp curtains' jaunty frill;
Inside, a cheery welcome waits,
    For all who enter through its gates;
A glowing fire, an easy chair,
    With books to banish daily care,
A house where all who enter see,
    Its owner's personality
Reflected in its atmosphere,
    And feel its all-pervading cheer;
These things and more make up a home,
    A house where people love to come;
Of all the things that make home blest,
    Home where love abides is best.

Mable L. Ferguson

CROSSROADS

Your hand slipped
I knew even if I clung
you would leave

my heart's rope spun out
and tied
making a bridge
for you to cross.
Your haunting eyes
as you took the first step,
the bridge swayed,
red oil dripped
from a twisted fiber wrenched
beneath the weight,
a braided fragment tore
you leaped, reaching
the other side.
The frayed rope recoiled
tears cannot wash away
the stenciled footprints.

Carol E. Wolf

ACCEPTING FATE

Only a trace of a smile remains,
    Vanishing as the wind steals it
    from your bewildered face.
Time once given to you,
    Now is slipping from your eager
    grasp.
Battling an unknown force,
    You don't know your rank
    yet the gun surely fires.
Carrying withered remains,
    You treasure the rose of yesterday.
Crying in the night.
    You regret the disappearance of
    a song you had once sung.

The questions unanswered are many,
But — listen!
The wind is approaching.
Leave the memories with me.
Let the wind gently take you away.

Carolyn McGrath

WHO WILL TEND THE FLOWERS

The little house sits empty now
Staring with naked haunting eyes
At the frequent passers-by
Who give it but a glance;
Few see the lonely tears
That fall from a broken pane
To the rotting porch below.
The tiny yard, now overgrown,
Is strewn with fallen boughs —
All speaks of gross neglect.
E'en the mighty oak that towers
Over all seems to know that life
Has gone from the old homeplace
And droops his heavy head;
Will no one tend the flowers now
That once bloomed in little rows
But now helter-skelter grow?
Now that the wizened hand that
Cared for them is gone,
Who will tend the flowers?

Jan Wolfe

CABERNET AND SWISS

Dazed;
Beneath a cloud
A shower of thoughts
Indicative of our present path
Whetted my appetite.

Wine, a bite
It began to rain.

Dewdrops upon the iris
Traced remembrances
of one former love where
Once he had placed
Long and tender kisses.

Another bite soaks dry the well.
I drink.

Soon the thundering cloud passes
Revealing a shapely,
Cantaloupe-slice of a moon;
Wedged between shooting stars
Aimed at these cheeks,
Your target for icy acknowledgment.

I am drunk; I am famished
No more.

Vivian J. Verstoep

VERSTOEP, VIVIAN J. Born: Newburgh, New York; Education: Vassar College, Poughkeepsie, New York, Class of 1978; Occupation: Marketing Representative for major multi-line insurance company for which I write a trade-oriented newsletter; Comments: *I write my best poetry when I am depressed and/or frustrated about a specific issue or circumstance. I am thankful that my poetry portfolio is limited and balance it out with character sketches, short stories and novellas.*

A Wise Man once said
One picture is worth a thousand words
But I say
Not a million pictures
Can equal the Warmth
The completeness
Of your embrace.

C. Robertson

THE WHIRLPOOL.

BIT OF HEAVEN

After a busy day,
Let us kneel and pray,
Then I sit and recall,
God's wonders large and small,
This is a bit of Heaven.

To watch a blazing sunset,
Seeing the first fall of snow,
To know peace and never war,
To be rich and never poor,
This is really a bit of Heaven.

To have seen a man walk on the moon,
To really be loved by your fellow man,
Putting one's dreams into action,
To smell a rose after a quick shower,
Feeling a cool breeze on a warm summer night,
This is a bit of Heaven.

Hearing the ringing of a church bell so near,
Never again to know the meaning of fear,
To hold your loved one close to your heart,
And being sure you'll never part,
To knowing one's children will always be safe,
This really is a bit of Heaven.

Carrie L. Como

BIRTH OF KNOWLEDGE

Horse nebula birthing stars,
They're points of lights from where we are.
Earth itself a birthing place
For man, who struggles to find his face.

The gift of light is many things,
To warm, to see, the knowledge it brings.
A door is opening, *dare* we step through?
The future awaits, it's all up to you.

Diana McGlynn

McGLYNN, DIANA MAY. Born: Kansas City, Kansas, 8-23-47, Deceased 5-6-85; Married: 2-27-81 to Robert M. McGlynn; Education: Junior at California State University, Fullerton, A.A. in Liberal Arts, emphasis, Anthropology; Occupation: Police Officer; Memberships: California State University, Fullerton; Anthropological Association; Awards: Mt. San Antonio College Faculty Association Award for Outstanding Scholastic Achievement, First Place. This award included her work: "Data Base: Earth, a Student's Guide to Physical Geography," a tutorial, May 1984.

CUMBERLAND FALLS

The odors of damp earth and pine
wrapped around us like a lover.
We discovered a stream
and swam, naked,
in the icy water.
At dusk you saw the first star
and we followed its glow down the path.
You walked ahead
and when I stumbled behind you,
you knelt to pick me up.
And when you swept the spider webs from my eyes,
I could smell cool mountain water in your hair.

B. L. Clemmons

CAPTAIN

The Captain's very first love is his boat,
    Happy is he when they're afloat!
        The Captain and his boat

The Captain's other love is his 1st mate,
    For within her he puts his fate!
        The Captain and his boat

The Captain masters all kind of weather,
    Deep inside his heart is light as a feather!
        The Captain and his boat

The Captain has great respect for the water,
    There he finds peace as if it were his father!
        The Captain and his boat

Gloriann Mclin

INSIGHT

From the top of the hill stood a tall tower.
Down a steep, narrow road.

All the cars went in to see a sight, birds gathering
into the sunset.

There people swim out into the open. And the meadows
were so grown up.

In daytime grass smells so green. I laid down along
the way.

Sundown came and brought the sailboats to the shores.
Across the lake lights yelled to the owner of the bay,
come in . . .

Betty Williams

FAREWELL

You offered a night, it turned into time
    That filled my heart, my soul, my mind
We shared our thoughts, frustrations and dreams
    I fell in love, for the first time it seems
The time in measurement was small
    Yet emotions spent it was eternity's all
I offered a feeling, I called it love
    But not returned, it fell short, not above
I offered a growth, like a plant when new
    You took it, you knew it, you gave it back used
My growth, this love, for you now is gone
    Friendship remains, no regrets, to me my heart belongs
I now move on, like a road, so do you
    To new horizons, to new feelings true
We'll pass each other, we'll offer a wave
    We'll smile our thoughts, as we go our own way

L. D. McKay

EPING CHILD

sound of the leaves
ustling in the wind.
He was
a million miles away
doing the impossible.
He was
the mightiest
in the universe,
a master of slaves,
yet
       a slave
         to all matter.
Every desire of his
was fulfilled,
every thought
    materialized.

He stirred.
A hint of restlessness
flashed
      across his face.
A sigh.
The long,
      yet momentary,
      struggle
         was fragmented.

Nimet Mawji

SOUL FLIGHT

The isolating, limiting parameters
Of life,
Constrict me and bind me
With unbreakable ties,
To a prison of responsibility
And repetitious tasks.
My soul within shrivels
And longs —
To shed its earthly shell,
To flee to the freedom
Of ethereal realms.

Meg Gibson

UNLOCK THE DOOR

Unlock the door, with this
               key to my heart.

Take hold of a dream
            that you'd like to start.

Unlock the door, before
            years pass me by,

And dreams I hold closest,
            fade in the sky.

For dreams have a way of slipping,
            as life closes in,

While we search to find out,
            where our dreams have been.

Then someone came along,
            taking hold of my dream

That a heart still held tightly,
            with an ageless gleam.

He unlocked the door,
            and made confetti of my life.

Barbara L. Light

YOUR CHOSEN ONE

For Carle

A single golden band
radiates the sensuous
immortality of love.
So shouldn't I wonder
what blessed me with
this metamorphosis?
Shouldn't I already know?

Thou truly are.
(The Renaissance of my life).
And Thou truly gifted me
with an eternal glow of love
and the one that makes
it possible —
your chosen one for me.

Martha Hayter Peterson

WINDS

The wind comes in a rowdy crowd of gusts
it pulls at your clothes
checks your pockets for change
and swallows your umbrella whole.
It dances with leaves a disco ballet
then hurls an empty can at your car.
The wind is a prankster
overturning what it can
it plays in the trees
flips over garbage cans.

John E. Madden IV

FOR MOTHER

I was your most precious child,
Or so you said.
Then why did you scar my crib
with outlandish sallies?
Cripple my flight to hope
With cries of foul?
I made my way delicately
out of the womb.
To see what was about,
Here, there, everywhere.
Always I tiptoed to cause no pain.
I found overturned troughs
of the heedless.
The rabble of convention.
The gumminess of words.
Where is the God you promised
Would be what you could not?

A. L. Morgan, IV

A POEM

I saw a poem in the air.
It did not make me wonder.
But in the light of my despair,
I sat alone.

I wrote the words I saw out there
And quickly gave them thought.
Each word a different meaning was to bear,
No match for any other.

The poem was a breeze, a moment,
For whomever chose to share, to care,
Observe and then to ponder why.
As fingers pit pen and journey,
I'm not alone . . .
But keeping company with my words.

Deborah Lomax Hall

A NEW DAY HAS DAWNED

As I open my eyes, a new day
has dawned, awakened from night, with
a melody of song.

A bird I hear, singing happily
with glee, a world of wonder, is
waiting for me.

I live each day as it comes
to me, for tomorrow will come, only
the past to be.

Lessons to learn, challenges
to meet, careful not to choose, a
dead end street.

Darkness draws near, day's at
end, tomorrow will be, and I'll
start again.

Joan M. Frascella

THERE YOU LAY

There you lay, so soundly dreaming
About the many love-filled days
We've shared together,
With a blanket draped
Lightly around you.
I patiently watch you
Putting every part of your face
Under my fingers' touch.
You quietly breathe and a smile
Suddenly comes to your face.
Do you sense my presence?
I am here to protect you from harm.
How could I have been so lucky
I think to myself, to have met you
That bright, sunny day
On the empty, isolated beach.
You, my love, bring so much to my life
And I could not think
Of not having you
For the rest of my life.

Mary Jeanne Russell

YOUR EYES

Your eyes are there,
  I see them.
And it makes me think
Of the time I held a cow's eye
  In my hand.
It felt moist
Like a boiled egg without the shell.
It looked up at me, sunny-side up,
Blank, thoughtless only eye.
It makes me think
Of that dog you keep around the house
  As your mirror;
I wonder if the dog
Sees the same in you.

Your eyes are there,
  I see them.
Two boiled eggs,
You without your shell,
Barking out at the world.

Adrianne Saunders

MY LADY

Fly my lady, fly away;
    No more fear the night.
Spread your wings and meet the sky;
    Free yourself in flight.

I, my lady, I must stay;
    Stay and face the foe.
No more tears, my life, my love;
    Spread your wings and go.

Soon my lady, we will lie
    Somewhere in the light.
Somehow we will touch again,
    Where the day is bright.

So, my lady, turn away,
    Or my heart will cry.
I would beg you then to stay;
    You and I would die.

Fly my lady, fly away;
    Fear not for my life.
I will love you for all time,
    Lady mine, my wife.
            Mark White

SNOW DOG

I saw a dog this morning,
of which I did not know.
He was a little rambler
but where is he to go?

He seemed so lost and
yet so bold,
but then, of course,
so very cold.

I wonder if the owners know
of what they had done.
They let their pet loose one cold day
for them it seemed like fun.

The owners then forgot their pet
and let him out off-line,
and now that good and fluffy pet
is one they cannot find.

I hope the people doing this
are somewhat so-called smart.
I know they lack of one good thing —
that's what's known as heart.
            Mrs. G. Smith

And she glistened as a diamond
As she stood there, center stage,
Waiting for her entrance
As she turned the final page.
The script was at long last ending
And she heaved a glad relief.
The act had been long in rehearsal
And the scenario was filled with grief.
She turned for the final curtain
And awaited the applause and cheers,
But she found the stage was empty
And dissolved into sobs and tears.
Had the play been all for nothing?
Where was her just reward?
Broken she looked around her
For the gold and silver sword.
Shaking she reached to take it
And holding it to her chest,
Screamed for heaven's mercies
As she put herself to rest.
            Cynthia Lynn Godwin

TRUE LOVE

Life gives us a measure of encounters to endure,
There are some we cannot overcome, I am sure.
Then, there are those that pull you and push you until you are no longer you,
And the love you had slips away and leaves to find you in the blue.

Yes, life has its ups-and-downs, this I know,
And with it are the glories and sorrows to take in tow.
But true Love has a different quality to see,
For it never comes nor ever goes forcefully.

Consider for a moment how an eagle soars ever so sure,
Steady and certain is True Love that waits patiently to endure.
For, if an eagle can soar to find its prey,
How much more shall we if we simply kneel and pray?

Yea, I say unto you whose heart beats to a tune,
Fortunes are not made of ambitions careless and soon.
Nor is life wrought in the flight of a love,
For many have fallen and many have cried to the One above.

So, let us be patient and listen to our hearts.
For it is there that the Master speaks and never departs.
Let Him in, my friend,
For he is True Love, to love you alway to the end.
            Frank E. Rocha

THE OTHER SIDE

Some say it's a gift, being able to wait like I do.
Often it's some of my feelings, — that are trying to break through.
It seems to lighten my load, writing what's on my mind.
Relieving some of my pressures, leaving attitudes behind.
It's kind of hard to explain, when I start writing I disappear.
Putting myself with the words, that soon will end up here.
Maybe I'm with a man, or on a big cloud's knee.
Drifting through a meadow, and out of reality.
It usually doesn't matter, any place or time.
I can sit with a pen and some paper, to write a few more lines.
I can write about a mountain, or write how to pretend.
Write about a mysterious life, and write about a friend.
I have written about death, because we all must go.
I've written about life, the parts of it I know.
I have written about myself, a side that no one has met.
Hiding behind my face that you see, another that is unborn yet.
She only comes out in words, telling me what to say.
I write what she feels, I feel it too, then we go on our way.
            Marla Cuellar

A HELPING HAND

As you walk down the darkened path of life,
A small ray of sunlight glows warmly upon your face.
You reach out for it, because you know if you try hard enough,
It could be yours.

All the years of uncertainty
Now are all contained within this one small thing.
As you strain to reach it,
You feel life's hardened standards begin to pull you down.

Just as you begin to weaken, and lose all hope,
In the distance you see a helping hand.
Through combined eforts you struggle,
Just to touch the thing that means more to you right now than anything else.

Darkness falls once again
As you lie resting upon life's beaten path.
As you stand,
You feel hurt, and disappointed.

You have lost to life just as many others like you,
But in your heart you know
Through that helping hand,
You have gained an everlasting friend.
            Teresa M. Wheeler

GOD MADE THE BODY

God made the body,
each separate part. He
even gave us a heart;
some parts are large,
yet some are small.
Just think of our toes.
We need them all.
If we keep all our
parts it makes us glad.
If one is lost it hurts
so bad!

Our church has members
not all are smart; yet
some are great like the
heart. The weaker ones
are needed too, even if
it's just a few.

Minnie Earp

THE ROAD SOUGHT

At first, methinks, we pacify
Those souls who would protest

For Passion's plan is never clear
To he who fears unrest

And if wits are gathered with Pride
And kept as to stay fresh

Then the burdens of the future
Become today's Success

As with trees of silenced echoes
Whose stumps are left to rot

Hope is forever beside you now
Patience is the road sought

J. M. Hill

WHY DO YOU?

Why do you snap at me,
Tell me I'm too childish,
Then moan for your younger days?
Why do you slap me,
Tell me I am awful,
Then command me to kiss you
goodnight?
Why do you make me go away,
Say that I'm a nuisance,
Then complain that I'm never around?
Why do you scream at me to be still,
Then shake me because I'm a statue?
Why do you yell at me to be quiet,
Then cry because I never speak to you
anymore?
Why do you do these things?
Are you angry and confused,
like me?
Why don't you answer me?

Vanessa E. Beach

CINQUAIN

Concert —
aging Maestro
and vibrant performers
become as one with Beethoven's
breathing . . .

Helen Olsen Snead

TOGETHER WE WATCHED

By flickering candlelight we sat
    Watching shadows in the dark gray night
Holding on to one another
    Lest we forget the springtime of our lives
All is quiet now, the only sound is the wind in the willow
    Tomorrow we will work the ground and prepare the fields
But for now we'll be content to listen to the mockingbirds twill
    The aroma of fresh-brewed coffee fills my senses
My heart beats like a big bass drum
    My mind races back, bringing up old memories
Our dog wags his tail as if he understands
    Together we'll sit, watching each other and renewing our love
        for we love one another
Eye to eye, then cheek to cheek, silver and gray atop our heads
    No need to speak
Life has been good, full and plentiful

Calvin E. Tyrrell

TYRRELL, CALVIN E. Born: 1941; Married: 23 years, two children, a boy, 21, a girl, 18; Occupation: Real Estate & Financial Planning; Hobbies: Song Writing/Writing Poetry & Short Stories; Poetry: 'New Poets of Summer,' Poetry Anthology, 'Lawrence of Nottingham,' Poetry Anthology, *Poems by: Calvin E. Tyrrell*, Other Writings: 'We're Going To Tampa,' Song, recorded.

GROUND RULES

How was I to know when we met what the ground rules were?
They were never laid out for me.
I couldn't guess that you wanted a soft, purring kitten to warm your lap,
Someone for you to stroke and to entertain you until you told her
    it was now time to get down.
That you had to visit the person you loved.

I didn't know I was to be a prize to be shown off to parents and friends.
"Look what I captured, isn't she cute?"
That I was to be regarded as no more than this,
Certainly not to be taken seriously,
That another was on your mind through it all.

I didn't think to question your envelopes of sweet words —
    I thought they were from the heart.
The anxious embraces of such deep longing —
    I thought they were from the depth of your soul.
The light from your blue eyes reflected back at me with such intensity
    and unexpected warmth —
    I thought it was a white light from your spirit.
The response of your body when I explored its wonder —
    It all seemed very real to me.

I feel deceived and shattered and betrayed.
The ground rules were never explained.
You never told me I wasn't supposed to fall in love with you.

Rosemarie Bem

THE MOUNTAIN

Towering here before me — The Mountain,
A picturesque Speck in God's hand.
But to me a mystical monumental giant —
A symbol of Life on the Land.
Just the weight of it humbles my
fragile being, but He can move it with ease
If only to crumble or re-form it or
cover it with the seas.
Like a high note struck on the piano
in the midst of a floating, dreamy melody
it stands — awaiting a new formation
by the strength of the Master's hands.

James E. Loeffert

ABUSE, THE NEXT GENERATION

In the twilight of my mind lurks a shadowy figure.
Tall and lean, with purple nails glittering against a fluorescent
moonlight.
Eyes annoyed at my quivering frame, gaze through my hollow soul.
   Now the pain comes, sharp waves of pain; Each new blow echoes
against an old one unwilling to die.
   The shadowy figure fades, purple nails disappear into their
hiding places.
I float in and out of madness, agony toying at my bones. Horror
whispering to my heart; "Until tomorrow my dear, tomorrow."
   But time heals all wounds they say, and fluorescent moons are
eons behind me now.
   I like the purple nails glittering in the night, as I lash
out at the trembling little body beneath my claws.
It seems justifiable somehow; as if a gift, handed down through
generations of fluorescent moonlights.

Janie M. Porch

WHAT HAPPENS TO LOVE

What happens to Love when it wears out
Or isn't it really gone?
It seems it's here, but then it's not
It used to seem so strong
What happens to Love when it wears out
I thought it was here to stay
It's supposed to make the difference
I guess Life deals it that way
Maybe it's up to us to try to keep that Love alive
In everything that we do and say, we've got to make it thrive
Love is Life and without Love, we would surely die
We've got to give Love that honest-to-goodness try
Give of yourself 100 percent and bend over backwards, too
Walk that extra mile, it really will pay off for you
What happens to Love when it wears out — it never goes away!
It's lying dormant within all of us, so get it and use it today!

Nancy L. Fantom

THE WIFE

She has done something that very few women
In this day and age would do. When her husband,
Lost his job she said that is no excuse for a divorce.
Then the wife turned right around and found
A job for both herself and her husband. The average
Woman would run to a lawyer at the first sign
Of trouble. This woman is not average and she does
Work her marriage problems without the use
And discretion of a lawyer. This woman is special,
Very special because she just wants to be married
To her husband. The average woman must have a lawyer,
Because they do not want to be married over a long
Period of time. All you have to do, is to pick up
Any newspaper and you can read about some woman
Who is going to a lawyer or court against her husband
                    or ex-husband

Michael R. Swartwood

AND IN ALL

All that blooms is not a rose,
Not all dark clouds bring rain.
The young that strive shall be successful.
Forgotten woods are not walked by man.
From the mountains a mist shall be summoned,
And a sunset from the sky shall be born.
Memories shall be remembered once more.
The heartless again shall take heart.

All that is lost is not forgotten,
Not all mortal men possess mortality.
The spoken one who is wise shall be heard.
Deep waters are not touched by foot.
From the sky a light shall stream,
And a sign from the hawk shall flee.
Free shall his fellowship flow.
The powerless again shall gain power.

Rhonda L. Oligney

THE STAND

Silently he does make every stride that he takes.
Silently here I wait,
silently I anticipate.
With every breath we both take, closer here he does make.
Quietly, without a sound, he stops dead still on the ground.
With head held high and nostrils flared,
inspects he the October air.
Motionless here do we stand, the animal and the man.
Time passed by, I held my gun.
"Damn it, God! Why don't you run?"
One loud crash, the deed is done.
First light now, the morning sun.
Surrounded now by all of us,
an open fire, we drink robust.
Feigning pride, I wax disgust.
This senseless slaughter, a bloody lust.
Ashes to ashes, dust to dust.

Mack Hamiter

IN MY MIND

In my mind I can still see you lying next to me.
I can still hear you tell me that you love me.
Then one morning I wake up and realize you were gone.
The teardrops fell like a waterfall down a mountainside.
In my mind I can see you and her, walking hand in hand
Down the street.
You were once my friend, my love, and someone I could turn to.
I close my eyes, and picture you once more.
But in my heart I know it will never be the same.
Now all I have are the memories of you and me in my mind.

June McRae

SHATTERED PIECES

My life feels like fine, blown glass — shattered,
Thrown against a wall — tattered.
Serrated fragments,
Shattered,
Scattered,
The fragments are retrieved,
Piecemeal —
just parts,
only pieces,
having no meaning,
waiting to be fixed,
but nothing fits.
Too much hurt,
Too much pain,
For things to ever be the same,
My life is glass — shattered.
Thrown against a wall — tattered.

Sister Frances Weber, S. L.

THE RED MAPLE

Walking through the woods
I lingered
Near a magnificent red maple,
In its shade
Numberless moments
Of heaven-ordained love
Had enmeshed us.
A pile of ashes marked the spot,
On top of the heap
Lay a pair of dark-rimmed glasses
Which had framed
The undefined color of his eyes;
Were they steel blue or slate gray?
Again — the answer eluded me . . .
Did it matter?
I shuddered
As I recalled
The shallowness of his caring,
Limited to the shade
Of the red maple.

Ruth Grande

IF YOU WERE HERE WITH ME

If you were here with me,
We could walk away,
Along the coasts to nowhere,
Watch sunsets to our west,
Wishing on stars come to rest.
The wanderer and his ways,
Has yet to anchor a place to stay,
You've mended my heart when broken,
We've been apart,
Since our last token.

I'd take you to places of the sea,
That's a big part of the one you love,
In places low, in spaces above.
Across each breaker to lands unknown,
With every ebbing tide and foam,
One day the sea will return,
With shells and drifting wood to burn,
Along with sailors that long the shore,
And all the women you have in store.

Paul E. Cheney

SOUL

The soul, an embryo in time,
Carrying a program for the mind.
Of time and other places,
The revealing of other faces.

The soul reveals through the dream,
Of lives before, it would seem.
The dream, a window to the soul,
Allows a look through this hole.

A glimpse of life, lived before
From the soul, the living core.
The soul, an essence of life,
The mind in constant strife.

Have you had that feeling?
That sets your mind reeling.
Have you set your goal?
Have you consulted your soul?
    Have you?

Richard E. Laubengeyer

WHY MUST YOU GO SO SOON

I've sat waiting
for many an hour
And watched the wilting
of many a flower

I went to pick the rose
precisely at noon
For you: I have returned
why must you go so soon

When unleashed
our hearts collide
Why now
do you suddenly hide

Dark does come
I stare at the moon
Under the beams I sit: wondering
why must you go so soon

Jill Anderson

PASSING THOUGHT

While I was lying in bed last night
I pondered all life's questions,
Considered the world's problems
And came up with some suggestions.

I had conquered world hunger
And devised a plan for peace,
Cured the ills of society
And even stopped crime in the streets.

I was about to write them down
As I finished thinking deep —
A beautiful world I'd created —
But just then I fell asleep.

I woke and tried again to write —
But it was not as easy as it seems,
To capture in words what I was thinking
In one of last night's dreams.

Dan Barch

Let us walk together
    hand in hand
To share our lives forever
    for our love is our band.

Kimberly A. Putnam

FREE . . . (SOMEWHAT)

Farewell, you Jill, it's reached its end:
    I'm now free from your obsession.
I no more need you as a friend:
    I've escaped from your possession.

I've loved you as no man dare love,
    You who lives without compassion,
You whom I once begged the help of
    To exorcise my madd'ning passion.

But you'd not deign to come to me —
    Me whom you viewed with such disdain.
To me you'd give no charity:
    Why heed my cry with nought to gain?

My love for you I can't repeal,
    But you'll not haunt me day and night.
Those wounds from you can never heal,
    But no more odes to you I write.

John M. Andrews

THANK YOU PRAYER

Thank You Lord for all good things
Thank You Lord for the joy You bring

Thank You Lord for the love You share
Thank You Lord for the load You bear

Thank You Lord for suffering our strife
Thank You Lord for giving Your life

We love You, Lord, this we pray
Thank You Lord for showing the way.

Brenda Joyce Read

FRIDAY AT 5:30

She pointed across the street
and sipped her drink. Upstaging
a crowded sidewalk cafe,
cherry blossoms bloomed; pink petals
placed on bare branches.
She had an old friend in Washington, D.C.;
I watched to see the petals fall.

Robert H. Berg

REQUIEM

Vietnam, what did you do to me?
    You were so cruel to me.
I seem to have lost all hope;
    I can no longer cope:
with the stench of death,
    and the feelings of 'lost'.
What is the cost:
    The price to pay?
My sanity? My soul? My life?
    I have lost all hope.
I will forget what you did
    to me.

Robin A. McGuire

GROWING DOWN

I long for compassion
and forgiveness
from myself
as I grow weary,
almost broken down,
from the onslaught
of painful memories
and regretful tears
which drown my hope
and nourish the illusion
that pride was more valuable
than love.

Joy Breckenridge

WINTER

Winter brings freshness,
A nip of cold in the air.
Winter brings crispness,
A wave of snow flurries your way.
Winter brings depth,
Snow encrusted castles to your dreams.
Winter brings vastness,
Icicle canyons sending echoes of beauty.
Winter brings distance,
Time for your mind to wander.
Winter brings adventure,
A time for escape.

Teresa M. Tribbett

LIKE A LOVER OR A FRIEND

The wood doves call and call
Through this soft century
And the honeysuckle sends up its perfume
To our window here,
But we sleep on.

Wild rose and celandine wake for us
In these meadows. From the elm
An oriole repeats his clear cadenza and
The hummingbirds sing too,
But we sleep on.

We do not hear them, though the far-off sea
Talks to herself and murmurs through our dreams
Her endless love, we do not hear,
Who, in careless sleep, live on,
Hearing not the sound nor understanding
The meaning behind the sound.

The Soul knows her own loveliness, but she
Sets the Truth far from her, and attempts
This way and that way, as a friend to a friend,
Or a lover to a lover,
To cause us to see for ourselves
The beauty that is not only outside
But in.

Raymond H. Clines

NO MORE PROMISES

There is no ball and chain, you know
Binding you to my side
And there never will be.

So you do your thing and I'll do mine
Without those promises which make you feel
Too constricted, so confined.

You are free to go or stay
Me? I'm here — at least today
But this is not a promise.

Because I don't make them
When I intend to break them
No matter how large or small.

This is why I don't like you very much right now
No, I don't
Not at all.

For you broke a promise to me
And that I don't forgive so easily
You've hurt me inside, don't you see?

But, I still love you . . .

Melissa Baldwin

HOME

Home is where you go after school
Home is where you can relax.
Home is where you have lived most of your life.
Home is where you can go crazy without anyone seeing you.
Home is the place you find love.
Home is the place you find peace.
If there is any place I'd rather be
Home is the place for me,
Our home is the best for me.
It may not have all the luxuries
Of many other homes,
But it is enough,
Everything I really need
Is at home. Home.

Richard Kratzke

SPRING WORK BEGINS

Beneath dark mouldered leaves pink mayflowers bloom.
We clear away the doubtful rusty brown;
We give exquisite pleasure light and room.

Old withered last year's leaves posture a tomb
Of counterpoise unless we know that down
Beneath dark mouldered leaves pink mayflowers bloom.

The spring-wood breathing of these plants assume
The veil's spices. Slurring dark's renown
We give exquisite pleasure light and room.

As individual digging deftly lifts the gloom,
Moist pungence rises from each clustered crown.
Beneath dark mouldered leaves pink mayflowers bloom.

The wistful searching for this rare perfume
Dissolves insidious doubt and lets it drown
We give exquisite pleasure light and room.

Fine-fashioned on its underhanging loom
Each blossom whispers freely with her gown.
Beneath dark mouldered leaves pink mayflowers bloom;
We give exquisite pleasure light and room.

Rachel Sanderson

A ROCK CONCERT

I have seen a rock concert
I have known the trance
I became one with its dance
Music, oh how it is good

However, on my head it can act as a hood
Yes, a hood
Not because of itself, but because of me

High on anything can be the greatest separation
    between birth and life's expiration

Loosing oneself to meditation
Is not meditation, but concentration
In meditation there are no highs
In meditation there also are no lies

I accept you for you, I accept your music too
Do you see what you must do, you are lost and I am too
If you love me and you do, accept me and yourself too

Don't leave out the world as you get high
This my friend is the greatest lie
If you do I may cry, yet my work will not die

Gregory J. Paul

TO MY SON

Hey there, my little man, who investigates all things. I
wonder if you realize, the happiness your little smile
brings. The tears you cry, when you hurt, melt my heart
in a burning pain. I will always be there for your
comfort, just to see your little smile again. When at
first, I laid my eyes on you, my wondrous little man; I
was so proud, I proclaimed to the world: "It's a boy; he's
my little man!" I look at you, as you work hard in your
play. Knowing I'll love you, forever and a day. You tease
all who so hard, try your affections to gain. Giving in at
last, to a kiss and a hug, when thought the love offered,
was spent away, in vain. I dream of so many things for
you, though your life I cannot live. I must say right now,
while you're but a babe, I'll let you have anything, in my
power to give.
Love Daddy

R. L. Barclay

MACHINE AGE BLUES

It could have come upon us
With a pounce and a prayer for survival

It came upon us
With a gradually increasing breath of fresh air
Until we were used to it
And then suddenly it suffocated us

Winners or losers we are playing the game
Our thoughts may travel to a village in South Africa
Where villagers work with their mother, Earth

We are computerized, machine age monsters

DEMORALIZED

By numbers, tickets, tapes, impersonal people
Talking to all of us the same
When our goals and fears are never analyzed

Let's go back to being people

Perhaps unsmiling, unfeeling voices
Were fine for a time

Perhaps it's time to change

Eric Kuklick

ISSUES OF LOVE

I know that you're down and not up to par,
But remember I'm here. I never go far.

Ending issues of love isn't always easy,
It's funny how the heart can make the stomach feel queasy.

The only relief I can hope to shed,
Is that everyone's dealt with the thoughts in your head.

Others have come and others will go.
You just have to learn to go with the flow.

I know it sounds easy for me to say,
But you're better off single 'cause life's meant for play.

The people we meet and the feelings we greet,
Will all form to prove that just living's a feat.

Any hurt you are feeling or wish to spare,
Over time will vanish right into thin air.

You'll find that time is the ultimate master,
I only wish he'd sometimes go faster.

So if it's of any help at all,
Your friends are all here, just give us a call.

Carol Roberts

NIGHT MOODS

. . . floating images appear before me as the
        night slumbers on.
the velvety darkness enhancing the theatrical
        sequences . . . one by one like pieces
        of jigsaw puzzle . . . forming, re-arranging
        bittersweet memories of you.
with all the efforts i could muster
        i shut my eyes too tight . . . till they hurt.
yet sleep eluded me.
the faint tinged dawn appears and i arise
        to face another day without you.

Rowena P. Gaad

FAERIE

Many years ago in an enchanted time,
I met a faerie of the woodland.

His gentle ways claimed my heart,
and his songs of joy bewitched my soul.

Fair to gaze upon was he,
and I spent many an enraptured hour under his spell.
But, elfin hearts rarely linger long in one wood
for they seek a prize called wonder.

Now in rare moments of solitude
when the hush of twilight   falls on a midsummer's eve,
I remember the enchanter's nightshade.

And I wonder.

Beverly Van Allen

*"The President has decided to stockpile
neutron bombs." (From a news report
on Friday, August 5, 1981.)*

Let's go down under the Oak Tree for awhile,
The world just took a step closer to crazy.
Madness seems to be the prevailing style,
Let's lie in the cool breeze and be lazy.

I've got a "let's drop out" kind of feeling,
My "hope wick" is burning quite low.
It's neutron bombs with which I'm dealing,
Protecting buildings, while people must go.

So let's drop out for an hour or two.
And watch as birds drop by for a drink.
Eyes may get heavy, and if they do,
Let's sleep! Let's sleep! What do you think?

Ronald D. Soucy

A THOUGHT

Life without meaning,
is a meaningless life indeed,
indeed if one should crave living,
the living should be worthwhile,
while most lives qualify as worthwhile, that
is in the eyes of the beholder,
as beauty is in the eyes of the beholder as well,
beauty does not always satisfy the onlooker,
as each onlooker is looking for something different,
different in all aspects, and yet the same,
the same in spite of what others might say,
but what others might say doesn't really matter,
it's what you yourself believe in,
So say you do not believe in God, that's
your choice,
as well it will be God's choice not to believe
in you!

Waunder Oshinbanjo

GIVING

The way I feel towards you is difficult to
    put into words.
You care so much and give until I feel you
    can't give me anymore.
I try to grasp and capture a bit of what
    makes you this way, but I can't.
This generosity comes naturally for you.
It is something that can't be taken away
    from you but oh, how wonderful you
    make me feel as I share in your happiness.

Jennifer L. Morris

ODE TO HITLER

A god tore out your soul with a pitchfork.
It hangs on the town church steeple,
dripping maroon blood on the churchgoers.
but it is only you.

They lick the foul congealed blood
with their holy tongues,
hoping to reach eternal heaven,
But it is only your blood,
they can only hope for hell.

You murderer of many.
You have hidden yourself well.
Many thought you dead; I did not.

For I see you hovering above the church,
asking for forgiveness,
from the god who put you there.

But you will never be pardoned.
For you forget Christ was a Jew.
And isn't the bond between Father and Son
as deep as the bodies of your victims?

Elsa Moura

OF LAYLA AURORA ON HER CHRISTENING DAY

Sparkles of light coming white
From your eyes
To light up the lives
Of all that are here.

Waves that soothe
The very troubles of time
By just being near you,
Holding you,
Smell the scent of your hair . . .

Iridescent beauty;
A goddess of grace
One fine turn of your elegant face
Will thrill us with the flash of your eyes
And stop all of time
And send us away
To a place

Where only dreams still exist
In delicate moments of infinite bliss
To grasp and hold on to
For as long as we wish.

Suzanne Lanza

CHRISTIAN UNITY

May there be Christian unity,
Now and through all eternity,
Distress from sinless shall disperse,
Saith Savior of the universe.

Many unto belief comply,
Christian union shall justify,
Life of happiness does prepare,
Regarding world goodness and care.

Christian praise to God shall exist,
Faithful homage as an assist,
Bless the realm whose master is Lord,
God forever being adored.

On earth various folks gather,
May we all praise God together,
May friendly brotherhood increase,
Remain in unity and peace.

Andrew Benkovich

THERE'S SOMETHING ABOUT THIS ROOM

There's something about this room . . .
With its mini-shag carpet,
The stack of dry wood,
One lonely Christmas card,
Up on the mantle
Between the picture of my dead Aunt,
And my live one.

The world can't reach me here . . .
Neither the hookers on the corner,
Nor the child flunking Algebra,
Can steal the warmth
From the cracked, blue hearth.
I come here on my scary days
To build a fire and hide.

Barbara Grasselli

GRASSELLI, BARBARA SUE. Pen Name: Barbara Taylor; Born: Evansville, Indiana, 11-20-42; Education: Indiana State University, Evansville, 1976-78; University of Utah, 1978-79; Occupation: Dispatcher, Jefferson County Police Department; Poetry: 'Cry of the Wolf,' *Moving Finger*, Indiana State University, 1977; 'Gently to the Moon,' *Moving Finger*, Indiana State University, 1977; 'Snatching at the Pieces,' *Moving Finger*, Indian State University, 1978; 'How Many Ways Can You Cook Macaroni,' *Moving Finger*, Indiana State University, 1978; Other Writings: "Magic Mountains Loose Their Power In A Rainstorm," short story, *Moving Finger*, Indiana State University, 1976; Themes: *Personal feelings and experiences about single parenting, divorce, recovery from alcoholism (I have 4 years sobriety), etc.* Comments: *I write to dump feelings for myself, and often write poetry for friends as gifts. My poetry is real, honest and often shockingly raw with emotion.*

TIME

Time,
Like tiny grains of sand,
Sifts through my fingers.

Days turn into weeks.
Weeks into months.
And so on and so on and so on.

Time's memories fill my heart and mind.
Wonderful memories of days long past
When time mattered not at all.

Youth mattered.
Love mattered.
I kept time with the world.
Drifting and floating
On the wings of time.

Love found.
Love lost.
Affairs of the heart
On borrowed time.

Phyllis Moore

WATER, WATER, EVERYWHERE

Water, water, everywhere
and none suitable for drink.

Streets of running rivers,
Lots of water,
Rushing water, dirty water,
Water all around.

Clouds stalled overhead
unwilling to continue their journey.
They like it here,
so they stay for awhile
dumping their entire load of rain
in one place.

The overpasses are flooded.
The streets are flooded.
The yards are flooded, and even
the living rooms are flooded.

Water, water, everywhere
and none suitable for drink.

Helen Heyder

CHILDHOOD

I needn't know
How the wind blows,
Why the grass grows.

I needn't know
Why the sweet flower
Will someday sour.

I needn't know
Why the sky is blue
Or cause for rainbow hue.

But now to know I must,
Oh! How unjust.

I have learned,
Now I know
But the wind doesn't blow
And the grass doesn't grow
Anymore.

Paul Birrer

FROLIC IN THE TREES

Frolic in the trees,
Laughter shed by all the leaves
Whose proud branches lie patiently awake;
Anticipating the path that they might take
While engaged in the playful scurry
That is hope — and without worry
For the life that we must live,
And the pain so relative
To the heart that knows the most: —
That we are born, but not the host
Of the Majesty that is God's,
Or the seed beneath the sod.
Nor the keeper of the years;
Light that shines both far and near.

If all of you could look and see,
And learn the rhythm they taught to me;
Then, like to the merriment abound,
The mind at ease, the spirit found.

Darrin Little

CHILD'S PLAY

Another day has come
And we are not ready
As far as I can tell
The missiles grow restless
And the east is not steady

The children grow old
As they play in the field
They too are busy
With words of their own
But the powers won't yield

The struggle is ours
And yet theirs too
We build the walls
Of their prison cell
For something they didn't do

The worst of it all
Is what we have taught
They look in our eyes
For guidance but see
The wars we have fought

Vernon S. Beausoleil

SENSUOUS STORM

Unfathomable, unattainable, unpredictable
   You are my cloud.
You are amorphous and cannot be contained.
You block the sun.
Irregardless, I love you
   Sincerely and Passionately
With a love that must never be.

Delightful, detrimental, destructive
   Your love is the rain.
It is natural yet tantalizing.
It purifies my soul with poison.
Irregardless, I love you
   Sincerely and Passionately
With a love that must never be.

Colorful, capricious, charismatic
   I am a rainbow.
My promise is to One you do not know.
Your realistic eyes are blind to my gold.
Irregardless, I love you
   Sincerely and Passionately
With a love that must never be.

Mitchelle James

AS I LIE SLEEPING

The cleaners of night
take my mind
as I lie sleeping
they sprinkle me with laudanum

They brush the scraps of day
into the dark net
they switch currents
tie the senses

Their silence wipes the cylinders clean
they dust the tapes
polish the keys
and discard symptoms of diseases

They scrape away
the pinned light
pieces of scattered love
yards of trivial words

They take over without noise
and are kind to me
as I wait for the claws of morning

Gladys Bean

FORSAKEN

Ever strength — never fear,
Always knew that God was near.
Felt the sun and the rain,
Never thought to complain.

Often strength — seldom fear,
Had the feeling God could hear.
Saw the moon and the stars,
Knew the world was still ours.

Little strength — tremendous fear.
Why, oh God, aren't you near?
Dark clouds seem to fill the days,
When there's sun, there's still a haze.

Gone the strength — only fear.
Now a mind no longer clear.
Can't feel the sun or the rain,
Must find the time to complain.

No more strength — no more fear.
God did neither see nor hear.

MaryAnn Cronin

THE CANDLE

The moment subdued. It reigned.
The candle flickers. It dances.
— tells me something that I need to
hear, so solely magnificent to me as it
tells me in a counsel about myself. So
warm. So very warm.

It heals. Splendor is the candle's
wavering. — beckoning me in a rapture
of heat. Fastened to its gaiety, its
poetry is revealed to me. Only to me.
Here. Tonight.

The candle's halo is markedly happy.
A merriment. Such frolic it displays.
— musical Sabbath in the candle's glow.
Tenacious. Heart. Soul. Its
exuberance has turned my heart to a
warmed peach colour. And it sings in a
hymn. Hummmmmmmm. Heart.

Anne Marjatta Sakkola

AFFIRMATION

It rained today.
   gentle drops,
falling upon the earth,
   tenderly nourishing God's creation.

It rained today,
   torrents,
beating, bruising, maiming,
   devastating God's creation.

It rained today,
   with floods,
and fjords overflowing,
   rushing to destroy God's creation.

It rained today,
   birds were singing,
splashing in puddles,
   enjoying God's creation.

It rained today,
   above it all the sun was shining,
a rainbow arched,
   affirming to all God's creation.

Joan M. Woodrick

RODEO HORSE

Untamed,
   unbroken,
      Wildly free.

Penned up,
   exhibited.

Fierce beauty,
   with every move.

One man,
   after another,
      lands on the ground.

Away he walks,
   prouder than before,
      much greater.

C. S. Bean

KEEP ON BELIEVING

On golden ledges once I held
Never letting go —
Never letting go —
To Satan's gimmick I was felled.

No longer can I hang
No more do dreams recur
The Serpent's shown its fang
And caused my inner stir.

Secret doors have opened wide
Slowly moving in —
Slowly moving in —
I was told Christ's on my side.

When will He make me whole?
How can I feel the touch
Into the darkness of my soul?
The desperation is too much.

Silent whispers echo to the sound
Keep on believing!
Keep on believing!
In God's World the answers will be found.

Ellen K. Leech

SO GRAND A THING

Love — so grand a thing.
  Fragile, yet 'tis strong.
Like the fine, fine chain You gave to me,
  With the little heart upon.
Then one day the little heart broke,
  It lay quiet on the floor.
I picked it up so carefully,
  Thinking to restore,
But it was beyond repair.
  The little heart refused to die!
So, I took a bit of the fine, fine chain
  And put the heart upon,
Then placed them in a golden frame.
  Now on my table sits.
And Love remains — so grand a thing,
  Fragile, yet 'tis strong.
Like the fine, fine chain You gave to me,
  With the little heart upon.

  Ruth M. Shores

A SPECIAL FRIEND

Today is not a special day,
  Compared to many others,
No holiday to celebrate,
  Not set aside for Mothers.

But as I woke this morning,
  To face a brand-new day,
I counted all the blessings,
  That life has sent my way.

And after I had finished,
  What stood out from the rest,
Was a loyal, faithful friend,
  The kind that is the best.

One to share the quiet times,
  The tears and laughter too,
Who understands the inner me,
  I show to very few.

My wealth lies not in money,
  Though it is nice to spend,
But in the strength that I possess,
  Because I call you friend.

  Judy Hopkins

WHERE THE RIVERS FLOW

O take me where the rivers flow,
And I shall stand, and I shall stand,
Along the banks of River Time,
And dip my hand.

O take me where the clouds fly o'er
The sun-baked land, the sun-baked land,
And I shall crest the waves of air,
And make my stand.

For life is but a fleeting moment,
Drops within the stream,
Which swells with each new birth of man,
In God's creation dream.

O lift me to the highest heavens,
'Mongst the stars, amongst the stars,
And I shall look upon the earth,
In heav'nly pause.

O grant me time to find my peace,
Of restless mind, of restless mind,
And I shall sing a song of life,
In this, my time . . .

  Psyaih Bennett

A JULIE

Julie.
She thought she was so cooly,
strutting her stuff as she done.

But what she did
was what she did.
And what she done, she was.

  Dan Buck

NIGHT DRIVER

It's shameful!
Blasting through this sweet spring night
Tires humming
Soft city lights flickering
Blurring.

Radio music
Pulsin' finger-poppin' hip jerkin'
Pleadin' cryin'
Marvin Gaye . . .
Other brothers . . .
Gone too soon.

Big rig passing . . . WHOOSH!
Taillights blazin'
Blinking alive
Gone over the hill.

Headlights glaring
Blinding . . .
SWOOSH! into the violet night
Moving together over the bridge
Crossing the dark river.

  E. Carole Woods

WOODS, EVELYN CAROLE. Pen Name: E. Carole Woods; Born: Springfield, Missouri, 12-17-43; Married 11-7-65 to Marvin R. Woods Sr.; Education: Studied Art briefly at SMS in Springfield, Missouri, 1962; Graduated from Mercy School of Nursing, Ft. Scott, Kansas, 1966; Occupation: Registered Nurse; Co-owner of Ft. Scott, Transfer and Storage Co.; Have written several poems; Comments: *I like to write about the thoughts and feelings of everyday people, and of the beauty that can be found in commonplace things.*

LOST LOVE

The Doctor said, "I'm sorry,
But we did the best we could,
We've known for weeks, however,
That her chances weren't too good.

Grandpa turned his head away,
And tried to hide his tears,
As he stood beside the woman,
That he'd loved for fifty years,

He took her fragile body,
In a final warm embrace,
And I could feel his anguish,
As he bent to kiss her face,

His rough and calloused fingers,
Softly stroked her hair,
And he whispered that he loved her,
As if she were still there,

And I stood there watching, helplessly,
Not knowing what to say,
As they gently took her from him,
And carried her away.

  Kristina Dabney

A PLEA

The Earth Mother cries
In agony and torment . . .
Who will listen now?

And lend an ear to hear . . . how
To heal the Earth and Mankind.

  Vicki R. Davies

DAVIES, VICKI ROSEMARY. Pen name: Neeniaa; Born: Brisbane, Australia, 7-23-48; Education: University of Queensland, Bachelor of Commerce, 1969; Canadian Institute of Chartered Accountants, Chartered Accountant, 1977; Institute of Psycho Structural Balancing, Massage Therapist, 1985; Occupations: Former Chartered Accountant; Currently Holistic Health Care Professional; Poetry: *The Adventures of Gingerbee,* children's poetry, Vantage Press, 1985; 'Butterfly,' *Lyrical Fiesta — A Poetry Festival in Print,* Fine Arts Press, 1985; Other Writings: *Footprints in the Sand, an Odyssey into Ancient Egypt,* poetic, photographic travelogue, self-published, 1985; *A Journey Back in Time to Ancient Mexico,* poetic, photographic travelogue, self-published, 1983; Comments: *I write about the feelings of the places that I visit. I convey the images so that the reader can visualize him/herself being in that place and feeling the spirit of that particular place. This I have done in both Egypt and Mexico, and with Gingerbee. I have a strong sense of Earth Energies and feel I channel poetry in the places I visit.*

GRABBING FOR STRAWS

(Straw Vote)

Grabbing for straws that will free us from destruction.
Hoping to gain a new start.
Grabbing for straws, of thoughts for a new creation.
And continuing to drift apart.

Now that the voice of the multitudes,
Has made their choice plainly.
Time has come for all the great leaders,
To continue the great plan for unity.

The task at hand is probably impossible,
And the answer will certainly be unsuitable.
For those forces that would prefer,
Disruption would be more workable.

No place to turn for help from the earthly opposition.
And talking of a plan for peace,
Searching the heavens for extraterrestrial civilization.
Weapons of mass death standing in imminence.

Grabbing for straws that maintain peace,
Reaching out for the right solution.
Grabbing for straws . . . anything, any straw,
Looking for a Savior from the "Heart of Creation!"

Wayne A. Shock

FROM RED FRIENDS

(if we could talk)

To East you glean the bleeding czars we fell;
 Rose horticulture, pruned by Mao and Stalin,
 With proletarians who nursed their pollen —
Purged red, you call our bed, "communist hell."

You see hatred-tempered hammers, sin-beat
 Sickles — hostile tools of Thor and Cronus,
 But they're *your* Western gods and they don't own us;
Our implements seek only nails and wheat.

Though Capital or Social *isms* weave
 To Left or Right and possibly to flounder;
 Their hammers are as peaceful as their pounder —
Their sickles harvest what the wielders cleave.

Now Mao and Stalin's dictates aren't with powers;
 Is Hitler's right-wing worshipped in the West?
 Can you judge evil? Put it to the test —
Though ours killed ours, your Reich slew yours *and* ours.

Propaganda pokers stoke up quivers,
 Inflamed on Eastern tongues till they rise dumb
 With cindered Western voices that set numb,
As silence bores at dams on nuclear rivers.

John Balkwill

WADING AND ME

Burning sand beneath my feet,
Knees knocking afraid of the deep.
Wading, I reluctantly go;
Will I return — I do hope so!

Step by step I entered the sea
With a hundred bathers in front of me
Splashing and pushing amid floats galore;
I slowly retreated to the line of the shore.

But Mother's grasp was awaiting me
As I made my way almost free;
"MOTHER, P-L-E-A-S-E," I did implore,
But it was back in again as before.

Helen Casale

JOE

We take my father's body for a ride
Outside; he sits supported in the front
And watches trees, a girl — who knows? — stream by
On either side. His mind remains inside
With debutantes and gin, some crazy stunt
that friends at college pulled, the cloudless sky
Of summer when he played a tennis game
With lemonade and flannels in St. Paul:
The farther back, the better to recall
Details which barely serve to brace a frame
That's come unstrung with Parkinson's and time,
That's left him sticks for arms no thicker than
The shafts of all those racquets which he swung,
Now lying dustily on attic floors.

C. Webster Wheelock

FEARS

Reaching deep into the dens of darkness
A slow eerie chill creepingly tickles your spine.
A gut-shivering shudder gropes through your body,
Leaving an abounding emptiness in your stomach.
Silky beads of sweat glisten along your brow.
Blood courses pulsingly through your veins.
Frenzied fears linger listlessly with your loneliness,
'Til days and nights are but infinite beads
Each being strung on life's incessant chain.
Day by dreary day, night by noxious night —
The days evolve to years as each minute dies.
A lonely, lone soul enduring the darkness
Awaiting the arrival of a soul-saving light
To relieve the fears in the recesses of your mind.

Dee Ann Carey

BLESSINGS OF FREEDOM

Freedom is to be cherished by all,
Resulting in love of God and Country,
Many blessings being bestowed upon our Nation,
Ending in total commitment toward total freedom.

Blessings of Freedom brought to our Nation,
Through many conflicts and many tough decisions,
Brought about by many patriots and clergymen,
Testing freedom as being bitter and sweet.

Many years of hard thinking and planning,
Shaped the course of Freedom's best Country,
As truly as it began only yesterday,
In the minds of men years past.

Vincent T. Vinciquerra

NORMA'S FINAL ROLE

Frail wings of sympathy, I am profound —
Come, fly your feathered skeleton; surround
And softly strum reality away —
Sleep — I will not hover one more day!
The atom particles have filled the room,
Draw the shades and blind me to their doom;
Release the maggots, let them have their prey,
You *know* there's nothing comforting to say!
My lips are cast in bronze their last display;
My kiss to *all* — unseen — Touché, Touché!
A bit of drama? . . . too late, pathetic tear . . .
Silence, now — there's no one here to hear.
 Somewhere, vague, a beating, rhythmic drum —
 Lights — and a steady, piercing, high-pitched hum . . .

Carol A. Waldvogel

CARMEL BY THE SEA

When azure sky shadows
Into ceruleous hues,
And crowd of noises cease,
The strength of God's prominence
Journeys through my soul's
Vast inner awareness:

I hear rhythmic sighs
Of melodic tossing sea waves,
And fluted voices of meteors
Above earth's security belts.
I see the blending colors
Of nights' nature sounds.

I smell unmatched fragrance
When the caressing breeze hums
Through soft moonlit boughs,
To lullaby cradled leaves.
And below, I feel the presence
Of gentle growing violets.

Alessandra A. Poles

THE ARCHITECT

I was the Architect of Vision.
I had the dream, you brought the
materials to build on.
We built together, but without
a master plan.
the opposite directions became real.
I must now follow my own plan.

I am the Architect of Destruction.
I have destroyed what is,
for what could be.
And in spite of all
I have done to you
for what little
it may be worth,
I do
still love you
like no other,
and I think
I always will.

Al Mitrevics

GOOD MORNING TO MARCH

I'm looking at dawn,
Not caring for rest,
Or darking of lawn,
To blacking of west.
Good morning to March.
I'm turning to draught.
No feeling of starch,
For sliding my thought.
My being is here.
My sailing is where,
I'm seeing in tear,
Not raving in swear.
My living is yet.
I'm moving in time.
My dying is set,
To ending of line.
I'm telling my soul,
My speaking will parch.
Still, knowing my goal . . .
Good morning to March.

Gerard Klusak

OUR LOVE

Our love started as a tiny seed dropped into the cold December snow. As
the snow melted, and the winter slipped away, the seed was nourished by precious
words and wonderful memories. As the early months of the year dragged on, our love
grew little by little, till, in early spring, our love was finally allowed to
start to bloom. Spring has come and gone, and the bloom, so tender then, has grown
stronger and stronger with each passing day. Now it is summer, and the bloom still
is as fresh as it once was, only more beautiful than ever. As summer slowly dies
and autumn comes ever so gently, the bloom looks toward the harvest, and the time
when it is realized that all the rain and growing were worth it. The final fulfillment
of all that pain and pleasure pulled together to bring extreme happiness. Then the
bloom will be welcome to all, and will fill everyone with its beauty. For many
seasons will that bloom continue to flourish and grow continually, until, when
the end of our lives come, we both drop the seeds back into the cold December snow
for two more people to come upon, to find, to cherish, and to experience the
wonderful feeling of true love.

Heather L. Dempsey

WINTER

'Tis the season of joy called winter, winter wonderland,
  Snowy meadows, drifts pile high against the old red barn —
Howling winds, icy cold, whip 'round the corners of the dilapidated frame house,
  Ashen grey, dull drab, hang heavy the clouds ever so low.

'Tis the season of joy called winter, winter wonderland,
  Icicles form on glassy trees as droplets of water drip below —
Silence grips the air, as if the world stopped to gaze in wonder,
  Silver streams gurgle, and bubble, as they flow beneath puffs of snow.

'Tis the season of joy called winter, winter wonderland,
  A holy hush fills the atmosphere, as one reflects upon this wintry scene,
And feels the presence of the God above, so near, so serene —
  'Tis He who is the Master Painter, the sky his canopy, the earth his
  canvas — for you and me to enjoy.

M. William Trott

A LITTLE GIRL'S PRAYER

One night as I went in to hear my little girl's prayer and tuck her
into bed,
She looked up at me and said these words before she bowed her head.

  "Mommy, I bet God's awfully tired, he never gets no sleep.
  He sees us no matter where we go, and hears us when we speak.

  I bet he's awfully sad; he only smiles when we do right.
  'Cause there's more people in the world doing wrong than
  there is right tonight.

  He watches over us Mommy; he does his very best.
  So Mommy, why don't the world set down and let God have
  some rest?"

Barbara Swiger

HAPPINESS

If only I could wave a wand and spread some Happiness,
It would be so pleasing not to see people under stress.

But life today is filled with so many difficult things
Such as tension, hate, lust, and all the sadness that these bring.

To achieve this happiness we must set a moral goal,
One true to ourselves, and that is alike for young and old.

In the past, we have guided ourselves by the "Golden Rule."
Now we have forgotten this and learn other things in school.

Whatever time of year it is, we should keep this in mind:
Happiness is how we lead our lives — never look behind!

Emily Sabatino

AUTUMN LEAVES

Summer has passed
With its wide-eyed face and boyish grin,
Tempting all of nature to frolic and rejoice,
Before the autumn leaves begin to fall.

Now the leaves are falling, gently fluttering and pirouetting,
Joining in the dance of Nature.
Each one comes to rest, with a million others,
To form a tapestry of lustrous color and royal grandeur.

Soon, the icy winds of winter will trumpet forth,
And all of Nature will shiver in anticipation.
An age-old ritual repeats itself,
As all things prepare for sleep, beneath a snowy blanket.

Winter will come as a watchful mother,
Gazing out over the linen-white nursery of sleeping life.
Silence — so intense —
Broken only by the sound of a single snowflake falling.

And then, the Prince of Life will come,
To awaken all the world by His gentle touch.
Until, again, Nature goes full circle
To a time when autumn leaves begin to fall.

Paul David Vollmer

AMERICA, WE LOVE YOU

America, we love you, we love you, we do,
America, to you, we will always be true;
America, we love you, with your red, white and blue,
America, we love you, we love you, we do.

With the coming of the pilgrims
Up to the present day,
Our nation has been successful
Never faltering, on the way.

Through wars and revolutions
This nation has stood firm,
With the faithful and the loyal
Our freedom to proclaim.

From the days of the great depression
Through thick and through thin,
America has come through
Always, again, and again.

America, we love you, we love you, we do,
America, to you, we will always be true;
America, we love you, with your red, white and blue,
America, we love you, we love you, we do!

Marjorie L. Halada

MIXTURE

The cosmic pull of the universe
Unites with the liquid essence
And there you have man.

His thoughts transcend
To the outer reaches of the heavens
And his soul, the brilliant fixture
To which all things are whole.

The tie to the planet that holds him
Lets him taste fulfillment and despair.
All the while his thoughts escape to amorphous
— Drifting, sifting, mingle with air.

Yearning for clarity and lasting satisfaction
One will have time to look God in the eye
And the wisdom to *know* that which is good.

K. Coogler

ON THIS YOUR GRADUATION DAY

On this your graduation day,
There is so very much I'd like to say.
As the door to your future opens wide,
Walk tall and never look on the bright side.
Use your abilities and talents to be your best,
To strive for excellence will be your test.
As tomorrow's leader, you face the new day,
Be strong in courage, come what may.
There will always be changes and challenges to master,
As technology accelerates the world faster and faster.
When others say, "It can't be done,"
Just think it through . . . and you will have won.
The knowledge we've shared is a stepping stone.
To give sure footing in a world of unknowns.
Your struggles and strides have been my concern,
As I've done my utmost to help you learn.
When I see you stand there, diploma in hand,
Prepared to contribute to our great land.
I'm thankful for the opportunity to have been a part
Of this joyous moment that fills your heart.

Clara Ann Foucht

FOUCHT, CLARA ANN. Born: Dayton, Ohio, 3-11-40; Married: 4-19-60 to Millard Eugene Foucht; Education: Ohio University, B.S. Ed.; Ohio State University, M.A. Ed., 1985; Reading Supervision Certification, 1974, and Masters in Early and Middle Childhood Education; Occupation: Reading and Library Enrichment Teacher, Kindergarten — Sixth Grades; Media Experiences: WSFI TV, Programs on Learning; WCLT radio, Local History; Memberships: President, Land of Legend Chapter of the International Reading Association; board Member, N.O.T.E., Newark Chapter; Licking County, Historical Society, Art Association, St. John's United Church of Christ, YWCA, Newark Garden Club, Symphony League; Awards: My Bicentenial song, President Ford, 1976, 'Anthem to the City of Newark,' 1980; Other writings: "Elementary Serendipities," teaching ideas, Licking County Schools, 1976-79; "An Apple From the Teacher," newspaper articles, *The Newark Advocate,* Newark, Ohio, 1983-85; 'Anthem to the City of Newark,' patriotic song, Old Town West Society, Newark, Ohio, 1980; *The Mary Ann School Yearbook,* Annual, School Annual Publishing Co., Coshocton, Ohio, 1980; *Licking County Historical Guide,* Ohio State University, Newark, Ohio, 1976; Comments: *My writing has been concerned with two important parts of my life, the past and the present. As a descendant of Francis Scott Key, I wrote a Bicentennial song and an anthem to the City of Newark, Ohio, which is sung to the tune of "The Star Spangled Banner," and was presented on the Newark Square on July 4, 1980. My writing of late has concerned itself with my life as an educator and helping parents and students foster positive academic growth, through articles in my local column, "An Apple From The Teacher!"*

Narrows near Lewistown.

INCIDENT AT MULAZZANO

(The Gothic Line, Italy — September, 1944)

Today we took the corporal in
leg gone
lead-gray from loss of blood
up the tack and sapper team had taped
onto the hilltop road
where tanks entrapped against the sky in full display
were turning
burning
caught by eighty-eights in ambuscade.
      They held their fire to let us pass.

For a moment there the enemy was not the enemy
and we were linked to him
in that belonging of the blood that comes of battles shared
that rallies men to flags
and bids them stand to death on the arena's sands
joined in a high reality
beyond that of the world that cheers our wounds
that tells us we must fight
but does not bleed
      or die with us.

James H. Brewster

PEARL OF WISDOM

There once was an oyster, whose story I'll tell,
Who found that some sand had got under his shell.
Just one little grain, but it gave him a pain
(For oysters have feelings, professors maintain).

Now, did he berate the unfortunate fate
That led him to such a deplorable state?
Did he blame Uncle Sam and ask government aid
To revamp the floor of the sea where he'd laid?

"No," he said, as he lay on the sea shelf,
"I'll improve my condition, and all by myself."

So, the years rolled along (as the years always do)
And he came to his ultimate destiny — stew!
But, the small grain of sand that had bothered him so
Was a beautiful pearl, all richly aglow!

Now, this tale has a moral, for isn't it grand
What an oyster can do with a small grain of sand?
What couldn't we do, if we'd only begin
With those little things that get under our skin?

Bob Shinn

THE LORD'S LITTLE FLOWER

When we pray for the Lord's power
   It blossoms upon us like a flower.

It opens its petals for all to see
   That its beauty comes from His Majesty.

The stronger the faith and love,
   The sweeter the scent from heaven above.

The Lord works in mysterious ways
   Upon His flower as it grows each day.

It stands so proud and tall
   And during droughts, it does not fall.

Faith and love fertilize its soil
   And to the Lord it is forever grateful and loyal.

It is the most beautiful flower in all the land
   Because it was raised with the Lord's gentle hand.

Brenda S. Marble

THE SAGA OF THE SOUL

What did the day have to gain
Would it snow or would it rain
And send the tears unto thy heart again
Would the sun be bright and warm
Or would there be a sudden storm
What will the winds have to say
As they play upon heartstrings for the day
What will the petals of the flowers play
Loss of thy love that they will say
What will thou ask of the trees
As they kneel upon their bending knees
What will thou ask upon thy pillow at nights
That the love of thy life be unto thy sight
What will thou sing upon thy wing
That I have lost my everything
When did the lonely willow weep
Upon the day or unto its sleep
What did the Golden Angel have to fling
An arrow through thy heart that pings
And crimson blood it will flood upon the snow white of the bud

Elvie E. Bryant Keller

ONLY IN MY MIND

As I walk, along by the sea,
I wonder where you've gone?
And if you are watching me?

For it seems, as if someone's here,
Although I'm alone,
I know it's someone I need not fear.

The sea is so lonely, but yet I'm not scared.
For I have a feeling,
That there's really nothing there.

It's there to protect me,
I know it's a friendly soul.
Even thou I cannot see.

For I am blind,
As far as seeing you,
For you are only in my mind.

Dawn D. Perrin

THE BLUE CANDLE

On rare pearls once worn to the grand opera,
I count off the prayers as on a rosary
For Baby Blue, now the big Bon Bon
Bouncy on smokes from the dream factory,
His years punctuated by periodic sentences
In mind-boggling sprints of Kafkanesque trials,
Subdued in chambers of quiet. Like Lon Chaney
Quakes in medieval corridors of cells,
The series of chillers, the stalk of old shake-o
The ever-looming black of the last draw,
The loser. If I had been the ad writer and not
The model, I could have spun and sold a tale to
Hucksters, had more than medals for my time —
Money to spend on diverting cures, offset the
Offenses. Only the Teddy Bear could bear
The tears, the severity of silences,
The ritual of our prayers sung as by habit
Of Carmelite Nuns offered up for others. In
Our veins the wine of love, I take the daily bread,
Then send a letter to my son, the drift from mother . . .

Chris Hollingsworth

HERITAGE

A wondrous sight to behold,
mountains standing proud and bold.
Whispering wind, howling cold,
harboring secrets never told.
Ancients following memories of old.

Plains of gentle waving grass,
holding onto memories fast.
Hushing tales of long lost past,
delving into nature's cast.
Years of heritage made to last.

Rivers rushing to the sea,
eternities made for you or me.
Will we ever truly see,
what the meaning is to be;
Shall all living things be free?

Mikki Neuwerth Garding

TO THE SUNSET

Oxford of rugby and jewel of the learned,
of towers, green gardens; of books and
    good wine.
Prophets, gowned, bearded, of quaint
    simple manner,
Teaching through nature that life
    is sublime.

Traditional bulwark; old windows of glass,
Sans classrooms, lectures, quizzes
    and strife,
Candlelight, tea time, great scholars
    of fame.
Chaucer and Homer all mingled with
    Life.

The old yet so young, the young
    yet so wise,
All things of good humor; a
    creed for the living.
To learn to approach then, the
    sunset of life,
With a heart of good joy and
    of unselfish giving.

Jeanette Bryant

THE GIFT

Once upon a starry night
'Neath a full moon, shining bright
In a barn all snug and warm,
There a little babe was born.

'Round the infant, gazing on
Came the oxen, sheep, and fawn,
Hound and cat and rabbit wild,
There to see the newborn child.

Since the fall in Eden's wood
Beasts of burden, beasts for food,
Sacrificial lamb and dove,
Where was their Creator's love?

Yet one sparrow ne'er did fall
That its Maker noted all
Gifts of service through the years
To mankind, and without tears.

"To my creatures, great and small
This I've promised to you all.
For your work that you have done,
You are first to greet my Son."

Nancy C. Coleman

FANTASY

Sometimes it's hard to sleep
Thoughts keep leaping through my mind
Some I don't want to think
Others I slow down to savor
the feelings they bring
And fantasies are woven
to make reality more bearable
Aloneness sometimes turns to loneliness
and fantasy helps to ease the ache
along with memories
of love, laughter and joy
out of the past
Sometimes from yesterday
It's easier to make fantasies
than take the risks to make memories

Lea Winchester

A MOTHER'S LOVE

A mother's love is beyond compare
Nothing can take the place,
Of a smiling face and loving care
And a warm enduring embrace.

A mother will do whatever she can
In every possible way,
To see that things go right for you
Come what may.

After your mother is dead and gone
Her love will long endure,
Because there is no other love like a
Mother's love
A love that's sweet, loving and pure.

Brenda Johnson

BRILLIANT DEWDROP

Only an inanimate object,
    One might thoughtlessly say;
And, thereby, miss completely
    The joy of its ray.

Although this fragile beauty
    Endures but a moment or two,
It can brighten life's monotony
    And inner strength renew.

Yes, every brilliant dewdrop,
    Can a precious gift bestow.
Concealed within this tiny bubble
    Is God's majestic rainbow.

Vernald Barnhart

STRAY PATHS

Our paths have crossed again
As stray paths often do
Which makes me think we're bound
For Nowhere, sure as true.

Maybe all paths are stray
And none gets anywhere —
So what if we arrived
At Somewhere, bleak and bare?

How comforting to know
We're always on the way —
That process is accomplishment
And paths are best when stray.

Grace Patrick Madigan

LOVINGKINDNESS

There is a beautiful garden and the
Lord God dwells there every day.
To bring hope to His children that
others have cast away.

To wipe the tears from our eyes that
we see and believe by working together
that the Good Lord is pleased.

So, don't worry about the time or what
the world has to say.
Just love and fear the Good Lord and
trust Him every day.

He will never leave you or send you
away.
For His lovingkindness is still the
same as yesterday and every new day.

Deborah James McMahel

NO LONGER US

Doors once open
now locked against our cold
no keys fit
the sound of ice
the rattle of bones

Keith E. McGaffin

BY THE POOL

We were sitting by the pool.
You were the fool.
Me to be your bride!
My eyes got wide.
I was so surpised!
Me to be your prize!
I thought I would die!
So I let out a sigh.
My, oh my, oh my!
He wanted me to be his wife.
I know; I'll get a knife!
Then I won't have to say no,
Even better, the pool!
We'll go swimming.
He'll accidentally drown.
No, I'd have to be a clown to try that.
Oh well, I guess,
I'll have to say . . .
YES!

Rhonda Whitaker

BARB STRILEN

Half mutant, half human,
She was copper lightning.

Barbara Strilen's eyes were
deep green, cold, and frightening.

Black wristbands gave her
fatal fists bomb-like qualities.

While the giantess also possessed
vast mental abilities.

Atomic mutant whose blood
flowed not iron red,

Had no mercy on criminals,
so many of them she made dead.

Mary Streblow

WHEN THE FIGHT IS OVER

When I'm with you I feel warm,
    secure, wanted, and most of all, loved.

It could never be expressed with words,
    but when I'm away from you . . .
    I feel alone, confused, and most of all
    without you.

It's as though I'm in a dark room stumbling,
    searching for a light that's not there.
        These feelings sometimes overcome me
        and make me want to give up my fight
        of what I'm to become, but my feelings for
        you are far greater than my feelings for
        giving up.

So each and every day I carry on the fight
    of what I'm to become for I know,
    for all the bad times there will be good times.

Our day will come when the fighting
    will stop and we can love, live,
    and have happiness together as one.

Duane D. Norris

AMERICA

America! a World by Herself
America! a World of Freedom and Justice for all
America! a World of opportunities and hopes
Art-craft embellished, enchanting symbolic statues,
Culturally rich, and economically stable.

Your beautiful, touching, star-studded banner I crave;
As it flies endlessly through the smooth sailing winds
Your majestic mountains and valleys, rivers and trees,
I watch, as their shadows fall amber on my shoulders
Then dissolve into purple evening light.

Give me a pen America
And I'll write your name on my heart.
Oh! America, give me a touch of Winter
Or I'll go for Spring
Oh! America, give me a feeling of Summer
Or I'll go for Fall.

Indivisible America, whose power's unsurpassed
Yet, one Nation under God.
Irresistible America, in your World I dreamed
Your World of Hope, Peace, Freedom, and Justice for all.

Isaac R. Frank

ODE TO A LEGAL SECRETARY

Per the Office Manual, I work "NINE TO FIVE."
    It must be a typo! (Or SOMEBODY lied . . .)
I go to work early (miss lunch) AND/OR stay late.
    (What IS a "Social Life?" When WAS my last "date?")

There's no TIME to "go out," not EVEN one day.
    (And CERTAINLY NOT on my meager pay!)
When the weekend begins, and it's time to "PLAY,"
    I can't turn myself off, at least not TODAY.

There's the budget, the house chores,
    The laundry, the shopping . . .
(I MUST keep on going —
    There will BE no stopping!)

I'm tired; I'm drained;
    I feel "all used up."
(Is there SOMEONE out there
    Who can FILL my CUP?!?)

Eliza Tea

A CHILD

A child is a marvelous creature
        so simply, yet adequately designed,
From each lovable, innocent feature
        to his inquisitive growing mind.
With fingers at first for sucking,
        then dialing a telephone,
A child makes many changes,
        but he can't make them alone.
He needs someone to show him
        the wonders he can learn.
He needs praise from someone who loves him
        for the reward he is to earn.
If growing up were easy,
        with no pain or grief,
Then life would be so breezy,
        but, oh, it would seem so brief.
If you have a child at home,
        watch him as he's asleep.
Thank God for this miracle of your own,
        and all life's joy you shall reap.

Lanette Sikes

WISE DECISION

    Dear Club Officer, forget not thy duties, but let
thyself keep thy commitment;
    For growth of club, great strides, and achievements
shall they acknowledge thee.
    Let not work and endurance forsake thee; honor thy
code of ethics; remember thy promise to serve diligently.
    Trust in the members to help thee, and lean not upon
thine own inexperience.
    In all thy ways include them, and they shall aid
thy meetings.
    Dear Officer, hold thy tongue when things go not
thy way, neither criticize alternate decisions;
    For what they chooseth may be the best, the gain of
the project be profitable.
    Happy is the officer who leadeth wisely, and the
members who worketh together.
    Surely thou shalt not scoff at opinions, but giveth
grace to sound reasoning.
    The wise shall achieve praise, but slothfulness
shall be condemned.

W. Gail Langley

UNSUNG HEROS

Oh! You bold ones who think you're good news
You're not the only ones who have paid their dues
There are many out there who have paid the price
Many who have gone through much suffering, turmoil and strife
It may not show like a bright shining star
But they are out there, both near and afar
When you see them you can't quite tell
What they have conquered, how they've been through hell
They may look timid, seem soft and untried
But when you learn of their story, you hang your head, you hide
They've been the object of ridicule and scorn
They've been made to wish they had never been born
But they have survived, they have made the grade
Some remarkable roles in life they have played
The world knows them not, but all the world feels
What they have done that shall remain real
Real contributions to the American way
Solid gold treasures forever to stay
With us to bless us, for all to share
'Tis only right to thank them, 'tis only fair

Thomas E. Ross

OUR PREACHER

Dedicated to: Aunt Janet Stanford

She stood in the pulpit, hands raised toward the sky,
There was a rattle in her voice, as she wiped a tear from
her eye.
Remarking, "What is life if you continue to live in great
sin?
Take Jesus into your life now, don't wait to the bitter
end."

She was a family woman, yet served her community and all,
She was our lay reader, preached the Gospel until God's
final call.
She often remarked, "Never call your parents 'Old Woman'
or 'Old Man'."
For her it was a lack of respect, and she always took
that stand.

I still recall her kindness, her prayers, her reaching
to the sky,
Reaching for her hankie, to wipe many tears from her eyes.
I visited her warm home often, with those she loved
so well,
There was no end to her caringness, in heaven, I hope
she dwells.

Frank Blackwood

BLACKWOOD, FRANK MAURICE. Born: Wesleyville, Bonavista Bay, Newfoundland, Canada, 1-1-44; Married: 8-14-82 to Louise Cyrenne; Education: Montreal Universities, mastered in the fields of Psychology and Psycho-Social Rehabilitation; Occupations: Behavioral Modification Psychologist, considered one of the pioneers in Behavior Therapy at Canada's first behavioral therapy unit founded by Dr. Ernest Poser of McGill University in 1967; Free-Lance Writer, former Radio Announcer and School Teacher; Memberships: Printers and Writers Association of Canada; President, Montreal Softball Association; President, City of Lasalle Community Civic Council; Canadian Representative for World Runners Club in Montreal; Writings: 'The Open Door,' 'Merry Christmas To All,' 'The Lobster Trap,' 'Fond Memories,' 'Long Rubber Boots,' *Down Memory Lane*, my first book, to be published in the fall of 1985, is a collection of all of my work, which includes poems and short stories; Comments: *All of my work is written in good Newfoundland flavor. It all reflects back to the past, memories of my childhood, family and friends. I am proud to say that I have Newfoundland at mind and heart throughout all of my works. Thanks to my parents and Aunt Maggie Feltham for permitting me to see this great period in my life.* Editorial Comments: *As one journalist remarked: "Frank tries to reach the realness and goodness of people whom he shared his childhood days with. From the local storekeepers and wharf keeper, even able to recall friendly remarks of the older folks, or to seek out lively thoughts of walking hand in hand with Aunt Maggie feltham as she put a small lantern on "lighthouse head" at Braggs Island. His wandering mind is truly sprinkled with great Newfoundland spices of real down-home flavor."*

TEDDY

It's lonely without you, Teddy,
But we are always ready
To wait a little longer for those
Whom we have cherished and chose
For the dearest things we want
To have and to hold;
When the supermen cease to haunt,
And the enemy has been made to fold.

The days are sometimes long,
And so many little things seem wrong,
And yet, there's always a sureness
That without flaw or unawareness
That soon there will be a solution
In spite of a wintry outlook,
And with love and inspiration,
We, like in any good book
Will know the true meaning of life and love
And happiness.

Mary Louise Cable Miller

MILLER, MARY LOUISE CABLE. Born: Murray, Kentucky, 2-15-21; Married: 12-5-42 to Ted Ralph Miller; Education: Murray State Teachers College, 1940 and 1941; Occupations: Dental Assistant, and secretarial until 1948; Poetry: *Poetry of Love During World War II*, Collection of Poems, 1945, 'Jenny,' Short Poem, 'A Christmas Prayer,' Religious, 'Her First Fur Coat,' Humorous, 1945; Comments: *Sincerity and the wished for ideal lifestyle were the theme and idea in my poetry. The poem lines began going down on paper to express feeling. All the above were written in Washington, D.C. after a year and a half working there doing secretarial work in the State Department, which inspired me.*

LOVE IS

Love is
   The white of a dove
      The red of a rose
         A gentle kiss
            An emotion, an emotion between a
            Man and a woman
Love is
   So pure
      So tender
         So strong nothing can destroy it,
            But so delicate a touch will bruise it.

Christine Krauss

COLLECTOR'S ITEM

You had the canvas
I supplied the brush
And together we painted a picture,
It wasn't all that complicated —
Just simple lines
With vivid colors —
I guess you could describe it
    as an abstract . . .
In the beginning stages
the colors seemed to clash,
But as we progressed
they all began to blend in . . .

I'm glad we took the time
to form this "masterpiece,"
priceless indeed!

Teresa Lewonder Simmons

MY FRIEND

U R my most treasured possession
& i do not price U
nor R U owned
yet, i prize U.

i give 2 U w/o loss
but gain is mine.

4 U i would die
& U would not ask
but beg 4 my life
that U've restored so many times.

Love 2 U my friend
B yon' eternity & returned again.

Laura Ludwick

IMAGES

Black whirlpool . . .
    Dizzy confusion.
Sea storm . . .
    Blaring noise.

Sightless weight.
Struggle . . . light . . . tunnel.

                    Rainbow,
                    Breezes,
                    Bird song,
                    Soft melody.

Me 'n God is buddies.

Henry A. Dux

LET'S COUNT OUR BLESSINGS

    To count over many blessings, Lord!
where would we start?
    We must start them all with Jesus,
Yes! Within the heart . . .
    But to count them all from day
to day, this could never be,
    For so many blessings we receive,
that we refuse to see . . .
    His blessings so abundant, as we
carry on our way,
    His blessings go unheeded, as we
live them day to day . . .
    For the many blessings we do see,
we try to show we care,
    If we could only count them all,
Praise God! for our fair share . . .

Sally G. Woods

IT'S GONNA COST YOU MORE

Day after day, the costs we pay, still continue rising;
And things we buy, get up so high, it's shocking and surprising.

The news we hear, brings shock and fear, about what lies in store —
Day after day, we hear them say, — "IT'S GONNA COST YOU MORE."

Rent increases — it never ceases — there seems to be no end;
No hope in sight, things don't look bright, up around the bend.

It's hard to know, which way to go — it worries and perplexes,
Unless we hold, a pot of gold, or oil wells down in Texas.

That's how it goes, and no one knows, just what awaits in store —
Yet comes the word, too often heard — "IT'S GONNA COST YOU MORE."

Here and there, and everywhere, misfortune may prevail;
Crops may be lost, due to the frost, or floods, or winds, or hail.

Nobody likes, when bad luck strikes, or ill winds start to roar,
"It will go away," that's what they say, "BUT IT'S GONNA COST YOU MORE."

And so the bills, rise like the hills — the companies seem to figure,
Though costs are rough, that's not enough, they should be getting bigger.

And this applies, to what one buys, at market, shop, or store —
What do we hear, both loud and clear? "IT'S GONNA COST YOU MORE."

May we keep coping, and also hoping, to keep the wolf from the door;
But yet, I fear, we still will hear — "IT'S GONNA COST YOU MORE."

Wendell Ehret

A MOTHER WITHOUT CUSTODY

A mother without custody is always wondering where her child is.
A mother without custody lives with oh so many fears.
    Is he fed? Is he warm? Is he safe, and secure?

A mother without custody never knows whether her child is learning
What she wants him to know.

Is he learning self-esteem and pride,
Is he learning to be humble and not to lie?
Is he learning to be moral and value life,
Is he learning the things she would teach him herself?

A mother without custody at the close of a weekend visit,
    Hates to say good-bye,
But never lets her child see that she cries...

A mother without custody waits and anticipates,

Just to know she is loved.

A mother without custody always is wondering if her child is getting
                Enough love and discipline?

Is he getting kissed and hugged?
Is he feeling independent and self-assured?

A mother without custody, fears never seem to subside
    But a mother without custody must keep them inside.
A mother without custody just because she's not always there,
Doesn't mean she doesn't truly care/she does.

Trudy Adler

THE SOURCE OF STRENGTH

The prophets of the human race
Attest that God is love;
And where mankind applies the tenet
Peace flows from above.
But when we find our fellow men
Opposing what we think,
Love is past. Before we know it,
We are at the brink
Of mutual mass murder, known
As war and then our brothers
Tell us that we have no choice
But maim and kill "those others."
If God is love, this cannot be,
For God must have the power
To straighten the affairs of men
And bring real peace to flower!
So we must learn to turn our backs
Upon the weapons-shovers
Who prate of "safety born of strength,"
For safety comes from Lovers!

Robert L. Montgomery

I MISS YOU

The morning coffee together.
I miss your smile,
All the while.
The twinkle in your eye,
        I miss you.
And that special touch,
That meant so much.
I love you more,
Than you could ever know.
        Oh! How I miss you.
Because you are not here,
Just to hold me dear.
I will hold all the memories,
Of our being together, forever.
        I sure do miss you.
You are watching over me,
Giving me strength to go on.
You will always be beside,
To lead and guide me.
        I will always miss you.

Ruth Robertson

PIPE DREAMS UNDER THE SOUTHERN CROSS

(another)

Leaving in a sampan,
For the island, Siapan.
Searching for the king's daughter,
Daughter of waters,
Queen of Eastern tides.

Her tears bring the monsoons.
Her fury brings the Typhoons.
Her nod lures the tide to shore.
Her beauty draws men to war.

Our vessel lands,
We touch foreign sands.
Proffering gifts of incense,
To the king's princess.
Offerings to the daughter,
Daughter of waters,
Queen of Eastern tides.

Curt Moore

She slouches sunken in the sofa
staring at the crazy man
barred by the box with its
broken antenna and "color" knob
on the side

Like the seven-year-old's face
pressed to the greenhouse's
plexiglass window as he watches
and watches but the plants
don't grow in the yellow-tinted
pots.

Jeffrey A. Greenfield

HURRY UP SPRING!

Snow is falling, covering the ground,
Lovely white softness all around.

I watch as a bird walks about,
Searching for food . . . An eager scout!

With the awareness of a hopeless plight,
My little friend continues his flight.

A second bird, as red as fire,
Perches himself on a telephone wire.

He watches over the winter scene,
Seemingly puzzled by the absence of green.

Unimpressed with the glistening white
The red bird, too, continues his flight.

I look around and what do I see?
What else . . . Bird number three.

This little bird displays great wrath,
As he frowns upon a frozen bird bath.

He shakes a fragile, angry wing,
As if to say, "Hurry up Spring!"

Joi Sigers

WHY?

Feeling of emptiness
A need to be caressed

Something is wrong
To where can it belong

Never knowing what it is
To whom it belongs, hers or his

What can it be
No one can see

When will it go
Why is it so

Where did it come from
What is the total sum

Is there a cure
No one is sure

What can be done
Who can help me, there is none

There is no one I can send
Really, this must be the end.

Isaac N. Horiuchi

SPRING

Spring is light;
Spring is bright.
Rabbits hop;
Others flop.
Crickets chirp;
Crickets sing.
Others have
A very, merry SPRING!

Patty Knudsen

SPRING LIES

*Dedicated, with much love,
to all the Karens in my life.*

Rolling, wet tears,
Glide down
Frozen, red cheeks;
A white snowflake
Falls.

Kim M. Hudson

NATURE GIVES

The mountains with their running springs,
The beauty of the trees;
Here we find a peace of mind
That only nature brings.

Lie back and listen to the wind.
Please let yourself be free,
To experience what life can give
In a forest that is green.

Teri Arismendez

As time marches on
I have begun to lose the meaning
    of minutes, hours . . . even days.
It is all one long time span
that I have been lucky enough
    to enjoy.

Deborah C. LaVeglia

IRIS

Tuberous bulb, dry and cracked
Clumps of earth clinging,
Moist pale yellow tendrils between
Invite bright green spikes
To flower in tissue paper white.
Three amber worms of fuzz
Fall on its triune form
And celebrate the joy of May.

Ruth W. Pettee

TAPESTRY

Woof and warp of life unspun,
by what hand guided fro and to?
Whose dream the pattern yet undone —
Who chose the scarlet, green and blue?
Why here and there a thread amiss,
a knot or ravelled spot to see?
Where beginning, middle, end?
Why so much love in tapestry?

Barbara K. Greene

THE VIEWPOINT OF THE ROCK

Listen well and learn
To be wise turn to the viewpoint of the Rock
   For the Stone alone sees the world as it   Is.
Observe: The comic opera, the Burlesque show, the Shadow Dance
Nothing is as it Seems.
Day and Night melt Away years melt Away in Twilight Gray
Time   is a whispering breeze, Man a leaf blown,
     come full-bloom only to fall Away in due season.
        We see the long-lived as Eternal but the Rock KNOWS!
Behold History the Nickelodeon flickering far too fast
   oneEventblursintoanotherEventuntilallislostin   Shadows.
And Lo! another marvel majestic Mountains are but
   ocean waves crashing across barren Lands,
     The Fleeting Grandeur of Empire the Crystal Spire of
City NOTHING BUT boiling, festering froth in the Tide.
   Civilization — whalebone to radio in the span of a Rockblink.
And Rock the Great Headstone Monument of our Mortality,
   What will you do in the great Silence, when Man,
that Ragin' Contagion has finally run his Fever-Course?
   Shall you then watch the Waltz of the stars?

     Terrance K. Harrington

HARRINGTON, TERRANCE KEITH. Born: Anniston, Alabama, 10-15-58; Single; Education: Jacksonville State University, Jacksonville, Alabama, B.S. in Business (1981), presently seeking a degree in Math; Occupations: Former Computer Programmer, currently Lab Assistant; Memberships: JSU Math Club, Art Guild, Kappa Delta Epsilon Honor Society, Rhinegold German-American Club; Comments: *I like to study the human condition by imagining how people must look to other beings, because this point of view can be entertaining as well as illuminating. I hope by writing that I can talk at least one other person into seeing the world in a new way.*

MOST MALIGNANT PLAGUE!

How readily we speak of our Freedom
While tentacles of slavery hold us fast;
How shallowly we think of THE KINGDOM,
Knowing that any Day could be our last;
How deep the Mystery that binds a Man
To his reverential concept of Hope,
Knowing that since he is only Human
This can be lost in a battle with dope;
And with it Theological Virtues
Of Faith and Love, making triumverate,
Without which his faculties cannot choose
What is real from What is false for his fate.

     Francis J. McGeary, M.D.

A SALUTE TO BREA-OLENDA'S FOOTBALL TEAM

Thanks so much to Coach Brown and his boys,
For services rendered to seniors in need.
It brought expressions of gratitude and joys,
From recipients of their good will and deeds.

Thanks for a reconnected water hose, now I can wash.
The banana tree and bushes reveal a groom.
Now the garage, the bear of the chores — "Gosh,"
"Let's get ready and clear the way for the broom."

Ruth's refrigerator has to cross the room, right boys?
So let's tug to the alley the rolled carpet of Tom's;
Then Tracy's contribution of books and toys;
John's ladders go up and I can use the chairs of Mom's.

In less than an hour the change-over came.
Thanks again for a marvelous look, not a mirage!
with replacement of everything by name.
Fantastic! Our Nova, "No-go" in Spanish, will go in the garage.

     Edith Wood Jordan

TRAIN MUSEUM: ENGINE 4500

I am so cold yet still I stand
   A monument to man
Within this yard, upon this track
   With ice-box wheels and algid stack.

And the north wind will be my steam
   The south will ring my bell
And the winter sun will warm my box
   That burned like the pit of hell.

It is so cold, yet still I wait
   My cabin seats are bare
The weeds between the rods grow 'round
   The rust flakes fall and coat the ground.

And the west wind will be my brake
   The east will whistle me by
And the winter sleet will stoke my fire
   That glowed like the northern sky.

     W. Wells Reese

PARADISE ON THURSDAY

A promise on Tuesday of Paradise on Thursday.

My soul sours above the pinnacles of reality
and drifts as the mighty eagle.

His feathered wings swept by the warm summer breeze,
His wise and ancient head lower than his heart
Searching for a fleeting glimpse of truth in his valleys below.

A flash.
The eager eye is alert.
He swoops, talons blazing in the sun.

Silent wings now, the object of his desire a possibility.
The strike is made, tearing flesh, as it must be.
The prize must not be lost or shared.

The world need not know — yet.

     E. Lee Smith

CHANGING PEOPLE

As I walk through the old neighborhood,
I can see that they are talking a new
Language!

And as I pass the burnt out building
And see broken glass.

I remember the younger years of my life.
Seems like it was yesterday that everything
Was so beautiful!

I see a church with bars on the stained
Glass and
   The doors are locked what a shame!
As I glance back at all the human
Suffering, I can remember, the old gang
   I wonder what they're doing now?
   Seems like it was yesterday that
Everything was so beautiful!

   Joe Guardino

HEARTBREAK

I hear the waves lap on the shore,
Hear the gulls cry overhead;
Hear the distant ship's horn,
Realizing that I'll never see you anymore.

I see the lighthouse through a haze of tears,
See the cottage where we spent many lovers' trysts;
Eyes misted over with pain,
Throat clogged with fears.

Onward I walk,
Leaving footsteps to follow;
Hoping in vain that they will be followed by another,
Wishing that we could talk.

If only we could set things straight,
Instead of letting our hearts break;
If only wishes came true,
I'd be here loving you.

   Ramona Tart-Beasley

A CORPORATE ENTITY

As I once sat pondering over the elements of stress
I realized it became a situation of more or less.
A policy or procedure became a daily quote
And I had enough gall to ask for an antidote.

A call to headquarters to ask for help
Became a plea from within and felt,
The many anguishes of an employee's soul
Didn't receive the very act of console.

Barriers are placed and walls are built
Because there are attitudes not meant to melt.
So, now learning to deal on a factor of consensus
Maybe they're prepared to forget the sale losses.

I, myself, want to flee from this society
Go on to a new job, new people and a new place to see.
Become once again the individual with feelings of passion
'Cause as most of us know what's done is now done!!!

   Harriet L. McDonough

Oh, I saw the monkey,
   and the monkey saw me.
The monkey said to me,
   "Come climb into my tree."
So, I climbed up high, so very, very high,
   that I could almost touch the sky.
Oh, would you like to know,
   Would you really like to know,
   how it felt to be
   way up high there in that tree?
Well, it felt so grand, so very, very grand,
   to be up high, so very, very high,
   that I could almost touch the sky.
Oh, we had fun, the monkey and me, playing all day,
   way up high there in his tree.
I think I would like to play again
   way up high there in his tree.
Oh, I saw the monkey,
   and the monkey saw me.
   Ruth Kirk

CLARALEE, MAIDEN OF THE SEA

Forever and always, two words so simple, and
In my mind's eye written in a violet sky. The
Indelible carving; the cornerstones of those
Lofty peaks where the heart's truth speaks.
They were not words but the solemn pledge
Ordained. Take them not away from me; let that
Moment remain as you promised it. For as you
Spoke and wrote so did my soul repeat those
Vows; not as an echo but as the waves rushing
To the shore; as the foam maiden Venus that I
Adore. And those waves can never cease or their
Love release for though the shore may change in
Lines and time, it is eternally in the embrace
Of the wave's tear-stained face. Forever and
Always like the land and the sea; different
In texture and grace yet together. Today,
Tomorrow, forever — and always.
   William D. Sachse, Jr.

WE LIVE TO LOVE

It's *we* that make our circumstance
   deciding down which paths we dance . . .
It's *how* we think and what we *feel*
   that sculptures what our lives reveal;
And what we feel about the "now"
   creates our future schemes somehow . . .
We either waste time feeling blue,
   or just decide to change our hue.

So search for truth — for visions strive;
   CREATE your life . . . become alive!
And find the beauty everywhere —
   it's in yourself . . . it's always there.
Just smile a little, laugh a lot,
   and love all those you touch — why not?
For those of us that love to live,
   we live to love, to share, to give.
   Kathy Fox

MORNING LOVE

I awaken,
You are next to me fast asleep.
Gently my fingers begin to caress your warm, inviting body.
Your eyes meet mine.
Our lips touch —
Soft, moist, longing kisses.
Slowly but passionately we become one.
Love, ecstasy, love, joy, love flowing
From one another to one another.
Morning love becomes you, my love.
   Judith B. Whiteman

MY QUEST

O Boundless imagination
O Endless yearning for all that is good;
   all that is forever
Come, enter into this box and make it
   end its fruitless search for satisfaction!
Let it be still and quiet
Let it free me from its gluttonous appetites.

Then would I soar through a cloudless sky
Play tag with the mighty eagle
   Until one, or both of us, are declared victor
Then setting my sights toward heaven
   And never looking back
Alight on its golden shores
Never to return to this greedy box
   and its neverending desires.

Juanita Iversen

TIME AFTER TIME,

   Time after time,
I think I'm losing my mind;
Always thinking of you,
And not knowing what to do.
Something inside of me keeps turning like a wheel,
And it seems so terribly unreal;
Every time I hear your name,
My heart jumps and I don't feel the same.
I long to hold you for just a while,
And see your beautiful smile;
You I cannot resist,
I'm really happy that you do exist.

Antonella Gulia

THE EARTH IS WAKING

The earth is waking
Listen closely to the rending river gliding to the spouting sea
As the sun peering from the east
Dusts the valleys with dawny fingers,
And bluejays' calls pierce the silvery night
Unveiling the dewy morn to the sleepy sky yawning
Stretching its red-blue hue to a tensiometric tune
Whispering, cooing
Hushing the rustling mind
Giving voice to the wind.
The world is waking
Listen closely to our worldly manitous
   Chanting . . .
Homo homini lupus, homo homini lupus, homo homini lupus . . .
As the world's darkly knit tendrils avail the stilted mind
While we cradle time's immortal hand.

Mrs. V. Sargis

WALK WITH ME

He took my hand within his own
   and led me far away.
Upon a path unknown to both
   with no certain words to say.
His eyes were set upon our trail
   as if he knew the road to take.
So sure was his stride and bearing
   I knew there had been no mistake.
This man that now pulled me to his side
   would watch my life with care.
He had reached out for me to share his love
   and had found me standing there.
My step grew even stronger beside this man
   and caused a smile to cross his face.
No turning back would ever come
   for my heart had found its place.

Celeste A. Prater

HARD JOURNEY OF THE HEART

A splash of coins in the cold
Haunting memory of Easter.
The look of spring
In the false climate of February.

A good day to stay — the best day to leave!
Forgotten and trapped in the wilderness,
Only the fox can run on three legs
After he has chewed one off for freedom.

Beggars on the street, beggars in the mind,
Picassos of the back alleys and gutter.
How silent the screams when the voice no longer works,
And the heart is so dead with pain.

Evacuation pain plain heroes,
Princes and paupers, vagabonds and clowns
Struggle on Aftermath Avenue
Holding only lost beginnings unnoticed.

Even in the best of all possible worlds,
It would still be a hard journey of the heart.
Simplicity of misdirection and incorrect priorities,
The old dog barks and the caravan moves on.

David C. Olson

TELL ME DEAR POET

The poet, of course, is an expert on love,
set in blissful surroundings, or on the wings of a dove.
He equates it with Beauty, with Power and Grace,
then wraps it in ecstasy, satin and lace.

But what can the poet say to one's heart
so burdened with anguish, and so torn apart.
To give one a reason to laugh and to play,
and to forget of another who is far, far away.

He'd better not talk of the ultimate gain
that tomorrow will bring from this longing and pain.
And none of his nonsense about the wings of a bird,
for what is love, but a four-letter word.

A four-letter word, that's what love is,
a detour to the gutter on a road meant for bliss.
A game for fools, and makes fools of the smitten,
but what do I know, it's the first poem I've written.

So tell me dear poet, in your ultimate wisdom,
how one in the gutter may find honor and free form.
And where does one search to find dignity lost
to the acts of a fool, caught in love's holocaust.

Paul Shannon

PEOPLE

They say
Depression   These feelings?
Is a figment of imagination.

They say
Loneliness   Tears, tears. Drowning.
Is self-pity, passing.

They say
Anger   Black.
Is foolish and avoidable.

                  So. Am I
      Imagining   This Dark world of Water
                  In which a Child
                  Drowns?
                        Grinning.

Laura Plimpton

LIFE

I wish i had my own knowledge
I wish we'd understand
How much we have unrealized
In our own mental lands.

It's a bitter pill to take
When we destroy what we need
We don't seem to care
That we starve what we should feed.

And then there are some
Who were born without certain facilities
They cannot talk, walk, or think right
They are talked about as having disabilities.

There are also certain people
Who cannot relate to others well
They don't do so good in school
They aren't stupid. They just live in private hell.

Each type of person
Struggling just to stay
Both had no say originally
But both continue to pay.

Valerie Burke

DEPARTURE

"I was not put here on this earth to fail;
Nor to exist in a mediocre way.
I am the hammer and life is my nail;
To achieve success — any price I'll pay.

Success — a journey, no destination;
Learning with vigorous intensity.
Power gained with great fascination;
What will be my ultimate destiny?

Committing myself to utmost limits;
I will never give up — one step further.
Obtaining information, minute bits;
Dismissing failures — confident future."

> Departing grey herds — the white elephant;
> The ultimate trek, long but triumphant.

Christian J. Pettersen

EASTER

How sad and gray, that Easter Day,
When Mary went to the tomb to pray;
And found the stone was rolled away.

An Angel was there, garbed in snowy white,
His face seemed to glow with a Heavenly light;
"Don't weep," said he, at Mary's fright.
    "The Master Lives!"

Now hear the cry ring loud and clear,
Passed along from ear to ear;
The joyous news we wish to hear;
    "He Lives — He Lives!"

And just as on that Easter Day,
So long ago and far away,
The news is still as true today!
    "He Lives — He Lives!"

Jesus died on calvary.
For us He died to set us free.
He shed His precious blood for me.
Proclaim the news!
    "He Lives — He Lives!"

Edna Cowan

ISLAND OF LOVE

As I entered into your island of love,
It seemed so vast and wide.
My soul felt a peacefulness, yet, I wondered
Why I felt a slow, restless, rising tide.

Now I know, your love had no anchor.
It wasn't solid, nor strong and sure,
Yet, even though I knew, I kept reaching out and
Hoping that soon there would be more.

I'd hoped your love would be my fortress,
My harbor with a light.
For I needed to feel the security,
Of safety during the lonely nights.

I realize now and clearly see, that from the beginning,
My need for your love was only a wishful fantasy.
One that I will always hold locked in my heart,
And secretly kept in my basket of memories.

Marti Moore-Barnett

MOORE-BARNETT, MARTHA I. Pen Name: Marti Moore-Barnett; Born: Waynesburg, Pennsylvania, 5-14-40; Married: 12-26- 70 to Samuel H. Barnett, a career man in the U.S. Navy, killed in Vietnam, 1-21-71; Education: Graduate of Penn-Commercial College, Washington, Pennsylvania, with Steno-Secretarial Degree, 1959; took courses in writing from the Writer's Institute, Maramack, New York; Occupations: Legal Secretary for the County Solicitor, A. J. Marion, Esq., in and for the County of Greene, Pennsylvania; Memberships: Member of the Pennsylvania Association of Notaries, The American Museum of Natural History in New York City, Greene County Council of Democratic Women, Gold Star Wives of America and a Charter Member of the Young & Restless Fan Club; Poetry: 'Reason: Insane,' Depicts the justice system and 'By Reason of Insanity' used in the Courts, published locally, 1981; 'He Gives Me A Song (Within and Without)' Spiritual, 1984; Comments: *Writing poetry is a great enjoyment to me. It helps me to express my feelings about life, my heartaches, my joys, the love I've shared, or just to write about a person who has been a very special part of my life. It's like giving a gift all wrapped up in a beautiful package. I also enjoy writing lyrics and jingles to commercials or to a special event or person. Being a direct descendant of Stephen Collins Foster, it may just come naturally. I wish it were possible to devote more of my time to writing.*

COMPETITIVE CREATION

Upon a thousand parchment worlds,
The same, yet differently unfurls,
A song, a soul, another dream,
A butterfly, a silent scream.
Varied yet identical,
One body, many a tentacle;
A poem is a universe,
Some built better, others worse.
Pens, creators, strive in vain,
Forever paper bears the stain.
Beauty and paper are never one,
Poet's compete, but God has won.

David N. Wilson

THE RETURN

The speck is getting larger and larger
It is now beginning to take shape
At last the distance is near
The object of my determination is here
The sky is getting brighter
I see shades of red and white
Around a form
That I have often dreamed about
The void is being lifted
Heaven is a face with golden skin
And eyes deep as the heavens
We now seal our future with a kiss.

Bill Russell, Jr.

BORN TO RUN

I was born
to run
from everything

until I had
outrun
everything

then I began
to run
for myself

Ulrich Stange

DAZZLING STAR

When I ponder on a star
And gaze out on its hues
I often find that what I see
Are visions clear of you.
I see the wonder of your smile
In its bright and gleaming beams.
I hear the softness of your voice
Enchanting all my dreams.
I reach to touch and bring you close
But like that dazzling star
I cannot hold within my arms
What reality holds afar.

Mary Rousselle

THE MACHINES

The machines are here to take and destroy.
Like a small child they will roam in a
    forest of tomorrow,
For no one will be there to see the things
    they have created,
But will surely feel the pounding at dawn,
From the graves on which they stand.

Ross Patrick Smith

WILD FLOWERS GROW

I escaped the noise of town that day
Surrendered myself to the forest sway.
There was before me, wild and sweet,
A host of violets near my feet,
Wild Irises standing brave and true
With rain-washed blossoms of dainty hue.

"Why here?" I thought,
"Oh, what a shame.
These are worthy of
Some road of fame."

A girl and boy came that way
And lingered near the bright array.
A hunter came with harsh gun,
He left, a richer, gentler one.
I stayed until the sun went down, then
Refreshed and calm, returned to town.

Ruby M. Newman

I'LL JUST THINK

Would you like to come over?
Sit down. Have a drink.
If you leave me alone now,
I'll just sit and think.

I'll think about life
and the way it should be;
and I'll sit and I'll stare
at the birds in the tree.

I'll imagine the children
and the way that they smile,
while I pull petals off roses
for a long while.

I'll dream about beauty
and where it has gone.
Please don't leave me here
by myself for too long.

So, won't you come over?
Sit down. Have a beer.
But don't feel too saddened
should you see a small tear.

Jacqueline Currie

LOVE IS

Love is like a flower, it grows more
            every day.
Love is like the Bible, we know it's
            here to stay.
Love is like a rainbow, colors that are
            true,
Love is like a winter coat being close
            to you.
Love is what I feel when you're by my
            side,
Love is what brings me so much joy
            and pride.
Love is like the wind flowing gentle
            and free,
Love is in our eyes when each other
            we see.
Love is in our pain whenever we're
            apart,
Love is our whole being starting
            with the heart.
Love is what my words are a symbol
            of,
Love is you and I in our world of
            Love . . .

Danny Ensch

A CHOICE

The ground already white with snow,
What better thing can you propose
Than a flurry looking in.
It wasn't always so.
More like an invitation out.

I stir my coffee laced with cream.
Can you suppose a better thing
Than warmth and ease
To realize a dream,
Or find what it's about?

A thought can do as much with tears
As snow does melting on my face.
The cold will penetrate and crack
My carefully put on veneers.
The wind may be too stout.

The sun may take away the chill,
But then the glare affect my sight.
What if I fall? Will someone note?
Must I remain out there? Until
I'm covered with snow, no doubt.

Naomi Gist Cox

THE ARRIVAL

lined in lines
a hundred long, a hundred wide
captured in a moment.
recognition sounding in the heights
and in the depths.
a figure alone — pacing
retracing thoughts
escaping from the moment.
faces — silent and solemn
eyes searching
breath quickening
turmoil within
without — immobility.
hard, cold pavement beneath
and a flatness exciting the nerves.
self-denial, self-delusion
self removed

        for the moment.

Deryl D. Browning

MOM

She sits and stares, with toothless gape,
        Thinking evil deeds of me.
And, as I work within the room,
        Telepathic hate is free;
        It flies to touch my soul.

I give her care, a bath, some food,
        Bringing flowers bright to see.
She takes them all, and asks for more;
        Neverending servility
        Is mine in daughter's role.

My mind must send my thoughts in turn.
        Acting ever outwardly
As love is all I have for her,
        Keeping all I feel in me,
        She knows I want her cold.

At night she lies upon her bed,
        Praying soon for dead to be.
I cannot help but pray some, too;
        Freedom needs a blessed key
To furnish both a dole.

Nancy L. Fuller

MOTHER O' MINE

February 9th in Eighty Two
A day so sad, empty and blue
My heart with grief was filled
Your life gone as God had willed.

He knows best I must confess
For years our lives He has blest
We give so little, He gives a lot
His Son He Gave our sins to blot.

Your life spoke well for you
To your Savior you were true,
I asked you once if you dreaded death
"I'm not afraid" you replied in one breath.

These words of yours comfort me now
Helps me strive to go on here,
Reading His word, obeying His voice
Knowing some day, with you, in Heaven I'll rejoice.

Rowena Bragdon Holt

HOLT, ROWENA FERN. Pen Names: Rowena Bragdon Holt, Robert Endicott Bragdon, or initials R.E.B.; Born: Merom, Indiana, 10-29-14; Married: to Louis J. Holt; Education: High School, Home Courses in Interior Decorating, Showcase Writing; Occupation: Mary Kay Beauty Consultant; Memberships: Community Concert Association; Awards: Church Bulletins, various years; First Prize, 'Thanksgiving', *Cynthiana Argus,* Indiana, 1927; Poetry: 'Falling Leaves,' nature, *American Poetry Anthology, Vol. III, Nos. 1 and 2,* American Poetry Association, 1984; '50 Years of Love,' love, *Hearts on Fire, Vol. II,* American Poetry Association, 1985; 'Heartaches and Blessings,' 'Old Age Alone,' 'Only Jesus,' Summer Poetry Anthology, American Poetry Association, 1985; 'Daughters Three,' love, *American Poetry Showcase,* American Poetry Association, 1985; Comments: *I write about nature and religion mainly. My love for writing poetry helps me bear a physical problem. I hope to help others who read my poems. Many poems of others have given me joy. I have many unpublished poems, some are soon to be published.*

A FANTASY NIGHTMARE

There she is by the ocean side,
reaching to a man.

He knows he has been defeated, it is not denied,
and an unsure heart just wishes to hide.

Both warmth and coldness riddle him with her touch

Pleasure and comfort caress the hand she holds,
while misery and restlessness strangle his hand,

It bonded by a ten-year-old wedding band.

Kevin Cooper

THE MASTER QUELL

Love was singing through the air
With passion upon the heart so kind and fair
The flaming passion was out of control
And sweep through the depths of the very soul
It cried upon the dark of the night
And whispered softly unto the morning light
The singing passion cannot be filled
But unto the power that possess the quell

Agees

BRAVE MEN

Death comes on the shoulder of peace,
Had they one more day, the war might have ceased,
Compassion for loved ones in their grief,
Please, God in Heaven, help them find relief.
From daggers and swords, to guns and bombs,
Histories' battles are fought, while life succumbs.
May they not be forgotten, for the price they paid,
as we look upon, where their tombstones are laid.

Terri Reddick

JOHN WAYNE IS

A man of greater stature, a king among the common cowboys,
A lady's "Man of Men"; he's the hero for a damsel in distress.

A dusty saddle, a rope, and a worn down pair of boots; a six-shooter with not too many notches; a slow, smooth southern drawl to his voice —

All these things portray John Wayne as America's #1 Cowboy.

Debby B.

KITTEN

in this kitten there is a tigress
Just waiting, lurking below the surface.
No one knows she's there for certain
But I know.
He feels her stare and turns to look, but all
he sees is the kitten there.
She must plan and wait to stalk her mate.
The tigress.

Janice Sue Wenning

REJECTION

Pain
Rejection
Empty chairs all around me
Empty words spoken to me.
Alone.
The room is filled with people, but I am alone
Silence rings in my ears.
I cry.

Wendy Works

LOVE IS . . .

Love is what you feel for that very special someone,
Love is what makes him or her second to none,
But love of course is not always good,
When things don't work out like you hoped they would.
Love is so many things, one of them is complicated,
But another thing about love is, it can never be duplicated.
Love is, daddy rolling over to hug mama,
Love is, if you're in love with Debbie . . . not mistaking her for Donna.
Love is, walking into a room and knowing your loved one has just been there,
because you smell that special scent in the air.
Love is the last to know, because love is blind.
Love is staying, if it means leaving a loved one behind.
Love is sometimes a point we have to make,
to make sure our loved one's feelings are no mistake.
Love is not holding back or cutting slack,
Not when you know the one you love, loves you back!
Love is something that takes over your heart and soul,
Love is a definite feeling we can't control.
Love is when you're a thousand miles apart, and your
loved one calls, just to say "I love you sweetheart."

Louise Franks

BEDTIME

Can you see them creeping
'round the blankets?
mean little creatures
they're stealing his sleep
but he waits
for the savagery trapped
in the closet
and he waits
for the huge formless spiders outside
to crawl in
when he slips
from his watch.
Sleep drags on his senses
creeps gray 'cross his eyes
'til he freezes — and shivers
they came close that time
and the soft droning hum
of his parent's t.v.
only pushes them farther away . . . monsters hoping for sleep, and
— don't be a foolish little boy — and he waits.

Karen Laidley

TRUE FRIENDS

A friend is a person with whom I can think out loud,
And with them I can be sincere,
Because a good friend is one of life's treasures.
They share your tears, as well as your laughter.
They help you see things in new and different ways.
They really understand you even better than you understand yourself.
Countless are the reasons we have cherished friends.
For the smiles when they're most needed, and the helping hands they lend.
For special confidence they take the time to share,
And for all the little loving ways they show how much they care.
For their joy in our successes and their comfort in our sorrows.
For these and more, it's true friends who make our lives complete.
Thanks for all the special ways you have brightened my days,
For the times shared with friends make the nicest memories,
Because friends like you are precious and few.
And I will hold the memories of you, my friend, in my heart,
And I'll always treasure beyond compare the special love you and I have shared.
Which is deep and strong and will last a whole life long.
For the times we shared just have to be the bonds of true friendship.
And how lucky I am to have found a friend like you.

Zandra Darnell

I WISH . . .

Hands to hold in my old days
Smiles to share in my old days
Memories to treasure in my old days
Dreams to hold us together . . .

And when everything is over
Face to face, hand to hand
Take time to tell others
What life gave us to share

And look back through the years
Remembering all the dreams that
Came true, all the happiness we had

And let it show in our face
Let it show in our lives
That we are so thankful to God.

And let this be our treasure
To give to our children
And if the time is not over
Let us keep our dreams and
Smiles still in our life

And keep holding our hands . . .

Eva Primero

MOVING ON

Riveted in awe I watch him . . .
Illuminated, sun-struck limb
He used as anchor very well,
And tethered to the garden bell,
His home of silken moorings, fine . . .
All built to set the stage to dine.
At first I thought it was complete,
But then I saw his many feet
With tightrope walker's stance, indeed,
Yet magically, with utmost speed,
He gathered strands, a one by one,
Until his joyless task was done
And unspun, as it were, his home . . .
Then left me standing quite alone.

Sandra Correnti

IT'S TOO LATE

You came into my life,
   when it was dark and cold.
And gave me your sweet loving,
   to gently soothe my soul.
Your beauty brought me sunshine,
   and your smile warmed my heart.
And I was soon believing,
   our love, no one could part.

My love for you grew stronger,
   with each new passing day.
I couldn't wait to see you,
   and I'd hope that you would stay.
I know I never told you,
   the way I felt inside.
I know I never showed you,
   my love . . . I seemed to hide.

Now time has turned its pages,
   from the love that we once shared.
And turned it to another,
   where you no longer care.
Now it's too late to say I'm sorry,
   and try to start anew.
Too late to say I love you,
   for you've found . . . somebody new.

Thomas R. Wien

WHEN I TOUCH YOU

When I touch you,
The clouds wave rainbow
Kerchiefs in the sunlight.

When I touch your face,
I find starlight to guide
Me through the darkness
Toward magic mountains
Where my journey ends.

To hold you is a gift
Of music in my arms
And blest with sound,
A symphony of joy
Sings within my heart.

When I touch you,
I'm eager child again
Running in summer fields
Bright with light and laughter
Because I've found you real
And not just a dream.

Walter W. Price

ELLENSBURG GOTHIC
THE GRANDFATHER TREES

The wind whittled
those trees
a long time

In a permanent
curvature of the pine

Slouching and muttering
together as though

they'd been
rubbed the wrong way
for too long a time

Leaning feather ruffled
in a querulous Row

made buzzard hunched
and grumpy by the
constant blow

Lisa Warren

ENCHANTED CITY, GENTLE LADY

Enchanted city, rising from
Your blurred amorphous bubble bath
Of foamy clouds, what raggedy
And roughly torn unravelled seams
Of tattered lives do you conceal
Within your hidden alleyways
And splintered darknesses? What dreams
Lie shattered in your gutter streams? —
The ones that no one sees except
Police or shadows they pursue?

Or should we only seek to find
An artistry to please the eye —
As in some charming portraiture
Of long-ago delight and grace?
We know the gentle lady's skirts
Are trailing in the mud, and yet
We only see within her face
And smile, her hat and gloves, her lace-
Embroidered dress and parasol
The loveliness that meets our eyes.

Mauricia Price

I've seen the moon in all its splendor.
A quiet, pale light that speaks of its
gender.

Moon of the night, so unrevealing of the mysteries that glow beyond You.
Mysteries of Man and Woman and what is true.

High on a mountain I saw You as You pulled the sparks from the sun, down
around Asia's eyes as its work here is done. As a gift to exchange day
for night the sun burst into colors and rid my eyes of light.

Then, peaceful was the gloaming that the moon promised to bring. A flight
to my mysteries and I pondered them 'til Asia returned light to my world.

We all must sleep, but God is never still. For when we see Him rise and
set, we know He hopes to give us thought.

A Vision of Light, A Changing Day, A Child who must Be Taught.

Audrey Albrecht

DRIPPING

Faucets drip incessantly when sweet slumber's kiss is lacking.
Night meditations of a restless heart, day's hopelessness it's
tracking.
Though his soul desires night's sweet caress, his heart will not
give rest.
Though blessings abound on every hand — in this he's not been
blessed.

Drip, drip, drip, drip, the waters, they keep speaking.
Yet never addressing the answers that his troubled heart is seeking
Regular, constant continuity is the water's intermittent flow.
The lack of night's stillness on his breast — the world will never
know.

Why does the incessant water flow stream toward streams of
thought?
Primal thought from deep within this wretched soul are wrought.
Wrenched before he could run away and find solace in sleep's embrace.
Wrenched while he lay sleeplessly — coldness in his face.

Sleep finally overtakes him, and he settles in her arms.
Giving in completely to the sweetness of her charms.
Wakefulness' resistance into unconsciousness is slipping
While the world around him fades — with its constant dripping.

William Arnold McLeod

TRULY DESERVING

tears of loneliness can only explain how I feel for you,
and I wish I could tell you what is here, in my heart.
but being away, time is the thing which keeps me blue,
and I can't really let it begin to make me crazy, and tear me apart.

as I write to you, do you see what my heart has in store for you?
it's the strength and sadness that makes me know what I truly deserve,
and surely do deserve your love, which in turn isn't just a lonely two.
I am always here, and my mind has thoughts only of a young love, preserved.

it's only once in a lifetime that a person can feel the way I do,
and I hope that the pressures of time don't change our relationship any,
because it has taken me this long to realize that I need you,
and letting you know how I've tried to grow inside of you each day,

makes the love inside of me swell with the triumph of winning a marathon.
as I continue to examine my protected feelings, I know the thought is shared.
I guess it's the blocking of thoughts of you, which weigh more than a ton,
and I don't plan on having this feeling for a long while, because I do care.

maybe this is just young love,
but I want this feeling to last as long as I have breath to breathe.
and the minor noted songs that go on in my mind from up above,
may take me away, to another dream, still I never want you to leave.

A. Kevin Wade

The Brides Vail   The Oyster

The Tower of Babel

The Ghost Chamber   The Shell Room

CHAMBERS IN WEYER'S CAVE.

Gentle ocean breeze
rushing past the tide.
I thought I would see you again,
imagined here it would be —
just you and I, side by side,
loving by the restless sea.
But thoughtless was I,
how foolish I can be,
to think that you would care —
to think that you could love me.
Well — maybe someday I will learn how to choose,
between a lie and the truth
and a love I shall never lose.

Joan Freeman

A PROMISE

I stood beside the sea today
And felt the gentle touch of God
Upholding me — quietly — with great love
    and tenderness.

Beyond surf and spray and wind and tide,
An overwhelming sense of thankfulness and joy
Flooded my very being and my soul
As I plodded through the shifting sand,
Along the wave-tossed shore.

A sea gull, swooping, darting gracefully,
Pierced this thunderous, salt-filled din
With plaintive, haunting cry.
And in my heart re-echoed a reply — a prayer,
    "Lord — lead Thou me."

In the gathering dusk — alone —
Surrounded by sea and mist and fog,
Came forth a sure and welcome response —
    "Trust Me."

Smiling and secure —
I walked on.

Thelma Sturgis

STURGIS, THELMA MARIE. Born: Boston, Massachusetts, 12-20-18; Married: 6-19-53 to Herbert S. Sturgis, Jr.; Education: University of Hartford, Hartford, Conneticut, B.A., 1950; Massachusetts General Hospital, Boston, Massachusetts, R.N. 1940; Occupations: Visiting Nurse, P.H., 1941-43, Captain U.S. Army Nurse Corps, Tyler, Texas, 1943-46; Teacher, Harris Elementary School, Needleham, Massachusetts, 1952-58; John Eliot Elementary School, Needleham, Massachusetts: Tutor, 1971-74, Resource Teacher, 1974-80; Awards: Magma Cum Laude, 1950, University of Hartford; Listed in *Outstanding Teachers in Exceptional Education,* Academic Therapy Publ., 1975; Comments: *As an artist uses pastels and oils attempting to capture the life, beauty, and various moods of our planet; so, too, in a small way, I attempt to portray the beauty of our earth and living things with words, knowing that the bottom line is — God lives and moves in all His creation, and when we love, we are able to take His proffered Hand and be led.*

DADDY, PLEASE TAKE ME DOWN TO THE SEA AGAIN

Daddy, please take me down to the sea again.
Where all sorts of creatures, fish and fin,
Swim and dance in the shifting tide,
In waves as white as unicorn's hide.

I want to breathe the salty air,
and let the wind caress my hair.
To run along the stretch of sand,
holding a sea shell in my hand.

I want to listen to the music of the waves,
and the sea gulls' cry.
Here I will spend the rest of my days,
Here is where I will die.

And when night comes,
you will find me asleep,
Beside the sea,
The ocean deep.

Felicity Dreamer

A NEW SENSATION

The stars were shining brightly, love,
When you came to me.
And I've been thanking God above,
For letting our love be.

I never dreamed I'd find someone,
That's everything you seem.
You've filled my life with a new sensation,
And lent my heart a new dream.

I thank God every day,
For letting our love grow.
And showing me another way,
Of letting my love flow.

I want to thank you too, dear.
For loving me like you do.
And holding me so close and near,
And letting me love you.

Anna Jane Potts

END OF THE RAINBOW

If one could touch the rainbow
    and all its majestic colors so true
Then one can touch the sky so deep
    with the wonder of its heaven so blue

Yet the beautiful rainbow mystifies all
    for at each end there can be found a pot of gold
Down through the ages many times it's been said
    that believers of this include both young and old.

The beholder of the rainbow and its magic
    is he who ventures and tends to roam
Following the rainbow behind the mountain
    where his pot of gold awaits him, which is home.

If you pray each night and wish upon a star
    then look upon the rainbow as your own;
Happiness is simply where you find it . . .
    Not hard to find, for there's no place like home.

Mike Trevino

THE UNICORN

Oh Unicorn, Oh faithful steed!
Animal of fantasy,
Where will you lead?

You are always just a step away.
I reach out to touch you,
But again you tease and play.

Take me to your childlike land,
And I'll play on the beach of
        golden sand.

And if one hurt or tear should come near
The tide will erase it,
Never to reappear.

The road of reality is sometimes hard to walk,
The friend of imagination
Glistens in the dark.

So follow the unicorn if he ever comes your way.
Hold tight to your daydreams,
You will laugh, and love, and play.

Charlene W. Wikel

SOMEHOW . . .

Somehow . . .
You opened my eyes to make me see,
how much love could mean to me.

You gave to me the love I have longed for,
and your love causes me to want you more.

You have given me love every day,
and do it with your special way.

You bring me up when I am down,
and have completely turned my life around.

You have made all my dreams come true,
and have made me see I will never be blue.

You give to me a special kind of love,
and sometimes I swear it was sent from above.

Somehow . . .
This is all true
because of you!

Charlene G. Crain

MY ADVOCATE

My dearest brothers and fellow men, the time has come
for a moment of truth and recollection.
Emotional Crisis, Identity Crisis blocked our pathway
to liberal freedom and greater glory.

There is a new and prevalent Emotional Instability
sweeping across the land of plenty and blessedness.
For we are men of Insatiable Character destined never
to be satisfied. We are born with Insatiable Lust for
greed and power.

I must admit to you the frightening rate of Criminal Activity.
The violent behavior committed with impunity against people
and personal property.
But do not despair, my brothers.
There is still hope for those who thread the other way;
Universal love triumphs over the negative will.
Knowing our real human nature is the key to self-improvement.
So be it.

Alan Badilloh

MORGAN'S LAST POST

Rattler Morgan's eyes are staring,
Rattler Morgan's eyes are glaring,
Rattler says to grab a broom,
Rattler says he'll troop you soon.

Rattler's breath smells strong of whiskey,
Rattler's breath smells strong of gin.
Rattler's breath smells strong of parsnips,
Let the bloody work begin!

Rattler says the navy's changing,
Used to be all wooden ships . . .
All the men were made of steel,
All they drank was scrumps and snips!

Rattler says standards are slipping
And the men are always dripping . . .
Now the ships are made of steel,
And the men are bloody wooden.

Internal phone, it rang this morning
Says Morgan killed himself . . .
Still he was an alcoholic!
Let's all practice reverse arms drill.

W. F. Jones

THE HOSTAGES ARE FREE

The hostages are free, after such a long time
They are cheerful and witty and say they feel fine,
A rescue attempt was ill-afforded
Ending in death and finally aborted.

Stopping in Germany on their first leg home
They went shopping for clothes and ran for the phone,
They told of coping with abuse and violations of their rights
The days grew longer and so did the nights.

Yellow ribbons and bows were seen far and wide
To show that Americans were still on their side,
The halls of West Point were filled with family and flowers
Where they became reacquainted and danced for hours.

A meal of steak and lobster was part of the activity
That replaced bad memories of 444 days of captivity,
An ecumenical service, about 100 in all
Thanked God for America, let nothing befall.

Then President Reagan signed a proclamation
Declaring Thursday a national day,
For 52 Americans who gave so much
Thank God they are here to stay.

Lorene Wayne

ILLUSIVE INTERLUDE

Moments in the opera of life —
The sanctuary of daily ritual
Wraps your shoulders in a cold wind,
A performance viewed for many seasons
Entertained the audience.
Unexpectedly,
Hearts betrothed to others
Touch at a distance in the balcony;
Desire —
The fire of fantasies and dreams,
Heaven and hell curtains the stage.
Anticipation permeates the theatre, and
The orchestra plays a wondrous song of promised beauty —
A melody of passion laced with the pain of betrayal.
The opera glasses
Lost in this musical drama;
A scene portrayed by lovers of another time,
Another place.

Laura K. Turman

R. MERRIL

I watch the man bend to his work.
It's that palm sweaty push towards the finish.
Constant. The white shove of space
is pure gut, fresh off the street.

He begins, is always beginning
to scrawl & beat time. He feels for
the center, for what talks. It's real to need.
He knows it all like the ending ash of a cig,
a spectacular moment to forget.

Susan Lorraine Madonich

SILVER BIRCH

Stately and majestic she stands tall
The lady of the forest
The silver birch, she is called.
She stands slender and fine
Reaching to the sky
The rays of sunlight pass between the leaves,
To the path below.
The feeling is golden, the smell, it is clean
Nothing is out of place
The moss is on the stones, and everything is green.
There is a silver pond beyond with waterlilies everywhere
A green frog is sitting on a leaf, he croaks as he sees me
God's earth is pure
Everything is serene, day has begun.
A rabbit runs across a walk
A squirrel is climbing a tree
The ants are scurrying along the ground
The butterflies flurry, the dragonfly goes by
A bumblebee is buzzing around
A flower he has found.

Marian Kelly

O'SHEA, MARIAN V. Pen Name: Marian Kelly; Born: Glasgow, Scotland, 3-23-32; Education: Johnson & Wales — College of Business, Certificates in Switchboard and Reception; Occupations: Dressmaker, Copy Designer; Awards: New York Poetry Society, 1985 National Anthology; Poetry: 'The Great Sea,' New York Poetry Society; 'The Silver Birch,' American Poetry Association; 'America,' 'Street of Dreams,' 'Enchanting Forest'; Themes: *Nature, anything that lives and breathes: people, plants, animals, landscapes, moral themes, true adventures of people, places in my travels;* Comments: *I see something to write about in everything: love, emotions, death, mourning, joy, hate, good and evil.*

OPPOSITE WORLDS

To you so endowed with talents galore
But whose values I do sadly deplore
Then I remember with a great deep sigh
That you are a dreamer and a pragmatist am I
And, alas, the twain shall never meet
Except in matters quite aesthete
You float on clouds much of the time
I'm fixed on earth with all its grime
You envision the world as a joyous sight
And all its wrongs you attempt to right
You revel in sun filtering through trees
The gentle wind creating a breeze
The intermingling of time and space
Locked in the bosom of earth's embrace
Wealth to you has a special measure
The essence of nature is your greatest treasure
Spiritual and material keep us apart
Only the mystical captures your heart
The fabric of life that I designed
Comes from a loom of a different kind

Grace Ditzion

MELANCHOLY MEMORIES

The old bitch cried all the day
We gave her pups away
And wandered in her perplexed grief
From shed and barn out to the ditch
She would wander back again
But none of us could come to her relief

Which calls to mind Big Bessie
Bawling at an empty field
From which she was sure her newborn calf would spring
She couldn't comprehend the silent wolf
On his midnight haunts
Or all the grief and sorrow he could bring

Like me sitting in this damned old shed
With Jim's harness in my hands
Its fine leather stained with my tears
For I'll never feel his nudge again
Or him my calloused palm
My dearest friend and partner through the years

Floyd B. McKenzie

THE ETERNITY FAIR

On a winter's day when the snow is falling down
I'll be on my way and leave you behind
I've listened to the sound of your crying out
And I've thought of you each day in my mind
But please don't you cry. Don't mourn for me my dear
You still have to try to be kind and care
For you know that truth will lead you to better things
This life is just youth not the Eternity Fair
I'm getting old and my life is passing on
To something I'm told that's waiting for me
Just what lies ahead I'm not so sure about
It's something that's said and not something you see
It's believing that death cannot stop someone who's good
When you breathe your last breath your life won't be through
And it's knowing that life could not die so easily
And that you my wife will one day come too
So please don't you cry. Don't mourn for me my dear
You still have to try to be kind and care
For you know that truth will lead you to better things
This life is just youth not the Eternity Fair

David L. Miley

SLEEPY HEAD

Oh! It's hard to get up in the morning,
When it's dreary and dark outside.
My covers feel so warm and snug,
Here forever, I'd like to abide.

Why must my alarm clock ring so loud?
I'd like to finish this dream.
But no, it just dings and dongs again,
Till I feel I should like to scream!

Now that I'm up, I can't find a thing,
Though my clothes were in order last night.
And I feel all around with my eyes half-shut,
Till I step on a tack — What a plight!

I think if I ever get wealthy,
I'll sleep till eleven A.M.,
And will laugh myself sick, when I hear ding-dong
From the depths of old Baby Ben!

Joanne Gallagher

GALLAGHER, JOANNE McCARTNEY. Born: Philadelphia, Pennsylvania, 8-2-58; Married 8-2-80 to Lawrence J. Gallagher, Jr.; Education: Springfield Senior High School; Roxborough Memorial Hospital — Nursing School; Currently attend Eastern College; Occupations: Registered Nurse, Mother of two boys; Memberships: National League for Nursing, Childbirth Education Association; Awards: Top English Trophy Award, grade school graduation; Bulletin Spelling Bee: dictionary and certificate; Poetry: 'Grandmom,' dedication to my grandmother, 7-84; 'Confession,' about being alone, 10-82; 'Depression,' serious, 4-80; 'Eden,' happy — appreciation of life, 6-79; 'Strangers,' breakup of relationship, 2-76; Comments: *I mostly write about relationships (people to people, time to people). Most of my poetry is my* heartfelt *reaction to things; I use poetry as a release of emotion (when I'm sad or confused, or happy) This is the only work ever submitted for publication!*

A NEW BEGINNING

This is the first day of the rest of your life;
Now that you have become man and wife.

Never let your dreams go;
Just plant the seed of love and watch it grow.

Now you are as one, no longer two;
May your problems and troubles be few.

Wishing you the best of luck and love;
And guidance from God above.

Donna L. Haas

VICTORY

The sun was high, 'twas nearly ten
My meager troop and I across the glen.

We saw our change, a mighty gamble
Strode we through muddy creek and bramble.

Like Henry Five at Agencour'
Swift action made our works secure.

U.S. Grant himself would've scarce been able
To more handily win that last picnic table.

August Marshall

PEACE

Cast off to the wind
Set sail for the stars
Reach for the heavens above
Set your mind at ease and flow with the breeze
Let your thoughts ride with the waves
Hold your dreams in the calm of the night
Let your fantasies wet your appetite
Fulfill your emotions in the squall that's in sight
Release all your tensions let them fly away in the wind
Let the peaceful quiet sea relax your every nerve
Let your mind visualize the calm of desire
Let your every fear and worry wash away in the rain.

Donald A. Gaeden

WINTER'S MYSTERY

There, the snow falls,
    winter calls,
You feel the hush of the snow
    soon winter must go,
The trees are bare,
    but they are beautiful there,
The birds are huddled in a nest,
The trees are weak, they don't
    sway with zest,
Winter's Mystery is all figured out with me!
    winter is the best
Better than all the rest.

Priya Rangaswamy

CHILD DEVELOPMENT

I love to listen to the simple babble
Of prattling infants. From the life of children
I draw sweet pleasure to note
How reason dawns towards a perfect day.
How the brain kindles and impels the mind
To all the useful purposes of life.

Benjamin Pasamanick, M.D.

LIKE A MOTE IN THE EYE
(or poem of a rejected idea)

Like a mote in the eye . . .
    A cancerous idea spreads
    Like a prancing dancer,
    What God knows, promoting.

Like a mote in the eye . . .
    A destructive storm passes
    and is rampant in tasking emotions
    and tearing

Like a mote in the eye . . .
    you think of me as weak.
    for I am small and passive
    not massive.

Like a mote in the eye . . .
    my spirit will be here.
    my presence will linger
    In your dreams,
    how impossible it may seem.
    Resilient am I, bounce back I will.
    For I am a product of hurt and pain.
Like a mote in the eye.

Aaron Huff

CHANGE

    Change has covered life like a
cloud ready to burst. Realization
of a new today caresses us like
darkness.

    Darkness sweeps across life's
past so fast rejection is lost.
Acceptance is taken by wind.

    Hidden behind darkness emotions
creep out to argue with change.
Forbidding future to accept change
with devotion.

    Slowly life's past is swallowed
by persuasion. Change evades the
past.

    Clouds of change burst; washing
a pattern into emotion to fit
change.

    Yesterday is swept into darkness;
change unfolds into a new day.

Tina Marie Nutt

GALILEO OVERTURE

I watch the hues of twilight,
Amber, rust, and sapphire
quickly elude to black.
Stars peer through
from the other side
of the looking glass.
I see them
in awe and wonderment,
as the first clear image
to a baby's eyes.
In vision, I move among them
and grasp them
with my heart.
Truth becomes evident.
Galileo Overture
is mine.

Dawn Braack

POSITIVE PAST

Never say, "What is wrong with me?"
Instead, find what is right.
To concentrate on past mistakes
Can make your life a fright.
So when you reminisce, my friend,
Don't search back through your life
And pull out all those rotten things
That make your life pure strife.
Remember past accomplishments,
Your ego will be fine.
The point of power is right now,
It's all up to your mind.
So use this power and see the good
From your past history.
Your life will be more bountiful,
Because you chose to see
The positive past that's part of you
Through all eternity.

Jackie Miessen

BEAUTY

Once I had beauty
Beauty of skin
Now I have beauty
From deep within

Older I've gotten
Skin beauty I've lost
But the beauty I have
I've got without cost

The beauty of love
Of God — of life
Of goodness and faith
Of a family without strife

Of animals and children
Of sun and rain
Of the Creator's promise
Of a world without pain

A world without sickness
A world without death
A world where a baby's
Not deprived of his breath

Carole Strickler

WIND

He came at sundown, hesitant,
As though he were afraid of light.
A mere suggestion of a breeze,
A timid traveler, seeking night.

Lightly touched, I thought I felt
Curious fingers in my hair.
Curious fingers touched, retreated,
Stirred among the tresses there.

Curiosity now whetted,
Wind decided to explore.
Rattled windows, lifted shingles,
Not so timid anymore!

All night long Wind played, enchanted,
Seeking, peering everywhere.
Not a thing escaped his notice.
Drunk, he was, on midnight air.

With the dawning, he retired.
He will sleep throughout the day.
Do you think he'll be returning
Once again to nighttime play?

Lois Schmidt

TO MAKE A GO OF LIFE

Be complete in yourself.
Be in tune with nature.
Be in harmony with the Infinite.
Be in rhythm with the perpetual motion
of our universal system
for therein life holds a basin for us
with drops of wisdom, faith and love
falling into it from the faucet of life
With wisdom as your Guiding Light,
always have it filled to the brim,
with life's preparedness within you,
to instill good guiding thoughts
in the hearts of needy others,
adding another blessing
to each new day.

Isabelle Goldsmith

GOLDSMITH, ISABELLE. Born: New York City, New York, 1892; Married: in 1920 to Lang; Education: Teacher's College, New York City, 1916; Occupations: Poetess, Author; Awards: Honorary Award, World of Poetry Press, for 'Thoughts Unsaid,' 3-13-85; Poetry: 'Thoughts Unsaid,' World of Poetry Press, 3-13-85; Other Writings: "Message to the Elderly," prose, *December Rose Magazine*, Winter, 1984; Comments: *Born in New York City 1892. Later spent forty years in Europe. I embarked on my first career as concert chamber music pianist. Keeping pace with time, I went on from there and forged through two more successful careers; and became an author and poetess later in life. What could be more rewarding and meaningful than a poet's and author's human approach to the elderly. So purposeful to instill hope and encouragement via my poems and messages, that it became a ritual. Then whenever the belief in themselves also emerged, it elected them that it is never too late to put the message across which lives after them and if they get to be as old as I am. With thankfulness in my heart, I rejoice whenever similar possibilities emerge from their impossibilities. Five novels, my memoires, stories and poems I have written now await publication. Still going strong at 92, young at heart with spirits uplifted. Each new day is welcomed as a gift from God, adding another blessing to each new day.*

'TIS NOTHING TO BE RIGHT

Since I am always right,
And you are always right,
It follows, then, as day the night,
That anyone is always right.

William K. Carr

LIVE IT

I am a mere existence yet with purpose.
    Guide me. Continue to be with me.
I yearn for your nearness.
    My Redeemer, my Best Friend, my All.
I listen when you speak. I listen when you do not.
    I know your love. I know your touch.
You grace me with the Holy Spirit.
    It fills my every need.
All understanding abounds
    And understanding reveals.
To know and to believe.
        To believe and to live it.

Glenda J. Donley

TELLING IT LIKE IT IS

I may have told you many times "I LOVE YOU"
But that was in a passion.
I may have whispered lovingly those words in your ear
And that was in a passion.
And now, Sweetheart,
When I draw you near
And say you are sweet
And, Oh! So sincere.
It's not in a moment of passion
But from a heart which has known
Right from the very first moment that I could not let you go
Even in a Passion.

Valerie D. Whittaker

TEENAGERS

Life is rough for people our age,
One day in love, the next in rage.
Instead of accepting the way that we are,
We try to be different but we never get far.
Trying to succeed in every way,
Making mistakes that always pay.
We never listen to the people that know.
We think that adults don't go with the flow;
Little do we realize that they were here, too.
They had problems just like me and you.
When the years pass, we'll look back and say,
The problems we had "ain't nothin'" today!

Janna Warden

BECOMING COMPLETE

I know you're somewhere waiting for me
Just like I'm waiting for you — so patiently
For the Lord has our lives already planned
And He'll let us know when we'll walk hand in hand
He'll whisper it softly in your ear saying —
"That's the one, right over there.
She's the one that has your rib and to her,
of yourself, you shall freely give."
And then our knowing eyes will meet
and He'll tell me it's you that I seek
And later in life we'll look back and say —
"Praise the Lord for that fateful day."

Joanne Hoston

AUTUMN GLORY

There is nothing more beautiful that time of year,
    As autumn sets in and winter draws near,
Than the colors that nature gives to its trees,
    Forming a majestic kaleidoscope with all of its leaves.
It looks as if someone had taken a paint brush and went wild,
    To color this world anything but mild.

Emily A. DeStefano

ME

When I look into your eyes
I want to see
All the things of my dreams
But your eyes are empty
They hold only lies
I sit in despair
Wondering — Hoping
Will they ever see what I want them to see
ME.

The life I want, the love I need
As days and years go by
I feel myself losing
An endless battle of hope
I often think the day may come
When I might find someone to share my dream
And when I do I will look into his eyes and see only
ME.

Dottie Pederson

CHIPPING AWAY

Chip, chip, chipping away
each day I play at chipping away
the doubts, the fears of bygone years
and how these led to me — Today.

A hollow sound my efforts make —
to whom? to what? who cares of faith
no longer there and nothing to replace
as I continue to chip, and chip, and
chip away.

Be gone the fears, the doubts, those years —
let me be, let me rest, I tire you see,
and wish to be
                someone building and hopeful
of me.
        Instead? I continue to chip, and chip —
Damn! the chipping away.

Elaine Jordan

THE PROMISE

The life you gave me so
marred with pain, hatred and bitter words
Will no longer sting my soul.

I forgive the mistrust and slanderous words
Though the memories are still there
Forever etched within my mind,
The pain within my soul.

Every bit of yearning; the visions all too clear
Time has healed the hurt
BUT

For the longing of love that you never gave
I promise to my children
No pain but love complete
AND that
For your soul I will not weep.

Julie Spears

IMMORTALITY

Time and a river
running down.
Gurgling, sparkling,
twisting and turning,
arrayed with vigor and youth.

Shimmering in the glow
of morning.
Effervescent at twilight.

A marriage at the fork.
The river widens,
slower, wider still.

Eroded in time.
Brackish and buffeted
and very weary now,
it pushes
against the saline slough
where it is gone
in the entrails
of the immortal sea
to run forever.

Jack V. Diamond

FALSE SMILE

I was thinking back over my life one day
Of all the torment and pain.
And all this time I wore a smile.
What did I have to gain?
One day my mother died on me,
My father was already out.
But yet and still I wear a smile
With nothing to smile about.
Yes I'm alive and well today
But it's not my choice, you see,
If I had my choice right now
Dead is what I'd be.
But yet and still I wear a smile.
Why? I do not know.
I guess that all this pain I'm in
Don't want to let me go.
I wear a smile that shows no joy
Or no contentment to me.
Just a smile that shines out there
That only you can see.
I wear a smile oh yes I do
But only for a while.
Until I find a way to win
I'll smile, and smile, and smile.

Pamela Whitson

THE STARS WILL BE OURS

Silently I dream
But it's not like it seems
Thoughts keep coming back to me
It will be as it will be

Looking 'round at all I see
It's all looking back at me
will you try to understand
will you take me by the hand

Can you help me make it through
I must do what I must do
Tonight I'm here
But full of fear

Just like the sun will rise
The moon will shine
The stars
will be ours

Mary Theresa Cahillane

THE ARGENTINE

The lion's roar was confident.
The eagle screamed encouragement.
And so John Bull put out to sea
To annihilate the enemy.
They sailed afar to a lonely isle
To fight a modern war in style.
The punishment one will not take
When so called honor is at stake.
A futile effort, win or lose,
These issues we so oft confuse.
When many lives are lost —
Impossible to count the cost.
Perhaps pride comes before the fall.
At least it does not help at all.
In such a war no one will shine —
The lesson at the Argentine.

Ivan L. Coe

ETERNITY

Seasons come, seasons go
Playful springs from mountains flow
Mysterious eternity

Seasons come, seasons go
Milder winds in summer blow
Whispering eternity

Seasons come, seasons go
Colorful is autumn's glow
Painting of eternity

Seasons come, seasons go
Field and forest white as snow
Glistening eternity

Inge C. Hill

LOVE FROM YOU

The love from you
was what I'd been waiting for,
for so long!
You are sweet and gentle, tender,
Peaceful, loving and caring!
The love from you,
that might have been mine
is hard to find
another of its kind!
I'm thanking you for this
lovely moment in my life!
I shall never again see you
but to say hello.
I'm sad though glad to store
our moment in a spot
at the bottom of my heart!

H. Jety Quarton

When the path you walk is lonely
And the days seem oh so long
Just look ahead and I'll be there
I know that you are strong.

When the light you see is dimming
And the darkness starts to grow
Just open out your arms to me
I'll never make you go.

When the way you feel is hurting
And you need someone to care
Just open up your eyes, you'll see
I'll always be right there.

Terri McDevitt

The falling petals . . .
   it is snowing in my yard
      Spring is where you are.

Deon Davis

DAVIS, WYNORA DEON. Pen name: Deon Davis; Born: Hereford, Texas, 10-26-31; Married: 12-14-51 to Roy Lee Davis; Education: Chemeketa Community College, Salem, Oregon, AA Degree, 1983; Occupations: Homemaker, Writer, Poet; Memberships: Mensa, Intertel, The International Society for Philosophical Enquiry; Poetry: Two Poems, Haiku, *Chemeketa Literary Magazine,* 1983; Comments: *When life distills itself, when the glory of creation bubbles up and I want to express its essence, then poetry, especially Haiku, is the ideal form for holding the precious nectar. Writing equates with creating, so that is why I write. There is no inspiration quite like watching your thoughts and feelings come alive — in full color — on a black and white page. I write to express human nature, emotions, and the ambience of aliveness that is in all things. In my writing, at present, I am creating a new world of my own in a series of fantasy novels.*

Once again the time has come
Laugh and dance, have lots of fun.
Then at the bong of hands upright,
Leave this world in winged flight
And go now to a better place,
Where no one knows of color or race.
The cares of this world will fade away
To where the nights emit a warming ray.
But don't despair for more shall come
To live like those before had done,
They'll come and go 'til time does stop,
Rejuvenated by a precious raindrop

K. R. Greenwood

CHALLENGING LIFE

We try every day to do our best
And sometimes it ends for the worst.

Whatever job we do, and we are feeling fine
But then something goes wrong
It turns out bad but I don't mind.

I know there's someone bigger than
all of us, that will bring us through.

Living here is not easy, but we have
no choice you see.

From childhood to adult,
Memories good or bad are left.

Until the closing of eternal sleep,
Many people are left doing their best.

Challenging our lives whatever we do,
Faith in God is the answer to the rest.

Jeanette E. Logan

There was a child,
a lonely child.
Who fell in love with a rose.
She had finally found a home,
a lovely home.
Where she remained with the rose.
She shared and cared her life with the rose,
and promised never to part.

There was a storm,
a raging storm.
Drowning her home away.
She saved her rose,
her lovely rose.
But, with her steal, the blossom had died.

There was a heart,
a broken heart.
In promise, her life she took with melancholy.

Blossom and child became as one in spirit.
The child had reborned her beauty,
and forever remained the Blackrose.

Joseph L. Ochinero

THE CONSUMMATION

The foam-encrusted waves lap tantalizingly at my feet,
covering first my toes, ankles,
then my soul itself
with their bone-chilling desperation
Then, quickly, they draw away,
As if beckoning me to follow,
to be consumed in their frigid,
bottomless eternity
In apprehension, I draw back closer to their entrance
see the path of my mortal footsteps,
and wonder what kind of mad, fitless passion drove me here
to be helplessly enveloped by those merciless waves,
Until all that is visible is my brown mane swirling
near the surface,
A tangled mass of seaweed parted from its sandy depths
Leaving merely a shell,
A pitiful mockery of the vitality once held within it,
Like a hollowed-out ship,
The loser of too many battles
Atop
the fathomless, eternal sea.

Debbie Petersen

LOVE (AND DESPAIR)

I hope you call and I don't answer
I wanted you . . . and you weren't there
Where were you when I needed you
You said you would always be there for me . . .
always   Where are you now
Why don't you call   Let me know you are there
Why have you gone away like this
I hope you call . . . and I don't answer
THEN when you need me
I won't be there for you
You shall know how it is with me
The heaviness . . . the despair . . . the gloom and doom
and all that   You will taste it
the zombie-like feeling   Waiting to live again
The waiting going on forever
Someday when the golden moment comes,
and the hurt is gone, the void filled
with love again   This shall be an echo
But for now, I hope you call . . . and I don't answer

Darlene Todd

THE CHANGE

In the serene surrounding
I dare not pause to let my mind wander
Over the objects of life,
Nor the feelings which dwell among me
Whether they be of passionate love or
Intangible hate, which no man
Could change or make pleasing.
I shall ponder not upon the many things which
Make me whole or even those things that destroy
Me and tear me down while ripping the standpoint
Of my heart and leaving me with an
Endless sorrow.
Somehow my mind stops to wonder why
Things were and why they had to be.
Yet there has been found, a place —
A place for acceptance and rest from
That which has chosen to be one way
Against my will.
Where is the change?

Keesha Marie Gibbons

GRANDMA'S SONG

I have loved for so many years yet time swept by so quickly.
I sit alone now ripe in age; will death come soft and swiftly?

I think back now on time gone by;
There is no need for me to cry.

Our family was one and we were two;
Tender nights came when days were through.

So many years we spent together;
Now he is gone but our children live on.

A room full of pictures, a box of love letters;
These are the things I'm left with.

I have loved for so many years.
Has it all been lost, or found again and again in the letters?

Donna Jean Evett

COMIC WALTZ ON AN ICY KNOLL

Soft movement of bulky dresses,
Your hands and breath made misty spirals.
The winter snow,
The northern light,
Made comedy of your grotesqueness.

Soft shadows from your golden cabin lights,
Said nothing of the gruesome lonely nights.
Your clownish smile,
Your comic style,
Could only emphasize your sadness.

Your movement was like a pattern,
Woven in the snow of ancient winters.
A child's delight,
A father's death,
The sorry void that was tomorrow.

William S. Dockens III

DOCKENS, WILLIAM SILVERINGTON III. Pen name: William Silverington; Born: Baltimore, Maryland, 5-19-36; Education: Ohio State University, B.Sc., 1954; Howard University, MS, 1971; Stockholms University, Ph.D., 1969; Uppsala University, Ph.D., 1974; Occupations: Associate Professor in Psychology, Classical and Flamenco Guitarist, Tai Chi Instructor; Memberships: University Teachers Association; Awards: "Improving on Shakespeare," 1984; "A Biobehavioral Approach to Treatment of Amphetamine Addiction: A Four-Way Integration," 1984; Comments: *I try to suggest solutions to the constant conflict between our concepts of what is happening, the emotions generated by what is happening and the consequences of our actions toward shaping a life governed by the unsympathetic principles of chance and necessity. I write because for me writing is a compulsion.*

I was in the circus
I had run away
I was juggling knives and throwing them
at the person with you at your new friend
I heard the audience clap
I juggled and never slipped and threw
daggers into the void and into the separation
I ran away from the circus

P. J. L. Brown

IMAGE

Gazing down into innocent eyes,
Miracle of youthful love . . .
So new and fresh in her arms he lies,
A gift from God above.

Her thoughts race to another day,
When she was wild and free . . .
When they watched the sun set down by the bay,
And dreamed of what could be.

They loved and lived without a care,
Dreams were so easy to see . . .
They lived each moment so precious and rare,
Basking in the joy of being free.

A call to duty one cold December eve,
He's off to search for glory . . .
A man comes with a message: "To the bereaved . . . "
She's left with just a memory.

Gazing down into that innocent face,
She leans back and sighs . . .
Prays that he never learns to hate,
He has his father's eyes.

Elena Schmunk

JOEY

Fingerpainted cheeks
            with yesterday's chocolate,
Shoulders hunched over
            last night's homework
                        at recess,

Eyes that have seen too many "Mom's,"
            too many heartbreaks,
                        hostile homes,
Veil shadowy present with bewildered stare.

A daddy's tears of depression, despair,
            resolve to make a car their home
                        — even for a night or two
Till someone's found who'll care.

Now his desk sits empty there.

Lola C. Tate

BACKWARD JOURNEY

Yesterday I journeyed back to the place
    where I was born,
In place of the woodland that I loved, were
    rows and rows of corn.

The old house still was standing, but was
    sadly in decay,
The only inhabitants were rats and mice and
    a few scrawny bales of hay.

I couldn't find the spring of cold water,
    at the foot of the big red hill,
Gone was the wild plum thicket where I
    used to eat my fill.

Gone were the wee folk and fairies, that
    I chased among the flowers,
Gone was the shady pasture field where I
    spent many happy hours.

How can all these changes be? I asked
    as I turned away,
Has it been fifty years? Seems like it
    was yesterday!

Ina Price

FACES OF TIME

It's sad to be so very young,
    Too young to ever know
The faces in the photographs,
    From whom my roots did grow.

The faded pictures hang, so loved
    And cherished on the wall,
Reminding me that I am part
    Of a time I can't recall.

The faces hint of harder times,
    Of which, I know not well,
There's so much more I'd like to learn
    From the lips that cannot tell.

Their end did come to pass, alas,
    I guess you'd call it fate,
To ask about their unique world,
    I came into it too late.

Although I know, when my time comes
    And my death I can't outrun,
I'm sure I'll see that bright, bright light
    And I'll meet them, one by one.
    Les Watkins

That shattered window you saw
Lying outside today
Each splinter came from my mind
I tried to pull them away.
The bloodstains on the grass
and the ones on the window
came from the pressure
of trying too hard to know
where each faded line would lead
I'd have to etch them in on my own
I don't really mind, I'm just afraid of losing time
'Cause the little girl has grown.
The jagged edges still pointing up.
from the side of the windowpane
are sharp so don't touch them
you've nothing at all to gain.
That one splinter hanging
from the cracked and paint-peeled wood
is the very last one left
I'd save it if I could.
    Roberta Serra

FAREWELL MY LOVE

I stared into her eyes,
  as her hand caressed my face,
the words she spoke so softly,
  felt cold in her embrace.

I pulled her closer,
  trying hard to hide the pain,
so many things she wanted to know,
  so many feelings I couldn't explain.

She smiled and said, "don't cry,"
  as she wiped away my tears,
"a part of me will always be with you,
  to help you fight any fears."

She said, "just hold on to the memories,
  'cause it's the sweetest thing we own,
and look back on the happy times,
  to find you'll never be alone."

I kissed her gently,
  and said, "you'll be all I'm thinking of,
until we're together again,"
  she whispered, "Farewell, my love."
    Bernie Felix, Jr.

THOUGHTS FAR AWAY

As I look out and gaze on the city lights
The palm branches sway in the cool night
Wondering how long will I be able to cope
With every passing day there brings new hope
Looking up into the sky at each star put in its spot
Knowing that if I were a star this ole place would be a dot
The fragrance of your perfume lingers on
Yet somehow my love I know you're gone
The sweet and gentle music that whispers in my ear
Cradles each and every thought of our love which I hold very dear
Now I will sleep to dream of you
When once again one and one will together make two

    Joan Weaver

WEAVER, JOAN ARLEN. Born: West Milton, Pennsylvania, 9-27-59; Occupation: Radioman in the U.S. Navy; Comments: *My poems have no common theme or ideas just emotion and thoughts put on paper. I write poetry to relax and get what I feel out into the open. I feel poetry is one of the best ways I've found to express my true emotions. It's fun to create. Like crossword puzzles, once you start, it's addicting.*

DEMISE OF ANON

Toward the end of the day,
When he had quite accepted the grey.
Where the evening was still,
and he had set firm his will.

"These bind me not, nor those, nor I."

So innocent, so guarded, so perfectly complete.
A bubble, effervescent, yet dripping with meat.
With stones in his pockets and visions in his eyes.
Walking into the ocean, reaching for the sky.

"Nor that I should wish it gone.
For with it, with me. I need it as such."

There came on the edge of the cover
The faint but growing points of another.
It pushed and it pushed under the wall.
The sun shone through and it covered all.

The sun-flecked ocean filled his view
and lungs.
The hard gravel of the bottom was muted by water
and death.
The world was green
and gone.

    James D. Friedly

70

KNOCK THE BARRIER DOWN

Knock the barrier down my love
   Let's never let us lose
Think as I do darling and we can
   Make our life as we choose

Knock the barrier down my love
   For we are stronger than they
This thing we have found together is
   Worth the fight and here to stay

Knock the barrier down my love
   When at times I make a mistake
For without your care and love
   My heart might surely break

Knock the barriers down my love
   Now that we've so much to gain
Forever will I love you — even
   When beneath the ground I'm lain.

Michele Daune Polito

POLITO, MICHELE ANN. Pen Name: Daune;
Widow; Occupation: Writer of novels, short sto-
ries and poetry; Poetry: published in previous
American Poetry Anthology, 1985; Other Writ-
ings: *Uneasy Veil,* novel, Winter 1983; *Chicken
Town,* novel, Exposition Press, Summer 1985;
short stories and articles in popular magazines;
Comments: *For me, being a writer is a small
curse — as well as a gift — You cannot stop!
No matter how you try, If? the talent is there,
it is indeed a deep part of one's soul — Just
there!*

GIFTS

I stopped people
From buying gifts for me.
Although they buy
A gift for me,
They are not thinking of me.
They are thinking of them.

When you buy your gift
With the thoughts of me,
Let it be for the thoughts of me.
And not let the gift for me
Be with the thoughts of you.

Carolosue Wright

MAYBE

Can anybody hear me talking?
Sometimes I feel so alone.
Can anybody see my crying?
Not if I'm hiding at home.

I need to get myself together again,
And cut out the self-pity.
I need to find a reason for living,
Maybe I'll leave this city.

I think I've found someone to love,
To share my hopes and dreams.
I think I might just be okay,
Life isn't as bad as it seems.

Maybe I won't leave after all,
He makes me want to stay.
Maybe I can make it work,
Tomorrow is a brand-new day.

Now everybody hears me talking,
And I don't feel so alone.
Now nobody sees me crying,
And I'm no longer hiding at home.

Davena Smith

THE GULL

A gull flew by so gracefully
Its nature on the wing.
He caws at you then soars away.
Its beauty with a fling.

He is so sleek, so free and wild
It's lovely to behold.
If only man would search and seek
Its mysteries all so bold.

He only hunts for food to eat
And leaves the rest to God.
Somehow he knows he will survive
And never will be trod.

If man was free as is the gull
Our world would better be.
Yet God does know what has been done
It's up to us to see.

So like the gull let us be free
And live a life of love.
Forget all hate and selfishness
And act just like the dove.

Robert Lovelace

LIFE

In our time we see,
Why we must understand,
What our lives will be.
Why we must grow old,
Before we see that,
We have reached many goals.
Sometimes to succeed,
We must climb many hills,
Begin where we must,
Battle all kinds of hells.
And have you noticed?
When you stop and think,
Where have we gone?
Does something have to link,
Where we did begin,
To what we shall end?
And what will become,
Of the message we send . . .

Joseph W. Trusty

BRANCHES

And when the branches of our love
Grow, and reach out,
They will be filled
With the leaves of tender moments;
And nestled in them,
Will be the feathered caresses
We have shared.
And the wind blowing through them
Will carry with it,
A medley of love songs, we have spawned.
And our branches will be covered,
And protected by the bark of truth.
And the roots of our love
Will stand firmly rooted,
By our passion for life,
And for each other.

Robert F. Vitalos

FIRST SURRENDER

She would have to pick the day
That she was willing to say
I surrender

He would have to pick the place
To use calfskin and lace
To accept surrender

She must pick the hour
Strong she has to be
In giving surrender

He has to know when to enter
And gentle he has to be
When accepting, first surrender

Eddie M. Hendrick

THE CHILDREN'S TABLE

How fortunate are we
Who knew the magic and majesty of
The Children's Table.
Exclusive we sat,
With personal cuisine and napery,
Enjoying adult attention.
But as all things must end —
Came the fateful hour.
Cousin David announced with hurt dignity,
"I'm too big to sit at the Children's
   Table."
Although we who remained in our sanctum
   sanctorum
Still held court,
Somehow, the Children's Table lost a
   piquant flavor.

Sara Katz

Time after time
We look at the world
To see a coldness
It grips the heart
It drowns the soul
Taking them down
Into the silent pools of despair
Yet in my heart
You will find warmth
You will see compassion
For I am unlike
Anyone before
I am me
A part of forever

Tim Bass

PA

See the figure at the top of the ramp
Eyes searching the crowd with strain
We wave and shout but he hears not our cry
That old man debarking the plane

His face is sun-browned, his hair streaked with gray
His body rebelling often in pain
He stands less tall, takes a slower step
Descending the ramp from the plane

He is nearer now to the turnstile gate
He smiles and waves. Have our thoughts been profane
He is warm and joyful, bent, yet proud
Greetings Dad, dear Pa, how was the ride on the plane

What secrets does he hold behind that tinge of a smile
In his eyes a sharp sparkle remains
Gentleness, honor and pride show forth
From this perky man from the plane

Through all the tomorrows yet to come
With the sorrows and joys which remain
We will cherish the remaining time with Pa
. . . He just came in on the plane

Paul J. Korson

COOKING MONSTER

It's hard to imagine the weather
Affects how a person may look.
Yet I could be light as a feather,
In spite of just loving to cook.

If weather would never be gloomy,
And rain would remain "on the plain,"
My clothes might not need be so roomy.
I'd be slim and haughty . . . and vain.

As long as the sun shines I'm okay,
And normal as neighbors next door.
But then when it's cloudy, there's no way
To hold back the danger in store.

The Wolf Man, when wolfbane is blooming,
Turns into a monster, it's said.
I pray that I'll stay meek and human,
But something strange happens instead.

When rain falls and greyness reigns grimly,
Though on a strict diet I be,
A mad beast arises within me,
And goes on a wild cooking spree!

Jeanne Gale Wilkinson

FAREWELL, MY SWEETS

I went to the Lab, for a blood test
Their report showed, I was not the best,
They said that my case was, "Border line,"
That meant, I'm not bad nor am I fine.
They said my test was not a dud
That there was some sugar in my blood.
Of what all they said, I got this gist,
That I should go and see a Dentist,
That he could extract or maybe treat
Any tooth of mine if it was sweet.
This too is what the Lab, seemed to think,
I must give up sweetened food and drink
That I'd make a very big mistake
To eat some three-layered, frosted cake,
Or candy, griddle cakes or cream pie
To all such food, I must say, "Goodbye,"
'Tis said my sweet taste I will outgrow,
'Til then, sprinkle on some, "Sweet and Lo."

Bill McDonald

THINKING OF YOU

We knew it was love at first sight
We were made for each other
And despite the quarrels and fights
We would always be together

Thinking of the present, future and past
Dreaming wild dreams, planning wild plans
Wondering whether this was too good to last
And yet hoping that it somehow would

Of drinking together from only one glass
And looking deep into each other's eyes
Asking questions we were once afraid to ask
And cherishing those warm replies

And then it started happening
We started to drift apart
The bond was somehow breaking
Just as we feared from the start

So we couldn't make it despite our tries
We decided we were better off apart
You had tears in your lovely eyes
But then I, I had them in my heart

And now when I reminisce
I hope you feel as I do
That there's only one thing I miss
And that is you.

Sandeep Mehta

ME AND GOD

This battle within me I'll never win.
For too many years I have turned towards sin.
I am not ignorant, nor am I a fool.
I am just a sinner a devil's tool.
I am wise and smart indeed.
This battle within me I'll never win.
Until I open my heart and let God in.

Vivian Sprinkles Nyberg

THE WIND

The wind is unseen but can be felt
To be sometimes like a gentle breeze
The south wind blows strong and warm
While a sea breeze is so moist it can tease

I see and feel the fog as a cloud from the sky
Coming to visit the earth below
It hugs the mountains and touches the trees
Spreading moisture where it should go.

The west wind blows strong and wild
Blowing the dust from side to side
Picking things up and blowing things down
Scattering things like a playful child

The east wind has a rolling sound
That blows the water against the rock
Giving sweet music to our ears
Like a lullaby that others can mock

When it grows stronger it can shock
The farmers and sailors with boats and stock
The north wind blows up a storm
No one knows just how it will form

There are lots of surprises in store for us
As we huddle in shelters and shiver and fuss
And wonder how much damage is done
But we all know that the wind has won

Eva Cook

EPITASIS

And there, in the wee hours of eternity,
Eve's smile, a birthing in her opened eyes,

breaks out in glitters of desire
(as though it were a rising fire
of fever rivaling the sun's)
blinding the wakened nakedness of man

that's Adam bedded in the dust of night,

who sleeps a longing faulted at the loins,
a knot of sap unraveled to run free.
He arises from where his slumber joins
the brooding shadows of the Tree

of Good and Evil and of Choice.
He hears Eve long before she speaks
of pleasure tumbling in her voice,
of valleys plumbed and soaring peaks.

The first sin is the innocence of rite.

They fall: a bruise of ashes on their thighs,
the pungent air pulsating the heart's mortality.

Carlos Angeles

WHEN CUTTIN' WAS ROUGH

The country was wild, the cattle were too
Cowboys were many, cowhands were few
The cattle were longhorns, bred to be tough
Life was not easy "when cuttin' was rough."

There wasn't much money, enough to get by
Loners and drifters, they couldn't be tied

They just got by as best they could.

Days eatin' dust, nights in the rain
Never complaining of weather or pain
Few words were spoken, unless swapping tales
About busting broncs and rough riding trails.

Possessions were scanty, only a few
Pleasures were whiskey and maybe a chew
Chaps and a saddle, boots and a hat
Not many men traveled with much more than that.

North went the cattle to this virgin land
A trail drive demanded a top-notch cowhand
Brave was the man, hearty and tough
Who earned his keep riding, "when cuttin' was rough."

Caren Halmes Low

Chance,
A timeless date with the distant stars.
One magic dance to soothe an aching heart that time
Has failed to heal.
A final chance to feel,
To be the name we seek,
To have the love when in dreams is lost before the dawn.
A chance before we die
To tell the world we lived,
To have unrelenting vigor which made our youth
Make us young again.
One last chance to win,
To play with fire and not get burned,
To take the dive into deeper water
And leave a final breath.
Chance,
A path so narrow,
A rapid rarely braved.

William Lawrence Woods

FATE

He travels the paths of a maze
Writhing in the grips of the mist
Vacillating between sanity and madness
Possessed by the turmoil in his mind
He looks outward for a solution to the mystery
Seeing the city as naught but a human menagerie
He recalls no happiness from his memory
But feels, though in a crowd, he is marooned

Mary Ellen Hartman

BARREN SOUL

In Memory of Ronnie . . .

To lose a friend is hard to bear
To lose someone you care for, harder still
To lose someone you love with all your heart
Takes the warmth from your soul
And leaves you with but a shell
This feeling I have felt
This is my soul

M. S. Dellinger

A WINNER

She died! — Taking her little shroud and cape,
She hurried, lest she be late.
God knew she was coming;
He waited by the gate.
Clasping her hand, He led her to the Angel's door.
Only Saints had entered there before.
In awe and wonder, the Angels attended.
CHRIST'S Mother had ascended!

Ruthe Wooden Graham

TRIALS AND TRIBULATIONS

'Tis bitter taste these trials and tribulations
which may whirl of winds from within oneself or from
that which is not held within the grasp of reaching
palms. Thus, sweltering hearts toil to preclude
gentle breaths of beauty from twirling into blustering
gusts which may tear the silken soul. And that which
has been tested, or that which has been lost, seeks
its strength, its appreciation, through love.

Susan A. Tanous

CRUCIFIXION

Droop, sacred head upon Thy gentle breast,
  Bleed, blessed brow by crown of thorns oppressed
Quake, slender limbs Thy quivering nerves laid bare
  Part, parchèd lips receive the vinegar
Gush, precious blood from Thy piercèd side
  Close, lambent eyes the ghastly scene to hide
Weep, blessèd mother to see Him hanging there
  Moan, all mankind, the awful guilt to share.

Vivian E. Farr

AS NIGHT TURNS INTO MORNING

To the night and darkness comes,
as lights go out in each house,
one by one.

As the air is quiet and the ground is damp,
waiting for the hours to go by and a new day begin.

Just waiting for the quiet to become noisy,
the dampness to become hot and dry
and the calmness to become anything but calm.

To the morning,
the sun is shining through the kitchen window as the
radio plays.

William David Payne

DETACHMENT

So, you've crossed another generation
    and strewn hibiscus in your path.
You think life's full of simple answers;
Made so simple, you've failed to see
The beauty in the complications —
    intricate webbings, delicate silken threads
which catch dewdrops dripping, but
always hanging on precariously, somehow
aware of their contribution to the beauty.
So strong those slender threads of life, that
    winds do not disconnect, but in their
vulnerability they bend. In their flexibility
they arch, in their elasticity they regain shape.
Come forth from the cocoon which covers your
eyes, and get entangled.

Sindi Schloss

THE PINE

I love to dream of days gone by,
When on a bed of pine needles I lie.
Evening campfires brightly burning,
Thoughts to the active days returning.

I dream of a home of pine in a secluded spot,
And a peaceful solitude is my lot,
Acorns dotting the pine-needled forest
As the flaming sun sets in the west.

I see pinecones in the woods so quiet —
Gone, the noise of the day and the riot.
Swaying gently in the breeze — no worry,
There I see it standing in all its glory —
    The pine.

Felicia Gwozdz

A MILD REMEMBRANCE

Sometimes when I am sad, I think of you . . .
And I remember well.

Your sentimental smiles that you have shared with me . . .
I remember.

The caring conversations that we have ventured . . .
I remember.

Our quiet moments of sharing . . . .
I remember well.

And you, at this mild moment . . .
I remember.

April L. Parker

STORIES

Anyone can do scribbling,
about any kind of quibbling.
To write about any kind of act,
even if it's not a fact.
Anyone can talk about a sibling.
Words can be played with, or classify,
then re-arranged to re-classify.
It can be autobiographic,
or even written to be cinematographic.
Words can be played with until one will pacify.
Writing about a cribbling,
takes a bit of dribbling.
It could be written distastefully,
or just ultra-wastefully,
try a little dibbling.

Laurel J. Hinderks

BEAUTY OF DEPRESSION

Depression — emotion;
Emotion reserved for humankind,
Think of it: reserved for humankind.
Depression — we hate it, dread it, loathe it;
        it adds . . . so much.
                Emotion.
We give it so much,
                tears,
                anger,
                frustration,
Never satisfied.
Please, don't run!
Bask in it; the beauty of emotion given you!
And when the clouds break,
                Savor the feeling.

Deric Weiss

I'LL WALK FOR CHRIST

I'll walk through the grass to get to the water
I'll walk down the aisle to sit by my brother
I'll open my heart for another
I'll walk to the church to sing God's praises
I'll fall on my knees to ask God's forgiveness
I'll always have God's lovingkindness
I'll walk down the aisle to help my brother
Open his heart first to God then to another
I'll be there when my brother's troubles hit
Then he will understand God is with him yet
I'll hold my brother's hand while we sing God's praises
I'll always love Christ for he died for me and from
His grave he did rise
I'll have room in my heart for one more brother
Because Christ died for me and all the others.

Shirley Ann Thiry Cullmann

EATING TAINTED FISH

At her hinged house I perch myself on
a wicker stool overlooking the television
of black and white reruns.
"This is delicious" I yell out to the kitchen
keeling over embracing my stomach as
a commercial tans the back of my neck.

Now grinning she trots between me and
Rod Serling removing her apron getting ready
for nighttime retirement. When she snores
I will feed the bulk of what remains to
her clawless cat who seems to like me
as he rubs up against my leg purring
in a Musak tone. I like him also but
it doesn't matter because I'm allergic.

Chris Connolly

VIEW FROM WEST PARK.

WORTH THE EFFORT

So I will disassociate,
with the undeserving,
they only facilitate,
my unnerving.

I will, redirect my forces,
to obtain my goals,
wisely manage my resources,
and allow destiny to take a hold.

With confidence and vigor,
I boldly assert myself,
and challenge the odds that figure,
in favor of someone else.

To allow your course to be altered,
is to lay plans to abort.
I'm not one to popularize falter,
so to stay the course is, "WORTH THE EFFORT."

My venture will bear fruit,
of the successful sort.
Fertile are my roots,
and the harvest will be, "WORTH THE EFFORT."

F. E. Jackson

JACKSON, FREDDIE EARL. Pen names: Julius "J" Damian McLamore (J. D. McLamore); Born: Shreveport, Louisiana, 12-26-54; Single; Education: Western College, Yuma, Arizona; Pima College, Tucson, Arizona; DeAnza College, Cupertino, California; San Jose State College, San Jose, California; Occupation: Operating Room Technician; Memberships: U.S.A.F., stationed in Germany; American Heart Association, Teach: first-aid and C.P.R., refresher courses; A.B.C.; Other Writings: *Thoughts From The Heart,* collection of poems and song-poems, Vol. 1, 1981; Vol. 2, 1982; Vol. 3, 1982; Vol. 4, 1983; *A Book of Poems For The Moment,* collection of poems and song-poems, Vol. 1, 1984; Themes: *Emotions of the heart: love and hate, shades of passions. Inspirational, with occasional dives into religion, politics, and sex. Revolution and liberation.* Comments: *Writing is an outlet, my way of reaching out to the world, more than just a hobby. It's a passion!*

THOUGHTS OF THE HEART

The things in life you love so well
are the things in life most likely to perish,
But when they perish, you realize —
they're the most precious things in life to cherish.

Vickie Postell

A CORNER IN TIME

It's a place that you go to
and know very well,
a place where you know
the people who work there;
you've known the people who work there
for a long time.

You come in to purchase one or more items,
to say "hello" to the familiar faces
behind the counter.

The people who work there
that you see are quite friendly;
you know their names
and maybe even them personally.

For some, it's a place to visit
with familiar faces, and to talk about
current events, news, etc.
For others, who see it somewhat differently,
it's just a store.

But it could be any corner store,
just around the corner in your neighborhood.

Ron Alfano

ALFANO, RON A. Born: Elmhurst, Illinois, 2-24-62; Education: College of Dupage, Glen Ellyn, Illinois; George Williams College, Downers Grove, Illinois, B.A., Humanities, 6-15-85; Occupation: Student; Poetry: 'The Love of Adam and Eve,' Randall House Publishing; 'Man Needs Love,' Randall House Publishing; (These two poems will be published in a third annual college poetry anthology); Themes: *My themes vary, but a few of my poems have dealt with "Love" and "Time."* Comments: *My work expresses an emotional outpouring of thoughts and feelings, to which I have given a poetic voice. My previous works are also "labors of love." I basically hope that what I write is well-liked by any reader.*

OUR FOREVER FRIENDSHIP

Only around you am I free to express
my feelings, my hopes, my desires,
my strengths and my weaknesses.

You'll never know just how much you mean to
me. One of the things I cherish most in my
life is the everlasting friendship I share
with you. The happiness, the sincerity, the
feeling of total comfort in each other's presence.

I hope maybe someday, sometime soon, when I
think back on all the good times we've shared,
that in some special way, I can show you
just how much your friendship means to me.

Dawn Rodgers

AS BLUE AS BLUE CAN BE

Black is as black as obsidian, deep down in a dark underworld
White is as white as pearl, submerged in the depths of the sea
Red is as red as fiery flames
and blue is as blue as blue can be.

Black is as black as ebony
White is as white as ivory
Red is as red as mercury
and blue is as blue as blue can be.

Black is as black as the Lady Night
White is as white as the dove that flies free
Red is as red as the delicate rose
but blue is as blue as blue can be.

Cherise Fong

Maybe the waves *are* unicorns
playing at discovering the beach
than doing their sand-vanishing magic

Not shyly, you understand,
but in the spirit of game
contestants glorying in secret strength

Aware of the universe watching,
too proudly involved to acknowledge
the hovering, limited humans

Who wonder if the waves *are* unicorns
riding within the curls of surf
that rush the beach and leave whispering foam.

Ronan

I DO

You're the only one I need today,
A feeling that I had, each yesterday.
Each part of you has blossomed like a tree,
And all that branches out, enlightens me.

You're the only reason for my thoughts;
A present to the mind which can't be bought.
I'm spellbound to your touch and every glance,
A prisoner of love; a lifetime trance.

Together, we can smile away the fears,
Look forward to what comes with every year.
You inspire me to say the words, "I do,"
For I'm forever, this day forward, in love with you.

Ann Updegrave

And in dreams, when I close my eyes to sleep
Why must you arouse each of my senses
Twisting emotions of inner thoughts deep
Causing my heart to let down defenses
If you love me as your whispers confess
Then don't invade my solemn daydreams now
Though time pretends, the love shar'd is no less
Or life as cruel as lonesome thoughts allow
Just let me escape but once from your hold
That torments feelings of love ever true
To feel once again the life in my soul
To be free and strong and outside of you
You left me but chain'd me so I exist
With only life in memories we kiss'd

Tammy Reo

THE HOUSE ON THE HILLSIDE

The house that was built on the side of the hill,
Stands today so solemn and still.
There is hardly a soul coming or going.
There are no bright lights or no flowers growing.
How sad it is to stand here and see,
That the laughter is gone, it's not what it used to be.
The shades stay drawn and the well has gone dry,
The house is so desolate, it makes me want to cry.
The lawn needs a mowing and the rose bushes trimmed.
There is no sound of music, and the lights stay dimmed.
A little old lady with apron so clean, can be seen,
As she comes to view the flowers and sweep the walks clean.
She pauses a moment to enjoy the beauty and the sunlight.
For she never ventures out in the darkest of night.
Her children are raised and gone separate ways.
Her husband was called Home in his earlier days.
She is biding her time, until she can too,
Join her Saviour in the heavens of blue.
For she knows not how many seasons this might be,
Before she too drifts off into that Eternal sea.

Dorothy America Boat

BOAT, DOROTHY AMERICA. Born: Belle Plaine, Iowa, 5-1-18; Education: Belle Plaine High School; Occupation: Retired Cashier; Poetry: 'Friendship,' Quill Books, 8-3-84; 'Word of Comfort,' American Poetry Association, 8-16-84; 'House on the Hillside,' American Poetry Association, 4-85; Comments: *I have written for a number of years. I do not remember the year I first started but I do have about 150 poems, some short stories also. I love to write; it is a great inspiration, a way of expressing your love for your fellow man. I have written poems for political men never had them published but I enjoyed expressing myself through my poetry.*

LOVE SALAD RECIPE

Assemble two people who are in love.
Mix caring with love.
Blend with unselfishness
Add a pinch of companionship.
Stir in patience and understanding.
Put in a liberal amount of sexual passion.
Sprinkle with common sense.
Stir in a lot of religion.
After mixing well, add faithfulness.
Add a touch of responsibility.
For spices, add humor, laughter, joy, games, hopes, and memories.
Sprinkle lightly with courtesy and politeness.
To thin the salad dressing, add a cup of perspiration (from work) and
a few drops of tears.
Spread friendship all over it.
Serve the salad as often as possible.
If served often enough, this Love Salad Recipe will make enough salad to
serve two people in love for a lifetime.

Dr. Roosevelt Gentry, Ph.D.

Dr. William T. Henderson, Ed.D., CSP

HENDERSON, WILLIAM T. Born: Sardis, Mississippi, 1-12-42; Single; Education: Alcorn State University, B.S., 1964; University of Illinois, M.Ed., 1968, Ed.D., 1974; Occupation: College Professor in Educational Psychology; Memberships: Phi Delta Kappa, Mississippi Psychological Association, Mississippi Association for Psychology in the Schools; Other Writings: *Handbook for College Success: A Psychological and Practical Approach*, Research, Crescent Publications, 1978; *Micro-Encyclopedia on Mate Selection and Romance: How to Make Things Start and Go Right;* Research, to appear, 1985; *Effects of Immediate Positive Reinforcement on Undergraduates' Course Achievement*, Research, *Psychological Reports*, 1976; Common Theme: *Using the intellect to assist one in achievement and solving personal and social problems.* Comments: *Why I write: I write to encourage people to use their God-given resources and talents to help them live better lives.*

GENTRY, ROOSEVELT. Born: 11-18-47; Married: 12-20-75 to Eula Frazier Gentry; Education: Jackson State University, B.S. in Mathematics, 1968; Rutgers University, M.S. in Mathematics, 1970; Ph.D. in Mathematics, 1974; Occupations: Professor of Math, Head of Math Dept., and Director of Engineering Program, Jackson State University, Jackson, Mississippi; Memberships: American Mathematics Society (AMS), Mathematics Assoc. of America (MAA), National Association of Mathematicians (NAM) Phi Beta Sigma Fraternity, National Institute of Sci. (NIS), NCTM; Awards: Cash Award for Written Plan to Reorganize Kennington Co. (now McRaes), 1966; Selected as a Scholar for the School of Liberal Studies at Jackson State University, Jackson, Mississippi, 1979-83; Other Writings: *A Micro- Encyclopedia on Mate Selection and Romance: How To Make Things Start and Go Right;* Book: Mate Selection Points, to appear, 1985; *Inspirational Words to Help Everyone Live and Work*, Book: Witty Quotations, to appear, 1985; "Fun with Calculators While Learning," Educational Game, to appear, 1985; "New Diagram Proofs of the Hausdorff-Young Theorem and Young's Inequality," Pure Math Research, *Pacific Journal of Mathematics*, 1981; "A Generalization of Theorems of Krasnoselskii and Juberg," Pure Math Research, *Journal of Mathematical Analysis and Applications*, 1980; Common Themes: *Caring, unselfishness, common sense, religion, responsibility, humor, politeness, hard work, and friendship;* Comments: *Why I write: I write to make people think, and to help others realize the joy of living.*

THE WORLD WAS STILL

The world was still, the guns were silent,
The soldiers stood in calm defiance.
The passions of the greedy hearts
Had not a soul to play the part.

The nations stood to face one another
And finally embraced each other.
All the wars were finally done
And they realized, no one had won.

The world was still, on every side,
And they wondered why so many died.
And in the mist of that great war
They knew not what they were fighting for.

The world was still, no more they fought.
But peace had come at this great cost:
Devastation across the land —
The price they paid for their demands.

Sue Broadt

LOVE TRIUMPHANT

A cross hung high on Calvary
Purpled with blood and fear
It stood alone on Calvary
Washed by a mother's tear;

This cross bore the man of sorrows
The sinner of men that day
Had shed His life for others
Who travel along life's way.

They buried our God in darkness
After the fashion of men;
But no sepulchre could hold Him
The Living Christ shall rise.

Death is swallowed up in victory
Christ is risen! 'Tis God's plan
Sing Oh Earth your song of triumph
Love hath broken Heaven's span.

Margaret E. Danielson

CHANGING COLORS

I loved someone today
But I did not love myself
And as a consequence to what I am
The relationship was set upon the shelf

Every time I love this way
It happens all over again
Another disappointment, another heartache
I wonder if I will ever win?

Why do I feel so worthless?
Why do I have to hide?
Why can't I just look out from under?
With my self-worth and pride

If I ever want to be good for you
I have to first, be good for me
And realize that I am truly special
Even with my faults and insecurities.

Paul N. Klock

HEAVEN WAITS FOR ME

Up above the clouds,
Heaven waits for me.
Where all my cares here below,
no longer bother me.
Loved ones and friends have gone on before me,
waiting there to greet me,
when I enter the pearly gates.
Day by day I ponder,
what a glorious place up yonder.
I know Heaven waits for me.

Mary Rothmeyer

UNCLAIMED

Who is no one's child? Who has never felt pain?
 Indoctrinated into oblivion and fear,
 Little child who is no one dear?
And who is the child who ages in vain,
Whose prayers are for no gain?
 Where is the justice, the love so sincere?
 Is such only found upon a funeral bier?
Who is no one's child . . . who feels no pain?

No one's child came and went without heed,
 Like a bird lost in a narrow fjord of life
 Succumbing to the loneliness of being disdained.

Never to fruition grew the seed,
 Unable to be lifted from the strife,
 No one's child, who was vanquished and unclaimed.

Kathleen M. Sullivan

TO THE AUTHOR

 Dear Gibran what shame it brings
to wish you back here now.
 The heavy woe that it would bring
in wrinkles on your brow,
 that you should see the gifts of God
so twisted, so ill-used,
 and see the world that you loved so,
so desperately confused.

 You've shown the ways of life and love,
that pleasure is one with pain,
 that we must find our strength above,
this that we lost, we must have again.
 Your words a spiritual truth has wrought,
as a net to capture all.
 Bring again, what you once brought,
to save us from our fall.

Peter Jerome Mangles

FOR EAGLES ONLY

As the prism of the present
bends the fading glow of the moldy past;
diffuses it through dreams and hopes
into the radiance of the future,
tomorrow's adventure still waits
for men struggling with riddles of today
to boldly pick up their backpacks
filled with lessons of the past, and march on.

In the valley of what has been,
old homesteads grow ancient and woodwork rots.
Look up through the mists of what is;
spread new wings and soar to what is to be.
Leave tired ghosts and shadow spectres
to the drab, dull haunting that they know best.
Ride high on the rising thermals
to the Valhalla of the courageous.

Robert H. Dyer, Jr.

STAR DREAMS

I yearn for sights I will never see:
 Skies of red and seas of gold,
For friends unmet but who also burn
 To know the deep space cold.
They, too, on their distant worlds stand alone
 With the chill of loneliness
Fueling their dreams 'til their minds flame out
 Across the emptiness:

To know, to hear, to touch, to taste
 The shoreless seas of space,
The limitless reach of the far stars' light,
 A kindred alien's face.

Few can fathom these secret dreams.
 "The stars are pretty," they say
While they sit with hearts and minds of lead
 And wait for yesterday.
Oh, a star is a bright and shining thing
 But it lights the galaxy's span;
It warms those worlds of which I dream
 But will never touch with my hand.

So still will my mind try to pierce the blue,
 Resisting other's disdain;
Cheered in knowing that there is One
 Who does call each star by name.

Janice Beurling

My love cannot be found in loud, dimly lit places
Nor does it reflect the years of my life
In its sacredness
It nurtures that which it surrounds
And surrounds that which it nurtures
It touches many
But encircles few
Withstanding the ridicule of man
And does not wither with time
Like the fleeting moments without it
It stands on its own
Untouchable
Beyond the range of those who do not know its joy

Courtney Willis

THE COMMERCIAL PILOT

He's flying from San Francisco,
due in: 2:00 a.m. Holding

weariness at bay, his cool, sensitive
fingers play across the instrument panel.

His eyes have trapped the ice-blue sky.
Crow's feet make tracks to his ears. He

would prefer to remain airborne, but his
wind-polished jet has other ideas. He seems

taller than other men, his shoulders are
broad and strong, steady as the runway
he lands on. His hair

resembles cumulus clouds streaked with
silver contrails. He wonders

why his passengers complain of
bumpy landings and bad coffee, when
he has been jousting with lightning storms.

He lands his plane gently as a settling dove,
sees the woman who loves him, turns and
kisses his plane.

Cynthia L. Corbett

THE SEA

I stand and stare ahead of me
At the everlasting, endless sea.
The sun beats down on shores of white;
Harmonic sounds of gulls in flight,
With waves that crash on rock and land,
And winds that blow, seem to demand
The rightful freedom for which they stand.

Though I, alone, stare face to face
With the sea and all her grace,
She steps towards me as if in dare,
Then withdrawn in seemless care.
Oh, so much power, so much might,
If not restrained, if not held tight,
Could end the world in one, lone night.

Vivian M. Strong

OKEMOS

What stirs this wheat field
On this windless night?
To whom do these heads bow?

To whom do these insects chant,
Their phosphorous cant,
On this windless night?

The sky sings tales
Of man's infancy
On this windless night.

My pen is a mighty rushing wind,
On this windless night.

Renusch

The minute I saw him,
I knew it was true.
My heart he could have,
that was the least I could do.
I loved him so well,
From the first time I saw him
The gleam in his eyes,
let me know how he felt.
He told me he loved me,
and he held me so tight.
We parted with a tender kiss,
and a soft "I love you."
The night was long,
with many pleasant dreams.
Dreams of me and him,
being together . . .
Forever.

Becky Hughes

SELF-EXAMINATION

Upon close inspection
There is no detection
In mirror's reflection
Or during introspection
No paragon of perfection
Am I.

Therefore, never again
Will I cast glances of disdain
Utter words of pain
Which my friendship strain.
Rather than keep score
I will ignore
Faults of my fellow men for —
By actual count, *I* may have more.

Sara Lee Skydell

MAX KNOWS HIS GROUNDS

Max is dependable!
Wise to Freedom's facts,
Dogs may be individuals,
But some travel around in packs!
Rats are squealers!
     When they're cornered and caught
     Hard to overpower, until you've
          Fought and fought!
Birds are a different story
As they fly about in glory,
They'll pluck you on the head.
If you're near their feeding station.
When they know that Bird seed
Is *not* my daily ration!

Eulalie L. Steward

STEWARD, EULALIE LOATMAN. Pen Name: Yula Lee, Molly Martin; Born: Dutch Neck, New Jersey, 6-13-10; Married: 12-25-47 to E. Emerson Steward; Education: Glassboro State College, 1930; continued studies to shift from secondary to primary grades; Occupations: Farm Worker, Antique Shop, Teacher; Memberships: NEA, NJEA, Legislative Vice-President of Cumberland City Teachers Association, (Retired 1985); Awards: Distinguished Alumna of Glassboro State College, 1983; Weekly Reader Teacher of Year, 1974-75; Writings: in various newspapers, little magazines, local papers and poetry readings; Themes: *Religion, moral dignity, fun, nature, animals, "for enjoyment";* Comments: *Poetry was a great motivating tool for a newspaper,* The Trumpet Vine, *published by my second grade students.*

The country air
Is clean and fresh
Unlike the city type.
But as I see the days go by,
I thought I'd let you know:
The best place in the whole wide world
Is good old Buffalo.

Caroline Witkowski

HE'S ALWAYS ON MY MIND

My thoughts, my hopes are all for him
But when I pray, I stop and realize then
My son is gone, I must not pretend
As I know, he can't come home again.

I know he's in God's presence there
Now, he does not need my prayer.
I wonder though if he can look and see
Just how much he means to me.

Does he see each step I take?
Can he know how my heart does ache?
I wonder if he can understand
How I long to hold his hand.

Or is my son just sleeping
With a rest of peace divine,
Or does he know I miss him so
And think about him all the time.

Maybe he's my guardian angel
The Bible doesn't say it would be so,
But perhaps that's one of God's secrets
That, in this life, I'll never know.

Eunice Lake

TRUE LOVE . . . (A LOVER'S FANTASY)

How far the distant starlight,
When spirits of two soar in flight.
Burning fantasies of joyous delight,
That dwell within my girlish sight.

True Love, I learn the meaning,
As my mind lay dreaming.
Of silent rapture screaming,
Beneath hot love is steaming.

For loving eyes that caress,
Tender hands that undress.
With all his soul and nothing less,
Sweet lips against mine press.

One touch and I shall soar,
Hoping and wishing for more.
Of the man I so adore,
To open wide his bedroom door.

From you, my only desire,
Is for, your burning love of fire.
Set deep in a mystical satire,
That holds me with a single wire.

Ester Lena Smith

THE REBEL

Got caught speeding
got a ticket, it's a law I couldn't bend
Didn't want to do my taxes
so the forms I didn't send
didn't do anything
that might end up as a trend
Didn't wear the same clothes as the others
so with them I wouldn't blend
I'll never be drafted
because I don't want a war to happen
I'll never kill for my country
but for my country I'd defend
If I see someone in trouble
my help I'll always lend
If you're hurting
I'll try and help you mend
but don't turn your back on me
If on you I depend

Scott Spore

SENILITY

My mind?
No longer a possession.
Crumbling, drifting?
Stolen I say!

How can man, alone or severally
Command the dissolution of another's?
Statistics?
A toast to your health and longevity!

Idiots!
All of them — Bastards!
Only I can hear my thoughts.
Only I can appreciate the brilliance of . . .

Pardon me for staring,
There's a spot on your coat,
A fly! Greetings my little friend!
Perhaps you will listen. Perhaps you will . . .

Dear God Almighty — Please help me!
Is it better this way?
Was I really such a burden?
Why is everyone smiling?

Victoria A. Hopperton

THE CHOICE

How in those silent moments when I let my memory flow,
back to the greatest act of love
this tired heart will ever know,
I see myself saying what I must to make you go.

I wonder now as years and longings pass,
if you had turned but once and looking back,
Did see that every part of me was holding fast
the urge to call to you.
The die was cast.

There is no peace for those who love as I,
only the hope that as the seasons fly,
the choice that had been made so long ago
was right, and just,
But time will only know,
for you have gone as I bade you to go.

Stephanie Moore

LAST WORDS

Oh my child please hear what I say,
'tis the day the Lord chose to take me away.
For in this world of pain and sorrow,
he gave not one of us a promise of tomorrow.

As memories of you as a child pass by,
I lie in my bed unafraid to die.
For my pain and suffering is gone you see,
it vanished as the angels were singing to me.

And when the singing stopped and I opened my eyes,
I saw your tears, I heard your cries.
As I felt my soul being lifted above,
I knew in my heart I was surrounded with love.

I know as a father how this love comes to be,
and I shall not be dead when you think of me.
Yes life goes on, though not always fair,
reach inside your heart, I'm living there.

So this is not goodbye for long,
just till the angels sing you their song.
And I leave you a promise, a last gift from me,
one day we'll be rejoined, eternally.

Teri S. Pratt

PHYSICAL EDUCATION CLASS AND THE CHOIR

The gymnasium floor glistened
under the bright lights
as the class stretched and pulled their bodies into
strange contortions. It
was silent, no breath
could be heard and the instructor's
words echoed
hugely in the expanse.
The choir, with their
Latin chants and hymns,
could be heard throughout the building.
The sound was glorious and
pure, and although the poor
souls out on the waxed
floor couldn't be aware of
it — **through the thudding**
of their own hearts and
thoughts — it lent a
frailty and crystalline
quality to the atmosphere.

Bobbi Blackwell-Taylor

LET THERE BE LIGHT

Staring out this empty window,
Down on a vacant street,
No one knows the feeling that's locked inside of me.
No one's seen my tears running their race down my cheeks,
Searching for something inside the people I see.
They huddle together in darkness, in the shadow of a cloud,
Not knowing what lurks there with them,
Demons laughing out loud.
They're blinded by the darkness,
Like in a soft comforting womb,
But the pleasures of their ignorance
Won't stand in the light of truth.
A light that shines in darkness
Is shining down on me,
And I know it's not for what I do,
But for what I really believe.
It's the light of truth in the midst of lies,
The light of hope in despair,
The light of grace in the spirit of God
And the faith that holds me there.

B. J. Hays

IN A FABLE

It was somewhere, not too far from here
Where I met you.
Under those stone arcades
Winding through the doorways
Of period-piece courtyards.

The diseased pigeons fluttered
In and out of gaping windows,
Then dispersed suddenly, from a shower
Of pebbles, thrown by street boys.

And hooded monks passed by
Like night foxes, their mutterings
Lingering long behind the dust
From flapping sandals.

Remember, we saw the bell tower
Of Corpus Dei, and listened
To the thudding toll of village life
Where women baked bread to sell before the gates.

Katherine Markiewicz

AN EVENING RAIN

A tiny face
pressed against the windowpane.
Hollow eyes
staring into the evening rain.
Six o'clock . . . he should be here.
But not tonight
I know you miss him, dear.
A tiny face
so sullen and sad.
A little girl
who misses her dad.
A dad
no loner here,
'cause he had to stop
for one last beer.
Now, a tiny face
stares out the windowpane.
Tears on her cheek
and an evening rain.

Richard B. Thorson

THORSON, RICHARD B. Born: Minneapolis, Minnesota, 6-25-52; Married: 5-26-84 to Nancy; Occupations: Starting my 10th year as an Insurance Salesman with American Family Mutual Insurance Company; Poetry: 'Eleven Roses,' 'The Winter Warrior,' 1979; 'The Eternal Flame,' 1982; 'The Little War,' 'Words,' 1984; Comments: *Occasionally, I try to make a statement, regarding a current political or social issue, through my writings. But most of my poetry is directed towards human feelings and emotions. I try to write the words we all need to say, but words we don't often hear.*

ODE TO A TOAD

Oh thou slippery slimy sluggard,
Burping in a tone so harsh:
If you're handsome, I'll be bugger'd,
Yet your loved one o'er the marsh
Feels the urge for springtime mating,
Croaks an answering refrain.
Through your song I'm sleepless, waiting
For the day to dawn again.
Ain't life marvelous — Heavens above! —
When even toads can fall in love?

Anthony C. Smith

ANGER'S ARROWS

Brownie is cute
angry/hell-fire bursts out
of her darting eyes
piercing my heart
with flame-tipped arrows of poison.

"Joe, let me tell you —
I'm going to get really angry now"
she says look out — here come
the arrows piercing
my heart burning intense
desire flowing forth
from open wounds I joke
she laughs make-up.

Brownie is cute
angry and fighting is fun
making up-out-and in
love pouring forth from
my opened heart.

J. Butkovich

THE AFTERMATH

The purple lining of the mountain
is all that can be seen,
and emptiness has invaded
the destructed violent scene.
A soft white cloud has risen,
as a surrender to it all,
and somewhere in the darkness
there is evidence of the fall.
No human race is present.
No emotions can be sensed.
This earth has been destroyed.
In control — such false pretense.
Yet somewhere in this emptiness,
a child's cry is heard,
and although he's just sobbing,
his sobs are full of words.
He knows he never chose
to be a survivor of this place,
now he must recreate
the whole damn human race!

Kim Elise Sherman

THE DAY OF THE FIRE

Almost five years ago
The fire came.
I was at school,
Terrified by what was happening,
The teachers wouldn't let us go outside.
Later a neighbor came,
To pick us up —
My sister and I went home,
My dad was in his office,
Gathering important papers.
My mom was at work,
On the other side of the fire.
Up on the roof, we took pictures,
Three rolls!
The fire crept up on the houses,
The sky turned black,
All I could see was the sun.
A few hours later the fire was out
And we went to the Fotomat
To get the pictures developed.

Diana Ostrowski

LIAR

If a man lies
about himself
and that around him,
he has then created
an unreal world;
and all that he touches
or is a part of
is unreal.

I do not want a man
who is not real.
I do not want
to be unreal.
Even if reality
means living alone,
means losing you,
my unreal love.

Rosemarie Ann Carpenter

MAY GOD BE WITH YOU

May you find what you
Are looking for.
May the sunshine find
Its way into your life.
May you see the fulfillment
Of your dreams.
May your dreams lead you
Back to home's light.
May you find happiness, wherever
You may roam.
May you find peace, to ease
Your soul.
May you never forget you
Have a friend.
May you always remember,
That you're not alone.
MAY GOD BE WITH YOU

Robert K. Maki

THIS IS ONLY A TEST

This is only a test
I heard the T.V. say.
Thank you Lord, that it is only a test
For we all know it could be true.
Bombs could fall on me and you
Or a tornado could drop from the sky,
And people could even die.
I want to thank you T.V.
For the warning you give each day
And I hope folks out there too, will say
Thank you Lord, that it is only a test.

Sybil Goodwin

HOPEWARD

Is there any hope bound here
To lend to a man
Of little cheer?

Are there any words to speak
To nourish the heart
Of a fainting meek.

Let me see a smiling face
Which with a meal
Would add it grace.

And let there be evermore
A hope unbound
To call you o'er.

Gary Fredrickson

NIRVANA CALLS

A place to go
where I can be free
Moving to unreal
I leave reality.

I see things I want
And do as I please
None to follow!
None to appease!

I await the time
I can forever stay,
In this fantasy world
So very far away.

I feel ready to leave
My soul heeds me go
Again to such bliss?
I can not say no . . .

Leland Putterman

MY LOVE FOR YOU

As the Evergreen Tree boasts
Of its greenery
And the sky claims of its blueness,
My love for you needs no proof.

For my love, as branches of a tree,
Reach out to you for acceptance
And my lips, with your lips, embrace
As a seal of my love for you.

Let the winds of love
Blow deep within your heart,
Allowing the melodious music
To start.

Come dance with me the dance of love
Let us twirl in circles so large
That makes our heads spin
As you become one with me.

Ted J. Seachord

NURSE'S DAILY PRAYER

Dear Father as this day begins,
  I offer it to you,
And pray that thou shalt help me serve
  Thee well in all I do.

Safeguard the lives and being of,
  Each human I may touch,
Endow me with the knowledge and the skills
  I need for such.

May I be kind and gentle,
  May I understand each need,
Please keep my mind and hands alert
  To perpetrate each deed.

And though I fail in doing
  All I really wish I could,
Help me to learn by each mistake,
  That failure may serve good.

Peggy Stewart

TO THE AMERICAN POETRY ASSOCIATION

I have struggled for hours
to write the perfect poem
but nothing seems to happen,
my talent is suddenly gone.
There is no inspiration,
no precious words to speak,
I don't think there will be
if I sit here all week.
Just a lot of scribbling
of anything that comes to mind,
a very pitiful, little bit,
considering the amount of time.
My weary brain longs for a rest
it's time to bring this to a close,
and all I seem to have produced
are these several lines of prose.
It is not really worthy
of your poetry contest;
but for now it seems,
I have done my best.

Sandra Burgin

A DAILY THOUGHT

A beam of light leads the way
A road of sunshine every day
A precious stone shines so new
Tiny raindrops, morning dew
A casted shadow from afar
A twinkling quiet from a star
A rushing water from a sea
A gentle love is found in he
And yet stern hands, a peaceful grace
A tranquil heart, a rested place
A glow within a humble heart
A binding spirit never parts
As never seen a golden dove
But felt within his perfect love
An added strength from where not known
A caring though has been shown
A mellow cry, a cheerful praise
For from the dead, did he raise
A ruling king, he's seated right
Forever glory, eternal light.

Andrea Gross

EACH TIME THE MOON IS FULL . . .

Each time the moon is full
I make the vow again
I remember most distinctly
the white lady
Each time the moon is full
I can close my eyes and
I am there wrapped in my
Indian clothes/smelling Agra
tasting hot sweet tea
from glasses
seeing dazzling jewels
soapstone tajs
the white lady and her lover
each time the moon is full
I stand transported in the
darkened night to the quiet
stillness of a hundred muted
tourists sitting in awe
each time the moon is full
I am there

Michelle Dutch

THE GATE

There is a gate at Graceland,
  with musical bars,
and a rock and roll star,
  strumming a wooden guitar.
And with a little imagination,
  one can hear a voice say:
"The king, he's not here today!
  He has gone to a place far away;
To that beautiful city foretold,
  with streets paved in pure gold;
Where no one ever grows old,
  and is bestowed riches untold;
A city that has no need of the sun,
  where there's room for everyone,
When their course on earth has been run."
  Before that gate I stood,
One glorious day in spring;
  and I heard the star,
Strum his wooden guitar
  for Jesus, the Heavenly King!

Lois E. Wood

A CENTURY FROM NOW!

The scientists will call for rain
To help earth's seeds to grow.
All pavements will be heated
To melt the ice and snow.
Computers will keep clicking,
While robots work with ease,
They'll babysit for Mamas'
And tend the plants and trees,
Accomplish chores in households,
And shop and cook and sew,
While parents lads and lassies
Are happy on the GO.
His motor wings will carry
A man up to the sky.
Where he will board a planet ship,
And visit Mars on high.
He'll build a moon-house out in space,
Where he can work and play,
And nose-dive zooming back to earth
To pass a busy day.

Margie Zimmerman

TRIBUTE TO LITTLE CARL

There were trout,
  so he'd be fishing.
There were dreams,
  so he'd be wishing.
There was night
  so he would sleep.
There were treasures
  that he would keep.
There was family
  that he shared joy.
There was love
  for this little boy.
There was so much
  he left undone
when his world
  had just begun.
There was Little Carl
  whom we miss so much
and long so hard
  for his special touch.

Margaret V. Olds

GRADUATION DAY

A bird song awakens
A heart overtaken
With summery spoil
of youth.

Ceaseless youth,
How vast his wisdom
This wooer of destiny.
Exuberance unexcelled, clean of spirit,
Liveliness unhumbled,
A lonely jewel in stony field.

He dares the task
of Life's undoing,
Tromping meadows of scholarly pride
Searching for kinship amid worldly saga.

Linger 'a yet in guarded innocence
Or now choose to brave the upheaval.
A seeker comes, is bidden pass through the
Gate of Dreams.
Ceaseless youth with joy unshaken
Steps through.

Betty B. Jones

JONES, BETTY B. Born: Roswell, New Mexico; Married: to Phoenix businessman, Art Jones; Education: University of Texas; Occupation: Writer; Comments: *Gathering the words of an experience, a feeling, or a memory and setting them to verse, — to me, is poetry. I have a great fondness for the writings of Robert Frost. Among some readily quoted favorites of mine: 'Stars,' by Sara Teasdale, 'Moonlight,' by Berta Hart Nance, 'Here Is the Sea,' by Arna Bontemps.*

BETRAYAL

She called to him teasingly,
beckoned for him to come to her.
She reached out her cold dark arms
and when he finally came she embraced him.
She pulled him down deeper and deeper
promising him peace and serenity.
When it was too late he knew she had lied.
After she had taken all he had to give
she tossed him away to float like so
much driftwood on her devious waters.

April B. Ramburg

EXPERIENCE

My thoughts fly like the breeze, and reach
unbelievable heights, and burst into
flame, which rage through the night.

And then come the showers, down from
the heavens above, and extinguish the
fire like a turned-off love.

Passion flares again, vibration giving
of rhythm to the air.
A flowing, constant, pleasant feeling,
leaving absolutely nothing to spare.

Calm winds are blowing, caressing
the hair, sending around tendrils
softly moving nowhere.

Sunlight burning in through every
crevice and pore.
Glittering like diamonds through the
windows and door.

Snowflakes that fall and melt on the
skin, pile up on the doorstep if
not let in.

Gloria Gambale

REMEMBER ME

You broke my heart a long
time ago
We had that silly quarrel so
long ago
My love for you has lasted
all through the years
My memories never end: my
love for you never dies.

Love and be loved is the greatest
joy on Earth.
Was it desire and youth? Or was
it just lover's moon; A walk among
the flowers? Deep inside love is
Everlasting love.
I guess I loved you always, dear,
I just learned the truth.

Deep inside love is everlasting
love.
I guess I loved you always, dear,
I just learned the truth
Remember my love will last
forever in my heart.
Remember my memories will
never die.

Elva M. Hull

A BOOK

A book is a bore.
It bores into the mind and soul.
It bores into a blooming hole
found in the brain's core.

A book pulsates with life.
With the history of man.
Some were crass enough to ban
books that can suppress strife.

We should learn to soar,
As written words must.
Or, writers should have just
written their books to bore.

Alton P. DeRoche, Jr.

REVERIE

I'd like to walk
where Jesus walked
Beneath an azure sky,
Hearing the bleating
of the lambs —
His Holy Presence
caressing them
when He quietly passed by.
I'd like to see the little
children
He held so tenderly
As side by side we walked
along the Sea of Galilee
Hearing His voice conversing
with me —
Like a heavenly melody
As side by side we walked
Along the Sea of Galilee.

Pearl Bennett

BENNETT, PEARL BELLE. Pen names: Pearl Belle Krelwitz, Pearl Belle Bennett; Born: Duluth, Minnesota; Married: 8-5-43 to Joseph B. Bennett; Education: Music: violin, 1910-15; voice, 1920-22; Portland Opera Association, Roberto Coruccini; Occupations: Colatura Soprano, Violinist, Nurse (World War II); Memberships: MGM Pictures; Awards: Satire, Reader's Digest, 1924; Poetry: 'Desert Nights,' 'Soliloquy,' 'A Little House,' 'Two Rings of Gold,' 'Carrot Patch Patch'; Themes: *Satire, religious, children;* Comments: *I have always loved poetry — most any subject that comes to mind — time to write comes spontaneously.*

THE BREEZE

See the breeze as it flows in the sky;
Sniff the limbs as they bow to the wind;
Feel the lark as the gusts urge him nigh;
Hear the cod as the gales now descend;
Taste the bear as the storms are now high;
Sense the world as the whirls come again;
Know the earth now makes a new cry
For love, fellowship, and peace among men.

Deborah Alysande

OKAY, VANQUISH ALL THINGS AT ONCE!

O if I had the wings like an eagle's,
   I would fly to the universe,
   Wandering and drifting as I flew to see galactic civilizations.
Long since, I've loved the mysteries of space.
   I often gazed into the outer space in spirits,
   Yearning that I could visit my superior planet friends.

Some day, I would fly alone in my spacecraft — Phoebus,
   With only the great space
   And Jupiter, Pluto, Venus . . . as my companions.
I knew I would not be lonely, because there would be the music of the spheres
   Humming to me a sweet romance
   And carrying a cosmic dust onto my face.

The red sun flings bright beams on the stars,
   A gale from the heavens,
   And even when there was a magnetic storm's force,
I would face it bravely get to grips;
   I should prove myself an Atlas.
   Okay, vanquish all things at once!

Liu Shi-yue

LIU, SHI-YUE. Pen Name: Joseph Liu; Born: Tientsin, China, August 2; Single; Education: Correspondence University of Logic and Language of China, Beijing P.R. China, 1983; Occupations: Teacher of English, Writer of Poetry, Musicologist, Pianist, Interpreter; Memberships: International Council for Traditional Music; ICTM Study Group on Music Archaeology; Poetry: 'Mother Nature and Man,' January 1985; 'My Dreams,' February 1985; 'Okay, Vanquish All Things At Once!' December 1984; Other Writings: "On Music of P. Tchaikovsky," article in English, *Moscow News*, U.S.S.R., 1958; "A Chinese Translation of Plauen's Vater u. Sohn," article in book, Tientsin P.A. Publishing, 1981; Themes: *The universe and human life, unity of brains and brave. I write for humankind, because I loved them with my whole soul. The great value of man, especially man can conquer nature! The bright future of the human race.*

DO YOU LIKE POETIC DEVICES?

Alliteration, Assonance, Consonance —
Caesura   with the tintinnabulation of an Onomatopoeia —
a false Paradox walking across the lines allowing for Personification of just a small Hyberbole —
and the Metaphors you are and the Similes you are like —
this one is FOR YOU!

Bonné

CARING

Spread your little wings my child
For tomorrow ye shall fly
Into the dangers of tomorrow
And the fears of yesterday
Take special care to greet
Each day with gusto and
Reminisce at each passing dusk
Walk slowly that ye don't stumble
Stride not into the arms of temptation
Reach out for the hands of success
Take with you my love, my respect
My gratitude of having shared your being
Hold me close to your heart
For you will always be in mine.

Starla Saunders

STAND TALL

Stand up and be counted!
Stand up one and all!
Stand up and be counted!
Stand tall!
The American flag is waving!
Waving for one and all . . .
Stand up! Stand tall!
The Christian flag is waving!
Waving for one and all . . .
Stand up! Stand tall!
Be proud of our flags!
Never let them fall . . .
Stand up and salute!
Stand tall!

Shirley R. Salyer

I'VE BEEN GIVEN A MEMORY

I've been given a memory
That contains a special thought
Its meaning enlightens me
Because it cannot be bought

I've been given a memory
That will always make me smile
You shared that memory with me
And I'll carry it down every mile

I've been given a memory
Because time was there to share
I'm happy for that memory
And for you I'll always care

Maureen J. Downey

LOVERS

In the shadows of the muted light —
Of the flickering, fervent fire,
Creeps the romance of the coming night —
The warmth of love's desire.

Two bodies intermingle — one
Emotion dancing in their eyes.
Their dreams and fantasies let run —
And nothing is disguised.

The lovers in the calm of night,
Share secrets never told.
Whispering of their weaknesses —
About the one they hold.

Anita Torielli-Fenley

EVENING PRAYER

The full moon shines brightly in my window,
Shining on my rosary, on which I pray.
Before I go to sleep, I think of this,
Of the little babe once asleep on the hay.
Over the bed I have the crucifix,
The cross on which one day that babe must die,
To make amends once and forever,
For all the sins done by you and I.
Before I go to sleep, I place the rosary
Side of the crucifix to shine all through the night.
And the moon is still shining in the window,
Together they throw an extra lovely light.
And as I drift into a world of dreams,
I say a special prayer at close of day.
Bless all my friends and keep them safe,
I guess that's all there is to say.
Give us all sweet rest all through the night,
That we may praise you with the morning light.

Kay Grady

DADDY

You know Dad, of all the men I've known or know
You are the greatest of them all, you're my hero.
And all the things I attempt or try to do,
I guess I am just trying with all my might to be like you.

When you smoked, how contented you seemed to be
And when I got a chance, a pack of cigarettes I got for me.
Daddy I knew smoking was the thing to do,
For you see dad, I had to be just like you.

The social drink that with your friends you were drinking,
And the drink you gave me, not even thinking.
And when I grew older the hold it got on me,
I just had to be like you. Don't you see?

Doing things like you was a habit I got,
But I went from tobacco to "pot."
And I went from whiskey to hard drugs too,
Though you didn't use them, I got the pattern from you.

Daddy you were luckier or more cautious than I
Else I can't see how you could have gotten by.
Now they have me here in prison, trying to dry me out;
Somewhere I went different from you; no doubt.

Eli Young

SUMMER OF OUR DISCONTENT

I wish . . .
we could make this magic night last forever.

I wish . . .
I could always see the stars
that shine so bright in your eyes.

I wish . . .
I could hold you in my arms
and drink in all your gentle love
like a fine white wine.

I wish . . .
you could see the possiblities
and endless dreams that could be;
if you would just leave
and run away forever with me.

I wish . . .
I could show you so many beautiful places
that we could stop and share.
We wouldn't have to worry about anything else
because there would always be just you and me —
forever running wild and so free.

Charles Walter Rudolph III

WE

We are long together —
Through stormy, through sunny, weather.
The many days never apart
The many nights heart to heart.
The babies came, they grew with loving care,
They grew up and are gone; we are here.

He died in early summer and is away
He died in early summer; I cannot stay
No place other than with him can I be
No place other, is never for me.

How can one live, who so long was two?
The world all dark, no light shining through
Dear God, let him linger at Thy gate
Let him linger, I'll not be late.
No place other than with him can I be
No place other, is never for me.

Madalene Middleton

YOU LEFT ME HERE

We were together for a long long time;
But then you moved and said goodbye.
I cried for months — so many tears;
I thought the pain would last for years.
You moved so far — many miles away;
I looked forward to when I would see you again,
Some other day.

Some months later on the late night news,
I heard what I did not want to hear.
A young man is killed at the age of eighteen;
Then the name, it could not be,
The boy was killed who should have married me.
It shouldn't have happened.
Just three more months,
And you would have been here with me.
I can't believe,
The boy was killed who should have married me.

Dennise Shaffer

MY FADED LIFELINE

I look at my hand and see my faded life line,
Your days are numbered as the hairs on your head.
I wonder after the flesh rots off the bones
where goes the portions of the soul.
I think of my gone and spent youth when I was
a spring suckling.

I know I am fading one day at a time,
When I awake the slumber is like being dead.
I am fading, I wish I were as spry as all the
flowering youths that conquer the world.
I am fading, degenerating, emaciating, I am
fading slowly away.
I am fading one day at a time,
You die one day at a time.
My life line traces into the graveyard.
Cherish the minutes and days of the precious
gift of life.

Steven J. Smith

BROKEN BLOSSOMS

Broken blossoms fallen and adrift —
all too soon they fade and die —
blown by the wind, like beggars they drift, no
permanent roots to hold them fast.

Robert Dureson

ODE TO AUTUMN

A burst of color
A roar of thunder
Nature beckons us to ponder
Her seasons gay and grave with wonder
Like sons and daughters tuned in choir

Autumn sweetly sighs from yonder
Twixt summer gay and somber winter
With arms outstretched from one to other
She takes and gives from nature's blender
To fill our falls with skies of amber

One hand sweetly warmed by summer
The other nourishes cold winter
Her leaves she bathes with raindrops tender
The countryside she paints in splendor
With colors only she can muster

oh Autumn! A friend of old September
Let's not forget your virtues dear
With golden days and nights so clear
and songs of love so sweet to hear
Your season is a spice so rare.

Melva Bracchi

BRACCHI, MELVA AURORA. Born: Jamaica, 9-25-38; Married 6-19-65 to Francesco Bracchi; Education: West Ham College of Technology, London, Advanced Level GCE; Occupation: Scientific Laboratory Technician, University of Milan; Comments: *Poetry is one of the many expressions of the "inner self" of man, that part which needs to be nurtured and safeguarded just like the body. Poetry, art and music have proven to be vital in taking care of that "inner self."*

APOLLONIE SABATIER/LOVE FOR THE TOY DOLL

Let me caress your hands in cold embrace.
Oblivious to their mercy pleas
Let the fallen souls scream around us.
Breathing scent is now so past
Days of agony for your warm touch to return
But knowing it never shall.
Gone now are the tender tears
With bright smiles of silly games
Laughter of the shared thought
Is but echoes in a hollow shell.
And my life shall now be interrèd
As I return to my velvet grave
Where corpses sing of pleasures dead
And where memories are all that breathes.

Mark Jocasta

GUIDING STARS

Two little stars in the vast space of life
Special in all that they do,
Learning life's wonders day by day
What shall they learn from you?

Were you honest that they might know
How harmful a white lie might be,
And were you consistent in praise and fault
As you daily change twig into tree?

A boy and a girl both reaching on high
For ideals to be handed down,
Did you help guide their tiny minds
With twice as much smile as frown?

As grandparents you are liable
For seeing they are all they can be,
So if you must spoil them rotten
Please see if their parents agree.

Gladys M. Case

ACT I

I am but a smiling face,
A clown on the stage of life,
Who will make your eyes sparkle
And make your heart sing.

Admission is free
And when you're with me
You can become anything you want to be.

I have learned my act well
And I know you will be pleased
By this painted grin and silly suit
And nothing up my sleeve.

While it's true my performance is not one to be missed
And I really am a star,
There's just one thing that you must know
Before this goes too far.

Everyone loves a clown
So that is what I choose to be
But the pancake make-up is hard to wash off
And my costume almost a part of me.

Starr Cochran

ST. AUGUSTINE'S ABBEY, CANTERBURY

The day had a spacious effect about it.
The ruins of St. Augustine's Abbey sank
back gradually inside their shadows
like sand castles melting in the lifting tide.
We waded through the soft black pools as they rose,

taking the darkest possible photographs.
Suddenly you swung through a ninth wave, great red
weeds of November wind streaming out like kelp
from their holdfasts on your wing blades. I still
have that photograph of you facing the yelp

the wind made, like Queen Bertha with windy wings
and the golden fur from the treed sun blurring
the black hair-threads that haloed your head. I held
your hand as you stood down from the wall, then freed
it, letting it swoon back to place like expelled

flowers too old and too faded to arrange.
You were another man's wife. That hindered me.
But for a moment, I confess, your face
was eyeshattering, suggesting not so much a saint's
as your own face in a distant time, a distant place.

Roger Finch

BENEVOLENCE

A tearing heart makes no sound from without.
The reservoir, that held so much, can hold no more.
A futile fight, a loss of love or bested bout,
It matters not the reason why, only that the heart is tore.

The tears do glisten as they leave their salty trails.
A sign of seas hidden behind the vulnerable levee.
They show the dam's custodian, his job he fails.
Allowing the ocean of one's soul ebb outwardly.

Who can save this disaster from destroying the source?
Only one who has felt that pressure subside.
For the engineer who has known and felt the force,
Knows well the cement that must be applied.

Neither text, nor book or lecture of understanding
Can mend a torn heart, nor stop the tide of tears.
Only those whose heart shows cemented scars of yearning,
Will dry up the pool of despair and put away the fears.

Norris S. Pendergrass

THE SAD ENIGMA

Within the space of a sigh,
one discordant heartbeat
signals the onslaught of despair —
your familiar, but impatient visitor —
a mongrel pup that nips at your heels
crying, "Pick me up, take me home."
Your heart then slams in submission.
Its weight holds you fast from flight.
And the roots of your self-doubt
anchor you firmly in foolish pain.

You have no freedom now.
Your body controls you in a
mutiny of flesh and bone.
Your blood knows its journey well.
Coursing along scarlet banks,
it carries you in a race you can never win.
And at the finish line
is the razor's sharp edge.

Deborah Dasch

MY NEW SNEAKERS

I passed the cashier my bucks for sneakers new,
She gave me the shoe box — shoes of deep blue.
I scraped them, I stomped them, and kicked up dust,
Wear 'em down; break 'em in — a definite must.

Finally, after a month, it took no more,
The sneakers had my mark. Man, what a chore!
I woke up one morning. My shoes! They're gone!
I looked under my bed, saw not even one.

Under my oak dresser, then all around,
In every dark corner, not to be found.
Then I saw a new pair with not a fray.
Mom came in with their fate, "Tossed them away."

All the tiny nicks, every last hole,
Chucked in the garbage, left without sole.
All of that energy, all my work gone,
And Mom didn't understand, "What could be wrong?"

Janet Lopes

SECOND DATE

I felt like writing you a poem.

I wanted to tell you all about me.
In one word
Inamillionwords
Spoken at once.

How lucky you are
To meet me
At this   precise   prime of my life.
How lucky I am to be
                              Me
At this precise moment:
          Not growing past
          Not distant future.

I wanted to describe in complete and loving
detail
The amazing complexity
That I am.
That I am discovering.

And I don't want you to be frightened.
And I don't want to be afraid.

Terry P. Teague

JUST A DROP

I was just an ordinary person,
          Exploring the ways of the world.
But alas, I explored too far and too deep,
          God's standards, I sadly ignored to keep.

So I reasoned with God, conveying my desire,
          "Please Lord, could you forgive my past?
What must I do? What is the price,
          To grant me blessings that eternally last?"

"My child," said God, "there is no price,
          For the solution is: Just a drop."
"A drop of what?" said I, "What could a drop do?"
          "A drop is the answer," said He, "a gift for you."

Yes, without this drop, you cannot be forgiven,
          For it is divine, and no one can comprehend;
This magical formula called Redemption,
          Through which God's agape love transcends.

Accepting it, you will have an abundant life,
          Joy and Heaven and oh, so much more.
Because that SPECIAL DROP — that DROP OF BLOOD,
          Was the touchdown at Calvary's final score.

Gladyce E. White

THE WORLD WE KNEW

The world we knew together, destroyed forever,
By the changing world of hate, hope in it's not too late,
The swift blowing wind, taking you astray,
To a world I knew nothing, but you found your way,
The sweet birds were singing, you thought it was heaven,
It grew cold with horror, not hell could it be even,
It was a dungeon away from civilization,
The world you became a part of,
You were abused for all sorts of reasons,
While I looked from above,
Is it too late to bring you back up?
Can you find your way with a little luck?
Do you still hear me calling out your name?
All these years have passed, I'm still here the same,
The sweet birds are here singing your song,
They're waiting for you to come back and belong,
To this world we knew a long time ago,
Maybe we can begin again, or maybe we'll never know.

Peggy Zeaphey Nerl

TIME

Stillness of time
passes without echo . . .
For only man, not time, records.

Time is untouched by rain
Unmindful of sun — passing by
tumult of war and dirge of death.

Time can't be held in your hand
. . . It holds you in its grasp.

Winnie E. Fitzpatrick

FITZPATRICK, WINNIE E. Born: Atlantic City, New Jersey, 10-23-26; Married: to James P.; Education: St. Matthew's High School; Santa Rosa Junior College, 2 years; Occupations: Clerk/Typist, City of Santa Rosa; Writer/Poet; Memberships: California State Poetry Society, California Federation of Chaparral Poets; Poets of the Vineyard; Awards: 78 Poetry Awards; 3 Prose Awards; Poetry: *Happy Time Poems,* children's poems, 1979, 1980, 1981, and 1982; published by Minute Man Press; Comments: *I wrote the children's books to help children to learn to enjoy poetry.*

AUTUMN

A willow fills the lake
In a sad farewell to her summer love
And swans gather in the air
To escape the wake.
Everywhere,
Mounds of tarnished leaves
Give off incense
As they return to the trees
That bombard the rooftops
With their wooden eggs.
Squirrels wait for the fallout
And squadrons of geese
Retreat in the evanescent blue.
Somewhere,
In the navel of an oak,
A legged sage weaves himself
Into a silken refuge,
Away from the stench of death,
alone with dreams of flight.

Roberto Ruiz Galván

IMPRESSIONS

When I take a walk on the beach
And in the sand are the impressions
    of my feet,
The ocean water comes along
And washes away any impressions
    upon its beach.

And in my mind
That is the way my heart
Would like me to see you.

And if anything remains
It is only what was valuable
For my heart to keep.

Cathy Lyn Steinert

RESPECT

One day the silent night did fall,
And the love was gone forever.
It pinched the heart to a whispering call,
For familiar ties were severed.

A sadness and wondering gathered there,
A longing to know life's feelings.
Then confidence crashed the swelling fear,
And opened the world to new meaning.

Happiness filled the heart once more,
For now the truth was known.
Love for another isn't life's core.
It's respect for yourself alone.

Susan R. Stephenson

FIRST CROPS

Purple and white
tassels
of fireworks
spring
into the green sky

Soon
they'll turn
to red
and glowing
embers

Hey hurray!
Mom's gonna bake a cherry pie

Jana Suchy

LOVE

Love cannot be forced
    nor can it be bought;
it is free as a summer's breeze,
    gentle as the April's rain,
joyful as the nightingale,
    bright as a starlit night,
warm as the radiant sun
    and sweet as a flowery ground.
Love is intangible;
    until it touches the heart of o
                                    n
                                    e
                                    '
                                    soul.

Maria L. Canales

FRIEND

Friend
            this is where we p a r t!
Our end has finally come.

But, when we meet in the next world,
I promise you friend
With all my heart
It will be beautiful.

Our friendship was worth
It all!

Believe me as I say:

I wish all others
Were as friendly as you;

I wish that I had more
friends just like you!

I hope that in the new world
You will still remain
my friend.

Now as we p a r t ,
I'd like to say
once again
That our friendship
Really meant the world
to me!

Clara Sidloski

CREE FEVER

An Indian man
Captured my heart — rode away
Erotic — my dreams.

Yolanda Queen

BRIEF SANCTUARY

High on the mountaintop I stand
    to contemplate
Relaxing in the sweet embrace of
    silence

Where huge sequoias lift their
    thick green branches to the sky
I rest beneath their shade and
    realize how insignificant am I

And breathe the pure and pungent
    air that smells of cedar, pine
    and manzanita brush
So far and high above the unclean
    air of the hectic city's rush

And wish I didn't have to make
    that journey back
To noise, pollution, smog, and
    sooty grime
Of streets so full of fear and
    hatred pandering and crime.

Looking down upon the valley once
    so green and fertile,
Now torn and raped with steel and
    concrete, chemicals, ill health,

Is man destroying all the natural
    beauty on this earth
In his greedy quest for wealth?

Lawrence A. Souza

Under Trinity Rock, Saguenay.

FADED AWAY

You said you loved me
with all your heart;
  That never again,
would we be apart.

  Look at us now,
so different and strange;
  Who would have thought,
that things would have changed.

  Today when I saw you,
I remembered the past;
  We shared something wonderful,
it just didn't last.

  I can't tie you down,
you've got to be free;
  And I can't make you love
only one girl, just me.

  I have changed so much
with each new day;
  That the love we felt
never died, it just FADED AWAY!

Denise Duncan

INK-SMEARED DREAMS

Poetry pieces written down
about you written by me.
Those daydreams I remembered
only my eyes could see.

Fantasizing while I wrote
on a piece of tear-stained paper,
I thought of you and wished
we could always be together.

Laughter and tears when I think
of times we have shared;
Are proof to me to show
how much I really cared.

All these thoughts about you
are stored in this notebook of mine,
In the bottom of a shoebox
to be opened later in time.

Even though I've only been
just a good friend to you,
I wish for something more to come;
If only you knew.

Cynthia Windheim

A quiet hide-out all alone.
A secret spot to call my own.
Flowers swaying with the breeze.
Blossoms budding on the trees.
Colored pebbles in the brook,
sparkling in their little nook.
Willow branches hanging down,
brushing softly against the ground.
Butterflies and bumblebees,
birds sharing sweet melodies.
Fluffy clouds up in the sky;
The sun winking as they pass by.
The haunting beauty of it all;
Endless, like that waterfall.
Dewdrop kisses everywhere,
everything without a care.
Whispering wind through the pine.
Wishing you were truly mine.
I come here often, to sit and dream,
on my bed of grass beside the stream.

Cindy Greene

As I look into your eyes, I see,
Poverty and unimagined desolation.
I am aware of the terrible hunger
        of your starving little frame.
I cannot understand man's hesitation,
        in reaching out a hand to you.

Unable to turn my gaze aside;
Drawn to look deeper as we commune.
I see God's love waiting to consume.
Yea — the road to Him —
        is through such as you.

It is no longer impoverished man I see,
But crucified Christ, gazing back at me.

Marvice H. Archambeau

ARCHAMBEAU, MARVICE HOECHERL.

THERE THEY GO

She's a dilly of a filly
And she rides her bike quite fine
He's a can man and boy will he
Rev his three-wheel right behind

On their vehicles they peddle steam
Dust and gravel always fly
On this trip around the block they seem
So grown I want to cry

Dere Welch

WELCH, DERE TILL. Born: Mobile, Alabama, 12-20-56; Education: McGill- Toolen High School, Mobile, Alabama, May, 1975; Occupations: Housewife, Mother of three.

YOUNG, URBAN, PROFESSIONAL

Although we work
on the same project
you might as well
be Marie Antoinette
and I might as well
be George Armstrong
Custer for all
the profit that
these transactions
clear will not
bring us closer
to the wind that
waves at the sun.

Frank Turgeon

THE LAKE

The Lake:
Cool, deep,
Wide,
Soothing, freeing,
Tide;
Swirling, sweeping
Strife;
Giving, taking
Life.
Illusions, dreams.
Wake!
Cool, deep
Lake.

Mercurion Suladdin

HEATHER

The purple flower snuggles close
        to the ground,
    seeking security from the
            moist spring winds.
The delicate amethyst face cuddles
        next to a staunch pearl stone,
        awaiting the abatement of
                nature's ferocity.
The sun shyly peeks out from
        behind a voluminous cloud,
        calming the air
            and bestowing a glowing hand
            upon her lilac-tinted ally.

Kenneth G. Geisert

All the years spent struggling with
tangled emotions.
Fighting, tearing, waiting
for the confusion to subside.

Much as a flower blooms
a sense of serenity has unfolded,
quietly,
gently,
        in its own timeless wonder,
I stand breathless,
hypnotized,
by the beauty and color
of my now
freedom wings.

Doreen Johnson

ICEBERGS

Icebergs melt when the warmth embraces them
and flood the land with their tears
    So cold, so frigid
    How can they exist?
When you give them warmth, they cry cold tears
and melt away into nothing

Which is all they are worth anyway.

Larry Frank

FRANK, LAWRENCE ALVIN. Pen Names: The Rock and Roll Buddha, The Man From Japan; Born: Boston, Massachusetts, 10-6-60, A.D.; Education: Montgomery College, Rockville, Maryland, to graduate with A.A. degree in December, 1985; Occupation: Ad. Art Student; Other writings: *Pieces of Mind*, book of poems and prose, 1980-82; Comments: *I write because it becomes a "permanent" document of my thoughts. I wish to contribute to the wisdom of the human race. Anti-war themes, cosmic consciousness, personal testimony, love, and word punnery are common in my works.*

THE REASON AND THE WHY

(For Marita)

Perhaps one day
I'll know the reason and the why of your smile.
Perhaps if time permits I'll learn the secrets of a heart
I know has died many times over,
But that still beats strong.
Resurrecting love within the hearts of others
Who have likewise been wounded by life and by love —

Tell me, is the blue of your eyes
The reflection of a sea of tears held inside,
Or is it the reflection of an eternity
Seen only by a heart torn free of its human limitations —

Is it by bleeding that we are healed,
And is it by seeking to touch others,
That we ourselves are touched.
In your moments alone do you laugh so much,
Or do you also seek the answers to questions
Too often asked by a heart afraid of finding —

So often we seek but never find.
Reach out but never touch.
Our minds grow tired and our hearts they grow so weary.
But within your words I have found a place of rest,
And have drawn strength from within your smile —

Genn Chryst

THE PRAIRIE

There are legions walking with me as I
Stroll this land. Those who were captured by her
Beauty long before I became. Friends I
Have known a lifetime but only met today.

We speak many tongues in a common silent
Language. Hope, fear, drought and cold rustle through
The grass. Despair, laughter and love ride upon the
Wind. All todays are yesterdays and all
Tomorrows today. Her harsh beauty binds us.

Pat Wood

OZARK INSPIRATION

Many things inspire me.
I stand in awe when I see

    rocky knolls, wooded hills,
    little valleys, crystal rills,
    limestone bluffs, pools of blue,
    sumac, sassafras' golden hue,

    purple violets, forget-me-nots,
    saw briars, sacred spots,
    meadows filled with new-mown hay,
    cattle returning at the close of day,

    the big brood mare with the frisky foal,
    the mighty oak, or the old swimming hole!

Fertile valleys, fields of corn
Fill my heart with hopes newborn.

To breathe the pure fragrant air
In a home in the Ozarks is my prayer.

Jessie D. Atkinson

ATKINSON, JESSIE DAVENPORT. Pen name: Nana Atkinson; Born: Roy, New Mexico, 12-10-17; Married: 10-23-43 to Glenn M. Atkinson; Education: Southwest Missouri State University, B.S. Education, 1939; Occupation: Retired Teacher; Poetry: *Fairy Airplanes*, children's poems; Other writings: 'Lord We Know,' gospel lyrics; "The Wisdom Tooth," short story, ; "Lisa's Alligator Cake," short story; Comments: *I try to express the joys of living. I write for readers' entertainment. Most of my works are drawn from thirty years of teaching experience and antics of young children.*

SPRING CLEANING

Set my life upon a table
That's what I should do
To dust it off
And polish it up
To make it shining new
The laughter are symbols
Of times once enjoyed
The crying is all the junk
I have no purpose for and must destroy
I will rearrange all that is kept
Into some new scene
So my new perspective
Will be sharp, new, and clean
Spring cleaning is a strenuous task
But it must be done to clear away old masks.

Sandra Riggins

WATER

The water is as summer air after rain:
sun-touched, sticky honey;
suffocating, stifling fire . . .
Yet it flows
The water is smooth as rich liquor going down.
Going down
A weary traveler.
It flows.

You atop a mountain
A cross-legged Buddha
Contemplating Water.
Watching it,
Making it
                    Flow.

Myrna Washington

Sometimes I look at these children and wonder why
they have to suffer so much. It's bad enough that
they have to deal with the everyday pressures but to
have to go home and be abused by their parents is
unfair. Home should be a place for them to hide; a
place for them to be able to unwind and relax. Parents
should be available for their children to talk with
them; to learn how they feel. Children shouldn't be
ignored or pushed away.

There are times that when I see abused children, I
wish I could open my arms and hold them tight; never
letting them go. Just letting them know that someone
cares; that someone loves them; that someone is there.
I wish I could have a place for abused children to run
to; a place where they would feel safe; a place they
could call home.

Rachel Wallace

LOVE AND WAR

I worked so many years on this wall —
Piling the stones, chinking, plastering,
MX-ing myself into Safety, Peace.
Finally safe from hate and love,
Old painings amputations gone,
Walled out.

How you slithered through this tech-tight wall
Dumbfounds me!

Stunned, raking up slags of flesh
From this bombing

I thought I was so safe from.

Laura Beheler

It wasn't the last time I swam in the ocean
While you photographed me from the shore;
It wasn't the last time we walked down the strand
Or raced up the steps to your door.

These pictures hold dreams of a future
And we're out on the pier, holding hands,
Watching the waves down below
Beating rhythms out into the sands.

It wasn't the last night I stood on the deck
Looking out at the lights in the bay
And you haven't forgotten the way that you felt
The first time you asked me to stay.

Tonight we'll be walking back in from the pier
And I'll sing while you play your guitar,
And I'm going to wake up from this bad dream I'm having
Of driving away in my car.

It wasn't the last kiss, a kiss of goodbye;
Please tell me that this isn't so.
I'll turn back the time to that moment again
And you'll say you're not letting me go.

Hollie Ridenour

GOD IS STILL ON THE THRONE

When all hope is gone,
God is still on the throne.
Hope not in this world; hope in Christ.
For he paid the sacrificial price.

When all joy is gone,
God is still on the throne.
Joy cometh in the morning, after the storm is gone.
Remember, God is still on the throne.

When trouble comes, things go wrong,
God is still on the throne.
The trouble we have just may be,
We fail to put our trust in Thee.

When we are in a battle just about gone,
Remember God is still on the throne.
The battle is not ours; the Lord's instead.
Kneel down and bow your head.

He's just a prayer away.
God is still on the throne each and every day.

Annie Smith

THE WANDERERS

Who could imagine
In the vast longings
in the pit of Creation's stomach
We, would emerge?
(a subtle essence strung out on Creation's sigh?)

The Semitic strain
A cadence and a cacophony.
A spontaneous evocation of plea,
and praise.
A kneeling at the altar of perpetual "Why?"
and a whispered invocation for Grace.

God, our God
A force so inextricably bound
to our every move and consciousness.
A meandering into a privileged past
That leaves us in confusion
and awe.
To be. To be a Jew
Caught in the Clasp of the Century.

Roberta Sherry

PORTRAIT OF AN IDEAL FAMILY

A family is having a wonderful wife
A woman to cherish the rest of your life
A partner to love with the greatest of pride
A mate to adore you and stand by your side

A family is having an ideal boy
A son who can bring you a bundle of joy
A spunky companion . . . an athlete too
A lad who will be a great credit to you

A family is having a daughter to raise
A child who will add to your happiest days
A girl who will grow to a lovely young lass
A boon to the family with plenty of class

A family is having a "Dad" who is strong
A father to turn to when everything's wrong
A friend and adviser all rolled into one
A man you consider as second to none

A family like this is a beautiful thing
A blessing of riches no money can bring
A lifetime of memories for someone like me
A part of this family I'M HAPPY TO BE!!

Al Milanette

WENTWORTH PLACE

In the house and yard where John Keats used to live and write,
there is a sense of enchantment that gives and lights up
any true poet's soul with deep romanticism,
a kind of fanaticism with the ways of the past.

Musky letters and one gold ring
tell the story of two lovers' love.
Picture portraits and locks of hair
tell the glory of two lovers' fate.

One who left, and one who stayed.
One who crossed an ocean, and one who prayed.
One who died, and one who cried.
One who was buried, and one whose love tarried.

An image is painted inside my mind.
And what do I find? John Keats sitting
in his chair underneath the plum tree
with a soft breeze blowing through his hair.

The birds are singing sweet melodies at dusk — while —
church bells are ringing sweet harmonies at dawn.
All the world is at ease, as John Keats writes his masterpiece:
An Ode to a Nightingale.

Randy C. Pedersen

SUNSHINE OF GOD'S LOVE

Look at the ray of sunshine
   Shining down on those trees
The ray of sunshine is also shining down
   on me . . . Oh what a beautiful sight
to behold, I feel the Holy Spirit down in my
   Soul . . . yes the ray of sunshine is
also shining down on me, that's the way
   The Heavenly Father shines down his
Love . . . It seems the Heaven is shining
   down, I will shine someday in Heaven
When I receive my crown . . . Nothing
   gonna stand my way I'm gonna get
to Heaven some sweet day . . . It just
   seems the Lord poured out a ray of
Sunshine down on those trees and it seems
   that he didn't forget you or me . . .
The Heaven opened and God let down his
   Sunshine of love . . .

Ramona and Danny Benoy

RAINBOWS

Today I saw a rainbow, it made me think of you
and all the little things we used to love to do

The times we spent together when we would sit
and talk, or maybe in the evening we would take
a walk

I sat and stared at that rainbow and thought
it just might be that, that very rainbow
you could also see

It's little things like that rainbow or a song
that I hear play

That keeps you here so close to me while yet so
far away.

Lida Daubert

A PAL

I need a pal, to relate to
Another gal, just to talk
To reminisce, to visit, ride a bike, take a walk
Anything that's company
A friend, maybe someone just like me
Who would understand sometimes I get lonesome
And sometimes I need to be alone
Maybe we could talk on the telephone
Are you listening Lord?
I need a pal, another gal
Who understands sometimes I'm shy — I don't know why
It's hard sometimes to talk to strangers
But there are times I meet someone
Lord, just like you, that I can tell my thoughts to
And they can see what's in me and understand my needs
And love me just as I am.

Elva Goldhersh

FATAL ADVANCEMENT

Ignorance and Stubbornness arm each other
      while childishly prevailing;
Ranting and raving and provoking
      constantly failing!
Time moves in, an unwelcomed fact,
      smashing edges with blows leaving wounded tracks.
Meanwhile, Painful Humility is discovered in their souls
      by shots of heartless attacks!
But when Time becomes unquestionably
      a respected enemy,
Lofty Life laughs at the Proud
      who dared to act in such foolish mockery;
And those hopeless Youths wilt through
      these blunt hardships because of harsh sin.
But if any uncrushed Virtues remain,
      these bow as Wisdom walks in!

Patricia Agardi

A BEGINNING OF A NEW LIFE

The joy of love is seeing it grow.
The fun of wondering what it will be;
The color of hair and eyes,
The smiles they bring to young and old.
A mother that's filled with hopes and dreams;
A father that cares and wants to name it,
Sisters and brothers that don't know what to
      think.
As the delivery day is upon us;
Mom and Dad waiting to see what it is;
A new life appears to all.
This is a new beginning of life.

Dee Ann Wilkins

LIFE'S PICTURE GALLERY

As I look back over my life,
Through pathways traveled
Some not smooth
Along jagged mountain peaks,
Along all kinds of paths I've moved
Some rugged and some smooth,
Some so rough I can't recall
But I know I've traveled all.

Life is like a great big canopy
Full of pictures for us all to see —
Different pages of our life
Has now become just history.

Each of us has played a part,
On the stage that we call life
And buried deep within each heart
Memories lie like works of art.

Hope Young

THE YET TO BE

Upon awakening
In a dream half-spent,
The creative forces of life
Blending to form
Manifestations of reality.

Passing through time,
Interludes to eternity,
Those encounters of presence,
Everlasting memories set in place,
Crystallized by emotions.

Unique moments,
Fragments of existence,
Materialized perceptions
Of one's own space;
The here and now
Of the yet to be.

McRobert Scott Parker

DAWN

Light came —
Spilled its being
Across the desk.
The flowers tilted
Their heads —
In response;
A cascade of warmth
Brushed —
My hand . . .
I smiled
As the sparrow,
Fluttered under
The eave;
Somewhere —
A dog barked,
Footsteps shuffled,
Day emerged —
From the blanket
Of night.

Maryanne Zugarek

THE ARTIST

You sat home on weekend eves
and colored canvas for a frame,
the wildest dreams you could sketch,
I'd prepare paper from a book
and break the end-point from my pen.

Robyn Reade

FRIENDSHIP RISING

I remember,
Hours we spent
Sitting on the floor
Looking at the Christmas tree
Talking and laughing
Petting one cat
And brushing the other.

We disagreed about —
The threatening cold and snow,
What to put on the stereo,
What pictures should be on the walls.
We disagreed on just about everything
Except
That we liked being friends.
And we enjoyed each other's company.
But that was more than enough.

Kim S. Wakefield

THE SANDPIPER

A busy life has he,
Who pecks upon the sand,
Awaiting still another wave,
To leave a harvest land.

He lives his life from day to day.
He scampers with the breeze.
He times each rolling, churling surf.
He flits about with ease.

Another world has he,
Each time the ocean roars,
He rushes to each morsel found,
Along his treasured shores.

He envies not the high sea gull,
Nor yet the pelican.
His kingdom grows with every tide,
He gathers all he can.

Russell Troutman

TROUTMAN, HOLMES RUSSELL. Pen Name: Russell Troutman; Born: Beckley, West Virginia, 7-27-33; Education: Marshall University, B.A. 1955; University of Miami, L.L.B. 1958; Occupation: Lawyer; Memberships: The Florida Bar, The American Bar; Poetry: 'Summertime,' Poetry Press, 8-20-81; 'Why The Ocean Roars,' *Florida Bar Journal,* 5-9-82; 'Exeter Chapel,' *Outlook Newspaper,* 7-27-82; Themes: *Feelings.*

THE CHRIST

His father a carpenter
From hated Galilee,
His mother, gentle Mary,
A virgin saint was she.
Bethlehem the city
Where Jesus Christ was born,
A stable served as birthplace
On that December morn;
And though this birth seems lowly,
It rose to high estate —
For 'tis this baby's birthday
We Christians celebrate.

Inez S. Macha

SOMEBODY

I have somebody in my life
Someone I thought I'd never find
The one I want to keep forever
Who's warm and gentle and kind
He always has a shoulder
Whenever I get down
And if I have a problem
We'll search until the answer's found
If that isn't all that he can do
He'll always find some more
Of his ways to make me happy
Forever and evermore!

Richelle Geiger

HERE AM I

World of turmoil,
You know me not,
Yet here I am
For all to be sought,
Hope my name to give you
Courage to toil
With faith none can despoil.

Janet Z. Silberstein

ON BIRTH

My blank eyes probed 'round on pivots
Looking for something pure.
But mistaken for a telephone pole,
Someone attached wires to my head,
And transformers,
Which threw up the voltage
And started a constant humming in my ears.
Later, as a stamp collection,
Someone hung magnifying glasses on my eyes
And their image became the only one I saw.
Or maybe they were colored glasses
That someone assured me were clear.

Eric Green

I'M SOMEONE ANYWAYS

Someone who knows
What it means to go home
All alone but never afraid

Someone who cries
Only on the inside
All alone but never lonely

Someone who gives
From where they live
All alone but never free . . .

Mary L. Norus

MY BETTY

Her hair of red and eyes so blue,
her voice so soft and heart so true . . .
no kinder soul this world could know —
than My Betty.

Her tenderness and loving ways,
the way she brightens all my days . . .
no lovelier a woman lives —
than My Betty.

Her helping hand and comfort deep,
tell me I need no longer weep . . .
no dearer one in all this world —
than My Betty.

Her love of life and will to live,
her generous heart to always give . . .
no sweeter woman could exist —
than My Betty.

Our memories will always be,
a part of her . . . a part of me . . .
long after death I'll not forget —
My Betty.

Leonora V. Williams

I was wondering as I watched you,
Princess with shoulders squared,
If that was a tear that lingered,
On your cheek so petal soft fair?
One of such preemptive beauty,
That walks with head held high,
Do you linger in your garden,
So that no one sees you cry?
You're clad in crimson,
Trimmed in lace,
Adorned in emeralds,
The finest made.
Satin ribbons to tie your hair,
And others to lace your shoes,
And the sparkles that your diamonds cast,
Illuminate the whole of you.
So tell me, pretty princess,
Why are you filled with gloom,
When all of heaven's riches,
Have filled your every room?
Cynthia Lynn Godwin

LEARN TO CRY

The feelings that you're having, dear,
Are nothing to be afraid of
For the world that we live in
Is nothing to be proud of.

The emotions that you feel, dear,
Don't have to stay inside
Open up your heart, dear,
And please learn how to cry.

Anger is just a feeling
You feel deep down within
If you don't let it out, dear,
It destroys and always wins.

Sorrow is an emotion
That eats away your heart,
Dig down deep and lift it out
That's the place to start.

So let your emotions go, dear,
Lift them to the sky
For the world would be a better place —
If we all learned to cry.
Susan Haga

MOTHER'S LOVE

When I was a little girl, I tried
To think of life without my Mother;
But I could not see how I would
Survive without her.

My Mom was the world to me,
Its beauty and its dignity.
But now that I am grown and
Have a life of my own, I wish
Mom could see and get to know
The real me.

We live far apart but she is
Always in my heart, even though
We do not always agree, Mom,
You still mean the world to me.
Diane R. Boudreault

WATER IN THE LIGHT

In dark forest,
I stood alone.
        Lost
The night seemed like eternity.

The Son kept His promise.
        He arose.
Silvery, living water flowed.
I drank of His deepness.
Peace and joy banked.
Sr. Arlene Casey, OSF

AN EVERLASTING SORROW: THE DEATH OF OUR BABY

Tears in deep black rivers flow,
        there are no words
                only silent sorrow
For the death of one so fair,
        so fragile, so small.
Unmercifully leaving living full of pity,
        of sadness, of anguish,
Desperately reaching for something
        to hold for strength, finding none.
Alone to suffer, to dwell, to weep.
Sorrow is here and mine to keep.
One perfect rose laid upon her tiny breast
To make sweet this eternal infantile rest.
For Babe there will be no 'morrow,
For we the suff'ring, eternal sorrow.
Tears in deep black rivers run,
        for so quickly ended, life begun.
Laurie Blankley

(IM)MORTALITY

Immortality seems
(at best)
To be just a procrastination
Of the definite end of
Mortality.
I will not try (as so many do)
to make immortality with
My words.
I do not mean for them
To live forever in time.
I only wish to have them
Live at the top
And at their best
In the small amount
Of forever
I have been given
For them.
Lisa Brant Deck

WILLIAM TREMBLETOE

William Trembletoe,
He's a great gentleman;
Catches hens,
Puts them in pens.

Older than nutmeg,
Crafty as cradles,
William paternal
Eternal clinchman.

Wire, briar, limber lock,
Three geese in a flock.
One flew East, one flew West,
One flew over the cuckoo's nest.
O . . . U . . . T . . . spells OUT,
Get up and be gone,
You old dirty dishrag you.

Dance out the quadrille,
Trembletoed gentleman,
Snap out the cadence and
Tap on the ebony.

Hit the will gingerly,
Soften its fervor. Let it be harmless
Old marker symbolward.
Old manor folded, groan,
Old spikenard leavened,
Upward, above all.
Robert M. Reed

FOR A VERY SPECIAL PERSON

I just can't remember
When you weren't there.
To help me through my problems
And show me you care.

I was there too
When you needed me.
I hope I helped you
Because you sure helped me.

You sat there and listened
When I needed advice.
I trust you again
I wouldn't think twice.

I love you like a sister
And also as a friend.
These feelings I feel
Will never end.

The love I feel
Cannot be explained.
Only we understand it
Yet its meaning is plain.

Remember the good times
And the serious, too
But never forget
That I'll *always love you!*
Scott Becker

TASKBOUND

Tomatoes know why they were born.
All higher roles they seem to scorn.
As mission-oriented plants
They flaunt no magic that enchants
Like varied fragrances and hues —
Just a juicy yield to use
In salads, sandwiches and stews.
Albert D. Hatcher, Jr.

WITHIN REASON

Nature is a realm outside my mind appearing to my innate senses . . .
My eyes capture the beauty of scenic paintings.
My ears behold the movement of tonal airs.
My hands express joyous wanderings among the touch . . .
    within the reach of nature's joy.

My mind creates an atmosphere of astonishment . . . for once . . .
Reason becomes blinded by the light of the unknown.
I turn myself now towards my emotions,
Hope to escape the bondages of a life without feeling.

I seem to dwell on the spirit of loving . . .
For that is the most difficult to portray to another human
    being.
Physical sensations despair upon unrequited passions . . .
Sentiments within my heart cry out to be savored.

At night the moon shakes among the stars that glow
  like sparklers igniting on the fourth of July.
The hidden clouds sway around the sky — darkness so inviting.
An anticipation of unknown forces within my limbs.
       But why am I afraid?

It's too late to reverse . . . but I must behave within reason,
For now, my mind has begun to dictate my desires.

Christine Byczek

POEM OF THE WORLD

God with his wisdom and knowledge made our galaxy, he made each planet
to be used by you and me. In all his wisdom and knowledge man does not
understand why God used the world for his paradise for each and every
man. He made Adam and Eve for his perfect man, and then Satan stepped
in and upset his plan but before the end of time man will surely see,
that God is the controller of the universe and is there for you and
me. He gave Adam and Eve, Abel and Cain, and then Cain slew Abel and
that really changed things, although everyone did not come from earth
I am proud to say, that God made each and everyone in a special way.
And as the world turns on its axis and men sail from sea to sea, we
should be proud of the world that God made for you and me. And in our
travels every day we should be proud as can be for the world that God
gave us in our galaxy.

Nathaniel Morrison

MORRISON, NATHANIEL. Pen Name: Bud Morrison; Born: Bruce, Virginia, 6-25-35; Married: 9-20-62 to Katie Morrison; Education: One year of college; Poetry: 'Ode to a Writer,' 'To Someone Special,' 'Hold On'; Other Writings: *Human Roots: Fact or Fiction,* novel, Carlton Press; *Eternal Life After Being Lost in Bermuda Triangle,* novel; Comments: *I write poetry because it gives me a way of expressing my feeling in rhythm and I find it is a good way to tell a story.*

DEFEATED BY TIME

Aged
Existing on borrowed time
Rich with memories
Blessed seer, your knowledge
Clever, your recollection of life.
You have maintained your dignity
With an honest reputation
And a warm heart
It was you, to clearly define living
By an example of your own existence
Sadly, your only battle
Was the struggle
To obtain youth
And you lost it
With time.

Nancy J. Trudelle

HOW I LOVE YOU

From the rising sun
To the setting
I know I love you.

No matter how terrible
A test you put me to,
Or the things I see,
Or the things I hear,
I'll always love you.

But that love,
Although unchanging is also
Protective of itself,
Not willing to be hurt or scared
But to be enriched and everlasting.

Jo McLavey-Collins

WITH DAWN SHADOWS COME

The lone bird
sings a brighter song
as morning begins.
I've seen dark blue
turn golden
in the sky.
Don't cry my love,
don't cry
in love we'll live this day,
for Autumn's touch
feels far away;
and a song of departure
is but a sigh of the wind
leaving tracks in the desert
as twilight ascends.

William Hartell

WHAT ARE CHILDREN MADE OF

Dedicated to my son, James

What are little boys made of?
What are little girls made of?

  . . . The wind in the trees
    A bright tune on the breeze,

  . . . A breath of fresh air,
    Playful cubs in their lair,

  . . . The warmth of a song,
    And the will to be strong . . .

And that's what children are made of!

Linda H. Rhine

ANGEL

They say but what do they know?
"Lynx, minx, jinx" . . . finks all of them!
Stand a-while you speak:
Painful twisting through channels
Where others run so free.
Smile
        breasts aggressively
                hips suggestively
(Stay awhile and hear)
(Yes, you are beautiful)
If Chance were
More human than divine.
Instead you smile invitingly
Ramble aimlessly
Gaps of many spans cutting, smothering, troubling
But never crushing,
They who say have no ears.
Eternally innocent
Your name is your humanity.
                Angel.

Dolores Hartwell

PENDING

You left
And I was overcome with
The *despair*
Which says I've *lost* again.
Two lives that will not *synchronize*,
That will not *mesh.*
The puzzle is a *failure.*
The pieces refuse to fit.
I sit *tightly*
While
Despondency
Fills my body . . .
It won't work . . . *won't work* . . . won't work
Swirls around me,
Like
The *endless* whir of a
Merry-go-round.
I could end this
Morbidly
If I knew how.

Paula K. Butt

To you Bryan Cravens, I dedicate this dream.

In the still of the darkness, and the calm of the night,
sometimes I sit and ponder, its perilous plight.
When man first saw it, I wonder what he thought,
maybe a God, or: maybe not.

When first it appears, on the horizon at night,
its only sliver, of shimmering light.
But as the days pass, and the nights grow long,
its body grows fuller: its light grows strong.

Its magical light, casts an essence of love,
yet it does nothing special, but glow from above.
Though cherished by our ghosts, from centuries ago,
it still has a magic, mystery untold.

Though it's touched many hearts, from here and afar,
it loves not a thing, not even a star.
So when I stare at night, from my world apart,
it simply makes me cry that the moon has no heart.

Jay R. Willows

THE PRINCESS AND THE SEA TURTLE

I took my horse and raced to the sea. Watch the sea gulls
flying so gracefully. Then there I notice a giant sea turtle
looking at me. Would you like to take a ride around the
mountainside? he asked. I said why of course, but wait until
I tie up my horse.

I took off my clothes so they wouldn't get wet. Hopped on
the back of the sea turtle and held onto his neck. He said,
there is a place that I've been told, to take you to where
it is cold. Here we are as you can see, this is the cave that
needs no key. Go in the cave and look around and you will
find the emerald crown.

Place it on your head my dear for the magic is powerful
I hear. Watch that the crown doesn't fall in wrong hands or the
devil himself will be in command. Now I'll take you where
you can dry and see you again someday
but now it's goodbye.

I gave the sea turtle a kiss and told him how much he'll
be missed. When I got upon my horse she grew beautiful wings
with such force. The sea turtle sure was right, the power
in this crown will bring me pure delight. Now my father
the king can see, my horse and I fly so heavenly.

Lynnette Capriotti

TO A DISHEARTENED FRIEND

Whatever be the purpose of our life,
        'Tis best that we be good.
To try to be right and keep out of strife,
        As often as we could.

To lend a hand to those who are in need,
        To be humble and kind.
To subdue our faults; mitigate our greed,
        To throw sins from our mind.

To love our father, to love our mother,
        With all our might and heart.
To pray that they'll never be a bother,
        Enough to let us part.

Every evening 'fore going to bed,
        Let's bless the day and night.
To heaven let's pray that the morrow's bread,
        May come with the Morn's light.

Let us say a prayer for one we love,
        And ask especial care.
For I know the King of Heaven above,
        Is lovable and fair.

Albert N. Lane

THE PINES OF GOD

I
The stately pines so tall and straight,
  Reach up their arms to Heaven's gate,
They seem to say "May we come in?
  Oh please, dear God, forgive our sins."

II
Their roots go way down in the ground,
  The swaying branches make a moaning sound.
They are singing their little ones to sleep,
  While placing them in the dear Lord's keep.

III
I wish that I were tall and straight,
  I'd reach my arms to Heaven's gate.
I'd also say, "May I come in?
  Oh please, dear God, forgive my sins."

Alta Alger

LOVE ME BABY BLUES

Want that be one happiest time darling, just you and me
Now want that be one happiest time
Your love so kind and true
We been together for a long long time now
It's too late to turn back now.
Yes, I want you to love me; love me baby, just as I am.

Think of the good times that we had together
Now your love leaves a place in my heart.

Yes, I want you to love me; love me baby, just as I am.

You promised me that you would love me forever
But now you are leaving me with all those memories

Yes, I want you to love me; love me baby, just as I am.

Sweetheart you are mine forever and
I am never, never going to let you go, oh.

Yes, I want you to love me; love me baby, just as I am.

Into each life some raindrops may fall
But just remember the one that loves you all.

Yes, I want you to love me; love me baby, just as I am.

You better believe it, love me baby, tell it like it is,
Now love me baby, nothing like the real thing,
Love me baby, oh how sweet it is,
Love me baby, right on, right on, love me baby.

Yes, I want you to love me; love me baby, just as I am.

Joseph Lewis

friend

there was summer melon on your hands.
always it was early, and still barely dark.
warm on morning's wedge
i have embraced the fruit
                              and you.
we slumbered off
                    and on,
once until eight . . .
                    it mattered so.
                    it was enough.

Sandra L. Nelsen

NELSEN, SANDRA LILLIAN. Pen Names: Sandi Nelsen, Sandi Jo Carson, Lilly; Born: San Diego, California, 12-24-50; Occupations: Medical Office Nursing, Private Nursing, Model, Mother of two children; Memberships: Association for Alzheimer's Disease, Huntington's Disease Foundation of America.

Walking the street,
covered in only a bandage of morality;
hiding her youthful voluptuousness behind
a Madison Avenue polluted naiveté.

Cracked country lips unable to voice
the frustration,
welling from misconstrued attentions,
fostered by magnetic movements
of lost and lonely loins.

Brain and body scream for a mother's caress,
only to be answered by
a sordid impersonal pawing.

Expectations melt as confusion mounts.

Her only fault —
tourist adolescence.

Darrell Jepson

CONCEPTION

And there is man.
And there is woman.
Mankind, Manevil.
And there is Mother Earth held within her planetary cradle.
The sun. The stars.
The universe with Orion standing nearby.
And God waiting also, as Terra Mama sleeps
Restlessly through the darkness of life.
And crying rain beats the world with sounds of strife,
The mother holds the cradle and God disappears,
Smothered in her loving bosom.
The baby awakes and Terra Mama sheds a tear.
Satan awakes to the music of fear.
The mother now lies in a coffin; so near.
The baby is here, breathing.
And there is man.
And there is woman.
And here am I, being.

Norman Dyce

ONLY IN THE DARK

Your face haunts me.
I see you late at night,
when I settle down to sleep.
Your blue eyes, pleading me to come,
your hair, thick and gold
as the first time we met.
Your body still lean and strong.
I sense your need for me to follow, but I resist.
As if my dreaming of you
betrays the man I love.
And so you haunt me.
Ever on my mind,
Playing out my fantasies,
safe within his arms.
I dare not meet you now, face to face,
in the harsh light of day,
for fear the eyes I see at night,
would not remember mine.

MaryJayne Reeves

God of the great outdoors,
Why must I seek You there?
Why can't I find You here at home
Asleep in my easy chair?
Why? Because You're God of the great outdoors
And You live in the open air,
And You're never known to the man at home
Asleep in his easy chair.

Hamilton L. McNichol

DELIVERED ON HEAVEN'S GATE

Thank you — for this
life deemed my own
here in a galaxy
to all other's unknown.

But why? is the question
my brain always asks,
why are we hidden
our existence so masked?

How can I answer
believe and accept
this given Reality
so truly inept?

There should be a purpose
to this unspoken Vanity —
keeps me alive
in this thing called my sanity.

Bruce R. Thompson

COUNT

Count the blades of grass you see.
Count them apart, one by one.
Count the leaves on a tall tree.
You'll find it won't be much fun!

Count all the stars in the universe.
Sing all the songs you know in reverse.
Count the grains of sand on the shore.
Count and count and still there's more!

Count waves rolling in from sea.
Or the fishes down below that flee.
Try counting snowflakes that fall.
You're good if you get them all!

Count on 'til infinity.
And in all sincerity
If you can count all these things,
You'll count the joy your love brings!

Phil Peagler

TEMPTATION, GO!

Why bother me temptation
as I travel on my way,
trying to do what I think is best
as I go from day to day.

Here you come snooping around
interfering with this and that
trying hard to make me unbalanced
with your naughty little chat.

You know you make me nervous
and my mind begins to twirl
when you keep on pestering me
trying to upset my world.

Why don't you go your way
and leave me to go mine
Bother someone who wants you
without you I am fine.

Eutora M. Butler

SPRINGTIME LASS

Oh Springtime Lass fresh Divine pride,
  Much love and joy your face unfolds;
In bosom warm my lone heart hide,
  Come soon oh please lest I perish.

With warm rain tears my soil please wash,
  That I be pure as snow on mounts;
With perfumed breeze my love refresh,
  That I be strong and frail no more.

Your green gown with love freedom sign,
  All ways to romance land she opes;
Like bright stars brilliant flowers shine,
  All Venus fruits your heart unfolds.

How pleasant thrills sweet melody,
  Of your celestial choral song;
As gay birds sing in harmony,
  To me they preach love gospel more.

In seasons all no Lass I found,
  Full so much manna dew and charm;
From nunnery with milk I'm fed,
  That I be mighty strong and firm.

Napo David Moloi

MOLOI, NAPO DAVID. Born: Pietermaritzburg; Education: Metric, 1980, Teachers Certificate 1976-1977; Occupation: Teacher; Songs: 'Jesus is Our Savior,' 3-9-84; 'Raise Your Eyes to the Cross,' 1-11-84; Columbine Records, Inc.; 'Oh Sing Me Please a Song of Love,' 3-23-84; 'Blow My Soul,' Sunshine Records, Inc., 10-12-84; Themes: *1. To appreciate nature and try to find the message she conveys to man. 2. To encourage humanity to look to Jesus as an answer to salvation from sins. 3. To appeal to humanity to discourage the evil of victimization, oppression, exploitation and racial discrimination.*

REMEMBRANCE

Though we have walked a million miles,
A thousand years or so —
Thy memory lingers near me;
Wherever I shalt go.
And whilst thou know not where I am,
Or givest not a care;
Wherever you may wander,
You will always find me there.
For love is not a fountain
That floweth in one place;
My love is like the sunshine,
That gloweth on thy face.
And when the sky is black with rain
And clouds are at their peak,
My love will be the rain that forms
A teardrop on thy cheek . . .

Sandra Crawford Porter

DEAR LORD TO THEE I PRAY

Dear Lord to Thee I pray,
Thanks for each and every day.
Bless my family and my friends,
Keep them safe till the end.
Give me the knowledge to understand,
The pain I must endure to be a man.
Keep me happy and free from sin,
And let me fight evil and fight to win.
Blessed are you God of most high,
Who reigns supreme above the sky.
Let this and all my prayers be heard,
With each and every solemn word.
Let my faith ensure the day I die,
That my soul soars towards the sky,
To be with You in Your Heavenly Home,
At the right hand side of Your throne.

Kenneth Hajek

NOone can
teach(
the dead
LOVE

you

   only
when you
are
INVOLVED)
you
learn to
   sing

Christopher Jones

DISILLUSIONMENT

Wish there were a dream left,
one to be reached out for;
one that could be touched.

None remain.

They are all gone now;
scattered to the winds
like leaves in a hurricane;
Shattered like fragile crystal
dropped on cement.

And here I stand
with a broken heart
and an empty hand.

Linda Bleser Hunt

CHANSON*

In the silence engendered, the chord of the song is heard.
Bestowed to each an origin and legacy of mankind there known,
The venerate cup of ourselves that is the mold, then the supplication and the
      bourne.
Now illuminated with the perceived striving and the dedicated, solemn vow,
Ere the hour of truth and reason will become a rejoicing triumph,
An echo from the voice of time of the saddened savant and the warrior.
A cry and word, assailed to understand in anguish and a mantle worn in pride.
Veiled destiny, no lament, but a heralded, alleged encounter of valor.
A measure of manifest duty, a measure of the unity of reason, a measure of devout
      faith.
And the human odyssey renders and unfolds the promise of the sacred victory avowed.

And contend the eternal cry of civilization arose to confer truth as a shrine.
There in ancient Hellas, amid solemn columns of stone, the story is told,
The hour of thought and reason that became and has remained an ultimate testament,
Held as a noble declaration to philosophical laws and statecraft,
Not seeking line or ornate ornament, but the vestigium of form.
The voices of Plato, Aristotle, Herodotus and Homer resplendent,
The dominance of Athens, the culture of Corinth and the harbors of Rhodes,
The Parthenon, the Temple of Poseidon and the Winged Victory of Samothrace,
A quest of virtue, an apologia to understanding, an attempted redemption,
When the still vase is about to curve to Eternity.

*Song — French
    Jeanne C. Mac Nider

three summers long

           our strength we test, off Greenport's shore
           with swells so high, we rock and sway
           but calm within the cove once more
           together through the night we stay.

        and hold and touch as once we had
        we huddle close against the chill,
        with tenderness no longer sad.
        i've loved you and i love you still

    forever riding seabird's wings
and leaving all of time behind;
we're living just what loving brings
    us, whole of heart and peace of mind.

        three summers long we've shared the sun
        and opened wide our eyes, with sight,
        to life, if there is only one;
        to love, to laugh, to hold on tight.

           you quench my void, my emptiness,
           my yearning heart i've longed to fill.
           you soothe my soul with one caress,
              i've loved you and i love you still.

    Annemarie Bettica

EASTER PSALM

My Jesus is not a face.
He is a feeling I accept.
He is God made man
To walk the hill of pain for us.
The hunger to know Him is in my heart.
I can feel the pain of the nails on His palms,
Of the crown of thorns on His mortal brow,
Of the taste of vinegar on His fevered lips
While His mortal body cried for water.
And the ultimate pain
To be surrounded by the coldness of human hearts.
Ignorantly and wantonly I did waste the treasures He so freely gave
I am unworthy of him in my conceit.
Greater than a mother's love for her child is His love for us.
His mercy, His patience is infinite.
His strength is strength eternal.
I put aside earthly desires and love Him alone.

    Alys Roach

THE CONTRADICTION

I am Dante's inferno,
    My surface is covered by clouds,
    My temperature is 900° F.
    My surface pressure is 90 atmospheres.
I am no lovely goddess,
    raining sulfuric acid,
    Trapping blistering heat,
    Circulating noxious gases.
You silly human — calling me Venus.

    Edna Mae Walker

YOU HAVE TOUCHED ME

I see you,
but you are not near me.
You linger somewhere,
    far from sight,
I can feel you,
you have touched me,
but from the inside.

I sense your presence,
    and you come,
but not in body.
When I need you —
    you are there,
in the shadows.

You live within me,
and will never die.
You see right through me,
    and always will.
I could not
erase your memory.

You remain inside —
the depth of my soul,
and the very heart
of me.
You will live forever,
for you have touched me.

    Antonette Daniar

AS ONE

You plus I equals two,
That is how it is in Arithmetic.

But, in love, you plus I equals one.

For if one of us falls, so does the other;

But, together we will help each other up.

If one of the pieces of life
That we built together falls out;

Together you and I will pick it up
And put it back together again.

As we grow older together,
Learn, Love, and Live together,
We will be as one.

For you and I shall stay together
as one
Till death do us part.

For only HE knows,
That when that day comes
We will soon be together again,
For we are AS ONE.

    Sandi Jean Mann Robinson

An easel stands
Unencumbered by hands
The hands of an artist
A pen quiet
Laid to rest
From the writer
Who wrote it
In twenty lines or less
No sound
From this stage
We're through, done, finished
Cameras are down
No action needed now
So you don't have to go on
Calling yourself
Artist or thief
You're never wrong
What a relief
From belief in defeat.
        MaryJane Powell

I LOVE YOU!

I love you — the boy told the maiden
    so fair —
She had a bright yellow ribbon in
    her hair.
The words "I Love You"
Made her smile with delight
Her heart was so happy,
Like a bird off in flight.
I love you, too, was her reply —
As a happy tear fell from her eye.
And as it dropped it shattered his hand
With a caress that only true lovers
    can understand —
He embraced her gently and caressed
    her lips
I love you, I love you
Echoed in the mist —
        Earl Hopkins

HE CAN'T BE A DREAM

I close my eyes — and I still see,
The smile he gave — was just for me,
I close my lips — and I still feel,
The tender kiss — that is so real.
I opened my heart — like the gates above,
And he gave to me — his precious love.
I opened my arms — to reach out too,
He came to me — out of a sea of blue.
I closed my hand — and found it to be,
Around the hand, that just touched me.

Let time stand still — so I'll never see
What I will do — when he's not with me.
So I close my eyes — and I still see
He's standing there — his arms around me.
He can't be a dream — he just can't be
Because he feels so real — so real to me.
        Lillian E. Nyen

THE CHINESE EXHIBITION

Was he priest or soldier, faceless king
In the reign of fire?
He painted riders blue and battle-red,
And touched their steeds with war.
To shrilling pipes they fell, parading
Two thousand years
Before the guests in granite halls would
See them, brushed and free;
The horsemen of Qin.
What task an earthen army but to be?
        Xenia Argon

LIBERTY

I have often wondered
When I was very young.
If God knew what would happen
When he gave us different tongues.

Could he have predicted
Our riots in the street,
And was our choice of freedom,
Then our country's greatest feat.

For God and Country
Let our spirits soar,
Our country stands for equality,
And for the Golden Rule God roars.

His fear of judgment
Is electrifying.
I will gather all tongues
And nations for my glorifying

        Mick Barrett

SPRING

The flowers are blooming,
the grass is so green;
The Springtime is glorious,
with things bright and clean.

The snow has all melted,
the cold winds are over;
The trees are all budding,
the grass is all clover.

The birds are returning,
the robins that sing;
Their songs help to cheer us,
before they take wing.

The Winter is long,
cold, windy and gray;
There's nothing more sweet,
than a warm Spring day.

        Jan Calkins

LORD, MAKE ME A BLESSING

Each morning when I rise I say,
    Lord, let me bless someone today!
Let me in act or word or deed,
    Plant some of your eternal seed.

Let me speak truth that sets men free
    And impart life and liberty.
Hide the self that might show pride,
    In Thee, O! Lord, let me abide.

I claim no credit for your work,
    Each duty I'll try not to shirk;
But put you first in everything,
    And as I serve I'll smile and sing.

And thank you for the joy I know
    As onward through my life I go;
Growing steadily in thy Grace;
    Learning to reflect your face.

        Gladys Burd

GRASPING

Searching through the smoke
    of misunderstanding
For the shining light
    of perception.
Brushing back the tears
    of endless frustrations.
To feel the warm caress
    of relief.
Breezes of realization
    ruffle the feathers of new ideas.
And there in the ashes
    is a new beginning.
        Annie M. Bunch

The loving touch of a hand,
A warm smile on a face,
A thoughtful word said
At the right time and place,
A friend's kind help when needed,
A morning flower wet with dew,
A young child's trusting gaze,
This is the true —
        Beauty in Life.
        Phyllis A. Strand

WASH ON GENTLE CYCLE

The
    fabric of life
    is woven it seems
    with troubles and trials
    mixed with pleasures
    now and then.
If
    taken care of on
    a gentle cycle
    it will last much
    longer, as it passes
    by slowly.
        Josephine Copenhaver Thomas

POE-EMME

O the Art Institute!
Let the Prudential sign reflect
brilliantly in your windows
Go into a snotty "art" café
Ask them for coffee . . .
You pay!
It's your fuckin' first-born!
Write on poets of the dirty streets
Paint on artists unknown until they
hand out their ear on a platter
Yes! this café was built for you . . .
But is not going to let you in.
        Sheila Bitts

LAUGHTER

If a person smiles he needn't be
    especially happy and gay
And even though the sun will rise
    there might not be another day.
The ocean breeze will wash ashore
    aboard the morning tide
But who knows of the future
    that is left for man to guide?
Life is an illusion
    in which we hide behind a mask
Scenery is painted brightly
    but surviving is a task.
        Jennifer A. Malin

DAFFODILS

There are so many days when sunshine dwindles,
and cares jostle to take a place in my line.
My heart is heavy with longing
For a different place and clime.
I cry silently as I walk through the small crowded rooms
That make up my world.
My footsteps sound hollow on the well-worn floor;
A square of glass catches my eye,
Drawing me to the picture it frames of the outside world.
Daffodils peeked from under every shadow;
Their golden sunshine shouting "Have a happy day!"
Violets wave beneath their glow,
Smiling at me from dewy faces.
My heart lightens, I turn back into the kitchen with
The borrowed smiles and sunshine reflecting from my face.
The Lord, in His infinite wisdom,
Has put enouragement in the strangest place.

Ileene Peterson

"WHO?" "ME, OWL"

A cat and an owl met at three.
The owl perched in his favorite tree.
The cat sat below in the leaves.
The intent was to exchange pleasantries
Since they'd sailed over the seven seas.
The owl spoke first with his, "Whoooo?"
Answering, the cat replied, "Me, Owl!"
"Who?" "Me, Owl!"
Louder came a "Who?' Declared the cat, "MEEE, Owl!"
The owl dropped the "h" and out came a "Wooooo!"
It was more like a dove's "Coooo."
The cat grabbed the "h" and out came "How?"
There were no new vocabulary words
For this cat and for this bird.
It was the owl's same "Who?" and cat's howl of "Me, Owl!"
The owl was no wiser, the cat no more brilliant
Since the last they had met.

Yvonne Hale Salvador

WHAT IS HEAVEN LIKE

What is heaven like, they want to know.
Are the streets of gold and the gowns of snow?
Are there real jewels in the wall?
Are there real saints both short and tall?
Is there never sorrow or never fear?
Is there never shedding of a tear?
Do we have no worry or no care?
Do we know everyone who lives there?
The answer to these questions will soon be known.
As we go to meet God at his royal throne.

Rita White

THE SOUND OF LAUGHTER

Laughter has such an infectious sound.
            It seems to vibrate through the air.
It has no language barrier —
            It is contagious everywhere.
I've seen dragging footsteps, quicken their pace —
            At the sound of bubbling laughter;
I've seen a bedraggled, hardened face,
            Look up and smile and grow visibly softer.

Mother Nature, is filled with laughter.
            Our Father God made it that way:
The laughing wind, caressing the trees.
            The beautiful flowers, dancing in the breeze.
The rippling brook, laughs at the rocks.
            Over which it must ever run;
The swaying shadows, liltingly laugh —
            When the beautiful day is done.

Joy S. Pearce

A TRUE FRIEND

Good friends are hard to come by these days.
Too many people are wrapped up in their own
problems to even care about anyone else's.
But I know this will never be true of you.
You have always been there to smile, laugh,
or even cry with me. When all the world
seemed to go out, it was always you that
came in. When I wanted to cry, you made
me laugh. When I wanted to frown, you made
me smile. When I felt like "throwing it all
away," you were always the one who helped me
put it back together. You are a special
person . . . a true friend. My only wish is
that I, too, am always there for you . . .
like a true friend.

Angie D. Hufford

MORNING WALK

Walk through wilted grass parched brown to the roots,
Past withered vines long strangled in their reach.
Winds snatching dry syllabic leaves ripened
To fall, on loose wreckage thirsting for rain.
Hear your feet murmur through squelch of canvas
And sunwards, the mimosa pleads for shade.
Hear the aches of dry branch groaning aloud
Rumbling in the cold tumble of your colon,
As the stiff nutgrass curving with the track
Stretches up to the rusting metal gate.
Now come windrows in a Payne's grey batik
Lustreless, waxen decay in dyed patches.
Salt trickles free, runnels along your cheeks.
Windblown, your hair tangles in a frenzy.
Across the stands, the sky brightens with heat.

Willi Chen

MY SPECIAL VALENTINE

You're the sweetest Valentine that I could ever find,
You fill my life with happiness of a very special kind.

You pick me up when I am down and try to make me smile,
You comfort me when I feel sick by holding me awhile.

You like to bring me little gifts to laugh at my surprise,
The special way you feel for me shows deep within your eyes.

Your love surrounds me like a glove — you make me feel complete,
My mind is filled with thoughts of us — a poet's dream retreat.

You're like a brilliant star at night — the others you outshine,
For in my heart you'll always be — my special Valentine.

Melody Olivo

THE SAPLING

From sturdy sapling to majestic giant,
spreading its tentacles with seeming
defiance.

Brother to the flower, son to the soil,
offspring of a family to which he deems
royal.

A sentinel in the kingdom of nature's
weald, protecting the fruit of his mother's
yield.

Growing old and strong in silent grace,
engaging each season with a changing face.

Deborah Currey

VOICES OF THE UNIVERSE

How can there be in so few a rhyme
Prophetic kingdoms down through time?
And how can souls so vanquish death
And soar to depths of unguarded breath?

And when on each fine thought arrest
The gathering plumage on the phoenix's breast
The flowers of each rampant age
Lend their mean to the eternal sage.

In moments of rending solitude
Through flashes of heart-enchanted mood,
Instrument exquisite-toned
Senses rapt, magnetic-honed

Mind and soul given pure by choice
Yielding, bestowing to the inner voice
All to in shining vision see
Glimpses of immortality.

And when in golden climes there be
Unmeasured song in cosmic symphony
Find you the poet's resting place
Freed by time and found in space.

Rhoda Summitt

HOME PLACE MEMORIES

I guess the dogwoods are in full bloom
On all the mountains around.
I know the creeks must be overflowing
From the spring rains that have fallen down.

The apple tree on the side of the hill
Must be covered with beautiful blooms
And I know the air is surely filled
With a fragrance as sweet as perfume.

The willow trees along the creek
Are beautifully dressed in green.
I can almost see them now
If I just close my eyes and dream.

The old house is probably still the same
With the changes oh so few,
I guess most of all would be paint on the wall,
It's worn out a coat or two.

The old swimming hole where we used to swim
So many years ago,
Has filled with sand and leaves and limbs
And memories that are left untold.

Benita Gibson McCampbell

THE GETTING OF A YOUNG LION

Persuasion . . . to entrap!
Using the eyes, creeping close
        to the prey . . .
watching for a flash of friendliness
        or a snarl of hatred.
Silent amber clouded by
    night's dark force
two sets of jaws tightly clenched:
never a hint of emotion except disdain.
    (him watching her watch him)
a slight drum of pads
    on crushed, yellow grass
teeth grinning suddenly in a feral grimace —
        Both cunning creatures
        finally separate in the velvet night
        strange feline eyes moving off
                to meet
                    separate worlds.

Laura Ladds James

THE ROSES OF LIFE

It's the cry of nature to want to win,
    The lovely roses of life;
But you earn those roses along the way,
    Because of thorns and strife.

It's the way of nature to bud and bloom,
    Replace the roses that die;
Let there be more roses in nature's aim,
    Before the time goes by.

Let there be some roses for everyone,
    So keep that always in mind;
Leave enough nice roses along the way,
    For those who come behind.

Let us share the roses with those we love,
    Keeping that Eternal Rose in mind;
It's that precious rose that will not wilt,
    It bloomed for all mankind.

Sterling Holt

HOLT, STERLING. Born: Gray, Kentucky, Knox County, 3-10-10; Married: 7-4-37 to Nellie Mae Harrington Holt; Occupation: Retired Surgical Technician; Memberships: Buck Grove Baptist Church; Awards: Commendation Award from American Red Cross for presenting play, "The Spirit And Not The Age" during Christmas 1962 at Fort Knox, Kentucky, for the soldiers' entertainment; Other Writings: "The Spirit And Not The Age," play (dialogue), 5-61; "Fingerprints," song, 11-74; "Mustard Seed Faith," song, 4-74; "Condition My Heart God To Your Will," song, 5-61; "The Day They Call Tomorrow," song, 6-60; Comments: *Since my retirement in 1959, I took up the hobby of writing poetry of a spiritual nature. I like to spread the Good News of Christ around through poetry and song.*

MY FREEDOM

I have finally learned to fly;
Allowed myself to try my wings and soar as high
as they could take me.
As I fly, I spread the joy I feel for my new discovery.
For so long I feared these wings my God had given me.
The life he'd given me and my ability to love it.

Rose-Kathryn Young

CLIFFS ON THE YELLOWSTONE.

LOVE HURTS

When you kissed me with burning ardor, I believed in you.
When you held me in outstretched arms, I believed in us.
When you touched my soul with sugar-coated words, I believed in love.

Promises of a rosy future danced before my eyes.
Promises of an undying love blinded my vision.
Promises of tomorrow dazzled my mind.

But then, too soon, your warm eyes grew cold as ice, and love hurt.
Then, too soon, your soft lips hardened, like a rock, and love hurt.
Then, too soon, poetic words of love sharpened to steely insults and
recriminations, and love hurt.
Then, too soon, you turned your back on me, and now love hurts!

Once, your heart opened up to me, and I held the key to its secrets.
Once, your heated body sought mine and ignited the sparks of a passionate love.
Once, your soul met mine and, united, we were one.

Now, the light of love is dimmed.
Now, the flame of love is chilled.
Now, the taste of love is soured.
And love hurts!

Dianna Fiks

PLUCK

Superman!
    You flew up and away and never came back.
    I've read that long ago you held the sky upon your shoulders
        (stealing apples for the king) and threw your enchanted
    hammer at the clouds, flashing fire
        and pulled the sword from the stone.
    But I remember you best wearing Sherwood green
                arrows zipping
    and wearing white hat and guitar
        saddled   singing into the sun ever setting.
        And coon caps and fast guns   silver bullets   silver badges
    masked or cowled   but always it was you.

I stand under the night
        a screen after the movie.
    Broken arrows   tarnished badge   tattered cape
And I reach into emptiness
    searching past pinhole stars past the screen
        needing that bed and blue and silver and white
            and that smile that told me
                            I could be you.

J. David Kiser

REFLECTIONS OF LOVE

Reflections of love are soft in your eyes.
You radiate a beauty that you don't realize.
But love shines bright from the life you hold within.
And it's a reflection of love where it all begins.

    When it's a blessed feeling, but it's too the greatest pain,
    Do you remember what you're soon to gain?

Reflections of love — just to feel the baby move.
Soon to lovingly caress baby's skin — so smooth.
Arms long to hold you; you're in momma's loving care.
The masterpiece is near completion — yes, it'll soon be there.

Reflections of love stream softly down your face.
Oh! the precious moment of the first embrace.
All questions answered; the perfect beauty can be seen.
And in this baby's birth are many a fulfilled and beginning dream.

    Reflections of love will last for all time.
    So this poem reflects the love that is mine.
    The love that's reflected is my love for babe and you.
    Thankful for reflections of your love — a love that is so true.

Sharon D. Novalis

THE BLACK DRESS

The black dress binds the wound.
A happiness so brittle
that it died long ago.
But she will not see it,
dead.

Her hands are swollen, arthritic
and bruised
by the continual covering
of her eyes and soul . . .

The illusions that have lived within
for years
are now realities of her own.
No one shares them.

A loving wife? A lie
that hides behind
her mourning clothes.

The black dress binds the wound
that decays within.

Joyce Matula Welch

God is the Universe
A ceaseless enigma to man
Mysteriously diverse
Existent when time began

Bask in the splendor of His charms
Receive His warmth and grace
Find instant peace within His arms
Which welcome every race

Take pleasure in the innocent joys
Surrounding all who live
Those of the world; the girls and boys
Which only He can give

Yearn to become one with the Lord
Yield to His gentle hand
Seek the wisdom of His Word
Obey its wise command

Spread His Spirit through your ways
As a servant of His Will
Waste not the minutes of your days
Waive no wish you can fulfill.

Patricia A. Quinn

'TIS HEAVEN ON EARTH

HIGH HIGH above the earth's realm
where all tender minds meet
somewhere above the universe of thought
Masters seek and greet
their esoteric kind (E.S.P.)
Dare to be so bold
tools perched within the hand
as to launch the ship and glide
across prolific land HO!
The journey's treasure: G O L D!
'twas so ages ago
wooden artifacts held the key:
The blessed Captain maneuvered SOULS
as Freudian as we
fears unladen voyage begun
earthbound solely by fleshly means
helms to the wind SOAR smooth little ones
eternity awaits heaven beams thee
WELCOME to her shores
'Tis Heaven on Earth:
The keen deep mind of a poet

Doretha Williams

THE MIDDLE KINGDOM, 1984

The misty mountain backdrop's green and gold,
The red and yellow roofs ornately scrolled,
And weeping willows mirrored in the lake
— A real-life Chinese painting comes awake.

His light-blue jacket sewn with bird and toy,
He clutched his grandma's hand in awe and joy,
His dirty, white-knit cap with bright red star
— A child, with smile, so near and yet so far.

The Wall's great teeth embossed against the sky,
Grand halls of red and gold rise, soaring high,
Two-thousand-year-old soldiers stand their guard
— A past revered, so ancient and so hard.

An old man, stooped, in Mao cap pulled down low,
The workers pedal off, go row by row,
The woman, bowl-cut hair, in clothes of grays
— a billion different faces, different days.

A thaw, more hope, with buildings on the mend,
And peasants selling wares, a brave new trend,
The Chairman's dreams retouched, so fresh goals soar
— Or next year, "eating bitterness" once more?

Jackie Fooks

TIME

Time, how precious its fountain in which we dwell,
For although we live within it
We cannot buy it
Nor can we sell it
And neither can we lend it away
To gain it back in brighter days,
For it is a gift and it is not ours to hold
But it belongs to the Creator
Who within his hands holds all of the fragments of eternity,
Yet because of its generosity our hearts grow hard
As we cease to yearn, replacing it with gatherings
That in itself will wash away
But its beauty always seeks after itself,
Just as love always seeks after love,
And longs to be exchanged
With praises of laughter towards heaven
So let us no longer pursue the course of lesser things,
For now is time.

Charles Strozeski

SUMMER BARNS

The seasons lean the hollow summer barns,
Whose long, deep grains of drying barn wood fade
Along the untilled meadows' tumbling walls,
And wither into spreading avenues
That fall away in flakes and field dust.

I see the seasons in the summer barns,
Those ebbing citadels in Old Time's chains,
Whose siloed towers slip back from the sky
And tilt from side to side and fold within,
As petals closing out the long day's light.

I see all seasons in the summer barns,
Whose pegged-beamed shoulders shed their splintered
    skin
To open silent lofts and stanchioned halls,
For nesting swallows and the green-stemmed hay
That weaves its way throughout the timbered pores.

I see my seasons in the summer barns,
Whose falling members like the pulling tides
Return my yielding veins each passing moon,
To deeper soil where night's waking seeds
Will fuse our limbs back toward the morning sun.

David Lawrence Cole

IT'S VERY LATE

The jackal feasts on the winter's clover
and all the late summer long, the katydids
                    sang their song
                    sang their song
                    sang their song

sang it down the long long long
days. Nights are so swift in summer.

Did you not hear a child's wail at noontide?
Stifled by in at for before beyond nightfall

And if the jackal and the katydids and the wild mild child
are there
        Or are not there
One dares not ask
            forgets
            or doesn't care.

Betsey Mcgrath

THOUGHTS

What are thoughts?
Are they feelings? or are they something mystical?
I know for sure they are as beautiful
as they are horrible!
I know they can make you choose between
good and bad —
But, what are thoughts?
Do they make you cry?
Naw, that's emotion —
Only to have emotions, you have to think!
Do they make you laugh?
Naw, that's happiness!
But wait a minute!
You have to feel good about something
if you're happy —
therefore you're having thoughts!
What are thoughts!
I don't really know —
                Do you?

Deloris Jenkins

I AM — YOU ARE — WE ARE

Alone, I am a very insignificant person,
    allowing myself a chance to live.
My only purpose was to expand in any which way I can.
    But, since I had met you and you became my wife,
you made me feel there was another reason for being a man.

For you are the essence who has entered my life,
    making me feel the joys I have never known.
The reason is plain, you see, we have grown.
    The promises existing between us on our wedding day,
is a day I will cherish forever and ever, and another May.

Together we are one, with each other in the days to come.
    There are many barriers to pursue,
in the days ahead, hoping that they are not too few.
    With you in my life, there is no turning back,
and the love which grows between us, it is by far,
    making us feel that I AM, YOU ARE, WE ARE.

Jack Gerard Anthony

Dedicated to Vince Neil in memory of his friend,
Nicholas "Razzle" Dingley

Hold your head up high
And don't ever look back,
Fulfill all your dreams Vince —
Stay on the right track;

I'll be standing by your side
Through times good and bad —
Don't think to give up
What you know you could have.

Though my name is just a memory,
I'll still live in the hearts of all;
I want you friend to carry on —
Pick yourself up if you fall.

Please think of me from time to time,
We once were such good friends;
But remember you must continue on —
What you've worked hard for shouldn't end.

Your music is a taste of youth,
A breath of something new —
Play on for me friend and don't forget:
I am here — I'm standing beside you.

    Sonia Erfon

WHOLLY

Love is like a dream
masking need
or other elements in deed,
and true love twisted
through censored sinew bleeds

So is, as life
the source for substance, fluid in form feeds
there is no balance,
therein lies the blame

Irony, echoes; two sides and boundaries set

Symbols in braille, receiving what's sustained
if true vision given, in this division,
the face would be seen
with all in, its lean tissue

Plants are pleading, the grass isn't bleeding
sign language prevents mothers screaming

Not lost to illusion
my division has transposed,
exposed and at the mercy of
the centrifuge

    Charles W. Copeland

GOLDEN DAYS

The halcyon, golden days beyond belief
Are passing all too swiftly, and it seems
They're lapping at the shore beyond the reef
Of time, while we're imprisoned in those dreams
Of dear delight. Stop now — and take a pause,
While slowly savour our felicity.
These things I say are simply in the cause
Of furthering our benedicity.
How quickly do we count off all the beads,
Carelessly clicking them along the chain!
Here's love; there's joy, and don't forget our needs.
Love grows and flourishes, as though the rain
Was falling on parched soil and making grow
These wonders. It is too fortissimo!

    Miriam A. Arnold

CHRISTMAS AT GRANDMA'S HOUSE

During Christmas at Grandma's house
Anyone would agree even a tiny mouse,
That we had some wonderful times
We sang songs, told stories and many rhymes.

We would come in horse and buggies
With lots of greeting and huggies.
We would come in Model T's and Chevies
Wishing Merry Christmas.

After Grandpa would say the blessing
We'd have turkey and dressing.
We'd have candied sweet potatoes
And green beans and tomatoes.

Our mince, apple and chocolate pie
Would also bring a very close eye.
Devil's food cake, fruit cake, and coconut cakes
All homemade with custard and the makes.

Now no Christmas seems to last as long
Even when you might hear a favorite Christmas song.
But in the Good Old Days we had it all
With friends and relatives it was a ball.

    Carol M. Morris

MORRIS, CAROL MARIE. Born: Lima, Ohio, 11-7-68; Education: Junior Year in High School; Memberships: Girl Scouts of America; Awards: Girl Scout Gold Award and Silver Award; First Prize for English poetry project in school fair; Poetry: 'Christmas at Grandma's House,' and 'My First Love,' American Poetry Association, 1985; Comments: *I try to express my true emotions and feelings toward the subject I am writing about. I also use my surroundings when I write this way; I have more ideas and can go into details, putting the reader into an atmosphere of their own. In writing 'Christmas at Grandma's House,' I pretended I was Grandma so I could write the feelings of Grandma.*

SILENT FEAR

As I stand alone,
Contemplating the silence that surrounds me,
I shudder from the intensity of their fear,
The fear that creates the silence,
A fear that leaves me standing alone.

    Wendy Woodford

THE LAST WORD

After all that's said and done
She has the last word on everything
For quietly she silences each and every one
From staff-reclining shepherd to scepter-wielding king:
All, all march before her to the beat of their fate.
She dissipates all our vain debate
And pulverizes our most impregnable argument
By reminding us that we have had our day;
Now is the hour, the act that ends the play.
For the Lady is really an angel in disguise, heaven sent
To free us from life's dizzy passion parade,
Pride's inane game of hide and seek
And all the greed that makes the world so bleak.

Oh man charade, sad masquerade!
We rave, pant, plead, mask our naked face,
Foolishly we run to catch our breath,
Helplessly we grope to find our place
But the Dour Dame gently gestures "No More Time,"
Then who fails to hear the final, fateful rhyme?

Robert Casals

QUANDARY

LIFE seems at best . . . a bit of a JEST!
There is a choice . . . for better or worse
Should we strive to be happy or should we curse?
There MUST be an answer in this vast . . . UNIVERSE!
Shall we cheat or shall we play fair . . . even be underhand
Being dealt cards . . . the Gamblers say:
We cannot possibly . . . understand!
Now comes the question: How shall we play it?
Shall we forfeit . . . act the coward and secede?
What can we do but 'play it by ear?'
We dare not stop grinning as we fear
There is little chance of winning!
While the HURT burrows . . . deeply
And our heart is ready to . . . burst
We bravely figure: Things could be worse!
After all: We could be CHIEF passenger in a Hearse!
Like a brave Captain and his crew
Keeping 'Stiff upper LIP' . . . we blunder through
OR face the inevitable . . . DEFEAT . . .
GO DOWN WITH OUR SHIP!

Mabel Lagerlöf

ROGUE'S REASON

Canvas warps with wind-whipped hemp,
Bahaman palms still shadow the stars.
Crystal waters wash the deck of lost hopes,
Ten kilos of snow hide below the spars.
Friends seek answers to my ways,
To the guarded silence in my voice.
None know of my past lives or days,
Of the brown eyes that once were my choice.
I can't remember what she looks like anymore,
Only the way I felt when she touched me.
So much a part of my soul, my paramour,
That I was born with her face on my eyes.
And now the sea rocks my body,
Moist and warm like her fluid form.
But deep in my depths all passion still broods,
Lie coral reef piers below the foam.
Nature, grant me that gift again,
To know the touch of nourished heart.
Before law enforcers discover this game,
And my dust flies to the lands apart.

Mark Richards

THE SYMPHONY

A symphony stirs within me with all its crescendos and accents.
Its beauty and thrill are impossible to describe.
Of its strains I never tire.
Its humor and serenity are exquisitely exciting.

The elements of mystery keep me ever watching.
The fullness and gentleness of its melody
Are like soft fingers upon my skin.

There is no monotony in it for me.
The silences are as emphatic as the swells.
I err by not listening to interpretations, wanting only mine.

It touches my innermost self with excitement and anticipation.
The tones of joy are without end,
Although, at times it threatens
With the ominous notes of finality.
There is hope that it will not disappear —
For without it lurks the silence of an empty stage.

The symphony has a spirit wild — not to be restrained.
But maybe, by some tethering strand
It will always come back to me.

Jolene Hamel

PEBBLES ON THE BEACH

Smooth and slick the permeable layers do lie
Basking in the open air amidst a temperate, turquoise sky
Edges once jagged, primitive in design
Shimmer in the ocean's pool now rounded and benign
And at night when up at the stars I might reach
I recall the twinkle of the pebbles —
The pebbles on the beach.

Rough winds may tumult the vast, blue calm
And dappled skies infringe upon the sun's assuaging balm
As darkness skirts the wonder from my sight
Ever-yielding beauty with all its blinding might;
And when the hope of love life appears to breach
I recall the promise of the pebbles —
The pebbles on the beach.

But warmth of day soothes the sands beneath my feet
While the ocean's breeze courts my nose with aqua perfume sweet
Scratching your name into the golden, grainy floor
Lapping tides partake the morsel from the shore
And when in absence of your love, I beseech
I recall the nearness of the pebbles —
The pebbles on the beach.

Mark Wells

THE WALTZ OF THE FLOWERS

Old Mister Wind, on his stringless violin
Played a waltz for the dancing flowers,
They bowed and swayed in gay promenade
As they waltzed through the morning hours.

The pale mignonette and the blue violet
Swayed to the rhythmical breeze.
While the pink wild rose on tiny tiptoes
Tripped lightly beneath tulip trees.

Sweet-scented phlox with lavender locks
Swung cowslips of bright golden hue,
Sweet Williams kept pace with Queen Anne's lace
Waltzing in warm morning dew.

Green-carpeted hills where morning sun spills
Set the scene for this formal ball,
Where the musical breeze echoed through the trees,
For the flowers waltzing in their spacious halls.

Cora Layne

FIRST LOVE

I still think about you from time to time.
I feel as though you are a part of me.
Even when I know we are miles apart.
For I shall always feel your tender love
in my heart.

Sue Barker

METAMORPHOSIS

Bear with me,
The change has just begun,
Though I'm lowly and burdensome now,
Someday I'll be fun!

It's a long and painful thing
From this lowly estate
To the spreading of wings.

The process can't be hurried,
It takes time
From lowly estate
To creature sublime.

Though I struggle on the ground
With many a care,
Someday I'll sprout wings
And soar through the air!

Linda Waak Beasley

GET INTO TOMORROW

When this life is hard and cold
Or dull at best
Gather all into a heap.
Curl your thumb in,
Get it warm,
And sleep
Some wine-delicious slumber.
Forget the day, its number.
Mix your worlds together.
Create a scheme
Or two!
Drink a sweet and gentle night.
Relax inside of you.

When the light comes dancing
And your eyes it's met
Waken to a new time
Undiscovered yet!

Steffanie S. Douglass

MEDITATION AT THE SIXTH HOUR

Then gasped the thief upon the left,
in tortured hate and rasping breath,
"How can a God, or Son of God,
Be hung by man on mortal rod?
And why should He, if a divinity,
Cry to heaven forsakenly?"
so shrill and fierce he spat his scorn
It drove pain deeper than the thorn.
"Come down, oh King, this little thing
Should not be hard for God!
Release us with a nod!"
Now turned the thief upon the right —
His vision clear with sudden light —
"Oh, man, called Christ, I do believe
You have the power to reprieve,
And though I hang deservedly,
I still would ask, "remember me!"
Christ looked at him with dying eyes —
"Today you shall see paradise."

Frances Pangborn Morehead

SEND NO MONEY — GET NO PRAYER SHAWL!

A man from the tube
Smiles with a God-like stare,
Asks for my money,
Leads us in prayer.

I change the channel —
Different faces say the same;
They pray for my money
Mouthing God's name.

The words I hear
Are sweet and runny,
Syrup from brains
whose God is money.

All pray to Jesus
With the same refrain,
In His name send money,
We've a church to maintain.

Then smiling faces sing,
Their eyes aglow,
They have the answer —
It's the question I don't know!

V. E. Opincar

MY MIDNIGHT TALE

I rushed along
The star shade night
Astride my white mare
As we galloped so high,
Chasing the paired
Butterflies
That rose with grace,
Then descending
To the sands
That cupped the black sea,
Where I watched Aphrodite
Sing to the mermaids,
As she flew in the rippled
Moonlight
With silver angelic wings,
Blessing my enchanting world
With harmony
And peace . . .

Jim Asch

REMEMBER THE GOOD

We read it in the papers
    And hear it on the news —
Violence, bloodshed, fighting,
    And murders without clues.

Depressing, frightening statistics
    Of people ruled by addictions.
War and unemployment —
    These are the dire predictions.

But what of people sharing
    By giving all they can
Of time and money and food
    To help their fellow man?

And what of autumn colors
    And the laughter of a child?
The new cures found by research —
    The animals in the wild?

Wouldn't the bad be easily faced
    If the good were remembered, too?
Instead of partly cloudy skies —
    Why not partly blue?

Brenda Janish

HOUSES OF MYKONOS

White doves
voyager of the islands
asleep on Aegean shores
nestling tenderly.

Peter the Pelican is asleep.

Astride straw-covered
chairs, only inches
from the sea.
Calm.

In the summer's heat
locals are
seasoning lobsters
lazily.

Street strolling in the shade
undercover, the ancients are watching.

Homes, in their
guiltless white domes
smoothed by the winds,
houses of Mykonos.

Sleeping white birds.

Prof. Salvatore Galioto

DANCER

Flowing like a wave,
Motions,
Silk in the wind.
Music carries her off.
Oh dancer,
See the dancer.

Off she goes,
'Round and 'round.
Going to eternity.
Oh dancer,
See the dancer.

Toni Beckwith

PROGRESS

And this is the way we grow,
    we little children,
    watching our elders.

And this is our mother,
    the oldest eldest,
    dressing and eating,
    like this.

And we do it that way,
    and we make mistakes,
    and the knitting ravels.

And this is our teacher,
    the smartest eldest,
    one, two, three we
    do it that way.

And she smiles,
    no, no; this way,
    and we learn.

And Diane cries,
    she can't tie her shoe.

Watch me, this way, like this.

Francena Goodine

JOURNEY TO THE UNKNOWN

Exploring a journey to the unknown with the
imagination of the mind can be a frightening
experience.

An experience beyond your wildest expectations.

I sit, wondering and sighing
What's on the other side
Is there life or death in store.

Will there be songs of birds
and humming bees.
Will there be flowers of every shape,
color and size growing above our feet.

Will there be the beauty of blooming trees
And fragrant air and a cooling breeze.

Will there be flocks of the air, beast of
the fields and aquatic animals of the open
seas.

Trees, so tall with branches that spread like
the wings of an eagle.
To shade me from the heat of the day.

Will there be a night or a day.

Will there be stars in the darkness of twilight.

I wonder about the seasons of the years.

Will time cease to be no more.

A journey to the unknown is an endless expedition.

Audria M. Edwards

MOTHER

This is the reason for what we have become,
for no one knows until our lives are complete.

The becoming of our true selves is started even
as we are a mere child; and we behold with our
own eyes the beauty that shines forth as one sees
their mother for the first time.

The powerful calming as she brings you to her breast,
and you draw from her again, just as you have from
the very beginning of your life.

She is in you as you were in her, and the bond that
is created will be.

Upon life's road in the early years you will venture
together; learning to become a person and a love, and
a life.

The bumps and bruises that will come with time, as they
surely will, become the reasons for the character and
confidence built from the way your mother instilled her love.

As she goes, a deep part of you is surrendered to the
memory of the love that was once shared;

But will now be remembered with the fondness she gave you,
the desire of hers for your life to be good;
and the depth of her love that will share forever.

Because that love is forever.
                    Thank you, Mother,
                        Your son,
                            R.O.V.

Russell O. Varner

IN A MIRROR OF ICE

The dryad combs her hair,
Glad to be free of root and leaf;
Glad to breathe the morning air.

Suddenly an intruder comes
Upon the snowy embankment.
The morning ritual forsaken,
The wood-nymph barks silent.

A human form glides upon the frozen effulgence,
And unaware that he is watched,
He skates before the silent audience.

Steel upon ice, the music of the spheres,
An everlasting melody to which
Eurydice, with lyric, volunteers:

"Oh Steel-footed Orpheus,
Whose instrument is a cold device,
Play on, play on, my love,
No matter how hard the sacrifice.
And when the Maenads make you cease to skate,
Your music will live on: For lo,
Infinity will be etched upon the ice."
            Robert M. Hill

MUGGA DEE

He's flashing brown eyes and wavy blonde hair
With a smile that could win anyone.
A ray in my world that's more than sunshine.
A bright one, this child of mine!

He loves planes and trains and great big balloons.
A chance to do it his way.
How many times he's refused to be rushed!
"No no Mommy, *Mugga* do!"

A little man set to take on the world.
A blur as he runs through the house.
Half a baby, half a boy —
Never too far from worn Mickey Mouse.

As I trip on his toys that fill up the room
And feel like I'll never get done,
I think of the day they'll be gone from my path
Along with my loved little son.

Someday he'll be "Mike," then "Mr. McDeed."
Someday he'll fly from my nest.
But for now he's all mine, my sweet son of three.
And I think I'll love "Mugga Dee" best.
        Patricia Power McDeed

TRUTH OR LIE

They call him the piper
bearing warning of earth's end.
Heed the warning
of the colorless sunset,
and a man bearing the silvery-gold pipe
of ages.
He speaks not a truth
but of all truth.
He speaks not a lie
but of all lies.
Who is this piper who gives warning
of earth's end?
Who follows the rainbow to her end?
He walks with us wherever we go
and he plays the leading role in our dreams,
he's anyone you'd want him to be
yourself and,
even me.
            Richard G. Hamm

GOD

God, can you hear me?
It is nine o'clock
I am at school
I had a wonderful night
I felt good in everything I did
I enjoyed being with this man
I feel calm, fulfilled
Some people cannot understand me
They consider me a sinner
They say I am going to Hell
They give me a taste of hell on earth
They are judging me in your name
God, I am not afraid
If I am going to Hell
I will go walking, on my feet
I will go smiling
God, do you hear me!

Pedro Pereira

DANCE

Society, that wretched black crow
with forked tongue screeching necessity
from its hungry festering mouth,
exhorts, nay commands! participation in
its death dance.

— (Round and round they go,
the twin tunes: produce, conform,
spinning in their hollow skulls
like angry bones;
humanity's macabre loaded dice.) —

Trembling, the soul draws its curtain
over dry agonized eyes —

weeping, it is alone.

Simone Dubé

THE INVASION

The sun emerges
the new day approaches
beams of light invade the room
and march across our faces.
Warm beneath the blanket
I fight off the sun's warning
that I must learn to brave it
and start another day,
My eyes adjust to the piercing light
worse than any torture I know
I dress myself
step out the door
and sink into the snow
I glare up in the sky
shivering, and wonder again
why, every morning
does the sun have to win?

Cathy Curran

PRAISE

Dogs love it,
People want it,
Plants need it,
But try to buy it
Unless you can supply it.

If you cannot buy it,
Then why supply it.
Who needs it
Anyway?

Michele Coviello

ALL BECAUSE

A secret kiss
A stolen night
All because he's dark
And I happen to be light.

I don't understand the fussing,
Why all the fight
All because he's dark
And I happen to be light.

J. J. Lawrance

YOUR DREAMS

A Want
A Need
A Dream
Strive for it
Believe in it
Then turn it into Reality
Hold it
Treasure it
For a moment or as long as
there is a need
Then reflect back to that first
thought of it
Which now has become
a heartwarming memory
Smile . . . then Rest
Be content with your success
Then . . . set it free
from your thought
Start again to accomplish
yet another of your fantasies

Gayle Symonds

SYMONDS, GAYLE LYNN. Born: Geneva, Illinois, 10-19-48; Married: 6-17-72 to Richard Rae Symonds; Education: Iowa State University, B.S., June, 1970; Occupation: Teacher; Poetry: 'Happiness Radiates,' *National Poetry Anthology,* New York Poetry Society, 1985; 'Looking for the Rainbow's End,' Poetry Press, Anthology — *Moods and Mysteries,* 1985; Themes: *Reflecting on words of wisdom, wonder, feelings and faith;* Comments: *I believe in the expression of poetry for it is one of the few communication tools where so few words can say so much.*

CALL ON ME

I pray that I'm the kind of friend
Who means the world to you,
And may you be aware of me
In all the things you do.

Please feel free to call on me
When I may be of aid,
I'll help you out, and keep you safe
So you won't be afraid.

I want you to be mindful
That wherever you may be,
I promise I will serve you
In whatever capacity.

I offer you my knowledge
And what strength I may possess,
To assure each day, along the way,
A time of peaceful happiness.

It surely is a joy to me
Whenever I'm allowed to do,
A favor that can smooth your road
And help to make your dreams come true.

Caye Hurst

HURST, CATHERINE ELEANOR. Pen Name: Caye Hurst; Born: Ingham County, 3-7-19; Married: 3-27-40; Education: Sienna Heights, Adrain, Michigan, Commercial Science; Occupation: I took care of the sick in their homes; Memberships: I belong to a bowling league in Ovid, Michigan; Poetry: 'Autumn,' 'This Above All,' 'Fond Memories of Mom,' 'Hallowe'en,' 'A Tribute to General Eisenhower;' Comments: *Whenever an idea comes to my mind, I have to write it down. If I don't, it bothers me all day. I have six children, thirty grandchildren, and seven little grandchildren who supply me with the incentive to keep writing.*

PARADOX

Now the puzzle is nearly complete,
lacking but a single piece.
How I long for you to find it,
yet dread the moment when you do,
For then Your Picture shall be cast,
and nevermore in it a place for me.
Ever again.
Love seems
Always
Painful

Christian W. Zauner

TIME PASSAGE: A REFLECTION

The sheer thirst of wind rolls
out hours, flattens constellations,
their tiny clarities shift
through the night.

Darkness crowds, the sunken moon
is a flat blemish, behind the eye
tender memories grow, ring on ring.

Round bubbles, words in the throat
of an unvocal sea twist a message.
Smiling blue lightning heats the pulse
of black ink, till the voice of a poem

melts grief. Childhood's secret body
opens fresh scars, where pride
longs and presses every star
against the lonely voice
of sound.

Lori Beth Sackett

SACKETT, LORI BETH. Born: Washington, D.C., 12-12-57; Memberships: The Writer's Center, Bethesda, Maryland; Poetry: 'Fireflies,' Freestyle, Helderef Publications, Fall, 1982; Themes: *The forces of nature, concepts of reality and our bond with the universe.* Comments: *I write because of the possiblity that one person may be touched by a thought or idea I can share with them. My goal is to embody a feeling with words in a way that won't be forgotten. Whenever that poem crosses your mind a little light will go off in your head.*

MY HUSBAND

Sometimes, early in the morning, I awake and marvel at the man who lies beside me. Others may not find him handsome, or even attractive, but they don't see him through my eyes.

These shoulders, so broad and strong, powerful enough to carry all the burdens placed there by the world, but gentle enough to cushion a sleepy son's head.

His arms, well-muscled and manly, with strength to crush all opposition, but used only for building dreams and chasing nightmares. His hands, large and calloused, strong enough to pick you up when you fall, tender enough to wipe away a daughter's tears.

And his face, such a fearful countenance when angered! With black furrowed brow and stormy eyes. His are the most beautiful eyes I've ever seen; sparkling with happiness, glowing with love, or shining with unshed tears; the messages they send are too special for mere words.

But those lips with the power to burn your ears, can burn with an even fiercer passion. Bitten in pain, or split wide in a smile, they have a thousand things to say without making a sound.

No. Others may not find him attractive, but when I look at him, I can truly believe that God made man in His image. And I'm eternally thankful that *this* man is mine.

Susan M. Russell

TWO WOUNDED

Hell's burning fire consumed us, many had died —
again and again that day, old warriors cried.
We had no way out, no place to go —
trapped and bleeding we fought with our weary souls.

Then finally the battle ended, we slipped from the demon's grip —
the retreating march was long, our blood would painfully drip.
The living carried the dead and dying —
and I saw two wounded marching and crying.

As we struggled along bearing our bloody brothers —
these two wounded carried each other.
Arm in arm they painfully limped —
fear in their eyes, from death's cup they had sipped.

I could not help but watch these two from under my lifeless burden —
with strength and courage; life for them was certain.
As the gruesome march came to an end, they fell to the steamy ground —
the two lay there together not making a sound.

We rested in despondent quiet, but the two wounded broke into
fearless laughter —
together they had made it beyond death's cold lonely rafters.
Now we the living can learn from those two wounded trying —
it is far better two are holding, than one left dying.

Wayne Standiford

EVE

I wonder how Eve felt without any clothes —
Without any bra, without any hose.
What did she do when she had to go to town?
Instead of dressing up, she had to dress down.
I wonder what she'd do if she wanted to wear a pin.
If she wanted to look fancy, she had to pin it to her skin.
She had not any colors to brighten up her face.
And what would she do if she had some pretty lace?
What would she do if she wanted to wear a hat?
She'd look rather strange in no more than that!
She never seemed to notice till after the first sin.
The awful sensation began to sink in.
The famous words were spoken when Adam began to stare.
She cried in a voice heard by all, "I haven't a *thing* to wear!"

Rosemary Beecher

THE HYATT — 1981

This was the Hyatt
That spot of light-hearted gaiety
Frivolity on a hot summer's eve.
Amidst flowers, laughter, and music
Those mighty girders of concrete fell
Creating a living tomb for some
A final concrete tomb for others.

Those massive concrete skywalks
So firm to see
Those happy smiling faces
Full of hope and fun
One brief quick moment
And the falling pieces of concrete
The dust
The smell of blood
The moans of mangled and trapped
Filled the air.

Can we a few short years later
The dramatic statement they made
Forget so quickly.

Mary Welsh

You are my sweetheart,
That's why we cannot part,
Let me start.

I want to take you on a journey,
Please follow me.
Time could only stop us,
We must leave today.

Along the journey,
We may experience
Pain, joy, faith, and maturity
For these four things make reality
          real.

For we must remember to stick together,
Whatever happens,
Just be glad we did it in time.

There my sweetheart,
Let's start,
And take our lasting journey
Before it's too late.

Debbie Anderson

MY CHILD MY CHILD

My child my child
So beautiful
So wild

My sweet little girl
With one blonde curl

My dear little boy
You bring me great joy

I want to take your hand
Walk in the sand

I want you to feel the breeze
Walking through the trees

When you're gone and grown
I'll be all alone

You give me simple pleasure
That I will treasure.

Debbie Best

SILENCE IS SINCERITY

To be a faultless mortal
Difficult but of much necessity
Is a concern to humanity

It's because man hears all
It's because man says all
It's because all are criticized

Think about the beautiful flowers
Imagine the new babies
They are all sincere and innocent

Look at the moon and stars
Remember the sun and heavens above
Sincerely they all appear

Imagine if a new baby speaks
If the beautiful flowers talk
Their grace will fade away
The only sincerity today is silence

Let silence show the innocence
And the grace speaks loud
Into the ears of the deaf.

Onyemaechi Emmanuel Okoro

OKORO, ONYEMAECHI EMMANUEL.
Born: Umunumo Mbano Imo State, Nigeria,
12-31-53; Single; Education: LL. B.; Occupation: Legal Practitioner; Memberships: International Bar Association; Poetry: *My Emotion and Passion,* Collection of poems, Luiz Copiadora, 1984; Comments: *I write more about love and fear of life and nature in general. While I try to expose my personal feelings, I make efforts to represent other people or things that may share the same interest with me. That is why most of my poems are dominated by "I," "You," and "We."*

BY PIGEON AIRLINES

Twenty-two cents for a letter
That's for the birds!
I'll get a pigeon,
To carry my words.

Ruth Voss

ILLUSIONS

People are walking, walking
Walking and talking
Talking and talking
Talking and walking

Lies, it's all lies

Look at the skies

The ground is hot, sultry and hot
A sleepy maze
Of white blue reflections
Enfolds one's gaze

Slowly the water's edge creeps coolly
Beneath your feet

Awake, arise
The time has come
To refresh yourself with the nourishment
The sun has given you
Move off and run
Tell the good news to one and all
But
Careful, do not stumble and then fall.

Ilse Kleinman

TO BE RICH OR THE RICHEST ONE

The richest one
has good health.
It is not someone
whose only thought is wealth.
The richest one
has freedom.
Not acquiring possessions,
and then some.
The richest one
has independence
Not high living
and carelessness.
The richest one
is a lucky one.

Lilly Kucharczyk

PROGRESS

The whir of machine in continual sameness
Steady beat steady
'Round and 'round not missing a stroke
Never higher never lower

The coruscating grinding of rim on rail
Sudden shearing shrieking
Marrow-piercing halting rending

The gearing of cog on wheel
Clutching meshing braking

The hum of fan over and over
Exact jerk measured spurt
Controlled hot mechanical chill

The streak of jet thrust high higher
Loud roar straight far far
Farther farther

A thousand more ideas still brain-existing
Will come
Intrude sensations dull
Or dirty or noisy
Or wrench muscle from bone

H. Lieblich

GOOD FRIDAY: APRIL 1, 1983

A madcap scrambling
of the planets,
stars
contrives this doomsday,
spelling a jackanapes
to Pilate's court,

a flim-flam king
in draggled tatters
squat
on a footstool throne
sceptered,
salaamed
in ribald mime,

whose lens of bloody rheum
targets the sottish ragtag's
caps and bells.

Poor April fools!

Sister M. Immaculata Muldoon, C.S.J.

HIDE

as the day of your love
is passing by
Every time you see him
you want to run and cry.

If your love doesn't realize
how much you care — so dear
but maybe he'll realize
whenever you're not here.

On the streets
when he passes by your side
You look for an escape
But there's nowhere to hide.

So now that you've learned
          just how to act
Don't be sad
Because he'll be glad
And all of this is a fact.

Becki Willey

THOUGHTS WHILE FOLDING SHEETS

I wish I had a man
on whom I could depend;
at the very least, to hold up
the other end.

Yet, how nice to be my own boss
for the first time in my life!
I keep telling myself.

I eat when I please
choose what to wear
whom or what to see.

But when I watch T.V.
there's no one to poke
in the ribs at a joke.

Laughing alone
is a one-handed clap.

Bobbie Goldman

MY SEVEN-YEAR OLD

Why do you dawdle
And swing on the gate?
You must hurry to school
Or you will be late.

I wish I could analyze
That look on your face;
What do you dream about
As you stare into space?

Are you looking forward
To orbiting the earth,
While I look back on
The day of your birth?

Oh, please don't hurry
To grow up, Little Man.
I want to keep you with me
As long as I can.

Marilyn E. Harris

WET SEPTEMBER

Dripping water
Falling water
Potter potter everywhere

Flooded yard
Leaking roof
Snoring mom
Crying child
Water dripping on the floor

Market woman's headtie wet
Taxi driver soaking wet
Crazy man feels no cold
Falling water on them pour

Empty streets
Bulging buses
September sun's dimple cheeks
Sinking in the weeping clouds

Dripping water
Falling water
Potter potter everywhere

Walter C. Savage

I DREAM OF MY ISLAND HOME

I have a rendezvous
To sail my canoe
To a small motu
And catch a fish or two.
To dream of my island home
I must return there soon
To a blue lagoon
Where I can sing a tune
'Neath the southern moon.
I dream of my island home
I must hurry back
To a little grass shack
Where I can eat a snack
Or just lie on my back.
I dream of my island home
Far across the sea
Someone waits for me
And I know that she
Will come to me.
I dream of my island home
Far across the foam
To a place I call home
I'll never more roam
From my island home.

LeRoy F. Oates

Yesterday, the good and bad memories
Today, the life you live and grow from
Tomorrow, the future and what it holds.

Dwell on the past, the feelings that
make you happy.

Dream about what happens tomorrow.

But learn and grow today, from the
life you live.

Before your dream of tomorrow
becomes today, and almost suddenly
turns into yesterday

Kim Koester

TWILIGHT

Shadows glimmer
with secrets untold.
Time stands still,
Its presence bold.

On wings of darkness
a hush sweeps the land,
tempting all,
to grasp its hand.

A whisper of light
dancing, teasing,
fading slowly . . .
ceasing

Stephanie D. Lestenkof

A POEM

Of the things called to mind
Whenever I'm at repose
One is a blood-red candle
Burning alongside a scarlet rose

Another a fine china tea pot
With crumpets by its side
A vision of my sweetheart
When she was no more than a bride

A tapestry of delight
In envisioned memory
A beautiful moment in respite
Just my soul and me

Pamela McKenzie

A MUSING OWL

That I be wise
   Few can dispute;
Where silence sins,
   I give a hoot.

When screeching proves
   An unwise choice,
I humbly watch
   With muted voice.

Best hush, to hear,
   Than being heard;
'Tis vain to flaunt
   The final word.

Warren B. Howe

MODERN HOLOCAUST

Should it happen to begin on this day
It would be advisable not to wake
For I would rather die dreaming I'd say
Because this shall be worse than any quake
"But our great leader will protect us, right?"
It's doubtful — most likely he'll flee and hide
"Won't our nation put up even a fight?"
Of course — when it's all over — *killer pride*
"We will rebuild and be great once again
as it is done in all movies I see"
Political propaganda my friend
This cannot be stopped — what will be will be
    Those who live by the sword — die by the sword
    There was once a time our great eagle soared

    Timothy Holman

EVENING'S VOICE

Feel the joy —
Sense her presence-fragrance —
Hear her voice —
See her face —
    the fierce and innocent,
      sad and sincere eyes.
Feel the excitement —
    the cool and warm ecstasy of a nervous heart,
    the relentless shafts of piercing eyes.
Laugh inside the feelings of a joyful childhood world —
Watch the light of its impending dawn —
    a fading morning star.
Feel the silent vibrance —
Feel the brisk warmth of the Indian summer —
    the calm red sky and mellow gold on grassy hills.
Feel the cold of a wind-swept cliff —
    the lonely pulse of a dying heart.
Cry the tears of a weeping soul shunning its natural love —
See twilight dreams,
    beyond diamond eyes of a sleepless city . . .

    Derek Brewer

BREWER, DEREK EMERSON. Born: Chattanooga, Tennessee, 9-25-67; Education: High School Graduation, 5-28-85; plan to attend institution of higher learning; Occupation: Self-Employed Artist; Poetry: 'Patricia,' 1983; 'Crescent and Guitar,' 1983; 'Evening's Voice,' American Poetry Association, 11-84; Comments: *Just started in poetry a few months ago, although I had experimented previously. I try to relay my own adolescent feelings of loneliness and being in love. I try to incorporate the element of passing time, and the feelings that seem to endure forever.*

OUR LOVE

I've got a blank sheet before me,
So what can I place here for thee,
How strong our love will ever be,
That's always been between you and me.

We'll be together on love's great sea,
And travel the roads of hardship with glee,
To make our lives worth living you see,
That's always been between you and me.

So let's be free, let's be free,
To do what comes naturally,
For you only live once, that's all, you see,
It's love between you and me.

    Nancy Jack

AQUARIUM

The natives casually glide within the borders
Of a glass-lined interior;
Some, swaying like milkweeds in a summer breeze,
And others . . .
Dancing in the dark
To the child's delight.
Grandfather's warm eyes follow the boy
As the child runs from the room.
The elder turns a brief glance to the aquarium
Only to see a smiling face
Out of place;
And, like youth passing in a moment,
The child disappears
Between the slate and flora.

    Robert Tatigan

LIFE THAT ONCE WAS

Do you remember me?
The dreams we used to dream,
Of you and I together,
When our lives were better.
Now I cannot see,
The reality of the dreams,
Of you sitting near the base of a tree,
Praying for the lushness of the leaves.
It hurts when I remember, how we used to be,
Happy with a lot of glee.
But now that is gone,
For you took our fawn,
And said, "Farewell,"
Leaving me to dwell.

    Jennifer Biggs

A PROPHECY FOR WINTER

Dark, light, and medium grey,
The trees will be bare
Of leaves.
And sprinkled with fresh snow.
That will soon make icicles.
That will reflect the cold, bright sun.
Sometimes, break up the aberrant ray
Into a whole spectrum of jewelled colors
That will hang, suspended in rarified air,
For a minute.
Unappreciated by people scurrying away from the cold
Shielded by their dark,
Light,
And medium grey, winter coats.

    Krishna Thangavelu

FADED MEMORIES

Time has passed
And dust covers the picture
I once held dear.

Memories have faded
In the silence of our hearts.

You've gone your separate way
And left my love behind.

I've watched you from afar —
Afraid to touch or share
Your inner thoughts
We once so eagerly exchanged.

Time heals all wounds —
Or so they say . . .
My heart has mended —
It is true.

But hurt raises its ugly head
From time to time
And reminds me of all that's changed
And how I miss your smile, your laugh, your love.

Samye Hill

HILL, SAMYE CAROLYN. Born: Bartlett, Texas, 5-4-46; Education: Baylor University, B.A., 1968; San Diego State University, M.A., 1981; Occupation: Teacher; Memberships: California Teachers' Association, California State Poets' Association; Poetry: *Sand at Sea*, Chapbook, Ursus Press, 1985; 'Christmas,' *Moods & Mysteries*, Poetry Press, 1985; Comments: *I write about the aspects of my life which others can relate to: friendship, emotions, education, and religious poetry. Some of my poetry relates to various holiday themes.*

CAGE OF RAGE

There's this anger down inside,
a deep and silent rage.
Sometimes it swells to a burning fury,
and she rattles the bars of her cage.
She screams into the silent darkness,
cursing the cold night air . . .
Her screams are swallowed by the night,
for there is no one near.
And she doesn't quite control her rage . . .
it lives in her, as she lives in her cage.

Mary Kelly

UNTITLED

I am safely protected here, inside my insulated shell.
Protected from evils and pain, protected from myself.
Should I take the chance, emerge . . . ever so slightly,
to face what might lie beyond the walls of my shell . . .
    No, I feel safer inside with only my imagination.

Julie Pajares

BELOW THE SURFACE

I have looked across the ocean
Watching breakers crest and fall.
It seemed that in that water
There was no peace at all.
A constant noisy battling —
Waves rose with speed and flow,
With a fringe of foam to top their crest
As they hit the shore below.
Going back to where they started,
Again to play their scene,
Repeating every restless trip
With motions not serene.

Who could know — beneath the surface
Moved the sea in quiet calm
Where fish could swim and plants could grow —
A gentle kind of balm.

Emily L. Moore

MOORE, EMILY L. Comments: *My poetry is very diverse. I do not follow any one theme, but write material as my conscious thoughts dictate. My hope is to express depth of thought which will speak for many people. I am an avid writer of personal and family history, including childhood memories, and recordings of my nurse's training about fifty years ago. Since my children grew up, I've devoted much time to the artist side of me, creating untold numbers of art pieces which I have framed and displayed. For many years, I have held weekly art classes for children, to help them to "really see what they are looking at." Many of them have won school awards. All of these things are the history from which my children and grandchild, Jeff, sprang. Many years have gone into the making and selling of gift and craft items, most of which have been originals, old-fashioned woodburning especially.*

FREE

The sun turns orange on the horizon
Ever onward
And I listen.
Pen glides swiftly across the page
Thoughts appear to mirror soul,
Who has been so long hidden.
Questions rise, orange and glow
Increases and releases
Answers . . .
Abstract void to clearly written prose
I understand
And I listen.
Speak to me soul, sing to me of sounds
I yearn no further beyond.
A part of me balanced three
Mind thinks, body does, soul sings
Increases and releases
Answers . . .

Kathleen Fuller

CROUCH, KATHLEEN FULLER. Pen Name: Kathleen Fuller; Born: Seattle, Washington; Married: 8-2-69 to Dr. John Charles Crouch; Education: University Puget Sound, B.A. in Art and Elementary Education, 1970; Occupations: Children's Book Writer, Freelance Writer, Lecturer, and Publisher; Memberships: Florida Freelance Writers, Society of Children's Book Writers; Comments: *Poetry is said to be the language of God. I talk with God through my poetry and from the soul words come.*

TO REDRESS THE GOLDEN THREAD

Common place hardly exists
Compulsion has greedy hands,
It stalks; it binds; it climbs;
Forward, encircling one's vision;
Destroying inhibited innocence;
Latching itself onto the will,
And burning all inner senses.
A link is broken by enmity
A dream is shaken by howling temptation,
But which incubus is surviving;
And are they not both the same —
Disarray cannot repair the severed line;
We must put hatred on the shelf
If love is the book to read.

James Wesley Duren

WINTERSOUL

Steps so brisk with winter aire
not one brings hesitation.
To stop on frozen land so bare
with warmth's anticipation.

Across the hurried realm of frost
our feet do ofttimes scurry.
Forgetting that with winter's loss,
springs birth, in all its fury.

O. Felspar

GREEN, DAVID LYNN. Pen name: O. Felspar; Born: Sedalia, Missouri, 11-19-51; Education: University of Texas at Arlington, B.A., Communications, Journalism, 1975; Poetry: 'Soft Sounds,' *American Poetry Showcase,* May, 1985; 'The Love of Trophy Great,' American Poetry *Hearts on Fire,* February, 1985; 'Oceanography,' *Our World's Most Beloved Poems,* March, 1985; 'Wanting Words,' *Our World's Most Beloved Poems,* March, 1985; 'Amongst the Gale,' *Lutheran Digest,* 1986; Comments: *I've always had the deep desire to be the wise old sage, and writing my poetry helps me to know I'm not.*

AN ATTAINABLE GOAL

While flying high above the clouds,
So near the Face of God,
Away from noise and motley crowds,
Where never man has trod,
I mused, "How grand must Heaven be,
Where all is joy and bliss?"
And then this thought occurred to me,
We all could strive for this.

What must one do to gain this peace? —
It's easy to acquire.
See that your zeal's daily increased,
Endeavor to inspire.
Just work for God, and say your prayers,
Help a needy neighbor.
The One who's up above and cares,
Will reward your labor.

Sister Mary Neumann Spuhler

TWO LOVES

Through the years we've come together.
Met and parted. Met and parted.
Gossamer the thread that binds us,
Leaves us free to roam and wander,
Till again we come together
Drawn by this silken strand.

Not so with the other union.
Passions wove their swift strong ties,
Bound us with a thick sure band.
Surely such a band would hold us
Keep us close all through our lives.

In relentless grasp it held us.
Left no room to grow and wander,
And the tighter that it pulled us,
More the chafing and the fraying,
Till it all was rent asunder.
Every tie let loose its grasp.
In cataclysmic shock we huddled,
Knew not how to live unfettered
Shattered as our broken bands.

Mildred Guadino

I TOOK A CHANCE

Strangers — or are we?

I see him sitting there.
I don't know him, yet I want to.
I wonder who he is, where he lives,
What he's thinking.

We look and turn away,
As if frightened or guilty.

Do I dare smile?
I take a chance.
I smile.
He smiles.
We speak.
I made a friend.
Others follow our example.

Silence turned into conversation.
Strangers turned into friends.
No more lonely quiet bus rides.

Jennifer Lee Sager

THE DISPOSSESSED

(On building a house on a hill in the country)

The deer are there, behind the trees.
They peer at us from a fringe of brush
Goaded by their timid curiosities.
The grassy knoll, where they at dusk
Their paths had carved, is no longer
Theirs to traverse boldly.

And we are disappointed,
For we thought that they
Would be an entertainment
As they ran the hill —
The floating grace, the flirting tail,
The young fawns, dapple-faced.

But we have spoiled it for them.
They do not come. Our house
They slyly circle out of sight —
One more encroachment on their freedom.
Our beagles bark them in the night,
Rousing us to drowsy guilt.

Sharon E. Lewis

AMERICA TODAY

Crime is a on a rampage
Morals are real low
People are complaining
There is no justice anymore.

Criminals are treated like
They are always right
and the victim is forgotten
By the courts almost overnight.

Our government gives money
To all the foreign lands
And cuts services to our poor
And elderly — isn't that a shame?

To anyone with common sense
It is easy to explain
If we don't change our ways
We are headed down the drain.

Wilson Molero

QUANDARY

A thing there is that baffles me
And makes my composure quite crack:
I can't tell indigestion from
A bona fide old heart attack.

I get this heavy feeling of
A lump of lead within my chest.
Is it my heart or something that
My stomach didn't quite digest?

Should I call up a doctor or
A nitroglycerin tablet take?
Or will some soda or a Tum
Quite dissipate this funny ache?

I guess from now on I should pass
Up onions, pizza, gravy, pie;
This would remove my problem, but
I think that I would rather die.

Janice M. Walser

THE INNER VISION

Living in a plastic world
Forgetting all things outside
If I had only felt
The emptiness going on inside

Spending precious time looking for fun
Hoping someday I'll find a girl
Like a dewinged bird
Looking for a place to hide

People think I'm truly a bore,
Never showing I cry
Inside rotting to the core
Wishing I could pass it all by

Gazing out at an imaginary shore,
The inner vision fills my eye
Wondering when to soar,
I think it's about time to try.

Greg Phipps

MARIAH

See me, I am Mariah, a daughter of the wind.
My lonely destiny was born, to love the might-have-been.
I walk the fields of golden youth, the starshine paths of love.
My eyes caress the mighty pine from cloud-swept skies above.
I tread upon the daffodils on silken slippered feet,
and wander over distant hills where dale and valley meet.
I have topped the mighty thunderclouds on golden eagle wings,
and skimmed the lofty rainbow, where sister bluebird sings.
Pegasus is the steed I ride through misty morning light,
he carries me and moonbeams in the silken summer night.
My father is the west wind, my mother is the moon,
and, when alone in midnight sky, a soft, wild tale they croon.
They sing a song of yesterday, a past not yet begun.
They sing of summer dawning, and warmth of rising sun.
They spread their love through summer skies on laughter-silvered wings.
and give to me the love of light, and promises it brings.

Julia Ann Reynolds

MY FRIEND JIM

See the little boy outside the window, who's playing all alone?
He doesn't seem to understand, why his daddy isn't home.
"I've never seen my daddy," I heard him say to his friend named Jim,
"He doesn't seem to care at all, so why should I care about him?"
And then he hit his friend with a forceful blow, and he kicked him in the dirt,
He seemed to be enjoying all the torture and the hurt.
But then he picked him up, and brushed him off, like a loving little tot,
"You may be just a ragdoll Jim, but you're the only friend I've got.
You always keep on smiling, you never seem to be down,
You always seem to have more love, even when I beat and kick you around.
You always seem to be happy, you never seem to be sad,
But I guess I'd be the very same way, if I only had a dad.
But I don't have a daddy, like the other girls and boys,
My mommy tries to please me, with stuffed animals and toys.
She says I must forget him, and I think she has already forgot,
I know my mommy loves me Jim, but you're the only friend I've got."

Carol Welch

CLOUD FORMATIONS AT SEA

A tiny ship bobbing along on the vastness of the sea,
While billowing clouds reached so high — Oh! God, to Thee.
The mighty cloud had a thin border as a ring of gold,
While shafts of light streaking toward the heavens so old.
The tiny ship was so small in view of the cloud so high,
And there we were, my friend, the tiny boat and I.
Had I been atuned to God as one really should be,
I still could have seen more of God's beauty out at sea.
When the sea was raging, billows did ever so high roll,
And there were other times we were fearful for our soul.
Once we were caught in a fierce storm not so very far from shore,
As the ship came down with a bang, we fear we could take no more.
Yes, the waves beat against the cabin and water rolled on the deck.
It was time of great fear — I'll never that experience forget.
The waves were beating one upon another and so very high,
And it was time for sensible people to turn to God and cry.

C. D. McKay

OLYMPUS REBORN

"Look over there," exclaimed archaeologist Prof. Agadorn.
How then this beauty beast looking so lost and forlorn
Who in the shrouded myths of earth's obscured history was born
To a world of endless ages by battles of credence torn
Offering up to him but a mere curious melange of reverence and scorn?
How indeed to behold this mystical creature of long solitary conical horn
An illuminating jewel vain human ignorance to adorn,
Mute testimony to faltering faith by weary centuries of disbelief worn?
Dreamily silhouetted playfully upon today's lovely misty Grecian morn
Regally prances the wondrous, marvelous equine, its mythological mask divinely shorn.
He is in princely living reality none but the fabulous fabled believable unicorn.

Allen Binckley

FALLS OF THE BLACKWATER.

THE DREAMER

I am riding on the sunset, looking for a dream,
I am a dreamer, gliding on a laser beam.
I cast my shadow on the ground,
And there is nowhere I belong.

Like the mountains reaching for the sky,
I am a man who can get himself high.
I am the river flowing down,
And I am even a circus clown.

The sea gull soars through the clouds,
and I am a man who stands alone in crowds.
It is like the wind blowing through the trees,
You see I can bend, but you can't change me.

Victor C. Massaglia

PROMISED LIGHTS

The forbidding darkness of the midnight sky,
Held over me a treasure of promised lights,
And all, I thought, I could do was cry,
About how cruel and lonely were the nights.
Of all the stars that were beyond my touch,
The dearest were those covered by the dark,
The very ones that always meant so much
More, but my eyes could not find their mark.
Believing that my dreams, the dark had killed,
I never thought the night could be a friend,
But then I understood, as in the field,
I sat in awe and watched the darkness end.
For as my new found friend, the night, waned old,
The sunrise touched the sleepy pond with gold.

Ellen Wetter

DREAM OF ESCAPE

I try to sleep but think of you.
Beside me lies a man I never knew.
I watch him sleep and wonder why
The dreams he talks of are never mine.

We fell together — two broken hearts.
It seems so complicated for us to part.
But now my heart belongs to you.
The times we've shared have been so few.

I hear you, touch you, feel you, see —
As if it were you lying next to me.
I close my eyes and dream of fate.
When it will all come true — my dream of escape.

Delene Nairns

THE LAKE

The cold blue expanse, set off by a wall of white,
Wildly waiting for the season to change,
As the gulls call urgently in their suspended flight,
And the scene is set, a windy and rugged range.

Neverending cessation of cobalt crashing cliffs
Laced at the breakpoints in angry white foam.
At the shore the spray uplifts,
As each pounding wave comes hitting home.

The contrast is the sky, now the blue of the fair season,
The gulls are ever content, white wings unfurled,
As in the wind-whipped day, they seek no reason.
The view: On the edge of the rest of the world.

Mary Elizabeth Rowan

TRIBUTE TO MOTHER: LIFE AS A LILY . . .

In the field the fragrant lilies grow;
And unto all those who near them go

Radiance and beauty they shed around
With each glorious velvety gown.

But the winds and storms their beauty mar;
And unhallowed hands their petals scar.

'Til tired, weary, and wanting to rest,
They droop their heads to the Maker's breast.

Our precious Mother the race has run.
Her work is finished. Her crown is won.

Her toils of life are forever through;
And now she has begun life anew.

Our own dear blessed mother, whose life,
As the lilies with fragrance was rife,

Has gone to that Celestial city afar,
Where nothing shall her happiness mar.

After awhile on Heaven's golden shore,
We hope to meet and part nevermore.

Eddie Hammit Strickland

STRICKLAND, EDDIE HAMMIT. Born: Athens, Texas; Married: to William Clarence Strickland; Education: West Texas State University, Wayland Baptist University, A.A., B.A., 1977; Occupations: School Teacher, Housewife; Memberships: Associated Country Women of the World: ACWW; American Association of University Women: AAUW; Alpha Chi — National Honor Society; National Extension Homemakers Council: NEHC; Poetry: 'Mother'; Other Writings: 'The City of Gold,' song; *21 Rules for a Happy Marriage,* book; Comments: *I choose to write about themes concerning the family, because marriage and the home are the life-sustaining cells of our civilization. Success in everything is governed by rules. Happiness in marriage is no exception.*

MY RAY OF SUNSHINE

Courtney fills my heart with love,
She's sweet as she can be.
She puts her arms around my neck
As she climbs upon my knee.

"I love you Grammy dear," she says
With a smile that's heaven sent.
How could I help but love this child
So full of sentiment!

She loves to sing and walk with me
And examined every flower.
We gather bits of this and that
And we read books by the hour.

I hope she'll never ever lose
Her sweetness and her charm.
"Please dear God take care of her
And keep her free from harm."

And as she grows to womanhood
If I'm no longer here,
I hope she'll treasure memories
Of the ones that I hold dear.

Phyllis S. Howard

DANCE ON

Dance my pen, on the pages below
Move with the rhythm of minds,
Record their thoughts, their sorrows,
and woes,
And leave not their laughter behind.

Dance my pen, to the beat of the mood,
No matter how fast or how slow
Though some may put you down
For the way you move 'round,
The words give us direction to go.

Never fear ridicule, for it always will be
And don't only seek praise from a few.
In the future they'll know
Just which way to go
By the words that were written by you.

George T. Diesel

DESERT WINDS

How can love come so swiftly
Like the blistering desert sand
Like in the bad times, it can soothe you
Make you think it will never end

Hot and cold as the desert
All things our love can withstand
Tall, straight or crooked as the cactus
And as pure as our wedding band

As from a beautiful cactus flower
From inside me our child grows
May he or she find a love
As we found so long ago

So let the desert wind keep blowing
As our years keep slipping by
Like the blowing sands of the desert
Keep whistling our desert lullaby

As the winds blow up a sand storm
And the tumbleweeds roll on their way
We will spend our life together
As we grow old and gray.

Ann Melford Cagle

SOUL OF MAN

Flying buttresses of faith
reach skyward to support
majestic walls of inner peace,
while resounding bells fill the air
with thunderous praise.

Vast windows of emeralds
usher in light from above,
bathing the sanctum in blinding,
cleansing, awesome brilliance.

Countless gleaming organ pipes,
tiered and erect sentinels of hope,
direct the way to The Cross, everlasting.

Great portals beckon
to those that seek the Lord
and would know His mercy.
And mighty spires race heavenly
to touch the Hand of God.
An eternal edifice — this Soul of Man.

J. D. King

KING, JOHN DAVID. Pen Name: David King; Born: Ferriday, Louisiana, 8-22-31; Married, Two children: Son — Michael King of Gulf Shores and Daughter — Nell Herron of Montgomery, Alabama; Education: Louisiana State University, Baton Rouge, Louisiana, BS in General Business, 1952; Occupation: Accountant for a Ship Repair Facility in Pensacola, Florida; Comments: *I write mainly for pleasure and this particular poem expresses the beauty and untapped strength of man's inner self.*

FOR MY SINS

His hands were scarred,
For all the evil deeds that my
hands had marred.
A nail went through his feet,
For all the wrong paths I beat.
A crown of thorns was put on his head,
For all the evil thoughts I said.
A sword went through his side,
For all the times I lied.
That's why he died. Who else but *Jesus.*

Ben Lanier

The sun peeping through the clouds
Watching the dewy mist sparkle
On the green grass, as people
Rise to a beautiful day.

Flowers awake as he gently
Warms their sleepy faces,
And they wave to greet the day.

The sky of blue, looking over
    The wonder of nature.
People going about their day,
While the sun shines on their way.

The sun goes down, the moon comes out.
The stars light the night.
All these were created by God
For mankind on their flight

Back to Him.

Carolyn Roberson

THE MEANING OF LIFE

Please wake me up in the morning,
As the baby just was born,
With the first happy birthday song,
Let me see the beauty of earth.

Please wake me up at noon,
As the strength of the teenager,
With the love of a human being,
Let me think to be an angel.

Please wake me up in the evening,
As the time for me to be married,
With a wonderful girlfriend,
Let me plan for my future.

Please wake me up at night,
As the crying sounds of my children,
With the loving words from my wife,
Let me enjoy the meaning of life.

Hai Nguyen

LITTLE MOUSE

Little Mouse on the window sill,
    Why do you sit so very still;
Why do you hesitate and wait,
    Why don't you go and eat the bait.

The little Mouse said to my surprise,
    But you do not see through my eyes;
I'm God's creature same as you,
    I want to live my life too.

Then a tear rolled down my face,
    As I thought of God's redeeming grace;
I gave the cheese and then I said,
    I have no right to want you dead.

Little Mouse I said go free,
    Yes! Jesus died for you and me;
It's through Eve's sin this entered in,
    In the beginning you were my friend.

Lorraine Medley

FOLLOWERS OF CHRIST

For all you followers of Christ you should be
proud of yourself which is very nice because now
you're walking after the footsteps of Christ and for His
love he charges no price. You do not belong to this world
of sin and now on Our Heavenly Father you can
depend. You are now expected to do and say the things that
are right in Our Heavenly Father's sight. You are now
expected to live each and every day by a way which
will not lead you astray and remember you can always come
to the Lord and pray. You now have a change in your soul
and in order to enter heaven on this earth you must
first finish your goal. There will be times that are not
easy and then again there will be times that are not
hard but remember you must make sacrifices to serve
the Lord. For the Lord you have now taken a stand to reach
your goal you must further expand. Be ready for persecution,
temptation, frustration, and fear remember the Lord will
always be near. For all the bad things you have to face
continue in the lord to have your faith. Believe it or not
but God always has a plan. Just remember to hold His unchanging hand.

Dexter McCrory

WINTER MORNINGS

I wake up early in the winter mornings
To the smell of fresh perking coffee and baking bread
Bacon and eggs are frying, the fire crackling
The family stirring with muffled sounds
I lie in bed snuggled between warm sheets and blankets
The snow is packed, frozen, and will crunch loudly underfoot
My breath will be drawn out of my mouth and hang cloudlike around my head
The stars shine brightly in the clear pre-dawn sky
The constellations shimmer on the snow and ice
Dim firelight casts a golden glow about the house
Through windows covered with fragile fronds of ice
The old chimney is puffing white smoke that rises straight up
Out of sight in the calm air like a tall cottonwood tree trunk
Winter morning is beginning
"Time to get up!" Mom calls up the stairs to my sister, brother, and me
The house is coming to life
The low winter sun is peeking coldly over the eastern horizon
The golds and reds of dawn are even cold
The chores await me
These are winter mornings

John Beer

RAINY SORROW

I feel no pain this rainy day
Because our love has gone away
Scattered words on torn sheets of paper
Written then, meant to last forever
What can it be, when we can feel so drastically different memories
And so we said fare thee well that hour
As the rain fell down with nature's power
I walked, she stayed, the air carried nothing more to say
I felt no pain that rainy day
Because our love had gone away
The crying stars knocked at my door that night
The clouds have no ears, they are out in flight
The sun shined hope, with the morning insane
With whispering dew bringing newfound pain
I feel unending heartrending sorrow
On this crisp, fresh sunny morrow
I look to my God for a rainbow of hope
But the sadness of dark will force me to cope
I am alone in my endless, mindful castle
Thrust home, I am free. I have won the battle.

Thomas Edwin Thomas

WORK NEVER ENDS

Intensity's wicked flame
Burns you out again
Sleep on fevered exhaustion
You have to go back
to work in the
morning

John O'Brien

O'BRIEN, JOHN JOSEPH. Born: Oak Park, Illinois, 12-28-57; Education: Wilbur Wright Jr. College, August 1976 to April 1977; Northeastern Illinois University, September 1977 to August 1980; Occupation: Bagger at Jewel and Circulars; Themes: *Love and romance, male and female, memory, loss, loneliness, and time;* Comments: *I write virtually because I have to get my feelings out and express important plus new ideas about the world; to see things in a fresh way and ourselves in a better way.*

LOVERS' DAY

I stayed in bed all day since dawn,
Sharing love with you.
And though in person you weren't there,
The loving grew and grew.

Your beautiful head lay on my breast;
I kept it there to stroke and rest.
We barely moved. Then in time,
I felt your body enjoin with mine.
A feeling I had never known
Happened beautifully without a moan.

(In streams of wine is such love bathed;
Its sparkling contents for lovers made,
And soft green banks serened in shade.)

Like a song our love went on,
Until the daylight hour was gone.

I never rose; I stayed in bed
by love emoted and jealously held.

If I am taken while I sleep,
The thrill is mine in death to keep.

Frances M. Ruchman

VISIONS

I let my mind go wondering
Through doors to me unknown.
a life of merciless of monism
To a place that's far beyond.

My mind will let me travel
Imaginative both near and far
Through the spectrum of a rainbow
Or meteoric of distant stars.

Clouds that are lined with silver
Frame the Gates of Gold
It could be hallucination
Or looking at my soul.

When my life is over
And time will be no more
I'll meet my friends and loved ones
On Heaven's Golden Shores.

Hazel M. Potter

THE WILLOW TREE

Weeping, the Willow tree watches
as menacing Morning-Glory tendrils
wind around its barren branches,
imperiled during the winter's ills.

Weeping, the Willow tree watches
as encroaching buds unlatch
trumpet-shaped flowerets,
filling the lonely silhouette.

Weeping, the Willow tree watches,
spellbound by its sudden stardom,
as the broad-tailed Hummingbird dashes
among the bewitching pastel blue blossoms.

Weeping, the Willow tree watches,
as enchanted Hummers
enjoy the fragrant summer flowers,
that have graced its barren branches.

Susan Hill

RUSTIC BIASES

If smiles are to laughter
Like words to the page:
As fox is to hennery
Is chicken to cage.

The chick locates fence
And the fox finds it too —
Our barrier for both
From dear you-know-who.

With hackles well-raised
A sly rooster can crow
As if chickens hunt foxes
That know where to go.

Our teen said her dad
Was "outfoxed by the fowl!
Every fur has its cackle;
Fine feathers must prowl."

Duane Frederick Jones

SNOW

Like a soft blanket of white
The snow falls in the night;
Changing the wintry scene
To one of frosty clean.

Then the silvery moonlight
Peeks from its cloudy bower;
To bring upon the shadowy night,
A sparkling diamond shower.

Debra L. Bradley

BRADLEY, DEBRA LYNNE. Pen name: Debbie; Born: West Palm Beach, Florida, 7-13-60; Education: Palm Beach Jr. College, AS Degree, 5-81; Occupation: File Clerk for Palm Beach County Clerk of Circuit Court; Memberships: Christian Education for grades 1-4; Comments: *I write because it's a way to express feelings felt and to let others know they're not alone in difficult times. Most of my poetry is written from emotions and situations from life, but my poem on snow was written on my impression of what it looks like, because I've never seen it.*

BLUE

Blue over the Guatemalan sky,
The Quetzal's feather blue,
The deepest sapphire hue,
An Indian weaving blue.

The lilies and the candles
Burning on the altar low
Deep in the Christian church —
No matter, consecrated to Quetzal.

All blue, the lake,
The weaver's thread,
Heaven and celestial fire —
All one, the weaver's thread.

The back strap loom of life,
Stop in the time of blue
Before the streams run red.

Joyce Jones

REVOLUTIONARY WOMAN

Because I was a woman,
I was not called to fight.
I sewed beside the fire
In the dimness of the light.
    My duty was of sewing,
    Not fighting hand and hand.
    I was not called to march
    or to listen to the band.
When the men were marching forward,
By the firelight I sat.
I could not add my strength to the
enemy they met.
    If I were born a man
    And the circumstance reversed,
    I would have led the bravest men,
    And let the enemies be cursed.

Kim Vinton

BEECH TREE SONG

What are you thinking, ancient tree,
Of the days you left behind?
What of the secrets in your limbs
That the years have left entwined?
Why do you look so pale and bare?
Was there a time gone by
When, looking through your foliage,
One could not see the sky?
What did the forest mean to you?
What animal sounds are lost?
What did you carry within your heart
From the springtime into the frost?
Or are you telling us something else
As we follow you into the sky?
That your heart is light and happy now
With people so close by?

Patricia O. Simmons

JUST ONE MORE TIME

Gee it's really great to get
together again,
Just one more time.

We are always happy to see and
visit each other —
Come rain or come shine.

As the years roll by our
School friends become dearer —
Now we find.

We are looking to our next reunion
Lord grant us —
Just one more time.

Medora L. O'Neal

In my mind
I came to you
Years long ago
An image you portrayed

I dreamed with you
Cried with you
Laughed with you
Loved with you

So much together
Days spent sharing
Nights spent caring
Now so far apart

Sarah A. Mattila

NIGHTFLIGHT

Do we stand still?
The bumps are gone, left behind,
A hundred miles down west.
At least with them one felt
A kind of movement, a thrusting
Through air made thick by speed.

Now, there's just the rush of wind
Six hundred miles an hour strong,
Sweeping the skin, the rivet pores
Outside this metal womb.
I cannot see the stars, not even up front
Through the flight crew's curving shield,
And I cannot read their other, Argus eyes.

So once again, safe back and buckled in,
I lay my head on your shoulder,
The black, ballpoint pen asleep
In my breast pocket, and believe —
And imagine I can hear your heart.

Paul R. Anderson

COME ON IN

When I start down my last lonesome valley.
Will I be afraid?
Will I have to keep on paying,
for all the mistakes I have made?
I know that I have made many,
and I have sinned a lot.
Will Heaven's gate be locked against me.
Or will my sins all be forgot?
Will I see my mother and dear old daddy?
On his face that same wide grin.
Will he put his arms around me and say,
"Welcome son, come on in."
Will I hear angels singing,
and see Jesus walking by?
Will he reach out and hold me,
When I start to cry?
Will I hear his gentle voice saying,
"I have forgiven all your sin.
The doors of my house are always open.
Won't you please come on in."

J. Lee Bragg

FREE BIRD

(Title from Lynyrd Skynyrd's Free Bird*)*

I love you
Do you love me?
For all of the times I've told you
Why can't you see?
You're the only one, babe,
And the only one you'll be.
I've tried so hard to please you,
But you just don't seem to care.
Now I see what you mean,
On how it would be,
And I know what you want now,
Just to be
A free bird.
Just promise me one thing
You'll never forget
How much I love and care for you,
And the fun times we had.
For you are
A FREE BIRD.

Vicki Thomas

SHARED SECRET

Here is a secret I'm willing to share; I'm watching you closely.
Your crossed leg, bent arm, shaking head — all show your response
    to me and tell me what I mean to you.
Our unspoken words are heard much louder than those verbalized.
Long after we've parted and I'm alone, fragments of you will
    remain with me.
Please know you've touched my life forevermore.

Essences of my friends and mere acquaintances, all cluster
    within me and become that from which I'm wrought.
Chances are you'll never realize what you've given me.
In fear of my eventual outcome — I caution you to impart thoughts
    of quality and joy.
You see, what you give me and others so freely, lives on long
    after you've gone.
My knowledge of your value in my life crystallizes in the hope
    that I too may remain with others.

All that I am, and all that I hope to become — is a reflection
    of the people who have shared my life for only fleeting moments.

Sally Contour

ME, ALICE AND THE OLD FIDDLE MAN AT 9:10 P.M.

Least of all was the notion that you were really Alice
Where were you then
When we were in your Potters' studio?
Strange that I should remember the "Old Fiddle Player" now
I made him of clay and music and right side of brain
It was our last real link
I remember when I rolled legs of clay and I laughed
Because you told me the fingers were too fat
So you rolled them for me while I heard the color of "Doo-wop"
I sensed the sound of pink — your color — as you worked — created
You turned the radio knob and suddenly said:
"Listen to Alan Watts!" it was KPFA
And I saw that ancient look of Egypt in your eyes
You were throwing a bowl
And I watched your fingers with envy
The way you watched mine
And said how could I memorize where my fingers were on the strings
what would you call it — juxtaposed synthesis
Or just plain memory
And another notion, was I in wonderland too?

Bernie Griff

TO MY RUNAWAY DAUGHTER

I wish I were as eloquent, as writings I have read,
to say the words that tell the tale, of how my heart has bled.
    Such heartaches, there is such a pain, as I have ever known;
to realize my teenage girl is out there on her own.
    Embarrassment and guilt I feel, is now my deepest trench.
For fear her life in danger be, my pillow, tears do drench.
    Misunderstanding, lack of love, or just forgotten how,
to hold and smile, as once we did, are all behind us now.
    My baby has grown up, they say. She thinks we do not care.
She ran away, because she thought our love was just not there.
    Some things were said, some acts were done, that hurt her feelings so.
We meant to help, but lost the way. Instead, we made her go.
    She needs our help, so late I fear, for time to heal the pain.
I pray to God her heart to hear, "Come home, and try again."
    I love you Dear, though troubles reign. I want to help you grow.
For all those years, my life was yours. It hurts to see you go.
    To run, will do no good, my dear. Your fears are by your side.
Alone, or in a crowd, my dear, from YOU, you cannot hide.
    Together, as we always were, my thoughts were honest, true.
Together Dear, our problems face, your happiness, for you.

Gail B. Gregg

AUTUMN'S FLING

I see the morning brighten,
I see the clouds unfold.
I see the sun now shining
On leaves of burnished gold.
The Oak in all her splendor,
Waves her wondrous leaves
Of rust, and red, and scarlet,
As if a quilt she weaves.
The Poplar, and the Birch trees
In suits of brightest gold,
Stand proudly in the sunshine
Like the shining knights of old.
And there's the stately Pine tree
In his heavy boughs of green,
Standing up so straight and tall
In his envy of the scene.
Yes; Autumn now has come again
To have another whirl,
At brightening up this dull old world.
Just like the "Grand Old Girl."

Billie Hatzenbuehler

ETHIOPIA

Dear Lord,
Bless the children,
Hear their cries,
An empty sound.
For many are orphaned
And . . .
Famine strickened,
While death is surrounding them
All around.
Give us your heart,
A heart of compassion,
That we may care
For . . .
Our fellow man.
Are we then
Our brother's keeper?
In answer to this,
Lord,
I will have to say,
Amen!

eva marie stover

THE LIGHT OF LOVE

The light of love,
    The light of peace,
The light
    For all to see.
Do give this light
    To everyone you meet.
The light of cure,
    The light that's pure.
The light of might,
    And, within reason,
The light's surpassing
    Every season.
The light of logic,
    And common sense,
The light to bring back
    True romance,
The light that we may
    Never disagree,
The light of peace,
    Love, and harmony!

Mario Castelli

PEACEMAKER

Blessed is the peacemaker,
For he will be called a son of God.
He has the heart of his Father,
Wanting to mend what has been flawed.

His heart is ever so tender,
Wanting to comfort and console.
He sees what has been put asunder,
And tries to make it whole.

For years, people have hurt each other.
Long has the world lived in hate.
But says the peacemaker,
"Let's stop before it's too late!"

He remembers lessons of history,
How blood stained the land.
He wants to end the misery,
So he holds out his loving hand.

He listens to the voice of his Lord,
Desiring reconciliation in his home.
He meditates, day and night, God's Word,
And praises Jehovah Shalom.

Melanie Shelton

ON THE OTHER SIDE OF THE RAINBOW

Somewhere over the rainbow,
Far away on the other side.
From all the people in the world,
Something is trying to hide.

Little Patrick Leprechaun
Came and sat down by my side.
He said, "Listen carefully! Watch me too!
And I'll tell you what does hide."

But of course that little Patrick
Was, oh, too smart for me.
I blinked my eyes and when they opened,
Nothing could I see!

Then suddenly my feet started walking
Towards the other side.
Can someone please tell me
What it is that's trying to hide!

Finally when I reached the end,
I sent my little pet dove
To tell all the people in the world
That it was only a promise of love!

Agnes Papanastasiou

RARE PAINTING

Sometimes,
I can see you
Standing
On a hilltop,
Looking
Out to sea,
The wind blowing
Echoes back and forth,
A perfect painting
Etched
Upon my mind
Although, there is no
Complete forgetfulness
Choosing
To go forward
Is reality,
This I must
And will.

Martha Ann Jones

THE ANGRY SEA

I watch the angry sea
As it marches ashore
Like a hungry giant
With gaping jaws
Engulfing its own.
Bits and pieces
Of man's refuse
Whirl about
In toothless foam,
Until they are sapped
By the fury
Of the waves,
And pounded into submission
Before being spat
Against the graying grains.
The wavering giant
Retreats into its own,
Leaving behind
Man's broken rejects
Shapeless and torn.

Julia Anne Mueller

MUELLER, JULIA ANNE. Born: Augusta, Georgia, 5-30-32; Education: Augusta College, Augusta, Georgia, 1967-71; A.A., B.A.; Medical College of Georgia, Augusta, Georgia, M.S.N. (Masters of Science Nursing), 1974-75; Occupations: Registered Nurse (RN), Free Lance Writer, Craft Artist: Memberships: Sigma Theta Tau, National Writer's Club, League of Utah Writers; Poetry: 'Reminiscence,' 'Eventide,' 'Clouds,' 'Awareness,' all submitted Winter, 1985; Other Writings: "I Didn't Have a Chance to Say Goodbye," non-fiction article, submitted 1978; Comments: *Poetry is an expression of life observations, feelings, occurrences, relationships. My poems are a reflection of innermost thoughts expressed through words. I try to draw the reader into my world as he reaps, relates and identifies similar experiences in his life.*

FORCES OF NATURE

Lying there in that cherished twilight plateau
of restfulness, I was abruptly awakened by the
mournful moaning of the majestic pine pleading
for protection and searching for support against
a white wooden structure. Trying to escape the
awesome elements. Her graceful web-like limbs
cry against the forces. Her screaming only to
be rivaled by the north winds. Her fragile form
outstretched to the sky begging for mercy. Showing
none cutting into her veins. Bleeding yellow and
thick down the husky rugged brown trunk that gives
her substance. Vibrations felt throughout. I lie
there, a puppet helpless and terrified. And unknown
spirit is pulling the strings that control all things
that are happening in heaven and on earth.

Mary Frances Hayes

HAYES, MARY FRANCES. Born: Baltimore, Maryland, 10-21-40; Married: to Thomas N. Hayes; Education: Twelve years formal education and one year college in Creative Writing and Poetry, Essex Community College; Occupation: Homemaker; Memberships: Secretary, Bird River Grove Civic Organization; Secretary, Inland Waterways Impr. Association; Poetry: 'Vanishing Love,' Fine Arts Press, 2-25-85; 'Frozen Wasteland,' Green Valley Pub., 3-85; 'Corridors of the Mind,' Yes Press, 4-85; 'What Were They Searching For,' New York Poetry Society, Inc., 4-85; Comments: *I create poetry when emotionally charged, although sometimes I use it to relieve outward worldly pressures, by going inward to a tranquil place to meditate. It comes out poetic.*

AN ODE TO A BEAUTIFUL WOMAN

You, Laurie, are a beautiful woman, far more beautiful
than any other woman on this earth. Nature herself tries
in vain to compare her beauty with yours.

Your eyes sparkle brightly, your face outshines the midday
sun. you are like a bright spring day, with fresh and
beautiful flowers everywhere.

Your beauty is intoxicatingly enchanting. I know of no man
but a fool, who could ever grow tired of you.

I know you have many men who match each other for you,
but I still wish to spend my lifetime with you.

David McElroy

GOD'S JUDGMENT DAY
Dedicated to the Lord Jesus Christ

The trumpet will sound — The earth will tremble
And out of the ground — Will come men to assemble
Alas every race will gather — All; men women and children
For from God's face — There will none be hidden

Sheep go to the right — Goats go to the left
Separated — like wheat sifted — out from the chaff
His footstool to be cleansed — His floor to be purged
Getting ready for God's kingdom — About to emerge

It is finished God will say — My will has been done
On earth this very day — The end of all things has come
Now time will be no more — For there will be no need
My plan has been accomplished — It's useless, now to plead

Virginia Ruth Marcum

INSIDE BEGINNINGS

Once alone
   the heartbeats shone
   of shivers of solitude.
Lonely without despair,
   isolated with little care,
   desires wane 'til nude.
Who cares for the one who shines so brightly
   all day,
   but so distant nightly,
   as façades of brilliance fade?
In truth the glow is real
   believing in life that others reveal
   and with others all joys pervade.
Scrutinizing betrays the strengths and joys that lie within,
   and communication with others causes
                              belief in oneself to begin.

Dale Charles Jore

HIS DREAM

Martin dreamed a dream, many, many years ago
About equal opportunity and freedom for all negroes
"We shall overcome" was the theme of his dream, with
"I am somebody" echoing loudly it seems.
Racism, bad slurs, and not being able to ride
Made Dr. King an angry man as he toured the countryside
He preached to multitudes from every walk of life,
Shouting "We shall overcome" without violence, envy, or strife.
Love, peace, and unity were among his many cries,
Throw down all your weapons, hold hands side by side
I have been to the mountaintop, I saw the promised land
The one God gave to Abraham for taking his rightful stand.
Blacks! Because you are Black, and all God's chosen ones
Can stand tall together and sing "We have overcome"
The changes that he spoke of have become America's goal
A legend in his own time with Jesus as centerfold.

Helen McDonald Jones

FOR US TO (ALWAYS) STAY IN TOUCH

   True friendship can be difficult to find —
It may even take years to discover that "one of a kind."
This friend also understands the meaning of "care."
   A close bond that is felt between two
Is, sadly, known between far too few.
   Although it takes a lot of work to make a friendship last,
   A person should not lose an extra-special friend —
For this type will be there for you until the very end.
   Before I go, there is one last thing that I would like to say,
And I want you to know it also comes from the heart, by the way.
   To me, it means so very much
For us to (always) stay in touch!

Beverly Painter

SUMMER WONDER

i could have driven up University;
but chose to take busy Embarcadero —
and the scent of the magnolia blossoms
filled the air with summer wonder.

i've seen the sun set many times;
but not as beautiful as beneath the fog.
keeping the nights warm and mornings cool —
the fog is much a part of a San Francisco summer.

i awoke one morning to the roars
of a thundering rainstorm.
to think He washes the earth just when needed,
and gives us another taste of summer wonder.

another day — crisp with sweltering heat;
but just enough Pacific breeze for comfort.
and the summer wonder in my mind
leaves me dreaming . . .

Karen R. Fultz

A DAUGHTER'S PRAYER

As I stood at my father's grave,
I thought of times we were often brave.
For anyone to face such a time
Was much like a serious crime.

Please dear God, please hear my prayer
Help us find the ones who care.
Give us concern for those we love,
Send the answer on wings of a dove.

Destroy the beast that kills so many
And heal the ones with it if any,
As I pray and often ask,
Help the physicians with this task.

Now as I stand at the grave and weep,
I start to think of the ones with this disease,
And how we all could make it stop,
By persuading smokers their fags to drop.

Sally Pace

LET YOUR HEIRS WALK

Whenever you feel like taking a cab
Though the distance may be for a block,
Get in that cab and relax, my friend
For once . . . let your heirs walk.

Perhaps you have wanted all of your life
To go on a trip or two,
Pack up your bags and go where you wish,
(That's what your heirs will do.)

Take time out to be good to yourself
Then only your heirs will be sad,
It's better to say, "I'm glad we did"
Than to say, "I wish we had."

Your kindness to others you'll never regret
But the years tick by like a clock.
It's time, my friend, to be good to yourself
. . . And let your heirs walk.

Dorothy M. Treano

NON SUM QUALIS ERAM BONAE REGNO CYNARAE

By Ernest Dowson
(1867 — 1900)

Last night, ah, yesternight, betwixt
        her lips and mine
There fell thy shadow, Cynara! thy breath
        was shed
Upon my soul between the kisses and the wine.
And I was desolate and sick of an old passion,
Yea, I was desolate and bowed my head:
I have been faithful to thee, Cynara!
        in my fashion.

I cried for madder music and for stronger wine.
But when the feast is finished
        and the lamps expire,
Then falls thy shadow, Cynara!
The night is thine.

Ernest Dowson

MOJAVE DESERT

The beautiful, the beguiling, the Mojave Desert,
California's enchantress beckons bewitchingly.
I surrender to the lonely stillness of her wilderness,
where centuries of nature's calamities of wind-driven sands,
eroded rocks and boulders have sculptured effigies of
medieval castle ruins painted by desert sun in vivid hues
of vermilion, rising above lavender and gold plateaus.

Grotesque Joshua trees — bearded desert sentries
thrust swords upward, inward and outward, stand stanch
guarding desert treasures. Giant Saguro cactus reaches
prickly fingers into abstract clouds to filch a feather
from spreading wings of the bronze eagle; to tickle
the purple dragon lapping flames from the blazing sunset.

Night falls — I am lost in the archives of ancient desert art.
My sandaled feet sink in hot sand, my moist hands tremble
as wind-blown aspen leaves. Phantom forms of baffoons
and bandits right out of dusty pages of ancient desert lore
sling arrows from ghostly shadows across the Mojave Desert floor.

Edna Densford

THANKSGIVING DAY

The harvest is gathered; the table is spread;
It is Thanksgiving Day, at the old homestead;
When we give thanks, and, to God we pray;
Indian Summer has gone away; the birds
Flying high, could no longer stay; friends
And loved ones gather together and become
As birds of a feather; we flock about the
Fireplace warm; we are not cold; though
Out of doors there is quite a storm; I recall
The story in my history book; how the
Indians made friends with the Pilgrims; as
Blessings from above, they took; the
Feast might have been near a babbling
Brook, or in a field; and, even the shy
Little hare came forth, from his well-hidden nook;
Our host raises his glass, and drinks a toast;
And, about events in our past, we naturally
Boast; so, come, my friends once again
This Thanksgiving Day; let us promise
To cherish one another; come what may.

Amelia E. Cabouch

AN EMPTY GARDEN

An empty garden is a space to walk in gladly.
  There is no shade, no flowering glade,
No trace of God-made grassy blade,
  But rather still the earth and sky
To only question why, oh, why?
  What is this foolish folly that is here to live and die?
An empty garden is a space to walk in sadly.

An empty garden is a place where freedom thrives.
  Where poor beleaguered bushes burned and tore
See searing stumps suppress their scorn.
  And all around no rose's thorn, no rose's thorn,
An empty garden is a space where naught survives.

Penny Tuminello

THE BARBER SHOP

It is an old fashioned sort of barber shop.
With only three chairs and plenty of magazines.
The counters neatly lined with
Containers of various lotions and concoctions.
Leather straps hang from the counters.
They haven't been used in years.
The afternoon sun reflects from the scissors.
The floors are spotless, clean from hair.
Capes neatly folded across the chairs.
Pictures of time gone by, family and friends,
Dot the walls.
The old barber sits in a chair,
Reads the sport page and waits.

Marie E. Davis

ODE TO A FELINE

I give praise to a four-legged feline
Who has never written a line
To be read by ardent admirers,
Those being the ones
Who hug him, pet him, and love him.

He lives in luxury in my humble abode.
He certainly thinks himself no toad.
He knows his place
Which is to live in a world of satin and lace
Forever pampered
And never hampered
From living a life of contentment.

Lucy Gibson

SPRING

Does it mean just IRS to you . . .
  Does it mean the paychecks have been too few.
Does it mean your bank account is too low.
  and your saving account is growing kinda slow.
Or does it mean New Hope . . . New Life.
  Time to forget winter strife.
I like to think of pleasant things . . .
  Like fresh rain . . . a bird that sings.
Flowers all colors of the rainbow . . .
  The evening sun as it descends low.
Apple blossoms' fragrance in the breeze.
  Children's voices rejoicing beneath the trees.
Welcome Spring . . . Welcome all the Happiness you bring.

Doris June Winkelman

Coke WAS it!

*(A protest from a true Coke drinker,
a caffeine addict and factory
worker at the local plant)*

Why change the formula for Coke?
Is this some kind of a joke?
It was the 'pause' that refreshed,
The likes of Ike and Bing.
It was the real thing back then,
But now it has lost its zing!
Why mess with success?
Loyal Coke drinkers ask . . .
The new formula Coke
Is like the Lone Ranger without his mask!
Would Dinah Shore have been a hit,
Without her kisses in the air?
Would Farrah be such a fox,
Without her long, blonde hair?!
And where would James Garner get his start . . .
If he wasn't Bret Maverick, to brother Bart!
I'll end this protest with one more line . . .
Starting today, an R.C. Cola, I'll find!
                    Coke! It ain't IT anymore.

Melinda E. Maybruck

THE COUPLING

In life to come, you cannot escape.
Tentacles of soul, my psyche, shall pierce
      and penetrate you;
Shall bond you to me before the star of
      aged days shall sink;
Young erupting lava sperm will fire you,
      fecundate heart and mind.

Your karmic face has faced me many days
      in the past Cycles of Time.
But in Past Times my grasp imperfect
      slipped my hold upon you.
Still, I will clasp you before the Cycle breaks;
And Union-Communion will gorge our days:

      with insensible sweetness of love —
      with incense intense of passion.

The Cycle fulfilled;
The haunted hollow filled.

Minds, Souls, Bodies meshed for ages hence,
And we will be coupled forever.

Joseph Coppola

A DEDICATION

The memories are so hard to forget.
I hope to god that you still remember.
No one could ever have what we did.
We were so young.
But really in love.

We'd walk together, not touching.
People would stare,
With mixed feelings.
But able to tell the love we held.

I still remember every contour of your face
Every muscle, your habits.
And mostly your soothing voice.

God, how I miss you.
Why did I ever let you go.
Lessons are too hard to learn.
But believe me I can't go on.

Brett Waters

watermelon song

say, hey can't you saw
by the sun's early light

what so loudly we chopp'd
until the moon's first beaming,

with wide stripes and deep scars
through the fearful flight

from the trees we watch'd
where so doggedly screaming?

and the hounds' hot stare,
the shouts bursting in air,

gave proof through the night
that we were still there.

say, hey does that
slip-noose rope yet wave

from the mind of the free
and the heart of the knave?

Artie Stewart

PARADISE

I see a place not far from here,
That's where we ought to be.
It's a place that's very near,
Where passion runs wild and free.

The sky is blue and sometimes cries,
Sweet tears fall from above.
Showering down into our hearts,
The rain turns into love.

Flowers bloom the whole year 'round,
Their fragrance fills the air.
Vivid colors that never dull,
The sun has painted them with care.

As the ocean sings its timeless song
Keeping beat upon the shore,
Lonely birds call out our names
To stay with them forevermore.

The sun has faded into the night,
Starlight dances within your eyes.
Say goodbye to this winter world
And let's spring into our paradise.

Ian Alan McManis

MEMORIES

I stopped and asked myself, where
did the time go?

So many memories held in a
single moment.

Time made us go our separate ways,
we found different interests,
leaving each other further and
further behind.

In my mind I remember things said,
and the time spent together.

If only it could be like before,
but we can never go back . . .
only forwards.

Joyce MacKenzie

As she lay
        dying.
I sat down beside her.
Slowly,
    Silently,
            she stared beyond . . .
She whispered . . . one word.
Then
        she was gone.

Dolores Ekstrom

EICHEL, GLORIA L. Education: Hunter College, New York City, B.A.; Brooklyn College, Brooklyn, New York, M.A.; Occupations: Case Worker, Teacher, Counselor, Career Counselor Consultant; Memberships: NYS Association for Counseling Development, President of NYS Career Development Association, National Career Development Association; Awards: National Chairperson for the Career Poetry Recognition (National) for the National Career Development Association since 1979 and currently National Chairperson for Career Guidance Week; Poetry: 'Fulfillment,' Vantage Press, Fall, 1985; 'Friendship,' Vantage Press, Fall, 1985; Comments: *My poems reflect my innermost feelings when I am touched, emotionally. They are a cathartic vehicle through which I am able to release inner tensions.*

QUOTE

I have this insatiable need for
quiet dreams which man has laid
to rest.

Within these dreams are quiet
scenes of places which have long
ago reached their crest.

Dreams are not one's personal
matter. But there is one, a dark
mind with a cellophane soul. For
he spins our dreams for jest.

Michael S. Lis

DEATH OF A SPIRIT

On a windy night
I went to him.
The forces outside railed
As I searched inside
Myself for reasons.

That same night
I went to him
    with longing,
Despair crowded within.

My spirit and my heart
Both open, each vying
    for attention.

Pleasing them,
Pleasing no one
Trying to be myself
I failed.

I wanted to get
Back that lost part,
But like the blind,
I missed.

Priscilla Talbot

WINTER WINDS

The thought of waking up to
a memory of us,
Leaves me lost, wandering in
the empty chambers of love.
The threat of winter is in the
air,
It will be cold and brutal
without you.
What will I do, where will I
go, alone?
With the dawn of each day brings
the fear,
That the winds will whisper your
good-byes.
And in the frozen memories of
yesterdays gone,
I like the trees will shed my
many colors and die.

Veronica Porter

MARY

Mary, the name given to my loving mother
I would not replace her with another
If you should know her in years to come
You'll find, she has love for everyone.

Mary, the name of the "Blessed Virgin"
My lifelong doctor and my surgeon
Should you really meet her; know her charm
You'll want to crush her in your arms.

All my life she's eased my pains
No matter how tiresome the strain
She emits an unending love
While asking guidance from above.

There isn't very much that she will say
But, for these things she will daily pray
Asking that guidance be given me
To make me strong like the old oak tree.

She blesses me each and every day
Giving me strength when I lose my way
Eternally, I'll be her baby
Youngest child of an angel named "Mary."

T. Steven Watkins

GOD'S HANDS

The hands that hold a baby
The hands that teach a child
The hands that work for a living
    Just think of them for awhile,
The hands that promote the laborer
The hands that hold yours in mine
The hands that soothe you when you're in pain
    Just think of them for awhile.
The hands that teach us to pray
The hands that wave to us from far away
    Just think of them for awhile.
The hands that comfort saddened faces
The hands that make us liberated
The hands that heal the hurts in time
    Just think of them for awhile.
They have one thing in common
They share a common bond
These hands belong to Jesus
Just reaching out to us from someone else's arms.

Barbara Ann Wissert

STARING INTO THE EYES OF MY SOUL

The bright, shine, lustre of Living
Permeates my sightful visionary Reflection.
Lyric sounds rush my mediocre mentality
Unseen, Unheard, but *Felt.*
The force of their light scorches my ignorant intellect
Into subdued spiritual comprehension.
I suffer Harmonious Satisfaction, out of Cosmic Confusion.
My body dies itself to sleep.
It can't be awake; it can't be alive;
'Cause it can't comprehend.
The Spirit comes forth from the *dead,*
Resurrected by the Mirror Image *"The Self".*
I am the "I" in the Eyes of My Soul, speaking to myself,
In Melodic, Metaphoric, Music of Enlightenment,
And I am saying:
Brightness fills the eyes with many good lives;
Unsuccessful lives dull the shine.
The *message* comes incessantly, loyally, lovingly, lividly.
I stare so I can see, no need to suffer, an eternity.

Michael C., Lord Randall, The Magnificent

CRIES FROM WITHIN

My heart bleeds for freedom
as I lock up my feelings —
    and laugh

My face yearns for air
as I throw sand in my eyes —
    and laugh

Loneliness leaves me in a darkened world
and tears me into pieces

Make a sound so that it can be heard;
no one hears the sound, because no one wants to hear it

Lying, deceitful, hateful laugh
making, breaking, shaking laugh
needing, falseleading, crying laugh;
inappropriate cry

Peggy Begala

IF I DIDN'T HAVE YOU

If I didn't have you, my life would be nothing;
Not worth a penny, nickel, or dime;
Not worth living or giving or trying;
Only worth dying . . . if I didn't have you.

If I didn't have you, my world would be empty;
No other people, no life or breath;
No voices speaking or singing or growing;
Only wind blowing . . . if I didn't have you.

If I didn't have you, my heart would be broken;
No leaping with joy, laughter or love;
Nothing but crying and sighing and aching;
If I didn't have you . . . but I do.

Gail Sacharski

SACHARSKI, GAIL ANN. Born: Milwaukee, Wisconsin, 8-5-52; Married: Single, daughter, Molly, four years old; Education: High School Graduate, One year of college, WSU — Whitewater, in Special Education; Occupation: Office Clerk Coordinator, Radiology Department, Elmbrook Memorial Hospital; Writings: 'The Other Woman,' Song lyrics, MSR Records, Los Angeles, April 1984; Comments: *I have always had a vivid imagination and, since reading and collecting books is one of my hobbies, I naturally began expressing myself in writing — from poetry to stories. It's the one medium where I have control over everything that happens.*

TRIBUTE TO LARRY

A dream made me wake
Its image made me cry
and my body shake

A memory of a very old friend
Appearing no longer as he once did

He sat so still in a harsh cold place
I wanted to save him, kiss his face

Dirty and old, lines marked the time
Derived from past pleasures and drinking wine

I wanted to lift him from his disgrace
Many people passed, but not a human face
None caring if he were to die
And I too turned away in years gone by

S. Flynn McDowell

WHEN THEY TELL YOU

When they tell you to work harder
When they tell you to count your blessings
When they tell you to listen,
to the clap of one hand,
you listen and think

When they tell you to go with the flow
When they say make it your business to know
When they say you have a long way to go,
look down the road and keep on walking

When they tell you you're not important,
remember you are totally unique,
A form who needs the liquid of life
so your dreams can float on the boat of success

Walter Thompson III

THOMPSON, WALTER III. Born: St. Louis, Missouri, 4-19-57; Education: Drake University, B.A. Mass Communications, 1979; Ball State University, M.A. Anthropology (still working on degree); Occupations: Urban Anthropologist, Fitness Instructor, and Part-time Model; Memberships: Society of Professional Journalists (SPJ — SDX); Poetry: 'Black Boy,' Vantage Press Inc., 1985; Comments: *Although a great deal of my poetry is written about the supernatural, I feel more comfortable writing poetry reflective of the human spirit as it relates to man's survival as a cultural life form. In the future, I would like to further explore some of the themes in my poetry through the video medium.*

FUTILE UTTERANCE

Phrases like "you know" and "see what I mean"
Keep rearing their heads right in between
Sentences, questions, exclamations, and more
Scattering intelligence with nonsense galore.

If you didn't know or understand, surely you'd ask
Why does conversation have to be such a task?
These meaningless phrases are a waste of breath
Yet people insist on speaking them to death.

Lest you be with guilt, let me warn you, beware!
People will tag you when you're not there
So think before muttering, speak words serene
"You know," unclutter your vocabulary, "See what I mean?"

Carolann H. Knecht

A POLICEMAN'S SONG

The night's cloak of darkness starts my day.
It seems there is never a good night,
    Like my children often say.

Disturbance party armed, is a common call of the night
Lord help us make it through this call
    Without the loss of life.

It's a man and wife that cannot get along.
Knock knock, Who is it? The police!
    That's the Policeman's song.

What we hate most is the glow of a full moon.
I used to think it fable,
    But there could be danger soon.

If people aren't fighting, they rape, rob or steal.
There's a shot in the dark, and breaking glass,
    And I follow the sound of screeching wheels.

I get out of the car because I sense something wrong,
Knock! knock! No answer
    A tragic end to the Policeman's song.

H. T. Smith

SMITH, HARDIE T. Pen Name: H. T. Smith; Born: Gary, Indiana, 9-5-51; Married: 8-18-73 to Susie G. Rudd; Education: Northeast Missouri State University, B.S.E. in Art Education; continued study at University of Missouri at Kansas City; Occupation: Police Detective, Kansas City, Missouri Police Department; Comments: *Poetry is indeed the best way to mirror emotions, provoke thought, and inspire the soul. It is through my short stories that I continue teaching the children. In my dreams, I am a champion. In reality, I never give up.*

UNTITLED

Iridescent rainfall,
Incessantly it falls,
All over,
Everything,
Leaving nothing really wet,
Catching bits of light on the way down,
Forming half-bead shapes on the ground.
Sitting in seething self-possession,
Leaving nothing really wet,
But us,
Two lovers in a foreign land trying to say goodbye.

Boyace Van Harlan, Jr.

IN DEFENSE OF BORING KANSAS

Kansas isn't boring; Kansas is you and me
Its beauty is not missing; Kansas is subtle;
    appearing only as a surface.
The screaming engines of yawning tourists
    race past the beauty of Kansas.
Only the gentle heart takes the time
to hum the whispering songs of the prairie grass;
Only the keen eye sees the stone posts
    or the single daisy in a sea of wheat.
Only the uncluttered mind comprehends eternity
    in Kansas' everlasting blue sky,
    or finds the almost invisible horizon
    where earth and universe become one.
And only trusting souls inhabit a land
    so elemental, so all-encompassing
    that only the great oceans rival it
    in apparent surface sameness
    hiding creation in their depths.
No, Kansas is not boring; Kansas is you and me
Hiding its beauty in its flat self.

Susan Swift

THE MAN WHO SWALLOWED THE UNIVERSE

a man came by my window   dawn dancing on the sill
the man took a deep breath and swallowed the universe
I stay here and I wait
I can wait a long time but cannot wait   always
the man who swallowed the universe
travels on long dusty roads gray and hard still and sterile
smells sounds are gone
he wrapped them with the wind and went away
he almost choked on a corner of my land
the red sea wine quenched his thirst
he licked the stars like candies
salads of trees spoons of grass
I know he'll come back   he left time in me
I am waiting in the dark   time pulsing in me
he will walk this way his stomach swollen   pain in his eyes
I will be here waiting
for a long time I'll wait   perhaps always
to catch the man who swallowed the universe
and take him to a secret place rock him   kill time
let him sleep in my lap and digest

Gisèle Villeneuve

JIGSAW PUZZLE

Experience has taught me, that life is just a game.
Nothing ever changes, yet nothing stays the same —
You set aside the wrappings, and strive to link each bit —
just to find at ending — you've lost a piece of it . . .

Each piece of you I ponder, each bond you help me coin,
Can only be a puzzle, 'til one and all are joined.
Will you let me know you? Will you take it slow?
For puzzles are my weakness, as surely you must know.
Am I the master gamester? Or do you possess this role?
When did I start seeing pieces without looking at the whole?
I fear to find the ending, I fear that what I see,
will be there for the sharing, but will not belong to me.
And yet, are you too searching, to find that central bit?
To help you find the answer, that makes sense of all of it?
And yet, what if that coupling, should snap before it fits?
Do we then make another try, or simply call it quits?

Are you my jigsaw puzzle? Am I your missing part?
Can either of us be complete, yet wield a broken heart?

Deborah Spaulding

THE MORNING AFTER

Whether our days are filled with laughter or
    with sorrow —
We always know there's another day,
And that day is called tomorrow —
Just like days have sunshine and
    rain —
We must have times of joy and of pain —
And so we have our days of tears and
    laughter —
And after night is "the morning after" . . .
    Ruthie Mac

OUR OWN FIRST CLASS

Today as I watch my first class daughter, my memories
are as clear as water.
It seems like only yesterday, but I remember well
that early morn, when I called her dad to say she
was born.
He answered the phone still half asleep, but woke up fast
and was on his feet!
The nurse had sent him home you see, because he could
not be with me!
As we viewed "Our Bundle of Joy," he said, "Are
you sure it's not another boy?"
God Bless our first-born daughter, and keep her safe
from evil.
She grew so fast, Our Bonnie Young Lass, and here
she stands before us.
So Straight and Proud, is this young Scout,
Our Own First Class, our daughter!
    Dolores Rey Partie

THE DREAM

I will be an author.
To write and be published . . . that's my dream.

But meanwhile, I have to make a living . . .
So temporarily I've been working in an office.
I sit behind a desk and write . . . memos for filing.

Yet the 'dream' goes on . . .
During coffee breaks I share my latest story idea with friends.

But at night the 'reality' looks back at me.
My typewriter has become a piling place for papers and books.
There's no overflowing wastebasket of wrong beginnings.

Tomorrow I promise I'll set aside time for writing . . .
The 'dream' goes on.
    Elsie Walker

THE PANDA BEAR

The little panda bear still waits, among the other toys;
These souvenirs I have saved, were once my little boy's.
It seems like only yesterday, when he sat that panda there;
It was his favorite "bedtime pal," this ragged little bear.
"Now you stay here 'til I come back." I heard him say one day.
"Wait for me, it won't take long. I'm going out to play."
And so the little panda bear so silently did wait,
To hear that old familiar sound, of the front yard gate.
Time drifted by so slowly, then darkness began to fall;
And with the little bear still waiting,
Moonbeams danced on the bedroom wall.
Though many years have come and gone since that panda bear
Was put upon the bedroom shelf — He's still waiting there.
For this ragged little bear had no way to know;
When he was put upon the shelf so many years ago,
That time would bring maturity to the blue-eyed boy,
Who put him there to sadly wait, among the other toys.
    Joyce L. Meckes

A TROUBLED CHILD

Center of darkness, coal black as the night
The wind whistles soft o'er the plains.
The mountains rise high in the stillness of time,
And a child calls to God in his pain.

Unsure are the words pouring out from the heart
As a soul tumbles humbly in prayer.
Lift burdens that break, heal wounds that they make
Is the cry to the Lord in despair.

Snow-capped mountains are high, the green valleys seem low
And the plains you can easily tread.
Yet each path your soul travels can be lit with a prayer
And its burden as easily shed.

Lola Yearwood

NO FEAR

The clouds are dark and ominous
        but I shall fear no ill;
            the lightning flash, the thunder crash,
                will only awe instill.

Though wind may gain tornado force,
        and I be in its path,
            I will not fear, my Lord is near,
                He'll shield me from its wrath.

The Master of the elements
        is ever very near,
            He here will stand and hold my hand,
                and I shall have no fear.

Nettie Nelson

THE KINGDOM OF WATER'S EDGE

Mauve warning,
Breathless shattering of crystal cellophane,
The howling meteor penetrates
The Kingdom of Water's Edge.

Virgin denizens caress.
The tidepool's sapphire countenance
Of self and shore
Vanquishes our silvery intrusion.

Wordsworth and DuChamp,
Exalted both. Riposte and Parc.
There is no dominance. Visions dance
With Revelation's cyclic obverse.

Stephen K. Hall

DIRGE AND DITHYRAMB

Poetic Truth must defer to Practicality.
Each weekday morning
I shall fail deliberately to take up my pen.
I shall raise a pencil to a 14-column ledger pad.
For the duration of regular business hours,
I shall forsake Apollo's golden flare
For the guidance of a bare light bulb.

I cannot renounce the Muses and the God of Light!
Let inspiration invest my routine!
May I see magic in the most mundane things!
Each workday
I will create and recreate
The illusion of the floating light bulb!

Kathleen Thomas

ELDERLY PEOPLE

They sit in their rooms all night and day,
With nothing to do or nothing to say.
It's a lonely world inside those walls,
When no one comes to see them or bothers to call.

Some wish their lives would come to an end,
For what's the use of living if you have no friends.
They need someone to listen and someone to care,
One to tell secrets they have been waiting to share.

Just because they are old and a little slow,
Is no reason why we should ignore them so.
They need just as much love as anyone else,
So just once think of them, instead of yourself!

Sue Rowland

PASSING STRANGERS

All the loves passed every day,
They never speak but through their eyes.
Yet of each they think in a different way,
For in such speech there is no disguise.
Some are bold, some are tender,
Before the fleeting union's lost.
They yield but little to every sender,
Thaw only slightly the outer frost.
Merely a look, then on they glide,
Never stopping to find just what may live,
Beneath the glass-like, placid tide,
In the lonely desire they have to give.
They'll spend their lives loving from afar,
And never knowing just who they are.

Nora St. Denis

HELL

It is a daily gift: she gave him hell
And, generous, he gave her hell in turn.
Something to raise or catch, a clanging bell,
To live in, land in, or a place to burn.
Hell is in Satan's tail, the Summoner said;
It is the preacher's lake of fire and brimstone;
It is a secret suffering alone,
A swarm of angry thoughts inside your head,
Sisyphus climbing up a slippery hill;
Hell is the atom bomb — the final blast,
Apocalypse, Four Horsemen riding still,
Ultimate ruin, poisoned dust at last;
Hell is the blasted earth, the poisoned air —
Ten thousand times Hiroshima everywhere.

Ivan Earle Taylor

SEARCHING

Here I sit,
Searching for something which I do not know.
Feeling as if my heart has been hit
By the blizzard and cascade of snow.

I often wonder why life is so short,
Full of hate, sorrow, and people pained.
Wondering why love is treated as a sport,
All lost and nothing ever gained.

Everything is taken,
But never returned.
Minds are shaken
From something never learned.

Dawn Molnar

SCENE AT THE MOUTH OF RUSSIAN RIVER.

CULTURE'S SIN

I hide . . . inside . . . my . . . cultural cocoon
peeking . . . outside . . . my . . . alienated . . . nature
the painted . . . illusions . . . dictate quality
    I tuck . . . inside . . . rehearse
     "The Script" daily
  the Mask . . . hides . . . the civilized evil
  I surrender my being to the Quasi-God
the umbilical cord of Legitimate Authority
they pre-cast the embryos, seeding inequality
  promissory notes pulsate the machinery
  reducing my essence to superficiality
the Toxic Cocoon has consumed my identity.

Dianne M. Tchir

TCHIR, DIANNE MARTHA. Born: Edmonton, Alberta, Canada, 3-27-47; Married: to Ronald H. Tchir (1967-82), to E.U. Mist (Joseph S. Stadnek) (no formal union), 1982 (no formal ceremony); Education: University of Alberta, Certificate in Recreation Leadership and Development, 1965; Pursuing Bachelor of Education, University of Manitoba, Major: English, Minor: Theatre; Occupations: Recreational Planner, Laboratory Technician, Mother; Memberships: Canadian Authors Association, Alberta Writer's Guild, Manitoba Writer's Guild; Awards: Poem selected by Athabasca University, University of Alberta (proclaimed prolific poet), University of Calgary for *Pegasus* Literary Magazine, 'Fingers of Gentleness,' 1984; Poetry: 'The Thirsty Trees,' 'The Passing of Time,' April/May 1982, 'Do They Know Love,' October/November 1982, Athabasca University; 'Burning Images and Illusions. Misplaced Illusion,' *St. Paul Gazette,* March, 1982;; 'Sunspun Earth. My Land Lost,' Rural Writings, March/April, 1983; Themes: *Injustice, alienation, our dying earth, our cheated humanity for a quasi-god, death and the mask of reality.*

CHILD SIGNAL

The world is full of beauty,
And the people of wonder.
Welcome child, for each day
You are here as a part of wonder.
The contribution and sacrifice,
The pains of labor and endurance
Are mortal experiences of growth.
Now it's an heritage, and a pride,
From first blessed couple.
Whether a bond of love or hate, dear child,
You are here for growth:
That's the Freedom we never had.

But a child's first signal
Is a loud frightful cry!
Why are the wonder and the beauty,
Caged in this spherical theatre,
Not caused a beaming smile
When the world is beautiful
And the people wonderful?

Michael Etok

DEATH

I am the hunter who roams in the night.
I am the evil one who can do nothing right.
I come for the sick, the young and the old,
with fear and destruction, deceitful and cold.
Legend has recounted that I haven't a face,
I walk in silence and leave not a trace. I
am said to be wicked, vicious and bold, I am
death, my friend, tattered and cold.

Patrick S. McFarland

WHEN I THINK OF YOU

When I think of you the sun shines bright
When I think of you unicorns fly through the night
When I think of you stars smile down on me
When I think of you rainbows are all I see
You are the one that makes my dreams come true
Because I'm happy when I think of you

Kelly Henry

LONELY IS THE NIGHT

I'm here although no one notices me.
I'm here when you might think you're alone.
Watching you with every minute as time passes
On.
Although you never see me, I am far from
Your sight.
and no one really cares for me.
I know loneliness . . . For I am the Night.

Maria Jones

FREEDOM

It soars on wings of unchained flight,
not with brute strength or force of might.

It views the world from the tallest heights,
It's an unbroken circle of love's delight.

A precious, fleeting, delicate thing around
the world may freedom ring!

Tena E. Howard

WORLD OF ONE

World of one, where other than me there is no one
World of two, it can happen when I get together with you
World of three, just you and me sowing seeds wild
And maybe some day we'll have a child
World of four, we can have two kids and maybe more
World of love, keeps your hopes shining like the stars above
World of song, keeps us feeling happy and feeling strong
World of fun, happiness to find when I leave my world of one

Rick Knudsen

DEER ON SIXTH STREET 6:40 A.M.

Tawny silver shimmering in day's first light
Hooves hitting hard on the pavement
Supple muscles in motion
flashing through the morning heat
A sudden stop
She turns her startled gaze on me
soft brown eyes questioning
Which of us intrudes on this pale green morning?

Karen Farr

DAWN

Morning has laid her lips
Upon the hills
And with the Dawn
Has kissed the World awake.
The tired stars have gone
Their silent way,
And Dawn has shaken out
The golden folds of Day.

Margaret Forbes-Robertson

FORBES-ROBERTSON, MARGARET. Born: Belleville, Ontario, Canada, March 22; Education: McGill, piano and pipe organ; degree L.R.S.M. and U.B.C.; Summer courses, writing, etc.; Occupations: Former Music and Primary Education Teacher; Memberships: B.C. Teacher's Federation; Awards: Orchids for a year, for writing about flowers; Poplars, Englehart, Ontario; various papers, *Pioneer, The Globe,* etc.; Poetry: 'Firefly,' *Poems for Half Pints,* gage, 1983; 'Reflection,' *Parasols (The Instructor),* Jacaranda Press, 1983; 'Autumn,' *Autumn Mists,* Australia; Comments: *I wrote poems for children and used them in the classroom. I have a great love for nature and have a yearning to be free of the cities. To me, the sea and the desert mean peace and aloneness.*

LOVE

Love is like the ocean, either
Calm and soothing or stormy and
Violent. Love is the substance
Of all human beings. Love is
Possessive. Love is giving.
Love is the unbearable pain one
Feels when they can't have the
Person they love more than any-
Thing else in the world. Love
Simply is . . . life.

Patti Morgan

SOUP KITCHEN

Alone, he wandered, aimlessly,
Across the cluttered, dusty street,
Shuffling in his ragged shoes,
As Autumn leaves fell at his feet.

He looked toward the golden sky
That soon would turn to clear, cold night,
He coughed and heaved a weary sigh —
The pigeons feasting there took flight.

A wiff of some enticing flavor,
Wafted by the evening air,
Came and went as other transients
Opened wide a huge door there.

Beneath a sign, in yellow print,
The word, 'WELCOME' shone on neon light —
Hot soup and bread, like manna,
Was spread on tables draped in white.

Shuffling in the leaves of Autumn
Came the old man, bent, but proud
To stand in line, await his turn,
Then offer thankful prayers aloud.

Gladys M. Olsen

SLEEPLESS

From my window now I see
Only darkness waits for me.

Chilling stillness, dank and deep,
Covers all that care to sleep.

But oh! Not I! I am no fool
for evening's lulling, velvet cool.

Wonders missed when eyelids fall
in day cannot be seen at all.

Wondrous tunes are played for us
if we've eluded Morpheus.

Subtle changes in the sky
sad, evade the sleeping eye.

A beauty never meant for dreams
when dawn and dusk are rival teams . . .

Why then sleep when I might miss
the tender prince of morning's kiss?

Meryl Johnson Taylor

I,
changing,
am time,
a spring-wound clock
god-driven.

Time,
measured,
is a life
and a remembrance
    of others
and a movement
    of sun, moon and stars.

I,
changing,
am time,
and this flesh
that measure.

George Klett

IN MY OWN TIME

In my own time I will
be everything you ever
wanted me to be.
Handle me with care for
I am only young but once.
I have dreams too, but
For now let me be.
Because in time you'll
see that I'll be
everything you ever
wanted, including me.

Jennifer Lauman

MY CLIMB

                Nobody knows me.
            Don't I play well?
          This silly game;
        This padded cell.
          Why go on?
        Why play the game?
      They like me fine,
    But it's not the same.
    I've found no love
    Nobody cares.
  I walk alone
Up life's stairs.

Diane C. Fleming

LOVE

Do not be afraid
for I am near you.
Do not cry,
for I love you.
If you fall,
I will help you up.
If you are left behind,
I will wait for you.
If you are left alone,
I will be near you,
For I still Love You.

Sonia Trillo

accidental night

cataracts blind out clouds
into neverending dread
casting us all into dark

over my fields of rice
lie cold ashy shrouds
echoed with voices from the dead

if the sun will ever rise
old one says not to watch
its beauty shall melt your eyes

Katheryn L. Boyd

A WORLD APART

Always split in two
    the world is.
Many intentions cold
    many warm.
Will the weather ever
    be alike
on opposite sides of the world?
Often the wishes of millions
Wishes that seem never to come true.

Mike Bennet

FIRST LOVE

I remember so well the young man in me
The pretty young girls were all I could see
The eyes of youth had a smile all their own
Alive with life's love I was never alone

My "steady" and I used to walk hand in hand
We'd walk and we'd talk and we'd play in the sand
The first time we touched felt like nothing before
So thrilling and sacred and yearning for more

Sweet memories remain of that friendship of bliss
But first loves soon fade with one last final kiss
Yet never forgotten and left far behind
They're always right there in the back of your mind

I suddenly wish there could possibly be
A way to suppress the "boy" dying in me
My first love is gone and accept it I can
'Cause yesterday's boy has become today's man

Alan Milanette

THE MAN & THE WOMAN

A man is responsible for his woman
and a woman responsible to her man;
They share their dreams and every hurt
and comfort each other as best they can.

When a woman gives herself to a man,
she knows her womanly life's just begun;
She realizes all the commitment she makes
and knows she'll have hard times as well as fun.

A man vows to stay with her and keep her safe;
His strong hands protect her but still wipe her tears;
He works 'til he sweats as God has commanded
and provides for her needs througout the years.

They are their family — The Woman & Man;
The children can come then they're gone;
But, the Man & the Woman grow old holding hands;
The Man & the Woman are One.

Lynda J. Mescher

A DOVE OF PEACE

The radiant whiteness brings beauty untold,
Wings covered with silver, feathers, yellow-gold;
Sparkling eyes to see sharp and clear,
A voice of compassion to those who hear.

Used as a sacrifice unto the Lord
A sin offering, burnt offering, cleansing all.
A trustworthy bird, and faithful, too,
Sent from the ark, quickly back he flew.

On Jesus' shoulder he quietly landed,
A sign to those who stood so near
As our Father spoke from Heaven above,
Confirming His Son He sent in love.

This Christmas, it's Jesus we remember
Who came to earth with love most tender,
Shedding His blood, our burdens He bore,
That we dwell with Him forevermore.

Darlene Hall

O, CHAMELEON

I'll start listening when it isn't me you're quoting
    Talk to me
I'll listen when I don't hear myself humming in the shower
    Talk to me

When your skin settles down and doesn't match mine,
Keep it up until you lose your breath,
Then talk to me through clenched teeth
Spit out the words, press your tongue through sharp teeth
So I can see the pink
Help yourself to my expression, but keep it off your own face
    Talk to me

Touch me, but don't put yourself in my lips
Kiss me with your eyes open
    Talk to me

Imagine yourself in a place you imagine yourself
When the nightmare is done and all you can hear is the sound
Of your sweat dropping from your brow to a place you can't see
Because your eyes are wide open, staring through the bedroom wall

Feel only the salt slick encrusted in your lips' corners
    Taste it

Robert Bové

THE CHEROKEE

"You are Indian," the old ones said,
the ones once living and now are dead.

"That was true of my fathers, but not of me,
my heritage is of the smallest degree.

I am not blood, my skin is fair."
They said, "Time faded your skin and hair.

Be proud of your blood of any degree.
Be proud of your fathers, the Cherokee."

"I do not carry the red man's bow,
If I am Indian, it does not show."

"Your body," they said, "returns to the earth,
while the spirit makes ready another birth.

The body may again have eyes of blue,
but the Indian spirit will be hard and true."

The words of the old ones have made me see,
I was and am Indian, forever Cherokee.

Jane Burger

THE BLESSING

I guessed his age to be around eighty . . .
and for once since I was very young
I wished that I were old . . .
for I am wiser now, and I could envy his wisdom.
and I viewed each mar and wrinkle on his face
as a masterpiece . . .
because they represented the strength and endurance
of his agelessness . . .
and his eyes glared off into the horizon
and I knew he had seen those things
that I would never see . . .
and his manner was content . . .
for he knew his weakening vision would not
allow him to see those things that will manifest in the lifetimes
of those generations to come . . .
and because of this . . .
we both knew . . .
he was truly blessed . . .

Barbara Jean Burrell

From the yet unpublished book of poetry and prayer, Going Home

The claw of suffering
within my soul
is forever gone

And only through
the blood of my Master
do I know this

Finally, He has come
to me, to my broken soul
and removed the sickness of my sin

And this freedom,   this freedom
this complete freedom
soothes me

I can rest now
I can sleep now
The clouds in my mind are gone

Forever gone
Forever Gone

Jacqueline Bridges

LIFE!

Life — that means: in never wearing
Manner drive to heights, bearing
Grief and sorrow — own and others —
Helping those in need, like brothers;
Holding weak ones when they stumble;
Leading, who in darkness tumble;
Facing facts with patient courage,
Sanctifying love and marriage;
See the own faults without linger,
Tell the truth, and ever clinch t'her;
Pardon others, when they ask to,
Judge unbiased after virtue;
Loving what is good and nice,
Praising always heaven's size;
And — if necessary — die
For, ideals without sigh.
Following that mankind's strife
To perfection — this is Life!

Hartwig Heymann

LOST FROM WITHIN

I was looking for something,
Just the other day.
And where I lost it,
I really could not say.

But I began to search my mind,
Body and soul.
And between the three of them,
They said they didn't know.

They said, if I wanted,
They would give me a clue,
Of where to start to look,
And what I should do.

They offered that Harmony had gone
In search of peace,
When I couldn't be reasoned with
And then couldn't be reached.

So I mustered all courage
And never looked back.
Harmony was to the right,
If I was on the wrong track.

Karen Lee Jones

BIZARRE REALITY

On the threshold of reality
In the doorway of bizarre
If you step into this world
It will take you very far
But if you stay inside and lock the door
Then you cease to exist
Because when living in reality
It's dreams and fantasies you miss

Christopher Kalmen

THE IRONIC MAIDEN

As many jilted will insist,
    Nature's an illusionist.
'Tis her fondest repartee
    to veil her banns in Simile.
And suitor seeking liaison
    Must bid betrothal of his own.

Michael Burian

I'm so proud of you,
The way you've changed.
In the beginning you were helpless,
And now you're strong.
Shy, then brave,
I would like to tell you
How special you are, but
There seems to be no right time,
To tell you —
I LOVE YOU!

Tamra Bartelt

The snow was falling fast
On hill and valley grass
The trees were bending low
To the fast falling snow
Snow, snow, cold winds blow
Days are dark and lonely
Bright and clear
When spring is near
For in spring there is
        sunshine only

George W. Rouse, Jr.

DESIRE SUBDUES DEDICATION

Just a silver moment born
On the edge of nearing dawn.
Ascending to a mountain, peaked.
Silent silver moment reached.
Beautiful, two shadows shaped.
Promised golden vows, they raped.
Love, the mightiest emotion
Conquered a once true devotion.

Danielle Sue Monroe

DADDY

I shuddered as he roared in.
Fists clenched.
Eyes cold.
Whiskey poured from his lips
As he slowly breathed
My name.

And I wondered what I had done.

Susan Sands

A SEASIDE PORTRAYAL

Along the seashore,
    the rays of the sun
        highlight intense color
            as it surges across the water.

Above the racing tide
    the sea gulls sail,
        adrift in the open spaces
            of the vast coastline.

Amidst the soothing sea breeze,
    the secluded cove,
        with the silence
            the crystal clear air
                portrays a peaceful hide-away.

Aligning the spacious horizon
    the vivid beginning
        of a vibrant sunset
            creates a spectacular scene.

Charlene Rust

I WENT TO HER

I went to her;
Gave her daughter's love . . . ,
    Became her daughter.
Gave her son's love . . . ,
    Became her son.
Gave her sister's love . . . ,
    Became her sister.
Gave her brother's love . . . ,
    Became her brother.
Gave her mother's love . . . ,
    Became her mother.
Gave her father's love . . . ,
    Became her father.
Gave her grandmother's love . . . ,
    Became her grandmother.
Gave her grandfather's love . . . ,
    Became her grandfather.
    I went to her;
Gave her human being's love . . . ,
    Became hers . . .

Jimmy Salinas

THE SKY

What if we couldn't see the sky?
It is so high.
I guess the earth would look strange
Without a sky; Without clouds.

Oh! It is such a beauty
To have a sky;
To see clouds forming and rain,
Snow, sleet coming out of it.

Sometimes I wish I were in the sky
To see what's going on in it.

It must be so beautiful in the sky
Because God lives in it.
The sun shines in the day;
The moon shines at night.

Oh! The sky, a beauty.

Maria Creighton

A HUMAN BEING

Poet's Point:
To such a one "Come right on in"
the Saints will say.

He reached a decent age,
Had lived as he saw fit,
Giving, taking fairly,
Then faced the end of it.

He begged no Lord's forgiveness,
Sought no pearly gates,
Feared no sinner's hell,
Peace did anticipate.

Demanded no salvation,
No self-continuance,
No immortal future,
No creator's evidence.

Thus in asking nothing,
He stood most in grace on high,
Whispers echo far in space,
"A good man, not afraid to die!"

He lived by no man's bible,
Yet did not evil thing,
He did what good he could,
He died a human being.

Pearl Ganz Brussel

LIFE'S CHOSEN

and in that growing path
the river's flowing back
and those burns are cooling off
so in impatient wait,
much after that dark gate
then Charlie will appear
to play his favorite song

Michael Pletz

SPRING

Spring approaching,
earth trembling,
ground rumbling.
Sun coaching

seedling's spring coat.
Soil still brown,
snows melted,
winter will tote

itself away.
Earth will turn
into green finery
on a spring day.

Season's migrant
robins return chirping.
Crocus peeping above ground,
air is vibrant

with spring smells.
Trees soon fully clothed,
nature is casting
magical spells.

So capture
when spring arrives,
nature's splendor,
a moment's rapture.

Elizabeth Hennessey

REACTION TO GOOD NEWS

Lower your windows,
Oh, body of mine.
The shining within
will darken the sun.

Leap, oh my heart
as a deer in the woods,
light and free,
leaps for joy.

Take wings my soul,
fly to the highest mountain.
And the waters below
will echo your happy songs.

Let the winds catch
the spilling songs
played on heart-strings,
and take them to the west
until they return
from the east
to rest in the heart
that sang them.

Nellie Lied

MR. MURPHY

It seems that I can hear you still
Your little bark so loud and shrill
saying, "Come on let me in."
We let you in dear little pet
So deeply we cannot forget.

Your button eyes so dark and bright
Yet soft with such a trusting light
Your Welcome-Dance when we came in
Wiggling clear from end to end
No greater love has any friend.

At night my feet stretch cold and bare
Expect to feel your body there
Snuggled in a wee warm ball.
Although you romp with angels now
It seems you're with us still somehow.

You taught us much wee little friend,
To give of joy right to the end
To show the love we feel to all
And from a plane surmounting fear
Take on the world for one that's dear.

Julie Treasure

LIGHT'S QUEST

Oh! darkness seeking to obscure,
All light deep within man's being,
Flee away, far from here,
Fly on dark flapping wing.

Shadows of creeping doom,
Touch not man's quaking breath,
Release your bitter tasting spoon,
Free man's anxieties from dark death.

Oh! dimming light far amiss,
Let not black fears stay your quest,
Seek a path forsaking risk,
Alight within man's budding breast.

Come enlighten truth today,
Enter man's gloomy soul,
Seek a path forsaking pay,
Restore to him his heartfelt goal.

Shirley A. Boeye

EQUINOX

Eastre, the goddess of dawn,
Ancient courier of spring,
Brings her freshness to the lawn
And urges the birds to sing.

Her service, sunshine and song
Fill to fullest all measures
With nature's breath, all spring long,
And seed the autumn's treasures.

From time immemorial
Reviving light in her eyes,
Never dictatorial,
Brings new life to land and skies.

With buds of life in her hand,
She opens wide winter's locks,
Throughout all the waxing land,
With keys of the equinox.

Gaylord T. Alfrey

TWO-WAY MIRROR

Looking through
at another me,
who could see but
a reflective glitter.
thought she saw life
in sharp images
produced by the
shinier facets
of disillusioned youth.

Now the glass blurry
from smudged fingerprints
of lost innocence
Trying to find a way through
I see a blurry face with
unsure eyes
of someone who's not certain
she's alone
And is afraid.

Betsy Meeker

SHADES OF SEVENTEEN

Light passes through the window,
Showing all the things you think you know,
Suddenly made to disappear,
Fading into your seventeenth year.

Shadows fall upon your faces,
Can't believe what anyone says.
Can't hide, can't be seen,
Confusion at seventeen.

Tiny slivers of light,
I want to inhale the delight,
How useless I had been,
Before belonging to you — at seventeen.

Darkness clouds my mind,
My memories are hard to find.
Adulthood pushes me on my way,
And seventeen just slips away.

Lyssa Flaherty

WHEN TWILIGHT FALLS

When twilight falls and evening breezes
Whisper sweet nothings through the pines;
It is music to the weary soul,
Who at the end of day reclines.
'Tis then we hear the cricket calls,
    When twilight falls.

When twilight falls we wearily turn
Our backs on the day just past;
And turn our faces toward the evening sky,
To find peace and consolation at last.
We forget the cares, the bitter galls,
    When twilight falls.

When twilight falls and the setting sun
Casts weird shadows along the way;
When birds call to mate in sleepy note,
And night things, whispering, seem to say,
"Take care, sad heart, no tears must fall,"
    When twilight falls.

    Drucile Reid Byrd

BYRD, DRUCILE REID. Born: Newton County, Mississippi; Married: to Judson A. Byrd; Education: Jackson College, Jackson, Mississippi; Tuskegee Institute, Tuskegee, Alabama; Occupations: Retired Teacher, Secretary; Memberships: Local, District, State, National Federation Colored Women's Clubs; P.T.A., YWCA; Themes: *To express my feelings, ideas on life*.

HIGH ON A WINDY HILL (A DREAM?)

High, ever high, on a far and windy hill
The sky with clouds and darkness did fill.
I viewed a scene most awesome to behold
For there were three in agony untold.
The scene was one of startling amaze —
My eyes on three crosses did sadly gaze.
I couldn't move . . . it's as if I were tied.
"I need to help them!" my heart cried.
The man on the right a calm reflected;
The one on the left rebelled and rejected.
Remorse and chills my heart did enter
For oh, that one who held the center.
He was so beaten, his flesh was bleeding.
"Please, remove this man," I was painfully pleading
Wanting to help this child of someone.
A mother must be torn . . . for this was her son.
For some reason I knew He must die.
"For me . . . not for me," an inner voice did cry.
My soul was engulfed by a tremendous chill,
Witnessing the sight on a far and windy hill.

    Beverly A. Morrissey

THE FRAGRANCE

"What smells so good" the small one said,
"here at the foot of the mountain?
What smells so good when it is dark?
What is it? Can you tell me?"

"It is a very poison weed
that grows high up in the mountain.
Don't ever try to find it, child!"
The fearful old one answered.

    Ruth Williams

INNOCENTS

The cruelty of children is as keen
As polished steel, a dagger's brutal blade.
Its thrust is deep; and yet, it comes out clean
And bears no trace of wounds that it has made.
Perhaps a youngster doesn't even know
How things that he or she might do or say
Can injure other people's feelings so —
By accident, or meant to hurt that way?

Though children might display but little tact,
Its absence taking devastating forms,
At least they are sincere in every act —
No sleek veneer of empty social norms.
They judge not in the way that adults do;
They're less discreet; — less narrow-minded, too.

    Susan Williams

WILLIAMS, SUSAN MARY JANE. Born: Calgary, Alberta, Canada, 8-21-58; Education: Diploma in Social Work, 1980; Occupations: Temporary Placement Coordinator, Word Processing Operator; Awards: Canadian Centennial Poetry Contest, Ontario School for the Blind, 1967; Poetry: 'How Much Can You See?' Canadian National Institute for the Blind, Summer, 1981; 'It Must Be Monday,' *Robinson Connection* magazine, July, 1984; 'Isosceles,' Media Products for the Blind, Winter, 1980; 'The Storm,' Media Products for the Blind, Winter, 1980; 'Our English,' Etobicoke Writers Group, 1983; Comments: *Interpersonal relationships — like to play with the English language. Appropriate form of self-expression. Permits exploration of feelings and ideas. Unlike a lot of modern poets I generally prefer rhyming forms which may or may not follow recognized, traditional patterns.*

TO KURT WALDHEIM

Secretary General to the United Nations
Bastille Day 1977

Did you hear the joke?
He visited the Pope,
The Austrian fox,
About the "Human Rights" issue!
Didn't he fool you?
And should he be so lost
That in a desperate hope
He pulls every rope!

He ignored these very SAME rights
    From FAO and WHO,
Believing he was ALL Might
    And Mikado,
Once his irresponsible bureaucracy
    Had created the story
Of "The Edelstein Sandwich,"
    In a twist,
And hoped it wouldn't reach the calendar
    OF OUR Jimmy Carter!
The night was long, but the day is at hand
    For such a gang!

Gisèle Guerre

GUERRE, GISELE RENEE. Born: France; Occupation: Legal Secretary; Poetry: 'Dearee,' American Poetry Association, 1983; 'Easter Dream,' *Hearts On Fire,* American Poetry Association, 1985; 'To Vice-President Patton,' *The Art of Poetry: A Treasury of Contemporary Verse,* American Poetry Association, 1985; Other Writings: "Pre-Rebellion Student Memoirs," educational human rights denial, 1969; "The Bushes," housing human rights denial, 1981; "The Edelstein Sandwich," pursuit of happiness denial, 1984; Themes: *All that which is related to human rights, law practice, New York City and New York State;* Comments: *I write about the denial of human rights, civic and civil rights as a cover-up for denials of educational rights and subsequent intervention to delay their process, combined with New York City government, New York State under Hugh Carey, Columbia University Housing Office persecution, involving now the State Division of Human Rights under Governor Mario Cuomo.*

Sometimes I sit alone
staring at the stars or the
many raindrops,
the petals of a rose or the
leaves of a tree.
There are so many of them
just as there are so many of us.
Hearts and souls thrown together,
Non-entities existing from day to day.
Nothing special, just one mass
able to survive if one body was
plucked away and thrown into
    the wind.
Just as raindrops flowing down the window,
we roll from one moment to the
next awaiting a final goal.
we as the waves rise only to fall,
we achieve only to fail,
But we will someday realize that
we are special and in that moment
we will succeed.

Tonia Caldwell

LOVE IS LIKE A ROSE

They say that
Love is like a rose.
Give it warmth
And up it grows.

Watch the thorns
Or hurt can intervene.
Its beauty can
Act as a go-between.

Our love has blossomed
Much like the rose.
We've nurtured it;
Its beauty shows.

We've tried our best
To watch the thorn.
And like a queen,
A crown of love adorn.

Jennifer Z. Salsbery

MONEY BEAST

Money is the root of all evil —
A quote appropos to us all.
For money is what we strive for —
Something we all should deplore.

Success is measured in dollars,
Not the goals we have attained.
It's too bad that wealth is power,
And fortune means more than fame.

Even notoriety for a wrong cause
Is not something to be proud of.
I think we should all take a pause
To contemplate our morals.

Happiness is what we should seek
Along with kindness, love, and peace.
To help not the strong, but the weak
Defend against the money beast.

Cindy Becker

THE GOLDEN YEARS

The years have swiftly come and gone,
since the path together, you started on.
Your love for each other, you knew was true,
so you set the date, and said "I do."
Now you've been together fifty years,
You've raised a family, and shed some tears.
Life's disappointments didn't get you down,
for in each other, new strength you found.
There were trials, troubles, and temptations,
there were joys, sorrows, and frustrations,
but would you trade one single day,
or change a thing in any way?
Now you take the time to reminisce
through your years of wedded bliss,
to look back on all that you have done,
and look forward, for things yet to come.
So take one another by the hand,
and walk on together through this land.
Make new memories, that are sure to last,
and someday, once again, you'll recall the past.

Loretta M. Renken

A NOCTURNAL CLOSING

I would ask,
                    "can words draw pictures?"
My drooping eyes,
                    they cannot see.
When will the drawing be finished?
                                        Endlessly my mind searches.
An imagination,
                    you with a smile.
                              Me with you.
                                        Can this be real?
My fantasy is coming to a close.
                              Sleep overtakes me.
I must say goodnight.
                    The portrait will wait.
Only the hand can touch another's.
                              The spirit sometimes knows.
Is this a dream that may come true?
                    If not today,
                              some other day.

Sweet dreams!

Andrew Jay Moore

REMEMBRANCE

I mourn for a valley, where a tree once stood,
Embracing a meadow, from head . . . to foot.
A meadow of flower and fauna combined,
With a mystical aura, I sense . . . a mind!
A mind of contentment that espoused with flair
All truth, condescendent . . . to be naked . . . there.
Yet . . . still in my mourning, I heard a scream,
That invaded the reverie, I thought . . . a dream!
'Twas then I awakened to realize a "rook,"
At the slope of a mountain, where I peered . . . to look.
Why . . . there in its chamber, reflected a sky,
As big as the mountain, that careened in my eye.
Then, "peace" did surround me with an odd refrain,
That stirred up the memory of a source — mundane.
I went up to heaven, (I think), one more time,
To discern the meaning, of a certain pine.
That echoes a rosary . . . instilled within.
The womb of sorrow . . . in my heart of sin.
A dualness in nature given me . . . to bear.
Adhered to the foot . . . and the head . . . we shared.

Mrs. Calmen E. Welan

UNTITLED

a street lamp shines from behind
as if history sheds light for the present's ongoing
a man struts forward
as if his shadow leads him toward light

Ho Hon Leung

THE FLEA FLEAS

Flea Flea Felicia and Flea Flea Flora Lee
Both got together to bite the Big Man's knee.
They nibbled on his ankles,
They noshed upon his shins,
They both had a big old time on the Big Man's skin.

Flea Flea Flora Lee bit with just one tooth.
Flea Flea Felicia says, "That is so uncouth!"

They passed by Flea Flea Frankie,
Who was sitting on a log,
He said, "I can't come out and play,
I'm waiting for a dog."

They had Tea with Flea Flea Frances,
Who served them bread and jelly,
She said, "You haven't lived until
You bite the Big Man's belly!"

Sue Ellen A. Kepley

THE FOURTH HORSEMAN

Where once stood splendor
Bathed in light,
Fringed with nature and kissed by the morning dew,
Where once the flowers bloomed
And music sang,
Dust and smoke rise up together
To greet the chaotic screams of
The devouring beasts.
Death takes its toll.
Where empires stood and fell
We walk no more.
Eyes that peer from behind the broken glass
We do not know. We do not recognize the sound of feet
That scurry through the smoldering rubble.
"World, your cries for help
Fell on deafened ears and blinded eyes.
We leave you now alone to heal thy wounds."
But through it all is the sound of thundering hoofbeats
And the cry of wild beasts.

Louise Huffman Shadel

I AM NOAH

I am Noah in an empty ark
Set to drift on a world of water,
Confined in a universe the size of a boat;
Upon the silence of God I float
And stand upon the lonely deck.
The hours of the day are filled with waiting
Tied to the night by a thread of hope
That land will appear to replace the waiting
And a mooring will finally erase the hope.
I pace the length of my wooden world,
Wear a pattern on its face
And time keeps walking on my brow
Its wrinkled failures left behind.
Forty days and forty-one nights
With only water in my sight
Has failed to silence the distant voice
That christened this vessel on the flood.
So I shall wait and watch the sea
The distant voice still calls to me.

Ronnie Vehorn

THE PEACE, THE HOPE, THE FREEDOM

The pale moon on the water
Slips silent toward the west
And the bright morning star
Tries on its soft blue vest.

As early warming sunrays
Make rainbows on the dew
The songs of life begin to
Welcome the day so new.

Another day to sail the skies
Watching over the kingdom
Loving all there is to learn
The peace, the hope, the freedom.

The fiery ship explodes and
Disappears in golden sand
Cool winds gently whisper
Nighttime's spell is on the land.

And friendly diamonds shining
Smile down on sleeping earth
Watching, hoping, waiting
For morning's blessed birth.

Counting stars above my aerie
Resting over the kingdom
Dreaming all there is to learn
The peace, the hope, the freedom.

John H. Wright

VEST POCKET PARK

*Omnia autem, quaesecundum
naturam fiunt, sunt habenda
in bonis
Cicero
De Senectute Ch. xix*

Heads bobbing like toys,
three pigeons flirt
with a saltine, mushed,
a puck on center ice,
along concrete. The
visored attendant stamps
them into flight, and
sweeps the crumbs of contest
          into his dustpan.

The waterfall soaks up
office gossip, indecisions,
syllables of infidelity flavored
with tuna fish and
ice cream cones.

Walled in, among azaleas and
rhododendrons,
the pigeons glide and swoop,
insolent, to reprisal on
a scrap of cheese.

Michael Greer

MORNING HEARTS

I awake to a haze
My mind in a daze
I use a knife to cut through
Many feelings to feel, too
It mends as it parts
Mine and yours, two hearts
I wave my hand, I see
Two hearts now one

William F. Berry

WHY

A woman walks the darkened streets afraid,
As someone hears her lonesome steps, and mirrors them to meet his own in
  lustful urgency.
        A woman dies.

A husband's eyes betray the pain of losing life's beloved light,
While angry words console his aching soul.
        He thunders . . . why?

Too soon the child in peaceful sleep will waken to demand a mother's breast.
And as clumsy hands uplift him, frightened tears consume the brightness of his
  smile.
        Her baby cries.

A tortured mind lies buried, deep within his frightened shell of human form,
Which threatens to uncover, the memories of recent hours past.
        Yet he survives.

Light breaks through the darkened sky, to waken and revitalize man's dreams,
Creation springs anew with every dawn, and time erases memories and pain,
        Still, man's eternal question why, remains.

Patricia M. Bishop

HAVE YOU

Have you died a thousand deaths, then lived them over again
and again? Have you ever cried a million tears and thought they were
over then cried them again? Have you ever been lonely so completely
alone, then looked around and you were lonely again?

Has sadness ever surrounded you, so very tightly no sun can shine
through? Then, have you ever looked up into a cloudy sky and the
sadness was so great you thought surely you would die? Have you ever
thought there is an end to the miseries we bear, then looked around
and found them everywhere? Have you ever walked into a cold drenching
rain, then turned around and did it again? Have you ever watched a
new fallen snow and wished you were a snow flake and everyone would
know, that you covered the ground gleaming and white, then you
melted and melted in shivering fright?

Have you ever watched a flower unfold, before your eyes like soft
spun gold, then saw it wither and fall from the branch, cut off from
life, it had no chance? Have you ever followed a tiny mountain stream
and it took you nowhere it was just a scheme, to get you lost never
to be found in a dark dark forest no one around? Have you ever longed
to be totally free, then realized, it could never be.

Rose M. Koch

MY DISCOVERY

School's not the life for me, with teachers' looks and big fat books,
Grades of C and D.

Think I'll take a look inside, see what I can find;
Stir the still, deep waters within; reveal the jewel that's mine.

Watch the golden evening sky; birds in flight — no plan in mind,
But to soar unhindered in thought and time.

Eternity, wish I could believe it; weightless, floating — letting go,
All I do is receive it.

This gift of God is mine I know; the price He paid was dear,
It's not found in many books this word called charactear.

The final test is coming, no classroom can prepare,
For Christianity in action; the cross that I must bear.

A, B, C, are meaningless grades to me when confronted with my life of sin,
My overwhelming will to win; in despair I turn to Him,
Christ, my fortress within.

Lee Hayford

THE OUTDOOR CAFE

An umbrella shades
the table for two
Lovers that clink wine glasses
in a silent toast to
nothing.
Classical music
features a flute and
floats across the air
to land
on the edge of an eyelash.
Words say she loves,
is it him?
or is it the umbrella-
shaded moment?
The carafe and her laugh
are empty.
Blurry eyes meet in soft focus.
And the lovers leave
as pigeons pick at their
leftovers.

Natalie Larkin

PLEASE DON'T GO

Darling, darling, please don't go!
You're all I've got and I love you so,
In this world I'll be so alone —
If you go away and leave our home.

But if you should ever need a friend,
I'm the one on whom you can depend.
I'll be waiting all alone and blue —
Waiting, my darling, just for you.

Please don't go, stay here with me.
I don't want to set you free
If you love me as I love you
No one else will ever do.

So let's stay together you and I
We can make it if we try.
We'll never be happy apart you know
So let's take a chance my dear,
Please don't go.

Opal Johnson

VISTA

My eye sockets exist on the dark side
of the moon —
Removed from sight and thought,
Buried in craters
Unslated for eruption —
Lost
In waveless dust.

One fills with crystal,
Its thousand faceted retina
Possessing the stars.

The other hollow —
Marooned in stone —
But not yet rock,
Extends soft, silicon veins,
Grows cavernous,
Stares below,
Stones
Untruths.

Sandra Wasko-Flood

THE BIRTH OF CATHERINE REGINA

Lovingly,
From seed sown on isle of saint and poet,
'Neath nurturing eyes of sacred sun,
Grew bright blossom of regal beauty,
In
    Quiet
        Careful
                Earthly
                        Home.

Gloriously,
After season sheltered from killing cold,
Wrapped warm in walls of mother womb,
Burst infant flower of spritely splendor,
One
    Breezy
        Joyful
                Shining
                        Sunday.

Daniel A. Speca

RAIN OF PURITY

The pristine rain of Autumn fell
  So pure upon the dusty trees,
Across the plains and through the dell
  Refreshing is the scent it leaves,
Gone now is Summer's heat, as well.

This cleansing of the atmosphere
  Of sweltering dust from yesterday,
The purging of *all* yesteryear
  We'll not regret it's gone away,
Nor that the breath of purity's here.

So exquisite is nature's plan
  And never does it ever fail
To purify the scene for man,
  To prove persistence will prevail
If, with patience all began.

Perhaps the metaphor's complete —
  In season is it ours to pray
That living waters so replete
  Will cleanse all error's dust away
And make our lives refreshed and sweet?

Alfred W. Hicks

THE TINKER

If you should ask me
Which of all my toys
I like the best;
I'd prob'ly say: "My Tinker Toy
Is better than the rest."

Why you should see
What I can build
With circles and with sticks!
In one tall can of Tinker Toy
There are a million tricks.

A windmill now,
Perhaps a church,
And next a tiny wagon;
I'll make for you most anything,
From bridges to a dragon.

I'll build them up,
'N break them down
To put them all away;
And so, it's with my Tinker Toy
I play most every day.

Betty M. Keith

ANO NUEVO

Waves are ghosts.
Their veils of white
shadow the sea
each time they rise
to haunt the sand
blown above their reach.
Handprints of waves
are unsounded
distances,
somewhere in air
or high on a dune,
spread, then lost.

Laney Iglehart

IGLEHART, ELAINE LORD. Pen Name: Laney Iglehart; Born: Baltimore, Maryland, 3-8-53; Education: Antioch International, B.A. 1976; Brown University, M.A. 1979; Poetry: 'Rounding the Cape,' *Works in Progress*, Brown University, January, 1978; 'Omens,' *Nexus*, Claremont Colleges; Comments: *In my poetry, I try to communicate complex emotions and states of being through the use of clear and straightforward imagery. My biggest challenge is to try to allow a poem to create its own identity, to present its own ideas or vocabulary, to transform itself into something new and unforeseen.*

AXTON

D & D 5-0-5
D & D 5-0-5

A victim of attempted murder
Afraid of being too slow

Freedom's right around the corner
If you feel the need to kill

What a strange world to be living in.

5-0-5 D & D
5-0-5 D & D.

Tom James

I looked up at the trees with branches bare
and thought of all the leaves that once were there,
I looked inside my heart that once was warm
but now was cold and brittle from life's storms.

The spring will bring new life to trees again.
Green leaves replace the lost ones soaked with rain.
Would God also give me a brand-new start;
create in me a warm and loving heart?

Hattie Barousse

PEOPLE SAY

People say the world is just a battle ground, someone's
killing someone every time you turn around

People say the children will inherit the earth, but who
can inherit something if there's nothing left

It's time to get up and start over again, before the next
war has a chance to begin

People say little children don't you lie and cheat, well the
children should say why don't you practice what you preach

People say "PEOPLE" let's talk it all out, but no one
wants to hear what you're talking about

Children starving over here, children dying over there,
We've got to join together this whole world has got to care

It's time to get up and start over again, before the next
war has a chance to begin

Rosalyn Hill

HILL, ROSALYN DENISE. Born: Lake Charles, Louisiana, 5-19-57; Education: Nursing Degree, 6-82; Occupations: LPN, working with children, Songwriter, Poet (my ambition is to become one of the great songwriters of my time); Comments: *When I write poetry or songs I have no idea what the theme will be. I just sit down with my pen and put onto paper whatever my heart and dreams are saying to me on that day at that time. If dedications are allowed, I would like to dedicate this poem to my mom and dad, Johnny and Kathryn Hill, my sister Reginia, my brothers Ronald, Rodney, Randell, Roger and Roderick and to Gary and our son Trevis — to all of you I give my love and devotion.*

THE CONSTANT ROAR

A shallow sound and yet, still deep,
Through the veins of time, a solitary weep.
The blood of clouds, on one hand,
Seeps very slowly now, through the sand.

But where is the filament of life?
Is there no end to this strife?
In the darkness there is some light,
How strange, so small, yet such might.

I endure that which must be,
The shell of opposition to see.
Still, vision is not the best,
There are choices among the rest.

Inside, I can feel the surge,
That once forgotten urge.
Hidden and hard to find,
Wake, my torpid state of mind.

Richard E. Laubengeyer

AN ETERNITY OF LOVE

If you are a sinner, I beg of you please;
Come to the altar and fall on your knees.
Ask the Lord Jesus to cleanse you from sin;
Open your heart's door and let Him come in!

Love Him and praise Him and serve Him each day,
Read from your Bible and learn how to pray.
He will be with you wherever you go
To lead and guide you to things you should know.

Your tithes and your offerings, the souls you have won
Will all be recorded as things you have done
To glorify Jesus and broadcast His fame
As you witness to others in His Holy Name!

When this life is finished, with Jesus we'll be
Our friends and our neighbors and loved ones we'll see.
The Lord is our Shepherd, our Saviour and friend,
We'll ALL be together for time without end!

Carol R. Mills

SOMEONE
SPECIAL
Dedicated to my parents

You make me laugh,
You make me cry,
You're the only person
That can put tears in my eyes;
When I'm all alone,
And I'll begin to cry
You'll come up to me, and calmly say
"Don't cry my sweet . . . Don't cry"
You're very nice,
Though mean and firm
You teach me life
And what there is to be learned;
You're very straight,
And very intellectual
And all of those things make you . . . Someone
                                        Special

Christine Frederick

TO LIVE AGAIN

Disbelieving, numb, I stood outside myself
and watched the fragile, eggshell foundation
of my life begin to crumble.
He turned and walked away,
My life lay in ruins at my feet.

The restless waves hugged the shore,
The sun turned the rippling waves
to glittering diamonds.
I saw it not, the numbness held me still.
Like a shattered mirror, the long jagged
slivers of pain stabbed my heart.

Compassion came on wings of love and care,
whispering soft words that pierced my shell
and eased the anguish that gripped me.
You held my hand with sweet understanding
as the waves of pain receded.
In your hand was strength, in your eyes,
tenderness, in your heart, love.
You took my life and carefully helped me
build again, and I lived.

Virginia M. Riley

SILENCE

What is silence?
If you sit back, relax and listen
you will know silence is in your presence.

Silence, it's the absence of any sound or
noise of any sort; it's the stillness around
us. It's a time for peacefulness, a time for
serenity, a time for study, meditations, and
a time for resting. With silence, concentration
can be accomplished deeper and faster. Silence
is in the darkness of the night, when the moon is
full and the stars twinkle high above.

Silence in a maternity ward is broken at the cry
of a newborn. Silence is filled in the room of a
little child, who's fast asleep. Silence is when
two lovers communicate with their eyes. Silence
fills the room of a dying person, who just looks
around to see for the last time; silence is that
person who cannot speak any longer, and who will
not utter another word again, and who will sleep
for eternity in silence.

Robert P. L'Hoste

OUR THREE SONS

I give of me to you, my sons.
You are my life, my dear ones.
May the three of you, whatever you do,
Choose in life what seems best for you.

As you live each day, do the best you know how.
For I shall always reward you with a motherly smile.
Be as enthusiastic as you can be
Observe as far as the eye can see
Always be kind and use forethought too.
Respect all people and they will see niceness in you.

This world of ours is big and great
Learn to live in it with knowledge and wisdom.
Think big and your goals will be reached,
Your life will become rich because you have sought.

I say to you, you are never alone.
You have a friend you can call your own.
We call him Dear Jesus, and loves you so much
So always, Dear Sons — do keep in touch.

Helen L. Merryman

LIE STILL

On the bed the woman wept.
Stillness would not contain her,
Beside her in the crypt,
laid her unborn,
with no life to spring forth.
Gone, Gone away, hours pass,
minutes betray.
Sorrow, Sorrow lay on the surface,
deeper than pain. Come melt me away,
hide me from sight, morning, morning light.
Distinguish the flame, bury me my soul,
lie still lady luck, father of sun smile
down on me. One may lie buried, another
spring forth free.

S. S. Johnson

THE PLAGUE

A peril as dark as the blackest of coal . . .
that shifts from the mind; to trouble the soul.
Spreading within . . . encouraging grief;
Inducing great fear . . . destroying belief.
Increasing self-doubt 'til faith is gone —
As sleepless nights . . . break into dawn.
Life becomes solemn; instead of bright . . .
One's days are conceived as endless night.
Resolution for most, gives way to despair . . .
When there's absence of aid . . . and needed care.
This "condition" it seems, leaves problems inside . . .
The avenues closed that were once open wide.
No way to avoid "the plague" unless . . .
. . . Never stricken with terminal *loneliness!*

Richard Champlin

I LOVE RAIN

I love rain. I love to dance with it on window sills,
laugh with it on sunlit hills — talk to her when I'm lonely.
I love rain. Love to walk with it on distant
clouds — cry with it on autumn days — nights.
I watch it fall from lonely skies — I feel its pain.
I cry with it.
We cry for sad, gray afternoons.
We cry for shrunken red balloons.
We cry for cracked and broken dreams.
We cry, but our tears bring wondrous joy!
We feel! All of it!
We love!
I love rain. Love to watch it from a window.
I fall with it from skies on sad, but beautiful afternoons.

Kevin Morrissey

MEDEA RECONSIDERED

To spurn me now and seek a richer bed.
Forgetting how I sinned for him — I schemed,
Betrayed, connived, to give him stature. I deemed
It worth his love to see a brother dead.
He's gotten sons of me, but now, instead
of honor, gives me scorn. Leaves me, demeaned,
To face the gibes of all. — Oh I have dreamed
Revenge — To slay — No, I'll not lose my head.
'Twere better to concoct a draught to fire
Them till they burn and ache for love. Bewitch
Him then, that he may never love's bliss reap,
But eunuch-limp and weak, endure desire.
Medea was a fool. Were I a witch,
I'd turn my skill to taunts, and laugh, not weep.

Delta A. Sanderson

THE SUMMER SEA HORSE

She carries herself high with pride,
With no competition;
Such deep golden sun on her curly tail;
So overly nice, young and frail;
Has many journey's yet to sail;

Like a piece of glitter that shines like gold,
It has love for us to hold;
She is the Sea horse of the sea;
Without chariots for you and me;

With delicate speckled lumps,
Rides the sea and jumps;
Straight to the top, without a drop;
With a touch of salt water air;
Breezes by without a care;

Solid coral and rocks to find,
She has left nothing behind;
Happy as can be,
The Sea horse holds the key;
With a need to settle down on her own . . .

This is what the Summer Sea horse has shown . . .

Seagie the Sea horse

MY SISTER SPEAKS AFTER THE CRIPPLING OF HER HUSBAND IN A SHOOTING: A CRY FOR HELP

why speak of Spring
when the Winter snows F
                          a
                         /
                        \

darkness
descends

yet i am aware that light is out there

someone please
help me grab onto one sunbeam
before the darkness c o v e r s
                 me

until i am unable to be seen

Keith T. Hoerner

ECOLOGICAL MOOD SWINGS

This winter has been long and tiresome and endless;
About three years in sighting a glimmer of relief.
With all its frozen moods and blizzardous dreams —
Inching up around my life, piling high its grief.

Drafts were welcome though, after the tedious scorch;
My ten-year summer kept up a snide, relentless burning,
Leaving a third degree scar to disfigure my wisdom . . .
Drying, defying my enthusiasm of love's own yearning.

There has been not one moment of any beautiful spring;
How I have missed its elusive and refreshing part . . .
Well, an isolated flower did bloom when I'd crash,
So hard its impact, I bounced higher than my heart!

As I landed face down, autumn befell me, crushing me
Under its swift chill before making a colorful escape;
No fallen leaves to burn — only fragments of my own,
Rendering me the victim of a seasonal emotional rape.

But I won't blame untruths and imbalances on the weather
Like others do whenever they despise what life brings;
For I can easily adjust to wearing a down coat in June,
While I tread the ecological tightrope of my mood swings.

Irene Manus Singh

WHAT'S UNDER MY HEART
— To Rodney

The first gift you gave was a kiss.
We laughed, danced, and then we did part.
But the kiss cannot compare to the gift
Which is now under my heart.

The second gift you gave was a flower.
You walked in, surprised me, and then you did part.
The flower was beautiful but not quite as beautiful
As the gift which is now under my heart.

The third gift you gave was your name.
We're in love, never to part.
And it's because of our name that I'm proud to carry
The gift which is now under my heart.

The fourth gift you gave me makes me laugh, and cry
Sometimes hurt, sometimes sigh.
The gift you gave was a part of you;
For me to love, nurture, to protect;
Until the day that the gift and I part.
The gift will be with us always
And I will never forget the special time
I carried our child under my heart.

Cindy W. Hatcher

NINETEEN FORTY-TWO

The malaria-breeding Cactus landing-craft
slowly drifted on the gentle Pacific swells.

In her heritage of tropical rainforests
the living went on living
as dusk gave way to darkness
dawn to light.

As the first rays beamed
Cactus sagged under the conflict between machine and machine
that blew breath out of breath.

In the mounting heat
fangs of hysteria stung the unwilling participants
as dust made dust
maggots flew away.

At noon
the sun went down north
as the stars littered the Pacific beaches
Guadalcanal had breakfast with my grandparents in Washington.

In the twilight
the bills were signed and forwarded to me.

George West

LOVE IS.

Love is a rose that blossoms in the morning and dies at
night.
Love is a brilliant dawn that ends in a tranquil sunset.
Love is what it is, a deep sentiment that takes the heart
and makes younger.
Love is simple, sincere not egoist it is to give the best
of yourself to another human being.
It is to receive happiness and pain from it, is know-how
to comprehend, know how to divide the good and bad as it
comes.
Love is a sweet breath that unites two hearts and two
souls and it makes them one.
Love is a sweet memory that is in the mind of the young
and the old.
Love is something of divine that existed from ever and
it will always exist.

Grace Aglira

GOVERNOR OF FLORIDA

The hour draws near. He thought of another man
Moving towards execution up a hill,
The strained face of the mother, learning long ago
The sword's meaning. He thought of the blue-skied days,
"Springtime in Galilee," and a single phrase,
To race like a frightened child in its cage of bone,
The instant of its final beat unknown.
He felt the power of God. Accountable
To none for either mercy or its foe,
He pushed away, hands trembling, the telephone,
Smashing four holy words, "Thou shalt not kill."
Outside the wren continued to build its nest.
Inside, the non-deed throbbed like a drum in his breast.

Sister Bernetta Quinn, O.S.F.

QUINN, SISTER BERNETTA. Born: Lake Geneva, Wisconsin, 9-19-15; Education: The College of Saint Teresa, Winona, Minnesota, B.A.; The Catholic University of America, Washington, D.C., M.A.; University of Wisconsin, Madison, Ph.D., 1952; Occupations: Writing and Teaching; Memberships: Alston Wilkes Society, Associated Writing Programs; Awards: National Endowment for the Humanities, 1967; National Endowment of the Arts, 1958; Black Studies Institute grant, North Carolina University, Durham, North Carolina, 1969; Triangle Association Institute, North Carolina Central, 1971; Linguistic Workshop grant, NSU, 1971; Fellowships at MacDowell Colony, Peterborough, New Hampshire, 1972, 1984-85; Fellowship at Rockefeller Villa Serbelloni, Bellagio, Italy, 1975; Fellowship, Virginia Center for the Creative Arts, Sweet Briar, Virginia, 1979, 1983, 1984; Weymouth Place grant Southern Pines, North Carolina, 1980, 1982, 1983; Honorary Doctorate of Letters, Siena College, Loudonville, New York, 1972; Fellowship to Yaddo, Saratoga Springs, New York, 1973, renewed 1983; Fellowship Ossabaw Artists' Colony, Savannah, Georgia, 1974; Fellowship Tyrone, Ireland (1984, 1984 — not used); editorial board *The Visionary Company: A Magazine of the Twenties;* Poetry: *Dancing in Stillness,* collection of poems, St. Andrews Press, 1983; Other Writings: "Randall Jarrell," criticism, G. K. Hall, 1981; "Ezra Pound," criticism, Columbia University Press, 1972; "The Metamorphic Tradition in Modern Poetry," Ruters, then the Gordian Press, 1955; *Give Me Souls,* biography, Newman Press, 1958.

LORD, I'VE MANY ERRORS

Lord, I've many errors and faults that do be.
Hear my confession now on bended knee.
I have not done what is good and true and right.
Instead I've done evil in your holy sight.

I've separated myself, dearest Lord, from you
And did not do things you would have me do.
Instead I followed in the wicked ways,
And I acted evil through my life today.

I broke your laws given many years ago.
I have been cold-hearted and, Lord, it shows.
'Gainst you only have I sinned, God on high,
So, hear me as I put forth to you my cry.

Forgive me from my sins which inflict great pain.
They cause me to shed tears which drop like rain.
Forgive me from evil things I did do,
And turn my desires back to serving you.

Suzanne Clement

THE FACE OF CHANGE

Do not be afraid of Change, my friend.
For she is only a frivolous young lady
who never quite makes up her mind.

It's true, she always gets her way
despite our wishes to ward off her influence.
And no, Change is not known for offering choices;
She flitters about, distributing her wares,
then passes on, oblivious to our outraged voices.

But, let's take a deep breath and dare to be open
to the challenge of her constant existence.
We may not approve, but we must face the fact —
the woman called Change, is quite persistent.

If we embrace Change, and even with trembling hands,
pull away that intimidating mask,
she could turn out to be, we might find,
merely a clever disguise for Old Father Time.

Patricia B. Keck

THAT FOOLISH OLD MAN

I met him one day last summer,
   that old man
He was grey and wrinkled,
   that old man
He told me that he was the president,
   that foolish old man
He told me that he was the Duke of York,
   that foolish old man.

I met him again this summer,
   that foolish old man
He didn't tell me that he was the president,
   that foolish old man
He didn't tell me that he was the Duke of York,
   that foolish old man
He was my only friend in the world,
   he was dead, he was my father,

THAT WONDERFUL FOOLISH OLD MAN!

Daryl Chesley

SOUTHERN SIDE OF WILLAMETTE FALLS.

A SMILE

A smile is a gift from God which you cannot
keep, it comes from within so very deep;

The smile of a child is more precious than
gold, you know at once that God made the
mold;

Those you meet in your walk of life, may be
having a battle with some type of strife;

We must forget self and think of others, for
those you meet may be your brother;

God does not give the same talent to all,
however the smile should go 'round the earth
like a ball;

There is no beginning and there is no ending,
we must all do our part as there is no
lending;

Just a little smile will go a long way, and to
the one you meet, please stop and pray;

We never know what burdens they bear, but
always smile and show that you care.

Yvonne Boone Deen

AS HAS COME TO PASS

As has come to pass, like so many things
the passing of a relationship is soon becoming
                                    a distant afternoon.

The falling of an autumn leaf
   gently ends
                the month of
   October.

As has come to pass, like so mkany things
A road . . . winding paths through
A forest of light and dark; time
                                in silhouette . . .

Passing moments
            frozen into a photograph
                    in the penumbra of the mind.

As has come to pass, like so many things
The reflection on the back side
            of a passing cloud
                        blown by gusting winds . . .

There is a chill in the air.

As has come to pass, like so many things
   so must I.

Neil Butcher

   For all the years of caring you've taken for your children —
The knowledge you have parted with so graciously — For taking a
whole world's beatings of hurt — being there holding out your
wonderful and giving arms — Hoping for a peace in this world
where hatred is around the very next corner — Wanting an
everlasting gift, called love — For having a faith in something
so complex the beginning is not there to find — For
giving a smile to a stranger who knows not of kindness —
Swallowing your own hurt for another's sadden pleasures —
Every day you give continuously from your beautiful warm heart —
For these things that come so naturally to you are of great
value — And for this I give you my foreverlasting and growing
love — God Bless

   Cathy Blaker

SNOW KISS

My pretty Snowflake,
So delicately adorned in white lace.
So briskly beautiful, yet so gentle
A slight breeze leaves little more than a trace.

Your kiss is tender, refreshingly cool,
And as soft as a blanket of snow.
An Angel has kissed me with frozen care,
And She left a teardrop, so I could know.

Dear Snowflake, dainty flurry,
You kissed me quietly, as a precious child.
Your softness, your gentleness, your frosty care,
Touched my eyes brightly, tearfully; but friendly and mild.

   Valerie Biddick

BIDDICK, VALERIE RUTH. Born: Oklahoma City, Oklahoma,
12-29-56; Married: 10-10-81 to Joseph Biddick; Education: Oklahoma
University, transferred to Texas Christian University, BFA, Theatre Arts,
1980; Occupations: Mother and Housewife; Comments: *I write poetry
about people, situations, and other things that I either love and enjoy
deeply or that hurt and confuse me. I express personal feelings in my poet-
ry. 'Snow Kiss' is about my two-year-old daughter, Laura.*

INNER PEACE

Ocean waves cascading against seaside rocks
The universal love spirit rests
Ultra vibrations ascend from above
When will beings become one?
A rainbow shines through the sea's spray.

Reach and find peace within
Focus in from without
Admit those things from afar
Release doubt

Take a breath
Feel the depth
Keep energy coming
Search not, seek not
For what is sought is already there

Remember —
Love has always been
Will always be
For who was born without it
Dwell within waves of yesterday
Tomorrow is here

   Marilyn Marshall

LOVE IS THE KEY

From the start everyone knows,
that love opens the door to
the heart.

And throughout life,
Love conquers pain and
strife.

Bonnie Hannan

THE MOON IS BLACK

Gray snow, red water,
cold winds blow summer's hotter,
and the moon is black.

Towering smoke stacks,
pierce guiltless skies.

Innocent fish gasp,
not knowing why.

Poisoned air, we all share,
doesn't anyone care what's up there?

Ageless beauty, of the stars,
hidden by fumes, of our cars.

While clouds of soot, hide the sun,
will we just go on, having fun?

Remove the factories, scrap the cars,
I'd rather see, than visit the stars.

Gray snow, red water,
all for the cause, of the American dollar.

Cold winds blow, summer's hotter,
we all know, our time grows shorter,
the moon is black.

Ralphiel R. Payne

LITTLE ANGEL

Sometimes when the night
is too dark

And the stillness is an
echoing cacophony

When solitude turns to
desolate aloneness

When hopes have grown to
gargantuan impossibilities

Sometimes when the angels are
far away

And God's not listening

When I feel so terrifyingly
ALONE . . .

I walk to your room and am
Suddenly overwhelmed with guilt.
I look at you and cry tears of
Gratitude.

The angels ARE near.
Sleep tight,
Little Angel.

Marie Harding

GRANDCHILDREN

the grandchildren are growing
each a prism
reflecting
faces of yesterday
today
mingled through
individuals
yet part of the past
how wondrous they are
bright eyes
full of love and laughter
each precious in different ways
how fortunate i am Lord
how blest i am
icing on the cake comes last
and covers all
with sweetness

Grandma Rice

THIS VILLAGE

Dogs barking 'round the lane.
And birds singing everywhere,
Someone sitting on his porch dreaming,
In the afternoon sun,
Waves lapping and rolling,
On the lake nearby,
Adds to the lullabye,
And sweet simple song,
Of this village I live in,
Trees grown tall and green,
It sure is a pretty sight,
I wish I could stay,
All of my days,
But when I leave,
I'll take a dream to dream,
And a memory to remember,
Of this little village.

Pixie Stevens

FORBIDDEN FRUITS

I came upon an apple tree
One sunny afternoon.
Its fruit all red and shiny
Like a midsummer's evening moon.
I stood beneath its tempting yield
My hand halfway held out,
When all at once across the field
I heard an angry shout.

He came upon me quick as sin,
And chastised me for coming in
And eating of his apple tree
That no one else had seen but me.
"I merely meant to touch it, Sir.
I have no appetite for her."
For well I know how far my reach is —
Besides, my favorite fruit is peaches!

Elaine Manger

HOW TO DO NOTHING WELL

We the willing
Led by the unknowing
Are doing the impossible
For the ungrateful
And have done so much
For so long
With so little
We are now qualified
To do anything
With nothing.

Peggy Hughley

LOVING SOMEONE

When you love someone so very much,
Let them know with a loving touch.
Show your friends that you're in love,
And let them know who you're thinking of.
For love is such a wondrous thing,
It will always make you want to sing.
Love is a beautiful thing to know,
So when you're in love, let it show.

Julie Jamison

TAKE TIME

Inside my mind, I see my time
  Moving faster than before.
Will I ever take the time,
  To understand my mind.
And see that life can hold
  So much more.

Douglas R. Smith

No one else seems to notice
The things I find
  in you
Is it only
  that I see
  through the eyes of love
Or
  that the rest of the world
    is blind?

Jo Glatz

CONSEQUENCE

Known is the risk.
Being human,
We must try.
Sometimes,
From the choice we make
We suffer . . .
We die.

Dakota

COALS

In our hearts and in our souls,
Burn the sorrows and the coals —
Coals of love and coals of hate,
Coals of fire and coals of fate.
When it's time for coals to die,
Then it's time to say goodbye.

Amber Gardner

UNTITLED

An oracle who lives by the sea
He knows the truth that others fail to see
Yet by his knowledge he cannot say
And by his knowledge they shall never say
That his truth is there for all to see
An oracle who lives by the sea.

John B. Franz

DRIVING THE URGE TO PUSH AHEAD

I met Rose Senia at a naval shipyard
One year later we got to know one another
We wedded, I begot a little boy child.
Now ten years later we are apart.

I have never ceased in the use of my ability
There is built in my being the urge to push ahead.
A force urging me onward; a given impulse to overcome.
A profound drive propels my mind to go forward.

Driving, propelling, impelling, compelling, urging,
pushing, and forcing.
              Driving the urge to push ahead.

Sauls Demento Suzzs, Suezs

PAUSE AND TAKE NOTICE

Life, that inexaustible turning of the cosmic clock;
Ticking away the few seconds, no, microseconds,
That a human life passes through on its journey
Of personal importance, but cosmic irrelevance.
And oh how we struggle within those fleeting moments,
Reaching out for that elusive ideal of love.
How much of life is wasted in that trivial pursuit?
Yet for each moment of happiness we are confronted
By a multitude of sorrows, pains, and ills.
We, who are just a speck in the universe,
Of no more importance than a feather lost by a preening bird;
Place so much relevance and importance on ourselves
That the universe must pause and take notice.

Lynn Gill

NEW DAY

Another workday comes to an end . . .
Greeted by a whisp of cool air as I walk
    out the door, I look up to see a
    gray mist sky closing in against the
    white light near the horizon.
Suddenly, I realize I've let my spirit
    become like the colorless sky I see;
Gray — that which allows only half the light
    into darkness, half the potential and
    half the feelings into life.
Let me clear away the gray I've put in my
    spirit, and welcome a new day.
       a life filled with many colors.

Cindy Triebes

THE DOOR

I don't let many people in anymore.
In fact, you're the first one to come
through the door in a long, long while.
I don't know how it happened.
I certainly don't know why.
I suppose I forgot to peep through
the window first to make certain
you weren't some dark, foreboding stranger.
So you'll have to excuse me
if the door squeaks and the doorknob
is a little rusty . . . A draft
of warm air followed you in
and I am accustomed to the cold.

Amy Warren

LETTER TO THE QUEEN

To the Queen of Diamonds, from the peasant,
this letter I'm compelled to write.
Run over, rejected, overcome by fear,
it looks like I've lost the fight.
Days grew cold and walls were built,
oh, I just couldn't take the pain.
Times got tough and it sure felt rough
but I hid my love just the same.
And the daydreams that numb the pain
are a shelter from the storm in my heart.
Seemed like my only defense was to offend.
Looks like I've dealt the hand that kept us apart.

Peter C. Coker

A SIDNEY SHELDON MORNING

RING! RING! Sevena.m.getyourselfuptogoagain.
But,
You have the worst breath of the day.
Rolling, you roll over, and chance to look
Outside.
The day dawns
Hot
and
Ominous.
But, that's from a bad novel
So you change your mind,
and go back to bed.

Marty Bell

MANTA RAY IN FLIGHT

Only destiny allowed me to glimpse such a wondrous sight.
On that beautiful day, I witnessed a Manta Ray in flight.
Leaping with such force that the ocean swirled
From what depths did it come to embrace our world?
It appeared determined to fulfill some inner desire
There was something of our world it seemed to require.
Desiring to escape the prison its world had to be,
It tried reaching out past its boundaries of the sea.
Finally obtaining an experience that was truly rare
For a moment it was free to soar through the air.
Then it returned to the sea from which it came
But the Manta Ray and I will never be quite the same.

Patricia J. Hare

QUEBEC ORCHARD

There's something nostalgic about a February orchard
    Trees in rows neatly pruned upon a hillside
Waiting to bear the fruit of summer
        Spring lines as yet unbloomed standing
Yearning to blossom forth with the hum
                      of it
        Branches arched in joyful servitude
Hoping for the summer sun to do
                      its thing
Bring fall's harvest cheerfully.
Winter night's diaphanous-winged moist prayers
Now a twigged silhouette against a rising full moon's glare.

Marie Tosh Bonner

LOVE

My thoughts about Denise are constant and loving
I tremble with joy thinking about her
And always want to be with her
Kissing, touching and whispering that I love her
Denise is very wonderful, and deserves the best
I wish to always shower her with pure love.

Leo Uzych

AN IDEA DAWNS ON THE HORIZON

An idea dawns on the horizon!
"There is one thing stronger than
All the armies of the world,
And it is an idea whose time has come,"
thus wrote Victor Hugo.
The time is now!
"Without Me you can do nothing!" *John 15:5*
And "I will come again!"
Thus spoke our precious Savior!
Three ideas!
But if combined into one, would work a miracle!
The world is on the rink!
Jesus is our precious link!
He could save us in a wink!
One prayer!
Jesus, save us now!
An idea dawns on the horizon!

Mary A. Briganti

TO GEORGE

My son you are gone but your spirit is everywhere

I see you in a shaft of golden sunlight filtering
through the trees. I feel you with the raindrops
on a warm summer day falling on my uplifted face

I hear you from the cosmos as I look at the
bright stars saying: "Mom, don't grieve for me,
I am not in a grave. I am free."

I see the transformation whenever I see a butterfly,
remembering our times chasing them
through the meadows.

Yes, my son, you are transformed. You are eternally
free. You are immortal. You are one with God.

Adele Campbell

LEAVES

Shedding our consciousness of sorrow and grief
     What a relief to be as the leaf
Budding in springtime unfurling in May
     Greeting the world in a pastel that's gay
Spending the summer synthesizing for food
     Just one little leaf can do so much good
     Making a tree of oakenlike wood
Soft summer breezes, we have it made
     As passersby lounge 'neath our ever-cool shade
All too soon autumn arrives
     Creating a riotous hue in the sky
Red, orange, crimson and brown
     These colors will soon carpet the ground
Though the youth of our season is now past and spent
     Wasted is not, to the earth has been sent
Mulching the soil for a whole brand-new season
     Giving our life a rhyme and a reason

Lawrence Robbins

PEGASUS

Pegasus, beautiful winged horse,
Pegasus, graceful and strong.
Many times I have seen you fly in my dreams,
You fly to the moon.
Pegasus, as white as a star,
Pegasus, beauty matched only by the Unicorn.
Come from my dreams,
Come Pegasus, let me ride on your back.
Fly to the moon, to the stars.
Come Pegasus, horse of my dreams.

Katherine Arnold

MEMORIES OF EVENING

Morning molds spring from night flowers
that once worshipped the moonlight;

an eastern wind came with the sunrise
and swept against the early horizon.

Spirals of golden skies and coils from
descant souls ride upon the face of dreams;

Soon life's broken image will mend
a recluse somewhere deep within dusk.

Dawn is filled with memories from an
untouched season's solace and reminiscent host;

Grievers of day will soon become spirits to
roam the earth and become evening dreams.

Jalane Rogers

YOU'RE AMAZING

You amaze me in so many ways,
No one ever cared about my thoughts before
I was amazed when you did
No one ever cared about my goals before
I was amazed when you did
No one ever dared to dream my dreams with me
I was amazed when you did
No one ever opened up to me the way you have
I was amazed when you did
No one has ever made me feel wanted before
I was amazed when you did
No one has ever made me feel needed before
I was amazed when you did
No one has ever understood the real me before
I was amazed when you did
No one has ever loved me before
I was amazed when you did
No one has ever made me feel the way you make me feel,
You are truly amazing to me.

Marianne F. Waugh

THE CAT'S MEOW

There's something warm and pleasing in a purr
Emitted either by a him or her
But, fearing fleas, one orders: "Pussy, beat it!"
And kit's response, alas, must be deleted.

Colette Burns

FREE PASSAGE TO THE STARS

'Tis a splendor of thine eyes to look upon
     the stars as they suspend in time
     awaiting yours and every casual glance

Longing to be called by name though be it
     from afar, so very far, that sight doth
     occupy the only means of touch one
     can enhance

Wait the moonless nights so's darkness be your
     guiding light to let your eyes aboard the
     starship and ride the heavens with your
     sight

For the beauty of thine eyes be passage free
     to voyage 'mong the stars and know them
     name by name as your brothers and your
     sisters on endless, timeless flight

Boyd Rahier

MOUNT ST. HELENS

Deep within the earth you feel,
The sleeping giant is real.
Awake, you giant, steam and roar,
Let the world know you sleep no more.

Smoke pouring,
Steam rising,
Lava flowing,
Ash gushing.

Fire and destruction are everywhere.
The giant is killing without a care.
Run, run for your lives while you can,
The greatest disaster known to man.

Forest gone,
Wildlife dead,
Lake filled in,
Gray ash everywhere.

The giant is calm once more,
Beauty awaits under the forest floor.
Sleep, giant, let sleep begin,
Let new life come to the world again.

Virginia Braddock

BRADDOCK, VIRGINIA ANNE. Born: San Antonio, Texas; Single; Education: Trinity University, B.S. 1956; University of Hawaii, M.Ed. 1961; Occupations: Teacher, Writer; Memberships: NEA, TSTA, Alpha Delta Kappa, Romance Writer's Association, River City Writer's Guild; Comments: *I have lived in many places and have enjoyed various cultures. My work is an expression of things I love. The ideas bubble forth and refuse to be suppressed.*

LONGING

I want a haven
    snug and warm
I want a man
    with a good strong arm
A cozy fire
    a little brew
More comfort, more love
    than I ever knew

Annie O'Dunlaing

A SPOKEN WORD

What has age to do
In the finding of friends.

What is time
Except something which never ends.

What is true beauty
When our hearts refuse to see.

What good are dreams
Without reality.

What becomes of a song
Which will never be heard.

What is life itself
Without a spoken word.

Peter M. Vingris

spinning vessels like poetry

the potter's hands aren't silky —
they were sacrificed for love
tiny glass grains cut her flesh and nails,
her hands are raw and bloody . . .
but she takes the trampled earth of ages
and summons beauty and utility,
she spins and pulls and pinches
and brings forth form and function
from crumbs that were once mountains.
the potter's hands aren't silky —
she puts them into intimate, fiery ovens
the way other mothers put their hands
on fat, hopeful bellies,
but this is her chosen labor . . .
spinning vessels like poetry
from the damp sludge of prehistory,
and grinding blackened stubs
that once were silky fingers,
gladly sacrificed for love.

Kellian Ehrheart

FOR KYNDRA
Written for my hearing-impaired daughter during eardrum surgery

Bless the child with a broken ear.
Make it whole that she may hear
The sound of puppies, kittens and birds.
The sound of stories — songs with words.
Hear the sound of Christmas bells,
Hear the special prayer it tells.

Bless the child with a broken ear
Make it whole that she may hear
The sound of words great and small,
The sound of a friend's special call.
Hear the words that people care.
Hear a mother's whispered prayer.
Bless the child with a broken ear.
Make it whole that she may hear.

Roberta Malone

THE AWAKENING

My name was written in the sand!
Aghast, I crept away.

My tongue is now more often silent.

Josie Goodrich Smith

AN OLD WORLD

I looked fearfully toward
Unknown wastes of wind and water,
Hidden by the departing sun.
A sighing wind blew
Through the void of evening.
I stood at the edge of the world,
Balanced on the brink of an abyss,
Staring into the sea-cold eyes
Of men who lay seige
To the mighty oceans of the world.
One ship lay at anchor,
Like an old woman resting in a field
While young girls labored at the harvest.
The ship's dark sails furled,
Weathered, unlovely, a hulk,
Yet she bespoke of mighty voyages,
With her gleaming deck awash.
Spindrift misting her pointed prow,
The sky awash with summer clouds,
And my soul adrift with her hull.

Mildred G. Alfrey

LONELINESS OF THE RUNNER

My sneakers striking the pavement
and uneasy breath,
keep pace with my quickening heartbeat.

I push my muscles forward, through
the darkness of night.
My hair slaps wildly, as if possessed.

Crickets sing while the wind screams.
The sounds ring
in my ears.

The headlights create living shadows,
that dodge the night
and me.

I am surrounded on all sides by
the world.
I am alone.

David Moody

THE NIGHTSTAND

Lying belly-down
on my Indian print bed.
I gaze at the nightstand.
A stubby brass lamp lazily
sits there
watching
over a plate of hardened
sandwich crust, an antique
soap dish, now a trinket
catch-all, and a
silent electric clock
whose second hand smoothly
glides in
a circle while
I absorb its
motion without
realizing until
it has made
three circles and
I catch myself.

Lance Horton

LIMITED

Forgotten thoughts, dreams, prayers, goodnights.
Remembered smells, tastes, feelings, sounds, sights.
Wanted sex, fire, water, air and earth.
Ignored call, letter, scream, death, and birth.

Earl R. Davis

HUMAN ORBITER

I go today without the common chains
hanging from my teeth, lobelias,
approaching i hear Camelot,
but no, it should by now be Cape Canaveral,
where astrolabes point
to the rockets of heavens,
at Mach 3.5
luna park of this bicephalous planet,
circular barrier of coral light
here we dwell,
on the frieze of iron with bacteria
closing forever the tiny globe
in the stellar soil, look,
walking with my antenna
in the ocean of eyes.
Your attention please:
Gold-anodized terrestrial embryo
successfully returning to the eternal
speck of earth
in the matrix with rings.

José Segura

SEGURA, JOSE. Born: Málaga, Spain, 3-31-44; Married: 1-23-76 to Annemarie; Education: To my dedication to literature, I add this passion for art, transpersonal psychologies, philosophy, mysticism, languages, and film-as-art. Occupation: For the past ten years, full-time independent researcher in the field of consciousness. Writings: My work (poetry, fiction, and essays) is presently in the process of finding its way to publication. Comments: *In my poetry, I try to reflect the debris left behind by the present Homo Electronicus as he travels through the narrow corridor of machines, flesh, slumber, androgynous reverie, and the nuclear perfection of planetary death. I believe that the poet's function is to generate consciousness through the relationship he may be able to establish between beauty and intelligence — via intuition.*

THE TREE OF LIFE

When the leaves begin to fall,
The tree of life begins to fade.
It's abused and taken for granted.
It becomes just a shell of a tree.
The trunk still lives
But the branches are dying.
It just exists from day to day,
Showing on the outside a beautiful frame
But on the inside a hollow hulk.
Unbeknownst to the tree,
One tiny branch refuses to die.
It creeps upwards, engulfing the tree.
Before the tree realizes what has happened
It has taken on a new form.
The branch has revived its juices.
Slowly and surely the tree begins to blossom.
The black emptiness fills with light;
A whole new life has begun to emerge.
The tree grows and becomes whole,
Taking on a new magnificence.

Dorothy B. Keane

REPRIEVE FROM EXISTENCE

Each time you smile at me,
                        or reach to take my hand . . .
I feel a healing warmth within myself,
                        to know you understand.
Each time we laugh together,
                        enjoying so much in life . . .
I feel trust and respect between us
                        And let go of sadness and strife.
Each time we hold one another,
                        and you gently touch my face . . .
I feel the honesty and sharing,
                        and know I've found my place.
Each time we share a memory,
                        for our future, to be held . . .
I feel a reprieve from existence,
                        and empty life I've led.
Each time we come together,
                        in spiritual moments of love . . .
I feel gratuity and peace,
                        with tender mercies from above.

Mary Ann Stamper

LOVE'S LAST BREATH

What a sadness to know love's last breath.
    To be caught
        in the whirlwind of its death.
The life of love that does remain,
    is lost
        in the agony of its pain.

The burden of the heart weighs much,
    and memories
        of bliss seem cold to the touch.
Loneliness burrows deep within the soul,
    as the years
        of sorrow take their toll.

Despair is felt, but drowned in pride,
    as we search
        in our minds for a place to hide.
Love's tormented spirit is sentenced to death,
    and ceases to fly
        with love's last breath.

Sara Kaden

NEVER REALLY ALONE

At last an evening all alone. My family had gone out.
"Household chores all done," I said as I looked about.
I'd sat not long in silence with many thoughts going through my head,
When I was startled by a voice — my name it only said.
It broke my train of thinking, as it was very loud and clear;
Interrupted by a summons to lend a listening ear.
I looked about the house. The voice had come and gone.
What was it, it had wanted? Was a messenger soon to come along?
I felt a certain presence, yet there was no one there.
If this was really happening not with just anyone, this I'd share.
It had gotten my attention. The Lord, I know it was.
I never heard the voice again, but now I'm certain of its cause.
He wanted my attention and He got it for sure that night,
For I had failed to listen to do to my delight.
I think He wanted me to know His daily presence, I'd failed to see.
So to remind me that I'm never really alone, He had to shout at me!

Francene Phillips

PHILLIPS, FRANCENE K. Born: Guthrie, Oklahoma, 3-22-48; Married: 5-5-67 to Larry Phillips; Education: Oklahoma State University, one year, Stillwater, Oklahoma, secretarial course; Occupation: Secretary; Writings: *The New Poets Yes Anthology,* 1985; accepted as student in the training division of Writer's Institute; music companies have accepted song/poems. Themes: *Inspirational in nature, with messages inspired by God, relating true- life experiences and observances.*

DRIVE A CAR

If everyone who drives a car could lie four months in bed,
With broken bones and stitched-up wounds and fractures of the head,
And there endure the agonies that many people do,
They'd never need preach safety anymore to me or you.

If everyone could stand beside the bed of some close family,
And hear the doctor say, "no hope" before that fatal end,
And see family there unconscious, never knowing what took place,
The laws and rules of traffic I am sure we'd soon embrace.

If everyone could meet the family, relatives left alone,
And step into the darkened home where once the sunlight shone,
And look upon the vacant chair where that person used to sit,
I'm sure each reckless driver would be forced to think a bit.

If everyone would realize pedestrians on the street,
Have just as much the right of way as those upon the seat,
And train their eyes for children who run recklessly at play.

And last if he who takes the wheel would say a little prayer,
And keep in mind those in the car depending on his care,
And make a vow and pledge himself to never take a chance.
The great big ads for safety, then would suddenly be gone.

Doreen Biefus

WHEN I AWAKE

I wake up every morning
To begin another day.
I need you here beside me
To get me underway.
You take me to the top.
And here there is no doubt
You're my all-time high
When I'm feeling down and out.
No matter what goes on
You seem to know my every need.
I never have to ask.
I never have to plead.
You're my favorite answer
When I'm feeling all confused.
Our love is but one blessing
And it will never be abused.
Our love, it needs no testing
In this game of give and take.
I have you when I fall asleep
and I thank God when I awake

D. Gayle Hart

CLEE

I see you waiting patiently
On the front steps
The wind chilling your fur
Snow packed between your paws.
Your eyes reflect sorrow
But your heart knows different
Waiting for afternoon to fade
Searching through rows of corn.
Then you see the yellow bus
Lurching down the gravel road
Your tail brushes the snow
As you scamper from the house.
I see you staring at me
Frozen like ice on the ditch
Then I chant your name
And your ears grow slender.
You come and rub against me
Climbing over my tennis shoes
I bring you close
Warming my skin with love.

Carmen Lubs

ode to the poem in the hi-tech era

no computer can render
your majesty into data

no floppy disc would contain
your boundless passages

no silicon chip could store
your divine energy

no program will recall
your mystic beauty

no telecommunications network
can transmit your magic

though a million bits of information
may be crammed on the head of a pin
a million computers could not possess
one fraction of your nature

Marc Stuarts

COUNTRY GIRL

Country girl driving down the highway
In front you see a skyway
But really in your mind
As you cover those white lines
You think of the country
With all the peace and quiet
That you love with all your might
Smells of greenery with beautiful scenery

Country girl walking those city streets
Wondering of those people you greet
Are their smiles for real
Do they have hearts that feel?
You can be so surprised
In their eyes if to realize
They have a sense of self-direction
Yet their hearts lack in affection

Country girl be what you are
With thoughts of country night stars
While neon lights are what you see
You know a place where love is free
Like rays from a soft moonlight
And memories of warm country nights

Charlie Howard

TOUGH

It is tough for two people
To sing a simple song
For one might sing too slow
The other too fast

It is tough for two people
To sit and eat together
Because one might eat too messy and fast
And the other too slow and too neat

It is tough for two people
To go and shop together
The grocery store might be for one
The flower shop for the other

It is tough for two people
To fall in love
Because one might want forever
The other might want for the day

It is tough for two people
To try to live together
Unless they are both willing
To share, and share and share

Bettye Jeane Van Buren

PHOENIX FIRE

Cradle my wounded spirit in your
lovin' arms, rock me slow, rock
me gentle 'til day's first light.

And when dawn at last arrives let
me be, set me free to fly. Let me
soar on the fiery wings of a phoenix to
heights unknown to me.

And if the night fog should cloud
my vision, and if the phoenix fire
should fall to earth, don't smother
the glowing embers . . .

Just cradle my wounded spirit in your
lovin' arms, rock me slow, rock me
gentle 'til the sun shines again.

Lisa Kopf

Almighty God, we thank you
For giving us this day
And for the many blessings
That have fallen in our way.

We pray you to bless the family
Around this festive board
And we pray that peace and harmony
To our beloved country be restored.

We pray you to bless the absent ones
Who cannot be here today
Because they are serving our country
And are very far away.

And now we pray you to bless
Our country in this war
That freedom, truth, and justice
May be ours as never before.

Amen

J. A. Lee

TIMOTHY'S SONG

Yes, I know you're leaving soon
you know how bad I'll miss your smile
still as the clouds pass by the moon
you'll be on your way tomorrow

The time we had together
seemed just too good to go on
I knew it couldn't last forever
though I prayed that I was wrong

So you became my night and day
when you walked into my world
now I'll watch you slip away
because you're something I can't hold

And someday as the summer's sunshine
wakes me to the dawning day
I'll relive our laughter in my mind
and smile back on the precious time
when we were both together

Cathy A. Rish

WHILE I THOUGHTFULLY NIBBLED ON THE ARM OF MY FALLEN COMRADE

"Billy Wordsworth buddy
Now
There was a fella
With his ear to the ground
Yessiree
A real nose for the ball

God
    In nature
Nature
    In man
God
    In man
Beauty in all things
    Tra-la-la"

Suddenly nauseated, I puked on my snack,
Inadvertently agitating the flies.

Richard R. Saltzer

THE HOPE

Still waters
    Running deep.
        Raging
Silent. Unobserved
madness —
    Sadness of the soul
Down to the root
      The Beginning.
It seemed it was always so.
    The pain. The fear. The Hope
Of Mother — of Motherlessness.
These silent waters have run
Red with wounds of love.
    But a young heart bruised black
Still will beat strong and push a Self —
    Secret bloody raging waters
Out to an open sea
    Of Self-Acceptance. Of Forgiveness.
Someday.
        When the heart opens to accept
The reflections of the past and present
From my mind's eye
            To make me whole.

Michelle Trovato

THE BALLET DANCER

My Nancy's fancy was to be dancey.
She swirled and twirled.
Our poor heads whirled.

On recital night,
We were filled with fright
But she was a sprite.

In magic spell —
She danced so well.
A fairy belle.

She wore blue costumes
With feathery plumes,
And danced alone to musical tunes.

Arriving home, we were so tired
But she, indeed, was really wired;
Did cartwheels till she was retired —
    To bed!

Olive Sahlin

Come sit here on my lap
let me hold you in my arms
This love is just too deep
to ever cause you harm.

I hate the sun to fall
because you age another day.
I fear that soon you'll be leaving
going very far away.

You know that I love you
though it sometimes may not show.
You are everything to me
And this love will always grow.

If you must leave me
then leave knowing that I care.
Promise never to forget me
Because that you know I could never bear.

You know that I love you
though it sometimes may not show.
You are everything to me
And this love will always grow.

Vicki Pond

MATTER OF IMPORTANCE

There are those that feel hopeless and their heart is
Weak, in a life they can't cope with and with no dreams
To seek.

Their heart knows not why, nor the rale of the lung for
This lonely cry that has been sung. This cry that's heard
Is in the mist of us. It is as small as a bird, but as
Strong as a rhinoceros.

This cry is the soul of what man has shattered. For the
Heart has been sold and replaced with tin matter*. And
Unless the time spent is taken with heed, from this our
Trees will remain dormant and the fruit will not seed.

*Tin Matter — slang for money

Adam L. Shaw

WALKING THROUGH PAST TIME

The mountains before us, the problems of life,
The valleys we pass through, we've conquered the strife.
With friends and our families, we've places to go.
From journeys, our mem'ries have something to show;
We are what we've made us, we're what we've been through.
We're products of struggles for good and bad, too.
What would you change, could you travel once more,
Through meadows of youth to the aging seashore?
For suffering we've been through, the pain you've endured,
Has made teachers of you, with wisdom assured.
So smile with the teardrops you've shed in the past,
But keep close a kerchief, they won't be the last.

Richard K. Morris

ONCE WAS LONG AGO

Once we talked of dreams and schemes and castles in the air
Now it hurts so much to think that you don't even care.
Once we were content to just sit and be together
Now we've grown so far apart the friendship's gone forever.
Once we thought we'd never be able to give up on each other
Since then we've had so many fights we'll never risk another.
Once we thought our friendship would last throughout the years
Since then that hope has died; we've shed too many tears.
Once we acted like we knew just what the future had in store
But that vision now has changed because of words that tore.
Once we thought life was great; it had so much to give
But the hurt had grown so deep we wondered if we'd live.
Once we were so sure that nothing could separate us
But we have not been together once when there is not a fuss.
Once we shared so many good times, we thought they'd never end
But now we know that we were wrong, the wounds will never mend.

Maria L. Stellabotte

SELF-PORTRAIT

I sing among the trees the story born of
    Ages past lost to time when those among us
Roamed in small groups and talked of love or
    Death and sin.

None remain now but me — old as the tree and
    twice as wide; wild leaves have fallen on
My carpet where feet of another shall pass.

Eyes coldly stare at yellowed pages from worthless
    books that reading is impossible to do.

Now I prepare the Journey upon new hills and over
    walls to somewhere that accepts the Way of an
Old man whose Gift has gone away.

Barry J. Crabb

A ROSE AND A DOVE

God gave many wondrous gifts
To His children on the earth,
And countless are the ways to measure
Their beauty and their worth.

But two wee gifts He gave to man
As symbols of His Love,
'Tis the fragrance of the rose,
And the grace of His snow-white dove.

In all its beauty as it unfolds
The rose will bring a smile,
To one whose eyes behold its wonder
Of velvet peace for just a while.

While soaring high within the sky
Or coming down to rest,
The dove has been God's sign of peace
At the Jordan or in Noah's test.

But together they are Heavenly ways
Of God to show His Love,
In the serenity brought by a single rose
And eternal peace in the flight of His dove.

Linda A. Hamilton

HOW FAR WILL THIS RUBBER BAND STRETCH

With both people pulling;
        slowly increasing the tension
        through words and actions
        for and against each other

Neither are able to let go
        as if it were their life-saving energy
                    . . . life-taking energy

Strong is their hold
        but their grip is slipping
        and the rubber band is getting
                    thinner and weaker

How far will this rubber band stretch
        before they let go
                    or it breaks

Kristine D. Koch

ODE TO A PINE TREE

There it lay in the falling snow, discarded,
Severed from its food supply,
Stripped, broken and dying,
And everyone passed it by.

It had been placed in a prominent position,
Dressed up in grand array,
Showered with present and glory,
And light up in bright display,

It had gladdened the hearts of the young ones,
As they gathered around in glee,
It even attracted the grownups,
But only for one day,

The gifts were shared between them,
And the grand array put by,
It was stripped and dragged to the doorway,
And thrown out there to die,

Now it lies in the snow, forgotten,
But this is a pine tree's lot,
After CHRISTMAS, forgotten,
And thrown outside to rot.

R. G. Goddard

GOOD FRIDAY!

Let me tell you about Good Friday,
  people thinking on what has passed,
    but still have not given their lives,
      that they might last!

My Jesus is risen in my life every day,
  and He is more alive to me today . . . than yesterday.

My remembrance of His death is life unto my soul,
  He has risen from the dead,
    so on Good Friday I have only to praise Him,
      for His blood that He shed.

I can truly say that I know Him,
  and of His wondrous love.
    What about you?

So as the world on Good Friday . . . looks to the past,
  (and still does not understand what Christ has done),
    I look forward to the good day when Christ will come.

"And this gospel of the kingdom shall be preached in all the
world for a witness unto *all* nations; and then shall the end
come." Matthew 24:14 — *The Holy Bible*

  Deborah A. O'Neal

O'NEAL, DEBORAH A. Pen Name: Don; Born: Chicago, Illinois, 1-6-56;
Occupation: Outreach; Themes: *Eternal life in Christ, salvation plan,
body, soul and spirit, the world today;* Comments: *I write in order to let
people know that there is a living God who cares and that there is hope
for tomorrow in Jesus Christ. My work is a total reflection of the peace
of mind and satisfaction of my soul that I have found in Jesus. My work
is an outreach to all that do not know Jesus as their personal saviour and
protector.*

AGED WARRIOR

The sun passes before my shadowed eyes,
as I look upon my old and wrinkled hands.
Once they were strong and smooth,
but time has passed and I have changed.
I know not why.
Once this hand held a mighty sword,
now it holds but a crooked staff of wood.
Once these hands knew joy and beauty,
now pain and sorrow wrack their every joint.
Have the gods no mercy, for an aged warrior?

  Scott A. Hicks

HAND IN HAND

Today my heart was filled with pride,
As I watched my sons standing side by side.
Hand in hand, they ran up a hill,
To play in the park as children will.

Up the bars and then to the slide;
The oldest boy laughed; the little boy cried.

From the top of the slide, my oldest son called,
"Come on up, you won't fall."
"I'm scared," cried my little son, trying to stall.
"That slide is too big, I'm sure I'll fall."

Today my heart was filled with pride,
As I watched my sons coming down a slide.
Hand in hand was a simple must,
As fear was conquered, replaced by trust.

My oldest son laughed, my little son smiled,
As they neared the end of that big old slide.

And as I watched it seemed to me,
That this is the way that life should be.
Today my heart was filled with pride,
As I watched my sons walking side by side.

  JoHanna Lynn Hendrix

THE CHILDREN ARE MATURING

"The Children" are maturing with contented smiles
The love we have given is now part of their style
The energy we displayed has helped a lot
They are emitting a love that cannot be bought.

Our sacrifices and understanding, have given them a boost
They know and understand, honesty and truth
The worry and care, endured day and night
Is making us proud, since they now see the light.

"The Children" possess what we put into them
If we pass on our honor; they will not offend
They are our clones; so, let's show them style
Keep them content through every worried mile.

  T. Steven Watkins

THE BLUE BOTTLE
based on a short story by Ray Bradbury

Crystal towers fall and crash
A million years gone in a flash
Searching . . . searching . . . evermore
'Til my mortal remains are nevermore

The Blue Bottle holds it all
Questions, answers; life and death,
Whatever it is you're searching for

I run, stumble . . . fall,
I see it lying 'gainst the wall

Trembling fingers reaching out,
I finally work the stopper out
I drink deeply of the bourbon of life

I feel myself slip away
I cap the bottle and put it away
To leave it for another searcher, another day
I feel myself slip away

I had the answer to the question
I had drunk the bourbon of life
Now the bottle gave me what I desired most: Death

  James Falkner

FUN?

The blood-soaked merganzer,
Huddled in safety near the dead tree.
The warm fluid slowly trickling down,
From a crack in his head.

The ski boat — spraying the shore with water,
While shouting from nearby fans,
And sounds from high-pitched motors —
Add to the excitement at hand.

She stands off from the injured duck,
Hoping for a sign of life.
The life-giving fluid continues to flow,
Once black and white feathers — now red.

His head slowly drooping — never to rise anymore,
He gives a last shudder — to the motor's roar.

Burton L. Mooney

SUSAN

I love her,
That she is a sometimes child,
Exquisite in pertness and playful rage.
I love her,
That — with thought — her heart is mild;
Her kiss, her touch tender which show her age.

Joseph Campagnolo

SOPHISTICATION IN STAGES

I never was a youth
I was always grown up
Responsible, Adaptable
but I wasn't alive
Oh I cared for others
     and I truly cared
     and I cried and felt
but I lost my youth
Well
I never really had it
being always the kind
that questions
the reason for reality
and the need for fantasy
and how everyone escapes from the former
     but never really does
     but they keep trying
and I'm here crying   from the reality   of it all

Erin Patricia Kelly

INNOCENT, INNOCENT

Silently listening for steps from above,
Lonely he waits for the coming of death.
Loud is his heart as he hears someone close.
Threatening steps that could kill; but they pass.
Quiet again is the cell and his heart.

Killer accused as he walked from the court;
Innocent, innocent, knowing inside.
Often he cried in the court, but they said
"You are an enemy; killer, be killed."
Guilty the verdict, he could not believe.

Quietly, waiting for people to come
Down to his cell, he can tell it is time.
Calmly he stands as the priest says a prayer.
Shattering life, a thud is the sound;
Innocent, innocent, hanged until dead.

Kevin Gregory Misak

CONVERSATION WITH DEATH

I met Death last night, staring
    me in the face, beckoning to me,
        I refused to go.

I said, "I have a lot of love to share,
    but if you would come when it is gone,
        I will go with you gladly."

He agreed, reluctantly, saying, "I
    could barely squeeze you in this
        trip anyway, people have been
            begging me to take them.

Next time, you will have no choice.
    Until then spend your days wisely.
        I want to hear no regrets, see no tears shed
            for tasks not completed, words unspoken.

My arrival will be unannounced and unexpected.
    Time will be precious, I will not wait.
        Do be prepared to leave at a moment's notice —
            I shall not stop just to talk again."

I agreed reluctantly, longing
    for immortality, but awakened and
        accepting of my destiny.

Karen E. Drager

A SONG OF LIFE
A CHILD

A child is a curious and wondrous thing
He sees only the good that living should bring
He understands not, the strife his parents have seen

Children are pure and Godly beings
Incapable of lying and deceitful things
Until they are spoiled by parental schemes

A child is pure with fragile dreams
Dreams of God and Jesus and beautiful things
Things of heaven and angels and wondrous deeds

Then a child matures into an unseeing being
Full of pride and greed and ungodly things
Full of hate and lust and worldly deeds

Is there ever a hope, of his being redeemed
Through the death of a Man, through the blood of the Lamb
That is God's great salvation plan, coming through Christ
as a child once again

Seeing the truth, as only a child can
Singing for Christ in that heavenly band
Proclaiming the true gospel through Christ's helping hand

Dan M. Gisel

MATT

If I could stop time,
Forever you'd be mine.
For all the evil that I could keep away,
Forever for you love would stay.

Of all the times I've tried to start,
I will finish and give you my heart.
Take it; with all my love inside,
For my feelings for you will never subside.

I love you now and forever on,
I will until our last darkest dawn.

Sara Clement

NICE, NICE, VERY NICE

I said goodbye to her.
She said goodbye to me.
Now I won't be quoting the sonnets of Shakespeare,
I won't be quoting Keats nor Yeats
    for at least a year.

And if I should see her what will I say?
"Hello. How are you? It's such a lovely day!"
Now that it's over how will we behave?
We'll be discreet, prudent, polite and congenial.

That's how it should be.
It should be how it is.
It's nice, nice, very nice to talk this way.
It's nice, nice, very nice to smile awhile
    and walk away.

And if I should see her what will I say?
"Hello. How are you? It's such a lovely day!"
Now that it's over how will be behave?
We'll be discreet, prudent, polite and congenial.

Frederick Mansour

INSIDE MYSELF

Look at me
See what I see.
A person who's insecure
Someone whose life is a blur.

The trials and confusion of life goes 'round
Try to talk, but make no sound.
To say what is inside
Speak of truth, tell no lie.

To see through my eyes
No rainbow in the sky.
Hear not the hollow of a word
See how flies the little bird.

A touch, to feel of a silent hand
To guide, to hold in a hectic land.
Be of one, stand by me
Be my friend, hear my plea.

Cindy Sue Husted

HUSTED, CINDY SUE. Born: Hicksville, Ohio, 6-16-53; Single; Occupation: Finish Painter, Automobile Parts; 'To You My Friend,' 'The Joker,' 'Life,' 'Children,' 'I Am Me'; Comments: *My poems are my feelings, parts of my life that I want to express; parts of my life that mean something important to me and will always be there inside me.*

A LETTER TO A POETESS

Dear Poetess,
    I found your address,
    thought you could express
    a few written words of happiness.
    'Cause all that I have found,
    are these cold, cold sounds
    and I don't want to continue to live this way.
So I thought I would ask
    you to do a simple task,
    "Please send me some *joy* today.
    Just take a moment,
    and write me a sonnet
    something — I can listen to or I can play.
    It doesn't have to be long.
    just make it strong,
    strong, energetic and gay.
    Kassandra D. Capron

VOYAGE

   As I sit here
In what may be considered the Captain's chair
   I find myself relishing in a strange solitude
Choking back tears
   To make room for those pseudo smiles and
For those also genuinely depressed passengers
   I maneuver my gyroscope cautiously and intricately
In hopes of charting a more direct course for future voyages
   As bits and pieces of debris begin to surface
Along with mixed memories, I adjust my bearings with my compass
   Skimming across the waters with my daydreams
While cutting into waves with fresh new perspectives
   I head for unbleached horizons
My vessel is piloted with the greatest of confidence
   Full steam ahead! In quest of a paradise
That is logged in a hemisphere that has all the answers!
   Sara Katherine Hurley

POETS' PARADISE

The poet's life came to its end,
time when his soul had to descend.
A poetic angel dug him out of the sand,
Shook him off and touched him with his wand.
Up they soared, through stars and the moon,
Then they approached the heavens very soon.
The walls decorated with poems all along,
Many of them even matched with a song.
Till they reached the room bearing his name,
Just like the others, exactly the same.
A self-correcting typer, piles with writing paper,
Everything is rhyming, even the dust and the vapor.
"That's *unrealistic*," he turned angry to his host,
"I can't and won't take this," as my permanent post.
The angel smiled to him, and just had to say,
"Just like your poetry," and immediately got away.
   Jacob Moskowitz

HAVING SOMEONE NEAR

When the day seems bleak and you're all alone,
And your friends have all gone home.
When the time has come to face yourself,
Just turn and I'll be there.
You will find me in the simplest things.
In the breeze that softly blows by,
In the eyes of a small trusting child,
Or in the beauty of a new spring flower.
I cannot be there for you to look upon,
You will not see me as a man.
But I'll be there in a kind word or deed
And in the love of all mankind.
   Susan Vinton

SUNSET, RAINFALL

Now when the sun will set,
I will think of you yet;
And though I've tried I can't forget you,
For we shared the strongest of love, just we two;
I remember the day you left me,
When the sun sank low, oh see;
When you told me goodbye.
Now I wonder why you left me, oh why —
And something in me died.

Now when the rain will fall,
It will be your name that I call;
And when the nights are so helplessly cold,
It will be you that I no longer can hold.
And I remember the night you left me,
When the rain fell cold, oh see;
When you told me goodbye.
And now I wonder why you left me, oh why;
And something in me died.

Marcia Kuma

WINTER IS NOT REALLY AS LONG AS YOU THINK

Gray November no longer grieves for summer;
Cannot frighten with blustering gloom or
Grubbiness and grit whipped briskly skyward.
Hurry, hurry winter.

Pungent evergreen and pine cones pray for holiday white.
No storms, please, just prettiness and peace.
December pace is fast and fun and very very hopeful.
This really isn't winter.

January sparkles with reward for the sturdy.
The excitement of the snowstorm
And the sporty crunch under prism branches
Are the quintessence of winter.

Muddy, depressed and longing for hope,
The curse left by our pioneer forbearers
Is the maudling month of February.
Alone the longest season of the year.

Luanne Castle

IF

If there is not music can we still sing
If there is no world
Can the future still bring
If we lose our voice can we still scream
If we die in our sleep
Do we continue to dream
If the soul lives on is there still love
If nothing exists
Is there still a below and an above
If we were unable to remember would there be a past
If there is no food
Can we still fast
If there were no fire could there be smoke
If there is no laughter
Can there be a joke
If we were unable to give could we still receive
If there were no lies
Would we always believe
If there is no beginning
Can there be an ending

Bridget Harrison

FLOWER CHILD

It pushes up from the snow-covered field,
  Gathering strength from the sun.
It captures sunlight in its petals
  To give the first sparkle of color to Spring.

Strong and steadfast in the wind,
  It sways gently to entice the Bee.
It offers shelter from the rain to a Lady Bug,
  And soaks up the cool water.

A lonely traveler plucks the Beauty from the Earth.
  He soothes his weary brow with
Cool silken petals. His steps are livelier
  To the pungent aroma.

Soon petals are no longer silky.
  Sun cannot give strength; the bright colors wane.
It is tossed to the wayside, crumpled and faded.
  No longer strong or beautiful.

The wind has its way with this shriveled bloom,
  Once bright beacon of Spring.
In a corner of the world Mother Earth weeps
  At the selfishness and carelessness of Man.

Karen Little

SOMETIMES I WONDER

Am I going right? Am I doing right?
For the future — for here and now.
Where will I find whatever it is I still seek?
And more important — how?

We claim we know it will happen to us,
But no one really believes;
Until the years lay scattered around our feet
Like autumn's pretty, but long-dead leaves.

And then it's too late to wonder
If the years were wisely spent.
For better or worse, invested or wasted,
Still and all, they went.

Time waits for no man.
So every moment we must struggle, we must try;
To do what, or how, I know not —
I can only tell you why:

A lie well-spent is a life spent trying:
To build, to do, to know.
Achievements are autumn's pretty dead leaves —
Yet only by achieving may men grow.

J. David Sanderfer

APPEARING AS EVIDENT

A fleet began rocketing behind the mimic,
take-off, precedent of similar kind hereupon
Into operation, the way in which it orbits the mold,
the hitch inside, "what it takes," or failure
Do not ask for comment? The uncover is prodigious!
What is it then between the origin?
Helmsman fires every which way, a "straw in the wind"
Beyond the atmosphere, the trick, to compete in the onrush,
Anxious eyes, are concerned over rivalry, in horror
Cautious not, perils still more
              The "Asterisk Art" in an involved set-up
              By what safeguard gauge?
              Wait! is it whim or intimately put?
              A score by an eight-legged arachnid on
              As a ship's mast, like an upright askew,
              It was shown to be correct, in these tests
              Adherents via Ken, the will "as large as life."
              Facing and enduring bravely, for "on the morrow."

Rose Mary Gallo

AWAKEN MAN! AWAKEN WOMAN!

Awaken man! Awaken woman, to who you really are!
    Awaken to the duality of your nature!
That you are not alone and never have been!
Only you have restricted your horizon,
    enclosing your vision into a 3rd dimension
onto a physical planet called Earth.
    You stand, so to speak, on tottering legs
as a child learning to balance,
    declaring that he or she reigns over the universe,
and all things revolve about this center of instability.

Oh, ignorance of true knowledge
    of all that is and has always been.
Stretch yourself beyond your five senses!
Reach for the stars that beckon you into flight!
    Know there awaits other intelligences
for your return to logic and reason,
    to walk once again the path to strengthen
the progressive nature of mankind.
Awaken man! Awaken woman, to who you really are!
    Awaken to the duality of your nature!

Neosha

GAZEBO

Corridor after corridor, symmetrical maze,
earthen bricks overhead and on all sides;
red brick and tile, columns carved in amber hue
in between the sky shows through
its winking azure eye.
Circular fountains beneath a massive arch
square gray stones circumscribe;
verdant strips run narrowly
between the parquet haze
in and out
          in and out

through this myriad maze.
Archway shut out the sun
and block the warming rays.
A peace, and wanton rest lies in the shade.
Corridor after corridor, open path,
blue sky above and on all sides;
rich earth and brown, timber earthen hue
in between the dark shows through
its sinking sulking eye.

Linda M. Hawkins

GOODNIGHT LITTLE ROSE

Goodnight little rose,
Tuck your head beneath the snow,
Where ice-dancing fairies will caress you.

Your seed of life will be protected
From the blizzards that surround you,

And in the spring, the sun will wake you from your sleep.
So that you may evolve completely
And reveal the beauty deep within you,
Consoling the hearts of widows as they weep.

Your mighty shield of thorns will protect you
From the most insensitive invader,
As you kiss the eyes of artists everywhere.

You consume them and entrance them
With your delicate color scheme and style,
And your gently sculptured effigy
Causes their lonely hearts to smile.

Craig Allen Scarlet

A FRIEND DYING

The first spanking is like blue water
Washing over me only to drown in
A gasp of cold fear.
I am teaching myself to cry once more.

Paralyzed in the outer vacuum,
My friend is dying while
She is trying
To let me hear that I am alive.

Rituals we performed
Never to be
Heard or called
In these deep waters again.

She calls to me from webbing crevices
Within my whispering cave, and then,
Grasping loosely ten megaphones in her hands,
She announces

The times we went the farthest together.

Candace Corrigan

CORRIGAN, CANDACE COURTNEY. Pen Name: Candace Corrigan; Born: Los Angeles, California; Single; Education: Mills College, one year, 1984; Occupations: Production Assistant, Screenwriter; Memberships: Unitarian Universalist Association; Comments: *Sometimes I wish I were not a poet, but there is nothing I can do about it. I am driven to express pieces of the quilt of my feelings, and I suppose it is because I want to believe we all share something inconceivable, as it may be.*

MEMORY OF A CLOUD IN BOX

a dissolving thought
captured in a natural space
a prismatic space
an optical reality.

a transformation of an illusionistic space
there it sits before you
demanding a progression of your human awareness,
boxed within a non-reality.

always controlled
always indirect.

Man a secondhand perceptionist,
for a secondhand observationist, nature.

Cathy Kuntz

COAST SCENE, MARIN COUNTY

OFFICE MANAGER AT VALPARAISO UNIVERSITY

Today, I know my co-workers will not hesitate
to express our feelings about DORATHY — we wish to commemorate.

To say, not a word of heartfelt wishes, would be a total loss.

Because this woman we speak of is such a — *Special Boss.*

She is an individual with many talents, and I know you will
all agree.

But, the blessed salience about her — is portrayed a special
gift — another gift of God's sacred recipe.

This token that is given only unto thee — is a revealment that's
shown so compassionately.

Because God blessed her loving heart, with this special blessed
gift — this gift I speak of — is the gift of *Empathy.*

We all know the top man — R.P.K. — "The Brown and Gold Giant,"
will confirm this blessed gift — he said, "I can't deny it."

So, from each of us — and all of us — God's Blessing to you
DORATHY HEFFERNAN.

Who will always be: Our Special — Dear — and Loving Friend.

Anne Kalina

ON PASSIVE SAND

Some have wings and think of things to say to us who cannot hear
      Nor see, but only agonize between us
         in a language not so clear

A gifted throat can sing a note which soars so sweetly on the air
      that all could pause from mundane chore to listen
         but instead seem not to care

Some are free with eyes to see a vision that the rest of us
      Could know by watching where they point their fingers
         if we were more curious

The sculpted clay can seem to say what never was expressed before
      Displaying for our view a revelation
         which we manage to ignore

Some try to teach those out of reach while seemingly oblivious
      To reasons why the twain shall never meet
         in ways so obvious

But the surf's demand on passive sand is sometimes undetectable
      Until erosion slowly moves in time
         to make the change

So wise men sew, even though they may not reap their harvest now
      Except to know the song they sing is for the joy of singing.

Robert P. Foster

CASSIE'S DAY

Banging doors and toy-strewn floors, and Grandma what you got?
Candy, gum, or popsicle? An orange would help a lot.
Can I stay here? I love you so.
This picture is a fish.
Be careful now, my little doll, or you'll break Grandma's dish.
I'll bless my food and say my prayers if I can only stay,
And spend the night or week or so, or maybe just all day.
This toy just broke, my pencil is lost, and Grandma, where's my shoe?
My dress got wet when I washed my hands.
Is this color green or blue?
What time is it? Just one more kiss, oh how she loves to play.
A sigh of relief, it's a lot of work when Cassie spends the day.

Zona Robinson

I AM A POET

I am a poet.
I can run barefoot through the meadow,
Scooping up baskets of wildflowers.
I can weave a path
Through the blackberry bushes,
Chasing butterflies.
I can feel the sparkling, cool water.
Upon my bare feet at the brook.
I can climb to the crest of the mountain,
To watch the sunrise.
I can lift on the wings of the skyhawk,
And soar above the clouds.
With my "paint brush,"
I can create the portraits,
Of my soul.
I am a poet.

Janet S. Nieto

REQUIEM

Life goes on
    Though loved ones go;
You wonder why,
    Grief wounds you so.
But comes a day
    When it seems just
That they had gone
    When go they must;
The pain and heartache
    Quiet grows
And we go on
    Till comes our close;
The parting's tem-
    porary then,
And you can know
    You'll meet again.

Rose Gordon LeVan

THE DAY HE HELD MY HAND

He was never one to say
"I love you" in words so clear;
Although it's what he felt
To say it was much to fear.
I don't know what he's afraid of
Or why the words cannot come out.
I just know what he feels
And what it's all about.
No, he never said directly
The words that mean so much,
But I can tell just how he feels
By his tone and by his touch.
I love him like the world,
And this I'm sure he understands
See I know my Daddy loves me
By the day he held my hand.

Melissa Rae Beckermann

TIME

You stopped by to say hello
I needed a friend
    but I didn't expect you to stay

As time went by, I wanted you to
stop by and stay awhile
    but I didn't expect you to stay

Now I want you to stop by and
stay as long as you can
    I hope I love you enough not
    to expect you to stay

S. L. Soldan

THINKING ABOUT SUMMER

Water rolls the shells
Sweeping salty chatterings
To my beachhouse door.

The ocean spray sprinkles
Sandy seashells and starfish
Tickling the shore's soul.

On a gray jetty
A sea gull hobbles about
Teased by the white foam.

Distant sailboats drift
With summer's music forming
An ice cream skyline.

Cinnamon sunset
Serenely blankets the sea
Waves whisper to sleep.

Mare Whelan

HAVE I TIME NOW TO ENTER

a poetry contest?
In 2 years I'll turn
forty, and even now
it seems too late
for poetry.
I am a casualty of
poetry, and now
all I can love
are children.
Poetry contest?
What poem have we
not yet written?
And am I fooling
myself
with some good reason
to write poetry
in the kitchen — wait!
Listen
            it's the children
Hear them?

David Wilson

I'M BY YOUR SIDE

I'm by your side when times are
good and when times are bad. I'm
walking with you my man till eternity.
I'm hoping with you when things seem
hopeless.

I'm by your side when you least expect
any support, and I'm listening when
you don't have anyone else to hear
your woes. I'm here when you are
saddened, discouraged, successful, and
joyous.

I'm by your side night and day, and
through sickness and health. I was
by your side the day we wedded, which
was twenty-five years ago, and that's
why I'm by your side today.

HAPPY TWENTY-FIFTH DEAR!

Melanie Brooks

Now that death has been
visited upon my person,
An occasion to repeat itself —
In a final swoon

I cannot say for sure
but in the wildest dream,
That this is but a passage —
To some higher scene

But *once* the bright light
surrounded my interior,
Bathed to cut all words —
Short of explanation

I do not *now* know it
But by some hazy heat,
And pressed to impatience —
Frustrated to repeat —

I will not . . .
I will not . . .
I *will* not.

M. Scott Davis

FORSAKEN

I don't know why it happens
To the rest, and me too,
But every life seems to be single-handed
In its rest, in its tenseness.

Tilling with working minds
Not in what they would like to ponder,
But figures and X's
Excel in each day.

But when they think not,
The chance comes.
Take off! Be free! Come away with me!
Who is talking?

They either put their heads down,
Keep on with the pencil,
Or rise slowly but surely
And leave the chair pushed out.

They don't always forsake themselves.

Heidi Louise Hanssen

LIKE A SECRET

In the evening darkness,
My cat is like a secret;
A whisper on the prowl,
An ebony streak of lightning,
A wolverine's howl.

She creeps ever so softly
On her velvety paws
Looking like a shadow as
She wanders through the halls.

But, in dawn's early light
She sits on my window sill
Looking out with onyx eyes,
Not ruffled by the breeze
Her soft sleek coat shines.

She pounces on my bed,
Purring crazily.
She licks me with her pink tongue
Curling up lazily.

Tara Szuszkiewicz

SAID THE LATE MAN

My love is the straight man.
He keeps me sane.

When I talk to trees, he alone answers.
He alone can.

He takes my hand
and makes me feel the sky,
He tells me
that it is real.

We walk for hours.
We stand on the horizon.
We look back.

If we fall he is the first to rise again.

My straight man is love.
He keeps me sane.

Michael Dill

LEARNING OF LOVE

There was a time many years ago
When poems would come with ease
The words would rhyme and verses flow
Of things a young man sees
Poems of days and poems of night
And poems of things I sought
The words would always come out right
With just a single thought
But then my mind became confused
With thoughts of love and hate
I was so blind my heart was bruised
By lessons learned too late
But with this fact it came to me
That I could write again
The thing I lacked I then could see
Flowed swiftly from my pen
Experience in the ways of love
Had opened the final door
And ever since my poems are of
The things I'm looking for

Raymond Robinson

A RAINBOW

The eye sees a great spectrum
With a gentle meaning,
A multicolored array,
Keeping a covenant
To those who still believe.
Though distant
It's so close
Softly whispering
Of a promise
Meant to be kept.
An arc of wonder
With no beginning,
No end.
But with a special promise
Of love.
A rainbow is
Assurance,
And as long as there
Is a rainbow
We shall go on.

Heidi M. Stallman

RAIMENT

tenderness spins
clad in delicate daydream
soft gauzy layer
upon layer

melancholy waits
simply cloaked in coarse woolens
of smothering
nightmare

always passion streaks
white-hot and sweating
through vibrant and shifting
mirage

nostalgia lies weeping
draped with winsome delusion
carefully arranged
to fall

fantasy is how
we dress our emotions
when we cannot bear
their nakedness

Dee Galloway

GALLOWAY, DEE. Born: Omaha, Nebraska, 12-27-57; Education: University of Colorado at Denver, permanently since 1976; Occupations: Accounting Clerk, Actress, Calligrapher, Graphic Artist, Violinist, Seamstress, Singer, Songwriter; Comments: *Always the eclectic over-achiever, my poems are born of my many disappointments: Lost jobs, missed opportunities, tardy revelations, wasted energies, insufficient loves. The only literal evidence of my failures, my poems are, at once, cause and effect.*

The oriental season
Of intermittent colors
Drifts . . . pauses . . . circles
Toward a wintery grave
Lined with crisp brown stalks
Of now forgotten summer,
And covered with a honey dew.

Lynne Tucker Warren

PHANTOMS

I watch the candle burning down
To the final ash
Flickering in the dead of night
Enticing me into its silent dance
Melting, melting
  i fall prey . . .
To the phantoms of the dying flame
The shadow of the child passes on
To the ghost of a woman bound in chains
Following the path of charred remains

And so former lives of a spirit mourn
The destruction of the soul
As the heart seeks refuge
In the eye of the storm
Falling, falling
  far from grace . . .
To the phantoms of a life untamed
Fleeing the wrath of a condemned fate
Where the wide-eyed child went astray
a haunted woman walks in vain

Jolynn Mastandrea

DAY BY DAY COURAGE

I heard someone
  say today
"Courage is living"
  And in an
          odd sort of way
I started thinking.

Day by day
  Is conquered
By living each second
  The best we may

Day by day
  Means to be
Taking inch by inch
  Lovingly

Day by day
  Is so hard to do
But in the end
  It'll make a conqueror
Out of you.

Tricia Shanahan

SOMETIMES I CRY
FOR YOU . . .

Our love muse
Still wears
The fabric of you and I

He comes to dance
With opiate fashion
Stirring ancient tides

Currents still flow
Connecting our streams

In quiet moments
Your gravity pulls
Demanding the smolder
Of countless memories

This vestige symphony
Performs inside
Behind my ivory mask
And no one sees
The applause
Of intimate tears

Joseph Stevens

THE WILDERNESS COULD BE PARADISE

I'm standing on the brink of time,
Of stardust path and nursery rhyme,
When winsome girl comes out to play,
With secret thoughts and lissome way.

Whose fingers weave a trail of sighs,
Or broken hurt within the eyes.
The legend flask again is filled,
The bread and bough again is willed.

And we then scamper fast away,
To darkened glade or ocean spray,
We touch each other dark and fair,
I kiss the highlights in her hair.

Our stolen moments flit away,
As breathing quickens, visions sway.
We hold each other while there's time,
Uncertainty or fate sublime.

I think of golden years to see,
Or aching thoughts and lonely me.
Now, if old Eros shoots her through,
Will joy and happiness ensue?

David Nelson Baker

THE SONGS OF TRUTH

I wonder how the true story goes;
Of young Adam and Eve.
How at first they wore nothing at all;
Then began to wear the fig leaf.

I wonder how the true story goes;
of Noah, and life upon the Ark.
Why? Outside of Noah's family;
No other could take part.

I wonder how the true story goes;
Of Moses' mighty climb.
To bring back the words of a God;
For all of humankind.

I wonder how the true story goes;
Of Jesus' doomed last steps.
How one quiet midnight clear;
From a great tomb crept.

I wonder how the true story goes;
of life on this green earth.
How we know for sure, we die at death;
Born with a soul at birth.

Joan E. Devine

The malignancy of loneliness
Permeates the soul
Like swamp fog.
The sullen silence
Of a house that was once a home
Now decaying
Inside and out
From neglect and joylessness.
The tenacity of enchanted memories
Appear as unlived fantasies
In the never-land of now.
To live the numbered days
Without warmth and laughter
Grows tedious.
To never be loved again
Is a devastating limbo.
And the crush of age
Causes a poverty of psyche
That searches for validation of existence
From external origins — to endure.

June Long Freitas

WEAVER OF MAGIC

The weaver of magic
stood atop his throne
wraiths danced about his feet
commanded by him
who would be king.

Presented to his majesty
they played upon shadow
a ballet of light dance
for those who stood entranced.

The weaver of magic
commanded me to dance
clumsy mimic of grace
jester's serious foible
feeble substitute for dancer's beauty.

Evelyn B. Sayre

WISH

i wish i could
                    draw
                              a picture
                    paint
of your soul
              somehow capture
                  the essence
                    spirit
                          beyond emotions
                                    passion
into what makes
            you
            us
                particles
                        of
                      God's
                      dance . . .

Patricia Starr

THE MIRROR

Mirror mirror
pretty picture
not a liar
repetition.
Reversed perception
superstition,
seven years of
imposition.
Cannot bend,
can't talk
back, silver
color on its
track.
Always molding,
never scolding,
magic mirror
show me all.

Lesley Sagel

WINTERTIME

We look forward more each year
In making memories we hold dear.
Noting the cold, fog and rain
Till the sun shines warm again.
Enduring the cold with chills
Remaining well with cold pills.
The body covered with a sweater
In us, soup makes us feel better.
Motivated, we watch for spring
Encouraged, we listen to birds sing.

Edna Herstein

DISCORD

Eyes blazing, casting
angry darts at me —
you speak volumes
in your silence.
I do the dance of jousters,
shooting back your darts,
screaming in myself,
Stop! Stop!
How can I leap the chasm
of our anger? . . . call back
the darts of pain? . . .
Stop this and choose
to love again . . .
I can.

Karen Genzel

ONLY FIFTEEN

All she knows
She feels
This is ladled out in phrases
Round enough to roll around logic
And hold you in her eyes

She believes wind is a language
And suspects much more

She says there are mountains
Lost beneath the sea
Dreams about the sky
And takes the man in the moon to bed

If you ask her why
She tells you about vibrations
Flowers that heal
And cactus that gives vision

On the edge of her words
You can feel her world forming

You want to reach her
She is only fifteen
But will not allow it

Richard Cronin

I MADE A DEAL WITH MYSELF

I made a deal with myself

I wouldn't think of her, I promised,
No matter what,
No matter how hard it got,
No matter how many times
Thoughts of her popped into my mind.

I made a deal with myself

But, it's hard,
Oh so hard
To forget,
Her leaving,
Leaving me oh so alone.

I made a deal with myself

But then, deals are made
To be broken, to be forgotten
And thus, here I sit
Not only thinking of her
But also writing a poem about her.

I made a deal with myself.

B. J. Lisatz II

ONE NATION UNDER GOD

We are one nation under God,
Let's keep it that way,
Let's show the world our love for Him.
And spread His word today.

Let's do His will in everything,
And help our fellow man,
Let's lead the world to better things,
And do the best we can.

Let's find the poor and comfort them,
Less fortunate than we,
So God can hear our many prayers,
For peace and unity.

Let's show the world it can be done,
To gain the world's no goal,
But if we gain eternity,
It means our very soul.

For as one nation under God,
We hold the world in sway,
Let's join in prayers with those who want,
A peace on earth today.

Carol Jelinek

THE WIND RAGED ON

The wind raged over the sea
The trees on shore bent low
The white-capped waves crashed the land
Thunder was heard below

The season past grew bitter
As cold as the churning sea
No love for me could ever last
In such a sea

The dawn broke fast upon the day
Still the sea churned free
Tossing up the topmost wave
A wasted love to see

There it comes the season
For all true love to die
No love like mine could ever last
In such a sea

But the wind raged, and on it raged
Until the dawn blew free
The sea grew calm, the trees grew straight
To another love for me.

Terry N. Levesque

WRAPPED IN A WINTER AFTERNOON

Porcelain teacups,
Baby dolls,
And angels watching over me
Were folded away in a winter afternoon.
Pour me a cup of coffee
And we'll climb back to
Those days.
We thought it was
Tough to
Grow up;
Looking back,
Those trials are
My security.
Now I'll fold them back in
The winter afternoon
So next time I need to
Scream,
They'll be there.

Kim Oldham

GOD HAS A PLAN FOR YOU

Some are born to the rich
    some are born to the poor
        some have a chance in life
            while others know not which way to go
But God has a plan for each one
    To each He has given a gift
        Let not your heart be troubled
            Your help will be sure and swift.

Yes, God has a plan for each life
even before the world began
    It was all mapped out
    Clear and plain without doubt
Just walk in His Light
    All will turn out just right.

Susie A. Tonkins

YESTERDAY IS LOST

My solace expression has floated away,
such as the cotton on a warm summer's day.
Harlequin counsel abounds in I of all men
lend me your ear, I now know laughter again.

Ahead are righteous roads beyond my time,
diverse incentive is now mine to abide.
Present strength encircles my newborn soul,
forever my time, forever be old.

Talent enriched, contentment legibly passed
I am the idealist, though the thoughts are proven crass.
The line is reached, always to be crossed,
forever is tomorrow.
Yesterday is lost.

Ronald Harth

AS IN ONE

As the sun has warmed the earth,
So have you warmed my heart
As love has sheltered many
So have you sheltered me
As in time all things come together
So have you and I
To be joined with you in the bond of love
Is to make the greatest dream come true
To know the union between two people
Is the union I wish to share with you
To love and live as one,
A new life now begun,
A love not to be outdone . . .

                        . . . As in one

Susan A. Montelius

DREAM STATES

At night, slumber overtakes me.
Captivated in memories — the consciousness departs,
Alternating states of adventure and intrigue.
Releasing ancient visions, imprisoned in the soul.
Mythical spirits uniting dreams and memories,
Weaving visions into vague drama of shrouded reflections.
A revelation of time preserved in eternity.
Confined in heart and soul,
magnifying what once was . . .
Reverting the reflections to parallel lines of awareness.
Endurance of mystifying encounters,
logical daydreams of memories,
prevailing upon the mind.
Episodes of impressions,
echoing what once was and ought to be.

Brenda Skinner

THE DEEPNESS FROM WITHIN

My heart is full of sadness.
It lies heavily, in its home within my chest.
Suddenly, a lump rises.
As it travels upward from my heart,
My tear ducts begin to fill,
My mouth curves downward,
Uncontrollably.
It is difficult for me to continue,
So I cry.

Laura Sinclair

A BEDSIDE PRAYER

Slumber in peace, my angel,
Trustingly sleep, my babe,
Remembering in dreamland the arms of love,
Encircling your world, my dove.

Sleep warmly in comfort, my precious one,
Your soft breathing is my peace.
Sleep deeply and sweetly, my angelic child,
Feeling only my smile, my joy and my kiss.

Aubrey Fay

THE PATH TO FOLLOW

The dangerous pathways of life lead us to
believe in things we cannot trust,
    In things we cannot see or in things we can
never be.
    But for those who lead themselves learn to
believe in nothing else.
    Only the guidance of our conscience and the
stillness of our thoughts will bring us one
step closer to all our fears and faults.

Rusty Hampton

MORNING GRABS

Morning grabs, push away, push away
I am a crab,
clawing and gnawing at my prey.
Afternoon quietly touches,
I'm a bee.
Four-thirty hops along, I'm a rabbit.
Night has a habit of making me a dream.
Ideas knock on my door; I let them in,
but morning grabs them and pushes them away.

Suzan Kerpetenoglu

THE SEA

The sea, its calmness draws me near,
In the wind, I hear faint voices,
The children, playing down on the beach,
Their minds drifting off, lost in one another,
Shadows of them reflect in the nearby water,
then fade with the falling sunset.
They run away, their laughter growing softer
leaving behind only footprints in the sand.
Traces, memories, of a day by the sea.

Lynne LaForte

ONCE MORE

Once more . . . they loved each other . . . violating rules . . .
Once more . . . they chanted the secret hymn from the forbidden papyrus . . .
Once more . . . they stood naked in front of the god of their hearts . . .
Once more . . . they made love in the Temple . . . !!

Once more the earth was to hold in her breast that which was cast
off . . .
Once more; the smell of Sandalwood, myrrh and cinnamon, filled the
air . . . and hundreds of miles apart, they claimed to Infinity the
curse of an ancient rite: To Bring Back the Dead . . . !!!

Once more . . . sinister figures dressed in black, others in white,
were seen in the Temple . . .
Once more he screamed his passion . . .
Once more he screamed out his love for her . . . !!!

Once more . . . The Book of the Dead was open to bring together
two souls that defied the Laws of the Universe . . . !!!
        Once more . . . they were together forever . . .

Maria Brunilda Roman

ROMAN, MARIA BRUNILDA. Pen Names: Bruna, Isha; Born: Manhattan, New York, 7-3-49; Education: Hudson Co. Community College, Associate Degree in Human Services, June, 1984; Jersey City State College (present) Bachelor Associate, Sociology; Occupation: Assistant, General Biology Lab, Jersey City State College; Comments: *Through my poetry, I try to communicate with others (to others) my feelings of love, joy, peace and harmony. I'm deeply in love with the ancient form of Egyptian mysticism; and this is where I "receive" the source to write . . . my personal feelings for God, creation in general; and my boyfriend: Samir . . .*

HANDS

I see those hands lying limply on a satin sheet.
The swollen blue rivers pulsate through marble canyons — with rage.
Stony arches stiffened by age clutch at silk sand dunes.
One crooked bridge crushed in the slammed door of the roadster —
Haughty days — too proud to cry. "A real beauty," they said.
Another, sculptured by time, imprisoning a jewel
Behind an ugly, painful hump.
It can't come off. What a laugh! It has no shine. It never did.
Small and dainty, creamed, caressed — seldom busy at all.
Often roaming, always grasping, gloved to hide the greed —
Never roughed a baby's head.
So strange and unfamiliar now — these grotesque talons
Clawing in their slippery nests. They seek another's hand.
Fire red is suitable polish — it matches my gown.
So sloppy you are — careless and dreadfully boring —
Hold my hand steady! You hear me? I said, hold my hand.

Carolyn E. Campbell

LONELY LOVE

You are the love of my life.
The man of my dreams.
The happiness I once had,
I miss you, I need you, I want you,
But without you I'm terribly sad.
You are the passion in my life.
And without you I'm not whole.
A part of me left with you.
The rest is dead and cold.

Mona Faye Hankins

HANKINS, MONA FAYE. Born: Enid, Oklahoma, 4-28-51; Married: 1-15-83 to Thomas Mark Hankins; Education: High School; Experiencing life; Occupations: Waitress; Clerk; Owner, Manager, and Exercise Instructor for Health Spa, 1982-83; Children: Angela McNulty, 17; Jim McNulty, 14; Troy McNulty, 8; and one stepdaughter, Lisa Hankins, 9; Poetry: 'Mom,' 1974; 'A Life,' 6-5-75; 'Ocean Breeze,' 1974; 'Lilacs,' 5-19-75; 'Baby Love,' 5-16-77; Comments: *I write to express my deep emotions, it's like having a release valve. I find writing has a very calming effect on me. My poetry is something I will leave my husband and children to remind them of my love for them. It's a gift of love that will be passed down for many generations.*

SIRENS

Women circulate
Like struck silver
Throughout this peerless realm —
More mercurial —
Their voices echo
A pleasing, breathless sound.
"Here, fair Necropolis —
Come unto us now."
Sonorous promises overwhelm.
We sail in toward her,
Forgetting all;
Set forth
Without a helm.

Brian Hall

BABOON

These limbs are deformed. They move not well.
The mountain moved closer to the trees.
The brook ran still.
I saw your face.
My soul is alone. These limbs are deformed.
Movement ceases in my heart. These eyes do not focus.
My soul is gone.

My stomach does not hold my lungs.
My eyes do not focus.
These are not trees. I've had no leaves for days.
The mountains moved closer to the trees.

My hands can feel no green. The earth is out of reach.
The air is still and warm.
The meadow has lost its odor. The leaves are gone.

My ears are healing to the noise.
The dampness is dry. The meadow has lost its odor.
The breeze became a melody of time and space.

The green lights awakened the day.
The dew has filled my nose.
My hands grab no trees. The leaves are gone.

Bobi Jackson

EASTER STORY

There once was a man who walked on this earth,
Who committed no sin from the day of His birth,
He healed the sick, the blind, and the lame,
Who was this man what was His name?

He tried to teach people to love one another,
He taught the children to honor their Father and Mother,
To give us eternal life was the reason He came,
Who was this man, what was His name?

He spent His whole life to save us from sin,
To open our hearts and let Him come in,
Even wild animals around Him were tame,
Who was this man, what was His name?

Centuries have passed but the story's still told,
We hear it over and over, but it never grows old,
How they crucified Him and put Him to shame,
Who was this man, JESUS CHRIST was His name.

The story's not over, it's not to be ended,
He arose from the dead and to heaven ascended,
So we celebrate Easter and although we're apart,
This man called JESUS still lives in our hearts.

Delores Escue

I'LL BE THE KEEPER OF OUR LOVE

With a happy sorrow I take my leave
A smile remembering times so good.
Your gentleness which warmed my blood,
And the strength which won me to you
Now is mine and blesses my days.

I am glad to have been one with you —
For now we'll be so always.
And if you kiss the winds they'll speak
Whispering melodies we have heard.
Glistening effervescent love of fulfillment.

Face the sun and heed not unending Time.
Your shadows will fall behind you.
We'll meet again and be deeper still
I laugh to think we ever sorrowed!
And though I go, I'll hold our love forever.

Danielle Hazard

UNTITLED

Living in a world of a thousand gaps
Breathing the life of a million deaths.
How much it weighs in my soul
I cannot begin to explain.
How often it kills me inside,
  Over, and over, again!

I cry for the relief of many peoples' agony.
I sorrow for those who never came to be.

If all tears in this world were gathered,
Rivers of chaos would be revealed for those who care.

Visions of utopian worlds would be better understood,
But never part of us to share.

Barbara M. M. Machler

MACHLER, BARBARA MARIA MEDEIROS. Born: Lajes Field, Azores, Portugal, 6-23-64; Married: Joel F. Machler; Education: (13) College of Great Falls, Montana, Georgia Military College; Occupation: Airman in the U.S. Air Force; Comments: *I usually try to write on paper what to some people seems confusing, such feelings of pain and happiness. I do my very best to reach all types of personalities. Anything can inspire me to write. What would make a difference in my life is if one day my poetry will reach someone needing an uplift or understanding.*

SECRET LOVE

How I long for him to hold me tight
For him to tell me I'm all right
To wipe my brow and dry my tears
And say to me there's nothing to fear
If only he saw the love I hide
The feelings locked deep inside
If he could understand the reasons why
As he slept I cried
And how my tears on his sleeve fell
As I wept in the night
If I could tell, and know he'd care
All my heart's secrets I long to share
But a voice, full of fear, tells me, "No, not now, not here!"
If I could say, "I understand"
Reach out and take him by the hand
Explain to him I can see his pain, his joy, his strife
That I read his heart through his eyes
Only then (which will never be)
Would this burden of "Secret Love" be lifted from me

Sherri D. Todd

172

BEAUTIFUL MORNING

Raindrops keep falling
The sunshine is calling
A boat rides the tide while at its mooring
Into the blue all the birds are soaring
The sea takes in the mountain streams pouring
It will be then that during this beautiful morning
I will give to you my love
For your love like an endless warming
Forever keeps the candle burning.

Christopher John Musto

In my lifetime
I've caught glimpses of you

I've smelled your perfume in a springtime rain
And discovered your image in a campside fire.

I've felt your presence, hovering, protecting me
From the chilly spray frenzied waves hurl on an overcast day.

I've heard your voice in my mind, whispering
Gentle words of encouragement and love.

I've seen your smile on a stranger in the street
And turning to pursue, lost it in the crowd.

I've been bowled over by your laugh erupting
From a thousand youthful throats, delighted by
The antics of a circus clown.

I've drawn you and sketched you in the sands of
My mind and on the canvas of my heart.

I've held you close in my dreams,
Feeling your breath against my neck as your
body melts into mine.

I've experienced you and savored your essence
Countless times, never knowing your name
Until now . . .

J. A. Moore

A MOTHER'S TRIBUTE TO HER DAUGHTER

In Nineteen Hundred Forty-Two a child was born
That child was you.

A dream I'd had since I was five
Had finally materialized.

And now it's Nineteen Hundred Eighty-Five
And I am all of Seventy-Five.

That child, a woman grown
Gave me a present like I've never known.
A three-day weekend in New York.

I didn't spend a single cent
In all the places that we went.

The theatre, symphony and ballet
You certainly took me all the way.

The meals were super, super swell
Which I digested very well.

The weekend now is stowed away
Which I'll relive from day to day.

The years fly by and memory fades
But this I'll cherish for all my days.

Gladys Evans

SOLILOQUY IN BLUE

Even when I am alone,
                    inside my own world,
                              she is there.
If I walk in a dark place
          or if I am with many
                    masked city-people,
                              she is with me.
And when I escape to some lost hillside
          or walk on the beach
                    where the foam falls in a white haze,
                              she follows me.
I have learned to be with her.
          She visits my soul,
                    we taste the night together.
She is a moving, low at night, crouching being
          who stalks me and waits.
She is the always coming young stranger.
          She is my friend . . .
                    Her name is
                              Loneliness.

Jim Houston

UPTURNED

Frail green needles,
rubbery thin limbs,
thicker, rigid extending arms,
and the long,
enormous,
cylindrical
trunk
have been
felled
in the storm,
toppled
by the wind.
The upturned pine
bares its dark and dense under-veins
of countless hairy branches caked with dirt;
at the core
milky yellow sap
in crusted sticky clumps oozes frozen
from deadened, reddish-brown nerve bulbs,
raw roots ripped from the rich depths.

Thomas Matthews

A LIFE SHOULD NEVER BE THROWN AWAY

A gray sky filled with clouds,
a dream that has been shattered.
You feel so empty and cold,
you no longer care about the things that once mattered.
You feel like no one cares,
and you want to throw your life away.
It hurts when you tell your friends how you feel
and they turn the other way.
It's like they don't believe you,
they just can't understand.
You turned to them for help and support
and they didn't lend a hand.
Your friends aren't always willing to accept
that what you say is true.
They think that you're just saying these things
because you're depressed and blue.
Go get help when you need it;
when you're confused and don't know what to do.
A life should never be thrown away.
There are people out there who love you!

Cindy Peloquin

AUTUMN ALWAYS

Oh to be the breeze;
To caress your being and linger about your heart,
To toss your hair with my bounding joy,
To curl and whisper into your ear,
To capture your smile and contentment with me,
To feel the radiance of the glow springing from your cheeks,
To glide across the curve of your lips,
To wander about your lashes and shimmery eyes;
Moist from their resistance of my advance.

Deborah Ann Beery

NOTICE:
VIOLATIONS OF MY LAWS
MAY TERMINATE YOUR LIFE TENANCY
LEASE

I created water to quench your thirst.
You felt growth and progress should come first.
I created trees for your shade and shelter.
You squandered this treasure helter-skelter.

The skies I painted were blue and clear.
The smog you created makes all eyes tear.
The earth was fertile, the grass was green
but your use of it was quite unforeseen.

The planets, the skies with stars shining bright
are Mine . . . all Mine . . . and, try as you might,
because you ruthlessly waste the day and the night,
your tenancy will end . . . as will the blight.

My World will return to its glorious hue.
The skies once more will be clear and blue.
The streams and the rivers will run clear and free
of all your refuse and all your debris.

The trees will stand tall and straight
firmly anchoring the soil under their feet.
My World will survive and grow anew . . .
Regardless of the damage done by you.

Marion Arnett Ashley

FIDELITY TO VALUES

To create,
        Art — Music — Love — Anything
        You have to love what you do,
        and you have to be in love with doing it.

An Artist,
        must not judge himself on external success or failure,
        but must proceed, which provides the stimulus
        to further and truer self-discovery.

For one to create,
        what they create becomes an expression of themselves.
        An expression that is theirs alone.

By creating — we become more than ourselves.

The purpose of the artist — is to provide what life doesn't.

To be creative,
        you must allow yourself to be surprised.
        Forget any melancholy you may carry.

Art is a mystery,
        and all mystery has its source.
        Art's source is love.

THE LOVING ARTISTS' WAY MUST BE THROUGH THEIR ART.

Thomas Scott

FREEDOM

The freedom of democracy has usually been
Used and misused by men.
Perhaps the conflict of protection and destruction
Will result in firm construction.
Some will be convinced who simply cannot see
That all people are born free
"In the state of nature" as Locke has said.
But cold nature is a very hard bed.
So to be more comfortable and safely secure
Men made laws that will endure.
They agreed all would obey or a penalty to pay.
Yet youth must have their say
After we have first learned to dig
For grains of truth both little and big.
Spiritual and philosophical kernels of thought
Like the pioneers brought.
This did aid in increasing America's size.
And it made some of us realize
Wisdom should be the weapon of all in our society
Who love the freedom of democracy!

Alice De

MOMENTS

Moments we need
  Moments of serenity
    Moments of quiet and peace
      Where we may be alone
        Allowing all worries to cease.
          Moments to love
            Moments to think
              Moments to meditate
                Moments as fragile as a
                  Baby chick out on his own
                    Or newborn buds on a slender vine.
                  I have been alone at night
                    And known Serenity —
                  The only sound, wind soughing
                    Through branches of Tamarack
                      Soft hush of wings
                        Hawk soaring past
                          And I have wished
                          And I have wished
                          Dear Lord, may this moment last.

Mary Triplett

WINGS

Little boy,

Ride under your mother's wing.
She can guide you and joy she'll bring,
When disappointment falls heavy on your feeble shoulders.

Find young wings of your own that fit you best.
Wings like your mother's which give her happiness,
When you thought none could be found.

Follow your mother as you learn to fly.
Let her lead you and in time,
You too will know how to bring joy and find happiness.

Young man,

Take off and find your dreams.
Your mother knows what it means
To bring joy and find happiness using one's own wings.

Susie Austin

WALK A TIGHTROPE

I've given you the sky above.
You've taken every bit of love
That I can give you in my life.
Yet, still you cause me all this strife.

Devotion you take from my heart.
Picked up the pieces from the start.
Now that I'm yours, do what you will.
I've these dreams only you can fill.

I need a love to depend on,
A love so strong.
I need dreams that I can lean on,
Need to belong.

You walk a tightrope with my heart.
I risked a fall from the start.
A net below will catch my fears.
Hold me close and draw me near.

Mary Ann Pyle

CIVIL WAR HARDSHIPS

Young boys left their homes,
Young boys left their wives,
Some came back as men,
And some gave their lives.

They fought for the 'Blue,'
Or they fought for the 'Gray,'
They slept little at night,
And marched most of the day.

They had many problems,
They had many fears,
And most of their families
Shed many tears.

McClellan and Grant
Fought Sherman and Lee,
And this whole war was
to make all men free!

Wendy Parsley

IF

If I were a famous artist
I would paint a picture grand —
blue, silver-lined sky, sea, and shore
with Christ's footprints in the sand.

I would sketch a dust road winding
with sycamines growing high,
(where the blind, lame, and leper came
to see Jesus passing by.)

In the shadows paint a deep well
with Jesus communing there.
nearby, the penitent maiden
with countenance young and fair.

The living Christ beckons all
with His tender outstretched hand;
blessing each, rejecting none —
Oh! If I were an artist grand.

Lucille Skoglund

LIFE IS MY TEACHER

I'm looking at life through
Clouded eyes.
It all seems so hopeless
Yet I still seem to try.
Looking up at this mountain
Thinking, what does it mean?
I need someone by me to
Wipe my eyes clean.
How does one live?
How does one stand,
With this thing they call love
In the grasp of their hand?
Life is my teacher,
And mistakes help me learn.
Trying to teach me of love,
Life can be so stern.
So, come climb this mountain,
We'll do it together.
We may just stay friends,
But at least friends last forever.

Katherine Lodge

CARE JUST A LITTLE

Shadows in the dark.
What is it that I fear?
Being all alone,
Can't even shed a tear.
My heart it is so empty
And no one seems to care.
I just wish someone would listen
When thoughts I wish to share.
Sitting in the moonlight
Doesn't feel quite right
When no one sits beside me,
No arms that hold me tight.
Flowers aren't as pretty
And birds don't sound as nice.
Sometimes I just quit looking.
I feel as I am ice.
Just be nice to me.
Reach and hold my hand.
Stop and say hello to me
If only that you can.

Terri Weatherspoon

THE TEACHINGS OF SILENCE

Hail to thee O Silence
Thy ancient unknown friend
Whose teachings found their essence
In roots that have no end.
The truth has shown its presence
For behold, it comes again
To lay low the mortal serpent
And invoke the souls of men.
Expound to me a doctrine
From the dialogues of your love
Unroll the scrolls forbidden
From those who have not swore
To raise the treasures hidden
Upon thine ocean floor.
And ride waves driven
By winds forevermore
To guide a course to Heaven
And by their signpost sore
To bind forgotten legions
And find their long-lost shore.

Thomas Williams

AFTER THE STORM

Moments after such a florid
and unexpected drenching,
The old house having shivered once,
Or twice,
Settles down to inherit fitfully,
the cocooned dream
and reminiscence,
of cooler days.
Then like an old lady
Droning before her midday fire,
Taut with the wryness
of body and smile,
It sighs stoically,
Coping with the thought of
all those hotter days
to come.

Wayne E. Davis

DAVIS, WAYNE EDWARD. Born: 9-23-44; Married: to Maureen Angela Davis; Education: B.A., Special Honors, English; Occupation: Administrative Assistant; Awards: Third Prize, Poetry, National Cultural Council, 1975; Poetry: 'Old Oracle Timeless Dreams'; Other writings: *Vortex*, fables, based on Sufism and Zen Buddhism, self-published; Themes: *Man's relationship with nature, man in society, man/woman relationships, other philosophical themes.*

YOU'RE SPECIAL TO ME

*Dedication: To Larry Pasciak
the love of my life!*

I close my eyes
and see your face
I feel no pain
you take its place.

My heart is calm
when in your arms
no need for tears
no room for fears.

Just peace and joy
when you I see
I want you to know
You're Special to me!

Luz E. Medina

SPRING IS STIRRING

Spring is springing as a lamb,
So sweet and soft is the sound,
With a bird beeping a welcome,
As little dewdrops wet their beaks!

Spring is stirring with the sun,
Sun so bright and sun so warm,
Gives a feeling of happiness today,
As all the snow goes down the drains!

Spring is sprouting amid the breezes,
As sleeping tulips are all alert,
Awaiting a burst of golden sun,
To raise their heads and say hi!

Spring is showing along the streams,
Streams so narrow are now so big,
Leaving their banks in some spots,
As winter ice becomes only water!

Spring is showering us have no doubt,
As green trees and green green grass,
Gives our spirits a great uplift,
To walk outside amid the scenery!

Spring is stirring over our city,
As little boys with their bats,
All line up in their lively caps,
Awaiting the call, "Let's play ball!"

Doris Burleigh

REASONS

Love is realizing,
each has faults.
Love sorts the
thoughts. But, hey!
Remember . . .
God is love.
Beautiful love.

Donna Peterson

I REMEMBER . . .

I remember the day we met and
we were one.

I remember how we walked and
talked together, it seemed as though
we always were.

I remember when our lips met that
night that you had to be mine forever,
but were you?

I remember the day I said that I
loved you, do you remember?

And I remember the day I said that I
loved you, do you remember?

And I remember the day I left, I
promised that I would love you forever.

As I sit here tonight, I remember
that I still love you and soon we
can be one again.

I love you and my heart will always
wait, for it remembers too.

I love you . . .

Diana B. Nacchio

THE SAGA OF ELSELBORN RIDGE
(THE ARDENNES CAMPAIGN***1944)

Over our foxhole a banshee-like cry shreds the frozen mist and wounds
the wind. Endless madness holds the vibration against our ears as echos
sound stronger, clinging longer. Red hot shrapnel rips the ground asunder
with great orange flame. More follows, beheading the snow-clad tree tops.
The pine wood gives way to many corpses as steel plows into unwilling timber.
A Nazi 88, in countless melancholy sighs, plays these melodies of death.
Men in iron coffins pit ore against sinew and after life has been squeezed
from paper thin flesh, treads rumble onward as feet trudge in falling purity
down a sanguine road.
From this ravaged outpost in the inner space of our world we observe the
blackened towers of hell rise in massive violence like a red wind and merge
with God-given breath in a tangled morass of death.
We are not forgotten though a boreal draft blows against our combatant
hearts. In the gathering of this Winter storm, all know that peace will
spread its wings again.

George C. Koch

KOCH, GEORGE C. Born: Bronx, New York, 2-22-22; Married: 9-24-60 to Lucille; Education: Far-
mingdale Agricultural and Technical College, New York, Graduate, May, 1942; Occupation: Medi-
cal Laboratory Technologist — 37 years in Staten Island hospitals; Memberships: Staten Island
Poetry Society; Awards: Honorable Mention for war poem, 'Attack,' *Midwest Poetry Review,* 1965;
Poetry: *Voice from the Ardennes,* Poetry Booklet, Gaust, 1965; *Two Pens,* Poetry Booklet, Bell's Let-
ters, 1967; *The Endless Climb,* Poetry Booklet, Nutmegger, 1969; Comments: *I am mostly known
as a composer of war poetry, but write about all subjects; use all forms; but mostly free verse. Yours
truly enjoys composing poetry and is published in many magazines.*

WAR

Bombs fall everywhere, confusion is all around me.
I run and hide but the explosions seek me out.
How often have I wished the noise and death away,
The screams and moans to silence, but it is not to be.
No, I must sit quietly and hear the death, the anguish,
And feel the pain of friends and neighbors as they fall around me.

Later, I will walk among the death, dust, and rubble.
I will cry as I see my family being carried away to be burned.
I will see the effect of the battle on our lives.
I shall write it all down in my diary,
Preserve it for all the world to see.
So I sit and wait to be sent away to a new home, a new family.
                    So I sit, and wait, and pray.

Mary-Beth Brophy

There are three main courts to my castle. Walls and doors are strong and solid. Built from years past. Throughout this structure are passageways and rooms within.

The outer court welcomes any who wishes to enter. 'Tis easy to enter in. This court holds many people. Here they can relax in the Court of Friendship.

A gate greets the few that trickle onward. The court is smaller but there is much room for growth. Here lies caring and sharing in the Court of True Friends.

From this court the most daring would travel. Only one person can complete the journey. For I choose if the person can press onward. Treasures can be found at The Heart.

Dana Craig

THANKS FOR EVE

Look!
Just look a there!
Walking down the street
everything all in place.
You make heads turn
as you pass through the crowd.
You stand out and you
differ from all others,
maybe it's the Eve in ya.

All women are descendents of Eve.
It's something Adam had to have,
and so does man today.

They may talk about the woman
being a snake in the grass
and when it all winds down
they love it.
With a little Eve in your system,
you can charm the pants off
any legs
and pegs.

Dinah Henderson

CONTEST

Tarnished metal —
Golden harp —
Finding love within
Your heart
To mend the childish ways
Of mother's goals for you.

Without an invitation
To begin
To cast you to her mold,
You try your own
And to disown her jaded
Path for you.

This, despite
A mother's love
When it was right,
Sent me on my search
To find myself
Strong and apart
And not return
To mother's heart.

Sande Cawthon

A SPIRITUAL BATTLE

The Angel was honest and promised love everlasting.
She was soft and humble with no meanness in her being.
The Serpent had charisma and seemed very dashing.
He was intelligent, all-knowing and had eyes all seeing.
The Angel said, "Follow me, my way is good and true."
But the Serpent said, "Do not listen, goodness is only for a fool!"
The angel touched my heart, with her I knew I should go.
But the Serpent looked deep into my eyes and wanted my soul.
Oh, God, right now, there is a choice I must make,
Between Angel and Serpent, no looking back, with no mistake.
The Angel approached me and took my hand,
And said, "Follow me, you will be my right arm man."
        What happened to the Serpent?
        That I do not know.
        Not ever looking back,
        With the Angel I must go.
    Ian Manfrina

JOHN CHRISTIAN — GROWING — GROWING — GONE

I hold you in my arms, fresh from your bath,
your skin is so soft and your hair so silky, that I stroke and stroke.
I think this is forever — this sweet joy — it will never end.

I hold you in my lap — gone is the smell of baby powder,
replaced by the sweet sweat of young boyhood, tender baby curves have
been transformed into the sharp angles of a man in the making.

I hug you close to me, you say "Aw, Mom," but a kiss you give me,
You gather up your ball and bat and out the door you go, I think —
"Is it over now, finally over?"

My arms are empty — so I use them to make macrame, and plant flowers,
and make pottery — but in the midst of all these activities I remember —
Soft skin, silky hair, and over all — the haunting smell of baby powder.
    Vicky Wells

A HOUSE; NOT A HOME (UNDUSTED DESPAIR)

A bottle now lies beside me in my bed.
        The pillow no longer holds the impression of her head.
Love is found in rare thoughts, dreams and the past.
        In all my rooms the spider's web holds fast.
Within the mirror's realm no image is to be seen;
        Just red eyes glaring back at a broken dream.
In my bathroom there is the sink; in its possession something dear
        Lying at the bottom Van Gogh's tainted ear.
And now a farewell to danger —
        Because my house has become the stranger.
The gun that was used for protection —
        Will now send me in a new direction.
    James Shoemaker

Walking through some youthful thoughts upon the planes of yesterday
There passed me by a man of age
    who held my mind and eyes in sway
Deep lines — where thorns of disappointment had etched their cares
Crept from corners of his face and marched sometimes in pairs
To carve a monument where time stands still
For other men to read
    the pain of life
        the strength of will
Within his faded eyes was seen the vastness of living
Within the contours of his smile
    the want for giving
His was a time-worn face where gentleness abound
Where wind and rain had taken toll but silently had left their sound
And marked his love for all to see that others were more important than he
Yet — though I glimpsed his face but once
    I knew his memory would be
        A part of me
    Darwynne Pucek

FOUR SEASONS

Spring comes on us like a flash —
With sunny skies, budding flowers and green grass.
Gardeners garden, lawn mowers mow,
We break the ground where our plants will grow.

Summer is bright and remarkably gay,
We labor hard, but mostly play.
Beautiful beaches, or an old swimming hole,
Makes us young, eager, and truly bold.

Autumn is full of brown, yellow, red, and gold,
After the things of spring and summer unfold.
Falling leaves, withered flowers, and biting frost,
Pumpkins, corn, goblins, Halloween at any cost.

Winter brings the cold, ice, sleet, and snow —
A time to wrap up, light the fire, and let it glow.
Then comes Christmas time in all its glory,
And before you know it, it's spring again.

Harold James Douglas

JUST LIKE MAGIC

As I close my eyes and wait to dream
I feel the warmth summer nights bring.
Drifting away until your face I see
Just like magic, suddenly you are here with me.

Arms unfold to hold me near
As you whisper words I long to hear.
Eyes that carry me far away
With a look of love that beckons me to stay.

Our lips met with a kiss so divine
I knew I was captured until the end of time.
My heart to you I give
And only for your love that I shall live.

My head is spinning fast
For only the memory will last.
I awaken to find myself alone.
Just like magic, suddenly you are gone.

Tammy Holley

NAMESAKE ANGEL

In memory of: Joyce Anne Saner

If ever there were angels,
You must have been the special one.
For as I stood next to you,
A friendship had begun.
We went through trouble thick and thin,
But my friendship never came to end.
No matter what happened whether happy or sad,
My heart would not let go of this friendship we had,
I thought I'd go mad.
One way or the other.
Just then you would walk in,
And make me happy again.
We soon had to part,
But our friendship hung on.
I soon had a child who's named after you.
Although you're in heaven now I know you are pleased,
Your namesake shall know our friendship will always
Be special to me.

Elsie L. Karns

YESTERDAY'S CHILD

She sits at the window
    looking at the world
passing her by
    on the dusty dirt road

She remembers the good days
    the days gone by
days when horses roamed free on the range
    and the sight of a buffalo was not so strange

The one-room school
    that she attended
has now been abandoned
    and left untended

The "kids" that she knew
    are all dead and gone
she is old too
    but still very strong

She sits at the window
    looks up the hill
sees her love's grave
    and remembers him still
Jeane Johnston-Miller

AGGRAVATINGLY ADORABLE

Passing me by; looking adorable and neat
Your loveliness sweeps me off my feet
Passing, I gaze into your majestic eyes
You're aggravatingly adorable, you win the prize.

Aggravatingly adorable and you are not mine
I know that you are someone else's precious find
The fates did not allow me to know who you are
But, I do truly worship you from afar.

A mere mortal am I, who cannot reach the sky
An elusive heavenly body are you, that makes me sigh
Aggravatingly adorable with your queenly walk
Awed and tongue-tied, I am afraid to talk.

Being attractively beautiful seems to be your style
I'm hoping today to receive your warm, friendly smile
If my hoping dreams can really come true
Then one day I will be an inseparable part of you.

Having become an inseparable part of my life and me
No longer aggravatingly adorable will you be
Without aggravation I will lie at your feet
And whisper; adorable, precious, beautiful love; I did meet.

T. Steven Watkins

THE LITTLE OLD FARMER AT SUNDOWN

The battered old wagon creaked down the road;
Its wheels were turned in without a load.
The trusty old horse, with his head held low,
Was tired and dusty, and his walk was slow.
The wrinkled old farmer was bent and gray;
He held the reins loosely — his horse knew the way.
How many times had he traveled this road?
How many miles? How heavy the loads?
Was someone waiting for him to come home?
Or did he and his horse live all alone?
Did he have children and a little old wife?
Had he been working hard all of his life?
The sun was hanging low in the sky,
But as he drew nearer, I breathed a deep sigh.
His work-worn clothes were neatly mended —
And in spite of its tiredness, his horse looked well-tended.
I needn't have worried, for as he passed by
He waved to me with a smile in his eyes.

Eleanor Marsiglia

ODD SONG

When grayish silver pours down my somber head,
O Devil! and hot tears sweating my hard bread,
Wrath'll hammer along those macabre days,
Would you ever sing and clink your sadistic way?

I ain't expecting you, for long, on this rock,
Watching you pacing nearer, on chain, iron and havoc,
Smelling your fume of hell filling the mañana
With blaze and fear in stuffed brouhaha.

Here, my nerve of fire, my mind of thoughts,
My soul of dreams, and my throat of drought,
All of me, through that conscious hue
Of my memory, would sense your senseless You.

But alas! Lover! would you be alive or dead,
Or Ghost's partner, or creed errant, or sound, or deaf,
Or wounded, or orphaned, or hearth loser, or sick, or so?
I never run out of my saddened credo.

Yes, I would flee, in search for your steps,
Tumbling again and again down my instinct cliffs,
Because of your presence, of my lack of way,
Of my negative future, of my lack of prey.

Nam Duyen Luong

LUONG, NAM DUYEN. Born: Vietnam, 4-24-24; Married: 1950 to Chinh Thi Hoang; Education: School of Medicine of Saigon, Doctor of Medicine (1960) in Vietnam, reevaluated in the United States; Occupation: Visiting Fellow at the V.A. Wadsworth Hospital Center of Los Angeles; Award: "CUOI, the Liar," a children's story, (1970) in South Vietnam; Writings: *Tuoi Tho (Green Age)*, Stories, Sang-Tao Publisher in Vietnam, 1964; (republished by Song-Moi, Arkansas, USA, 1983); "Me-Linh Episode," Verse drama, 1972; "Pityless Pity," Movie script, 1979; Themes: *Emotions about life and its contrasts: Love and Hate, Beauty and Ugliness, Violence and Serenity . . . ;* Comments: *I wish that my poetry be an unreal but rich expression of something strong and mystic.*

WHERE HAVE THE YEARS GONE

Where have the years gone —
Since Valentines trimmed with lace,
First beaus, the smile on youth's face,
When did I grow old?
It seems only like yesterday
Many years have passed away.
What about the years between youth, and age?
They would fill a book written on each page.
Why did I hurry at such a fast pace?
Was I trying to win the race with time?
I was sure the world could be mine!
I really do not know where the years have gone
It does not seem that long ago
Yet the blue has turned to gold —
Please, tell me — When did I grow old?

Darlene Grice Hayward

LIFE

What is life?
The cry of a newborn babe,
    laughter of a toddler as he explores,
        excitement of the first day at school.
Moments of anguish in the adolescent years,
    the lively banter of teenagers in the home,
        first date, first dance, first heartbreak.
Sleepless nights waiting to hear familiar footsteps.
Joy and tears of high school graduation day,
    looking forward to conquering new horizons.
Meeting of that special one,
    the joining of two lives in the eyes of God.
The nest is empty. Time to rest.
The golden years when we look back and say it has been good,
    looking ahead to another generation of life . . .

Mary A. Amos

VICTORY

Onward they move, a solemn band and grave,
Baffled and driven, timorous and weak,
Up through the darkness toward a shrouded peak.
Blind, stumbling men, each with a broken stave.
How few with strength enough to stop and lave
A brother's wounds, or hope enough to speak
A word of fortitude; how few that seek
A fellow sufferer's ebbing strength to save.

O man, so powerless beneath the hand
Of unrelenting force, why do you weigh
Compassion in the balance? Recklessly
Give of your love; one moment yours to stand
Impregnable and free, holding at bay
The mocking legions of the powers that be.

Martha E. Munzer

A LOVE SO RARE
(To my husband)

True love's like a wine so rare
    And when it's found none can compare
        to its alluring beauty — the sweetness of spring,
    Making our hearts merrily sing.
Each tender caress entwines our hearts,
    Bringing us together when we're apart.
Truly love's like the precious fruit of the vine,
    Soaring us to heights sublime!
When days seem lonely and absent of fun,
    I daydream about you 'cause you're my sun.
Strolling on the sandy shore side by side,
    I trust your love, I can confide.
Like the thick branches of the luscious vine,
    Together we'll journey, together we'll climb!

Linda C. Grazulis

TOWER FALLS

When the crush of foolish past engulfs me
I empty the bitter cup on you.
You rinse it as the gentle rain a tree,
Left sparkling in a sunlit sky of blue,
Like diamonds, each drop a jewel true.
You fill my cup with words of kindness, tender —
"Sans peur et sans reproche" — I'll remember.

Anonymous

TOWARD A SANER WORLD

There are so many things to say, that time does not allow
When I stop to think of them, I can see
That all is what it should be, for what it is we do allow

We meet, we talk, we wonder what we're about
We find that there's something we see that we can't
quite figure out.

We let go just a little, and see it's not so bad yet,
With the fear instilled in us we hold back and that's sad.

I wonder what the stop is that holds us back from giving,
Have we been so suppressed that we forgot
that life was meant for giving.

I want that we break down the walls and alleviate the doubt
and give to each other the Love, Sensitivity and Warmth
we deserve, let's throw all the rest out.

You are the friends in my life, I can see it was
meant to be.
Now let's cross the bridge before us
So our dreams can become Reality.

Michael V. Lanza

LANZA, MICHAEL V. Born: New York City, 9-14-47; Married: 9-23-80
to Suzanne Lanza; Education: Fashion Industries High School, Robert Fi-
ance Beauty School '71' Cosmetologist; Occupations: Total Look Special-
ist, Haircutter, Make-up Artist; Memberships: Celebrity Centre Church
of Scientology New York; Poetry: 'Communication,' 2-24-80; 'A Dream
Come True,' 2-22-80; 'A Blow to Suppression,' 2-23-80; 'Question,'
2-21-80; 'Decisions,' 3-18-81; Comments: *I mainly write truths of life in
a straightforward way using rhyme, through realizations of my life I put
them in print to share them with all. My main purpose is to assist others
to go free from the "traps" that enslave us.*

a tray of sunlight rests upon the sill
a calm no man has known
ah, the sweet kiss of evening
with its swirling dusts and orchestra of light
for but a moment, perfection blossoms here
and I have to smile at the simple beauty
given me upon that sill
so glorious and overpowering,
a common little dash of sunlight
running frightened from the crush of night
which creeps ever closer,
stalking the shiver of golden wind
that has paused at my window's edge
to laugh aloud at our eternal frolics
then off again it leaps
staying just beyond the grasp of night

Dennis Dolan

MEN

A man is a strange thing
They now possess you, since he gave you a ring
If he's not there, he says you are untrue
If he is there, he's making you blue
Never does he want to be close
Just always trying to make things worse
Never there to joke and have fun
Always too busy, he's got to run
Then when you ask for some special time
He acts as though you committed a crime
He tells me, I just don't understand
He's got to go and talk with a man
He asked me to share his life
He could at least give me a chance to be his wife

Judy Kay Howard

THE BOUNDARY OF OUR DREAMS

Let me walk with you
along the boundary of our dreams,
where spirits merge
and hearts unite,
and silence reigns

Remove my mask
and let me stand naked before you,
without my shield
to protect me from myself

Let me see beyond your innocent beauty
and discover the brilliance of your soul,
and let me know the eternity of one moment in your arms

Kenneth L. Meredith

A DAYDREAM

I wonder what is beyond that hill —
The farthest hills that the eye can reach —
Is there a city of beautiful build,
An ancient city on a silver beach?

And is there in that city of old
A stately palace of magnificent mould;
And is there in that palace, for me,
A radiant maiden as I've dreamed there would be?

If the maiden be there, this I know:
To the ancient city I will go,
To dwell forever in her bliss,
To live for her smiles and perchance a kiss

A. Cambron

THE OKANAGAN WEDDING RECEPTION

Fruit trees were bouquets of fragrant bloom,
    Set in rows around the valley. What a sight!
And a chandelier, placed in the astral dome,
    Silvered the high and low benches with light.

They were centered by the lake, a crystalline bowl
    Of spiked punch, from which guests would dip;
Nearby, on a limb, sat an owl. He was droll
    When he toasted the bride, hooting many a quip

About: a groom who forgot to fetch the ring;
    A poor fish, someone hooked, but set free;
Newlyweds who slept naked, not wearing a thing;
    And fallen petals, that were tossed as confetti.

Then a nightjar winnowed before his mate;
    While, shortly after the feast, came a dance;
The revelry lasted until quite late,
    Spirits bubbling over with exuberance.

As night departed, the sun rose in splendor,
    And the crowd dispersed, with greetings tender;
Kith and kin were happy, without exception,
    At the Okanagan's spring wedding reception.

Cedalia Alice Tarasoff

A SOUL DESERTS

Drift with the tide in its merciless flaying,
Join in the chant of the lost souls now praying,
Blend with the shadows that found not the truth,
Weep with the bells that toll for my youth,
Heart of my soul, must you ever condemn me,
Ignoble escape can my memory defend thee,
Infinite wandering is my future now past,
While the din of betrayal in each heartbeat holds fast,
There cast in my vision a coward's damnation,
With death which I feared as my only salvation,
Grant me my past so again I may choose,
Convictions of courage, not cloaked in a ruse.
Eyes of my mind must you see it so clear,
My ideals once flowed from a fountain of fear,
Condemned by the deed that anoints me with shame
On this altar of anguish, mocking honor by name,
Though I've saved you oh life, you have caused me this hurt
What is gained in a breath when the soul it deserts.

Thomas C. Alfsen

SHE WALKED STOOPED OVER

She walked stooped over with help from a cane
Her face full of wrinkles and showing of pain
She shuffled along and carefully stepped
But fell to the ground as she stumbled and tripped

No one would stop to offer a hand
As she tried to get up from the ground and stand
Strangers passed by in the noontime race
They looked the other way and not at her face

We can't stop to help, they would say
Someone else can care for her today
Cars whizzed past as she lay there in pain
She cried out but only in vain

Finally there came a sweet gentle man
His legs were in braces, a cane in each hand
He knelt down to the ground by her side
Then reached out and her tears he dried

He was clumsy as he helped her out
But together they managed without a doubt
Struggling they finally stood to their feet
Then arm in arm they walked down the street

Louise Story Laningham

SOUNDS

Though we take them all for granted,
They're all around us . . . SOUNDS!

From the smallest of GOD'S creatures
To the largest of man's creations;
It's all here to convey an impression
Of everything that is found.

The galleries are like whispering echoes
Of music . . . with lasting visions that
Go 'round, 'round, 'round.

The fishes . . . birds . . . insects . . . all
Have languages of their own, portraying
Different signals and busily creating
Their own mound.

The sound of death resembles a silent
Summons . . . and yet, it is with the
Loudest thunder cast on man like a pound.

Jacquelyn Ponder

LOVE AND HATE

I had a talk with hate,
and he criticized the golden gate.
He said "down in hell with me
there is no need for a key,
the door of hell is open wide
and the wrong can always drop inside."
It can be a pleasure you will learn
that if you can hate, you can burn.
So my dear friend what will it be
the golden gate or to hell with me?

I then had a talk with love,
and she talked about paradise up above.
She said "I have watched you all along,
long enough to know that you are not wrong.
Let the doors of hell be open wide
but God will not let you fall inside.
You can climb the stairs of heaven with me,
let your love and honesty be your key
to unlock the gate and open it wide
so you, God's child can step inside."

Ricky A. Perry

JUST BECAUSE . . .

Was cold and rainy, also I was lonely.
    The flowers were dying in the vase, also dying was the fire.
The street was dark and desert
    only was alert my mind and my pen.

I started to sing, but I feel my tears falling instead
    only because was Sunday, without no one to talk,
laugh, kiss or even cry.

The happy planned wonder life, because of the sad Sunday
    started to disappear, and suddenly I find out
that what had left, was unhappy and unfulfilled dreams!

Today is Monday, beautiful sunshine day!
    The streets are bubbling and no one seems to remember . . .
That yesterday was Sunday, a dark and rainy day.

I replaced the death flowers, I sing and sing.
    the fire self-started, the telephones ring.
With my mind and my pen I finished my poem!

Ester T. Mirshamsi

182

A CEASELESS BATTLE

A neverending confrontation between good, and evil.
These elements were structured in nature during early development.
Weapons used to help the cause, are one of the problems.
For every situation, man seeks an answer,
whens, wheres, whys and hows are commonplace in higher forms
of life.
For every positive there's a negative reaction, and to every question
there's an answer, no matter how complex the reply is.
I have never ceased in the use of my ability, there's built in my being
the urge to push ahead.
A force urging me onward, a given impulse to overcome,
a profound drive propels my mind to go forward.
Driving, propelling, impelling, compelling, urging, pushing, and
forcing.

Sauls Demento Suzzs, Suezs

THE BEACH

The eyes see, but the mind absorbs as only a mind can
the rushing waves over the crescent sand
the aura of energy that it invigorates
as it rushes wildly to shore only to dissipate

Her majestic waves flicker and dance with a roar
seeking expressions of freedom, asking nothing more
breathtaking visions stretched out for miles
in the wonder of nature's infinite guile

The eyes see, but the mind absorbs the rhythm of the rhyme
the tide's ebb and flow, ineffable sublime
her spirit so wild and free, yet in harmony with man
the eyes see, but the mind absorbs the splendor as only the mind can

John H. Jones, Jr.

HUMAN

I am human.
I wander through the forests of my mind seeking clearings.
I must be free.
I reach out to touch the horizon of my dreams.
I must be me.
I cut through the thickets, thistles, and thorns of my imagination.
Creation belongs to me.
I linger on the banks of my fears.
The tide ebbs abducting my tears.
I stand in the valleys of other men scanning where their land
    ends and mine begins.
I linger alone and restless in my self-constructed world,
    my ego trembling in my hand.
I am only human.

Joyce Whiteside

PRAISE, YAHWEH!

I have been searching my whole life knowing that things were wrong.
And now that I've found You, Yahweh, maybe it's taken too long.
The knowledge I've gained has ended my search, but You are on Your way.
The gods are dead, You are not coming, You could be here today!

You know everything about me, from You I cannot hide a thing.
I only hope I am good enough, and goodness to You I can bring.
I would give anything, even our lives, if I could know I was going to You,
And if I am not, I trust You, Yahweh, to give me the judgment that's due.

I have known God and Jesus. I've even fought Satan, but I've not known You for long.
And now that I do it worries me some but I lift my voice up in song;
For now that I know that Yahweh is true it has taken all worries away.
Except for the one that makes me think I'll not sit with You someday.

Ruby Anne Walker Rider

THE GRAND OLD PARENT

To His Mother on her Birthday:
February 12, 1896

There is always a grand old
parent; what would you say,
but remember, she's never far
away. She always lends a helping
hand, and tries to do the things
she can.
Through God almighty; for
which she stands, she will always
hold your hand.
Pay homage to her, for she
also seeks; love and affection,
among the Meek.

Charles Lee Terrell

THUNDER MOUNTAIN

The crash of thunder broke
the stillness of a cloudless sky.
A beaver stops the hewing
clatter of an aspen bow.
The bluejay quickly ends
his tattle-tale chatter.
And juncos scatter from
the seedy knoll.
The crag high on the mountain
lost its hold and fell.
The broken pieces tumbling down
the bosom of the lofty peak.
As suddenly they stopped,
to snuggle, and to sleep and wait.
For centuries to pass again.

Cedric Bourboulis

FOREVER AN IMPRESSION

Dedicated to that someone

During the course of our life
we encounter a person that leaves
an impression that will last forever.

    . . . the way they walk,
    . . . the way they talk,
    . . . their laugh,
    . . . their smile,
    . . . even the texture of
        their hair.

In some way, large or small, they
alter the path of our life.

Cheryl L. Winn

THE CHILDREN OF THE FUTURE

Children should believe they can achieve
the very best.
Many children are missing; we wonder
if their souls are at rest.
It is a pleasure to treasure the
picture of the beautiful smile of a
child.
Unfortunately, the smile is there for
only a while.
The children today are being neglected
instead of being protected.
The children today are being used and
abused.
Children, there is still time for you
all to learn of peace, unity, and love.

Melvin Larry Anderson, Jr.

WHAT HAPPENED

There once was green grass growing
Now there's not a patch of green
The air is filled with dirt and germs
And the waters far from clean.

The people who have lived here
Are gone now from this land
What happened, what happened?
To this world that God had planned.

Lori D. Greusel

JUST SUPPOSE

Just suppose

There are no colors fleeter than the eye,
Sounds no ear will transcribe,
Paths the mind cannot follow.

Just suppose

Things seen are but
A symphony of the unseen,
And the nucleus of man's logic
Is most empty space.

Just suppose

A rock, a tree, a bird,
A man are common elements
In the same prime equation.

Just suppose

The universe is upheld
By a single word.

Just suppose

God.

David D. Richard

Precious Jesus, take me home,
    To be with you, is all I ask.

Precious Jesus, take me home,
    For I've completed my earthly task.

Thank you for my loving children,
    For the care they've given me.

Keep them in your tender hands,
    So that I can come home to thee.

Precious Jesus, I give you thanks,
    For your blessings here on earth.

Precious Jesus, forgive my sins,
    Especially those that gave you hurt.

Thank you for your loving heart,
    And all the blessings you did send.

I've lived a long and happy life,
    The work you gave me I did tend.

Precious Jesus, take me home,
    To be with you, is all I ask.

Precious Jesus, take me home,
    I want to start my heavenly task.

Peter A. Gregorio

A POET

Gentle, intimate, distant
And yet a powerful link
Between humanity and
Abstract eternity.
Exists in a special realm
Untouched by passing tides
But perceives constantly
Essences from another
Dimension and translates
These delicate perceptions
in meaningful verses.
Feels an anguished urge
of expression, a vibration
in the cosmos but does not
ignore the loving scrutiny
of Mother Earth to which
Responds emphatically
As a true child of her womb,
And conveys a special message
Echoing all forces of the universe!

Adriana M. Gibbs, D.M.L.

PREJUDICE

She was his lady his first lady and
he was her knight the black knight who
wore no armor.
He was her friend, her lover he was
all things to her. He was sometimes the
target for all the hurt and hate she
held in her heart for the world the
world that had done her so wrong.
He was her teacher of life for one
year he taught her well.
He was the black knight the black
knight who wore no armor.
One night the passion she felt was
more than she could bear she
conceived his child the black knight's
child who wore no armor. — But the
child was never to be because he was
the black knight who wore no armor
and she was the fair lady who
always wore her armor except once.

Barbara Spears Johnson

COLLEGE BOUND

I will be sad when you go
Even though my heart beats faster
When I think of your fertile mind
Nurturing and replenishing
The seeds cast upon it.

It is what I wished for after all
To see my bright young son
Ferreting out each grain of truth
From all that's false
Probing the fields of knowledge
'Til the rarest flower blooms
Beneath the rubble.

It will be lonely then
In the dark reaches of the night
And I will miss your brooding presence
Absorbing and distilling
The moods around you
Sifting emotions and discarding the chaff.

Kathryn Cahill

THE ROSE IS AN EARTH-BORN ANGEL

Each petal grows as the one before,
a friend of fragrance,
of beauty in form.
Wooed to life by bright sun
and warm spring shower,
her regal crown's craft in
rainbow hue.

Enthroned on a pedestal of
brocade thorn,
heralding glory of celestial
joy,
the rose is an angel,
an angel earth-born.

Rhya Noel Cawley

THE EGO-SELF

I am a professional rememberer.
I will tell you how things were.
The griefs, the angers,
And the pale and faded joys,
I hold them all.

I am a professional dreamer.
I will tell you how things ought to be,
Should be, will be,
Maybe.

But I will never,
Ever,
Tell you how things are.

Patricia Aubrey

MELANCHOLIA

Within my darkened chamber,
Each door I dare to feel,
Each knurl and nook existing,
Profess a present seal,

In all my supplication,
Disposing thoughts prevail,
And deem within an orbit,
A soft and silent wail,

Oh empty darkened chamber,
This pawn you have surpressed,
Make short the stay, expose a way,
Relieve these thoughts oppressed.

Jean A. Selman

WHAT IS LOVE

What is love?
Is it a word or a feeling?
I think it is a feeling,
For I feel it when I am with you.
but then I am confused.
For what is love?
Is it real or imaginary?
I think it is real.
For it feels real when I am with you,
But then again I am confused.
For what is love?
It must be something only two people
Can share in their hearts,
For I find no words for love.

Carolyn Mares

184

THE LOVING WAY

I sense her graciousness pervade the room
Her very presence is a sacred thing
In a haloed headdress like a lily bloom
She ministers to patients. Comforting
Each hapless body palled with fear and dread
And dark foreboding. Pensive she comes whose touch
Is gentle, cool and deft; from bed to bed
She silent treads, detached, yet loving much.

Her grave, alert concern is haunting me
Her gentle touch is healing in itself
And pondering it I find security
Against barbed pain and all earth's sordid pelf.
    For more like her the world's well lost today —
    They only serve who heal the loving way.

    S.C. Kavanagh

SAINT VALENTINE'S DAY

Valentine's Day is perfected, purely for love.
It's a time to express unrequited, sanguine hopes;
Fun day, soft, sweet, silky smooth as a dove;
Love day that gently guides all of life's many ropes.

Combined
    With . . .

That brown-eyed, athletic, solid, perfect man;
The unity of Apollo and Mars in Statute and profile;
Thinker and doer, so good, so tall and so tan;
An intelligent human, biologist by trade;
This is Man from whom women's dreams are made.

Combined
    On . . .

February Fourteenth — the moment, that flood
Of love incarnate for lovers, hovers
To still the terrified heart — Marked red in blood!

Joined
    Together . . .

The perfect man and the perfect day,
Combined in gruesome suicide,
Sets a sorely sad and silent marker along the way.

    M. Regina Auzins

AUZINS, M. REGINA. Born: Günzburg, Germany; Married; Education: Michigan State University, B.S. Science, 1972, MA Education, 1980; Hillsdale College, Management Diploma, 1975; Occupation: Teacher; Poetry: 'Time Love,' American Poetry Association, 1984; Themes: *Love, life, people.*

THE POET'S PROMISE

By sheer force of habit,
editors would rather reject than read.
Still, a rejection slip means, *ipso facto:*
Either your poem is not good enough
or you sent it to the wrong place
or both.
Suppose you say in a song:
"I" am
the hungry "I"
the center of a storm
the hole in a needle
through which the world witnesses
the wonders of my wit —
and the editor says: "bullshit!"
Still, that Muse is on your back,
so write you must
and submit you will.
Writing poems is like laying eggs.
Some hatch and some don't.
So cock-a-doodle-doo,
        Where's the rooster in your mind?

    Emerson Brown

BROWN, EMERSON. Born: Mississippi, 1930; Single; Education: University of Illinois, B.A., 1955; Memberships: Phi Beta Kappa; Poetry: 'Ode to Azania,' *Transfer 46,* San Francisco State University, Fall, 1983; 'Sweet Revenge, Never Again,' *Compages,* Union of Left Writers, Fall, 1984; 'The Grenada Invasion 1983,' *San Fernando Poetry Journal,* Fall, 1984; 'Our Free Press,' *San Fernando Poetry Journal,* Fall, 1984; 'The Last Negro,' *San Fernando Poetry Journal,* Summer, 1985; Comments: *I try to express the uniqueness and reality of my perceptions in order to placate my Muse. Poems that sing and rhyme, and say something at the same time.*

AFTERNOON DREAM

Elegant tabernacle where sinewy hemlock breeds
Racing stream, a mindless thought run flowing, forever free.
Stop the race, slowing pace, forgetting what I am
Star-spangled face, diamond babe, an empty space.

High upon a mountaintop, rise to praise the sky
See the valley hazing, blazing golden sun
Watch a marble river in spring arcade
Make its daily thoughtless run.

    Wayne A. Rhome

GIFTS

The eyes are the keys to
One's soul.

The mouth is the door to
One's heart.

The ears can hear the
Truth of the Good Word.

The hands can comfort and
Heal the tormented.

The feet can follow the
Path of the light.

The examples of actions are
The true visions of one's soul.

Ivano Vit

VIT, IVANO PAOLO. Born: Sesto Al Reghena Udine, Italy; Poetry: 'The Roads of Life,' 'A Friend,' 'America, My Country,' 'Blessings,' 'True Love.'

ANSWER TO ERNEST DOWSON

*Inspired by Ernest Dowson's poem,
'Non Sum Qualis Eram Bonae Regno
Cynarae'*

I am Cynara,
    who lives in your past.
    I count the embraces
    and touch you so lightly —
    you quake from my traces.

I am Cynara.
    Though I silently watch,
    I watch nonetheless
    for the nonce to invade
    your mislaid caress.

I am Cynara,
    the quiet rebel
    refusing neglect;
    taunt with a whisper,
    cling like a limpet.

I am Cynara,
    hovering, a spectre,
    who beckons for wine.
    I make my presence known —
    the night becomes mine.

Guada Woodring-Lueck

WINTER'S APPROACH

Swaying trees
in the breeze.

Animals scurry
in a hurry.

Gathering food
winter's mood.

Winter is coming
the birds are humming.

Amongst the peaks
the eagle shrieks.

The sounding call
for the end of fall.

Winter's hand
will grip the land.

Still as night
in snowy white.

Julien Rapp

THE MASQUERADE

Painting my face
    I see
A mask a lace —
    I be

If you could feel
    The pain
I just can't deal —
    The rain

The public knows
    Nothing
They see the bows —
    Smiling

"You're a star,"
    They say.
My face, no mar —
    Decay

But the charade
    I played.
The life I made —
    Who paid?

Lillie Kim

LOVE

Love, the strongest word ever heard
As strong as the wind
Still as weak as the bird.

It's as deep as the ocean
As high as the sky
Yet no one can touch it
Not you nor not I.

Love, the most desirous thing to behold!
Coveted both, by the weak and the bold
First can be warm and then can be cold.

It's the most mystic word
Since the world began
When God first gave
His words to man.

Nettie Rae Witherspoon

TWO FACES OF A TEAR

A tear is a quiet way
to help you say
the things you feel
when words are not there,
and you want to show
how much you care.

A tear is but a drop of pain,
the calm before the storm.
The blood of an open wound
not yet healed,
and still too soon.

A tear for cheer.
A tear for pain.
One a loss,
and one a gain.
Two faces of a tear
are feelings far apart,
but the path they take,
runs ever near,
and always through the heart.

K. L. Funston

WHAT IS LOVE

What is love?
Is it walking on the beach hand
in hand?
Is it watching the shore sweep
up the sand?
Is it looking at stars and
seeing his eyes?
Is it looking at the moon and
hearing his cries?
Is it thinking of him when he's
not at your side?
Is it wanting to be his only bride?
Is it being alone after he's
gone?
Is it thinking that you did
something wrong?
Is it the hurt you feel when
you call out his name?
Is it that you are to blame?
What is love?
Can you give it a name?
Or is hurting and loving one
and the same?

Carol Davis

LOVE HAS THREE FACES

    anticipation
If I were in love, I'd be
So high up in the clouds,
That I'd be wearing shrouds
Of snow-white filmy clouds,
E'en though I walked upon
This lowly earth.

    fulfillment
I am in love! And I can sing
Higher than any bird can trill,
In the treetops on the hill.
Because of happiness
My heart sings.

    reality
I've lost my love. And I
No longer tread those feather paths
On high; nor blend my notes
With the orchestra of birds.
My heart doth cry, and then
Be still. Oh! Why?

Alta Mae Bowman

A SPECIAL MOMENT

There is a certain time in every day
That the sun will always shine.
To lead and guide me on my way,
Giving me what is mine.

This new world came my way
And brought upon me contentment.
Before it left me it began to say:
Leave behind your hate, despair and resentment.

It left me with that feeling fine
Of all that brings me peace.
I simply leave you with this line that,
Memories never cease!

Darrin G. Kramer

THEN CAME DIEPPE

A sagging, haunting emptiness stands
as monument to carefree summer days
amid fields and flowers and country ways,
gaping, jagged-eyed, forlorn both house and lands.

Empty the rocker where my mother sat and read
my father's censored letters after chores,
praying for an end to all the wars
and his safe return, living in constant dread.

Unknown to us the fear as we swung high;
for Jack and me war was but a glamorous, glorious game
we played, chasing across the lawn, as we became
mock heroes. Then came Dieppe and taught us how to cry.

Kathleen Konkin van Es

EMERGING SEASONS

A tree emerging from a long, long, sleep
To sprout its blooms, and greet the new found day;
To spread its roots into the earth so deep
Through mud, and rock, and sand, and dark red clay.
Upon a branch, stripped bare by winter's cold,
A bird did sing into the morning air.
With hard times gone, his beak held high and bold,
He spread his wings with a dominant flare.
The days grow long, as sunshine fills the air;
The multicolored blossoms soon unfold.
Their sweet fragrance is smelled everywhere.
The memory fades when nights were dark and cold
Two young people, their hands in love entwined,
A lover's stroll from spring to summertime.

Julia Stiegelmar

MY LIFE

My life is a tapestry of deep blue velvet
With multicolored threads woven in,
Embroidered flowers of many colors
And light blue fringe for the trim.

My life is a meadow springing with violets,
Forget-me-nots, carnations, and rose.
Like a green carpet, it goes on forever;
And in the midst of it, a river flows.

My life is a song of love unreturned.
And a longing for a home not yet found.
A ship on the ocean seeking its harbor
But having no guide, I myself am bound!

Sharon Lynn Embry

YOU ARE MY FRIEND

Remember when we met?
    Were you as unsure of me as I was of you?
I was always worrying whether I said or did the right things,
    And you always seemed so perfect.
We became friends.
Remember when we got to know each other better?
    We both began to slip,
    And I found out that you weren't so perfect after all.
I guess we began testing the waters.
    SOMETIMES it was too hot and sometimes too cold.
But we worked things out anyway and became closer than ever.
Somewhere during that time we fell in love,
    We accepted each other for good and for not so good.
It seemed that our silly mistakes didn't matter anymore,
    I found you and you found me.
As time goes by we become even stronger,
    Challenging each day as it comes, together.
You are always there for me,
    And I'll always be there for you.
You are my friend . . .

Carmen C. Raddatz

BEFORE YOU GO

Before you go, I want to talk to you once more,
So let me sit with you and hold your hand
And tell you how much you really mean to me,
Just to know you, as I do, and be your friend.

Lovers come — stay awhile and then hurry on
Like quicksilver passing through your fingers.
But memories of love quietly burn within me
Like the last flickering candle flame that lingers.

So, before you go, I must empty my heart
And tell you that I'll miss you most of all
When the day is done and I sit here all alone
In the fading light and watch the shadows lengthen on
                              the wall.

I guess I'm trying to say, please stay, I really love you.
I always have, even though I couldn't tell you so
But now the lock is broken and I can say what's in my heart
You are my life, my love, my all, before you go.

Al Hanes

WOULDN'T YOU?

You did love me, didn't you?
Love me again please, couldn't you?

You touched a part of me no one has before.
Will I ever find another love like ours evermore?

It is difficult living my life this way.
Struggling without you, day after day.

If I knew you would try loving me again,
Then this uncertain condition, I wouldn't be in.

You have touched that part of me no one ever had before.
I will never find another love like yours and mine,
                    Should I love until the end of time,
                              or forevermore.

You did love me, didn't you?
Love me again please, "Wouldn't you?"

Terry Mathews

MIRROR MIRROR

Mirror mirror on the wall
At the far end of the hall
Can you find not one connection
Why I'm just a mere reflection
Of the person that I see
So very far away from me?

Mirror Mirror on the wall
Am I short or am I tall
Am I fat or am I thin
Whom do I see there within
I must know for this I plea
Is that image really me?

Mirror Mirror on the wall
Listen to me, hear my call
One more question I ask of you
Then I'll fondly bid adieu
Tell me please for I must know
Is this person friend or foe?

Judy Tuttle

LEAVES

Autumn
        Leaves
Once rustling
Now russeting
Plucked by a gusty breeze
Swirl
      Spin
          Flutter down
A tumbling flurry of brown
Mingling
With earth's mysterious rhythming
To disappear
Into the atmosphere
And reappear
Year after year
A bud on another limb
A moth's wing
Or, part of some other thing
Come
     Spring

Jacqueline Shiver

VOICE INSIDE

Filled with dreams, my thoughts awaken
and gently whisper back to me,
keep on going, always flowing,
fill my heart, color my soul,
bright as bending rainbows
illuminating the sky.
Fly into the night,
glisten and glide,
land upon a star.
Say it with your eyes
stay by me, fly with me.
Pounding heartbeat echoes with pride;
true friendship never dies.
Climb the clouds wondering.
running like thunder.
"I'll see you in everyone
who will be free,
and I won't be alone,"
they whisper back to me,
fly with me, with me.

Kate Traylor

TO MY PARENTS — SHIRLEY AND DAVE BROWNE

I am a lucky person to have parents so dear,
Whose love lingers on and grows more precious every year.
I remember when I was little, they would look at me and smile,
And buy me the things I needed to keep up with the style.

My mother baked the best cookies and made me soup when I was sick,
She used to let me frost the cake and gave me the spoon to lick.
My father used to play baseball with me from morning 'til night,
He taught me to be competitive and not to give up without a fight.

Every day I had to do my homework, it was never any fun,
But they made me sit there for hours until I got it done.
I couldn't understand why I studied while other kids went out to play,
But now I see the reason — I get a good week's pay.

Now I am much older and a lot wiser too,
Because of both my parents, my problems are few.
I'm a strong person now and I have confidence in what I do,
I resented it when I was younger, but if only I knew . . .

They have been good parents to me and have always helped me out
I feel they're the best parents around without any doubt.
    Nancy C. Caton

IN THE ROOM

Going through life like a twilight zone — hoping for a solar flight — in order to regain my
Total sight — by night — in the room — something did form — I think it was love that was born — but,
My heart was once torn — we both saw the light — that name our sunflower bloom — some people
Say it was around noon — But, many were fooled — looking through the interlude and seeing the
Real you — within the mirror of a total reflection — I bet you — it was your love that I capture —
But, your soul was in total rapture — within the final chapter — (of love) was it out of laughter
Only, we knew what happened — which was a main factor — then and after — at first — I thought, you
Were my precious nurse — but, your love for me wasn't a curse — in the room — your lovely voice —
(which wasn't my choice) was out of tune — but, it was the grace of God that set — the pace —
Which was base — upon a sure love case — which eventually, I had to face, now, I know.
Clear as the cold driven snow — real love can't ever be erased — your precious love only
Could have been granted from the heavenly stars above — "Rosebud" — please don't hold a grudge —
Because, I realize — by gazing up towards the heavenly skies of blue and seeing the first
Cry from you — from your teardrop stains — I could be the blame — from your precious
Eyes — So, I'll never defile — you are a sweet child — that's why, I'll always be by your side
Your love finally came into clear focus — It was real love that I heard without you saying
A mumbling word. With these notions — of true devotion — you are a true songbird — that nearly
Disturb the ocean — similar to poetry in motion — This reaction could have made our love join —
As one — because, after it all, love did call — me in the room — that left me in a total gloom — Maybe
Love came too soon — with the monsoon — So, I'll remain in the room and let Cupid really take an aim — until
The month of June — Then, I'll finally become your bridegroom — and on our honeymoon — love
Really and truly bloom — in the room —
    Larry Wright

SUBWAY PSYCHIC

Let me see your palm
Splattered with lines that criss and cross over the F, E, and G lines.
Your musical ability is running past the track
symbols of cymbals crack and smash the metal plated path

Let me tell you man, you're gonna have a long life
with a couple of children and one or two girlfriends,
Hey kootchie koo, want to buy my sisters —
over there in the orange ghanja dress,
she has it written on her palm she loves you too.

Read the calligraphy on your hand
You're a drunken driver on the line of Times Square.
Sounds like steering intellect is for the birds
breadcrumbs and pavement make way for his neon brain
tipped up and ready to wish all over again.

Goo goo eyeballs falling out of your head
I think you need glasses or don't you understand,
it says it in the stars and it's written on the walls,
time for you to get off hop onto another car.
    Elise Krentzel

THE COST

The day is bleak, a piercing scream,
not loud but inside out.

The room is green,
the table glares.
Such shine — SO CLEAN! SO CLEAN!

"Now count from 10 and we'll begin."
The needle prick is sharp.

And misery, with child, desists.
They both fall into dark.

A piercing scream, it's outside now,
and hate and pain and loss.

The child is gone, unreachable.
Free will extracts its cost.

T. C. Collins

THE STAR

I saw a star the other morn
Shining faintly in the sky,
As the sun's radiant gown was adorned
So the Earth could pass it by.

I looked upon that minute star
And it was revealed to me,
God places wonders in His universe
For all who would look to see.

The sun shone in all its brightness
While the star was but a glow,
Both were created by one God
So that each mortal man could know —

Whether he be a shining light or
One of the faintly glowing stars,
God's tender care has placed him here
In this great world of ours.

Jack L. Whenry

THE VISIT

She flinches
        as doors lock behind her
Careful not
        to see barred windows
Stiff smile
        plastered on her tired face
But eyes light
        at the sight of him.

One brief
        bittersweet hour to share
Souls fighting
        to keep hope alive
Before she
        must go again
He watching
        in guilt-ridden silence
That she, too,
        need serve his sentence.

Charlotte M. Edwards

PATHS

A path is
A tiny road
Made by feet
From point
To point.

Cows wend
Their way from
Pasture to barn
On a path.

Students make a path
On the shortest distance.
Soon there is
A concrete sidewalk there.

People follow
Paths.
Their lives take
Certain directions.
Not always planned,
Not always successful.

Maude Nold

KNITTING

Knitting along with the music
Making a gift that seems worthwhile
Working my fingers like magic
Trying to keep up with the style
Knitting a hat for a present
A scarf is a necessity too
A handbag will look really pleasant
As for gifts it will hold quite a few
I'll make a shawl for cold weather
I'll make a rug for good measure
I can sit by the fireside and smile
Knit curtains can look really pretty
Letting the sun filter through
A bedspread is really important
To be sure I will knit only a few
At bedtime my fingers are weary
I hold everything up in full view
All gifts are ready for wrapping
And knitting has made me sleepy too
I hope everyone will be happy
There is nothing more I can do
Another year is rapidly ending
Next year will be bright and new.

Eva Cook

I am a writer.
I write at night,
While others sleep.
I write their dreams,
As I listen to the
Sounds of their souls.

I am a writer.
I write alone,
While others love.
I write their tears,
As I mend the heart-
Break of their world.

I am a writer.
I write to live,
While others play.
I write their joy,
As I see my life
Pass through their eyes.

I am a writer.

Lillian Masch

MY KIDS

Until I surrender this life of splendor
        And give this body to the dust,
I will strive while still alive to give
        My kids my love and trust.

I have a measure of life's treasure
        In my kids so full of gust,
For when I'm down and with a frown
        They give me courage to readjust.

And when it's done and death has won
        My efforts will not rust,
For in God's hands my kids will stand
        In Him my kids, I intrust.

Larry Knight

MORNING

Early morning,
Sun just rising.
Life is still,
And just waking.
Birds are singing,
The tide is going out.
Sanddollars, seashells,
And memories.
Being washed away,
Leaving only the imprint
In the sand.
Memories of you,
Vague and distant
In the winds of time.

Charlene Key Riden

BROKEN WING

Soothing breezes, fragrant air
Mountain's stone, the eagle's lair
Shadow darts over frightened hares
Thanking Her of the flesh he tears.

Hanging brilliance in eastern high
Yesterday's moon opens wide
To Her of All he now flies
And presents, the starry sky.

Now mountains thin, trees collide
Oceans pale, land passes dry
Sling-shot stone, whistles by
She falls dead, the eagle dies.

John Stag

YOU'VE GIVEN ME

You've given me something that
no one else could give,
you gave me understanding
and a will to live.

You gave me hope
and much much more,
You came inside me
and opened the door.

You gave me love
and you gave it free.
Understanding is the lock;
but love is the key.

Robert Prather

GROWING WITH LIFE

You came that I might learn and grow,
You came that I might have to know
That life has hardships, ups and downs —
That life is learning as we go.

You found a way into my heart,
You found a way to make me start
To know that life is oh so grand
And that we all must play a part.

In living from each new day to day
We all must learn to find a way
To make every moment very special,
For, in life we are put here to stay.

Cheri Bodner

A child sits
awaiting his punishment,
knowing he's done wrong.
Tears fill his eyes.
His nose runs a little.
And he looks up,
expecting to find anger.
Instead,
the face is smiling,
a kind, understanding smile.
Forgiveness,
because she understands,
he did not mean to.
And it can be replaced,
but, this child,
cannot.

Donna M. Harriman

THE DISTANCE

Fresh out of dreams I waken
spread flat as a flounder
across our bed.
One eye open, I search the dark.
Your soundings echo
down the hall.
Deep in camouflage
blankets surround me like weeds.
I find comfort in the quiet smash
of silt and sand
the rubble of upturned rock.
Soon I'll surface to measure again
the distance in the waters
that helped birth us.

Carolyn Light Bell

SPRING

With the robin
Comes the spring.
Bringing from within
Many, many things:
Daffodils and Meadowlarks,
Lilacs and shady parks,
Grass and showers,
And all kinds of flowers.
Gone are the scarves,
And gone are the mittens.
Enter the puppies
And enter the kittens,
And enter the young folks
Enter in love.

Kay D. Kettle

TO LOVE MY HUSBAND

To love my husband, what must I do
Agree with everything he says to do?
Or, be his friend, to no end, to find the kind of man inside
That's the one I'll be the bride to,
For hidden deep within his heart
Are many things, with which he cannot part.
Desires are wild and free at times, unable to share, push them aside
Am I to judge, push away, or condemn?
Or accept this soul, till it can confide
In me all things, with none to hide?
Oh yes, my love, for then we'll find
The kind of love that is so blind
To overlook the faults we find, to cherish the soul for what?
The ability to be honest, at times could cost him all
But accept his truth, without harshness,
With understanding, love, care, tenderness.
Look to the sky. God's helping hand
Will guide me through this world so cold
Ruled by the devil, and his fold
To love my husband, as he is, will return that love to me, threefold!

Marilyn Ruth Barnette

OUT OF STEP

Did you think you knew me? You know nothing of me.
Nothing of my passions, of my loves, of what frightens me.
What makes me fall, retreat, and burst forth again with joy
over nothing.
What lives I have lived. What lives yet to come.
That the sun makes me gloomy, that the clouds, the spring breeze,
are my cover, my connection.
How my soul can pace the floor of the ocean while my heart
trips its waters. And how sometimes — on a clear night —
I think I see the Flag on the Moon.
I do not believe that you love me, for I know what you do not,
that you have no understanding of the word . . . nor know how much
I wish that you had loved me
        a little bit
or raised your voice in anger at me
        just once
or comforted me
        for awhile
or made me laugh   .
        one Sunday afternoon.

Mary McAllister

THIS LONESOME PLAIN

We ride down into battle, sword and shield in hand.
To repel the godless bastards who dare invade our land.
With banners flying proud, now we make our stand.
Here, on this lonesome plain.

The battle, it went well for us; so many of them fell.
In my mind I hear the priests back home toll the victory bell.
I swing my battle ax and send another foe to hell.
Here, on this lonesome plain.

The heathen turn and flee from us; their retreat, though, a charade.
For behind us come a thousand more, too many for our blade.
An arrow finds me through the fight, and unto death I'm laid.
Here, on this lonesome plain.

It matters not who won that fight, not the ensuing war.
And I don't remember who we were, or what we battled for.
I only know our souls are doomed to roam forevermore.
Here, on this lonesome plain.

Norman V. Veasman, Jr.

THE INTERIM YEARS

One bright dawn, in a world now gone,
Was birthed a man, a pillar of his fathers' land.
So fresh, so bright, his emerald eyes, open and devoid of lies;
His wavy auburn hair, smouldering intense with life in there.

Of him there would be written song,
Through him the word shall carry on;
From him I found boundless joy,
Love was his world, this wondrous boy.

Laughter was a ready tool,
Not used infrequently, but as a rule;
Spontaneously it came from deep inside,
A wholesome godly sound, no one could hide.

From every look and every sound,
I collected the music that gathered 'round;
And locked each and every one away inside of me,
To abide me as memories, till sapling turns to tree.

Through life I could not hold the things I wanted,
Though grip and grasp, I've come away daunted;
And though, even now, I cannot hold the things I need,
My hope, my life's still bright and burning in my seed.

Laurence L. Furlong

FURLONG, LAURENCE L. Pen Name: Larabee; Born: Redding, California, 6-14-50; Occupation; Horticulturist; Comments: *Through a poem the screaming voice of my inner sanctum hoarsely cries a liberation of my soul; in sharing my melody I bare not only my own soul, I touch the naked souls of others in my passing.*

ROCKING HORSE DREAM

Mount your rocking horse, and let's go away.
Imagine another time, another land, another day.
Pretend that it is perfect, no rules to obey.
We can do as we please, everyone will listen to what we say.

So get on that rocking horse,
And let's get out of this cruel place.
We will find a better world,
Where everything is perfect and beautiful,
And the land is made of satin and lace.
Where it is touched with love,
And of our own, we may get a better taste.
We won't have to face reality, we can go slow,
And work at our own pace.

But stop! Remember that it is just for pretend.
Because the only reason a rocking horse
Goes forward, is just to come back again.

Paula Bookout

SEEKING HAPPINESS

You seek a sight,
You thought you'd never see.
Happiness is a part of you,
and a part of me.
Let's be joyful,
though you have never been before.
Let's seek happiness, then shut the door.

Start a new life better than before.
Be proud of what you do,
And what you are.
Be happy like you always were.

Seek happiness so you can be true,
Seek happiness so you won't be blue,
Seek happiness, day by day.
You can even seek happiness for me,
and for you.

Come on with me,
be happy and true,
And I'll seek happiness for you.

Leanne Butterfield

ODE

Little girl,
    I never knew you.

I never knew you;
        If you would have had long, flowing hair,
            Frolicked in the summer sun,
            Become a superstar, loved by many,
            Become rich and wealthy, wearing fine clothing,
        Or if you would have gotten married,
            Settling for becoming a mother and housewife.

Little girl,
    I never knew you.

I never knew you;
        But I'm sure you would have been a good person,
            Your daddy's pride and joy,
            Confiding in and looking up to your mother.

Little girl,
    It is true I never knew you,
    And of that I am truly sorry.

Gena L. DelSavio

BILL

I have a special friend, you know,
    such a kind and gentle man.
With his ever-caring ways,
    he helps when, and if, he can.
His Maniac accent, I love very much,
    and the pipe in his mouth adds a great touch.
Most of the time, he keeps to himself,
    but when he speaks, he gives me great wealth.
I look at him, and I see
    just how much he means to me.

"I'd like to draw," he says,
    "I just don't have the talent."
But when he puts words on paper,
    I happen to think he's brilliant.
His poems certainly are a treasure,
    one's about me, and I'll love it forever.
So this one's yours, Bill,
    and I just would like to say,
That my love for you keeps growing,
    with every passing day.

Marie Louise Fournier

LOST FIRST LOVE

Where are You? I have looked everywhere!

Are you still in my midst? Or have You vanished from me forever?

Quick! Answer my call, for the loneliness that dwells within has no
place to go.

What has ever happened to us?

I can remember the fullness of love You brought to me;
The warmth of the sun rays You gave to me;
Your loving ways in which You could love beyond the unlovable.

Oh! How I long for You once more.

The words of tenderness which would only encourage any
who would listen;
My, Your sweet aroma that would fill the entire sky above.

Is it me? Are You right before me? Or have I lost You?

Call my name and I will answer; Tell me to come and I will come.

Let me see Your face once more.

I can remember how You made every bad thing seem good.
And the brightness of Your eyes which could see beyond
my own imagination.

Have I missed You? Is there no goodness amongst me?

Since I walked away unknown to me, I lost it all.

Bring back my first love for You and my life will be worth living
once again!

Judy Fasulo-Smith

TO LIVE BY NIGHT

Did you ever tire of daily routine, and seeing the same old faces?
Going to bed, just to rise again, to go to the same old places?

Did you ever dread "tomorrows" and be tempted to stay in bed?
Have you ever wondered what it might be like, to Live By Night instead?

If I could just reverse the time, and turn it the other way,
The things I'd do, if I could live, by night, instead of day.

When the light of day had faded, I'd come to rule the land.
And everything that's done by night, would be by my command.

I'd ride the Little Dipper. I'd shoot each shooting star.
The cats would see because of me, through nights as black as tar.

I'd start the crickets singing. I'd fill each sandman's kit.
Fireflies would fill the skies, with lamps that I had lit.

I'd lead the bats to havens, where they could hide from day.
Before sunrise, I'd pasturize, the famous Milky Way.

I'd sit and talk to the "man in the moon." He'd smile because of me.
I'd open the eyes of the stars in the skies, so everyone could see.

If moonbeams ever lost their way, I'd send them back again,
And I would know where daylight goes, when it's left the land of men.

I'd have a friend in every star, and every satellite,
Oh the things that I could do, if I could Live By Night.

Garryett Fortin

SUMMERS OF PAST

The grass is cool on my skin,
as I lie
on the bank
leaning over
and twirl my small fingers in the water
and watch
as swirls race outward
in rainbow ripples,
and I breathe deeply of maiden air
and lilac bushes
and fresh mown hay.

A dragonfly lands gracefully
on a cattail
and crickets chirp
as a summer breeze whispers my hair
from my face
in my childhood memories.

Linda K. Cope

Two, with the world outside, apart
Blinded to blemish by the heart
Overwhelmed and thrilled
A feeling with which the soul is filled
Enjoying a peace not easily expressed
Standing in time . . . motionless.

Carol Coury Hefner

HEFNER, CAROL COURY. Born: Oklahoma City, Oklahoma, 8-21-61; Married: 8-4-84 to Robert Alexander Hefner, IV; Education: Louisiana State University, graduated 1983; Occupations: Writer, Poet; Memberships: Oklahoma Society of Poets, Pi Sigma Epsilon Professional Business Fraternity, Sigma Omega Chi Honorary Collegiate Poets, Meadows Center for Opportunity Executive Board; Awards: Institute of Children's Literature (student); Comments: *My Poetry is a reflection of me. It is a source of stability for me and a way of recording the events, triumphs and milestones of my life. I adore this particular medium of writing, and the things it has allowed me to discover in myself.*

RAIN?

Here comes the rain,
Or is it tears?
The lightning strikes.
What is it we fear?
The thunder claps,
Did we scream?
The storm is over,
Was it a dream?

Angie Brewster

NIGHTFLIGHT

Sung on by the sirens of my soul,
I followed Minerva's nightflight owl
Between the Pillars of Hercules
Laughing through time's portal,
Fleeing love's cauldron and the fates,
Seeking serenity's secret
In the cold Tibetan lamasery
Where my third eye rests.

Shasta-Dawn Maloney

THE STORM

Waves of fury,
Wrath of God,
Do you see the lighted rod?
Beyond the grave,
Beyond the sky.
No mortal man can hear the cry.
And in the darkness of the night,
The meek are silent with their fright.

Lynn A. Cooper

STOP

Don't forget to fly
          to think
          to wonder why

Take a moment to breathe
     a chance to absorb
     a chance to enjoy
a chance to love, and be.

Susanne

MIDSUMMER'S DAYDREAM

When all the elves and fairykind
Dance whirleyround,
Stepping lightly on grassleaf
And acorn-bud
The tremble there seems a summer
Breeze kissing the blushing sun.

Heather Robertson-Rhodes

Fall's full feeling,
          deep earthy smell:
          another year in decline.
Aspens triumphantly flash a celebration,
     a rich, fruitful display,
          festive not frivolous.
Flourishing a sumptuous swan song,
          nature's cycle
          revolves.
Fire to ember to ash.

S. Ackerman

MY LAST GOODBYE

I was yesterday's child
Laughing, dancing, living life.
I was miles away
But you were close in my heart.
I was like a shooting star,
Unexpected wherever I appeared.

I am gone now
But do not mourn for me.
Instead, live out your dreams
For I'll be watching over you.

When you think of me
Remember the laughter we shared.
And when it rains
Look for the rainbow.
Think of me as a part of it
And I will see you as
The pot of gold at its end.

Angela Wounaris

I AM . . .

I am the keeper of the possible;
Keep me in your sight.
Shadows of deep and silent thought
follow you through the night.

I have the key to the impossible
follow me in the dark.
Through the mournful mist
to the door
that holds my loving mark.

I am your tomorrow.
Your passage to salvation.
I am the king of the unknown;

     I am imagination . . .

Gerald Dean Titchener, Jr.

TITCHENER, GERALD DEAN JR. Pen
Name: Gary; Born: 11-24-64; Single; Comments: *My work deals with the human soul; the unconscious shadowy part of man. I seek out the hidden spectres of dreams and nightmares; the black as well as the white side of the mind. I create a surrealistic world of sights with pitch, sounds with texture; emotions with flavor. A universe of the soul.*

SELF-CONSCIOUS

No contact, eye or hand
Turn away, sit or stand
The goal of touch, precious as gold
In the object's mind
Ripeness to bring the spread of self
To one's first choice, a right
Envied by all others
Wait, for new blossoms
Never to receive

Joseph Scholtz

On some wall
     on a hillside
          in the City of the Sun
Where all wisdom
     lies carved in granite
          forever unciphered
There must be written this —
     The Dream may be the only bread
          by which we exist,
     And yet, the one weapon
          with which reality can sting us.

James H. Delap

A ROSE

A rose,
Blowing gently
In a blue sky
floated through me . . .
Soft red petals
Brushed
Against my eyes,
and turned my blue sky
Into silver.

Terry Chestnutt

PERFECTION

Had you ever to meet
with "perfection,"
and were hoping
for a "perfect"
resurrection?
Then, beware of
faultless souls —
They only live in
ancient scrolls!

Ginette Morin

I'M IN BAD NEED OF A TRASH MOVIE

Oh, miserable antagonist!
Hammering me with subtlety,
Irony and complexity,
Rambling about human existence,
and the questionable joys of art . . .

. . . when what I really need
is a man in a monster suit
wiping out replicas of Tokyo!

Brian Marshall

LOVE HAS LET ME DOWN

Love has let me down
enveloped me in a blanket
of false security
and runaway hopes and dreams.

Love has made a fool of me
let me move unguarded
through the days
in oblivion
trusting, and never fearing.

Love has bound me
in warm robes of wool
before the winter wind
and snatched them from me
like a child at play
leaving me exposed
to the bitter cold.

Amy Nichols

RESTLESS FIRES ARE BURNING

The murderous freedom is staying,
languid, beneath stained evidence
of a dreamer's only solitude.
It's calling. Loud voices
of creeping silence crush
the ears like fear. Fighting
is helpless when freedom
stares, stirring your featherweight
decision. Turn out the answers
to questions freedom is shouting.
Lighten the hairs of the heart,
extinguish the fires of fear,
scratch the eyes of idleness.
Make a move. Watch freedom
strike, then call out, reach out.
Make your own decision.
But it won't stop calling,
it won't stop
calling.

Terry L. Persun

HE BELONGS TO SOMEONE ELSE

You can look, but you can't have.
Touch, but not take hold.
Think your thoughts and dream your dreams,
But never be more bold.
Just Cindy
Cindy Helferstay

VOICES OF LOVE

Listen to the voices of the wind
Voices of angels calling to us
With joy in their hearts.

How glorious it must be
In their eternal land
Of love and of peace.

I long to be near them
To be part of their world
And be able to understand.

I pray to be worthy
To start my journey there
To be guided by faith
By voices of love
And have wisdom
To know the way.

Debbie J. Overton

BABY TALK

It's dark inside here and there's not much room.
I wished I could find my way out, and real soon.
I keep hearing voices, though I can't quite understand what they say.
But they keep repeating the same ole thing, talking 'bout some special day.

Gosh, I feel all cramped up, I sure would like to stretch out.
Oh Lord! There goes that noise again, it sounds like a shout.
I see an opening, and a bright shiny light up ahead.
I feel something pulling me and voices saying, "Spread."

My eyes they hurt, and it's cold out here.
What's that man doing? He's feeling of my rear!
Why did he hit me and make me cry?
I'd go back to safety if I can get away to try.

That woman on the table, I know her from somewhere
Her arms are open. I think she wants me to come there.
She held me close and didn't hurt me like the other.
Her voice was soft and warm as she said,"I'm your mother."

Linda Tambourine

FLIGHT

freedom soars above, on the white-tipped wing of the gull flying overhead.
as it dashes across the sky, it goes neither here nor there for the moment.
like the pendulum of a clock, it makes its course on its own time.
flying out to sea, only to return in a few minutes
        just long enough to know it could go, to stretch its wings.
feeding, to satisfy that natural quest for hunger
only to return to that warm inviting sand and rest its head.
walking to and fro it looks out on all sides, absorbing whatever is
        presently there.
not intrigued with what it sees or perhaps felt intruded upon
        it begins a brisk walk, and then with a swift jump
        it glides flawlessly up into the air,
        spreading its wings . . . and departs.
soaring up, soaring away, with one glance back as if to say
"i spread my wings and i do soar, for freedom is my flight
but free is also he who finds his way, through his own insight.
apparent as it may seem that we shall never meet again,
take heed to what my flight stands for then, my friend . . .
                one's freedom should never end."

Frances Millas

A TRIBUTE TO MOTHER

The arms that used to cuddle me whenever I would cry,
A voice that whispered in my ear each night a lullaby,
Her soothing hand upon my head at night when I would fret,
They all bring back sweet memories of days I'll ne'er forget.

I used to look in wonderment at tears that filled her eyes,
When things were not as they should be she always thought it wise,
To ever keep her courage up no matter what the price,
Until one day her strength had failed — that was her sacrifice.

Her picture hanging on the wall looks down at me tonight,
Just as she did when I was small and knew not wrong from right,
She'd pull me to her and explain if I were never bad,
I'd find reward in Heav'n someday — that there I'd be with Dad.

This person everyone must know who someday must grow weak,
It should not be so difficult to know of whom I speak,
It is not hard to find a word — to me there seems no other,
The letters in it are but few — together they spell MOTHER.

Velma Russo

THE GEYSER.

CIRCUMVOLUTION

Querulous posture
Abusive quip
slip
slip

Broach concentration
Urgency's fake
mistake
mistake

Magnify trivia
Grumble — thunder
blunder
blunder

Demand perfection
Double the work
quirk
quirk

Routine disrupted
Tactics moot
— Does not compute —
— Does not compute —
— Does not compute —

Barbara Osier Hammond

WITH THE LIGHTS ON

Through half-closed eyes
I see your sweet face
flashing up at me.
Sometimes with soft summer sighs . . .
seconds later . . .
hot light in those eyes.
Inspired by my hands,
inquisitive as they are,
to low sounds
from your heart.

Through half-closed doors
we wander toward each other
and somehow come together.
As softly as the day when breaking . . .
seconds later . . .
violent as the earth in quaking.
Touching somewhere, someone
forgot to tell me
I could feel.

Through half my life
I've been in the dark,
but now,

I like the lights on.

Starlyne Smith

LISTEN WORLD

Far away,
Across the sea,
Children are crying
For you and me.

Their cries are pleading
For the world to hear
Of the sickness and death
That is always near.

So listen world,
And save a life
For then they shall live
Without hunger or strife.

Angela Edminster

DREAMER

Rain, on my windowpane
A light's soft glow,
Pillow, at my head
Embers — burning low.

A lover's embrace
A tender, burning kiss,
I close my eyes, thankful
Life had given me this.

Soon the rain will cease
And the light's softened glow,
Will be lost, in the rays of sunlight
At daybreak, no embers glow.

My lover, e'er must leave me
For duty calls today,
In my heart, a prayer trusting
God keep him safe, while away.

Of course, it wasn't reality
But just a bit of a dream,
I pretended it all, for a moment
A fateful attempt, I ween.

Mary Emmaline Meeker

ROCKING HORSE RHYME

Sweet candy kisses and apple pie
wishes
Strawberry memories, of loves so
delicious

Candy cane moments, in peppermint
time
Touching and holding, to a rocking
horse rhyme

Sweet gingerbread smells, that fill
the air
The sugarplum magic, of those who
care

Chocolate chip dreams, last long into
the night
Marshmallow hugs, make the hurts feel
all right

Lemondrop memories, of all the days, that
have passed
A million jellybeans, will make his child-
hood last

Joel L. Ulsh

A POEM OF DESPAIR

Though words not spoken
nor feelings expressed
your feelings for me
I have now guessed

Words were not said
for fear of my hurt
but a love such as yours
I've longed for since birth

Enclose in yourself this
for I leave you a kiss

To cause you no pain
I'll retreat and be still
for I love you now
and always will

Ray A. Jones

THE MUSTANG

The Mustang ran wild
His temperament mild
When man came he went on his way.

He led his mares through thick and thin
He fought all the dust and the wind
He went through the trees
With wild grace and ease.

He was captured one day
And could not get his way
He was broke and was handled
He fought, almost strangled
His freedom was taken away

He broke loose one day
And went again on his way
Not to be captured again

He was once again wild
His temperament mild
He ran wild and free
As always to be
Until the end of his days.

Darlene Cogan

SEARCHING

So many years have passed
Seasons changing right along
But those thoughts, they still persist —
"Where is it that I belong?"

Still searching for that star
That may light up my life
Although a lot has really changed
And I'm a mother and a wife.

But still a part of me keeps fighting
Wanting just to wander on
To find some real adventure
Before these years are gone.

As if to say, "I'm still myself"
That person from before
Who never seemed too satisfied
Wanting so much more.

And so I'll keep on dreaming
Searching, wishing too
Until someday it comes to pass
That I'll be happy too.

Helen Symkowycz

THEY

They are merely self-programmed machines,
Living, or surviving.
Programmed to question all,
To leave nothing for the sake of wonder.

Though when wonders do exist,
They're labeled miracles,
Created by "Him".
"He" whom they shalt not question,
For the answers are evident,
Embodied in the "Scriptures."
Twisted by systematic brains,
To substantiate their beliefs.

Unfrequented thoughts reviewed twice,
Could demolish the magical cornerstone,
Only to realize that "They" created it.

William L. Gordon

MULTITUDES, MULTITUDES, IN THE VALLEY OF DECISION

God does not add faith to an unrepentant heart,
No, He adds fear.

God does not add faith to an unrepentant heart,
No, He adds darkness.

God does not add faith to an unrepentant heart,
No, He adds separation from Him.

God does not add faith to an unrepentant heart,
No, He adds distress.

God does not add faith to an unrepentant heart,
No, He adds death.

God does not add faith to an unrepentant heart,
No, He adds judgment before and after death.

God does not add faith to an unrepentant heart,
No, He adds HELL.

Conclusion: These decisions are all within the
Sovereignty of God.

Estella M. McGhee-Siehoff

RICHES OF THE HEART

Gold and silver, I have none,
Nor diamonds, stocks nor bonds,
Yet riches of the rarest kind
And treasures by the tons!

Golden days and silver nights,
Children's eyes with diamond lights,
A country's home, where love abounds,
I'd never trade for yours in town.

Fields white with snow or green with spring
Every season its beauty brings.
And yesterday, I learned to know
That I was privileged and so,
Thank you God for wealth untold.

The breath of many flowers
Is carried on the wind
While birds from tree tops tall
Their message to me send.

God's graced this land with beauty
He's blessed us everyone.
So let us start with thank you God,
For riches of the heart.

Evelyn Necessary

ALWAYS

She fills my mind like a silent memory
Always there in all my unwed thoughts.
Being tied to her is like being free
Like soldier buddies in all their "caughts."
We penetrate the moods of all our days
Together now, we are true as two can be.
I've known the careless years when lovers stray;
My heart has placed those memories away.
We have a trust that time will not betray
and know our earth free eyes will always see.
She has her encampment within my soul
Where all true love will never flee.
My cup of life will always overflow;
The needs we share I know were meant to be.

Donald G. Finch

THROUGH PURE EYES

I'll never tell and my children don't know,
I hide in them when I'm feeling low.
When I tire of swimming against the tide,
I hold them close and I jump inside.
Closing my eyes, with my energy spent,
I lose myself in their innocence.
Basking in warmth and in soft golden curls,
I drift from the grip of an angry world.
And as love releases frustrations and fears,
I pull them in closer to hide the tears.
Looking at life through the eyes of the pure,
My faith is renewed, my will made secure.
Learning again when my life is a trial,
Nothing can soothe like the love of a child.
But I'm sure my children will never know,
I hide in them when I'm feeling low.

John W. Coburn

COBURN, JOHN WILLIAM. Born: Rexburg, Idaho, 3-21-55; Married: 5-24-74 to Darlene Nell Coburn; Education: University of Hawaii at Manoa, B.Ed. 5-79; Occupations: District Manager, Sav-A-Stop Inc., Freelance Writer; Poetry: 'Jeffery and Olivia,' 2-85; Other writings: "Next Time I'll Raise Chickens," short story, 7-84; Comments: *Loved by a daughter, encouraged by a spouse, inspired by a friend . . . priceless gifts that can never be repaid.*

VANISHED

shadows of grief fill the rooms of this house
with the absence of my child
through the darkness I reach out for his hand
it is unwilling to reach out to me
my child is no longer there

sometimes I see a bulky form before me
sometimes I hear the voice of a stranger
sometimes I feel the terror of confusion

but

I see nothing to fill the empty space
I hear nothing to fill the void
I feel nothing but pain and sadness

there is no substance
my child is gone

will the son-shine through the blackness once more
will I ever see my child again . . . ?

Sabina Angel

I don't believe it was from
Lack of giving
        Or loving
Though from their standpoint
It could have seemed that way

Still
I tried to do what I had to
Day meeting day
To ask no one for anything
They could not give

They drove me away
By not saying
Stay   just be
Nothing more

I was forced to
Heal myself
On deserted streets
That know better than I
The laughter of wind
Nobody sees
        Ron Stefanac

Soft rain
Gentle rain
Mountain-in August-rain.
Earth drinks while
Flower laughs
And summer plays
A symphony
of water drops
on black-topper road.
Evergreen nods a
gracious salute
to life
Bathed anew
like a soul refreshed.
Sweet essence to
store for
memory-keeping as
God's voice murmurs
through stillness
and calm.
Soft rain.
Soft, soft
gentle
summer rain.
        Jayne D. Pettit

POEMS ON CONCRETE

Chalk
      marks on the side-
walk,
        and two young poets ran.
    By habit I'd
have gone
      on by, not stayed to scan
        the scribbled lines between
the curb and lawn,
but drawn
    this time by tide
      of curiosity, I paused,
voyeur, assuming what
        they'd written was obscene.
But it was not.
      What caused
me then to blush, ashamed
      of my impassioned
preconceit? —
      (if not a talent, still untamed,
      for poems fashioned
on concrete).
      H. Wendell Smith

WE ALL HAVE THINGS TO GIVE EACH OTHER
From The Derek Jacobi Collection

No, the world is not pretty or nice
We will not all become brothers in three hours
There will be no world disarmament in twenty minutes
Dictators will not lay down their arms to strewn streets with flowers tomorrow morning —

But ladies and gentlemen, we are human beings
We eat, we breathe, we sleep to wake, pull to survive,
We laugh, cry, feel want, taste grief, experience color, taste, sensation —
Black and white, gay and straight, Christian, Moslem and Jew,

I.R.A. terrorist and Nazi, Millionaire and wino share this universal and unbreakable bond
Whether we appreciate it or not, it is there, so instead of tearing each other apart,
Let's give to each other as each and every one of you gives to me —
In just the course of your existence — the looks on your faces, the sound of your voice completes me —

It's my ambition to be a great poet, ladies and gentlemen — a great poet —

It is my ambition to be one of you — You!

    Dara, The Barefoot Poet

ON DAWNS AS FRIENDSHIP

Dawns awakened — shades . . . pinks, violets, oranges. The ground
illuminated, shining bright with the purity of its intercourse
  with the night.
Dancing, yearning for morning's affections — searching, making
love to the silence of your mind.
Slowed pace, rustling like leaves, wind-swept, fallen
across the fields of the soul . . . stretching, yawning,
    roused by the orchestrated medley of an early dawn.
Rising, waking, slowly, softly, greeting the day with hope, awe.

The dawn — nucleus of friendship . . . priming organism,
  giving of itself with honesty . . . complete, total, encompassing,
  lacking judgment, without claim, yielding its soul, nakedly,
  unremittingly, in absence of hubris
transposition   metamorphosis.
Friendship — expressions of intimacy exemplified, portrayed
  by infinite fractions of realities . . . reflected in dawn's awakening.
  brilliance   purity.
Created of a reciprocity engulfed in by mutual givings released.
  creative . . . magical . . . mystical
    as the dawn.

    Kathy Robinson

OLD MAN

    Old man, old man, why are you living way back in the woods?
Your house made out of bed clothes, you've nothing but can goods?
Why do you bathe in the brooks, and eat out of tin cans?
Haven't you any clothes? Haven't you medicine for your bleeding hands?

    Though I am only five, and a girl at that,
I would be glad to talk with you, I'll even show you my cat.
Those railroad tracks, I'll bet, stay busy at night.
The place where I live is always bright and daylight.

    Old man, old man, your whiskers are so fuzzy and long.
My daddy has whiskers, but my daddy is gone.
Are you all alone and by yourself in this place all brown?
I am not where I live, there are angels all around.

    Old man, old man, please do not cry.
You can come live with me, way up in the sky.
There are so many people, they would be glad that you came.
Oh, by the way old man, what is your name?
Why, that's funny, my grandpa's is exactly the same.

    Rhonda Chadwell

MOM

Well, it's over now
And my life must go on
There's not a lot that I
can do
but remember all the
happy times I had
with you
I think about you
all the time
I realize now you're
no longer mine
I'll miss you now
and forevermore
but I'll see you again
when I reach the golden door

Meg Turner

REFLECTION ON A RIPPLED POND

The modern world of intellectualism,
This slithering bastion of civilization,
Permits the truth to breathe,
At last,
Though the air is foul and stale;
Betraying contracts based upon some
Piqued devotion.

Ah, to know the redeemer,
Greet him face to face,
Or shut him up inside his room,
Decaying.
His lust and chastity, hate and love,
The model for our chaos,
Mixed emotions.

John Moon

Awakening from the silence

For madness approaches,

agony and defeat;

Sadness and sorrow,

leaving and staying;

Caring and sharing,

kindness and joy;

Just another day!

Joann Manzo

ART NOUVEAU CONVERSATION

"Truth,"
I said, "needs nothing
to hold it up,
but alas, it cannot walk naked
into a room."

And you said, "What the hell
does that mean?"

And I said,
"Exactly!
There you have it.
Art Nouveau Conversation
as enlightening and rewarding
as Picasso or Warhol or . . . "

Barbara Splan

PEGASUS

Oh, Pegasus with whitest wings
Who smiles and laughs, to music sings

With independence is so free
The entire world can always see

And he can also change his mood
And Pegasus remains so good

Of best ingredients he is made
Portrays the happy and the sad

We all have once to heaven go
With Pegasus it is not so

His immortality can stay
As nothing can drive him away

Luisa Kerschbaumer, M.D.

FOREST RAIN

It rains over all,
Downpouring destiny in the thick forest,
Calling cold wet leaves left lying
Fallen and forlorn,
Soggy torn forgotten nameless
Rotten under world of wood above,

A natural law enforced in forest
In quiet inquiries of Sylvan signs,
Of barren branches beckoning losing leaves
Forever falling drowned below
To leaf this earth,

And whispering whipping wind encircles
Tree trunks, whistling rustling 'round
An answer on the ground:

It rains over all.

Steven Moore

A BREAKFAST IMAGE

As we sit eating our cornflakes,
we fade away . . .
And as we're going, we remember:
yours are crisp — mine are soggy.
We all have preferences.

Gina Meskil

A POEM IS

A poem is black and white
    trying to describe colour,
A poem is the words to a song
    whose melody has escaped it.
A poem is a net of words
    that can only describe
Something wonderful
    that has just slipped through it.

A poem celebrates
    its own failure
To bind in words
What only failure to capture
Can liberate.

A poem is a little machine
Delicately manufacturing air
For ideas to fly in.

Patricia Vickery

A COMPLIMENT

I was feeling really down,
    a very rotten day.

He only said one sentence,
    "You look very nice today."

My "feeling down" was over,
    and a happier person I was.

Because of what one person said,
    see what a compliment does.

Vicky Marzocchi

IS GOD CRYING?

I wonder is God crying now,
Or is He mad as hell?
Looking down on us, His children,
Choosing eagerly to sell
His Most Precious Gifts of life and love,
To the highest bidder go,
There's no buyer too obscene, it seems,
To make us cry out no.
The hunger and brutality
As mankind versus man,
Must surely anger even Him,
Whose son we call, The Lamb.

Donna M. Houston

I ride despair
Like a bucking horse
Hunched in night rides
My imperfect thighs
Buckled to the rest of me
Hurting down
Where the ground
Is a large stone
To be mounted

Claire Rabe

STORIES

There are stories one savors
    time and time again
Of misery and happiness
And looking out from within
These are the ones recounted
    time and time again
The young ones over a bowlful
The elders around the fire
These are what life is made of
The happy or the sad
For what more do we live for
But the memories of times we've had.

Joshua Kaplan

LIPS

Your
        Lips,   so soft and moist —
            How gently they quiver speech.
        They kiss me when I need it   and
            Help my soul   to Reach.

        They speak to me in whispers of words
            That softly fall
        Echoing   I love you,
            When I need it Most
                                of all.

Linda Stembridge

THE FAMILY REUNION

This cancer brought us together,
To laugh and joke
    and see friends of yesteryear

    Unspoken I love yous and I'm sorrys
Were heard by all

    Grown brothers and sisters,
With children of their own,
    Playing games that were once put aside
Like the tricycle in the basement.

    This cancer, eating away,
Made my father's bravery stifle his fear

    Depression,
Hidden in the back of our minds,
    Slept with us at night

    We lived,
And relived again,
    Through the old pictures in the albums.

    Memories . . .
We all still had our memories.

Beverley J. Sorholus

ELUSIVE TREASURES

While your eyes can see, and your ears can hear;
store some happy memories to cherish through the
years; for precious life is short and sweet; and
as we try to make our lives complete; with count-
less wishes and numerous schemes, we try to ful-
fill all of our dreams.

But while we are dreaming, finagling and scheming,
years flash by before our eyes; and as we lie aged,
our beds become cages, and we remember those times
in our lives . . .

Year after year of rushing through life, searching
for elusive treasures; not living each moment in
time content with life's simple pleasures;

Like freedom and flowers, a star-filled sky;
laughter and friendship, a newborn's cry;
music and family, a loving touch;
THESE are the treasures that mean so much.

So before you look back on your life that's gone by,
and find your thoughts lacking in pleasure;
start building some precious memories today,
the kind you can always treasure.

Judith Genovese

A SONNET CONCERNING ABORTION

"The Right to Life! The Right to Life!" they cry
Marching the streets in wild affectedness,
Shaking their fists and holding banners high
Clouding the issue by short-sightedness.
They give no thought to over-creation
Which already threatens the human race;
Garbage, Pollution, where's sanitation?
People sleep by hedges, or any place.
Who will employ these fetuses when born
Men, women, youth seek work repeatedly;
And should atomic war leave the world shorn
Why pledge these babes to die abusively?
What is the remedy for abortion . . .
Vasectomy — never by ablation.

Maye E. MacKenzie

in response . . .

. . . speak to me of desire
with slavic intensity i remember all too well
    and of thunder
    that betrays the chaos of the heavens —

speak to me of hunger
with articulated words only gypsies understand
    and of love that is relentless:
    passion unfolding like the wind —

speak to me of midnight:
branded on the edge of immaturity
    and once again, of desire . . .
    impossible yet perfect
    tumultuous and broken

        vigilant —

            needy —

                unforgotten.

Andrea S. Hansen

SUNDAY NIGHT

The day of rest is over;
And all the things I put off again will wait until tomorrow —
Still, I worry.

Sunday night is when all the bottom pins begin
To slip,
Like the pieces of a Chinese needle puzzle
And fall into a heap
Of emotional-pick-up-sticks.
(You don't really expect me to deal with this,
Do you?)

And that's just me. You look like you have
Tapeworm.
Why do we get so catatonic on Sunday Night?
It's just another evening with all the essential elements:
Dark, moonlight, twelve hours long.
But for you and me there's an extra something sinister
Something subtle and damning,
And so we stand
Outside the circle of redemption,
Waiting for Monday Morning.

Amy Voss

HE KNOWS

Who put the dewdrop on each blade of grass?
    Who opened the bud of the rose?
Who caused the sun to shine warm & bright?
    Ask my Heavenly Father. He knows.

Who caused the clouds that bring the rain?
    Who caused the wind and the snows?
For that's what brings life to each grain
of wheat.
    Ask my Heavenly Father. He knows.

You ask, "Is there comfort from sorrow and
grief,
    When nothing but ill wind blows?
To whom can I go, and what can I do?"
    Ask the Heavenly Father. He knows.

"Where can I turn my sin-sick heart,
    As deeper in sin it goes?
Can one really conquer the forces of hell?"
    Ask my Heavenly Father. He knows.

Harry E. Kruse

MY BROTHER — MY DEAR — MY OWN

'Twas early in December
    When someone told us all
The news of my dear brother
    Whom God had swiftly called

It seems he had an accident
    And like a breath was gone
So much to me he had meant
    My brother — My dear — My own

The report was like a whetted knife
    That stabbed within my heart
The deepest sorrow of my life
    And forget it I cannot

It seemed he strode right by my side
    And helped to dry my tears
He tried to make me realize
    In Spirit he was there

I cannot touch or see him
    But I shall understand
He is here as well as heaven
    That far and better land
                    Mary Logan

I DID NOT KNOW

An accident of birth, my sister . . .
fragile, ill-fated.
I did not need doll children.
You were mine.

Endless hot afternoons I cooled you,
sweetened you, watched you sleep.
I did not know
you were becoming part of me.

Tangled curls, sea grey eyes
ever deepening with light . . .
I did not believe the dark side of you
would change and grow.

I could not know
that forever I was to search
for the pale child in you
and in others.

That it came to be determined
I should give . . .
bear my grief quietly
and give.
                    Flora Wilhelm Bush

In a place of many promises
Of the good things of the world,
Where temptations, expectations,
Could rule a weakened soul,
I faltered on this narrow road
Not knowing where to turn,
Understanding had left my senses
And confusion had returned.
Yet through it all, He never left me,
His love had always flowed,
A warmth, a touch, a simple sign,
Were all it ever took.
And when I didn't have enough
To make it through the night,
He'd come and hold me close
Until the morning light.
And when I felt so lonely
There was nothing I could do,
He'd whisper to me in the wind,
"My child, I love you."
                    Elaine Der

SUNFLOWER

sun flower sun
FLOWER
just
SUN
shine that
on
EARTH
took
ROOT

anything more
than enough
more than above
adds no fragrance
is my
arrogance

SUNFLOWER
                Frederick W. Tamminga

IT IS IN THE NATURE OF THINGS

It is in the nature of things
that she will fly
not away
and not forever
but always . . .

and trees will grow up
towards the light of Phoebus
Phoebus light of the sun
source pulsating rhythms within the bark
resonating hymns of praise . . .

and she will suffer the fluttering
winging heart upon her bough
and sing together daughters of the light,
under the moment passing,
till once again she breathes,
she flies!

        Jesse Teran

WITH A BOW TO JOYCE KILMER

I'm convinced that I shall never see
trees lovely as a poem can be.

A poem conceived in fertile brain,
alive with beauty that will remain.

A poem that feeds the hungry soul
of avid readers from pole to pole,

offering a magical potion
to touch every deep emotion.

A poem with fresh imagery
lives in our hearts eternally.

I know only God can make a tree —
writing poems He left to me.
        Norma C. Taylor

AFLOAT

My thoughts were traveling too fast,
Slow down, slow down, said I,
So, I took a boat out to sea,
and floated a free loan from
Heaven, early in the morning.

        Robert M. Weiner

EXPULSION

The poetry has gone from my soul.
Only weeks ago I begged it
to leave, sore from its demands, its
intrusions again and again.
Now this white blank space, a dull
exhaling wash of cloud, flattens
my evening sky where briefly danced
Gods in waterfalls of stars;
I was so full of their song!

Did He feel this way, tried with such
revolt by His most beloved
Lightbearer of the Day, that
in tired rage He hurled him like
an August night of comets towards Hell?
        Nikki Nelson-Crabbe

TASTE OF LIFE

At a certain time it stops
It's locked up from unawareness
Hanging from curtains
The cold air cools the walls
And the shadow brings a hiss
From the depths of darkness hall
A handful of wind
Can bring the life back again
And laughter captured
From behind a grin
Tasteful nothing can find a friend
For future sounds
Ring through my hands
And my taste of life
Has made its demands
        Monica Gilbert

REJECTAMENTA

A fan, a glove, a doll
And a piece of lace
All strewed about,
Filling the room
With yesterday's memories.
"We have been forgotten
And rejected,"
Came a soft, low whisper;
Or was it
Just the wind whistling
Under the door?
As I sit here
With the fan, the glove,
The doll
And the piece of lace.
        Vera C. Poole

MY CHILD'S HANDS

My child came to me one day
Patted me on the cheek,
Although yet too young to speak,
The softness of his little hands
Were words enough for me.
The tender caress that touched my face,
I love you, mommy
Was their embrace.
As time goes on he still comes to me.
The same gentleness in his face.
He touches me with loving grace,
Puts his hands upon my face.
Softly speaking,
Mommy, I love you.
Hands are made for loving.
        Judy Gayler

MANAGUA, NICARAGUA

Shimmering images soften the moon's harsh light.
Sharks' fins flutter on the lake's surface.
Rays of heat stir the sleeping bodies,
and love's yearning bursts through the web . . .
trembling . . .
Moans increase to the shaking beat.
The cracks are deep, penetrable,
their attraction irresistible.
Ecstasy and anguish fuse in dark fire.
Bodies and buildings convulse.
The earth is shattered by the force.

Nature, in its finite wisdom, has climaxed.

Charles Kargleder

COOL CAVERNS

A dark emptiness looms ahead,
While deep limpid pools stare blankly
At dripping stones hanging tight.
Ripples resound reproachfully.
Mocking with silent laughter,
And I walk by to see
Wet drops try to ooze from morbid rocks
As my wet tears sting and blame me.
In the dark recesses of my mind,
Unknown horrors creep forth,
When the cool slithering comes and engulfs me,

Then I feel no more.

J. Pauline Jen

RESURRECTION DAY

E — Easter Sunday, Jesus arose from the dead.
A — All creation redeemed, this good news spread.
S — Since His victory, Jesus returned to Heaven.
T — To intercede for us against Satan's leaven.
E — Enter into eternal life Jesus has purchased.
R — Reverently trusting that our sins are erased.

S — Salvation from GOD, His Holy Spirit accept.
U — Under His leading, obey Jesus' written precept.
N — Neither is there salvation in any other.
D — Deliver this truth one sinner to another.
A — Always giving Praise to the heavenly Father.
Y — Your soul is nurtured with scriptural Water.

Paul O. Carlson

THE JOYOUS SEASON

It's the time of the year when wishes come true,
As the season approaches, so do the dreams in us all,
The colorful tinsel and lights shine brightly upon the
Christmas tree.
A fresh clean aroma of a wreath is almost delectable,
Candy canes are strewn everywhere for children to find.
Ponds freeze over anticipating little ones and their
New skates.
The joy of giving, a feeling that cannot be outdone; to
Bring a smile to that special face is unforgettable.
This time of the year is an inspiration to all; by showing
Respect, love and other feelings and emotions.
It makes one thrive in a joyous state.

Cheryl Vatcher

EMPTY TEARS

How long ago was it we came to this place?
Your conscience was hurting, it showed in your face.
Your time was important. It seems mine was not.
With each day that passes, it's clear I'm forgot!
The folks here are cheery, their concern is so real,
They dress me and feed me and ask how I feel.
Their concern overwhelms me. Their smiles make me wild.
Love from these strangers, but none from my child!
You won't write a letter. You can't make a call.
I sit and I worry. What's the sense of it all?
It's said when you leave here, it's too hard to part.
But what of the pain that is searing my heart?
You don't say I'm trouble, but I know it is true.
So forget I exist — it's much better for you!
I don't want your guilt and I can't see your shame.
Your words seems so hollow. It's just not the same.
So go live your life! Forget I am here.
You are my child, and I still hold you dear.
Just do me a favor. Cry not when I'm dead.
Our words have been spoken. What's said has been said!

G. J. Macka

AUTUMN MYSTIC

There are not many things that cause
a stop . . . for reflection,
in those who walk upright, as Autumn Mystic.
Autumn Mystic speaks that which seems
hard
to articulate:
The first glimpse of daylight,
Shepherds gathered to celebrate,
the dawning of a new era.

The rhythmic sound of marching feet,
the burst of engines, trails of smoke
that soar . . . beyond our scope.
Autumn Mystic, babbling brook that
echoes
the history of the races.
How is it that it reaches, it reaches . . .
its greatest height when it reaches its
cycle of
descent?

Allen J. Shuler, Sr.

AUTUMN

I can see the Autumn leaves falling from the once green and
luscious trees, now golden, red and apricot; all colors . . .
the seeds of yesterday.
See the leaves in desperate flight not wanting to land 'til
they have found the perfect place to rest.
Hear the winds whisper softly at first, then violently,
as if trying to resist the inevitable.
I *feel* life . . . a new seed deep within, ever so warm and
comfortable, but aah, so quiet, so still.

But the nights howl for the bitter cold. Oh, where to hide?
I think *she* has found the perfect place!

And with each passing day, we come closer to the time we can
dis-arm and bask in the sunlight, sure-footedly, once again.
We can warm our hearts and minds. We see the trees come alive
and watch them thrive.
With the miracle of Spring comes the miracle of life.
We have made the perfect seed.
Our little Autumn Raye was born this day!

Autumn Raye Gonzaque

THE SECRET OF THE FLAME

I see a glowing light from a candle's flame,
In a window bright.
To whom it belongs
I shall not name,
But 'tis a woman
That sits before it, and reads
Every evening and by the clock.
In the early hours, I have seen
A woman burden a book with her soul and every need.
She is old and in worry.
I watch her in the candle light's beam
And it is with the precision of time
That the glow from the window does disappear.
By the look upon her face, I can see
The hours of time and desolation
Filling in her heart.
So it is not by the wind, nor her blow,
That the flame from the candle does cease,
But that of a sultry tear.

Michele Bailey

CRYSTALLIZED MEMORIES

Sometimes, my thoughts flow as sugar tumbling
from a bin into a sugar's bowl,

Particles of minute crystallization, lapsing one
onto the other forming mere speculation(s),

Their impact fills the sugared bowl to its utmost
overflow onto the tables of my mind, and so —

Memories and their consequences, breeding grounds for
hypothesis and reflections grow,

Mirrored in the here and now, memory takes an inward bow
collecting its reserves — with dignity

It pervades, prevails and personifies;
a jam, a gel, preserves, sweetened by thoughts quelled.

Nancy-Lee Farris

THE HOUSE OF GOD

The soft hush of souls descending into a deeper Hell —
The gentle intoning cries of those already in Heaven;
A Heaven they have made,
Safe, comfortable;
Like a warm bed,
Imploring God
Intoning the Lord's Prayer . . .
Strong hands,
Weak hands, bony fingers;
Genuflections like frenzied dancers,
Turning, churning;
Incense burning — acrid, sharp, pungent.
Flaming wax,
Shadows, shadows;
Hovering, looming,
Saying, praying . . .
Saints with imploring eyes,
Judging, judging;
Christ just in from Calvary!

Dolores Guglielmo

THE LOSS

The ache is lessening now as midnight meets the sun:
    the friends are home, the food is gone, the ground,
        the victory won.
The deafening silence makes me cry for one I couldn't keep;
    I look toward the selfish heaven and find I cannot weep.

Sherrye Harvey

TELEVISION TRAUMA

When advertisers call the roll,
What's next? You got it —
Birth control!
We've been through cures
For smelly feet,
For slipping dentures,
Ladies' heat,
For foul breath
And itchy skin,
Gastric acidity from within.

But now a whole new day is dawning.
These ads will keep the troops from yawning.
Madison Avenue will tell us how
To do a job we'd thought, till now,
We'd mastered. Apparently that's not so.
But, safely, soon to bed we'll go.
Let's not waste time, my precious pet,
Get up, and go turn off the set.

Virginia Stanley

MY SHEPHERD

The Lamb of God became my Shepherd;
He carried me in arms so strong
'Til we reached the door of the sheepfold,
Where all my sorrow turned into song.

He led me to the hill of Calvary;
Strengthened by His Staff and His Rod;
My sins were nailed to the cruel tree
Where I found refuge in the arms of God.

The Lamb of God became my Shepherd;
He leads me beside the waters, stilled;
He feeds me with the bread of Heaven
Until with peace my soul is filled.

Oh! Worthy! Worthy is the Lamb!
Sweet Holy Spirit . . . Sweet Heavenly Dove!
Rock of all ages . . . The Great I AM!
The Lamb of God! Shepherd of Love!

Ruth W. Brown

HARVEST

Come labor today with me my friend,
The Lord's work to do,
The harvest is ripe He tells me,
And the workers are so few.

Let's gather the harvest for our Lord,
His storehouse we should fill.
Sometime He is coming back,
Let's witness here until.

Search each corner for ripe grain,
Bring to his threshing floor
So every burdened, troubled soul
Can live with Him evermore.

We are His hands for every task,
For jobs He will say "well done."
Down deep there will be a swelling in our hearts
When we have served God's perfect Son.

William A. Glasgow

LIFE COURSE

We are as a skiff sailing through the stream of life.
With our spirits as the rudder which keeps us upright.
We steer with great struggles through the buffeting waters.
Determination, strength and discipline, help span the portages.

Heavy storms blast at our hulls.
Rocky crags scratch at our souls.
Gusty winds thrust us askew with force.
But — we doggedly persevere life's steady course.

Pain beats at our bodies. We strain at the helm.
With each new victory, we grow firm and calm.
And conquer obstacles as we find quiet inlets.
To discover peace, contentment and hope with few regrets.

Gloria Eichel

MEASURING RODS

The human system measures all.
You're good. You're bad. You're short. You're tall.
You're honest, or you're a sneak.
You're very strong, or very weak.
You're ignorant, or you're smart.
We categorize every part —
The sifting and the molding —
The praising and the scolding.
You're a sweet child, or a brat.
You're this, or you're that.
Put a name to everything.
Symbolize the songs you sing,
But, in giving Spirit true identity,
Attach no labels to the unique-singular entity.

Alyce L. Hubbs

SONNET

In anger my spirit breathes,
Frozen words; Shattered ice . . .
What is this game called life?
To dream; To plan; to dwell,
Upon love lost frustration quell'd,
Agonizing silence pounds within my brain.
From reaching out for you, I must refrain.
For the wind, hath said it so . . .
Treat love gently lest she go.
Solitary; Elusive as the black rose,
Passion rears; Ebbs and flows,
Alas, I fear to have sought in vain,
Lost amidst poetry and prose . . .
Softly, ever softly, I search to find my rose!

Alex B. Wilder

THE PAINTING ON MY WALL

A kaleidoscope of brown and tan
With hints of blue and gray,
A painter has given life to
A forest only a fantasy away.

Emerging in subtle creams and pure white,
Flinging liquid crystals in the afternoon light,
A unicorn dances through a secret stream
To wake his friend, the water sprite.

Drenched in glistening silver array,
She rises and bids him draw near.
Together they laugh and sing
To music I cannot hear.

M. Elizabeth O'Neill

A BACKWARD GLANCE

Clinging to love's last warmth
Unguarded as passion's pain,
The soul is accessible like
Trees shorn bare and vulnerable in the rain.

Autumn storms sweet redolent clouds away
Woven from a labyrinth of poignant memories.
Deep within, growth begins again
Cleansed by love's liberated mysteries.

How felicitous the parting
Nourished by changes overdue,
Washing away remnants of the past
With the onslaught of cobalt blue.

The trees seem taller — kindred
Amid a plethora of sunlit spaces.
Separation has lost its meaning;
No real love is ever wasted.

Frances DesLoge

A LONG WAY HOME

I want so badly to go back to that time and place

when words didn't hurt so much
and looks weren't so harsh;
when spring fever brought us closer
instead of pushing us toward our freedom;
when we knew our names in the sand would last forever
even after the tide came in;
when a hug was all it took
to make the pain disappear;
when dining in a fancy restaurant didn't mean half as much
as sharing a McDonald's hamburger;
when goodbye was only a word we used at night
when we hung up the phone;

I want so badly to go back to that time and place
when we told each other, "I love you"

and we both believed it.

Maria Leon

THE CHILD NEVER BORN

I remember the day when I learned you were there,
The child yet unborn; entrusted to my care.
The joy that I felt, I had never felt before,
The dreams of a child, I would love and adore.

My body was changing; a difference I could feel,
And with each passing day, I knew it was real.
Then something happened, I could not explain,
It soon would be over, I knew from the pain.

I knew I would lose you; I tried to hold on,
But my dreams were shattered of the child yet unborn.
I wanted to bear you, I remember I tried,
And the day that I lost you, I remember I cried.

You will always be special to my soul, then a part,
As you were growing so close to my heart.
I've picked up the pieces; my life has gone on,
But I won't forget the child never born.

Marie L. Sturdevant

St. Johns River, swift, wide and deep
Your tides and your times you faithfully keep!

Boats and barges, yes, big ships too
On a watery carpet they transverse you!

A bridge will be found of every hue
Orange, green, and red, even blue!

Yours is a statement, a legacy
For you share a bond with eternal sea!

Stately homes sit on your banks
As well as tall buildings and storage tanks!

Salty mud marshes, white sandy beaches
are found along your extensive reaches!

From stormy to tranquil, your restless spirit
Is part of the people that love to be near it!

Oh, mighty St. Johns, flowing north to the sea
You bring out the poet that dwells in me!

Jimmie Ford

Saturday morning
Television crackles with excitement
Bugs Bunny, Road Runner
Pretense

News break
Obstructs fantasy with urgent plead,
"Send X-amount of dollars and feed
This unfortunate Ethiopian family for one month."
Contorted, deprived faces
Reality

Commercials
New Chocolaty Coco-Puffs and Cabbage Patch kids.
Stomachs growl in anticipation.
No, not the faded Puffs, the fresh Chocolaty Puffs!
Satisfied?

Rainbows
Lollipops, dreamlands, cartoons
Picture is distorted — tune in better.
Famine, poverty, neglect
Oh, change the channel and pass the Chocolaty Puffs!
Denial

Tara Brown

THE MORNING AFTER

What wantonness the night can foster!
Inviting us to discard reality, she comes —
A naked beauty 'neath black lace —
Enticing us to abandon with her starry face,
Can we do else but shed our flimsy fears?
As man and woman, otherwise but a harsh show
Of bones and beliefs, now become candle glow.

What fires passion can kindle!
Feeding upon the wick of desire, she comes —
A hidden spark within the heart —
Igniting two blue-white souls that flame apart.
Can we do else but join our burning bodies?
As man and woman, otherwise but a cold entity
Of doubts and deceits, now become sincerity.

What delusions intimacy can evoke!
For flame must die and warmth depart.
With the sudden rush of morn,
Lovers, once liquid and flowing,
Have cooled to waxy death.

Rita Ann M. Bolecz

WANDERING MIND

There is a wandering mind,
Full of events, current to none,
Able to form pictures yet unable to tell,
The needs of the present situation,
How sad, how sad,
Said I, "Is it creativity or mere collection
of garbage?"
Whoever knows, must have wandered first.

Tan Boon Hooi

HOOI, TAN BOON. Born: 4-18-65; Education: currently enrolled in University of Wisconsin, Madison, in Industrial Engineering (Sophomore); Occupation: Student; Memberships: Institute of Industrial Engineering; Comments: *Poetry is a way of releasing my emotions and burdens as I put them into writing. It is not forced or thought upon but came suddenly, like a mystery solved.*

YESTERDAYS

Yesterdays are filled with many memories
From the carefree days of childhood
To the awareness of life that adulthood brings.

Each day something new is learned
That helps us through our lifetime
Love, disappointment and pain have touched us all.

Friends have long since come and gone
New friends are still to be gained and respected
We earnestly need and cherish those dear.

The love of friends and family is quite unique
The bond is one so solid and firm
A fortress could not be any more protective.

Love has many faces and meanings to different people
Tender love can be blind and somewhat careless
It can expose the heart and innermost being.

If love has been mistreated and misused
The consequences can shatter and destroy one's soul
I inwardly tremble at the thought.

As years begin to pass more quickly
Wisdom comes as experiences replace experiment
How sad it is for many to realize so late in their lives.

From the carefree days of childhood
To the awareness of life that adulthood brings
Yesterdays are filled with memories.

Chris G. Sanders

MAYBE HEAVEN BOUND

Often I dream of being an Angel someday,
For getting up to Heaven would all blessed be
But too many evils are leading me astray,
To be forgiven now, would be a gift divine
And I hope I may be saved in a special way,
For I long and pray Him to my lost faith anew
As the Lord doth gaze upon me, and knows my pain.
Should I be one to be chosen of the very few,
I'll wonder if He would then let His all join me
And we would all be cleansed with a small drop of dew.

Genevieve R. Morgan

MORGAN, GENEVIEVE ROSINA. Pen Name: Gen; Born: Township of Clyman, Wisconsin; Married: 9-6-47 to Wallace Richard Morgan; Education: 8th grade, 6-1-35; Occupations: Leader of a rhythm band in 7th & 8th grade, several awards for not missing school days. Before marriage, Inspector in war plant, Supervisor in a laboratory; Memberships: Poets corner of Beverly Hills and Florida State Poets Association and NFSPS — joined February 1985; Poetry: 'I Wonder,' Comic Poem, 'My Street Love,' love poem and 'God's Beauty,' Life Poem, Beverly Hills Anthology, 5-6-84. Read poetry in State Capitol Building on May 20, 1985; Comments: *I love to write songs, have 35 copyrighted thus far. Have been writing more seriously in 1985 — It is sort of a hobby. I have entered a few local contests — But no awards as yet. Haven't had the time to enter more as yet — But have written more poetry now. Read poetry at the state capitol 5-20-85 in Rotunda — enjoyed same.*

TIMELY

Season of Spring arrives, bringing warm air
                Trees budding
                        Grass turning greener
Colorful tall Tulips spring up, bursting
through dark, deep soil
Bearing beautiful bell-shaped Flowers
Birds flying high,
                flying low,
                        singing as they go
                Signals of Springtime

Minnie L. Johnson

IN A NAKED STATE

In a naked state there would be no pretenses.
We would be classed by our paunch or our muscle, not birthright.
We would be men and women without hyphens or adjectives.
Sexuality would be fact not obsession
In a naked state.

In a naked state there would be no money.
Men would walk unencumbered by weighty wallets.
Ladies would be free of purse paranoia.
There would be no taxes
In a naked state.

In a naked state, we would tan totally.
We would feel the wet soil squish between our toes.
The sun would bronze our buttocks.
We would run with the animals
In a naked state.

In a naked state, though, it would all hang free.
There would be no trusses or girdles.
The private temples of self would goose pimple in the wind,
And we would all be vulnerable
In a naked state.

Tom Gage

THE WANDERER

I came upon the traveler of early morn,
    Wanderer with minutes yet unborn.

Before me lived dawn, early morn,
    with threads of dew so delicately worn

by the tall firs, infinitely standing
    in the forest's rich ground.
Dawn waited, ready to descend upon this spot
    which the breezes had not yet found.

Silent trees hid a clearing scattered with tiny flowers
    waiting for dawn's touch of light
to rid the forest of the long hours
    held by the impenetrable night.

This traveler and I watched as the sun rose
    to send forth its first ray,
shedding light over the forest
    to begin the new day.

This traveler, watcher of the forest sublime,
    Wanderer among flowers and firs, was Time.

Laurianne B. Carlson

YOU HAVE DONE IT AGAIN
(In memory of Neale)

You are still in charge,
right?
The anniversary card placed
in your desk drawer,
discovery time . . .
exactly, two days before our anniversary.
Bold letters, "For my wife".
Coincidence? I think not.
You may be gone, but in your
quiet way, you are still around.
I like to think you planned
for one tulip to burst forth, in full bloom
on my birthday.
How special that was,
no April Fool joke . . .
and to think you planted it last fall.
You always did surprise me with
unexpected gifts.

Ann Thomas

WHEN WE MET

It was three years ago,
when by chance we met,
before my life was empty,
now it has new meaning.
Where it was once dark,
you turned it into light,
it was just a spark,
that flickered in my heart.
What was on your mind,
when you asked to wed,
give her all my love,
not expecting anything in return.
What was it you found,
someone who loves you,
with all of her heart,
plus more than was possible.

D. Mathewson

Shalako
Divine deity
Dancer, messenger, helper
Emissary of the gods
Kachina

Martha Janette Dorsett

DORSETT, MARTHA JANETTE. Born: Lufkin, Texas, 8-21-43; Education: B.S., Elementary Education; Masters Degree, Elementary Education, with Supervisory Certificate; Occupation: Teacher; Memberships: Delta Kappa Gamma (Treasurer), Gallup Community Concert Association (Board of Directors), Gallup Area Arts Council, and International Reading Association; Poetry: 'Yucca,' honorable mention; 'Infatuation'; Comments: *I have 21 years teaching experience in the primary and intermediate grades. I have taught 3 years on the Navajo Reservation in Arizona and 17 years in New Mexico for the BIA. I have a twin sister. I write mainly about the cultures, land, and people I observe daily. I try to express the beauty in everyday and often tedious tasks of daily living.*

OUR YOUTH

Lord, help us give our youth a dream,
A dream of peace and love,
Where all men work together,
Let their symbol be a dove.

Let their dream be one of striving
To make this world a better place,
Where all are like a family,
No matter what their race.

Lord let them see a vision
Of what this world can be,
And let them take You by the hand,
To calm the stormy sea.

And may they show the nations,
All geared up now for war,
That disarmament's the answer,
That killing — You abhor.

So guide them and protect them,
From this world's ugly face,
And help them build as You would want,
A peaceful, human race.

Jean McDavid

murmurs from the distance

the sky drools down
to surround the trees
phantoms dissolving
into the wood

they sink
into their dead leaves
rotting

the chill air reeks
of winter decay
and shrouds the demise
in palpable dampness

murmurs of exiled Spring
drip into the quietude
from the distance

Alexandra E. Holcomb

WHIRLWIND AT HEART

With a whirlwind of desire,
And passion in my heart,
    Dream's living in admire,
Beginning from the start.

    Never ending the stirring,
Never stopping the flow,
    Like rivers that calm during
An afternoon tide's low.

    It seems like forever,
Yet, it's only been one night,
    Since your heart's endeavor,
With mine, beauty lie.

    In nightfall's arrogant air,
I'll wait for your embrace,
    Our love we dare to share,
Is in its greatest face.

    The moon is full,
Its light shines the way,
    I feel a lull,
Until near me you lay.

Lorrie Ridley

WHAT WE HAVE IS RARE

We've been through everything it seems
    that life could throw our way.
But yet we always keep our dreams
    inside of us and say:

No one can ever take away
    the hopes and dreams we share
And knowing this it seems okay
    for what we have is rare!

Deborah Preble Leone

LEONE, DEBORAH JO. Pen Name: Deborah Preble Leone; Born: Trenton, New Jersey, 9-21-57; Married: 8-6-77 to Robert H. Leone, Sr.; Education: graduated high school, Nurse's Aide degree, 1975; Memberships: Songwriters of America; Poetry: 'Precious Moments,' *American Poetry Anthology;* Song: 'Yesterday (was lost) Today (has just been found), 12-84, Tin Pan Alley Records; Comments: *I write about the love I feel for my husband, family and close friends. Sometimes it's easier to express my feelings in my poems and songs rather than speaking. Writing gives me ultimate pleasure and satisfaction.*

TROLLS

He comes padding on
    furry soft paws,
Proudly displaying
    his prize.
It's a small, thin, black
    orange-bellied snake.
See the excitement
    in his eyes!

He can't understand
    my distaste
Or why I throw his
    gift out the door.
But as soon as it's
    gone out of sight,
He's down the stairs
    looking for more.

LuAnn Zieman

THE PRICE PAID

Fragments of a tissue-wrapped dream,
Never sufficiently lost,
Float through my gauzy consciousness
And I reminisce:
The effort spent
Wasn't worth the cost.

Penelope L. Ogden

OGDEN, PENELOPE L. Born: Minneapolis,
Minnesota, 9-11-48; Education: University of
Minnesota, B.A., 1972; Alfred Adler Institute,
M.A. pending; Comments: *I use my dreams
(both waking and sleeping) as inspiration and
as a vehicle inward towards the discovery of my
personal and universal mythology.*

SEARCHING

A floating soul.
Incomplete in its aloneness.
Searching alway for fullness.
Reaches out touching, testing.
Crying for its goal.

To find another
of a similar note.
A vibration brother
With whom to float.
To play a symphony.
In tune with the universe.

A soul is found.
Though searching never ends.
And friendship is bound.
In loving acceptance
And fragile tendrils
of awareness.

Communion begins —
and falther — on defensive walls.
Misunderstanding, need for truth.
Honesty — and the wall falls,
on the prideful tooth.
Communion in tune with the universe.

Peaks are sought
Which don't exist.
But lunch is bought,
The soul persist
To grow, to change, to become aware.
To have the courage to strip bare.

Cheryl Onweller

OCTOBER-LAND

caught between
Alps and Jura
swift-running watch
in an unripe
                poppy
chilling German-French-Italian
harmonize octet breezes . . .
two toes on the clock
depict Piedmont Corridor
fancy an ostrich behind
Roger Fry's African Mask

Linda C. White

DREAM WINE

The night is too short,
For all the dreams,
I want to dream of you,
Hell! I don't care,
If I didn't wake up,
Just as long as my dreams,
Are filled with you,
No matter how deep it is,
I'll dive deep down,
As far as I can go,
I'll drown myself,
And be drunk,
With dreams of you,
And when I wake up,
From an overnight dreaming spree,
My heart will surely ache,
Not my head of course,
For I will have to wait,
The night to fall and then,
Before I could dream of you again.

Ronnie Cueto

CUETO, RONNIE MEDINA. Born: Manila,
The Philippines; Education: University of Cali-
fornia at Berkeley, Computer Science Student,
through correspondence; Occupation: Manage-
ment Specialist, United States Navy; Com-
ments: *I write what I really feel, poems on love,
life and anger. Most of them are trapped emo-
tions within me and the only way I can release
it is through writing it out. I think writing or
reading a poem is like a sign that says "wet
paint," you don't just read it, you have to touch
it.*

UNICORN MYTH

The mythical unicorn,
image of dreams;
mist of hope.

Real or not;
her message is love.
The wonder of the innocent;
the joy of the believer.

She's the end of the rainbow;
the beginning of life.
With faith and determination
your life is free.

Let her soar within your heart;
to run rampant through your soul.
Without the light of the unicorn
you live in soul's darkness.

Let her gentle ways guide you.
She's the image of dreams;
mist of hope.

Linda Alford

HE'LL BE REMEMBERED

The kind of man who smiles each day,
Who takes the time from work to play,

Who's neither rich, nor really poor,
Who thinks a dream worth waiting for,

Whose gentle touch can mean so much,
Who gives himself, unselfishly,

HE'LL BE REMEMBERED.

The kind of man who stops to pray,
Who lends a hand along the way,

Who's neither weak, nor really strong,
Who plans ahead, who rights a wrong,

Whose quiet voice can still a crowd,
Who does himself so very proud,

HE'LL BE REMEMBERED.

Bill Schueler

DREAMS

Nourishment to the soul
Generators of action
A friend always
    How foolish to believe
in the truth of a traitor.
Causing acceptance to be so
    tormenting.
Pain aggravated by the futile
    chase towards betterment
Only to find a mirage.

She marches on
Like a docile soldier
Nothing but a charade
    of courage.
Defenseless
    against empty promises
Imprisoned
    in the hollow jail of hope
Haunted
    by dreams unfulfilled.

Sarah Simpson

SYSNOPSIS OF LIFE

When I was but a little lass,
I used to jig — for the high school class;
On Memorial Day, I'd stand straight and tall,
and spout, 'In Flander's Field,' in our town hall.

At an early age — I learned to read,
Of fear and poverty and greed.
In my heart I knew to overcome all,
We needed love and charity first of all.

In high school — I became immensely
                        funny,
I gave humorous readings — certainly
                        not for money.

I was in every home town play,
That even remotely came my way.
I frittered away my college days
And soon was married with a family
                        to raise.

Now as I sit in my twilight years,
I must smile through the many tears.
"As a lawyer — I would have been great"
But like so many — I found out too late!

Lorraine Rossow

POETIC REMEMBRANCES

When thoughts of you make you mine
Rhyme and verse become sublime
I cannot forget all the love you brought
You adorn my mind with loving thoughts.

When thoughts of you make you part of me
I'm able to espouse poetry
When the mind recalls past adventures
Poetry rears its head in ecstatic pleasure.

Writing you into poetic rhyme
Gives me poetic strength, I find
I remember you sweet and tender
Thus, I write, and contentedly remember.

T. Steven Watkins

OPULENCE

The cold and the wind reaches into the depths of me,
My soul shivers, I stand staunch.
And the fat Mamas drive by,
Never looking the wind-swept person in the eye.

If they rolled down their windows to see the poor,
A warm, perfumed smell of tightness would escape the car.
Their bright red lips would pucker,
Superficially implying sympathy, and they would drive on.

The cold burns my cheeks so bright red and the wind stings
The eyes,
The salt crust forms before my tears roll far.

Somewhere a child cries out in pain,
Hunger, bellies distended,
Eyes bright and feverish.
But, still with hope, they are pleading.

And the fat Mamas drive by.
Make-up perfectly applied,
Clothing loose and warm,
A smile on their lips, preaching generosity.

But they lied.

Doris Ann Johnson

THE JOB INTERVIEW

Put on your best suit,
Tidy your hair,
Polish your shoes,
And then invite the vulture to attack.

The vulture will first look you over.
If he finds you appetizing,
He will slowly begin to nibble.
Each question is as painfully piercing
As the sound of screeching hawks.
Just as the sound slowly becomes more intense,
So does the vulture's appetite.

The vulture will continue his feast
Until there is nothing but skeleton.
If you are lucky, he will find some use for your skeleton.
If not, he will leave you there lying naked in an open field.

Kelly Keele

HER BEAUTY IS IN ALL CREATION I SEE

Her beauty is in all creation I see
Complexion of the pearl; Grace of the tree
Her skin is like the newly spun silk
That draws me in like a babe to mother's milk.

Her eyes twinkle like the sun on morning dew
Her face reflects the colors of the rainbow's hue
A body that moves in rhythm to the waves of the sea
For me she's like a breeze that must blow free.

Hands that touch me like raindrops to a flower
A heart as strong as the sun's warmth and power.
A mind so complex, yet simple in thought
She knows only the things that nature taught.

You should see as her hair begins to glimmer and shine
As it's borne by a moonlit glow immaculately divine
When she speaks it's like a whispering breeze in air
That tells me she's lonely and is glad I'm there.

Her beauty is in all creation I see
She's nature's child who just wants to be
Subjected to all the season's constant change
But her natural beauty will never surpass your range.

Ralph Renna

HAPPINESS IS

An old lady stopped me one day
Asked why I was in a hurry along the way
I told her I had lots to do
She knew I was in a stew

I had to find happiness today
And I didn't have time to stay
Happiness couldn't be far away, just one more day
I'll hold onto it this time, it won't get away

No you won't she calmly said to me
You're not lookin' in the right place you see
It's not the things you have or do
'Cause happiness comes from within you

Stop chasing the wind and the pot of gold
You can't buy happiness 'cause it's not sold
Get in touch with who you really are
Then you'll find happiness is near not far

It hadn't worked when I tried it my way
So I gave some thought to what the old woman had to say
I found out that being me wasn't so bad
And the happiness I hunted I already had

Billye Frazier

NATURAL TOWERS.

A POEM

A blank paper longing for words
A crying soul wanting to be heard
A quiet day, a restless night
Our life is a battle, an endless fight
We live for others, forgetting ourselves
We hide our emotions upon a shelf
We look for answers never to be found
And wonder for by fear we are bound
An eternal search that started at birth
Continuing until we depart this earth
The search for truth with hope as our guide
Together we travel side by side
And though shadows upon us should fall
We'll journey on, brave and tall
As we watch the pages turn . . .
And with each new day we work, we learn
We try to reach our goals, our dreams
So . . . unsure the answer seems
So many people longing to be real
The final victory is learning to feel
But until we reach the great beyond
The battle just goes on . . . and on . . .

Marie Nokes

SUMMERING

Air conditioners drip ice water and chug.
Clumps of red and yellow cannas stand in front yards
summering. We pack an ice chest and some towels.

The sand so hot we run to shore sometimes
peel rusty starfish from rocks and watch
their little sucker arms throb and reach for water
before frisbeed back into breakers.

There are days the sun shines through.
Pierside gold and silver fish
float on breeze licked water.

A little wife looking up might know
that opulent feeling that making love craves
but only looks from a blanket or
binds fingers and blinds in light.

There are days the sun shines through
leaves of silver maple and birch;
Post card sunsets waiting to happen.

Timothy L. Knapp

NATURE

Nature is a beautiful gift given to us.
It is beautiful for you and me too.
Nature is the only really natural thing.
It is a beauty that can be seen from within.
Nature is everything.

Nature is the purest gift ever given to man.
It is the most beautiful thing ever made.
Nature is beauty within itself.
It is life.
Nature is everything.

The eye of nature beholds itself.
Nature has the great animals of the woods.
It is beautiful and green and shines in a sunbeam.
It is pure.
Nature is everything.

Nature, nature is the fascinating and thrilling world around us.

Enjoy and appreciate it!

Kesha Custke

Imagine the beautiful sky of blue
A love between us, you and I so true
Walking along the great lake's sandy shore
Holding hands but both wanting so much more
We stare at each other, eyes lit up bright
Knowing the bond which we share is so tight
Sharing the feelings and thoughts in our minds
Hoping that forever our hearts shall bind
The memories of you, I will cherish
In my thoughts forever will never perish

Julie Reyes

THE KEEPER

Let the wind gather me in her silence for I weigh
no more than a butterfly.
And let the ocean roll over or crush me in her
violent surf for I am part of the sand.
And may the rain make mud puddles of me or the
sun a desert, for the one who is able to under-
stand the timeless power of the earth becomes
wise to the keeper of life.

Theresa Ann Moore

THINKING

When I'm all alone and my mind starts to drift
I think of you, and my spirits lift.
Your memory holds a special place
Of a smile, a love, a trusting face.
A special memory that's renewed each day
Of someone that cares enough to stay
Thinking of you brings a happy thought
Of someone I love an awful lot!

Marie Piekarski

WHISPERS

So quiet, so sweet, so soft, so low,
You tell me things I didn't know.
I smile because I love to hear,
The things you whisper in my ear.
I can't express just what it means,
To hear your hopes, your thoughts, your dreams.
The closeness we've built between us two,
Is from three words, I LOVE YOU.

Rosie D. Long

FOR DAD

It seems like such a short time, since my dad had to go.
I sit and think each day of him. Why we hurt each other so.
I was so young and foolish. I didn't stop to think.
I wouldn't have my dad the following week.
All I wanted was his love, the only thing he couldn't show me.
Now I only have memories of the times we shared alone.
He'll always be in my heart and mind.
Until it's my turn to go.

Barbara Pennypacker

SILENT WISHES

To my child, whom I long to have,
from your mother, whom I hope to become.

May you grow in mind to understand that all things are not understandable.

May you always strive to understand all you can.

Look ahead always to a new day.

Look ahead always to a better tomorrow.

May you find your life in progress daily to opening doors and books.

May you set your dreams as goals and reach them.

May you love me without trying too hard.

May thinking come naturally and work come with readiness to tackle it.

May you always fall asleep at night and awake each morning refreshed.

May you have rest and quietness and peaceful dreams.

May you have excitement and joy and laughter.

May your eyes see great happenings, your ears hear the sound of love.

May your hands feel the warmth of friendship, and may life touch you with goodness.

May you know I Love You!

Susan M. Miller

HEAVENLY WING

I heard a wing of Heaven last night.
It came beating through my dreams.
It was only one wing, white and magnificent.
Its sound was a swooping happy moan.
It was strong right there at its shoulder curve, and
    dark eternity surrounded it.
But there was only one wing.
Did it represent one parent since two would be the whole?
This morning I stared at the telephone . . . at its early ringing.
It was my mother, whose heart recently tried to fail.
She had been to the doctor.
He talked of danger signs.
A wing of Heaven beats near, strong enough to carry.
Fly away! Oh, please! Fly away!
I want so many seasons with her yet.
If she climbs upon your back, Strong Wing, push her back,
    please push her back.
Let me enfold her with my wings.
For a while . . . for a while.

Cheryl Diane Westbrook

MY LOVE

I feel a surge come over me I can't explain
A sense of belonging within me, whenever I speak your name.
Why do we tear each other up with words and thoughtless deeds?
When I know in my heart how deep our love is to fulfill each other's needs.
Just hold me now, you're so strong and gentle, hold me for awhile
Then you'll lift my head and kiss my lips and warm me with your smile.
I need your love, like birds need air, and the mountain water that flows to
The sea
I want our love to grow not apart, but together like the seedlings of a tree.
For a tree that grows over the years can tell us of what growing means.
In the winter she dies and withers, but holds on to life patiently.
Then just when it seems life can no longer be, from the branch a bud appears,
Spring has arrived, making her alive, and she dances with the wind, and the
Sap on her limbs are happy tears.
And through the years, the stronger she grows, and no wind can uproot her ground.
For it is through patience and acceptance that she will survive the storms, for
The mystery of life all around.
So we shall be like the tree, you and me, weathering out our storms.
And seeking to grow, even though it be slow, for we are, our life, *my love.*

Renée Lebeau

CAUGHT BETWEEN

Poor fly — lonely, sad fly
Trapped within the windows.
Outside's the cold
You just wanted to escape.
Inside's the warm
You're trying to reach.
But on the way
You became trapped between
The two.
Both worlds are within
Your visibility, but neither
Within your grasp.
I'm awfully sorry, Fly . . .
We don't let strangers in.

Laura Gerry

CHANCES

At times so lucid
But constantly perplexed
A feeling of love arises
Though appearing forbidden
So hesitant of confrontation
Yet temptation comes forth
What could come of it
Rejection or intensity
Considering both
Which is better
Rejection; a temporary loss of self-esteem
An anticipation of a great friendship
Intensity; A beautiful experience
With an ever-growing fear of separation

Edie Goldberg

PERSPECTIVE

There are times when on this path I aim
    That I will stop and turn around
To look back down
    From whence I came.
So often do I find
    That there appears a different kind
        of path
    From this other point-of-view.
My footprints are the only trace
    That on this place
I had been and traveled through.
    Eventually the rains will fall,
And nothing will be left at all
    Of my brief passage to recall.

Raymond A. Wiger

IF

If Father Time came by to say
I'll give you what you want today,
But no tomorrow shall you claim;
Would you choose beauty, love, or fame?

How torn with anguish I would be,
If Father Time said that to me;
I'd wring my hands, pray, and then
I'd think of you, remembering when

We roamed the land in lush of Spring,
And you so shyly showed the ring;
Told me your love would last for aye,
And June was not so far away.

Velma Cole Earhart

As the wild rose
rambles over the hedgerows
relentlessly entwining
the yielding branchlets of honeysuckle,
its blooms amid the thorns;

As a butterfly
caught, on a summer's day
in a web of gauze a spider left behind,
fluttering against its hold
in ever-diminishing waves;

So have you
surrounded this soul
pure, defenseless, vulnerable and trembling,
resisting the need,
yearning to escape the bittersweet hold
of unrequited love.

Let go! The thorns are red
Let go! The wings are torn
Let go! The soul seeks rest.

Krystyna Ochocki-Czerwinke

THE FISH

When the winds increased, our tiny boat
    capsized.

With waves crashing over me, I grabbed
    the tail of a large fish.

I tried to help my friend, but he could not
    hold on when the waves grew stronger.

The fish swam towards the shore and pulled
    me onto the beach.

Then I looked back and saw that it was dead,
    but it had saved me.

I came back a few days later, and I saw
    a fish jumping out of the water.

I knew that it was the very same fish
    which had saved me.

T. J. Singleton

SPRINGTIME

As the winter chill begins to thaw,
A newness can be seen by all.

The buds of the trees swell and burst,
And young leaves absorb the dew in their thirst.

The pussy willow and its furry balls,
A month ago were only sticks standing tall.

The birds sing while building their nest,
For soon their young will hatch under their breast.

A newborn fawn lying in the warmth of the sun,
His mother feeding to nourish her son.

The flowers are blooming bringing the country alive,
Their scent attracts the bees from their hive.

These are all part of your life and mine,
I thank the Lord for a season so divine.

This is Me

MY MOTHER'S HAIRCUT

"How do you think I look?" you say.
I reply, "You're looking better every day."
"No, no," you say, looking very hurt.
"My hair!" You look at me like I'm dirt.

"Oh, your hair." I look and then I say,
"You're right, I think it's going grey."
Your eyes flash and then you splutter,
"Don't talk like that, I'm your mother!"

I look closer, and then I see,
Her hair is shorter, How silly of me!
"I'm sorry," I say, "you look great, it's true."
Why Olivia," you smile. "How sweet of you!"

So we're friends again and I cheer up.
Now maybe she'll get me that adorable pup,
Or perhaps a kitten, or an Arabian mare,
And all because she cut her hair!

Olivia Morgan

THE HOPE

The children cry, and the parents weep,
    In a land that is filled with sorrow;
What's happened to the flocks of sheep,
    That used to pray for tomorrow.

Our Shepherd, it's true, we cannot see,
    But we know He is truly near,
For all of His straying lambs are we,
    And for us He will always be here.

He made this world in which we exist,
    The grass, the flowers, the trees;
Too many are the miracles for me to list,
    For all creatures, from man to the bees.

So gather together all lambs of God,
    The happy and the forlorn;
For we're on the earth that He hath sod,
And without Him, we'd have never been born.

Marilyn Yenger

NATURE'S GIVING AND TAKING WAYS

Wild flowers grow between the blades of grass,
while birds glide down to drink their nectar.

Hearts beat fast with love,
while others die caused by hate's decay.
Butterflies flutter to the wild flowers,
amidst gusty winds surrounding earth.

Buzzing bumblebees fly through the air sometimes to sting,
but always to enchant us with their flight.
Worms wiggle deep and shallow, then they become prey
for men dangling food before them.
Squirrels scurry to hide their acorns,
for old man winter hurries after their tails.

Trees embrace the world with their arms,
while termites eat away at their roots.
Wild flowers grow between the blades of grass,
while birds glide down to drink their nectar.

Priscilla M. Ornelas

BEGIN AGAIN!

What makes poetry so hard to write,
When ideas come to me left and right,
Words come to mind but not to pen,
Often I begin to begin again!

Burning the lights late into the night,
Wishing and hoping with all of my might,
That words and phrases would come together,
So I can get back to my pillow of feathers!

Sitting here drifting to sleep and dreaming,
My mind is wandering, floating, scheming,
Why should poetry be so hard to write,
Even when my watch tells me it's the end of the night!

Nothing so far has made any sense,
Just me with a brain — clogged thick and dense
And keeping in mind all your talented wit,
I know you must think me an overgrown twit!

But what makes poetry so hard to write,
When these ideas keep coming left and right,
Words from my mind slip away from my pen,
So here I sit to begin again!

Deborah A. Davies

SUMMER SMILES, SUMMER SOULS

Summer has arrived once again
Seeking the smiles of human faces
The summer's sun will cover all
Afresh, old and young will share the season

Summer smiles will be found on many
Bearing them will be children playing by the sea
Also, old couples strolling in the park
But the summer smiles will not be on all

Souls of some will be sad
Summer's happiness will not be theirs
The season will find their lives in wound
Instance, a widow of recent

She will reminisce of better ones
For these thoughts will keep her patient
Because summer includes all
Some smile and some are sad

Faces with summer smiles ought to delight
And forever record their joy
Souls that are sad ought to remember past summer smiles
For if remembered, they ought one day come again

H. Hector Monge

THE SANDPILE . . .
    A place to sift the dreams of life awhile.
To mold and shape, to build and tower,
    And never care the hour.

In a world removed from care and worry,
    Free from pressure, free from hurry,
He guides a stick, a truck, a stone;
    Makes a tunnel, shapes a home.

And in this quiet place,
    Where time measures endless as space,
No matter if a tower crumbles.
    (So unlike us when we stumble.)

For it returns to dreams and sand
    To be sifted through in a summer's land
By a dusty-haired boy 'neath the poplars' gaze
    Where dreams dwell on in the summer's haze.

Phyllis J. Matthews

NEVER SEE THE CLOUDS

The singing of a bird in a tree,
and the freedom of being free.
That is what we all hope and pray for.
So why would we sacrifice that, to gain war?

Why do we have to be angry?
Why do we have to be an enemy?
There are so many questions that we need to ask.
Like why is peace considered a hard task?

We are surrounded by so much beauty,
and there is so much love, when we have unity.
So why shouldn't we share
this wonderful planet and learn to care?

Our greatest treasure lies in our young.
So why should we never hear a nursery rhyme being sung?
We must all change our way of thinking if we can,
because we have all entered the Nuclear Age of Man.

We should never take for granted,
the small seeds of life that were planted.
We should never see a mass of shrouds,
because we should never see, the Nuclear Clouds.

Jody Evertson

ONE OF HIS STYLES

"The porch light is on! The porch light is on!"
    Shouted James to his Grandpa K.
"'Tis true, 'Tis true, my sleepy-eyed grandboy;
    God's scheme for beginning this day.

If you and I are to catch any fish,
    We'd better be heading that way.
And knowing how your granddaddy stumbles,
Well! God planned that moon for today."

Guess which one beat the other one dressing? —
    The one that caught the wrinkled arm,
"I'll go get the lines and also the bait.
    Cover Grandmom so she'll stay warm!"

As Grandfather K stepped into the car,
    He saw a most beautiful sight.
James sat on the front seat with fishing gear;
    And the bait he held mighty tight!

They drove away from the house, to'ard the lake
    With the man in the moon all smiles.
Do you suppose he, too, has a grandson?
    Their happiness! — One of His Styles!

H. R. Krauss

MODESTY

I'd rather be free, to rise above the rest.
To have my cake and eat it too would be
My cup of tea; but my eyes won't let me hide
What's on my mind.

My spirit is proud, but my courage is very weak,
Desiring to become a stronger self.
But I can only be myself when I'm alone, or
In close company.

The confusion of crowds
The laughter that prevails —
Leaves me much in stress.
Discomfort soon sets in, a lying smile.

The world may be a stage, but I prefer
To play a role that's honest and unspoiled.

Wesley R. Montgomery

SEE WHAT I FEEL

If your eyes could see what I feel
    then I've achieved something very real.
Yet not in the hopes of my selfishness,
    but in the rights of my sharing.
These are things that gave me my bearing
    so that I could walk in the days ahead,
        shadowed without any regrets.

Words cannot always express what I mean
    for my heart has been singed by love's broken dreams,
        leaving me anguished,
            with a bruised and broken heart.

Yet I know this can't continue
    because there's always a new start.
So I'll always look towards todays
    dreaming of tomorrows,
        and forgiving the yesterdays.

If your eyes could really see what I feel,
        you would be mine . . .

Robert Harrison Berko

THE HOUSE THAT LOVE BUILT

This is a house that love built.

These are the walls that were reared too high.
This is the roof that shut the sky.
This is the vine all shriveled and dried
That climbs the house that love built.

And these are the rooms where the children bleat
And are lost to the years, and where moonbeams creep
Searching them still —
These are the halls where sun doesn't come

    That lead to the rooms
    That are sealed by the walls
    That are pressed by the roof
    That smothers the house that love built.

And these are the days that scatter and fly.
These are the doors that can't be pried.
While mine is the face in the window's eye
Locked in the house that love built.

Millicent Allen

WITHDRAWAL

She was a fragile flower,
wafted with the breath of life
and tenderly placed in the center of the earth.
As she grew, she embraced the beauty of nature,
and hers was a love for all people.
She was blind to evil; to her all mankind was good.

Instead of being nurtured
with the gentle raindrops of love,
she was bombarded with deceit and
the warped ills of the world.
Still, unable to accept this adversity,
and retaining her belief in goodness and love,
she slowly withdrew into her shell
to begin her spiritual retirement
from the present.

Innocent child of the universe,
could you not have weathered
the storms of this earth
and waited for God's decision
to call you to His eternal bliss?

Mary Christensen

WHEN THE BELL TOLLS

What shall I tell my children
When the bell tolls for them?

When the ghostly voice of Nostra Damus
Echoes a reminder down
The hallowed Halls of Time

And the post-war wail of the
Air-raid siren conjures up

Tortured visions of premature death
Unimaginable pain, and suffering?

When they run to me for comfort, their upturned
Faces filled with terror and vulnerability,
What shall I say?

When they realize even I, the Almighty Protector
Cannot save them, and there is no escape.

I who brought them into the world
For my own selfish reasons
To face their deaths TOO SOON

I who cannot turn back the Clocks of Time,
Or stop the hand that ends all human life forever —

Shall I say "I'm sorry?"

Jill E. Moseley

S.W.

Every once in a while,
A breeze rushes by and cools the afternoon;
A field is suddenly transformed by a single flower;
The darkest night is brightened by the glimpse of a star.

Every once in a while,
Someone shows up in your life;
Comes in without a word and draws you near.

The breeze brings refreshment.
The flower, its beauty.
The star, hope.
She brings compassion, love, and understanding.
Her friendship fills me,
It refreshes me; it holds me up.
She has indeed become part of me.

As with the breeze that must fade,
The flower that can be enjoyed for only a short time,
And the star that disappears,
So too must she leave.

Watching her leave brings a tear to my eye;
An emptiness to my life.
I will do well not to be saddened by her going,
But reassured by her existence
And gladdened by memories.

She will remain with me forever.

P. K. Morey

THE UNICORN

In the large dense forest, where rainbows grow,
As the sun rises and the wind starts to blow,
A unicorn appears, her large horn gleaming in the sun.
She rears up and starts to run.
Through the tall grass, her tail streams along,
And causes the grass blades to sing a song.
The unicorn, the only one.

Christy Mueller

MY BIG DAY

I jumped out of bed and started to dress,
Then looked in the mirror — my hair was a mess.
I grabbed my best comb so my hair would be neat,
Then went to the kitchen for something to eat.

Grabbing my coat I dropped all my keys,
And picking them up I scraped my poor knees.
Luckily, though, it didn't show well,
I made up my mind you never could tell.

So off I went to try for the part,
Hoping to win with all of my heart.
This means so much, so much to me,
And it's not too hard for people to see.

Getting there I thought I would die,
But when I was done I heaved a big sigh.
For what I had won was the very main role,
to which I would put my heart and my soul.

Sondra Lizotte

THE BIRDS AND OUR HOLLY TREES

The birds swoop into our holly trees
And hop through the mazes inside.
They seem to have such happy times
Finding new places to hide.

They hang on the limbs and peek under the leaves,
And give soft chirps which seem to imply —
Find us, if you can, in your holly trees
Before we fly out into the sky.

They are so happy in our holly trees
As they literally dance across the branches.
How can they land safely when moving so fast?
I guess they aren't afraid to take chances.

Come, sweet birds, in your beautiful colors,
Swoop in and out of our holly trees.
You are always welcome, whatever the hour,
To play in them any time you please.

Hilbert S. Collins

HAPPY CHILDHOOD?

Orphan at the age of nine,
Strolling along the streets,
Selling boiled maize on the market
            For a slice of bread —
Mother killed in the concentration camp
Father working for the "Nazi" machine —
Old Grandma at home — a little boy
                  Relying on me.

"You're not afraid to leave the ghetto —
No identification stripe on your sleeve?"
"No choice" I say — Walking out
                  Never sure to come back —

A creation of distress — a child of war.
Barefoot in the snow — a little torn coat,
Result of my escaping assault — barbed wires,
Turning around projectors — machine guns . . .
My happy childhood?

Ida Weiss

THE GIFT OF TEARS

Don't be ashamed of tears of pain,
   Of love,
      Of happiness
   That flow from you.
Let them fall.
They are as raindrops on a dry
      Parched land,
         Refreshing, cleansing,
Giving life anew,

Little boys are told they must not cry,
      So, as men,
They cannot . . . will not . . . wet an eye.
But why?
      Tell me why.
Tears are gifts from God above;
To ease our burdened soul
      To show our love.

         Remember, Jesus wept.

Mabel L. Bowman

THE TIDES OF CHANGE

The tides of change are rolling in
The cries of agony echo through cemeteries
But politicians still bleed their fellow men
And slime is where they lie
The tides of change are rolling in
Weeping women kneel near beds
While workers dream of being men
   In revolutions many will die
   Woman, why do you cry?
   Woman, are you their mother?
   Woman, why do you cry?
The tides of change are rolling in
So let us go to the wars
Let us fight and be men
Let us bleed and let us die
      In cemeteries men lie
      In beds men die
      Cry mother cry
      In wars men die
The tides of change are rolling in

Myron Shlapak

TWENTY-TWENTY HINDSIGHT

I did it again. I did it to myself.
I set up pain and just waited for the hurt to start.
When did I forget my own beliefs?
That today is for living,
Planning ahead is for fools?
I am, again, the fool.
I have at hand any number of tools,
To assist me in learning.
But, I allowed the yearning
To have my own family around me
To take over my senses
I knocked down all my defenses.
What is to be learned here?
A lesson is at hand . . .
I'll find it, I know . . .
I pray it will come to me fast.
So that I'll learn it and know,
And I'll keep it near
And make it last,
      'Til next time . . .

Jill G. McDowell

216

ILLUMINATION

Po Po Boy   there has been an insurrection
                    no need for interjection
                    won't be no counteraction
                    'cause you Po.

Po Po Boy   no cause for you to mention
                    there will be no intervention
                    your Mom don't get no pension
                    'cause you Po.

Po Po Boy   I have just one suggestion
                    don't bow down to oppression
                    perseverance is protection
                    'cause you Po.

Po Po Boy   You live in deprivation
                    this country is your nation
                    you need an education
                    'cause you Po.

Po Po Boy   don't cry for benefaction
                    you have to take the action
                    no basis for correction
                    'cause you Po.

E. Bernardine Bayez-Sydner

HOME SWEET HOME

Within these walls that are so new
my thoughts they center all on you,
For you bring out the best in me
and that is what the world shall see.

Our love has found for us a home
where we may rest, we need not roam,
and we shall give to it our color
so we may never fall asunder.

Home Sweet Home in you we live
with guiding lights we all do give,
Upon your walls dreams come alive
to give us strength so we may thrive.

And as our eyes do scan the place
we'll see where love did leave its trace,
And built for us an atmosphere
to keep us strong throughout the year.

Here we shall gain our food for thought
through our creations we have wrought
A world of opportunity awakened in poem
please grow us green, Home Sweet Home.

Karen Ann Kish

RESEMBLANCE

the fisherman sits
    anxious to set hook
anticipating movement felt by his
    finger lightly perched
    on the glossy line

the judge stoops
    finger posed on the net
preparing to voice his sensation
    upon feeling the slightest
    vibration at service

the spider settles
    touching a silky lead line
awaiting tremors set off by
    victims entangled in
    his clinging web

Susan L. Miller

Snowflakes
in sun —
Like stars
in space walk.

Pierre Martischang

TODAY

today my heart died.
it fell into the river.
as it floated away from me
it made me kind of shiver.
my breast no longer beats
with the passion it once held,
now all that remains inside
is a silent, silent shell.

today my eyes cried
like the moaning of the sea,
waves lingering over
lonesome memories,
teardrops fallin' down
like seafoam spray,
the weather was misty here,
on the beach, today.

today the clock
is ticking so very, very, slow
there's no place left now
for me to go.
i stand on the rocks
and gaze at the sea.
i guess this is where
i am supposed to be,
today.

Nancy Gallagher

GALLAGHER, NANCY RITA. Born: Boston, Massacusetts, 1-19-54; Education: Studied music at University of Massachusetts, Boston; Berklee College of Music, Boston; McGill University, Montreal; and in Calcutta, India; Occupations: Musician, Accountant, Mother; Memberships: one of the founding members of Eyes of Ophelia Productions; Awards: Music Award for High School Graduating Class, 1972; Comments: *I write poetry to express my deepest emotions about everything. The reason that I write poetry is the same reason for my living life.*

WHEN I AM AWAY FROM YOU

In the silence,
In the still
Or high upon some lovely hill,
A sigh escapes.
I hear your voice
Reminding me of you
No choice . . .
I smell the sea, the grass,
The dunes, the sky so blue.
I cannot get back home too soon.

In the silence I come to you.

        You are
          My love.
Barbara Joan Creator

BIG KIDS

Cognitive psychology dictates,
That as your thoughts change
So does your physiology,
So if you think about the edge,
Or racing speeds of light, very much —
Watch out,
Halfway to flirting,
With death, by dreaming,
Tragi-comic symbolic extension,
And kingdoms of churches
Leaving tracks, cinnamon pain,
The first time I had an audience,
The feedback nearly crushed me,
I stay near to the phone,
If you want to call . . .
Eric Webb Shaffer

A VISITOR

A little mouse peeked out at me,
from underneath my bed.
Its tiny head cocked to one side,
to hear what I had said.
"Hello! my friend do come out,
and play with me awhile,
You don't scare me one little bit,"
I added with a smile.
He sat real still and peered at me,
as safe as safe could be.
He seemed to sense I was his friend,
but couldn't quite agree.
He must have felt he didn't know my game,
for all at once he dashed away
as silent as he came.
Ethel Burch

MICHEAL WHY

He is a gift to all who view him,
seek him, survey him.
A tall wonder who entrances,
sparkles from corner to corner.
Many have experienced his blessed being,
yet many more feel they must.
All long to touch his life in the
same context in which he enhances
their own
He is a man too beautiful for this
earth, he is my lover.
Why was I so unfortunate to know
him?
Now I must suffer with the rest
Now I must feel unspecial, unexalted.
Angela M. White

Abuse holds the smell
of violent fear and huge
swells of rage/sadness

Catherine McCaffrey

SHADES OF BLACK

We are
the color
of a rainbow

Tan
Yellow
Brown and
Black

We are
a people

full of color

We are a

beautiful people.

We are
shades of
black.

Bettina Thorpe

THORPE, BETTINA. Pen Name: BT; Born: Oxford, North Carolina, 1-1-54; Single; Education: University of Maryland, B.A. Library Science, 1976; Catholic University North East, Washington, D.C., Partially completed M.L.S., 1979-80; Occupation: Assistant Librarian, Library Technician; Memberships: Law Librarian Society of D.C.; Poetry: 'War,' Fine Arts Press, June, 1985; 'Negro Spiritual,' Spiritual Pathways/Writer's Dream, August, 1985; *Thoughts of a Serious Woman*, A collection of 21 poems, 1985; Comments: *I write about life, relationships, experiences and things I see going on around me. Writing is a release, a way of expressing how I feel, a clearing of my mind.*

LULLABY

Robin Red-Breast up a tree,
Who will care for you or me
When the world is put to bed
                    permanently?

When heat gives birth to brilliant skies,
No wink or blink in children's eyes
Will see that we have nowhere gone
                    eternally.

When we spin as cosmic dust,
Will there be left no one to trust
To tell if we have lived or died
                    humanely?

The question flutters in the air.
Explosion wastes a final prayer
That Humpty-Dumpty chants, or rants
                    insanely.

Robin Red-Breast, fly away.
The sky is yours, at least today.

Christine Erenberg

CREATIVE DRIVE
(He sd.

This paper or
CANVAS
as you put it
is empty.

A word does not
exist for
a word
does not come to

Re: Mind
me about
CREATIVE THOUGHT
drive an auto
mobile down a high
way and words
flow like traffic yet
comes to stop at red
beaming lights and
CREATIVITY
ENDS.

Linda L. Schlee

BUSINESS AS USUAL AGAIN

Oh hell!
Life's gone
awry again.

Oh well,
Business as
usual again.

You'd think
I'd know
that all
this snow
(I would
say bull
but it
doesn't
rhyme)
is never new; just
business
as usual
again.

Julie Ott

It is in the latest hour of hours
I am angry with the familiar
Puzzled by the unknown
Tonight I see what I have seen before
Of this I am certain
I need not despair
It's in the name of love

Old man
Don't pass me by
I see your rage
Tucked beneath your old coat
In the humble style of your baggy trousers
I swear on my life and my love of it

Under the street lamp
You pass
Then continue
Headed for the center of town

Mara Stacy Colen

A BRIGHT THOUGHT

What can I write
Oh let me see
Something that's just right
Now what could it be,

Maybe a poem on dogs
No, that's not any good
How about a poem on frogs
Or a bear that lives in the woods,

None of these are right
It has to be something terrific
Something you see only at night
I'll try and be more specific,

Something that's very far
Up high in the sky
Yes, you guessed, it's a star
Holding answers to our whys,

Stars are about what I write
Something that just came to me
Thoughts that haven't any sight
Like stars, bright but can't see.

Charlotte Jones

THE EXPIRING AND RETURN OF MAN

The expiring of man on Earth
From nuclear power burning
A contaminated world population a few
And it continues turning

The ground is poisoned with nuclear flow
The scars of death upon a face
Once a man now a monster
Plagues the human race

The glamour is gone, the skin is puffed
A newborn will arrive
Then comes the Infant lost at birth
None, born alive

World population exists no more
From manpower and his creed
A wasted future will open a door
Nature will plant a seed

Once more on earth man can live
Nature looks down and smiles
A nuclear force in time will give
Long live the child.

Ed Lewis

YOU AND THE SUN

Sue, inseparable, are you and the sun!
Each of your needs are simple —
To have, to give to each other completely.
Your sun, Sue, gives that energy you so welcome.
As your body experiences the sun's sensuous warmth —
Your tantalizing skin turns golden,
Your reward for your body's intimacy with the sun.
As your body heats, your mind drifts — then fills
with beautiful fantasies, exciting dreams;
Things that only you and the sun — your sun, dare share.
As the sun comes off its high and ebbs, likewise,
So do you; you even pout, you are disappointed —
Yet you show happiness, as you have had a full day,
A day of beauty and ecstasy, and you show happiness
for you know tomorrow, or the next day, you will
meet again — Sue — so inseparable, are you and the sun.
Robert Mitchell

SPRING MANIFESTO

The universe changes hands in time
Sensitivity impels me to meditation
Clowns I number among my best friends
Patience disregarded still is a better virtue
Cats are parties to actual reincarnations
Spires rise taller subside to decay
Children are monuments to sincerity
Leaders guide us down a dead end path
Poets speak truths of inner beauty
Disenchanted capitals chant full despair
Magicians project the light fantastic
Pedestrians succumb to blues and apathy
Prophets proclaim apocalypse and resurrection
Countdown buildup relentlessly continues
I find meaning in silences
And take time to know wonder
Brian J. Groth

LOVE ME A LITTLE MORE

When I feel my world come crashing down.
When the best of friends
Can not be found,
                    Love me a little more.
When the ringing of laughter suddenly stops.
When you can see
My silent teardrops,
                    Love me a little more.
When my hopes and dreams start to fade away.
When I can not say
What I want to say,
                    Love me a little more.
When I become a little too demanding.
Or when I need
comfort and understanding,
                        Love me a little more.
Susan Kimball

MY GREATEST FRIEND

I have the greatest friend my eyes cannot see.
He keeps me company.
We walked by the park.
He showed me the muddy waters of the creek.
"That's like the sinful pleasures man seeks."
He showed me the sturdy oak tree with its age and strength.
"That's how *Spiritual maturity* is in souls;
Strong and fearless like the oak.
This is a speck of my *Creation.*
I want you strong in *Faith.*
You are greater than the oak,
'Cause you belong to *Me.*"
Olivia Cerminara

STORMY WAS HER NAME

There was an old man and his name was Grudge.
His spirit was mean and his life was a drudge.
He preyed on a baby, he used up her life.
He twisted her mind and cut with the knife.
He tore at her body and gouged out her cries.
She learned to keep still and believed all the lies.
He robbed her of parents, of childhood and pride.
He taught her to beg, to mourn and to hide.
She learned how to hate, but not how to fight.
Her rage was turned inward, she never felt right.
Her fury was proof she was spoiled and was bad.
No one could see she was wounded and sad.
Death was her sister, sleep was her hope.
Her young heart soon froze when she couldn't cope.
The little girl was split, his work had been done.
She couldn't remember why she hated the sun.
Janet Robison-Marin

HOW THE STARS GOT THEIR TWINKLE

Children, gather 'round me, let me tell you why
    All the stars do twinkle in the far-off sky
Years ago, the dipper was filled with diamonds rare
    The "man in the moon" was told, to handle them with care
Well up came the north wind, and suddenly did blow
    Scaring old "man in the moon" so badly don't you know
Wham! He dropped the dipper way up in the air
    Scattering out the diamonds all over, everywhere
The diamonds started falling, but on their way down
    They landed on the stars, now that's where they are found
And if you change to look up into the sky at night
    The stars will be twinkling like a million diamonds bright
Grace Spurlock Mattox

HAVE YOU HEARD?

Have you heard the stories of old,
About the streets that are made of gold?
Have you heard of how our Savior lived and died,
The terrible way He was crucified?
And how our Savior said no one is to blame?
Have you heard that our Savior's death made eternal
        life for all,
And if we accept Him we'll never fall?
Have you heard that He's coming again,
To see how many are still living in sin?
Have you heard that His true children will be
        taken home,
To live with God beside His throne?
Have you heard that the sinful will be left to die,
With no one to hear their pain-stricken cry?
Have you heard? Oh, God! HAVE YOU HEARD?
Charolet Brooks

In the hollow of my mind
                        Is the sound of time
                                            Passing slowly
Creeping, crawling by
                        The slowness is only
                                            In the eye
For in actuality
                    Time is passing rapidly
                                            Leaving me behind.
A whirlwind of doubts
                    And anxieties toss
                                        and tumble me about.
Eager anticipation
                    To experience everything
                                            Permeates throughout.
The struggle is exasperating
                    To divest myself of waiting,
                                            Time is passing by.
Nanette L. Carter

THANK YOU LORD

In having problems and letdowns during my day
I know you hear me when I say

"I know deep down that they will pass
For God is with me — that's all I ask."

Sometimes I'll slide, and feel lost and alone;
But then I'll hear a voice and know it's not my own

"Have no fear, my child, for I am here
It'll be okay for I am near —
Trust in God for I won't fail —
To guide and protect you in life's tested spells."

With words of the Lord I feel so relieved
That everything that was a problem is somewhat better at ease.

With trials and tribulations that come my way
I look up at heaven, smile with peace and say

"Thank you, Thank you, Lord
For this day.

Gay H. Mulik

SHOPFRONT BRONZE

Cosmopolite city of the vendor's
Song
Prophet, sage and memory
What do you know of somewhere
Called the past
Sequinned portrait, NEW ORLEANS.

Are you a myth of shuttered doors
And lonely city streets
Or, merely some lost urchin's prayer
In search of some lost dream?

Collage, designed in silhouettes
Of bronze
Shopfronts chipped and faded
From the sun,
Of cobbled narrow streets and livery-man
Shuttered windows, trimmed in drab-olive
Green.
Shopfront image of the past, framed in a looking glass
Femme fatale, I've heard you called
Shopfront image New Orleans
Borrowed from the portrait of the past.

Joan G. Canfield

PUBLISH A POEM? HELP!!

I write ditties with ease, and joyfully
As long as I'm writing my poems for me.
When someone says "Publish, they just might sell,"
I tense, and my "genius" goes all to hell.

My meter's erratic, my imagery faded,
My sentence structure stilted and jaded.
Free verse becomes costly, haiku a joke,
I look at my verse, I think I will choke.

I sit back on my chair with my pen on my lip,
Feeling as if I had more than one nip.
This is not fun, this is work, and it stinks,
Oh publishing world — you sure are a jinx

Stop it! I say, clear your brain of pollution —
Then you're sure to come up with a simple solution.
Of course! I'll pretend it's a freebie I'm writing.
Perhaps then I might have a publisher biting.

Dori Alsop

YES, I WAS ONCE A MAGICIAN . . .

Yes, I was once a magician (some said a Sorcerer)
Studied and was born into garments both wise and good.
I thought myself special, but knew I was ordinary,
Dreamed I was immortal, but felt pain too easily to be a god.
My tasks were simple: Heroes and helpless maidens abound,
To outwit wicked lords, turn aside befouled parents. Indeed,
I spoke words that spilled through others' skin, filled their
Hollows, cured the mad staggers and sorrows, soothed the
Bruised self, released trapped devils, placed more than a few
On the right road, cast some from cliffs
That they might be near the sun.
I feel the grains fall faster now: Smells slip by in ribbons,
High mountains with stone fireplaces, beaches wet with rain,
Wine and bread on streets filled with people,
Whitewater rapids, honey and walnuts, mint and hay.
In the end, I honored the person, however humble
Reached for the moment, however fleeting;
Found love is the barbed arrow that cannot be withdrawn;
I tell my story; do my dance; sing my song.

Dr. Douglas Smith

SMITH, ROBERT DOUGLAS. Knoxville, Tennessee; Education: Georgia State University, Ph.D., 1970; Occupations: Clinical Psychologist, Psychotherapy, Hypnotherapy; Memberships: American Psychological Association, American Society of Clinical Hypnosis; Awards: American Writer's Award, 1978, 1983; Best New Fiction Award, 1982; Poetry: 'The Therapist,' *New Yorker,* 1984; 'Picnic Upon a Precipice,' Self Press, 1985; Other Writings: "Unicorn and Last Christmas Tree," prose, Vantage Press, 1978; "The Paper Rose," prose, University Press, 1978; "A Collection of Endings," essays, American Press, 1985; Comments: *I write of the uncommon problems of common people who cling to universal concerns of human love and despair, of ravaged love and ashes of dreams. I have chosen themes that hopefully may illuminate pathways and lessons for a few who pass this way. I draw my thoughts and feelings from past and present friends, patients and assorted good spirits.*

LONELY DANCER

Some days I feel I've lost my destination.
The time goes by and I'm wonderin' where I've been.
Can't seem to find the road or right direction.
There seems to be a cloud over the sun again.

Some days I feel I've found the answer,
And midnight dreams that haunted me could live.
And stars up in the sky could shine forever.
And songs within my heart were mine to give.

When I can't see the sun or know the answer,
I think about the times with you that might have been.
A shining star, and lost and lonely dancer;
And find the strength to look above the clouds again.

Deborah G. Collett

COLLETT, DEBORAH GAIL. Pen Name: Collett; Born: Norfolk, Virginia, 12-1-53; Single; Education: Tidewater Community College, advanced writing, real estate abstracting; Surety Real Estate School, degree, 5-81; Occupation: Eastern Regional Leasing Office Manager, Ernest W. Hahn, Inc.; Poetry: Have had several poems published in local newspaper; Comments: *I have written poetry since grade school. I write of personal experience or perceptions and currently have a collection of poetry and photography which I hope to publish. Also, I hope to set some of my work to music.*

KNIGHT CASTLES

From the verge on the tip of a moment,
The second the sun lit our minds,
I took your hand and asked you to come;
There was a castle, not far, to find.

We walked in the silence of morning,
As love poured from my heart to your hand.
You asked if our road was upon us —
I whispered, "Our castle may be in any land."

As the night air breathed ever so slowly,
You released my soul from your heart.
You said, "Sail upward and onward,"
For you were tired and our paths now did part.

With each day I come back much stronger.
The horizon in view where I stand.
In the back of my mind is the castle,
Taken to dust on the touch of your command.

Janet Richmond

PLYMOUTH

Here I sit
In a tavern of misunderstanding.
Waiting for my love.
Will he be here soon or may he never?
I walk a back road, many miles of troubled stones.
The way I travel is a forbidden place
Where the rocks of destination sleep under me.
A white misery of love
A tour of no other accommodation
Where people rest in the wide spaces of the world
Where grass grows like wild flower
Where communicating people exist
The road to freedom
Thumbing, walking, running; where to next?
Music that really isn't there but where are we?
Time of endless journey
Wicked thoughts of home
I say I will survive
With God's giving
I will live.

JoAnna M. DeRosa-Pease

AGING DELIA

A wanton hussy was she once —
    strutting her stuff down the boardwalk
        to the delight of hungry men and boys.
Now just a bag lady;
    a side-show attraction on the streets of Olde Town.

Lips dyed crimson
    on an alabaster face
        created by Max Factor,
Rhinestone bangles decorate the
    furrow between still splendid breasts,
        reflecting the sadness of yesterdays
            and tomorrow's gloom.

Her dress is of silver lamé,
    only slightly tattered,
and clings to a well-worn body,
    ineffectively disguising
        a heart wracked with tears
            of the tragedy of living.

Kathy Crowley

A DEDICATION TO MY BELOVED SISTER

They say that time heals all wounds,
If this is true Lord, let it be soon.
For it's already been eight long, lonely years,
Since the passing of my sister dear.
The doctors said it was a massive stroke,
For 13 weeks she lay perfectly still, and never spoke.
I can still hear her wail out in excruciating pain,
Lord I pray, please don't take her, you've nothing to gain.
Why Lord, how can this be, she's only 32 don't you see?
As our dear parents knelt by her frail side,
They prayed to God to be their solitary guide.
Finally everyone had seen the light,
God had taken her burdens away on a cold, dreary night.
Her troubles from this cruel world are no more,
God washed them away upon his heavenly shore.
Please dear sister in heaven wherever you may be,
Hearken, and hear my untimely plea.
Somehow I wished your peaceful soul could see,
That deep in my broken heart I still ask the question,
Why couldn't it have been me?

Donna F. Bennett

A LESSON TO LEARN

There was a Christian that we'll call, *"I Can,"*
Who opened his mouth before the question began
He said . . . I would, I could, I did.
As he began to wind down, his spirit up and it hid,
Because it was not God's direction he sought,
He was defeated in battle before he had fought.
And so if there is a lesson to learn,
Instead of I can, I would,
We must say I'll seek God's counsel and see if I should.

And in a house adjacent to his,
There lived a Christian that can't, but he could.
He sat at home alone all day.
Saying I know it's from God, but still I'll pray.
And God seeking to tell him it's you that I need,
Sent visions and dreams of unplanted seeds
But I can't, but he could continue to pray
Lost out on his blessing as his dreams went away
And so if there is a lesson to learn
I can't really could but lost out on his turn.

Beverly Armstrong

UNTOUCHED BY TIME

Every day, she sits there,
Still as beautiful as the first
    time anyone saw her.
She never changes.
As time passes, it slowly steals our youth,
But she remains the same.
Her hair never tangles,
    her smile never fades,
She just sits there on her
    Victorian chair,
Lady-like posed,
Untouched by time.
Her smile is like a breath of fresh air,
Yet she is unreal.
She is only a porcelain figure,
    but to many she is beyond human.
She has many fans, they stare
    through the window of the gallery,
Just to admire her beauty.
Always she sits — Untouched by time.

Melanie Patrice Falina

TARNISHED HALOES

On the edge of yesterday I poise my pen
Flesh has passed the threshold.
On the ledge of tomorrow I wedge my tears
I pledge my heart to my pen forever;
My lover weeps 'cause I'm possessed by fingers and rod.

A halo cries in the sky.
A halo penetrates the skull.
A rainbow runs to the breeding earth
To redeem the unsanctified. To redeem the solitaires.
To whisper to fleeing hearts wedged on the abyss,
Ledged on the threshold of the pen.
The pledge of the bleeding heart is
To write the song of the heart
In the mud in the sky. To flash her for fleeting hearts
To sing. And to watch her slide the galaxy forever.

The song of a broken people is to clean the tarnish
From their haloes. To ride their rainbow to the earth
And partake of their pie.

Emerald S. Amory

IF THY LOVE

If thy love does exist in thy heart
Let it strum as if mellifluous music;
Springs forth wells in mine eyes
If thy love doth exist in thy heart
Go forth in Land which never dwelt
And find thee a tulip of pure gold
Let it dwell in my sight forevermore, Love
If thy love does exist in thy heart
For thus have I hastened in many days lonely
Letting my heart grow fonder by the wayside
Such longing to bear my eyes upon thee
In pure excellence draw nigh unto me
If thy love does exist in the heart
Reveal the true essence in mine ear
And until thy dying phrase let it sing
As if beautiful cherubims begin to play
Love doth exalt in many ways
None other though than God in heaven
Above all creations display
If thy love doth exist in the heart
Let your love overexceed as if praying to God in heaven
So in my sleep I will dream
And live each moment in love's
Splendor with you Love's Joy.

Bernice K. Will

MYSTIC FALL

Hey tree!
Out here again, finding me
Dew has kissed my toes . . .
Shimmering water of the lake overflows . . .
Just as I overflow with love for thee

I unfold . . .
Bird call by bird call
Thinking on this marvelous fall
Romancing the sky, the ocean, the sea . . .
So great is my love for thee

Birds flying high
Send a message from the sky
Freedom . . . a loftiness from above
Telling us how great . . . how pure . . .
How wonderful is His love

Tree agape . . . just like a face
Sit here as guardian over this sacred place
Everything silently shouts out His name
All seem to say . . . like a turtle dove . . .
Oh how infinite . . . how powerful . . . how supreme is His love.

Fikisha Cumbo

TRACY

The middle child is troubled
Or so the experts say.
In my experience,
It did work that way.

Tracy is my child's name.
She left home at eighteen.
I'd hear her cry for me at night
Though Roy said, "Sleep, it's just a dream."

In later years as we talked
She said that it was true.
"I called 'mama' countless nights
Alone and feeling blue."

I heard you darling, many times,
Why didn't you come home?
"I couldn't mom, my pride you know,
I had to make it on my own."

Fran Pinson Bergman

FEAR

Anger, hatred,
Born out of fear,
secret thoughts,
Hidden feelings of
Wary people.

Caution, secrecy,
Hidden messages.
Growing rebellion,
Increasing numbers of
Changing people.

People turn
to find Invasion
Secret thoughts no longer secret
Hidden in the open,
Hopeless people.

Shocked faces,
Pale with fear,
Men, women, children
ruthlessly slaughtered;
No people.

Lisa M. Freeze

SMOKE

Like smoke that comes from cigarettes
At night while in a quiet mood,
My mind begins to rise and spread
In hopes to find a place of peace,
To find a place of peace.

You gave my lips a tender kiss
That moved my heart into a state
Where life's true meaning seems to come
From deep within your eyes so brown,
Your eyes so soft and brown.

You do not know the warm and tender
Promises you made to me
With sweet and very silent lips
That could not dare express in words
A message only hearts can hear.

Young as a man I feel
Each breath and beat of life's uncertainty
With full and very open heart
That gives of love and asks for love
That's warm, sincere, and very sweet.

James E. Stodghill, Jr.

A WARM EMBRACE

A gentle touch — A warm embrace,
Should I — From my heart erase?
Or could it be this tender scene
Is mere fragment of a lifelong dream?

A voice whispers softly in my ear.
And brings to cheek a joyful tear.
Words engraved upon my heart so deep,
As to put my soul in tranquil sleep.

Do I dare? Do I dare? Quest to find
An answer to this puzzlement of mind?
Or let not my heart, rampant, abound,
To revel in this enchantment I have found!

Oh — that time would stand still
Till cauldrons of my heart could fill
With pretty words and joyous rhyme,
And one rapturous moment that was mine!

Carol A. McQuade

MIGHTSOME

In pleasure search
        my soul doth perch
Were verse of mystic flee.
I tend my rhyme
        lace echo prime
What certain pleases me.

My careful joy
        praise exceed toy
Remembrance prod
Both manhood gain
        lose none terrain
Seed set inside wet pod.

So hear my spend
        rhythmic ascend
Up like stars aware
Their symphony
        uncacophony
Dream so must play bare.

May my sweet coast
        beachcomber boast
Lookness pearl known
Than shore excite
        its mightsome plight
Dances deeper lone.

Orien Todd

GHOST OF STANLY PARK

Your ashes were spread today
Where children cry, and children play
Where young Mothers come to see the day
expire.

You've seen through eyes of life
the nature of God's land
You've seen through eyes of dark
the lonely and downcast
You've seen through eyes of glass
the way was not long.

Many years you've walked Stanly Park
for a million more, your ash will cry
when trampled upon
Your ash will feel the snow, the rain,
and warmed by rays from the sun
hear happy cries of the young
memories spun by the aged
Whispered secrets
The jubilant reconsideration
between two loves.

They will come and go —
You will remain forever
Your ashes were spread
In Stanly Park today!

Bernice Daigle

RUNAWAY

Draped across briar fences
Are sky-boxed bouquets
Arrived late on a Return to Sender porch,
Red, autumnal blossoms
Raising flag with the wind's will.
Wilting beside a barbed stoop,
I am another flower,
A spring and summer blend
Stirred by winter gales,
The rose that is the thorn,
The seasons' breaking spine.

Lynn DeShea Armstrong

THE HUNT

Eye contact . . .
Hiding in the ferns
Threatening eyes,
Hearts pounding.

Dew drops from fronds with
gentle insistence.

Electrically charged air,
Hunger . . .

Pungent smells sift upward
Mists shroud the figures,
They move in a primitive dance
to the rhythm of the dew.
Repeating traditional rituals.

Blood-thirst.
Stepping over steel,
Evil-toothed metal traps.

A monkey screeches,
Time passes . . .

Dearly beloved,
We are gathered here
Today
To join these two people
in Holy Matrimony.

Catherine Jackson

MY LOVE

Be my love.
It's you I adore.
Never have I felt . . .
Total love before.

You came into my life;
Giving me love — anew.
Turning my gray skies . . .
Into skies of blue.

Stay my love.
Through your eyes . . .
I see things brand-new.
I'm flying high.

Upside down, inside out.
In my life you came.
Never again . . .
Will things be the same.

Wonderful our lives have been.
It's now time to part.
My Love . . . remember this;
I've loved you from the very start.

Our love will never end.
No matter where we are.
We WILL always be as one.
No matter where we are.

Gloria J. Eanni

The laughter of a child
    The lightness of a smile
        The freshness of a rain
            The seeing of life reborn again and
                The freedom of a pain.
These are the things that let you know
        You are a main player in
                Life's own show.

Audrey L. Bryant

JUST WONDERING

All of our lives are a struggle.
Mostly for what we don't need.
But, we keep it flavored with good feelings.
To rationalize our greed.

We have many dreams to nowhere.
But in our feelings they're quite true
With them we're trying to make wrong right.
Then reality comes slipping through.

We really live a lot in fantasy.
The material is somewhat a guide.
It seems to keep rushing us on.
Without it life's a meaningless ride.

For us the best that can be done.
Life remains mostly unknown.
What was the reason in the first place?
   And we all keep wondering on.

Calvin C. Wilder

REFLECTIONS

Sun on the water reflects in your face,
   And then it's gone not leaving a trace.
Chased by a cloud that glides along,
   Not bothered by man and doing no wrong.

Mountains are seen in the clear blue lake,
   Reflecting their grace, like a picture to take,
But they disappear when the gentle wind starts,
   Like grief subsiding deep down in our hearts.

A mirror reflects your image to you,
   With a smiling face and a tie in blue,
But if the mirror breaks our reflection is gone,
   Like dust in your hand that's gently thrown.

Your life today is a reflection in kind,
   Twisting and turning the life lines that bind,
As we live our lives throughout our days,
   Will your reflection be worthy of praise?

Donald L. Shepherd

MEMENTO AMORIS

Crumbling carnations
      marking yearbook pages
         snuggle friendly faces
            once frisbee-free.

Haggard roses
      remains of melancholy dreams
         conjure the first kiss of
            a sophomore spring.

Tattered violets
      concealed in prayer books
         raising wistful incense
            recall a requiem.

Lost loves linger
      like pressed flowers
         decayed in crushed detail
            portraits in the heart forever.

Joseph Martin Hernon

HOLIDAY INVITATION
(for A.L.Y.)

Have you noticed the birds no longer sing?
Lovers wrap themselves in coats
instead of each other.
Tree limbs are exposed like last year's Fall.
Will you forget April when Winter says hello?
Christmas will be here in a month or so;
another holiday alone? Lord, I hope not!
If you promise to share it with me
I'll buy you gifts of peppermint candy
and Cherry Blend for your pipe.
I'll steal flowers from Mrs. Rocha's garden;
put away my Tom & Jerry mix for drinks with you.
I'll wear my best face and make you smile
and forget what was before.
I'll spend the night curled against your side,
and let your face see God's gift to me,
and your hands . . . the comfort found in the small of my back.
I'll do all this if you'll spend an hour with me
on Christmas Eve and promise not to mention my age.

Marge Harvey

SEASONS OF LIFE

In the springtime, I was very young.
Full of life and energy galore.
I was ready to face life.
And do so much more.

Then in summer, I went off to school.
To learn and study, and follow the golden rule.
Learning wasn't easy, and I had to study hard.
To face my future, and to leave my baby yard.

In the autumn, my life started to change.
Just like the leaves turn color, on the open
range.
I was now much older and on my own.
And I was put to the test of being alone.

And now it is winter and I am very cold.
I find that my body is very old.
But my spirit is like the spring.
When I was young and could do everything.

Edith L. Gura

FAST FROZEN FLAME

warm
fireshine man
loved . . .

in the beginning
alone
it was the fantasy of that one love forever.

in the dreamtime
together
it was the touching secret in our tangled laughter.

in the end
apart
it was the reality of a raped to death desire.

cool
fireshade woman
lost.

Lyon

MOUNT CHESTERFIELD.

ALEUTIAN SECRET

Out on the far northern islands
Hugging the cold Bering bays,
The winds blow so hard a tree can't stand
And buildings are blown away.

Tundra grass grows hesitantly tall
To perhaps the height of a foot
And even then it grows twisted in half
And bent before the wind's chilling blow.

We camped for awhile by water's edge
And never considered exploring.
No trees, no bushes, no hedge, no life
Except ravens and foxes and bent tundra grass.

One day through boredom I decided to hike
Up the hills to look down on the camp.
Halfway up I sat down to rest on the way
And there on the tundra discovered His gift.

Under the grass and sheltered from storm
Grew profusions of tiny bright flowers.
Rainbows of colors to set in gem-like bouquet
God gives us again His proof to embrace.

John F. Webb

WEBB, JOHN F. Pen Name: Jack; Born: 10-7-19; Married: 11-4-44 to Mary E. Webb; Education: Pasadena City College, University Of Idaho, majored in marketing and radio communication; Occupations: Navy veteran, served as chief petty officer in the Pacific during World War II and Korea; 24-year employee of Copley Newspapers: Reporter for Santa Barbara *News- Press;* On Advertising staff of the *Los Angeles Examiner;* After World War II, returned to *Examiner* as Retail Manager; Retail Manager, Advertising Manager, for *The Daily Breeze;* Appointed Director of Display Advertising for *The Daily Breeze* and San Pedro *News-Pilot;* Memberships: President of the California Newspaper Advertising Executives Association in 1969; Honorary Life Member; Patient care committee at Little Company Hospital; Former Vice President of Marymount College's Advisory Board; Charter Member of Del Amo Rotary Club; Served on the Los Angeles County Executive Board of the Muscular Dystrophy Association, honored with citation of merit; Advertising Club of Los Angeles, received resolutions of commendations from the city of Torrance and the California Senate after his retirement in July 1981; Writings: Book on salesmanship for the Copley Press; Sold a number of travel articles to various newspapers and books.

HARD DAYS

I've had my time of love sweet
flowers and wine.
Now I am alone living like a wayward
adolescent.
There is so much inside me it is
hard to distinguish between the flowers and
the weeds. There is a longing for all
that is good and natural but I find
myself drawn to the wild places of the
night. There are some good people out
there and some bad. These are the
hard days I am coming of age,
I must blossom through the thorns
and winter of discontent.
Many things have not changed I am still
alone in my field of thought alone in
these hard days, alone in the wilderness
of self-imposed exile.

Lori Singley

SINGLEY, LORI. Born: Philadelphia, 5-14-61; Writings: Article published by local *Express* newspaper on Northern Island, 3-18-85; Comments: *This is my first attempt at having my poetry published. My poem 'Hard Days' is a statement about the harsh realities of life, what it is like to be young making choices that are sometimes painful, and what it is like to be young and alone but yet filled with hope. I began writing at age 16, shortly after dropping out of high school. I feel that dropping out of school was a difficult choice, and would not recommend it to other young aspiring poets, but for me it was a choice I made without regret. I do not practice my poetry and I know little about grammar. I simply write what I feel. I never force my creative energy; I simply allow a freedom of flow. I feel that my life experience, traveling the world, being engaged, then surviving a painful breakup, losing both parents, being adopted and discovering a whole new family, all of this happening by the age of 22 has all contributed to my blossoming through the thorns, so to speak, both as a poet and as a woman.*

A LOVE POEM

Could you grow love in a nightmare patch,
throw back the fish and keep the catch,
open the gate and shut the latch?

Could you hide tomorrow under your hat,
hold cabinet meetings with the cat,
invite a rainbow in to chat —

Could you sleep in an egg that didn't hatch,
make fires with a tipless match,
kiss a butterfly right where the wings attach?

Some of these things you perhaps might do
in some private way, if you wanted to,
but if you didn't, I'd still love you.

Delight McColl

THE HEART NO CHANGELING

Only the bluejay and the cardinal
Come to the garden fountain, now, to preen,
And they but briefly; withering annuals sprawl,
But cling tenaciously to the final green.
These are the changeling days when mornings read
The white, imperial edict of the frost
In silver hieroglyphs of flower and weed,
Yet noon insists that summer is not lost.
Even as I, denying time and season,
And all intransigence, turn hopefully
Toward light footfall; credulous past reason
Of mind's deceit, the senses; trickery;
Holding that miles between may bind together;
Proving the heart no changeling like the weather.

Addie M. Hedrick

TEXAN INDEPENDENCE

Calmly walking through the street . . .
    it seemed we had it made
    in that pleasant Dallas heat,
    hand-in-hand, on parade.
A few embarrassed stares, but no hard angry glares,
    no more blood to be paid
                for our love.

Remember the day in '77?
Sweet Paul, pacifist, loved all,
    was martyred then.
Believing . . . or maybe just tired . . .
    gently firm while we ran
        from the christening rocks and bottles
      when the movement began.

'85 and we're together again.
Lovers lying side by side
         sharing pain.
But this time no commiserative gin,
    just cool IVs feeding purple spots
while frightened nurses adjust our cots
and we, like old soldiers, "Remember when . . . "

S. N. Noble

MIDDLETON, CARLTON F. Pen Name: S. N. Noble; Born: 8-15-58; Education: M.S. in Psychology from St. Mary's University of San Antonio; Occupation: Behavioral Scientist; Comments: *Empty and endless, the oceanic void drowns objective meaning — leaving islands of subjective tragedy. Fascinated, frightened, amused, I peer into the surrounding black depths — occasionally whispering into the darkness. And sometimes . . . sometimes I think I hear a reply.*

HUMBLY REMEMBERED

I sit, middle-aged, reading to my daughter,
Amused by her loquacious discern,
and am reminded of the Narcissism
       of my ineffable youth.

When, truculently studious,
espousing a sort of genital vision —
my idiosyncratic ways and sanctimonious opinions
led me to wear my hair in a bun
        and call myself a hippie.

Slogans marched from pores, while others were
treated to my brand of intellectual arrogance.
Contemptuously I dismissed all science,
the clergy, media, ad men, the doltish public,
      and (especially) sinister power complexes.

Sincerely successful in achieving the critical state,
practical solutions were not my concern.
Today, self-chastened, reticent, establishment,
I smile at myself then. May you, maidenchild,
       never encounter such a hairy prig.

Leon Walker

THE QUARREL

Warm silent despised tears, I will not let them touch. Weak outstretched arms, I will not let them hold me to feel the burning pellets. Soft whimpering pleading voice, I will not let it find my cold and cowardly heart, I will flee the aching pain that stares at nothing more. Lost and icy sun return at last to find the drops of life that have long since died in drought, the arms that no longer flail but have fallen to lie limp and still, muggy sobs that yet pilfer through the silence frantically rubbing against each throat through easily severed passageways where life is tugged our own tears now burn gaping trenches that deepen as stiff winter quickly settles in. Even as I gaze upon the small face the seriousness and concern for life flow slowly from within it. Multitudes of silken hair tumble gently softly down upon her fragile cheeks and slender neck. I plunge down upon my perishing security as it steals quickly out into the darkness of the night. Desperately I grope about and grasp cold stone where arms that I refused shall no longer embrace. Far-off I see two dull stars whose embers fade with each light breeze whose loving glow shall never soothe my ruffled pride again. I crawl onto the cool fresh mound. I lie still, exhausted and cry, Mother please, still be here in the morning.

Peggy L. Stewart

NOW I SEE

The exuberance of the sun I see
Whose brilliant splendor unfolds to all,
As His manifestation of vitality shines on,

I see a love no man can purposely deny
That distinguishes the Almighty's universe
As none others' wondrous creation,

Such hope I see in the dismaying hearts
To assuredly cherish and preserve until
His significant reversion to earth is nigh,

Now I see inspiration delivered from a single being
And is treasured in the souls of we
Who are so weak, but have strength enough to believe,

All restoration of goodness for the heavenly bound I see
With the abundance of my simple spirit,
Because my eyes are on the Lord Jesus Christ
And now, like Him, I see the world.

Burnette Geddis Ford

Dear friend of mine, I want to thank you for so many things, but most of all for simply being there during the times I've needed you the most. In my darkest hours of loneliness and self-doubt you've always been there, showing me you really care.

When my tears came you were there, not trying to stop the tears from falling, but rather gently wiping them away as they fell, and all the while holding me close.

In your infinite wisdom you seemed to understand, without my having to explain, that such pain was a necessary part of life, needed to be fully experienced in order for me to learn, and in order for me to grow.

Then when the tears dried you still were there, helping me first to smile, and then to laugh, and finally making me realize what a beautiful world it really is, after all.

It's for this joy of life I thank you most, dear friend.

Marsha Reid

CHILDREN

What do you see for the children of tomorrow,
Will they live in peace and love or will they suffer from the pain and sorrow.
Will they be able to see what the sun looks like as it sets on the ocean,
Or will they see what is left if the enemy should win.
Look at the children of today,
Confused with society and still they run away.
Thinking that everyone else is wrong,
Until they learn the hard way that everyone else was right all along.
The children of yesterday must have really been great,
Fighting for their country with all of their fate.
Families gathered around their radios at night,
Listening to the people stand up for what they thought was right.
We are all children to the father above.
And the job for the children of yesterday is to teach the children of today the true meaning of love.
Showing them how to free themselves of all of their sorrow,
So that they can teach the children of tomorrow.

Mickey Manning

MONTEREY BAY

From the hill where I live I can look down on Monterey Bay and watch as the bay, still entirely covered by its soft white blanket, peeks out here and there playing hide and seek with the sun as the champion and ruler of the day prepares to rout the fog and impart upon the valley life-giving warmth, and make ready for the return of night; and another day is born over Monterey Bay and I begin this day as I ended the last, thinking of you.

With the return of night comes a bone-chilling fog that once again blankets the land and adds more discomfort to an already moody, restless period when the loneliness in my soul intensifies as day flashes its last defiant burst of energy at the engulfing darkness and the clash of the battle bestows upon the western sky a gift of colors created by a supreme abstract artist; beauty that I hope to one day share with you.

From the hill where I live I can look down on Monterey Bay and watch as day begrudgingly relinquishes its hold on the valley, and the sun is drawn down behind the mountains and extinguished by a hungry night; and another day dies over Monterey Bay and I end day as I did the last, without you.

H. C. Jackson

THE OCEAN'S CALLING

I see the sea gull in the sky
waiting for a fish to die.
I see my love, my love to be,
walking towards the open sea.

I see him stop as if to say:
Should I await another day?
My heart is torn with love and hate,
I wander through the garden gate.

I cry his name, he does not hear.
I run and cry in love and fear.
I see my love, my love to me,
turning from the open sea.

Too late am I, he does not heed,
he goes about his gruesome deed.
I see him stride into the sea,
walking, Oh walking, away from me.

I turn away, I cannot bear
to see the life of one so fair
snatched before my tortured eyes,
while life goes on with all her lies.

Betty Lyman

GESTURE

My eyes meet yours.
A flicker of hope.

I extend my hand to you.
Take it if you care to.

A hand is the symbol of good will,
for all who accept it.

A fist clenched in anger,
can quickly relax.

To accept . . . or let it go.
One decision.

I greet you with my eyes.
I extend my hand.

Thus opening the doors,
to a glow you can feel nowhere else.

There is nothing more.
Take it if you care to . . .

Lorie B. Skubal

TEARS OF LOVE

I cried a tear for you,
I cried a tear for me,
And one for each year
We've been through . . .

We've weathered some bad times,
And have seen some good times,
With each one of the years
We've been through.

And now with each tear
I share my love,
And with hand in hand I give
My love, with faith in God,
We'll stand as *one*,
With each one of the years
We'll be through.

Donna L. Woods

HUNGRY

I am an octopus of ears
at
a party; I listen to all
that is, and I
muse
with long inner tear
for your
words, people,
like empty caloried
hors d'oeuvres
do not nourish
me.

Joan

A SEASON FOR TOMORROW

There is a season with sorrow,
Reason for faith's tomorrow,
Throbbing Resurrection,
Enbalming benediction,
My mind's surcease to borrow;

His joy shall proclaim reward,
His kingdom a sheathing sword,
Unchained of Love,
Arisen Dove,
Peace, sings the mind of the Lord.

Anne A. Burke

THE COMPOSER

Can you comprehend
    those bitter notes

Of yesteryear so
    long ago

Can you forget our love so sweet
    it violated the truth so dear

Consuming until the dark deception
    starts once more

Angela Kay Eagin

I WRITE POETRY

The dumb mouths of my pen
Gape soundlessly upon my toiling
As I tend towards a perfect harmony,
Of the thousand minds living
Within my soul.

Pounding, I set forth free,
The sounds of a thousand dreams
Living, new upon my altered reality,
And henceforth bearing boldly the witness,
Of thoughts, both Black and White.

Kendell Geers

Let your mind reach out
    Let it be free
But keep your views open
    And like the sea

Learn by your many moods
    Teach them beauty
Touch a flower and smile
    Cry a tear for me.

Candace Stowell

DRAW NEAR

Draw near, and gaze into His tender eyes,
    My weary heart, to Him for understanding cries,
"Do not forsake me, Lord, though I am lost upon this Sea of Life,
    In worldly sin and strife."

He replies, "My child, closer come to me;"
    Then I draw near; I seem to hear Him whisper soft and low,
"No matter whether tempests come, or stormy winds may blow,
    I'm always here, my child, draw near."

When I draw near, His gentle touch inspires,
    The things for me, His holy will desires,
Then I know, He calls for me to hear,
    "Draw near, my child, draw near."

He shares with me, His Father's kindly care,
    I feel His holy presence everywhere,
So at life's end, when I'm no longer here,
    With open arms, He whispers low, "My child, draw near."

Lucile V. Treutel

TREUTEL, LUCILE VERONICA. Pen Name: Veronica Dale; Born: Mobile, Alabama; B.S. in Ed., UA, Tuscaloosa, Alabama; Occupation: Former Teacher; Memberships: AGAC, many educational associations; Comments: *I write poems and lyrics to music from within. I love music so much, that it seems to be with me always. I have to concentrate on poetry because I find God creeps in to most. I have written a number of lyrics and poems.*

MIND GAMES WITH THE BODY

Paranoid in a hole, I scribble down fragments of desperate affection. Hoping to run home tomorrow but knowing I have to stay for another battle tends to eat away at my patience, my sanity, and my faith.

I sealed the letter — the ambassador of salvation love — and then frantically tried to recall her face. Horror and immediate reality had bombarded the part of my mind that her memory warmed.

Looking into "no man's land," I see the Generals' chessboard. Understanding that their strategy is through statistics, I assume the role of a number. The pieces are all set up and ready to be moved into the line of fire.

The reasoning here is as sane as any rationalization. We must protect the freedom we have, inadvertently, taken for granted by dropping our pursuit of happiness and becoming pawns for our government. This is basic . . .

The pieces are thrust forward. Memories are sent back. The numbers change. I am dead.

D. C. Douglas

FINAL CURTAIN

The stage is empty and the lights are dimmed.
The curtain falls to end the closing play.
The laughter and applause are over now
The last soft notes of music fade away.

And though I had a full, rewarding life,
And found the world a bright, exciting place
I shall be ready when Fate gives the cue
To exit laughing, in Death's solemn face.

Marie C. Lafrenz

CITY TREE

The crooked tree stands bent in the midday mosaic.
It weeps its leaves onto the street, into the gutter.
With no one to love or care for it,
it is covered by the monstrous shade of skyscrapers.

Though it stretches what life it has,
it cannot catch the sunlight.
As ancestors past, it will die with no love,
leaving no memories.

Robert Yedinak

THE FATHER

As an unseen veil of fog
The Spirit of God is with me.
He is the fog . . . He can drift
and even sift through my hair.
When I am His disciple the fog touches me.
He is thin mist when I am searching.
God moves in mysterious ways.
His greatest mystery being the obscure . . .
Elusive soul He gave me in the
Ambiguous time of my conception.

Anita Lisko Gaab

PARENTS

Who are these folks, Mom and Dad?
Always there, good and bad!
They remember the problems they had,
and help you with yours, when you're sad!
Up-to-date with every fad,
they do what they can to make you glad!
Every once in a while, they make you mad!

But who's always there when you need them? MOM and DAD!

Trlllp Bowen

BACK STREET

When Dawn steps on night and
street lights go out, no
longer leading paths to other paths.
When starry silence is broken by
ominous sensations;
Awareness distorts emotion,
beauty becomes reality, unveiling
truths discarded in the night air as
if a bouquet of roses fading in the sun's relentless rise.

Michele Angersola

I KNOW YOU CARE . . .

I speak above a whisper
to soothe your fragile ears
I walk on rugged waters
to calm your aging fears.

I stepped aside to let you pass
I seemed to be in your way
I sometimes keep our trials amassed
In order not to ruin your day.

The times I need your love, comfort and care
You assume I have no hurts and that I'm made of stone
Yet, when someone else cries or moans
You make every effort to atone.

I stand by you through ups and downs
You shove me aside in rebound
Yet, when you are lonely and friends are few
It seems all my time is devoted to you.

You see, I know through thick or thin
Your love for me never ends
My love for you though strange and rare
Says, "HOLD ON THERE, I KNOW HE CARES . . . "

Mabel "Pinkney" Charles

GOODBYE TO MY DEAREST FRIEND

Forced to part, best friends were we,
I wish you could stay with me.
But to whom I leave behind,
I wanted you to know
You've always shared my deepest thoughts —
Will you miss me when you go?
And someday, down the halls of time,
When they ask you if you knew me
Remember that you were a friend of mine
Now that memories are all that's left behind.

Now the light of my life is gone from me.
All the hopes and the dreams went wrong for me.
Is it always the same, the sorrow unending?
There's a smile on my face but I'm only pretending.
Still clinging to memories when we were together,
I can't think what else to do.
The days now are colder, we've parted forever,
My heart longs each day for you.

Would your happy smile still light up my morning?
Would your bright eyes still welcome me home?
Don't worry about me, I'll manage somehow
To get through my life on my own.

Brian K. Wasson

I WISH YOU COULD SPEAK TO ME

Oh, how I wish you were here once again
    To tell you I love you and just take your hand.
It's hard to believe I was so unaware
    Sometimes it seems more than I can bear.
If I'd only known you had too much strife
    I may have prevented you taking your life.
Now, if I could only hear you speak
    What joy it would bring, it would be so sweet.
The years passed so quickly, you just can't be gone
    Each evening after school I look for you home.
It seems only yesterday I held you to my breast
    Singing you a lullaby as I rocked you to rest.
I had no idea your problems were so great
    I wish I had noticed but now it's too late.
Seems we take for granted the time that we share,
    We don't always show just how much we care.
I didn't always listen when you were near
    But now you can't speak, and I'm willing to hear.

Brenda Floyd Smith

WATERS OF LIFE

I remember my childhood and youth days —
        Like clear, deep-flowing river fables,
        Coursing purely free and profoundly
        Across shoals and sun-speckled pebbles.

And I remember my womanhood's ways —
        Like a vast waterway pervading,
        Hiding much soil with tumid waters
        That disposed in foul pools standing.

I remember how it was when you came —
        All these watercourses you amassed,
        To pour gladly through a deep ravine,
        So that all things within me were washed.

I remember the sweet hours to proclaim —
        All heaven beamed upon me anew,
        And evil was smoothly whisked aside.
        For your sake, I quested for virtue.

Thus it was when you came, but now you go —
        The lucency also goes away,
        And I am a raven in wasteland.
        Thus it was, and thus it is today.

Lynda S. Elrawshdeh

MUSIC OF MEMORIES

The crisp green mountains are tall and filled with dare,
        And the Banjo man is echoed from above.
These are the last reminders of the town which stood so fair,
        Seen deep in the valley by the dove.

The dove saw it all as he roamed across the sky,
        The changes which would all come to pass.
The people made the changes as they all said goodbye,
        To a town now part of the past.

The little tiny town grew big and the dove could see,
        The love disappearing from their home.
And the bright blue sky is as dirty as it can be,
        the changes by the people made it so.

The Banjo man echoes the sorrows of the town,
        In his songs named *Memories of Thee.*
He sings to the town "You were worth a diamond crown,
        And will remain as such in me."

Tomorrow brings a world unknown to all of us,
        Our past is a memory forever.
But the changes we make and the things that we change — are just,
        Part of a world shared together.

Julie Holmes

A PERFECT DAY

A PERFECT DAY
    is waking up and thanking God for this day
    for seeing the sunshine, to hear a bird sing
    just being alive to help someone less fortunate
    than I . . . is a perfect day

A PERFECT DAY
    is to see a child at play to hear laughter
    free of fear and pain to know that somehow
    somewhere God watches each step I take
    makes . . . a perfect day

A PERFECT DAY
    is knowing that when night comes you will be there
    by my side, to share whatever there has been
    whatever I hope to be somehow sometime on
                     One Perfect Day.

Joy C. E. Wilson-Tucker

ATOMIC ASTROMIC

The blast was bungotchka,*
Bungotchka was the blast;
Eerie luminosity, luminous iridescency;
Bend back, bend back,
Unearthly flash which must not be seen.

Epochal, cosmical,
An unworld light;
Fabulous, forbidden, energetical expansion;
Sky-splitting boom-boom,
Smashing, ker-mashing poompf.

Down crushing finale,
Fomentation ghastly;
Fireball, doomsday, orangey burst;
Earth shouting thunder —
Man was there too.

Celestial wisdom, likewise an atom;
Split it Prometheus,
And side by side
Match atomic astromic
With guidance bungotchka.

*Bungotchka: "Over, above, and beyond
anything hitherto known."

Henry S. Patricoff

TO MY CHILDREN

I cannot be your father forever,
for I am a child myself.
Ever will we remember days that used to be,
but further and further we will want to see.
We are guests in each others' lives,
then we must leave to go home again.
Ever growing, ever learning,
children in the face of eternity.

William C. Bean

BEAN, WILLIAM CHARLES. Born: Lowell, Massachusetts, 11-3-42; Married: 1-14-61 to Maureen Bean; Occupations: Truck Driver, Writer; Memberships: Teamsters; Poetry: 'Under the Rose,' religious, 11-10-84; 'Forgotten Dreams,' mystical symbolism, 11-14-84; 'When Did You Ask?' religious, 3-15-85; Comments: *I enjoy writing poems that relate to the mystery of existence. I believe that it is an exhaustless subject that serves to stimulate an otherwise indifferent attitude toward a seemingly meaningless existence.*

MOTHER'S DAY, 1966

I went to a movie with you in my tummy,
You flailed hands and feet and I knew I was mummy.

Close to you then and close to you now
My arms are around you wherever, somehow.

Watching you grow, proud as can be,
Glad you're yourself and still partly me.

Waiting to see just who you'll become
Besides being Jeannie Weenie Winsome.

I value your honesty, openness, beauty,
Knowing you're still a giggly cutie.

From all the rest I'd pick no other
To be my favorite daughter. Mother.

Reva Sparkes

SPARKES, REVA. Pen Name: Reva; Born: Dixie, Washington, 5-2-28; Education: EWSC, B.A., 1951; Cal State San Francisco, M.A., 1966; Occupations: Counselor for 26 years, retired and now own and operate Reva's Calligraphy and Personalized Poetry on Vashon Island, also write personal living agreements, for people who are planning to move in together; Writings: "Catecstatic," *No TV for Stevie,* book, Nitewriter's Press, 1982; Comments: *My personalized poetry is full of love and humor. My desire is to support and encourage each person's celebration of life. There is as much joy in the creation of poetry as there is in receiving a special gift of a personalized poem.*

GROWTH

Ah! Sweet love
Thy heart lies within the petals of a flower
Battered and beaten
Tattered and torn
Thrown hitherto —
Mine is the allegory of truth
A misconceived love,
That which, like the petals,
drifted into despair and loneliness
into the forbidden garden of hope
in search of yet another seed to thrust and
feed upon

Susan Cohen

A ROCK

Sometimes I feel like a rock in the middle of a stream,
    I want you to know,
        Just sitting back, watching the flow.

I feel like I cannot move and I am stuck,
        Just sitting here with the worst of luck.

Sometimes I feel so sad and all alone,
        It makes me feel just like a stone.

No one to talk to, no one to speak,
        Just like a rock in the middle of a creek.

Hope the water will get high and roll me away,
        Hope it will roll me to a new place to stay.

It gets so lonely and dark at night,
        I'm waiting to roll where I'll feel right.

Richard T. Freer

O CHRIST, WHO DIED

O Christ, who died upon a cross,
My soul attests your sharpest pain:
'Twas not the spikes in hands or feet,
'Twas not the spear thrust in your side;
These were but instruments of death,
From which your spirit never winced.
No, Lord, the sword that thrust you through
Was in the hands of faithless friends;
Their gross indifference to your fate
Was sharper than the keenest blade.
To know that those you trusted most
Had failed you in your darkest hour —
This was the stroke that pierced your heart
And brought release to death's grim power.

O Christ, whose cross is ever new,
Alas, it must be so today,
As friends of yours still stand apart
And let you die with bleeding heart.

John C. Slemp

THE PUPPETEER

Elegant in manner, arrogant in demeanor
He holds her life in his hands.
Sensing the unfailing devotion, the script
Unfolds only when and where he commands.

Having no commitment of heart or mind
The strings can be picked up or dropped;
As nothing demanded means nothing expected . . .
How can the behavior be stopped?

He doesn't want any closeness it seems
For whatever reason is hidden under
The cool exterior mask he allows
To cover the raging thunder.

Is it fear of the truth or insecurity
That drives him in this role
Manipulating someone else's life so
He needn't face his own.

Barbara A. Youngert

THE TONE OF LIBERTY
At the Liberty Bell in Philadelphia

Thy speechless tongue was eloquent
   That day it summoned Man to claim
The priceless right which Heaven meant
   To make him worthy of his name.

The tones thy joyous message pealed
   Resounded far to all oppressed;
The bright, dear hope of life revealed:
   That Freedom makes the future blessed.

The world re-echoed to thy chords,
   And to the cause of Freedom thrilled:
Man's noble aims, by tyrants' swords
   Can ne'er be thwarted nor e'er stilled.

Thy vibrant chimes released the chains
   Of man's dominion over man;
They fostered strong and stirring strains
   Of binding Earth in kinship's span.

Man's record to be free is writ
   In blood; in pain, his triumph wrought.
Thy ringing did this truth emit:
   With sacrifice is Freedom bought.

Samuel H. Schwartz

THE GRAVEYARD

The graveyard is an
expanse of land which
is the permanent home
for every soul

The mass of land with allotted
houses of six-feet deep which
everyone dreads to live in
but cannot escape

Its sight at night is a horror
to the onlooker because of its
clean white tombs with crosses
upon but with corpses within

The graveyard —
the land where
perfect silence reigns
without a king

Oh!
how I wish you do not exist
you pregnant land
yet insatiable but
always hungry for human bodies.

'Deolu Obakoya

PEACE BEGETS PEACE

How can we expect great nations
To talk and come to an accord
If individuals with each other
Will not communicate a thought?

Why do problems need a battle
Which solves nothing at all,
But serves to hurt the innocent
In more ways than can be told?

If violence only begets violence,
Will not peace do just the same,
For in the final truthful moment
Peace will alone the victory gain.

Eva Marie Ippolito

VOICE OF TRUTH

Life has a moment, now and then
That's due some fond reflection.
A time when truth speaks pure of voice
Untarnished by deception.

We spend our frenzied lifetimes here
Like ants, that can't be still
Our world is but a mount of earth
Beyond another hill.

While all the thoughts we call our own
Are words turned 'round about
There's little new that's said or done
That's due the faintest shout.

There still is meanness, here on earth
and greed and hate still reign
And wars have come and some have gone
And much, is much the same.

So, if the truth seeks voice in you
Don't wait till time is done
Far better that the truth shall out
No better time will come!

Phillip A. Meissner

STARTING AT HOME

As I look behind me
I see even I've been a part
Of the troubles that burden
My sorrowful heart!

Unresolved differences
Between you and me
Resembles a small war
Between countries!

The nerve that I've had
To moan and complain
Of faraway crises;
Of children maimed.

When words that I've spoken
Have accomplished the same
To the pride of a loved one;
The heart of a friend!

So work must begin
At home, not abroad.
Than harmoniously together
We can change the world!!

Cathy Moses

THE WEATHER OR THE MAN?

You blow in with laughter
You tumble in with a roar
You fall on us with tears
You're moody
Changing as you please
Breezy and carefree, dark and broody
You disappoint and tease
You're mysterious
Keeping us on our toes and curious
Will you bring us warmth and cheer
Or cold storms provoking fear
You know no rules, follow no patterns
You possess the power to crumble the earth
And churn the sea
You determine the way we live
With your many tempers
Joy or sorrow
Oh, What face will you show us tomorrow?

Lori Lyn Narlock

LOVE'S PERIL

Tattered, torn, ripped apart,
a piece has broken from my heart.
Never to be whole again,
I gave that piece to you my friend.

Scattered, tired, is my mind,
I have lost all track of time.
for all my thoughts are filled with you,
my moments of peace are very few.

Lost, alone, is my soul,
my very being is paying toll.
For all that I had hoped I'd find,
my thoughtlessness has left me blind.

Sad, scared, is what I'll be,
when comes the day you set me free.
For all the dreams I've wished upon,
shall never be, when you are gone.

Love, cherish, is what I'll do,
all my thoughts I have of you,
and all the hurt and pain I feel,
will prove to me, that you are real.

Ruth E. Weaver

A SPECIAL BOND

In the sun, we laugh.
Forever talking about everything . . .
   and nothing.

Helping each other forget
our past loneliness,
we live for now;
enjoying our short time together,
but always looking
   for tomorrow.

We give to each other
only what we can,
never having to ask.
Apart . . . we exist,
   but together . . . we grow.

It's so simple just to talk.
Yet it's so difficult
to tell you.
We share so much . . .
   How do I say it?

My friend, I love you.

Nancy J. Higginbottom

DEDICATION
*(Written in memory of my son who died
when he was 23 years old)*

"They" say I ask too much
Knowing what the world is:
This poem is dedicated to the one I miss.
So . . .
Please let me fly,
Please let me soar
Let me go where there is no war.
So . . .
Permit me many hours,
Permit me endless time
To know life without crime.
So . . .
Do hug and hold me today,
Affection and love can't wait
For tomorrow may be too late!

Cecelia A. Berman

MY SECOND LOVE

I sat on a hill and looked at the sky
And reminisced of the days gone by
I thought of the past and our wonderful life
That we shared together as man and wife
As I reminisced the sky turned grey
And I thought of my loved one who had passed away

Then I saw you walking in this lonely land
You sat beside me and held my hand
We walked through the meadow where the grass grows tall
And sat on a rock by the waterfall
The sky grew brighter and the sun shone through
For my love and my life was now with you

Edgar Oswold Blore

CHILD ABUSE

There's a crime, being committed today,
Against our children, in a very bad way.
Do you see that little child, sitting over there,
He's been abused by someone, that's supposed to care.
Children are being mistreated, against their will,
They're beaten and tortured, some are even killed.

He wouldn't listen to me, he rants and he raves,
If you don't hit him, he won't behave.
His cuts and bruises, will all go away,
But what of tomorrow, will it be a better day?
They're crying for our help, what's your excuse?
Please, let's put an end, to this awful child abuse.

Jeanette Walker

SELF ILLUSIONS

I like to say
  I know myself
But reality knows better.

Ambiguity
  Cognizance, reticence, dissonance, equipoise
Identity or nothingness
  Acquiescence, counterweight
    I'm not who I am or I am who I'm not
      Disavowal, eclipse, recovery.

An onion has layers but no core.
I am.

Katherine Ramsland

TINY TREE

I
Saw
A very
Tiny tree: so
Insignificant
Amongst the trees so tall.
The beauty, God endowed it with
Is missed — it's just too small. The
Other trees ignore it, as they struggle to
Grow higher; yet the Woodsman's scythe cuts
Through their heart and they're heaped onto
The
Fire!

R. W. Unger

LISTEN

I listen to your voice but do I hear?
I harken to your words but is there understanding?
In silence I wait for you to speak
It only lasts awhile as other voices jar the stillness
I am alone but for my thoughts that come and go,
start and stop, drift and return.
The ringing comes from no bells, the voice comes from nowhere
But I listen and strain
For there is no hearing without inner vibration.

William S. Hodgetts

GOLD RUSH

so perfectly in order you
i would destroy your symmetry
watch your honest face
come clouded with desire for me
intend to mine your dark side
until
biting through the veneer of studied reaction
i hit a glistening seam
of unexploited passion

Vidya Heisel

THE MIND'S A MASTER

The sword won't match the tongue when loose,
The pain is less by far —
Most painful yet is spoken truth —
It leaves a deeper scar.

Bury the sword and it is gone,
The word lives on to haunt.
The mind's a master that can't be fooled —
A demon forever uncaught.

Emily R. Webb

REALITY AND FAITH

We cannot live in the world that might have been
Nor in the world as it might be,
We have to live in the difficult world of today
Which is called grim reality.

So thank God for each day as it is given to us
And do with it the very best that we can.
Let God in His wisdom take care of our tomorrows,
Trusting in Him and His Infinite Plan.

Dorothy O. Keeton

A TEAR'S JOURNEY

Have you ever watched a tear
roll down your face?
It creeps down your cheek
and falls into space.
Then it may land on a sleeve or a mitten,
or perhaps on a letter you have written.
It stains whatever it touches
and leaves an eternal scar —
so in a tear's moment journey, it travels quite far.

Linda J. Morgan

MAY YOUR LOVE CONTINUE

May your love continue as the Bible you employ
And peace be within you while . . .
Yesterday's creation you today enjoy:

Yellow butterflies and hummingbirds;
Overhead, His planets, moon and stars;
Underfoot, meadows — grazing herds;
Rivers clear with bends and bars.

Lakes of blue with waters calm;
Oceans wide and very deep;
Valleys rich with thriving palm;
Elevated plains and cliffs so steep.

Caves of wondrous origin and size;
Occasionally an eagle may hover;
Narrow stream at foothill lies;
Timber — vast areas cover.
Into the sky His mountains reach;
Nature's marvels — including the dove;
Undersea creatures and miles of beach;
Everpresent guidance and undying love.

Ralph Alger

FAITH

In days of old
when Noah was bold
the world was to be destroyed.

By God's command, he built an ark.
With the door open wide
won't you come inside?
But no one believed it would ever depart.

For forty days the rain came down.
Soon not a living thing was left to be found.

For Noah and his family
those for whom God surely cared.
Showing unquestionable faith
their lives were then spared.

That was the Ark and the flood.
Now we have Jesus and the blood.

His door is open wide.
Will you come inside?

David W. Johnson

I can never express
the joy I possess
when I think of you two
sharing a love known by very few!

You are bearing a child on this earth
and I am sure he will know his worth
because his happiness is assured
by the hard times you will have endured
— for him! —

If you want that seed of love to
continue to grow as it has since it was planted,
whatever happens between you,
never take each other for granted!

I love you both
and wish you the best,
and I know in my heart
that God will bless:
You, your home, your love
and best of all: your children!

Sandra J. Othon

THE HOUSE OF MEMORIES

My Grandmother and Grandfather built it
In the early eighteen eighties.
It was made of logs and square-head nails,
And was considered to be the greatest.
This log house had a stairway so steep,
Leading straight up to the loft
Where the children slept on their beds
With mattresses of straw, so soft.
In the kitchen stood a black iron range.
Where the cooking and baking was done.
A spinning wheel "whirred" in the corner;
All of the clothes were home spun.
There were seventeen children in all,
Growing up here over the years.
All but the youngest had lived
In this log house of both joy and tears.
One hundred years it stood there;
Its memories ling'ring all around.
Plans were underway to restore it —
And then — it was burned to the ground.

Delores M. Winjum

WINJUM, DELORES MARIE. Pen Names: Delores (Solwold) Jensen (name from first marriage); Married: Hitterdal, Minnesota, 9-23-29; Widowed in 1976; Education: Grades 1-8, Country School, Keene District #38, Ulen, Minnesota; Graduated from Hitterdal School District #43, Hitterdal, Minnesota, 1947; Occupations: Small Town Waitress; Farm Wife; Mother; Grandmother; Memberships: Salem ALCW; Salem Lutheran Church, Hitterdal, Minnesota; American Legion Auxiliary, Hitterdal, Minnesota; Clay County Farm Bureau, Moorhead, Minnesota; Poetry: Contributions to the following Centennial History Books: *Memories of Yesteryear, Clay County Family Album,* 1976; *1884 — Hitterdal — 1984, Hitterdal 100 Years,* 1984; Other Writings: "Reflections of the Past," Synopsis in booklet program for pageant for the Hitterdal Centennial, 6-29-84; Themes: *Pioneer life in the Midwest; events as they happen; people; religious; abandoned farmsteads, schools and country churches;* Comments: *I enjoy making a memory live forever — word pictures that come alive in the minds of the listener or reader. I like to record events as they are happening — in poetry.*

THE BIG RACE

I wonder who will finish first. (You may have already.)
I wonder if it's been quiet enough to start.
(Maybe it's been quiet enough for you.)

Silence:
        To start to try to forget
        What we cannot forget.

Tell me when you finish: I'll stop along the way to cry again.

My rules are different than yours and God only knows
Who gets the prize and where the finish line leaves us.

Loretta Olund

MY WORLD

My world is flat, you know. Flat like the open page of a book that draws me with a
fascination of reading what I don't want the knowledge of discovering.

Step to the edge and see for yourself the endless blue that pulls with unseen strings
that manipulate us with gravitational pull away from knowing who we are.

The sun rises, often in shades of red that shout out a warning of care for your
emotions.

Those emotions can fall off the edge of flatness, being swallowed up in a blue that
never ends.

The cooling balm of green ends at the limits put on our world by being flat.

Green, deep roots hold us onto a world of sensitivity in which green grows eternally,
expressing itself in hope.

Brown is the underlying of salvation. It embraces the eternal green with a
knowledge of growing into a world that is round.

It reaches up and hungrily grasps the green and pushes out to hold back the blue.

Yellow reaches down and pulses with the hope of love giving to a being unfilled.

The light of compassion surrounds us with finality, because my world is flat, you know.

Lynda Langseth Sahlin

NEVER MINE

Cease! for a moment,
   the refulgence of thine effrontuous verdure, O pageantic spring!
Withhold thou this imperious invasion of elegance — Stop this intimate disaster!
Take off that harrowing, heinous garb, that egregious sneer, that invidious masque,
   for just one moment,

   And behold, my wound!

For thy beauties all are haunted,
   and thy blossoms are but vaunted;
Ecstasy by her is daunted
   whom my fancy wanted near.

She never was; we never were. Yet, how excellent the year
of dreaming, 'til the screaming of the rage within thy psychal sphere,
O Season of elite espousals, mem'ry of a tear aroused.

She found not reason to concur. 'Twas but I, who wanted her.
Never mine,
The thorn is thine! O tender time of roses.

I lay alone the ghost of hope that never blossomed,
until now, when amidst a myriad of blooming,
I remember that one unopened flower.

Spring, get thee hence!

David A. Yeagley

A MOST CONVENTIONAL MAN

If ever you start thinking, that your prayers fall on deaf ears —
That God ignores your yearnings — that He overlooks your tears —
Well don't just sit there waiting, for an answer from the sky,
For if you do, the miracles will surely pass you by.
Consider God a carpenter — as practical as that;
He's building you a castle, and faith is where it's at.
He works through worldly means; He takes over where you fail.
Your prayers will be His hammer, and your trust will be the nails.
So analyze a moment — that's all the time it takes,
To see that miracles, are disguised as lucky breaks;
For He doesn't need a magic wand to do all that He can.
In answering your prayers, God is a most conventional man.

Michael M. Meyers

IT'S A PITY

I lost my shining innocence,
my face now grows old.
The flow of hair upon my head
is turning white . . . instead of gold.
Now I walk, grave and slow.
My head that once looked up,
now hangs low.
My skin, dried and weathered,
is no longer smooth to the touch.
This burden placed upon me
is really just too much.
No longer do men look my way
with eyes that seem to question play.
Instead they turn with disgust
and only speak if they must.
Somehow my youth has slipped away,
now the only thing to do is pray
that soon my time will come.
So finally, I can be led away
by the beating of a drum.

Linda A. Mayes

LACERATED LADY

She is slain
Pain lies
Pillow muffled
Misty amber
Sucks blank walls
She is comatose
Ill wills
And charcoal grills
Siphon the summer
The fuse has blown
Turning on darkness
Utility air — stopped
The plastic casket — sealed
Inside . . .
She smothers
Her soul
Cremated
Again and again
Celestial fires
Rise.

Lynne Kirkpatrick

QUESTIONS OF THE HEART

I can't stop thinking of you
because I know someday we'll grow apart,
How can I explain to you
the questions of my heart?
Right now I'm thinking
of our fate;
It's not right
to let us separate.
Will we feel the same way
when I'm gone?
Think about it because
it won't be very long.
I love you more than anything
I hope you'll remember this,
Remember everything about me
right up to our very last kiss.
I will go now
with this pledge to you,
Always I will love you and
Forever I'll be here.

Nicole Harding

I'M IN LOVE, I'M IN LOVE, I'M IN LOVE

Every day I am with him
I guess that I'm in love
My friends and parents say,
"Let go, that's an awful lot"
But I can't seem to let go
I'm in love, I'm in love, I'm in love
Let me tell you a little about him
'Cause I think you are a friend of mine
He is tall, dark and handsome
His special features are
His white teeth that shine all day long
But don't try to touch them
'Cause if you do "VOW!"
He'll burst into pieces
And will make a very loud sound
Can you guess who is my friend now?
He is my piano
A big black Yamaha
And I want to keep on playing
'Cause I'm in love, I'm in love, I'm in love

Sima Khatami

KHATAMI, SIMA. Born: Tehran, Iran, 10-19-65; Education: High School Graduate; Occupation: Student; Poetry: 'Someone Special,' 'War,' March 1985; Themes: *Almost anything.* Comments: *I wrote my first poem when I was almost eight years old. I started playing piano when I was ten years old. At the age of thirteen, I went to Arizona and I studied at Judson School for two years, while there, I only played piano once in a while and I didn't write any more poems. Finally I went to Spain and I finished my high school studies with the American School of Chicago. Now at the age of nineteen, I am working hard again on piano; I have written three poems in English. And I want to keep on working hard because as I said in my poem I'm in love with my piano and this wonderful world. I write because I want to let out the feelings that can't be just talked out, and I think when you leave an impression on people with your writing, you have done something special.*

STEALING SOFTLY

The dawn steals softly across the sky,
As I sit here and watch it, I wonder why;

Why I let you steal softly into my heart?
What will I do when we decide to part?

For I know you will never love me,
And I know what my future will be.

But for the meantime, I'll hold you as much as I can.
For awhile I can call you my man.

And when the time comes, I hope we let
The parting steal softly like a sunset.

Alice Vanderpool

KIMBERLY'S REQUEST, "SING SOFTLY, PLEASE, MOMMY"

Sing softly, please, Mommy, some nice little tune,
Sing softly, of stars and the man in the moon.

My dolly will sleep with a soft lullaby,
Sing softly, of dreamland beneath starry skies.

The air is alive with the whippoorwills' song
Oh, can you tell me, do they sing all night long?

The fireflies have been winking, their night lights are on.
My eyes are a-blinking, while you sing my song.

Sing softly, please, Mommy, some nice little tune,
Sing softly, of stars and the man in the moon.

Esther E. Farrington

SPRING

There is a season, a season that brings happiness
and pain; a season when love starts to grow, the
season to take walks in the rain.
A season for remembering how things used to be;
about the people you used to know, the ones you
never see.
A season when you start to realize what love really
means; a feeling you first experience, when you are
in your teens.
A season for remembering the good times you had long
ago; a feeling you used to have, for an old love you
used to know.
The season when the flowers bloom and the birds start
to sing; a season to start remembering — the wonderful
season SPRING!

Jennifer Rogg

OLE SNEAKY SNAKE

Here comes Ole Sneaky Snake.
Watch out, for he may grab you.
That slimy Sneaky Snake may appear at any moment.
So watch your toes and watch your legs,
For here comes Sneaky Snake.
Ole Sneaky Snake is looking for an opening,
Oh, any opening will do.
Just enough for him to get a bite.
Look out!
Here comes Sneaky Snake.
Ole Sneaky is as quiet as he can be.
And he always catches you unaware.
He's slipping up behind you.
Slowly, slowly, he comes.
Gotcha!

Sharon P. Evans

HELLO DARLING, GOODBYE

I met you in the evening, you seemed so all alone.
I talked with you that evening, then I was yours alone.

You weren't an everyday guy,
You talked, you laughed, you made me grow.

The weeks that followed meant so much,
the little things you did.
The talk, the laugh, the happiness, and most of all the rose.

You would walk with me, and share your moods.
We held hands, we kissed, we looked inside.

And the moments we spent together, two people and yet just one.
Riding in the wind, sailing through, and dreaming just a bit.

I know a lot of things that were, I made up in my mind.
These feelings that I give to you, I know are not returned.

And now I've come to say good-by, for now I leave alone.
I think of all the wasted time, we could have shared as one.

As I go I leave with you, something that you stole.
I leave with you my heart's desire, I leave you all my love.

Polly Fassett Olson

THE CRYING CHILDREN

We've got to know when to love them, know when to stop.
Know when to correct them, know how to not.

We've got to band together, and count our blessings, for
The new generation will need our support.

We've got to love our children, support them and protect
Them. Answer to their prayers, answer to their tears.

We've got to have strict laws, so our children can be
Happier. 'Cause child abuse is on us like a full-fledged
War.

We've got to put an end, to the abuse of a child. So
The new generation will have a happier smile.

Teresa Ceccarini-Lopes

A TRIBUTE TO THE ELDERLY

Touch not with tongue of scorn the elderly folk
Whose life has been forlorn
       For burdens borne,
Give them happiness, dry their tears —
                  The lonely folk:
For theirs have been scores of years
          And filled with fears.

I plead with youth to revere each elderly soul:
Since life's beginnings — endings are ever near,
              All can be sincere;
So love them, help them to ever see hope in youth,
For we, too, may live to be better than we can see.
Neglect them as you may — these dear ones:
For life has found a way in kind to repay
Us each, for every word and deed, yes, all we do
Returns, as sowing with good or bad seed —
              This is life indeed!

I see their furrowed faces — these older ones,
And grow anxious at their faltering paces
Yet savoring their imminent graces . . .
I bow and pray with face in hand,
        That I may stand,
And someday join their noble band.

Earl T. Gentry, Chaplain

AUTUMN

An invisible brush, an unseen hand,
paint colors of grandeur across all the land.

A bold touch of orange, and a dashing of gold,
a picture of beauty begins to unfold.

Magnificent green from warm summer days,
now changed by the artist in masterful ways.

Creates he a palette from yellow to brown,
and all in between painting country, and town.

More rapidly now to the grass, and the wheat,
a touch on all plant life, and autumn's complete.

David Bruce Turner

TURNER, DAVID BRUCE. Born: Minneapolis, Minnesota, 4-10-47; Married: 4-9-83 to Mary Beth Showalter; Poetry: 'MaMa Let Me Live,' traditional, on moral issue, *Pine River Journal*, 6-6-74; Comments: *I have only recently begun seriously offering my work for publication. I try to show the simplistic beauty of personality, and actions in children, and the perfect unity, and balance in nature. Also, man's own ineptitude at understanding, accepting, and co-existing with the natural scheme of things.*

HOME

The place is a wonder
with a very narrow road
that winds in a curve, at the corner.
There are trees, bushes, birds
and there is a house,
down yonder . . .
Full of memories from times past
and also the present, enough to last
one full eternity of reminiscense.
There have been stories
but it remains changeless.
The house stands old, but proud
after six decades of fighting
against nature's fury, the wind and the rain;
of seeing children growing up
and one by one moving away.
The years passed and one returned,
he was the little boy of yesterday.
Today he has two boys of his own
and just like he did back in the old days,
his children are calling the very same house, home.

Ana Sofia Howard

NUMBER NINE

A morning's glory weeping all is still
A child's spouting laughter as dawn makes its will.
A place so might tranquil its thought will instill.
A memory worth scripting intense with the quill.

Peter L. Mazzuca

UNEXPECTED GIFTEDNESS

So great His Love
He made "just for me":
    — the silent shimmering of the silvered trees
    — the careless croaking of carefree frogs
    — the pesky persistence of bumbling bees
    — the firefly flutterings dotting the darkness
    — the droplets of dew that dawn leaves behind
    — the bespeckled butterflies basking in beauty
    — the cerise sunset serenely surrendering
    — the pebble-pounced ringlets rippling the pond
    — the muted mysteries of majestic mountains
    — the unfettered flight of the yet fluffy fledgling
    — the cotton-like clouds capering contentedly . . .
The glorious God
    so gifts ME
    with His extravagance!

Sister Mary Charleen Hug, SND.

HUG, SR. MARY CHARLEEN, SND. Born: Sandusky, Ohio, 1-16-40; Education: Mary Manse College, Toledo, Ohio, B.A., 1967; Ball State University, Muncie, Indiana, M.A., 1974; Occupations: 20 years in Education as Teacher and Principal; presently a patient in Sisters of Notre Dame Infirmary, due to spinal disease; Memberships: Sisters of Notre Dame; Other Writings: "Two Precious to Keep," *Parish Family Digest,* Our Sunday Visitor, 5-85; "A Lovelier Day," *Cathechist,* Peter, Li, Inc., 4-85; "Spiritual Formation Through Suffering," *Review for Religious,* R. for Religious, May/June, 1985; "New Ministry," *Catholic Chronicle,* Catholic Press Union, 3-85; "Living at Home with Suffering," *Human Growth and Development,* Le Jacq Publisher, Inc., Summer, 1985; Comments: *Why I write: To lift spirits — to offer inspiration — to spread joy — to reveal the Goodness of God — to show that there can be joy in suffering and that that suffering can be meritorious.*

THE MOTHER

She touched me with her tenderness
A tear in her eye and a sigh on her breath
The mother to be
Who was never to be
Watching a tiny spark flicker and fade
As the life of a child passed forever away
The mother to be
Who was never to be
Years later she holds her second and last
As from her life he too will pass
The mother to be
Who was never to be
The grief in my heart for a loss not my own
Reflects in some way what she will not show
The mother to be
Who was never to be
On whom would I wish it, family or friend
We only endure what we can in the end
Said the mother to be
Who was never to be

V. Bert-Murphy

STATUS AND SUCCESS

When *we* were younger; (in our prime)
We didn't worry about money or time or
Our place in life.
Status and success? they were for others not
Us.
Big houses and fancy cars were things
We looked at — others owned and
We did not envy because
We had each other.
It must be the gray that makes
Us act this way, and
We; have
We forgotten what made these hairs turn gray?
A symbol of wisdom and age?
A mark of growing? Let
Us not squander
Our gray hairs and golden years on foolishness —
Status and success
We are together;
We already are both.

Donald E. Phillips

END OF THE DAY

We spun out on the highway this evening.
it was a wet road and the tired lost their grip,
and we spun two, three times
across four lanes and stopping a foot from a guard rail.
I didn't see any part of my life roll
before me, and there were no frozen
moments of horror, or any scenes in slow motion.
I tried to grab the wheel from her
but it tumbles across my fingers; no
Herculean feats of strength here, nor any mass rushes
of adrenalin. We were just spinning there
                    I was at least expecting
some dramatic last cries, but it was all
so routine, like two dimes tossed out
to the tollbooth machine. "ding-ding." "thank you."
no hearts beating faster, no red flushing faces,
no breakdowns into tears. It was too random,
too silent.
We looked around, started the car up again,
and drove away.

Tony Molinaro

PURGATORY.

AN UNANSWERED PLEA

A little child nestles into
its mother's breast,
undaunted, by the reality in
the street, total unrest.
Dirty faced terrorists shelling
mortars, throughout the
barren plains, amid the gaping
holes and tear-streaked faces
in a world gone insane.

Where are the smiling faces,
The helping hand? Where is
the free land that used to be?
Has our world found pleasure
in this bloody massacre?

Just a sleeping child, its downy
lashes closed,
Tomorrow, another day of
hatred,
Will the child live? Who
knows.

Lisa Cummings

MONA LISA

My long-suffering
Somewhat bored, haughty cat
All liquid brown and black,
Her prim paws crossed,
Stares benignly
At the looney world
As it lurches by.
She sighs heavily.

Sloe-eyed
She disguises
Harsh, licking fire
Behind dilating pupils.
An insulting zephyr
Disturbs her spotless white ruff
And she heaves
Another resigned sigh.

The mystic allure of Golden Samarkand
Hovers indistinct around her Sphinx head
In vague decadent twilight.
Ah! Leonardo, we perceive your meaning.

Norma Hull

QUEEN OF HEARTS
(The Plan)

He was a young boy
just a day ago.
What made him
want to change?
Who could possess
his soul?

As though twenty-one
was his final call.
He dealt his cards
with precision,
though caution
was never his friend.
He had a plan!

All cards were laid
on the table;
he played his hand.
And the Queen of Hearts
began.

L. Marie Allen

discouraging words
dedicated to m.j.

harsh, cutting words, colorful adverbs
have such immense power!
they can strike one down,
abdicate a royal crown:
leaving a once-strong person
running from himself,
reduced to a canine cower!
fine deeds and spices,
yielding a sweet concoction,
mixed with unrelenting hate
rapidly turn it sour.
stories misconstrued,
re-told to such magnitude,
they crush the public image
of the famous to infamous;
so callous the words,
so uninvitingly shrewd!
terminal hurts, inflicted
by razor-sharp words,
like no other universal weapon
is, indeed, the most deadly ammunition!
and yet,
no prison term served,
no court-ordered act of contrition.

m. kay slade

NATURE'S CHANGE

As the leaves begin their change,
  the leaves begin to fall;
As they scatter on the ground,
  the breeze will take them all
Against the wind they'll fly away.
Soon landing, there they'll stay

Jeanette Ullenes

ULLENES, JEANETTE. Born: Bay Ridge, Brooklyn, 7-21-63; Married: 5-13-84 to Mr. Gary Ullenes; Education: Attended Wagner College in Staten Island, Occupations: Nanny, English Tutor, Artist; Memberships: Alpha Delta Pi Sorority — Gamma Pi Chapter; Themes: *I usually write about nature and about love;* Comments: *I try to express inner feelings of beauty so that others could read & understand my interpretations. Along with everyone else who writes, everyone has different ideas which are enjoyable to read.*

CORSETS AND LACE
(To Adeliade)

Intricate patterns bind
our lives
keep us tightly woven
like old lace —

grown deep in southern hills
and stored in milk churns
with cracked mason jars
and other old things

like corsets
bind us in blues times
when our rose bushes
are sprouting wild chiggerweeds.

I've called you friend
since Ethiopia
where we danced for parading blackbirds
and weaved fine lace.

I'll call you sister forever.
Like corsets and lace
yellowed by time
you become more precious.

Barbara Cochran

RULES

when i was five
i went to school
at ten, fifteen and twenty
i was still at school
where will i be at twenty-five

all i've known is school
the rules, the regulations
the requirements

if you do this, pass this,
you may go ahead —
if not, you must stay
and pay the price —

the price of defeat;
the price of despair
the price of success;
a new set of rules

when finally free of school
free of rules and requirements
what will there be
I am twenty-two
and not ready for another set of rules.

Nicola Travis

SEEKING

The brink of it, the edge of it
I sense the thrill of it.
It's magic, it's confusion
The song of it, the rhythm of it

Over and over as the tide
I rush in to ebb out.
Ever seeking, ever flowing
Ever knowing I'll never truly know

Seeking yet ever seeking
I'll never stop seeking.
Made to follow the sun
As cloud, as sea, as man.

John A. Devlin

SEASONS OF LOVE

Have you seen the sky so blue?
Flowers fresh with morning dew
Trees are filled with leaves so new
Spring is like my love for you

Summer brings the morning dove
We set sail on an endless sea
Times together as we love
Sailing towards eternity

Colors fill surrounding trees
We are still together
We have sailed on all love's seas
And still love one another

Winter brings on the cold
Wisdom, grace, white hair
You are still my knight so bold
And I your lady fair

Louise Grenier

FIRST-BORN

This entity is mine —
        wrenched from my flesh
and bundled there
        in clenched-fist innocence,
wailing with fierce denial
        and loss
of recent warm-laved
        residence.

Smile at your mother —
        bending near in disbelief
that she should see
        such perfect fruit, plucked
from her imperfect tree.

Never was beauty witnessed
        quite so fair
as my first-born —
        in battered innocence there.

Flora M. Kosoff

WE'RE IN THIS TOGETHER

My friends and my lover;
  please see what I am.
Accept all the things
  that you possibly can.

Born to this world
  just like the rest
Experiencing the same feelings;
  we all try our best.

Never think that you're better
  or not up to par.
We're in this together,
  realize who you are . . .

Swarming like bees,
  building their nest;
the World is complete
  the day we can rest.

Sandra Hudak

COMPROMISE

The world is such
That we may never know
One tender touch,
As yet, in embryo.
So let us clutch
What Heaven may bestow,
Forgetting much,
And so, in Time, our woe.

Tina Iannaci

IANNACI, TINA. Born: Philadelphia, Pennsylvania; Married twice, now divorced; Education: High School; Occupation: Copywriter, Religious Publishing Firm; Memberships: I've been involved with Community Theatre for almost 35 years. Mostly directing. Comments: *As a child, writing poetry was my "escape." I have encouraged my daughter to do the same. It's a way of putting things straight and of trying to make sense out of chaos. I would like to say to teens: "Forget suicide . . . write a poem, instead! One poem always leads to another."*

THE BY AND 'BYE LULLABY

Lullaby, baby love,
Cobalt bombs are your bunting,
Radar beams guard your dreams;
There's a spy in the sky
That is constantly hunting.
Lullaby, lullaby,
By-and-by, baby, 'bye.

Lullaby, baby sweet,
The napalm is flaming
Like a light in the night.
Sleep and rest! At my breast —
Nuclear warheads are aiming.
Lullaby, lullaby,
By-and-by, baby, 'bye.

Lullaby, baby dear,
Death, a wind in the treetops,
Rocks you slow, to-and-fro;
Hush, don't cry!
By-and-by, lullaby!

Billie A. Heacock

OUR SON IS IN KOREA . . . TO LARRY

Our son is in Korea,
  Many miles away from home,
But his heart is always with us,
  Wherever he may roam.
So this Christmas just remember,
  Even though you're across the sea,
That *you* are all that matters,
  To your mother and to me.
And remember, Son,
  To us you'll always rate,
And we'll be seeing you in person,
  In Nineteen Fifty-Eight.

Charles Ernest Hollopeter

FRIEND?

A friend, indeed!
Where's a friend when you're in need?

If you seek will you find
The kind of friend you had in mind?

Patience is a virtue, or so they say
But I need a good friendship anyway.

If I give, will I receive
The kind of friendship that I need?

Paul Kluxen

To Love Again . . .
        Read between the lines, and love
    there you will find. The special love, a
    once in a lifetime kind.

        I've found love Again . . .
            Without I just survive,
    with love I come alive!

With happiness,
        And dreams I thought were lost.
To chance a heart broken, but
for love, I'll risk the cost.

Gretchen Schumacher

HARRIED HOUSEWIFE

Frugally, carefully
clipping all coupons she
hides all her treasures in
secretive pockets of
wallets and purses; then
loses them just when she
gets to the Mall.

Margaret Joy Borle

TRANQUILITY

A torn pillow lies sleeping
quietly on the bed.
Its heart is beating lightly
with the breeze from the open window.
The feathers of its soul
are rearranged in time,
Like our own.
The hall clock chimes dimly
as an afternoon shadow crosses its face.
And the smokiness of dusk
slips through the cracks
and settles on the coverlet.

Linda J. Bartlett

FAMISHED FINCHES

Seekers sow seed in sod;
Finders feed famished finches
Fresh food from flock's Father.
Sweet, soft speech
Sows seed,
Bringing forth branches, buds, blossoms;
Breathing beauty
And feasting from fruitful feast;
Flourishing forever
To feed famished finches.

Terrie T. Leonard

LEONARD, TERRIE THEA. Pen Name: Terrie Leonard; Born: Lansing, Michigan, 6-15-59; Education: In spite of terrible physical handicaps caused by cerebral palsy, Terrie passed the GED and has taken college courses. Occupation: Writer; Writings: *My Walk With God* book of inspirational poetry, completed in 1984, yet to be published; Comments: *I write as a means of self-expression. Mainly inspirational, my poems are my way of showing my commitment to God, since I can't get out and witness.*

BONDING

If love exists
   the "oneness" doesn't dissipate
     as we move in separate directions;
      it transcends beyond our beings
       and lives in our spirits
        wherever we are.

It bonds
   but never binds us;
     holding us close,
      yet allowing us to follow
       individual paths.

Through love,
   we often find that freedom
     can still exist
      even as we sit
       side
        by
         side.

Diane Greenway

THE RIGHT OR THE WRONG

The right or the wrong are always in prime
At times, it is hard to make up one's mind
Should I do this or must I accept that?
Can have one searching for primary fact.

Who is correct or who made the error?
Sometimes puts one into a furor
Did I forget something; a missing link
That can make me wrong, in what I think?

Did I lose a few truthful thoughts
That could alleviate the situation, a lot?
Did I procrastinate, without trying
To analyze facts that may be lying?

T. Steven Watkins

PEBBLES

Pebbles of my life
Make pictures on the sands of time,
And I am sculptured into walls of strength
Burnt by the many settings of the sun.

Pebbles of my life
Form shores which reach into the sublime,
And I am molded into roughness,
Baked with the crumbs as a new-formed bun.

Pebbles of my life
Sound against the mountains I climb,
And I am battered into a rock,
Hardened by precipitant battles won.

Janina Judith Piszyk

ZENITH

Exhilarated by the gaze of love
Soars my spirit, Purity's dove,
Past the moon, beyond above,
To land safe within a starry cove.

My heart sings, full of gratitude
At its present point in latitude;
For reaching Love's high altitude
And navigating my attitude . . .

It lists adrift above the earth
Fixed in a state of raptured mirth
Aware that Love wields wondrous worth;
Thine aqua eyes, my soul's new berth.

Marilynn Davis

I never thought it possible
To feel this way again
To love someone for what they are
A very trusting friend
   To see myself inside of you
   And know in my heart
   That together we'll see it through
   Wherever it may start
To feel like this
Whenever you're around
And know that with you beside me
I could never become down
   For in our friendship I can see
   How trust can make security
   Knowing that I feel this way
   We'll last throughout eternity

Caren Osborn

THRESHOLD

Alone, distant from time,
Shadows on the wall,
Pressure of time
Crowding on my distance,
Separate, isolated,
I want to remain.
Don't touch, it burns.
The snow is clean,
White, pure, safe.
I want to make snow angels.
My ice castle.
Keep away, it might melt.
Fire and ice destroy.
You are you,
I am I.
Understand.
And stay away.

Gina Bacon

IMPRESSIONS IN THE SAND

The waves roll
Relentlessly on the shore
Erasing my first imprints
In the sand
Forevermore.
They recede again,
At God's command,
To leave a space
Where my dog "Chip" can chase
The screaming sea birds,
To watch them soar
Into the sunlit sky,
And I,
Can place
My fleeting footprints
On the strand
Once more.

Charles Atkin

THE RIVER POEM

Sitting by the water's edge,
Watching the sunset,
And the white waves
Gliding gleefully downstream,
I wonder

Could it be?

That life is like this stream
Flowing ever into a greater sea
Out to join a greater force?
And will this greater force accept me?

As I am?
As I was?
As I wish to be?

Therese Ensley

LOVELINESS

There is a poem about a tree,
That states, nothing lovelier can be!
But, newborn babe, so small and wrinkled,
A deed, that caused an eye to twinkle,
Kind thought, that caused a face to smile
Kind word, that eased a long, long mile.
A way to lift a heart to sing
A thought that's worth remembering,
These things; nothing lovelier can be,
We make these, GOD made that tree!

B. D. Walker

GRIEF

When the doctor diagnosed her husband's leukemia,
      she wanted to cry but she didn't
            because he hated when women cried.
                When she was alone, the tears rolled inwardly.

When treatments to contain his disease were unsuccessful,
      she wanted to cry but she couldn't
            because he hated when women cried.
                When she was alone, the tears rolled inwardly.

Now that death has claimed his life,
      she wants to cry but she can't
            because she remembers he hated when women cried.

She damns the tears
      and implores God
            to release her from her grief.

Shirley David

LIFE IS BUT A VAPOR

(Taken from James 4:14)

Life is but a vapor, so short but yet so long,
that when I think of yesteryear, where has my life all gone?
But when I look at the years ahead, they seem so far away,
yet when I look back ten years from now, it will seem like yesterday!

Life is but a vapor, here today and gone tomorrow,
life has its years of happiness, and also its years of sorrow.

Life is but a vapor, so make every moment worthwhile,
don't walk through life unhappy, love JESUS and you'll wear a smile.

Life is but a vapor, so do unto all others with love.
Give, and it will be given from your Father in heaven above.

Life is but a vapor, so don't store your treasures here on earth,
store your treasures in heaven, where God will count their worth.

Life is but a vapor, don't worry about death's sting,
because of Jesus' death on the cross we'll forever live with our King!

Life is but a vapor, I can hardly wait till I die,
to see my Master Face to Face, and live with "Him" on high.

Freda Carrier

LEE OSWALD AND JACK RUBY

    Why look down on Lee Oswald so hard, or Jack Ruby for his part.
When deep in our hearts we know, someone greater was backing the
whole show. They got so much money and power, they paid to keep out
of the shower. Lee Oswald was a tool they used to do the dirty
work, thinking he would get away and paid the dumb little jerk.
they used Jack Ruby to get him out of the way, because they were
afraid of the things he might say. Jack Ruby was one of the gang,
before he'd sing he'd hang. There was talk about giving Ruby a fair
trial — he didn't give Oswald a little while. When Lee looked up
and saw him among the others, he tried to get under cover. The
detectives looked away and no one had much to say. Jack Ruby said
he loved the president — he grabbed his gun and out he went to
right a wrong that had been done.

    He had rocks in his head if he thought we was so dumb. Texas
is known for yellow roses, yet they sent Mrs. J.F.K. red ones.
At the last minute they changed the route, someone there knew
what it was all about. If Oswald had lived, maybe we would have
known more. With things as they are, no one can be sure.

    The whole world is in a confused mess; poor people are in
distress. The Secret Service men went out and got pie-eyed the
day the president was killed. People who loved him stood and cried.
The one behind it must feel bad — someday he will go mad.

Bertha Fisher

A POET'S PLEA

A poet's soul is soiled
A poet's words are a confession heard
Sometimes a joyful relief
Sometimes a painful relief
But always a price worth paying

They are the guardians of the heart
That enable a poet to keep living
Like a cleansing bath
The words wash over old wounds
And soothe the scars left standing
As the colors of sunrise
Cross an unmarked grave.

Mary Jo La Ferr-Cohns

TOGETHER

Concrete, small and cool . . .
is the porch on which we sit.
Watching the tide as it splashes . . .
over the rocks, onto shore.
The warm air quickly turning . . .
nippy as the sun sets in the distance.
The chirping of sea gulls . . .
as they head for home.
The loud whistle of a large ship . . .
far away and not seen.
Together we sit and admire the . . .
sounds and beauty that encircle us . . .
on this beautiful place before us.

Sandra Gober

LIVING

Are you living your life,
  or just drifting through it?
You can dream all the while
  and do nothing about it.

You can live or exist,
  do whatever you wish.
But nothing will be accomplished,
  by just wishing for it.

To live is to have,
  to share, and to mingle.
To exist is to hoard,
  and keep everything single.

Eglantine Lee Riviears

BUTTERFLY

Butterfly soaring through the air
Gliding along without a care,
I wonder where you are going today
Is it near or far away?
I wonder will you fly on by
Or stop for a moment to say hi.
Resting on a branch nearby
Fluttering your wings ready to fly.
I wish you would stay for awhile
So I can watch your beautiful style
And enjoy your beautiful, colorful marks
Of perfect shadowing of lights to darks.
Then be gone again on your way
So others too can enjoy you today.

Shirley B. O'Keefe

THE NIGHT OF EYES

This is the night of eyes I see,
and those I saw — saw doubly.
Those eyes my way saw two of me,
as interesting as it may be . . .
twice the picture they must see.

But many gazed so tenderly,
around the faces presently.
I wondered what those eyes would see,
as they stared into eternity . . .
seeing once, then twice of me,
The night of eyes watched curiously.

Mike Bradshaw

DYING TREE

Most of my life has been the same
Like a dying tree in a summer rain
The leaves all seem to float away
Just so many lovers who refused to play.

But I long for so much more
Than the dying roots at my lover's door,
Why can't I see a healthy tree
With leaves so green and branches free.

Or am I doomed to search for the key
Which is locked inside the dying tree

Michael Meaux

CASCADE

Methodic sad notes
cascade through this cavern.

Electronic waterfall matches
the rain through the window glass.

My friends and I sit idle
scattered through the place,
lost somewhere
the space between
gray wet autumn
and caresses from the past.

Elaine Pinckard

PUZZLE

To Julie

Mystery of womanhood
That's what you portray to me
Lovely lines of beauty
A face of sensuality
Unpredictable as the behavior of life
Creature of caring
Trying to correct all wrongs
An impossible task
But undaunted you try
Ageless charm and loveliness
But with the fragility of a butterfly.

Bill Russell, Jr.

RHONDA

Bouncing and glad,
Crying and sad,
You can wager
She is my Darling Teenager.

Margaret Rebrinsky

THE SANDS OF TIME

The sands of time run swiftly through the hourglass standing on the shelf
There's tasks that need doing I should help I'm always saying to myself
The whales are all being slaughtered soon they'll be gone from the ocean
Something should be done about it though what I haven't the slightest notion
Wild horses are slain for dog food what else people say are they good for
It makes me sad to think there is no one to even care anymore
Forests are being burned down that used to be so green with trees standing tall
Some are caused by arson but people don't care I guess there's no one at all

Boys and girls take their lives daily more and more it seems each day
How sad that ones so young come to believe that there is just no other way
Is it because we've lost sight of God that these things have come to pass
What's gone wrong I ask myself as I watch the sand falling in the hourglass
I can't help but believe there must be something we can do to change things
We can't just sit and wait not really caring what tomorrow might bring
So I for one will not sit by waiting for more bad news tomorrow
I'll work to change things while I can I've had enough of tears and sorrow

Ardis Kent

MURMURS

They held each other close against their breasts and gazed deeply into the other's eyes
Gently their tender lips embraced and as one they said "I love you."
A million stars shone brightly overhead while sweetly sang the violins.

The subway screeched on iron nails drowning out the wisdom of profanity
Muffling the screams of those molested by the wall inscribed with blood "I love you."
Clouds of swirling dirt and dust blew by and the violins played off-key.

The streets echoed with running feet as glass was shattered in crystalline snow
Shots rang out from somewhere in the darkness, shattering the stillness "I love you."
Terror roamed the deserted city as stretched violin strings cried out in agony.

Beings without faces held each other tightly staring dumbly into mirrored orbs of nothingness
Like so many animals they ravaged each other and through the sickness coughed "I love you."
Clouds of molten fire spread themselves across the world
And the violin strings, stretched too taut, broke, their final note "I love you."

Steven Jay Marks

FOR BLACK WOMEN ONLY

Four hundred years of misery has been your only claim,
Degradation and debasement have been synonomous with your name.
You've toiled from dawn 'til sunset, your work seemed never done,
And yet you tried with all your heart to make your men a home.
Nothing was too good for them, for they, they were your life,
You'd go through hell to keep them well, and then you'd pay the price.
To Mothers, and Sisters who cried for us, and watched us as we died,
Tended our wounds, and cared for us, and taught us how to survive.
Arise Black Women, and take your bow, too long have you been ignored,
You've saved us for this moment, and now, this moment is yours.

Abdul-Mujaahid Shakir

FOUNTAINS OF LIFE

The magician plunged
Three naughty boys
Into his ink well
To create a suggestive magic.

 Sea nymphs came from the ocean.
  to weep salt tears
 We stood upon the shore.

From the underworld
Sugared skulls at the feast
Of All Souls
Dancing people circle a bonfire.

 All in a Hallow's Eve
  to keep their souls free
 We lent hand and song.

Above angels in swift flight
Whispering runes carved
In jewels and swords
Told us
Travel the sky and sea beds.

 Hail salvation, our ship's anchor
  finely shaped like a cross
 We drink from fountains of life.

Jerry Kennedy

HE WAS ONLY TWENTY ONE

He gave his life
Like millions others.
But for me he was
My baby brother!
His life was short,
His mind was sharp;
At fourteen he won a prize,
At sixteen he saved our lives!
I'll never forget
The day he walked out;
We followed in silence,
And then he said:
"I have to go,
Don't cry, don't worry,
The war will end,
And I'll be back!"

He never came,
He was only twenty one!

Jenny Ghihtei-Siroker

GHIHTEI-SIROKER, JENNY. Born: Chisinau, Romania, 3-10-20; Married: 5-1-44 to Lionel Siroker; Education: College; Occupation: Teacher, Retired; Poetry: 'America, America,' 'The Hudson River,' 'What a Loss,' 'Feelings,' 'I Wasn't There'; Comments: *I'm writing poetry because of my sensitivity to human beings, to events, to life itself.*

STASIS

Amassing things
of this world,
I have lost
simple joys of life.

Pursuing once
The Unicorn,
I have settled for
bull and bear.

Daring once
to grow
I now stagnate in
the norm.

O God
that it should come to this:
kaleidoscopic color
turned static monochrome!

Jerrie Hejl Collins

EPITAPH

The coolness of the autumn breeze
drifts gently through my windowpane.
I see the colors of the trees;
they beckon me and call my name.

Your spirit seems to fill the air
I close my eyes to see your face
I move my hand to touch your hair —
it closes on an empty space.

I know we'll never walk again
beneath the shadows of the moon
or hear the warmth of a spring rain,
the silence of a lonely loon.

I know that I must change my pace
and turn my steps away from you.
I know I'll run a lonely race,
but loneliness is nothing new.

My dreams look brighter in the light
of autumn wind and morning dew.
Your laughter cannot fill my nights;
the trees hold colors without you.

Janet Beals

LOVE'S LAST STAND

I can't bear this dreadful feeling
Deep within my heart,
I thought you'd never leave me
You said we'd never part,
My life's so empty without you
My heart cries for your love,
The tears are flowing from my eyes
I feel like I want to die,
I think about you night and day
I don't know what to do,
If I could only call you
If I could only write,
If I could only see you
I know I'd make things right,
If I could only hold your hand
To tell you how I feel,
If I can't live my life with you
I know I'm going to die.

Mario Aguilar

I COULD HAVE BEEN

I thought I was someone special,
  I was very eager to arrive —
I was protected, safe and warm,
  And so happy to be alive —

If I'd only been allowed,
  I know I could have been —
As answer to someone's prayer,
  Someone's true and special friend —

I could have filled the void,
  In someone's empty arms —
I could have brought happiness,
  With my personality and charms —

I could have brought answers —
  To a troubled generation —
I could have brought tranquility,
  To a warring nation —

If I'd only had the chance —
  But I never did — You see —
I was aborted,
  No one wanted me . . .

Janice Reed Hamlin

CHURCH
Written over the Sea of Cortez

The church is old
It has no priest
It has no roof
It's still a church
People come some days
They bring their cameras
Their popcorn
It's still a church
The mystery is supreme
The roof is as far as you can see or can't
The wind plays the organ
Some days better than others
You can visit this church whenever
Stay forever
I once went to a church like this
I wish more churches were like this.

Jon Meredith

MEREDITH, JON MARK. Pen Name: John Th Krak; Born: U.K.; Poetry: *My Time*, Collection of 50 or so poems in book form, not published; Comments: *I write for soul's growth. My work continues as I am drawn into visual poetry.*

SILENT SADNESS

Your eyes they look so lonely,
I don't know what they're looking for,
But it must have happened years ago,
To leave such a terrible scar.
Sometimes I know you're really not here,
Even when I see you there,
It's plain to see your thinking,
Of something that happened somewhere.
The look on your face tells me,
You try to be so bold,
And hide your feelings deep inside,
Of a story never told.

Then I sit beside you,
We both begin to talk,
Oh how I try to understand,
The path of which you've walked.
And though we talk of yesterday,
And what happened in those years,
A silence comes over you;
And you try to hide the tears.
Oh! What happened to our men?
And why do they have such fears,
Of things that happened long ago,
In those Viet Nam years.

Ruby Lee Winslow

CHOOSING MY POEMS

Choosing my poems,
Facing a piece of unworthy old poem,
The reason to hesitate to discard it
Is because of the unforgettable poem
Like the flame whom I loved
When I wrote it.

After all,
My worthless awkward life also,
Because of the living affectionate leaves,
Cannot be discarded carelessly
And manage to get along
One way or another.

Sung-Yol Yi

YI, SUNG YOL. Born; Seoul, Korea, 2-14-46;
Education: GA. State University; Cal State
University, L.A.; Occupation: Pacific Bell Co.
Employee; Poetry: 'America Lyric,' *The Sae
Gae Times*, 2-2-85; 'To the Son,' Korean-American Literature, 1-1-84; 'Difficult Autumn,' Korean-American Literature, 1-1-82;
'On the Freeway of Parting,' *Korean Street
Journal*, January 1981; Themes: *Life in America, love of life, loneliness, and love for nature.*
Comments: *I happen to write poetry when I feel
extremely happy or lonely or in agony. For me,
writing poetry means falling in love deeply with
my soul.*

SOMEDAY

Sometimes it's not so easy
    for two people to say goodbye.
There's a part that's deep inside them
    that really wants to cry.
I never understood the pain
    that could possibly be involved.
I guess I never took the time
    to stop and think what might be mine.
Maybe someday we'll understand
    and ask the question why?
Why two people that were as one
    threw away a lifetime
That had just begun.

Kathy Asher-Parsons

Leaves
The color of sun-baked blood —
Tattered, frozen, caked in dust.
Leaves
Returning to earth —
This one night's grasping mud
In flight
Across the ghetto's lifeless street.

Will Mooring

APRIL'S DAUGHTER
(On a phrase from Borges)

Impressions wash over her, this child,
    not from hearing the violin
    but much older, simpler tunes —
    rustlings amidst the early leaves,
    the resonance of gentle rain.

Edward Pease

Just
    when I thought
poetry was no longer
a part of my senses.
        Your smile
        beckoned my feelings
        to become a
        Sonnet.

Laquetta Parker

TOUCH

The end of an evening
The beginning of a nicety.
Smooth hands over my breasts,
Softly,
Without demand,
Just to feel.

Christine Novak

POETRY

The human insight
comes from the mind,
flows through the fingers,
is written on paper, and treasured
by those who
read.

Becky Miller

REMEMBERING PAMELA JO

Roses growing wild in the fields,
    Sending their sweet scent into
        the country air.
Sitting together by a silent stream,
    Sipping on red wine and living,
        in a dream.

Marc L. Ridge

FREEDOM

The air is pulsing with identity
In precise outlines of a blur
Clouds form and fade.
I float with calm, smooth buoyancy.
Ah, freedom, freedom.
To do something wild and carefree,
In the confines of a vast void;
Filled with new found nothingness.
A smile dances and plays.
Flowing ecstasy, radiating,
Swallows up all form;
All lines meant to be followed
Why, where?
Soaring beyond
Light.
Fear.
A sorrow filled with sadness
Saturates personal meaning.
Illusions followed,
Ending.

Sarah Moseley

THE ROOM

Somewhere within the empty room
    lives a long lost dream
Forgotten now with one more day
    it's just a distant scene
Walls with haunting laughter
    used to hold the love
Words were written and burnt much later
    words were not enough
Lace surrounds the windows
    where ghosts still dance inside
A picture guards the musty dark
    where demons fear to hide
In the smoky mirror
    where sunshine used to flow
lies a past without reminders
    and no one else will know
The love that was but never was
    has turned to something blue
Thoughts I shared with a man
have disappeared without a clue.

Karen A. Holcomb

TO TASTE

I had you bottled up,
stopped away, dusting
the glass occasionally to
hold you up to the light
and remark at the clarity.
With age your color has deepened.
Your flavor is richer
and is giving great pleasure,
for I have touched the bottle to my lips.
I have since even taken a drink
and I am stepping
up the stairs again cautiously
but eagerly.
When I reach to take the bottle
this time, I'll pop
the cork and pour
your sweetness over me
every drop,
with no further regard
for the bottle.

Jacqueline Kealy

BUILDING WALLS

What is right and what is wrong?
For this answer, how I long.
Others sleep while I think at night.
To society they belong.

What is wrong and what is right?
To solve this I waste my might.
I've been hurt, my wounds won't mend.
Why do I continue this useless fight?

Who's an enemy? Who's a friend?
Who won't hurt you in the end?
Who doesn't cheat? Who doesn't lie?
Who's the enemy? Who's the friend?

I've been hurt. I've had to cry.
I looked towards the heavens and asked why.
But stars are silent. Their secrets they keep.
The pain remained as time passed by . . .

Over me cold feelings sweep.
Never again will I weep.
Something inside, somewhere deep
Says that's a promise I need to keep.

Benjamin Raley

DEAR MOM

(The Letter I Could Never Send)

The land is green and drenched with rain,
it's hardly fitting that so many feel pain.
    the highlands, the delta, the contrast is great
what happened to us there could only be fate.

I watch as a grunt in his teens passes me by
little do we know, in two minutes he'll die.
    The bush is so quiet, only the rain can be heard
then hell opens up before we say a word.

In a few minutes it's quiet like before
except for the screams, man this must be war.
    I pick up a man, and stare in his eyes,
my God just two minutes ago this grunt was alive.

His life flows through my fingers from a number of veins,
and then as he dies, he has no more pain.

    Now ten years later, I try to refrain
from asking myself. Did we *all* die in vain?
                                        Love,
                                        your son

Michael P. Howard

A TAINTED REALIZATION

As I watch TV at night,
I am overcome by overwhelming fright.
Horror from realms deep within,
Creating a tainted realization of the world I live in.
I am mesmerized by the dust on the screen,
Frightened yet fascinated at what I've seen.
Antiquated reruns of the Twilight Zone,
Each thrills me to the very marrow of every bone.
Of late night movies I am curiously fond,
Concerning outer limits and worlds beyond.
Although I sit gaping like an imbecile, I know one thing is true,
Something the producers thought I never knew.
All of television is just a slanted depiction of;
        "Another chilling episode in a shocking series
        Especially designed to force me to
        Scream out in sheer, unholy terror."
As slowly I lose the one thing I most love.
My sanity . . .

Thomas Le Compte

ODE TO LAURA
— a mother's reflection

A knock on the door; a grin on her face;
"I've come to get Heather; is this the right place?"
A sound so familiar, it happened for days,
For Laura was special in so many ways.

She'd always take time to greet one and all,
Then off with her friends to go have a ball.
The life of the party, the center of fun;
A friend to so many, I'm glad I was one.

She filled us with joy and brightened our days;
We'll all miss her smile, her fun-loving ways.
The shock of her death has been hard to take,
But now of the future, the best we must make.

For Laura's gone home to be with her God;
He beckoned her come, and gave her a nod.
We know not the reason He called her so soon;
Why call her in May when it could have been June?

No matter the reason, the facts are the same;
We waited all week, but she never came.
We'll ne'er forget Laura, my daughter's best friend;
But she'll live forever; for her there's no end.

Elizabeth B. Stirling

STIRLING, ELIZABETH BRETT. Pen Name: Belle Knapp; Born: Brockton, Massachusetts, 8-22-36; Married: 5-5-62 to William E. Stirling; Education: Brown University, A.B. degree, class of 1958; Fisher Junior College, Associate of Science Degree in Business Management, June, 1985; Occupation: Technical Writer/Editor; Memberships: NAFE (National Association of Female Executives); Poetry: 'Mother,' 4-23-80; 'Heather,' 5-79; 'Holly,' 5-79; 'Heidi,' 11-80; 'Golden Anniversary,' 6-10-80; all of these poems were published in the local paper; Comments: *All of the above poems were written about my deceased mother, my own three daughters, and my aunt and uncle. I usually write poems about people close to me. Putting my ideas down on paper helps me to sort out my own mind about problems, or situations of concern — sometimes sad, sometimes happy.*

CITY OF THE LOON

This loon beats
her wings like a heart
behind alabaster ribs.

Velvet neck, dark eyes,
baptized in a lake of breakage,
perched on bone,
drowning in the echo.

Her ribs cave in
under an avalanche of air,
who hears
the feathered spectre
the sound of her beating wings
whipping the air cracking it in two.
Who sees
the ghost gull rise
flapping madly out of her heart,
out of the skeleton of the loon.

Julia McCarthy

JEALOUS CLOUDS

Lo, the sun sinks down
  behind a mound of sand.
The desert winds begin
  to howl and moan.
The Moon will soon assert itself as
  Master of the Night,
And all its myriad subjects
  will praise its Glorious Reign.

Jealous clouds will sometimes
  try to hide it
From the view of those of us
  who care enough to try to find it
There within its Throne.

Yet, soon enough, it bursts into its
  Gloriously Illumined Self,
And shines down upon the faithful
  who have waited thus.

Eugene Howard Murrell

AND YET . . .

The quality sought seldom meets
  the quality produced,
And days begin and end
  with no dissimilarity.

Expectations are set forth but
  never wholly fulfilled,
While disappointments mount
  with each new day.

Dreams are dashed upon the
  cruel edge of reality,
Like so many soap bubbles
  burst by a strong breeze.

And yet there is new hope
  to be found,
In the internal solitude
  of believing in oneself.

Beverly Anne Startz

THE BIOLOGIST'S CHARM

Come little butterfly, don't be afraid
I only want to see you
and see how your wings are made.

But you flutter and you flitter
and fly where you will.
Why don't you trust me,
you little delicate creature, so frail?

Would I stab your heart,
and rip out your wings?
Would I dissect your limbs,
and leave you gasping?

But do come closer, my dear.
Let's not play "hard to get."
Just let me sweep you off your feet
and into my alluring net.

Aha! I've got you!
You see, it wasn't so bad.
But please don't look that way, my love.
Don't you trust me alone with you
in my lab?

Hallia Baker

WHAT I BELIEVE

I heard a leaf say, as it fell,
"I have no fear of heaven or hell!"
The birds compose a happy song,
but what know they of right
or wrong? or of the theme they
            tell?
But, man, from birth, he must
prepare for Death's benevolence
            or despair.
Sometimes I wish I were a bird,
Unchanged from all confusing word,
Or, dancing earthward like a
            leaf,
Unbound by either creed or
            belief.
But man must believe. Believe
            in what?
I have it! The forget-me-not!

Gertrude Weston Brown

FAR BENEATH YOUR MIND

Searching through your mind
You come across a block
Something you might see
A door you might unlock

Rather than go deeper
You choose to go around
Now you'll never know
Exactly what you've found

Far beneath your mind
Lie things you'd love to see
Perhaps a drug might work
Perhaps a hidden key

I speak of something real
Something you can hold
Not only in your mind
But also in your soul

Seconds, minutes, hours
Time is yours to take
Though you have the power
The key, you'll have to make.

Joel McElvaney

MY DOG'S FIREPLACE

Sparks, then the bright,
beautiful orange,
red flames,
of steaming warm fury,
logs crackling.

Covering the ice cold room,
with warmness,
pushing out the cold air,
farther away,
into the shadows.

Snow, outside the icy window,
melting from the heated fireplace,
my old beagle, Satch, then living,
cuddles up on the warm blanket,
for the long night, snoring away.

Morning, near,
the fire still holding its own,
with the few logs still to go,
Old Satch, has no thought on his mind,
but the warmth of his favorite blanket.

Kenneth E. Koepplin

THE DEATH OF TRUST

After the death great dullness comes.
The center of my being now entombs
My naked trust newly dead;
I encrypt the severed head
Of my naiveté.

Nerves now neither sob nor moan,
They speak in hushed funereal tones.
Limp fingers listlessly arise
To brush dry tears from wooden eyes,
For it is gone.

Killed quick by a careless blow
From His voice knife-edged and low.
Innocence reddening wide,
In a pool of tears trust died
Swift painful death.

Now interred in my being's core,
House of Pleasure for Him before,
Starched nerves keep their dull-eyed wake,
Too numbed with grief to make
My life resume.

S. H. Gray

SONGBIRD

Songbird
You're only here
For a short time,
And then you disappear —
Songbird
You never concern
Yourself with things
But what you're singing.
            Songbird, I wonder

Songbird
This world is changing
But you don't care as
Long as you're singing —
It's winter,
And now you're gone
But you don't care that
You left me all alone.
            Songbird, I wonder

Edward M. Luttrell

WHERE DO I BELONG?

I've dreamed so much of a long, long ago.
Sometimes there is sand and sometimes snow.
There's a house in Scotland waiting for me.
There's a pyramid in Egypt you should see!
My chalet in Switzerland is big and bold.
There's a castle in Spain all trimmed with gold.
Oh! Yes, there's a cottage in dear old England.
It's nestled 'mid flowers and trees.
Now on to Plymouth there's a cabin of logs,
When life was new in our U.S.A.
Oh! For someone to guide my steps
And extend a hand,
So I'd know just where I really belong.
Perhaps I've been dreaming again and
I'll wake up knowing
Just where I belong and get myself going!

Louise McPhail

WIDOWER HANGING CLOTHES IN OCTOBER

Among the amber at his ankles he moves,
Unfamiliar here,
As among shattered trophies, the leaves at his laces
Jaundiced with the time. The time-tyrant depletes him
The trees towheaded in autumn, his shirts alone,
His flannel, half the suit of his travels.
Unmirrored, they wave, bodiless, at gentler hands,
At heartbeats — the percussive of passion.
The linen of his hemisphere billows,
With sheets his script of sleeplessness.
Cats unrake the gutters, disperse his sculptures;
Wet leaves decoupage the curb,
Brindled and scrolled in the sun,
And fused among flesh he moves amber.
He's not the phantom
He believes he's become.

William Dubie

LONG GONE

During the beatific days in New York
he swore never to return
now he is halfway back.
Listen to your pa,
now he listens to the silence.
He'll soon be over the hill,
across the river and in the papermill town
with its logpond and lumberyard.
Not forgetting the Redi-Whip on the river surface.

Long gone is the N.Y. hullabaloo
now he is proud to be a yahoo
no more jabberwock.
Just do your homework,
he tells his pupils.
Never stray to big cities, don't sleep in the afternoon.

L. C. Helming

BACK TO HIM

One day my soul will soar into infinity
And I will know at last the mystery of it all.
The curiosity that served me well on earth
Will be agog to learn it all on Heaven's call.
The measure of my stay this time will be, I know,
Recorded in the Book of Books and tell me how
The improvement of my soul has been this time around
And how I've really earned they key to Heaven's Gate.
By learning every day to be what He would want,
I shaped my life around His tenets and His laws.
So, peace and love and happiness are mine on earth,
And I will take my faith and love right back to Him.

Elizabeth Orpin

LIFE
From a Bird

I once sat alone under the shade of a tree
Thinking of what life should or shouldn't be
Speaking my thoughts as usual aloud
Thinking nothing or no one was around
When all at once a small bird began to speak.

Life he said to me, is something you should cherish
For its earthly pleasures soon will vanish
Those are things that only pass the time
So enjoy the things that make life
And worry not about things that perish.

After the bird had ceased to speak
I realized exactly what he meant
And suddenly it was a beautiful day
For what the bird really had to say
Is that a happy life is what we make it.

Wayne Austin

FOREVER YOURS

Misty dawn glazes the steamed window.
She awakens softly and scans the antique room like a doe.
He sleeps beside her body in colored whirlwind dreams,
as his love for her in his dreams stream.
Soft like a lily is her touch,
as he hears her whisper, I love you very much.
She strokes his tan wine cheeks and speaks
to him lightly as he sleeps.
  "My love your breath as sweet as spring grass,
your hair the color of coal ash,
I would drown in a raging, murderous sea to love you.
I would give up everything old and new."
Suddenly he dreams of her running into darkness,
escaping life's harshness.
He rolled over and cried out her name.
  "Hush my love it is all the same,
for I am love sick and you are the one I pick.
A memory of a rose can never fade,
as my love for you will stay forever, forever yours."

Caroline Hovi

PATIENCE

I have an illness — this they're sure;
  They've found no cause — there is no cure.
Once I stood straight and walked so tall
  But now I'm weak and often fall.
I used to run and do all I could
  Love each day as everyone should
Now each step is harder than the last
  Each day seems longer than the past.
"Why me?" I ask, feeling really blue
  Wanting to cry, not knowing what to do.
When I need your help, you're always there
  to lend me your hand and say you care.
With this pain — I do endure
  We will survive, this I'm sure.
It isn't easy, hard times ahead
  Possibly the wheelchair — this they said.
When and if that happens I'll be strong
  and with research, it won't be long,
They'll find a cure — this I'm sure . . .

Shari L. Tyler

BOND OF UNIVERSAL LOVE

Out of loneliness and despair
To meet a new challenge of friendship,
From one of short meeting to grow
To lasting awareness!

The need of more than lover,
Comes the meeting of one unique person,
Passing of spirits in universal time
They join to conquer their lost souls

For words to e'er express the need
Of union beyond the absent presence.
The need of united thoughts, understand
Feeling. Bond of two to one.

From wandering night to togetherness,
From togetherness to awareness,
From awareness to lasting friendship,
From friendship to special meaningful life.

For love comes in many forms.
Love can grow in many ways
More precious is love of awareness
    friendship, companionship, understanding!

Letitia J. Arguellez

CARLOS

As the morning stars fade
And the sun fights for the sky.
He whimpers in his sleep
And bids the world goodbye.

Raindrops, snow, tropical storms
Kindergarten, childhood, junior high and dorms.
A ship glides through the water
And angels hide in books
Grass grows in the sunshine
And captains avoid the storms.

Shed no tears sleeping child
A boy becomes a man

Our world turns
Like a top in wet cement
A boy wakes in the morning
And weeps at what he's dreamt.

Ruler of thousands
Renowned Indian hero
A mountain never changes
A child becomes a man.

Victor D. Curi

RENEWED HOPE

All hope was gone; I saw my Master die.
    Life was despair;
    my Lord was hanging there.
Then . . . in the grave, why did He choose the cross?
My King was gone; it seemed that all was loss.

But hope returned that bright new Sunday morn.
    Gone was the gloom;
    I saw the empty tomb.
My Lord arose . . . a victor over death;
a note of joy now fills my every breath.

My life was changed, and yea, all history;
    new life unfurled
    for men of all the world.
'Tis now a joy . . . though trials are hurled at me,
because my Lord . . . o'er death brought victory.

June Browning

ONCE

The dancing lady came late one June
From a faraway mystical land.
A partnership born, in tandem we walked,
Exchanging her lakes for my sparkling sand.

But careless, muttered, misplaced words
Cast grace doubts in my love's heart.
With doubting eyes she only spoke
Of pain perceived, so thoughtless wrought.

My nightly muses, paradise-rapture,
Now are mere shadows of beauty once bared.
And though we've both surpassed that moment,
I often wonder just how she has fared.

Christopher J. Heller

THE SERVING GIRL

She welcomes me to the restaurant each time
we both are there and wonders that she sees
me once again, advises how a crime
would be committed if I order these
or those, but *that,* so tasty, would be right
and suitable, makes me recall the kinds
of pie because I have them in my sight,
and we relate the kinship of our minds.
One day she was exalted to cashier
and hostess, dressed so prettily I stared.
And when I paid my bill, she called me "Dear."
Each asked the other how the other fared.
She's gained position, I have sold my poems.
I know for Davids there are Ahinoams.

Gordon Mayfield

SNOWFLAKES AND ICICLES

Scintillating mounds of fluffy flakes
Draping the world's windows in
                transparent curtains of white,
Tantalizing mitten-clad children to
                sleigh rides, snowballs, and snowmen.

Glistening peaks of fragile glass,
Shimmering in the sparkling sunlight,
Edging pointedly to a disappearing drop.

Snowflakes and icicles — gems of unique designs,
Beautifully layering roofs, lawns and lines,
Blanketing my universe in a wondrous and
                fun-filled snowscape.

Cheryl A. Keenan

She advanced with graceful fleeting strokes,
Her flaming sword burning through the blood-soaked air.
With every ascent and plunging of the tempered blade,
A mighty foe did fall below its arching flow.
    Her sleek bronze skin shimmered with radiance
As a snowy steed charged beneath her curvaceous frame.
Her long sword pierced the endless hordes,
Until on the point of cold steel the last perished;
Trampled by iron hoofs and long lightning spears.
    She halted abruptly upon the bloody field,
As a flaxen sun drifted behind massive gray peaks.
As an unnatural silence once more enveloped the plain,
And billowed clouds blanketed the sky,
They slowly rode across the darkened greens;
The victorious legions of the Amazons.

Roger J. Santi

YOU'RE NOT KEEPING ME WAITING

"Do what you gotta do
I love you Suzanne" — Lou Reed

I know I'm lazy but I work too hard
blaming myself for not taking it easy
Going ahead and moving into a new house without you
where I listen to Jim Carroll and Oingo Boingo —
I don't care what people think —
I'm sober now, I'm spiritual, I have a job —
    Everybody has their faults, Suzanne; I know
    we all do, and you, and me, but

I don't feel right when I want to change you.
You don't have to tell me what you're going to do
It might work out I meet you over there later
Gotta buy some cigarettes anyway
I need to get a haircut and consider her wonderbra
I really don't get much mail
Sometimes I feel forgotten but it doesn't get to me
I go ahead and go about my life

It's real ok to take your time, Suzanne.
I've still got all the time for you.

Michael Creedon

DO YOU LOVE ME?

If you were staying here
we would think back on all the times we shared.
But now you're going,
how I'll miss you, but at least I know you cared.

I'll always love you —
but if you love me, that I'll never know.
But now you're going,
how I'll miss you. I wish you wouldn't go.

He just stood there.
He was speechless, his face turned toward the ground.
Would he stay or would he leave?
But just then he turned around.

Please don't leave me . . .
Then all was silent. I knew my love for him was true.
He turned around and broke the silence
by simply saying . . . I love you, too.

Jacquelyn D. Cibulka

NO CRIME'S BEEN COMMITTED

I sit by my window on 11th Street
Praying to God for something to eat.
It's grayer than Hell
The skyline is stained
What flowers could grow under acid rain.

If the sun were to come out where it once belonged
I might be an actor or a singer of songs.
I'd call my Grandfather and cry in his ear
But he passed away about this time last year.

I'd be in a world of glitter and gold
Where people are bought
Bought and then sold.
I'd be so respected, admired and awed
People would think of me then think of God.

No crime's been committed
I'm still in my place
Here on 11th Street with age on my face.
My trousers are tattered
My buttons all worn
Is this what God thought of the day I was born.

T. Bennett Hitchcock

CITY OF BROTHERLY LOVE

Stroll the historic streets of Philadelphia
The birthplace of this unique nation
Rich in history and incomparble cultural gems
From Society Hill to Valley Forge Park
Independence Hall Carpenter's Hall Congress Hall and Old City Hall
Elfreth's Alley Poe House Kosciuszko House and Graff House
Christ Church Franklin's grave Liberty Bell Powell House
And the red white and blue at Betsy Ross' House
Arch Market Chestnut Walnut and Pine Streets
America's past springs alive and you will never forget it

Experience the priceless paintings sculptures
Books and scientific and music treasures
Harbored in magnificent edifices along Broad
Street and Benjamin Franklin Parkway
Relax in splendid Fairmount Park
Upon returning to Center City
Look atop the towering city hall
Where faithfully stands that revered Quaker William Penn
Who in 1682 founded this great American city

Stanley W. Polec

POLEC, STANLEY WALTER. Born: Philadelphia, Pennsylvania, 6-9-30; Memberships: Poets and Writers, Inc. of New York City; Comments: *I prefer to pen poems that convey a specific message to the potential reader; poetry with meaningful content in lieu of fancy words only.*

DEBUGGING DE WHITE HOUSE

It was 4:30 a.m. at the White House,
Everyone was fast asleep,
Except for Ole Chester Cricket,
From within the walls he did creep.

Chester Cricket began to chirp
Which caused a crisis so great;
Had the President's bedroom been secretly bugged
By the opposing candidate?

First item on the agenda,
Spray the vents and under the rugs;
Decricketize the White House
Make sure to get rid of the bugs!

Maybe the opposing candidate
Chose Chester from a wide selection
To bug the President and make him cranky
Before the upcoming election.

Whatever the reason, be it known
The President is quiet relieved,
For Chester is no longer with us
Since the Debugging has been achieved!

Roberta Winarick

LOSS OF LOVE

How painful is the loss of love?
Much worse than death, I'd say
For death takes you away —
Far away from burning memories
The memories you long to remember —
But learn to forget.

Fragile is the loss of love —
Fragile to the heart,
To the soul.

Feel the sorrow deep down
As it fights to escape —
And the mere sight of his face,
The sound of his voice,
Drives you mad, so mad —
What is left?

Death — yes, death!
Come and take me away —
From the agony of
A love I have lost.

Maria De Rosa

COME SEPTEMBER

I and you
You're a dream in my reality.

When i shut my eyes
i see the amber glow
of when two worlds meet
and become one
if only for a moment . . .

i close my eyes
yet there is no sleep
no darkness
only the love between us

the feel of your embrace
the look upon your face
captures my every waking moment . . .

Come September
will you still remember
the way it used to be
I and you.

Denice A. Banks

HUMAN RESIDUE

The residue of truth comes
in a nether cloud that hovers
over his head like a mutated halo.
The residue of words
remains in his mind, a dark comedy
of language that slices
into his brain's cortex.

He lies on his deathbed,
recalling the residue of memories.
He speaks of regret.
"Oh, all the things I should have done,"
he moans, breathing erratically.
then his heartbeat stops
in its own tracks . . .

Stillness envelops his body
with the residue of death.
Soon death becomes dry and cracks open,
peeling away to expose the residue
of eternal life.

Donald Gastrow

POETS

Our minds remember
moments and symbols,
frozen in emotions,
of days otherwise forgotten.

Events are linked by
possibilities, wishes,
not facts,
or twisted truths.

No one can say
what truth is or was,
only memories confused
by fantasies exist.

Scars remain inside
and out, flags of the past,
they shape the present,
warp the future.

Words shift
around on pages,
elusive reminiscences
blur with perceptions,

we glimpse each
for only an instant.

trish bryant

WHO ARE WE?

Do you know who I am?

You stare a hole through
my body and soul but you're not
looking at me.
I talk to you but you don't
hear me.
You touch me but you don't
feel me.

They say the best mirror is
a friend's eyes — and you
only see yourself.

Help me identify *myself* —
observe, criticize, understand,
and believe. Then you'll know me.
I'll take off your "mask" as you
take off mine. I will observe,
criticize, understand, and
believe you also and I'll
know you.

We can create together to know
what we're made of, but do
you know me and do I
really know you?

Darese Weiner

I shed tears for my son's unhappiness —
a marriage gone wrong — she didn't care.
My daughter in college — looking, while
studying, for someone special.
She says: "Mom, just nobody there."
I, in the daily workplace, am looking too.
All these people who come and go —
Don't they know?
A wealth of love in these three hearts —
waiting, wanting, at the gates
for that hand to lift the latch
and enter and fill the space
with warmth, at last.

Betty L. Antin

WATCH

Watch the blue-black Pygmalion,
caped in beams of moon,
skip from turret to turret
chasing the silver broom
whose magic sweeps the stars
with wisps of golden talk
that all is not as it seems
before the sun comes up.

And through the baby blue,
that star between your eyes,
gaze upon the smile
hazing through the flute.
Watch reflections from the cape
and footsteps on the sun
and know that before the rise
the broom is on the run.

Richard Lee Armstrong

In my sense
of truth
I know
that I
know not
of it.
So buried
deep
beneath
to wade
it would
me choke.

Susan J. Hess

CANNONBALLS OF PASSION

Cannonballs of passion
through the heart of the lion
seeking the lustful prey
of his ancient desires

cannonballs of passion
through your life and mine
entangling the mysteries of love
across the silvery veil of the night

ancient cannonballs
anew bewildered passions
subduing inspired lovers
through time and space
changing custom
and revolting fashion

Yanina Brignoni

MEMORIES

There's a house that stands
    At the end of the land,
Weather-beaten and old
    Though it be,
Is dearer to me
    Than all else beside,
For it brings bygone days
    Back to me.

Oh the house at the end
    Of the lane,
How I long to be back
    There again.
The moon shining bright,
    Casting shadows at night,
On the house
    At the end of the land.

Mary Lillian Evelyn Rainier Thomas

WHERE TO RUN?

Hate, fear, sinful life . . . rejection, depression, envy and strife
Got to get out; losing my mind . . . Where to run? Where to run?
Call a friend; call my mother . . . busy signal, think of another
Get in the car, lock the door . . . ride through town, ride on through town.
Weather is bad, can't see my way . . . raining outside; can't tell night from day
Stop the car, wait awhile . . . rain soon stop, gotta stop.
Don't know where I am, can't see name of street,
Just see part of building, big white building;
Cars coming up beside me on every side, slowly moving, still raining outside.
A knock on my window, I roll it down a bit . . .
A voice gentle and kind saying, "Come on inside."
Car getting cold so up the stairs I go, to that building where no sin can hide.
Music, drums, tambourines, singing, shouting, soul-stirring preaching
At the altar, hair dripping wet . . . Calling on Jesus, my Savior I've met.
Start to speaking, tongue out of control . . . feels like fire in my soul.
I have found peace, joy, and love . . . Filled with His Spirit, a Gift from above.

Jocynthia McCoy

McCOY, JOCYNTHIA BUSH. Born: Waterbury, Connecticut, 9-6-58; Married: 4-27-79 to Ervin Ladell McCoy; Education: Midlands Technical College, Associate's Degree in Civil Engineering Technology, May, 1978; Occupation: Transmission Engineering Technician at South Carolina Electric & Gas Co.; Memberships: American Society for Certified Engineering Technicians (ASCET); Awards: Honorable Mention for 'Aunt Marylee Done Been Changed,' World of Poetry, 1985; Poetry: 'A True Man of God,' 1984; 'Aunt Marylee Done Been Changed,' World of Poetry, June, 1985; 'Where to Run?,' American Poetry Association, June, 1985; 'Another Year,' 1984; 'Death and Destruction,' June, 1985; Comments: *Through all of my poems, I try to share thoughts that, although the world is full of turmoil, through salvation in Jesus Christ, a soul can be comforted. Death is imminent, but by being saved, it becomes a joyful beginning of eternal life. I write to offer hope for all the turmoil through God's love for us all.*

WHAT OF YOU?

Can you believe in you?
Are you sure of who you are?
If not, what do others think,
For yourself have you looked far?

First you must know yourself,
Believe in what you do!
Then others will see you differently,
And they will trust in you.

Are you afraid to try?
Do you say, I think I can?
If so, you may be the only one,
To think that you can stand.

Others see the picture,
That we paint about ourselves.
Whether open, happy and useful,
Or lost upon the shelves.

B. Jean Swanson

COLOUR ME GRAY

Colour me neither black nor white,
I don't recognize the day.
Like calling stars, bound in motion.
Somewhere in the gray.

Prostitutes, robed with grace,
show us how to pray.
She found freedom.
He found bondage.
They just want to play.
I simply plunder, wandering.
Somewhere in the gray.

We've witnessed childhood innocence,
and still we've changed our way.
The wise men leave us two doors now,
just bleed quietly, and pay.
You won't find me to left or right,
but somewhere in the gray.

C. D. Panagopoulos

MY CHILDREN

My children, dear children.
Can it be that long?
Young boys and the toys
Sure didn't last very long.

Two young men, my children.
So big and so strong!
Remember to love
Always, for your whole life long.

Remain kind and be gentle.
Show strength in your mind.
Be slow to anger
Will show others you are wise.

Let it not become rare
To show that you care.
Remain children in heart
And you'll get your longest wear.

Terri Lynn Murphy

HARPER'S FERRY.

DARK REALMS

The journey into self
    Is the most difficult of life.
Deep are buried armor-plated
    Memories, fears, agonies . . .
Open the shutters of the soul!
    Understand that with
Full self-knowledge comes
    Full self-acceptance.
But do not lose faith with
    The rate of progress.
Do not be daunted by walls.
    There is nothing in the
Dark realms of the soul
    Which cannot be faced.
Face it! To do so is to defeat
    The paralyzing grip of self-doubt,
To open doors, windows —
    Gaining freedom of emotion.
Honoré L. Hillman

THE EAGLE, OUR NATIONAL EMBLEM

I read a parable about an eagle
And an oyster in the bay.
The oyster was entombed in sand;
The eagle could fly away.

The oyster's house was a shell secure
For protection from its foes.
But the eagle's nest was on a crag
Far from the earth below.

The oyster didn't hunt for food;
It just opened his shell-house wide,
And God provided all the fare
It would need to stay alive.

But not the eagle, proud and strong
Its noble wings flew high.
It battled hail and rain and sleet,
For food he had to fly.

Now the oyster is safe inside his shell,
A prisoner out at sea,
But not our nation's chosen bird,
God allows him to fly free.
Arline Ratliff

CHIQUITA BANANAS

Have some Chiquita bananas
Have a whole bunch
Eat one at work
Or have one for lunch

They are tall and yellow
And have a peel
If you look closely
They have a Chiquita seal

They are so tasty
They're even ripe too
They pop in your mouth
It's so easy to do

Chiquita bananas
Send for a bunch
Buy them right now
And have them for lunch

This is the end of my poem
I'll write again
But I can't write now
There's no ink in my pen.
Donna M. DelGuercio

SAILING

While sailing on the seas of life
Many waves are surging high;
I realize that other ships
Have swiftly passed me by.
Some have been driven by the wind
While others float on waves;
I hope to pass some of the ships
That forced my sail astray.
The bigger ships can glide right through
Though tempests rise and fall;
Other ships are smaller.
They cannot sail at all.
My ship has weathered many storms
Upon life's raging seas;
But now today I'll sail away . . .
To shores of victory.
God is the Captain of my ship
The Guide of this worn vessel;
No rival ships will ever pass
This sailor shall reach home at last!

Emily Gentry

GENTRY, EMMA LOU. Pen Names: Emily, Emily Kerri; Born: Cincinnati, Ohio, 10-18-49; Married: to Donald R. Gentry; Education: High School Diploma; Occupation: Homemaker; Comments: *I write about God, love, life and experiences of faith and victory through trials I have faced hoping to be of some help and inspiration to someone else.*

LOST

My heart's a confused piece of
misunderstanding,
mistrust,
an empty warmth of love
never to be known.

A sometimes want,
a never having,
sense of responsibility,
feeling of belonging.

An inevitable future of
loneliness,
a survivor,
an object
not to be sincerely touched.

A wall pleasant to look at.

R. Marie Harrington

IT FEELS SO RIGHT

From that first night,
I knew it was right.
From that first day
We spent away,
We knew our love wouldn't stray
From that first day.
It feels so right
To feel your love
In your own loving way.
It feels so right
When I take you in my arms
and hold you so tight.
It feels so right
To feel your warmth
as we kiss through the night,
into the morning light.
So, it feels so right
When I ask you to be my lovely wife.
It feels so right, tonight.

Albert Rania

RANIA, ALBERT NUNZIO. Born: Camden, New Jersey, 10-13-66; Occupation: Food Coordinator at York Steak House; Comments: *I write because it lets me escape into a fantasy world. I can let go and let all my feelings known. I also love writing because I love to entertain people who like to read. I enjoy hearing their comments about my work. Though I'm unknown, I like my work read because it's like an actor hearing his applauses, it's rewarding.*

TO KNOW YOUR LOVE

I see the sun's reflection in the dew
    on a flower at daybreak,
    and I see your eyes.

I feel the warmth of the sun
    as I lie on a beach at midday,
    and I feel your touch.

I hear the wind whispering gently
    through the forest at eventide,
    and I hear your voice.

I hold you in tender embrace
    in the quiet solitude of night,
    and I know your love.

Timothy L. Bishop

EDNA O'BRIAN

At the poetry conference we met,
she was beautiful to behold,
can see her image even yet
as I write these lines so bold

We sat at the very same table
The glance between us was fleeting,
How well she'd look in Sable
Everyone soon began eating

The lady on my left didn't mind
when asked who this lovely could be
In fact she was graciously kind
as she made introductions for me

Her gown was a pretty creation
as I stole a few more glances
A most pleasing sensation,
turning over in my mind, my chances

Now my one and great ambition
may it not be long of time
OH! Were I just a Magician
Once again, to meet "EDNA O'BRIAN".

Louis J. Bookwood

SEASCAPE

So many beautiful memories
Drift through my mind
Like the shells
We collected on the beach
Timeless and perfect
I hold each one
Inside of me
And touch them often
And if I can't caress you
Then I can' take out
Each shared experience
And touch the dreams
We once shared
And though we can't be together, my love
You have only to close your eyes
And think of me
And I'll be there
Forever . . .

Nicole Pachey

A MOTHER'S LOVE

I pause this day to recollect
With heartfelt thoughts and deep respect;
What hours of happiness I've shared,
What pain and sorrow I've been spared.

Because one friend stood by my side
With so much love, and God to guide;
So many trials I have faced
That time and change have near erased.

The many highways I have run
Through winter's rain and summer's sun
May not have proved all best for me,
But pathways to my destiny.

My mother's prayers and loving care
Have been with me 'most everywhere;
So much she gave — so much I owe,
I truly feel I'll never know.

Though one life only I can give
To share with others while I live,
May I in parting hope to be
Cognizant of my frailty.

Wyman H. Lord

ONCE UPON A TIME

I knew that person once,
But it's a once-upon-a-time story.
Everything I dreamed of, somehow,
Was in that person;
Happiness and love.
Yet the story ended
And the characters all lived
        ever after.
All happily?
        Well, that's another ending
                For another story.
I knew that person once . . .
        But now I don't.

Noelle Ferris

PEACE

The times that I spent with you
let me raise among the stars,
let me reflex in the oceans
as clear water goes by.

The times that I spent with you
taught me about myself,
taught me about the world,
taught me about hostility and peace,
and I chose peace in my heart
just for the pleasure
of watching your eyes shine
as much as a beautiful sunrise.

Alice Levy

THE IGNORANT GUEST

Irving died when he was 22,
I read it in the paper.
He died at a party.
He had a big funeral,
all of his friends were there,
They cried.
Poor Irving, whisked away
in the prime of his life.
Poor Irving must have been in a hurry
to leave;
he didn't even say goodbye
He left right in the middle of
a beer.

Therese Doyle

A THOUGHT

What are they
But attractive images
Lustrous, vivid, glowing
Many exciting words
No flesh behind them.
I hear
I see
They smile, or gaze passionately at me.
I love them.
I hold out my hands
We touch.
I feel
Paper.

Lily Principe

THE WINDBIRD

'Twas alone was I,
when this windbird
did soar,
beyond the barren land,
to a distant shore.
My eyes saw
the distance, and
thought it too far,
but the windbird
took flight, and
called from afar.
Come my child, come
spread your wings,
reach out for
the land, where
harmony sings.
Be brave, be bold,
put life to its test,
soar above the clouds,
reach over the crest.
You're a windbird now,
proud and free,
riding the winds,
minus me . . .

Laura Garrity

HONEYMOON HOPES

I hope you'll always love me
I hope you'll always care
I hope you'll always be
The one with whom I share

I hope you'll bring me flowers
I hope I seldom see your wrath
I hope that you'll always be
The one who always makes me laugh

I hope you'll always respect and trust
I hope you'll always be there
And when I burn your favorite meal
I hope you'll just grin and bear

I hope we're together through the years
I hope these wishes all come true
I hope we stay forever bound
I hope you know I love you

Julia Brock

SEASONS OF LIFE

Vernal Equinox:
In saffron swaddling cloth
Tenderly is laid
The newborn babe,
Child of Sun, the Earth.

Summer Solstice:
With gentle love unseen
And joyous tears,
Adolescence nears.
Earth grows up green.

Autumnal Equinox:
Shortening of Earth's days,
The battle's won;
Earth looks like Sun,
Scarlet, amber, maize.

Winter Solstice:
Sun retreats to Heaven;
Earth begins the night,
Incubates in white;
'Til it's born again.

J. H. Genthe

MOON

sad moon
huge pearl
warm on my horizon
speaking my dream
grieving moon
your face is blemished
your tears are cold

Far
where you
watch him sleep
the rolling world
lifts you high
shrinks and smooths you
hardens your face
to platinum
a small mask
silent and shined

Be careful, moon
what tears you shed
They could fall
as fire

Marian Arthur

HOUSE CATS HAVE DIGNITY

Cats, cats, three dozen cats,
Dusty grays, strays, & striped cats,
Hard box-head cats,
Lean xylophone-ribbed cats,
Ears flexed to attention,
Cautious of broomsticks &
Hot water tossed at childlike
Shrieks in the night.

For a dime, an aproned grandmother
Buys them fish heads on Friday.
She turns a croaker sack raw — inside out,
Scattering bulging, glassy eyes
Across a backyard dirt floor.

Cats, cats, eight dozen cats,
Winged cats, falling from the sky.
Elongated, sneaking cats, bodies flattened
Against a backyard smothered in fur.
Cats, cats, & more cats, tearing,
Gnawing, heads tilted sideways,
Licking, lic king, lick ing, li cking,
L i c k i n g into the night.

Peggy Boozer

WHAT IT'S ALL ABOUT

Through all of the tough
times and the tears;
Somehow you both managed
over the years.

Making a promise and
together showing care;
Although it isn't always
easy or fair.

Sharing love and joy
with your very own;
Even now after they
have all grown.

Staying with one another
and sticking it out;
Makes it a pleasure to
realize what it's all about.

J. L. Carroll

HUNGRY

For all the hungry people of the world:
If you've ever been hungry — you will understand;
How you crave for food and need a helping hand.
Giving and sharing are the best things in the world.
My brothers and sisters, are you one of those who just doesn't care?
And there's no way you're going to share.
Remember, we can't live in this world alone.
You and me, we just can't make it on our own.
Yes I beg, I urge you, let's unite together now and support our brothers
and sisters here and all over the world and try to do the best we can.
This struggle for survival must have an end.
With unity and strength we will overcome and win.
United we stand, divided we fall.

Nan Blackshire Little

BLACKSHIRE-LITTLE, NANCY. Pen Name: Nan Blackshire Little; Born: Dawson, Georgia, 3-8-35; Education: High school; Occupation: Medical Switchboard Operator; Poetry: 'God's Gift,' 'A Visit,' 'The Wind,' 'Giving Thanks,' Religious, Displayed at St. John's Divine Cathedral, 'Unite,' union, 12-84, RWDSU AFL CIO; Comments: *On March 8, 1978, the inspiration to write was given to me in a dream. I have since continued to write as I have felt compelled to express my inner feelings.*

GEORGE'S INKING

Thus be that the new daying, as sunnings sliver through cracks of
windowing.

To the stool . . . I forth sit . . . to scratch inkings 'pon parchment gold!

Of such grace doth my hand glide . . . as markings of love flow atop papering.

For within each wording . . . I hide such feeling . . . that allows meaning to
come alive from spirit past!

Oh, thus from sunlight . . . there be of such warmings . . . as its voice speaks
from within . . . deep:

"Be that with me . . . this day . . . forever!
I long forth to touch thy heart as it beats beautiful rhythm!
It's like birds of the air that hath sweet songings to share!
It's as sweet winds . . . blowing . . . whisperings spake unto me!
Oh, heart for it is love . . . that longs . . . as thine beats in
melodies with mine!
Just as our tearings fall to touch each beautiful sonnet."

Oh, thus be that the new daying, as sunnings sliver through cracks of
windowing.

Of such love . . . thus I script in inkings . . . so that the world shalt be
touch'd with God's gifting!

George D. Kovach

A LOVER IN LAMENT

I felt this hand against me
your hand, supple and strong
had weathered, and tanned,
can it be? Has it been? . . . so long?

Through the mirror of my mind I see
reflected fragments, of a voiceless song,
and I feel this pressure build . . . love, demands
all that I will, all that I have to give —

            in the twilight of dawn;

From the heated sill, I hug the breeze to me
useless, to still this pain against my face.

        I mourn

for a grain of truth, sifted, through time's hand
and quietly placed, where it belongs . . .

I felt this hand, no stranger to me
but memory stirring, has stirred me . . . so wrong:
I search the eyes of this man
and find not love, but a love, now gone.

    Holly Murray

FREEDOM

Freedom's definitions are numerous
As the many hearts of men wherein they rest.
Countless are the counterfeits, the spurious,
That through impotency have failed to crest.
Those freedoms without office are no freedoms,
They venture nothing but their empty claim.
They're whispers of a different form of bondage
Masquerading under Freedom's name.
Just one there is that we can hail as Champion —
The one that spurns the greed of personal "rights"
While hugging to itself its obligation
And in its productivity delights.
For Freedom knows it is not self-sustaining.
To be continued it must interlace,
Must seek protection in the arms of duty;
Freedom's life depends on this embrace!

    Cindy L. Bauer

TO MY ICARUS

Daedalus in ancient Crete,
a labyrinth built
            to hide the sad result
of god-wrought lust,
            rose high on waxen wings
with young Icarus
            who chanced the sun and fell,
ablaze with dreams.
Now it is you
            who seek the sun-flamed heights,
from pained desire
            to prove a denied worth.
And you are like a god
            hell-streaked toward glory
who needs not love,
            and seeks no mortal goal.

But oh, my love, beware
            lest in this hour,
at summit of your power,
            like that young Thracian
in mock rapture's thrall
            — wax wings spread wide —
you, too, are come to fly
            too near the sun!

    Marjorie Holtzclaw

IN A CITY PARK

Stop here and trace the leaf on its way
Descending into this marginal forest;
'Round and 'round, it weaves each gentle turn,
A faint whisp reflective in the dim,
It twists among buildings and vanishes.

This is about the way it could be
On some cool evening, if by chance, you
Paused here on your way elsewhere;
And amid cavernous buildings
A leaf floated into your shadows.

This is neither fanfare nor a drama.
This is solace in an unnoticed descent,
A faint whisp reflective in the dim;
A leaf drops onto the surface,
The quiet surface shimmers and receives.

    Dan Sakach

THIS IS AMERICA

Americans,
The mighty offspring of the Indians,
No relation to any Gunga Dins,
The greatest country with the greatest men,
America!
With people beautiful,
With people strong,
This is America.
with rivers many,
With mountains tall,
This is America,
Where no one's ever too small.
America!
Where one is free to roam,
Where one can be a postman or gnome,
This is America,
My choice and chosen home,
This is America.

    Christopher Paul

GIFTS OF THE HEART

Two special people joined by love
Surely blessed by GOD above.
Always giving all that you could,
Sharing our sorrows; giving as you would.
Created by a love the two of you shared,
Raised to always feel and to care.
Safe and secure our home is and was —
You've taught us well, and given so much.
We've learned from our childhood with you Mom and Dad
The importance of love and closeness we have.
Now that we hear tiny feet in our home,
He too will know the love that you've shown.
For, you've given so much and shown us so well,
Your love lives on in us and ours as well.
For gifts of the heart are kept and stored,
Untouched there by time, cherished and adored.
Healing our sorrows, giving us joy;
Which we now pass on to our little boy.

    Sue Ann Myers

IN THE SUMMER NIGHT

I cry as i ask him for help.
He sits with his bare back to the open window,
feeling the breeze on his sweaty body.
He smashes with one big finger the shell of the egg he ate,
holding a can of beer in his other hand.
He tells me i exaggerate,
as the sweat falls from his fat face onto his belly of beer.

    Cristine Nice

LIFE AWAITS YOU

Let no acts of oppression
    nor thoughts of defeat
hold you back in life.
    when you believe,
you can defeat the largest obstacle
    for it is only in your mind
that life stands in your way.

March on
as young men and women would,
For you are tomorrow's future
    and yours.
Be not bound by insecurities
    and boredom.
Reach out and find excitement
    in your life
It awaits you!

Rosemarie Falcone

FALCONE, ROSEMARIE. Born: Washington, D.C.; Education: Montgomery College, Rockville, Maryland; Occupation: Sales Representative, Communications Systems, Tel-Plus Communications, Inc.; Comments: *I like to write because it gives me an opportunity to express my ideas to others. Because of this fact, when I converse I sometimes do not take time to communicate clearly and am like the person who winks in the dark — I know what I said, but nobody else does. Depending on what ideas I want to convey and what emotions have been aroused by experiences in my life, determines the themes of my work and I enjoy a captive audience.*

MY MIND

The turmoil of my emotions,
Always locked in my mind.
Seeking a means of escape,
Bursting forth,
To be repelled,
By a wall, of my own making.
And to regress even further,
Into my mind.

Donna E. Lazier

A BLIND MAN'S SIGHT

Though some may have five senses, I have even more; for though I'm lacking one of yours, God gave me many more.

Like you I feel, I smell, and hear, I taste of many things; but my senses are all stronger, than yours could ever be;

For I see with my heart, not with eyes alone. My heart sees the same things you do, but sees also things you don't.

Yes, I am ever grateful for those things that I can do. My sense of touch is so exact, and my hearing is so true.

And I can smell and taste, my friend, as no one ever could. For a blind man finds so much that is so good.

I feel the summer breezes blowing gently across my face. And I can tell when one hair on my head moves from its place.

I hear the flaps of little wings, when one bird tries to fly, and I can hear each bumblebee when I don't even try.

I smell a thousand clovers in the meadow 'cross the way, and I can tell each flower by its fragrance; I know its name.

My taste buds are so strong at times, I taste the morning dew; its sweetness much like honey, makes my taste sense ever true.

So, you see my friend, I may be blind from the visual point of view, but take a good look at yourself. Do you see as much as I do?

Hear ye deaf; and look, ye blind, that ye may see. Isaiah 42-18

Debby Bradshaw

BRADSHAW, DEBORAH KAY (FOSTER). Pen name: Debby B.; Born: Ralls, Texas, 12-18-50; Divorced, mother of two daughters, Mary and Missy; Education: Interior Decorating and Design Certificate, 1934; Occupations: Driver/Dispatcher, Passenger Assistance for elderly and handicapped people; Key-Punch Operator; Awards: National High School Poetry Award for 'Fireflies,'; A copy of 'Blind Man's Sight,' hangs in the National Congress Library Service for the Blind and Physically Handicapped, Washington D.C.; Driver/Dispatcher and Passenger Assistance Award for elderly and handicapped, 1981; Poetry: 'Colorado Fever,' nature (lyrics), 1984; 'Know This,' religious, 1984; 'Country Boy,' comedy, 1984; 'From Dreams to Reality,' true-to-life, 1983; 'There is a Place,' religious, 1984; all copyrighted; Comments: *I love working with the elderly and handicapped people. It's been my life. I've also been a social coordinator for senior citizens for about two and one-half years. I have always written by inspiration. Sometimes in the sound of sleep, I'll be awakened with a strong desire to reach for a pen and a scrap of paper. In the morning I'll go over the piece I've written, to recall what it was about. Then I ask myself: "Did I do that?"*

MEMORIES

Memories are such precious things . . .
Like stardust sprinkled on angel wings . . .
Loves of old, and friendships true,
Times of joy, and sadness too.

Bursts of passion, heartbreak, woe . . .
Breathless thrill of a girl's first beau . . .
Years of little, days of much,
The exquisite pain of love's first touch.

As life grows shorter and the days grow cold,
My precious hours, worth more than gold;
I live them over, each a treasure.
Life has, indeed, for me, full measure!

Fleeting, as on gossamer wings,
Memories are such precious things!

Marie Suzon Thomas

NESCIENCE

We drift full of motion and energy
Caught in the web of time — the void of space.
 Touching and Speaking;
  . . . Never to really communicate.

Sensing the knowledge of the gods.
Feeling the power of the stars.
Beholding the beauty of life.
 . . . Never to really comprehend.

Man: all-powerful, blessed creature.
 Planning and Designing;
  . . . Never to really create —
  . . . Never to really perfect.

We see so much,
 yet feel so little.
We experience so much,
 yet use so little.

Man: fool-hearted, blind creature.
 Existing and Surviving;
  . . . Never to really live —
  . . . Never to really love.

Cheryl Weller-Beck

IN NEED OF A FRIEND

When skies are gray & filled with gloom,
When sadness and despair fill the room,
When you feel as though you just can't cope,
Remember there's always a ray of hope.

When the world gives us its *very* worst,
There's a Friend who will put *our* needs first,
He's everpresent in our pain,
When to get relief would be our gain.

So "*Who* is this Wonderful Friend?" you ask,
"And where can He be found?"
"He's present with us all the time,
He lives *within* our hearts."

His name is Jesus Christ, our Lord,
A Friend who's always there,
To share our problems, sadness, and pain,
and to give us hope again.

We all need a friend nearby,
Especially when skies are gray,
So turn to Jesus without delay,
He'll help you more than words can say.

Linda Lewis

TOTAL CARE

When you are out of sight
Too far from touch
The stirring of my heart keeps you here.
I haven't forgotten your best expressions;
Upon those phrases I endure
The cold, unshattered silence.
Though my day is rushed, my breathing exaggerated,
Every second completing the work of two,
I still have loneliness conglomerately dispersed
Throughout the entire sequence of activity.
That's why the impact of your return is so intense,
A welcome smile from you becomes immense.
Your hearty greeting brings me full delight.
The warmth radiating from your hands
Is as melting snow teasing a parched earth.
I'm well contented now that you're at home,
I missed you perpetually today.
With each departure, may the reunion thrive
To dawn upon our hearts more love
Than time itself can hold.

Sharon Rasmussen

GYPSIES

I would be a gypsy and you a gypsy man.
Wandering free and happy as only gypsies can,
Not caring for the World's way,
Forgetting strife and pain,
Bareheaded in the sunshine,
And laughing in the rain.

Listening to the birds' songs, singing with them too,
Bathing in the cool stream, beneath the sky so blue,
Eating wild strawberries
Sweetened by the sun,
Dreaming by a campfire
When the day was done.

There would be no discord, but silence all around.
We would be so happy in peace that we had found;
Clover blossoms' fragrance,
And crickets' song of joy,
Were I a gypsy girl,
And you a gypsy boy.

Mildred I. Reeve

POETRY

In this way I express my feelings,
Although poetic thoughts are some of the most fleeting,
I find excitement with these words meeting,
It's a feeling priests sometimes feel while kneeling
It's been here awhile, nothing that is new,
Expressed mostly as feelings that are true,
Or of great and worthy deeds;
Or of gallant men on burly steeds,
But mostly it just plainly leads
To insights and literary pleasure,
Upon it there can be put no measure,
Of the value of thoughts deeply treasured
All a poet really ever needs
Is inspiration so his spirit can be freed
By and by it all boils down
To far-sighted people, their feet on the ground
There will always be poets who write
Poems about truth, about dreams and insights
For the world is there for all to see
And nothing is always as it may seem.

David Harris

LIFE

Life,
Yarn spun,
Twisted and coiled into immeasurable skeins of limitless time;
Then,
Knittight
Into strait jackets
So knotted and tangled,
We cannot escape
Until we realize that —
Although the stitches of our past cannot be unraveled —
They need not fashion our future;
For the knitter
Chooses the pattern
And controls the tension
Of life.

K. V. Skene

IF I WERE A PENCIL

If I were a pencil, and you were a pen
We'd set an example for women and men

We'd work close together, and both do our best
With no jealous feelings to cause us unrest

And though we were diff'rent, we'd feel our own worth
And know there's a reason for all things on earth

Then I'd learn the value of durable ink
And you'd find I'm precious to those who must think

If I were a pencil, and you were a pen
We'd write out our message to women and men

Shari C. Smith

WAVES

The Book says, "dust thou art . . . " etc., but
I'd swear from my experience, it was sand.

I was born waiting on a beach for the next wave
To wash me to a new spot downwind.

Where next? I seldom ask that — it's easier to
Let the wave decide.

You might say I'm uninspired, well
Where has your struggle left you?

A step behind me —
And out of breath.

Ray A. Stevens

MY ABATTOIR

In this my Abbatoir
A child shrieks,
Cowering from the one she loves
While acid seeps through the stem of my soul.
The silent pleas will not be heard
As severed limbs are sucked through stainless steel.
Neon lights flash, glare, blare
Out pleasures to be found inside,
All for the price of a soul,
And bile blisters my throat, yet I stay still.
But what does it matter?
The Beast has dined on human offal,
And even He has had his fill.
So stay, and play among the bones,
In this our Abattoir.

Shirley Lovatt

UNDEFINED

Forever marching forward, never ceasing.
Perhaps slowly or leaping and bounding eternally.
Returning not to paths behind. Used foolishly or wisely
determines the value. Experiencing joy and sorrow, love
and hatred. Yesterday is no more, tomorrow too distant.
Leaving invisible footprints; always present, never late.
By the old may be cherished, in youth misunderstood.
Though ancient as the heavens, as young as the first flower
of spring.

Waiting for no man, nor catching the fleeting. Having no
favorite, yet a necessity to mankind.

More precious than jewels never properly appraised. Treacherous
or faithful. Untouchable as twilight, never harnessed or im-
prisoned.

Grand marshal of every being, from the cradle to the grave;
no man escapes TIME.

Mary C. Hoyle

PIANO BAR

There's a guy who's sitting at the end of the bar
Who keeps putting money in my jar
He says son can you play me a tune
That doesn't end too soon

He had far too much, and I told him such
He said play one more, and I'll hit the door
So I said it's a deal heck I play for my meals
So everyone sat around the bar and when I got done playing

They stuffed money in my jar, they said kid you shouldn't
Be here, they made that very clear
The manager looked at me with a smile, because without
denial, I'm the guy who packs them in

Soon after I left for Hollywood, I signed a contract
And after that, I opened at the Ritz, and I was a hit
So it was the piano bar gave me my start
I shook up the place down on West Eighty-Eight

Mitchell Beamon

MY SON

Protesting, raging you made your entry
    into this mixed-up world.
Your body grew like a sturdy tree
    and in your mind curiosity swirled.
"Wizard of Math" was your name . . .
    bowling strikes was your game.
Time passed, your life you planned,
    then Uncle Sam made his demand
    and sent you to an eastern land.
You felt that you must go . . . we agreed and
    understood your patriotic stand.
Back, at last, you came . . .
    but never again the same.
Broad of chest, hard of jaw,
    eyes reflecting things you saw.
All this I noted and felt sad.
    In my mind this thought ran,
    you went a dream-filled lad
    and returned a troubled man.

Jeannette Goodwin

262

GRADIENT DENSITY*
(Or ode CON UTI)

When you think of BUSINESSMEN and TEACHERS;
Someone without EMOTION first comes to MIND.
THEY are from the "HARDY STOCK" who SHOUT;
"We CAN do it; So why can't YOU?"

ALL the while FAILING to see;
The many SHADES of COMPLEXITY that,
Make YOU so UNIQUE an INDIVIDUAL.
How I wish THEY could see YOU the way I do?

However their minds are CLOSED against,
The lights of REASON and COMPASSION:
That make TEACHERS and ADMINISTRATORS alike,
Not only more EFFECTIVE but more HUMANE as well!

There is a lot of TALK going around the GROUNDS:
PEOPLE claiming THEY'VE tried to aid YOU in SOMEway,
It INFURIATES me so because when YOU needed them:
THEY hid behind RULES and REGULATIONS!

*Geological term used to GRADE the THICKNESS of ROCK formations!

Rick Perna

WHERE IS THE "ESTABLISHMENT"?

"Watch what you do," they said,
"or the Walls will tumble down.
You can't ignore our yesterdays
to make room for your todays,
for there is order to all things;
a purpose perhaps not yet manifest,
but there nonetheless."

We heard but did not listen to their warning cries.
Our hearts were swept to action, fire in our eyes.
En masse we formed and stormed the foe,
fighting for our civil rights,
and once the Walls' weak chink was found
we attacked with unbridled might.
Fury fueled our strength, indignation on our side,
and as the Walls were crumbling
we exulted in our pride.
For the Walls came tumbling down.

But when we finally reached the other side,
when the Walls were at last laid bare,
we learned that the foe never did hide;
the foe was never there.

Steven O'Brien

HANDYMAN OF LOVE

A handyman can fix most anything,
From a backed up sink, to a broken ring.
He'll work hard and steady on his task in sight,
And he won't give up 'til he gets it right.

But there is one thing he can't repair,
No matter how hard he tries he'll end in despair.
A broken heart and ruined dreams.
A life once together, now split at the seams.

The only man that can mend these things.
Is the man at the heart of all these dreams.
He must have knowledge of a special kind,
A heart full of love and an open mind.

His job when done has no guarantees.
His only promise will consist of these,
To love, honor and cherish and do the best that he can.
He knows his mistakes, but he is just a man.

Shawn D. Ball

LIVE AGAIN?

If I had my life to live over again,
Would I feel more joy? Would I feel less pain?
Would I shed fewer tears? Would I laugh more too?
Would I sing more songs, or would chances be few?

I know there is one thing I surely would do,
I'd love you again the way I now love you,
I'd treasure your laughter, cherish your smile,
I'd love you much longer, not just for a while.

What could I accomplish if I lived again,
Could I move mountains and feel no pain?
What would it matter if the world changed a lot,
Could moving the stars make me somene I'm not?

Why should I worry about the way it could be,
Could changes I'd make really change me?
Would I be better off or just wish in vain,
That I'd like a chance to live over again.

Deana Campeau

HEALING

It was in my giving that I was made
      whole.
It was in my search for Him that I became
      bold.
Bold enough to dare to give of me enough
      to become one with all.
All that was, that is, and that will
      come after my fall.

It was the giving of myself to him, to
      them,
That made me want to live.
      To live fully, joyously, and well,
And made me forget to fail
      To love, cherish, and give to them well.

It was in my giving that I became me,
      Another Eve.

Blessed and wholly healed
Of all things that would have made
      me Eve,
And forget to give of me.

Dorothy H. Mink

MY FRIEND

I've lived a year now, as your wife,
And can honestly say, to you and myself,
It's been the best year of my life.

Through you I've learned the real meaning of living,
All because of your easy, gentle way of giving.

You've made me appreciate what others don't see,
Like animals in the forest or a hawk in a tree.

We've sat by still waters and crossed mountains above,
while enjoying each other and the places we love.

You're my partner, my buddy, a true friend to me,
And more of a lover than I dreamed there could be.

Words haven't been written to express the love that I feel,
The peace and the comfort that is ever so real.

I love you so much, with all of my heart.
Our tomorrows will only be better,
Thanks to this first year's start.

Pat Pearson

THE HOUSE ON THE HILL

The old house stands silently, high on a hill and nobody
    cares anymore.

The porches are sagging, windowpanes broken and hinges
    creak on the doors.

Birds build their nests in holes near the eaves, an alley
    cat lives 'neath the floor.

A lone flower blooms where once was a garden, but nobody
    cares anymore.

Bright fluffy curtains once hung at the windows, now spider
    webs dance in the sun.

Laughter once rang from walls that are crumbling, 'cross
    the floor a mouse quickly runs.

The old house stands sadly, high on a hill, like a soldier,
    wounded, but too proud to fall.

The yard once well-tended, now deserted and shabby, the weeds
    grow, rambling and tall.

A lonely sentinel from out of the past, all that remains of
    an era now o'er.

The old house succumbs to the passing of time — and nobody
    cares anymore.

Mary Jane McGuire

McGUIRE, MARY JANE. Born: Bridgeport, Illinois, 10-16-33; Married: 10-14-50 to Robert (Bob) McGuire; Education: High School, Mt. Carmel, Illinois; Occupations: Homemaker, Writer; Memberships: Beta Sigma Phi International Sorority; Petroleum Wives Corporation; Awards: Elected to The Outstanding Young Women of America in 1968; Writings: Large collection of poems, all unpublished; Themes: *Nature, past memories, animals, children.*

STAGE FRIGHT

The jester's gesturing on the stage.
It's a very strange move that life has made.
God and the devil went hand to hand,
Locked in the mind of a solitary man.
Strangely enough, the devil won.
He's got a deathly hold, that son of a gun.
And now he demands his duly wage,
So the jester keeps gesturing on the stage.

Jim Dunion

A FLOWER FOR YOU

I send you a flower today
Not in a vase or bright bouquet —
But in words so kind and true
I send this beautiful flower to you.
I will give you your flowers today
While you can enjoy them and under-
stand what they say.
Your sweet smile will brighten the day
Your look of kindness reflect the words
you say.
The Christian life you live here below
Certainly lets everyone you know, yes know
Who reigns Supreme in your life
Who helps you win the battles and strife.
You are a friend, a friend indeed
Willing to help when there's a need
So these flowers of thoughts I give to you
May you enjoy them your whole life through.

Thelma H. Sherrill

MY TIME

As I lie there looking down at myself,
I begin to see a light. It draws closer and closer and then!
Almost without a sound, the light speaks,
I hear the low tone voice, but not with my ears.
I just hear it.
                                        Strange . . .

Then I see my loved ones, but wait!
I have not seen them for years, at least,
that is, I cannot remember . . .
                                        Strange . . .

It's almost like I'm floating, suspended in space, I
drift and drift. I feel at such great speed . . . Why?
                                        Strange . . .

My mind I can think so crystal clear.
No error . . .
No twice thinking,
I speak without talking,
Hear without listening,
See, without looking . . .

God, is it really my time?
    Thomas L. Mullins, Jr.

GLEANINGS OF THE ELDERLY

About the time man learns how to live, it is time to die.
Religion has come to be known as death psychotherapy
by postulating the idea of continuance of the "I,"
after the known death of the temple, called the body.

We should all be interested in earth's husbandry
to create healthy, vigorous, self-productive old age,
where every person can live out life with dignity
and safely continue to grow into the next stage.

The tragedy of old age is reinforced by inaction.
We do not kill the elderly, like a primitive tribe.
We bury them alive in some type of rest institution —
the human junkyards or warehouses the aged describe.

These institutions, where untrained help is incompetent,
use tranquilizers as chemical strait jackets,
and keep food costs down to point of malnourishment.
There is no privacy, memorabilia, or pets, just regrets.

Seniors, disillusioned, live in desperation and dread.
Machines and drugs sustain with no conscious activity.
Thus, through these means, the living dead are created.
The dying should not be in a dehumanized Gethsemane.

Vivian Sangston

EXPOSED LIFE

Rough waters . . .
Rough times . . .
Rough places . . .
Rough things said.

Hearts broken,
Unmended.
Unpleasant memories
Restlessly linger.

Unfrilled belongings.
Unruffled thoughts.
Calm sea ahead!

Untouched mercy . . .
Unveiled faces . . .
Unmeasured joy . . .
Fulfilled dreams.
Ecstasy!

Ada V. Cotten

WHITE MONTHS

Spears of white crystal,
land of milky sands.
The rains have turned to ice
and drifts across the land.

The white months have arrived,
to deaden all life about.
Though the sun still shines,
not even the grass comes out.

It saddens me, there is no life.
All trees around have darkened,
and the leaves have all disappeared.
Will the white months ever lighten?

No, wait, life is emerging
from the houses caked with ice.
Children from all around
gather to see the flakes of ice.

Hours have gone by quickly,
now all has been overrun.
Garbage litters the layers of snow
but the white months have just begun.

Keith Madden

MADDEN, KEITH EDWARD. Born: San Francisco, 1-15-71; Education: First year student, Saint Ignatius College Prep., San Francisco; Comments: *Keith wrote this poem in the seventh grade. He was twelve years old.*

NO HOMECOMING

In the distance I hear the Guns.
In my mind I see the jungle;
the mud.
I imagine the darkness;
the fear;
the loneliness.

I didn't want you to go,
but you had to fight for your beliefs;
your country.

I cried in your arms that last night.
I wanted so much to tell you, then
but I decided to wait.

You promised you would come back to me
And, I promised to wait forever.

But, you won't be coming home,
and I never got to tell you
about the baby.
Debra Whitehead

Wander
emerged in such vagrant gypsy life
natural elements
      my entertainment
to find
      silent brooding seas
      or perhaps
chaotic splendor,
the ebbing and flowing
as tumbling crests plunge
in sheer spontanaiety
      pure rhythm
my mind to follow the turmoil
enslaved, a victim of
my melancholy,
yet tranquility
      pure undulated patterns
      sand.
I wish to design also — create,
the power of the sea
crushes in upon me
I sway to its rhythm
no longer
      the entertained.
Rena Burns

RESTRAINT, AND THE ONE I LOVE

In my longing for you
    I've cried away
The formless bits of life,
    to reach the shape
Of your kind loving heart
    caring nothing
For me.

    Now the floor is littered;
torn apart.
    The dreams I had of you
murder peace.
    And the charm I painted,
I once loved;
    Now despise.

Some other fool will sculpt
    in you — love.
Still another may paint life
    for your smile.
Though my heart searches pain
    for some other — like you.
Kim Chamberlain

STARS

Blessed Redeemer is
Jesus above
May we always and forever
Abide in his love

Jesus, my Saviour
My Lord and my Friend
The stars in the heavens
May I comprehend

Mona Lee Brock

BROCK, MONA LEE. Pen name: Ramona Lee; Born: Oklahoma City, Oklahoma, 2-27-35; Married: 2-3-54, presently single; Education: attending South Oklahoma Community College (Major: Psychology); Occupation: Medical Technician, Occupational Medicine; Memberships: American Clinical Radiologists Association, R.T., National Association of Physicians Nurses, National Emergency Technician — Intermediate Paramedic; Poetry: 'SORROW,' religious; 'Friends,' general; 'Love,' general; 'Joy,' general; 'Appreciation,' religious; Comments: *In my work I am trying to convey my innermost thoughts and feelings regarding God and the universe.*

A LIBATION TO THE GOD OF PEACE

Lord, that I could capture
The flutter of every wing
Seizing all the rapture
Of each transparent thing,

Gathering to my breast
Without wherefore or why
The hearts of all the best
To raise up to the sky

    an infinite offering,

Then would I ever cease
To sleep with open eye
Having given tears of peace
To flood the Earth on high?

Janet Pembor

THE CALLING

He has heard the thunderous cry of the beast
He has felt the need to free it,
Yet 'til now he has ignored and avoided it
But this time the call to greatness he hears once more.

Deep within him it rumbles and grumbles,
Sending tremors through him to his very core
The yearning, the longing begin to reach for his consciousness
And the call to greatness is heard once more.

Though he may try to deny what he hears
And attempt to quell those feelings from before,
He must at last acknowledge his fate
And let the call to greatness reveal what it has in store.

Now having torn away the roots of his fears
He proudly feels the need and hears the roar;
To heed the call of the untamed beast
The call to greatness must always be heard once more.

Michael J. Fong

FONG, MICHAEL JOSEPH. Born: Amarillo, Texas; Education: Baylor University, B.B.A., 1983; West Texas State University, current M.B.A. candidate; Occupation: Assistant Office Manager for Dr. Don Leon Fong, M.D. (father); Comments: *In many of my poems and stories, most of which are unpublished, I try to use my writings as a means to relax. In doing so, most of them are about upbeat, uplifting subjects, and in re-reading them and re-writing them, I get satisfaction in trying to convey happiness and success.*

CHANCE

One chance had gone and simply left in fear,
For what it saw and heard begat no care.
Vainly I sought to stop the quickened hare,
Yet nothing could I do to bring it near,
As chance had lent one bloom and would not hear.
To plead would give no fruit and just a stare.
So, poor I, threw myself to sweet despair,
Until somehow a soothing image should appear.

That is what thrashed my soul 'til I was found
Awash in grey of teary, moonless fright,
Waiting for the blow of enemy untold.
And even before I sought to find some ground
In which to sadly throw my tired psyche,
I saw the wingèd gleam of Death unfold.

Charles E. Klimicek, Jr.

SONNET TO MECCA

The sculpture of black hills against pale night —
a mecca for my sight, and bared to thought,
a pennon of delight. Rejoice the rite
of still gods, of large women freely taut,
laid down upon the earth in gestures proud
and sweeping in longevity — arms wide,
and singing sinuating songs aloud,
enshrining within time a spatial tide
of waves filled. Undulating mass enthroned,
fixed only fleetingly in eyes of time.
Space remains as time echos through wind-blown,
wind wailed or waffed or waived away in mime.
And centuries cascade on chimes of space.
And centuries cascade without a trace.

M. S. Musmecci

LIFE'S CHECKERED

Life is all checkered with light and with shade
As along life's shore each human doth wade,
Tiny feet with much aid toddle along
But soon he'll be strong and race with a song.

He meets many friends but chooses a few
Someday he'll meet one more fair than the dew,
She is true, she's loyal, she'll last for life
These two can master all possible strife.

When two are one the whole world seems aglow
But sooner or later sorrow will flow,
Plod bravely on, my poor tired brother
See, near is Christ, mankind's greatest lover.

Sister Bernadine Rusting, O.P.

THE MAN I HAVE COME TO BE

Just leftover feelings from yesterday,
We shared in the late afternoon;
Words were spoken that were all we could say,
And our parting would come too soon.

Wondering often of unspoken times;
Doubting our heart's deep intentions;
Songs sung of misunderstandings, in rhymes,
With melodies touched by emotions.

Speak words of love to my broken heart;
Your kindness is so good for me.
So often neglected when we're apart,
Is the man I have come to be.

Robert Ariel Keith

A FLOWER

A flower is a conquering beauty,
It's something to behold,
It's the theme of liberty,
It's as pure as gold.

With the fragrance of a seeding blossom,
That's budding with the flourish of Autumn,
With an order of freshness for its smell,
A scent we can distinguish so well,

Aloft a hillside it will stand,
Descending with a breath of wind,
To time indefinite it will be,
Like freedom, the theme of liberty.

Grace Camell

THOUGHTS OF BRAIDED HAIR AND FLOWERS

Braided hair and flowers,
Children's books and toys.
Life, love, and listless hours,
Where have they all gone?
Being young seemed so wrong.
The days pass and blend,
The wrong doings never to mend.
Now I spend my hours,
Longing for braided hair and flowers.

Leigh Hill

CHALLENGE THE IMPOSSIBLE

Time is forever challenging the
                              impossible
   as dark clouds survey silver
                              linings
appearing at a magic moment
   a starburst sprinkles stardust
                    on our shoulders
Impossible dreams and hopes
        search for moonbeams
                    obstructing
                    views of despair.

Rita M. Knecht

IN THIS WORLD

Flyers may fly home
Sailors have to roam
They have reached their
   Arms out to the sea
The same as you and me.
There are many wondrous
   Sights to see
The greatest, however,
   Is the sea.

F. J. Enright

WINTER WAYS

Such a cold time of year,
Yet clean and peaceful too;
With its blanket on the ground,
And a clear blue sky for you.

The wind it blows so fierce,
Sprays snow up in the air;
As we snuggle by the fire,
We watch snowflakes fall with care.

Jean Crawford

A CERTAIN MELODY

A certain melody
Brings back memories
Clear to me
Of time spent together
Enjoying simple pleasures
Though it is sad to say
That we ended this way
In a fond memory
Of a certain melody

Gary L. Davies

THE GIANT SNOWMAN

I made a giant snowman
   With eyes of pink.
He can make you smile
   Quick as a wink.

He has a round nose
   And a corncob pipe.
Five pink buttons
   That look just right.

He has ten toes
   Without any socks.
His feet are big
   And as hard as the rocks.

My snowman will need
   To stay where it's cold.
So he will be able
   To live to be old.

But I know very soon
   He will melt away.
I'll not see him
   Some warm day.

Charlene Carpenter Acker

SILENT OPTIMISM

Blue shades of a misty vision
Pouring out on sky-blue velvet —
Thrust within the wizard's hand —
All the secrets we may learn.

Crimson rivers running
Speaking splashes to the shore —
Coloring my true aggression
With melodies of faith.

Centuries upon a moment,
Correlating time with virtue,
Universal soldiers marching
Toward the day of recompense.

Love relates to those receiving
Promises of innocence —
Sheltering our soul's compassion,
Piloting the dreams we weave.

Here we stand against tradition
Fixing hope upon the moon —
Confident in those surrounding —
Justifying truth.

William Michael Terry

THE FELLOW LEADERS

To Orin and to Donna, I say
"Praise the Lord for you!"
You help enable us to know
What God would have us do.
He leads us to be who we are: His
Children, freed of greed.
By giving us, each Wednesday, just
Exactly what we need.

At first, I could but fathom not
Your basic motivation.
For groups like yours will likely never
Captivate a nation!
So how, then, does your ministry
Possess such life, such zest?
You're not afraid to be — YOURSELVES.
The Spirit does the rest!

Michael Herbert Shadick

WORDS OF A MIND

Words of a mind:
Invading
the psychedelically darkened depths,
desperately reaching out
with each aimless step,
triumphantly tormenting
every long crooked crevice,
fiercely piercing my skull
through each separate terrace,
a plentiful sea
of sedately called cries,
scratching in vain
they search distant eyes,
pouring profusely
into a destiny of light
to celebrate a reality
so blindingly white.

Alyson G. Bomhoff

YOU ARE MY WORLD

You are my world.
Orbiting in the great blue sky,
Universally known by all.

Always spinning so quickly,
Revolving around the sun so bright,
Equaled by no other planet in our system.

My wondrous world so filled with delight
You are my day and night

Waking to you each day is a gift,
Over and above what anyone should want,
Rightly so, all should be grateful
Love is my world
Deep within my heart.

Nancy Jensen

WISHBONE

Inspection passed;
I've weighed the odds,
And cautiously I choose,
The side which looks the strongest,
'Cause . . .
This wish I cannot lose.

It has to do with my whole life,
My future wished upon,
But should I lose this judgment now,
I know that life goes on.

And should I find another bone,
And this dream still holds my mind,
Once again I'll chance this wish,
And wish until I find.

Michael Pelitera

GOD'S BIG TEARS

Falling from the eyes of love —
On this world He created —
And it repented the Lord that He
Had made man on the earth —
And it grieved Him at His heart —
Yet, He loves His Children still —
And sometimes in the rain —
You can almost see —
God's big tears.

Gen. 6:6

Shirley Rhodes

WONDERER

I wonder if there will ever be a love that's permanent
with me? A love as deep as mine, a love so sublime.

I wonder if there will ever be, love that's eternal con-
tentment for me? Contentment made of love's undying bliss,
with someone's tender kiss.

I wonder if on this earth I shall find, a love like mine?
Not here, perhaps some other place, not within the human
race.

Shall I ever see someone who loves like me? I feel like
it's not here what I seek but in a world that's dark and
bleak.

Drew G. Myers

CARUNCHIA, DRUSILLA GARLAND. Pen Name: Drew G. Myers;
Born: West Palm Beach, Florida, 7-14-26; Married: to Pat Carunchia; Oc-
cupations: Restaurant Owners — Gulf Gardens; Writings: *To Kill a
Witch,* novel, 1985; Comments: *I write for self-satisfaction.*

THE PIED PIPER

How deep these memories occupy my mind
And unrelenting, hold me captive still
To all that had at once enthralled my heart
As yet it does, no matter what I will

I still envision the winsome form and face
Of one said Peter, who piloted our tour
Through all the Alpen regions of a continent
With artful skill to make us feel secure

How joyously we viewed the changing scene
Mountains majestic, forests, lakes and streams
Combined with melodies from his stereo
To vie with all the fantasies of dreams

What fortune brought this lovely lad to us
An image that enchants in all his grace
Of every quality that's meritorious
His aim — to draw delight to every face

We scaled the heights on winding mountain ledge
And smilingly he steered the coach with ease
One moment we were breathless, then intent
To gaze below, about ten thousand feet

Too often now, I wonder where this lad
Is bound, delighting folks on tour
Or with his magic skill he may be bent
On other fields, where magic is the rule

Laura Lorentsen

MY WORLD

And the raindrops do fall and splash outside my window;
I hear them crackling in the water puddles.
Yet I'll not let them into my world, no matter how loud
they cry.

'Tis empty and silent in my world, as I stand in front of
the window looking out at the raindrops, begging to come in.

The silence is so peaceful and calm that it seems immorally
wrong for there to be such a day in my world.

And the raindrops do fall outside my window, for I love to
hear them fall outside my world.

Mother Nature is so tempting when she weeps, it soothes me.
Yet is it not the same trickery used before? Alluring me out
into the cold, to dash me once again against the ragged edges
of reality.

No! I'll not leave the security and comfort, the peace and
serenity that inhabits me. For my wound is old, yet it still
hurts.

Can I not trust the raindrops enough to say —
I must be alone in my world.

Sheilda Holloway-Gillespie

I

"If the eye is the governor of the mind
And the heart the judge of the soul
If God is the Master of Life,
Then, Who am I?"

I am a being, a person of life
One who will live in this world and survive
I was created by the King of all men, I will
	trust my heart, my soul, my being within
My mind will rule me, it will warn my body
	of pain
If you let your mind slip away with you,
	you may live in vain
Your life depends on what steps you take,
	to learn of strategy in this world full
	of fate
Your eye is your governor, your heart your judge
	to begin
We will always be our master of our lives,
	and our creator of our own faith within
If we learn of our life and who we may be
Then I can say, "I am I, for I am a
	creation of God, and so proud to be."
For we take life as a gift, and use it with pride
Our mind is our ruler, a lifetime worthy guide.

Cindy (Kerns) Gartner

FRIEND

At your request sometimes command
Need only ask once I'll lend a hand
In time of trouble in time of need
Pushing and pulling, hoping you succeed
I listen, give advice and consultation
Always leaving room for inspiration
Not always understood — at times misused
I've been taken for granted — at times abused
In spite of advice I walk away from sorrow
Knowing understanding will appear tomorrow
Recognition of my face is only a start
My definition lies within my heart
From the day start to the day end
I remain always — truly a friend

Keith D. Wright

Moving slowly through a day wondering where and how I am.
Where is he and where is she or it or them.
That feeling of which I am uncertain follows me.
But there is another feeling which I am sure of.
This day like all others has its good and bad.
The Sun will set and the wind will still blow either way.
I feel happy when I see clearly, take what I can and move on.

Robert W. Frommer

"FULL-BORE!"

Someone has said:
"In the deed the glory" —
But actions spring from attitudes
And therein lies the story.

The mind is a wonderful producer of seeds —
It matches like thoughts with like deeds:
A little now
Will later be more —
As fear whispers "Hold Back,"
Positive thinking yells "Full-Bore!"

It's not only in the deed
Where the glory lies —
For "As a man thinketh"
Reveals the source of his prize.

After the deed is done
The attitude still proceeds —
Even the glory may be gone
But the attitude sows more seeds.

Steve Albin

ALBIN, STEVEN F. Born: Norfolk, Nebraska, February 6, 1949; Education: University of Nebraska at Omaha, Bachelor's Degree/English, May, 1980; Occupation: Free-lance writer; Poetry: 'Closet Magic,' October 1984; 'Everybody's Got Sumthin',' June, 1984; 'Somebody Had To Do It,' June, 1984; Other Writings: "Bubbles In The Milk," short story, March, 1984; "The Tomato Chase," short story, March, 1984; All sold privately by High Plains Services Marketing Company; Comments: *My objective is to bring to light the motivational, humorous and ironic principles which tend to guide our human nature. These little lessons on human nature, which are so often 'hidden in plain sight,' are not only treasures in themselves, but are even more delightful when said poetically.*

THE LESSON

I stand here fully accountable
for all my actions.
Palms held upward, eyes questioning
Where do I go from here?

I recognize guilt when it arrives
the pain it brings — instantaneous paralysis.
Peace, just be at peace
and the Universe keeps moving.

I can't hear you — speak louder
something is buzzing — down here.
Must be fear, anger, misplaced blame.
The finger turns to me — I have a choice.

Then out from the depths of my anguish
a little voice comes forth.
"You are an angel — move yourself and radiate."
All is forgiven — healing fills my soul.

I walk through the doorway — out into the world.
They are applauding now — banners are hung.
"Welcome Home Angel" — and with the sweep of my hand
The world is suddenly mine, I love it.

Peggy Lambdin

LAMBDIN, PEGGY GRACE. Born: San Jose, California, 7-7-53, Single; Education: San Jose State University, San Jose, California, B.A., Liberal Arts/A.A. American Literature; Occupation: Secretary; Comments: *I really don't feel that I have any basic themes, my poetry comes from the heart. Subjects range from unconditional love, forgiveness, God, to bees playing on flowers. Poetry for me is my ultimate expression of the human condition. 'The Lesson' is my favorite work, probably because it was written during a very difficult time in my life and has a vein of hope not only for me but for the reader as well.*

WILD AND FREE

The silent mist of the morning, is falling over the
   sea,
The waves are rolling in from afar, breaking wild
   and free.
For a moment your mind wonders, what it would be like
   to be
A wave upon the ocean of life, running wild and free.

Barbara L. Clark

OLD FORT DUMPLING

OUR NATION GRAND

Oh nation grand
    For you we stand
        On Independence Day.
            With ringing of
                Sweet freedom's bell
                    On Independence Day.

Through war and peace
    Your anthem rings
        We know you stand so true.
            With all its might
                Through day or night
                    Waves dear red, white, and blue.

From sea to sea
    With such beauty
        Stands our dear nation grand.
            Though masses from
                The whole world come
                    For unity we stand.

Oh nation grand,
    America,
        To you we will be true.
            Oh let there be
                Prosperity
                    In dear red, white, and blue.

Merle Ray Beckwith

UNEXPECTED LIGHT

A wealth of words outwits my pen
and I endure poetic poverty.
What makes a poet worthy of the muse?
What softness of the brain or sensitivity of the soul
will salt the clouds of image
to bring forth poetic rain
or saturate the logos to condense in bardic dews?
What, but that I work at it,
instructs me to the call?
What, but unexpected light,
keeps me interested at all?

Robert Brock

NOT THAT WAY

It's not the way that you
cheated, lied about me,
not the way that you went back home.
It's not the way that you
turned my friends against me
and when I called you hung up the phone!

It's not the way that you
wouldn't even tell me
about the others hanging in the shadow.
It's not the way that you
made me think you loved me,
then turned my heart into an aching hole!

        What did it was the
        way you pushed me under,
        ground your heel into my soul!
        What did it was the
        way you put it to me·—
        "If you love me, got to love me whole!"

It's not the way that you
cheated, lied about me,
not the way you sent me back home.
It's not the way that you
turned my dreams against me,
brought me out and then left me alone!

Joseph J. Simmons

SPINDRIFT

Spindrift is a summer-scented word, that sings
Of tall green waves, that lick the foamy clouds,
Fall back, grumbling, on themselves,
Gather strength, and leap to taste again.
It tells of salt-soaked branches, twisted, dark
Carved gymnasts posed on honey-colored sand,
Of dancing sails, white-breasted gulls,
Creaking hawsers, lonely clanging buoys,
Shell-fragments telling stories on the shore
Of little lives begun and ended, silently, invisibly.
It sounds of children laughing, and small sandpipers
Bowing, like Japanese gentlemen, to the sea.

Patsy Anne Bickerstaff

SUNSET OVER WATER

The sun is setting one more day;
The moon rips out from between the clouds
And shines upon the water
Like a lamp shines on a page of words . . .

The water is my page of words . . .

The words made by the changes
Of the motions of the sea —
The water is my page of words;
The water is my page of words . . .

Narayana Muraada

CHOREOGRAPHY BY M. NATURE

Shell-pink cherry blossoms
Tentatively unclench their pursed petals.

Tropical summer breezes
Tenderly whisper over the sleek surface of the lagoon.

Weary autumn leaves
Recklessly stumble onto the forest floor.

Vivid snowflakes
Radiantly bask in the cool moonlight.

J. M. Huston

NANA'S DEATH

The blanket is old, frayed on the edges,
tucked snugly to the chin, to keep the cold
without, the warmth within. And father says,
"She looks so peaceful lying there." "And old,"
thinks the son, "so very old." "Perhaps," says
father, "perhaps your mother should be told."

Lyle Witham

MY BRIDGE

There is a bridge I'll use one day,
It has a straight and narrow way,
This bridge of mine is infinite and long,
It will never weaken, it is always strong,
It leads to a land I'll see some day,
Beyond this world, far, far away,
This bridge is rock and has no sand,
It can't be repeated by the human hand,
It reaches from heaven, down to earth,
To use it you must believe and have spiritual rebirth,
When I die, I'll leave Death's valley, and climb the next ridge,
For you see, Jesus died for me, and he is my bridge.

Wm. Scott Hacker

Twined the twilight leaves
Wish the wind away.
Divine a separate space
For lovers safe.

World of nested sanctity
Crisscrossed a dream
To earn from day that steals
A plainer view by dawn.

Backward sliding, notching, breezing
Finding delectable crevices to wander
And whimper foolishly
This new or refound pleasure
Seals close our nighttime treasure
Infectious souls aslant
Invite to drift per candled lamp.

Lilacs sing and swell their time in clusters,
Toys spoiled beyond a bruise.
While trilling matched canaries
Pretend to weep.

Lynn Adler

ADLER, LYNN DONNA. Born: Binghamton, New York, 8-6-50; Education: Temple University, Philadelphia, B.A. English, 1974, M. Ed. Psychoeducational Processes, 1980; Occupation: President, Adler Transcriptions, Word Processing, Medical Transcripts; Memberships: Member, American Radio Relay League, Advanced Amateur Radio License, Association of Medical Transcriptionists, Volunteer Staff, Insight Transformational Seminars; Poetry: 'June, 1982,' March, 1985, 'Shabbat in Jerusalem,' March, 1985; Comments: *My current writing, though not exclusively, grows mainly out of my experiences while living in Israel from 1982-1983, coming to terms with the strangeness of another culture and our community. Successful writing for me is trusting my unconscious self enough to conjure its own images and sounds.*

LIMERICK

A trespassing hunter named Kotter
surprised a sun-bather, Miss Potter.
"Why are you here?" she cried.
"Hunting game," he replied.
"I'm game," she said. So Kotter shot her.

Nancy E. Jones

He should come again
He should wait as if it were the beginning
Maybe he was the man
who penetrated without asking
and saw in the garden a woman
whose body sparkled in the sunlight
with the water of purification
who stared long before she fled
let there be a Commandment that says
she owes him love, one embrace
that breaks down the arsenal of innocence
that separates him from her
that keeps him from dreaming of other women

Gerald F. Wilson

WILSON, GERALD FREDERICK. Born: Sault Ste. Marie, Ontario, Canada, 4-24-46; Education: Wilfred Laurier University, B.A.; University of Toronto, B.Ed.; Occupation: Teacher of English; Poetry: in: *IN*, anthology, University of Toronto, 1969; *Canadian Poets and Friends*, anthology, M. O. Publishing Co.; 1977; *Canadian Poets and Friends*, anthology, Laurentian Valley Press, 1979; Comments: *I write obsessively about loss, eternity, grace, love, women, beauty, pain, growth, death and the spirit. I work with every work I write. John Fowles, in* Daniel Martin, *says, "We write out of what we lack, not what we have."*

FOR T. N.

A touch —
    a hand outstretched to comfort, to reassure.
A hug —
    the closeness, the warmth.

So simple to express, so innocent the message.

Too often misunderstood, too hard to accept,
    Like winter's cold on a summer's day —
    the contrast, the contrariety.

Just to touch, to be understood as
Expressions of comfort, care, concern.

Arms around in shelter, a hiding place —
    a moment of precious silence.

So simple, so sincere, so misunderstood.

Just a moment to say, "I care, take shelter beside me."

Vicki Ann Buckley

TIME

I

Time enobles some faces with maturity and wisdom;
A quiet "knowing" reflects as if from a prism.

Time paints some faces with a subtle color,
And blends in mysteries you'd like to uncover.

The shade of peace and patience underlies
A golden dignity that accents the eyes.

A posture of purpose, health and grace
Floats like an aura from their body and face.

II

Time can rob all hope by slow degrees.
Despair and grief have roots like trees.

Bitterness and anger are the branches that climb,
And cover the eyes if given the time.

Selfishness and cynicism is the bitter fruit
Which silently drips,
And causes that tiny twist to the lips.

Carol Bailey

FRIENDSHIP

Friendship is a beautiful thing . . .
        It is a joy to give —
        It is a treasure to receive!

Friendship must never be taken for granted,
        'less it become lost forever.
        It must be treated wisely at all times!

Friendship can be brief . . .
        It can be once in a while
        or last a long time!

Friendship is special because
        It accepts everything about you —
        It doesn't try to destroy what you have.

Friendship is a great teacher . . .
        It is a healer as well —
        It often leads so others may follow.

Friendship is a special kind of love.
        It can hurt sometimes,
        but bounces right back again!

When you are given friendship, nurture it with respect . . .
        and strength — be glad you have it!

Linda Lee Haugh

REJECTION

or
(Take your medicine. It's good for you.)

It not quite kills.
A winded instrument that sounds the dirge.
A raven's caw.
A sinking urge.

Like poison pills.
The funeral leaves a black hole in the gut.
A monkey's paw.
The case is shut.

Kate Clark

CAN YOU TELL?

Can you tell I walk with Jesus, by the friend I try to be?
Or do you find, that I am lacking, as you take a look at me?
Can you tell by the way I dress or by the words I say?
That Jesus is walking with me, every step of the way?
Can you tell by the love of others; that I try to show;
That the Spirit is within me, and like a river flows?
Can you tell, by my faltering embrace,
That I have found HIS redeeming grace?
Yes, I am His child, this is really true.
Although at times you can't tell it, by the things I say and do.
I am HIS spoilt child, that wants my own way.
My selfishness often shows, in the things for which I pray.
I often argue and show my lack of respect.
Then my conscience fills me, with a feeling of regret.
Someday I hope: you can tell I walk with Jesus, in the things
                                        I do and say.
And that HE is with me, every step of the way.
        Linda Bishop Tadych

NIGHT DREAMS

How I long for sleep to fill this night,
                but it won't come.
It has left me exhausted.
Those stirring, whirling thoughts of guilt
                and unaccomplished projects left on a shelf
                waiting to be removed,
                are placed in the corners of my mind . . .
                tormenting me when sleep won't come.
I pray for the shadows of the night to leave me
                and let my mind rest.
Morning is an eternity from now and the creatures of the dark
                are still playing their night games.
Wake me from this dream of black and let the morning come.
Stirring, whirling thoughts of guilt no more,
                and unaccomplished work shall begin.
Take me to the brightness of the day,
                and push the night away.
        Cynthia Ann Cash

GANDHI

It was he!
The lean aged man,
Who sat with undying patience.
With his thick oaken staff in a nimble hand.
On this same stone he sits, gathering unmatched thoughts.
His silent advice guides us all,
through decades of turmoil and disgrace.
Watching us rise and fall by our own means,
He always seems to be in that same desolate spot.
Waiting and wondering.
        Kevin Woods

TOMORROW WILL BE BETTER

Let's talk about troubles.
No, no, not happy things.
Troubles.
Real troubles.
Like sickness.
No. Not death.
Troubles like worry.
Like fear.
Like anxiety. Like hunger.
Like meanness. Like cruelty.
Like a mind — like many minds with the wires pulled.
Let's talk about troubles. Real troubles.
Then again. Let's talk some more about,
whining and complaining and crying and sadness
And about howling pain.
Then, let's talk about who's listening.
And, how hard that is.
        Doris Flint

ME

As the rising sun marks each new day,
   I shall rejoice in the wonder of being.
      For I have found the one person
         I have looked for all my life.
            The one to carry me through,
To make me laugh and hold me when I cry.
   I am leaving the darkness . . . for a breath of fresh air
     Together, I can make it
       And I am at peace
         I found me.

Greg Hopkins

OF THE SEASON

One early winter day after a morning rain,
The sun broke through the clouds.
Some birds munched on seed from a feeder,
And a few ate seed scattered on the ground below it.
The shimmer of silver sparkled from the evergreens,
Which stood silently behind the bird sanctuary.
The twinkle was drops of rain,
Which clung to the boughs of the trees like tinsel.
Several birds perched in the conifers,
Appearing suspended like ornaments of the season.

Sandra B. Hortenstine

BRIEFLY BITTER

Know it
   where the wind caresses earth
   and the dust never settles
   but dances in the rain
There I will be found
   drowning china dolls
   with small black eyes
and wishing they were you

               Diana 4-22-85

Diana Evjen

LOVE REVISITED

I look out over the meadow
and the strains of a once-loved song,
long since forgotten,
float across the expanse to tease my memory.
Times of sharing laughter and tears
tumble from the trunks in the attic of my mind.
Softly
a shadow drifts through whispering trees.
     Is it you —
        or just a cloud?

Linda Fabert

THE TEMPTING CHEESECAKE

On a big table, in front of the grate,
sat a big piece of rich golden cheesecake.
As it so happened in the same house
there lived the cutest little gray mouse.
Its father had told him not to go near
but the little mouse approached the cheesecake without any fear.
He ate all he wanted then jumped to the floor
when in came the big cat through the open door.
If you do not know which one was glad,
just ask the big cat what kind of supper he had.

Betty J. King

EARLY SPRING SONG

From the trees
   about my house this morning,
   birds serenely call.

Suddenly
   red buds are out, a spattering of color,
   azaleas here and there,
   brightly red and pink,
   dogwoods blossoming snow-white,
   clusters of wisteria all over town
   in lavender.

But by
   the calendar
   it's ten days until
   spring properly should begin.

Delightedly
   upon the scene I fondly gaze;
   while amidst its perfume
   and its pollen-laden haze,
   my nose drips.

Dean Wentworth

DEPORTATION MONUMENT, PARIS, FRANCE

Two hundred thousand Paris Jews
Deported from this spot
Were never seen again

Is this King Saul beside me in the park,
Saul with pain-chiselled face?
What conflagration devoured this man,
Robbed him of all he loved, left him an outcast and alone?
He speaks to a child beside him —
A child that is not there!
The arm goes out to caress, a finger points,
The hand shapes the idea,
Explaining, cajoling, loving the empty air.
The voice rises and falls reaching into the past
Which is to him the present and now his only future.

Was this man left behind
When his whole world, sucked into captivity,
Was never seen again?
Like Saul, in his old age he lives on a dead love
Gone half a lifetime ago.
Why does he come here?
Oh, why does he come here?

Sister Agnes Nyland, S.S.A.

HILLS

Hills are important to little boys,
      When we find one,
         we explore its infinite possibilities.
Its slopes call us like sirens
and we carefully measure each rise and fall
like prospectors charting new territories.
Once familiar,
we laugh and tumble down the inclines
sliding, slipping, grabbing for handholds
all the while
       delighting in its contour.
As I do you now.
I love the gentle incline of your breasts,
      the smooth downward slope of your back
          and the soft ascent of your hips.
I love the territory that is you.
It calls me like hills once did
      and I delight in its contour
God made hills for little boys
but it was only a promise of better things to come.

Ben Cook

MY HEART IS IN MY EYES

My heart is in my eyes and I smile.
He hears . . .
. . . and looks up.
He sees the sparkle and is my prisoner.
He doesn't seem to mind.
He returns the music
and adds another note of his own —
a hint of laughter on his lips.
His eyes mirror my flash of love
with such INTENSITY
that I,
who began,
blush . . . and look away.
He starts to move, to reach out
and I wonder if he's real?
Or only another illusion . . .
He sees the question on my face.
His heart is truly in his hands —
he wipes the worry lines away
with one caress.

Julie K. Stover

SANTA CRUZ SEALS

The seals swam about,
as we watched
I wanted to save them
from the "seal slaughterers."
The young were saved
but
had to watch their parents killed.
They cried
and
here they are swimming about
as adults themselves.
We watched them
knowing their seal-fate,
we wanted to protest.
Shops sold signs of "Save the Seals."
As the seals swam away
we knew
the young would return
to Santa Cruz
as adults of fate.

Dorothy E. Rentrop

MAMA'S CHECKERED TABLECLOTH

There was something in the kitchen
That really caught your eye.
'Twas Mama's checkered tablecloth
That displayed her apple pie.
It also wrapped up loaves of bread
Just taken from the oven,
Or perhaps a fresh-baked gingerbread
For Dad — her 'everlovin'.
It also went on picnics
To a quiet shady nook.
Mama spread it on the ground
For all the good things that she took.
It dressed up the dining table
When company was comin',
Or with a glass of milk and gingersnaps,
The children all came runnin'.
For the many many blessings
And the pleasant memories,
'Round Mama's checkered tablecloth
Where we gave "Thanks to Thee."

Marie A. Unruh

WHAT IS A DREAM

A dream can be something
That you see in your sleep
They can be wild and crazy
Or the meaning's very deep

A dream can be something
To make time fly
It isn't hard to do
You don't even have to try

A dream can be something
That doesn't last a day
But a dream is yours to keep
No one can take it away

A dream can be anything
And that is up to you
But if you want them enough
All of your dreams will come true.

Lea Russell

GOD'S GREATNESS SHOWS

In things we take for granted
    God's greatness shows
From the vastness of the universe
    To the blooming of the rose

In the beasts that inhabit the land
    To birds on perch, in flight
In the early morning sunrise
    Which precedes the coming night

I see God's greatness
    When I look out on the seas
I hear him sweetly whispering
    In the gentle summer breeze

When the lightning flashes across the sky
    When I hear the thunder roll
In things we take for granted
    God's greatness shows

Ethel M. Johnson

DINNERTIME

Too many raindrops
Falling in my soup
The vegetables, soggy
The beef, a dismal grey

Not enough sunshine
To brighten up the placemats
The centerpiece stands alone
Against a plain table of brown

The puddles grow
Around the lonely flambé
Swimming away
Across an endless platter

The pot of gold is missing
Beside the sparkling candles
But — where is the salad?
It fell off the table

Linda Rosenthal

HOLDING HEARTS

I remember the way you smiled
When a tear would show in my life
I didn't think I'd see the day
when our love would be saying
good-bye

It's really hard to see the dreams
we've both created fade
We built our dreams on love
'cause that's how dreams are made
I don't know how you feel right now
but you know how I do
My heart will always hold the
past and my mind the memories
of you
We may go our separate ways
but I'll always be close by
It hurts a lot to see you go
but at least I know I tried
I don't want to fall in love
or find somebody new
'Cause in my heart I'd always
seem to be holding onto you.

Toni Dybala

YESTERDAY TODAY AND TOMORROW

People say "Don't think of yesterday
or dream of tomorrow. For yesterday
is gone forever and tomorrow may
never come.

Live for today for this is all that
you have and is true reality." But
is reality always truth?

God gave us memories for yesterdays
and dreams for our tomorrows. For
without our memories of yesterday,
our lost loved ones are gone forever;
but with it they live, forever. And
without dreams of tomorrow, we have
no future.

Today may be reality for some,
But remember — Today always slips
away into Yesterday and Tomorrow;
for without Yesterday and Tomorrow,
we have no Today

Ralph

SHADOWS
(The Moon Shines No More)

A withered paper blows,
Ain't nobody on the streets.
A little child's crying,
Mother's out of milk.

Attention, it's now five.
We hear the rumble . . . rumble.
Shadows loom larger, larger,
The moon shines no more.

Birds pick at a carcass,
A lonely boy beats his drum.
The fire's out of control,
Covered by darkness.

Oven's fueled by money,
My hands are about frozen stiff.
Shadows loom larger, larger,
The moon shines no more.

David R. Begin

LOST LOVE

I cannot fight these feelings I have inside,
For when I go, they only make me want to cry.

I wish I would never have met her that rainy November day,
But I did, and what is done is done, what can I say.

The hours I spent with her, were very special to me.
I want those hours back, for they are the only thing I can see.

Now I am lost and all alone.
I am as a drifter, with no place to call home.

I somehow think, I am to blame for ever letting her go,
Maybe I did not love her enough, or let my feelings show.

I cannot live in the past, because life must go on.
The only thing I keep is the memories, for she is forever gone.

Dwight Triplett

WONDERS OF THE PARK

Have you ever taken a walk in the park?
In the evening, when it's dark

And sat on a park bench and wondered why
There are so many stars in the sky

And that friendly firefly you see buzzing around
It's a beauty seldom found

You hear the wind go through the trees
They play their music on a breeze

You hear the chains of the swings
Even the teeter totter begins to sing

The merry-go-round squeaks just right
I thank you Lord for this wonderful night

Michael F. Brouillard

THE RISE OF A NEW KING

A war that has aroused this subtle land
Has borne its mark upon its troubled sand.
A new power has arisen from a land afar
And has descended out of heaven as a fallen
     star.
This conquering power has mounted its king
Of whose glory and power will the people sing.
Subject to his majesty shall Eskadore now be
As a slave to his master and no longer to be
     free.

Triumphant conquerors paraded throughout the
     streets
As victors of war having performed a glorious
     feat.
They reveled in festivities, prodigious and
     galore,
Throughout the captured cities of Eskadore.

Darren Dorsey

WEEDS

Caught in a tumbleweed mood
My mind slipping, careless.
Bouncing through memory-fields
Only to be trapped by a closing cellar door.

"What was I trying to say to you?"

Deep in a tumbleweed mood
Tripping over falls, icicles forming snake-like charms
To wear around my neck.
It's snowing now, perhaps, in New England.

"And — did you say something?"

The weeds are gathering, collecting me
Entangling, disarming my best attempts,
Caught in a tumbleweed mood,
Trapped with a tumbleweed mind,
Cluttered with formalities:

"Do you know anything about gardening?"

Ronny Ann Bohrer

ISHCABIBBLE

Said Ishca to the Bibble on a morning bright and new;
"I'm trying to watch the boat race but your head,
It blocks my view."

The Bibble was quite stubborn, this the Ishca knew;
For the Bibble kept his staunchy stance,
Thus Ishca's anger grew.

Again said Ishca louder still, "If you don't move your head,
I'll pull your hair and box your ears,
Until your face turns red."

"Look now!" said the Bibble "there'll be no violence here;
If you can't see the boat race, go in and have a beer."

"Bother!" said the Ishca "I do not want a beer,
Move your head so I can see, the boats are getting near."

With a sigh and a little sneer, the Bibble's stubbornness mended;
He moved his head and Ishca saw the boat race,
It had ended.

Jennifer Lennan

BEAT THE WRATH

The sunlight poured through the clouds and hit the
weary path —
     of bottles, glass and broken dreams, it SMILED at
the wrath.

It warmed the hopes of many, as it trickled through
shadowed screens —
before the slumbering alley bums, it displayed a new
day's means.

As birds awoke in chatter, and scavenged the soil
to eat —
this brightness made it easier, to forget last evening's
feat.

For once again, the world grew tired as darkness
set in fast —
The night took angry feelings of yesterday's tormented past.

To give life a new beginning, it came another day —
And we should make it simple, not throw it all away.

Katherine Olson

THROUGH THE NIGHT

Nocturnal cloak which shrouds the earth,
Womb of all that has gained birth.
What some may fear and some despise
Gives rest to weary, tear-stained eyes.

For in your barren void hue
I see my present point of view,
Such bleak and mournful, anguished pain,
Whimpering pleas for help in vain.

And in your icy, piercing breath,
I feel the grip of loneliness
But only you engulf my whole,
And hide my ever-wicked soul,
From myself which always sees,
A thousand cried hypocrisies.

New sunlight's beams interrupt your peace,
The turmoil doth no longer cease.
And once again I wait alone
For midnight's solemn, whispered moan.

David E. Jones

JONES, DAVID ERIC. Born: 6-13-64; Married: 10-12-79, to Brenda Gayle Armstrong; Poetry: 'The Towers,' 10-28-82; 'Geometric. Omni. Direction,' 2-2-85; 'Stars,' 3-15-85; 'Borderline Impressions,' 11-9-82; 'Wings,' 10-12-82; Comments: *I believe that poetry is an outstanding example of the divine spark which is man's soul, and is in reality one spirit, manifest in many forms; using the intellect as a tool. This I believe is the root of all inspiration in all forms of true art.*

BEHIND THE YELLOW WALLPAPER

the day wears on,
the heaviness, like
eating all day
and sleep,
sleeping to ease the pang.

morning pains, that
creep continuously, like
the flow of heavy traffic
in summer.

Joanne Giannino

THE SONG OF THE WIND

Hushing, gently rustling,
frozen leaves in the fall.
Moaning, ever groaning,
distant, swept of snow.
Crying, silently sighing,
in a moist breath of rain.
Whistling, joyously kissing
sun-sparkled waters.
Calling, while falling
over a breaking sea.
Roaring, soaring, gale-swept clouds
across an ink-stained sky.
Bellowing then mellowing,
a lull, then calm.
Murmuring, softly nurturing a breeze.
Quietly lying, not replying,
her song lingers on.

Carolyn J. Stienstra

STIENSTRA, CAROLYN JANICE. Born: Montréal, Quebec, Canada; Education: Canadian Coast Guard College, Nautical Science, Marine Navigation, 6-2-84; Occupations: Navigation Officer, Canadian Coast Guard Maritimes; Writings: Numerous works yet unpublished; Comments: *I write to inspire thought, and to explore the elements of man's relationship to nature, time, space, and himself. Poetry is a puzzle whereby each person searches to find a solution in the form of a personal meaning. Personally, it is a portrait of the self.*

THE SURFACE EDITION

It's all in the balance —
How you see me.
Checking no further
than your own reflection
in my eyes.
Content with the surface edition.
Could you grasp more?
Refrain from the usual, "Cool it!"
when I begin to bubble.
Shear the edge for once
and play the upstairs key,
take the distance, look —
My steps leave traces too.

Elizabeth Lachman

LOVE, QUESTION MARK

How is it
you are able to sense
who I am, deep down
where no one else can see

How is it
you bring me such joy
that I marvel and wonder
and hope I bring the same to you

How is it
my emotions can fear
as if on the edge of a waterfall
and then plunge in glee when I see you

How is it
this happened in a moment
so rapid, so sure, so overwhelming
it tears at me when we're apart

I wonder at all the questions
I know I miss you

Mary Hines Cady

Now and then come the tales of men
who fight but never wonder,
why their lives must be spent
in the jaw of greed and hunger.

And if they knew what they did
while their babies were screaming,
would they try to change their lives
or would nothing then redeem them.

Then if I could spy a lie,
could I hope to teach them,
right from wrong, friend from foe,
could I possibly reach them?

There have been men who tried to lend
their knowledge and their wisdom,
but after all they had to fall
to a life of death in prison.

For their ears do not see the tears
of life and its affliction,
they've closed their minds so many times
and caused Christ's crucifixion.

Phillip Nathan

MORNING

As dawn releases the cloak of darkness
And lifts her palate to paint the day,
I arise and stand
Within the shadow of His face.
And lest my thoughts should stray
To cast images of self etchings
That are stained with desires of me,
I kneel in that first light of morning
And ask for time to speak.
And as my soul absorbs the silence,
A gentle peace intervenes
To unravel the tangled webs of life
And set my spirit free.
And one by one the selfish thoughts
Begin to drift away
Until only a single need remains —

To allow my soul a glimpse of truth
And consider what I might say
Should I be required to stand
In front of Him today.

Joann Showers

ALIVE FOREVERMORE

Listen. Do you hear it?
Look about. Can't you see?
I wonder what it's like above —
With God over yonder trees.

I wonder what it's like from Heaven
To see a moonlit night,
But there there is no darkness
Just God's pure, loving light.

I hope someday to see it all,
The golden streets of God,
To hear the joyous singing
Of God's saints that never shall
    fall.

Oh, beautiful day it shall be,
When we meet on that shore,
Yes, with God for all eternity —
        Alive forevermore.

Kimberly Smith

#15

When rage from rage
Unto fierce fury blows
And all that's hidden inside
With swift force explodes

When madness crept in
Slowly ticks — endlessly
And life with hues divine
Shatters so breathlessly

Whence thought endless nightmares
Of hopes now silent screams
— Suppression — no longer reason holds
With firm blasts explode

Then say what I've said
And you'll see
All that's inside
Is but you and me;
Not you, but me.

Niloofar Razi

WINTER IS COMING

    Have the birds gone north
or flown south?
    The squirrels don't bark,
even before dark.
    No deer are in sight,
even in the late night.
    Don't hear the frog
croaking on the log.
    Trees have no leaves,
which is hard to believe.
    Don't hear the sound of the crickets
and no rabbit in the thickets.
    Don't see the chipmunk
running fiercely around the tree trunk.
    Bees are no longer humming,
so winter is coming.
    The ground is hard and cold,
which is near winter, I'm told.
    Trees are covered with snow,
so winter is coming, you know.

Richard E. Hibbard

YOU'RE HURTING MY FRIEND

I know you're hurting my dear friend.
You want the pain to finally end.
It's hard for you to live each day
In your very special way.
You say no one cares or knows how you
Feel.
But that my friend is not real!
Though no one can feel the pain that
You do.
There are others that are hurting too.
When you're in pain you think of just
You.
It's hard to see that others hurt too.
There's someone who loves you and does
Care.
It's hard to see that the love is there.
You hurt and I don't know what to do.
I can only think of hugging you.
And I want you to know my dear friend.
That the pain will finally end.
Then you can think how good that will
Be.
It will help you heal faster, you see.

Maryann Jokela

JOKELA, MARYANN PATTY. Born: Duluth, Minnesota, 7-3-55; Education: attended college for about a year, but have not earned a degree; Occupation: Manufacturing; Comments: *I write about feelings and what they mean to others. A positive attitude is important. I try to convey that in my writing.*

I cover sadness
In earth made damp
By cold tears;
I hide sadness
In a coffin sealed in darkness,
Like a corpse;
Dead.
I bury sadness
In graves marked with stones;
Fragments, like broken teeth,
Scattered throughout the gray dawn.
A smile is the shovel I use
To cover the hole left behind.
And the soul,
Once intertwined
In ecstasy and sweet torment,
Will never leap into the open arms
Of sunlight,
And sky
Again.

John R. Fontes

A BLUEBIRD PRISM

Life for three years among bluebirds,
    symbols of the world's happiness,
    magnifies each day of rain,
    each ray of sun-drenched light.

His brilliant blue flashes in
    awe-inspiring moments
    offsets her slate-blue camouflage
    blending into the tree bark.

Only through a drop of rain
    is it possible for a ray of sun
    to become minutely spectacular —
    a bluebird prism.

Were I to substitute a tear,
    heartfelt and sincere,
    for the insignificant raindrop
    will the prism last another year?

Patricia F. Gilbert

SOMETIMES

Sometimes when I look outside
and see the bright blue sky
I wonder why I'm not a bird
So I could learn to fly.

Sometimes when I take a walk
I wonder why squirrels can't talk
To see a squirrel climb up a tree
I often wish that could be me.

Sometimes when I feel the rain
Fall upon my brow
I no longer feel the pain
That holds me prisoner now.

Sometimes if you really try
And close your eyes and see
That feeling that you're wishing for
Is really to be free.

Sandra M. Martin

THE SUN

Wake the sun, open up wide
let me see your rays so gold
in your warmth I will confide
till the summer days grow old

Hold me in your warming arms
never let the day go by
keep me in your summer charms
let me hear your hottest sigh

Melt the snow and stop the rain
bring back the pretty fields of green
take away the winter's pain
alas, the beauties I have seen

You keep me happy when you shine
but sorrow shadows when you hide
how I wish that you were mine
wake the sun, open up wide

Kelly Oliver

THE WOODLAND CRY

Give me a tree, and I'll be all right.
Give me a forest, and that is my life.
A forest has mystery, it's deep and it's dark.
   Can you feel the spirits?

The forest gives power, it's alive and it's fresh.
   How quickly and silently I can run!

Oh forest that lives in my dreams,
Do not go into the forgotten land! Beware of man.

Oh great forest, accept me into your bosom!
Share with me your soul, and let me stand by your side.

Do not leave us, Oh forest, we have need of you!
Though many do not see,
Man's future declines with the forest,
Man needs room to be free. It is sad, so sad.

The spirits, they know, they hide and they await
the time that they will once again rule the land.
No man will there be, only forest land deep,
and my spirit will cry in shame.

What has my race done? They are blind, they can't see!
Oh spirits of the forest, come unto me.

    Scott Elliott Fricke

VILLANELLE:
GRACE

She wanders by in wayward discontent,
Her willful glance an existential freeze:
Aware but slightly of this world's lament.

We watch her pass and feel her steel intent.
Her face, her form, her motion seldom tease.
She wanders by in wayward discontent.

Her manner barely grants adult consent
To fling our hearts upon a wild trapeze:
Aware but slightly of this world's lament.

Yet would it come to pass, the prime event?
At least we entertain such thoughts as these.
She wanders by in wayward discontent.

Her virtue ascends humankind's ascent.
All reminiscence struggles to appease,
Aware but slightly of this world's lament.

Her precious pout appears to show dissent;
Though she accepts all destiny with ease.
She wanders by in wayward discontent:
Aware but slightly of this world's lament.

    Robert Cunningham

MY LITTLE BIRD DIED TODAY

He stood so proud with his feathers of blue,
and a crowned head that matched too.

He would puff his chest and prance around.
Then, toss his head like a little clown.

He'd watch me from his small domain, as he
walked his perch, but not in vain. And with
a foreign chirping sound, he picked his
food in gratitude.

My little bird died today.

    Raymond Vago

THE PHOTOCOPIER

Treat me tender, treat me nice —
If you don't, you'll pay the price.

I can't eat staples or paper clips;
The wrong grade of paper jams and slips;

My drawers demand a gentle touch
From loving hands. Now that's not much,

But if despite all, I need a fix,
Call the Machine Abuse Hotline, and stop the tricks.

    Sheila Insley

THE CARDINAL

Red Rocket shoots across the sullen sky,
And brings forth from my lips a smothered sigh,
Unfeeling, lies the snow,
But slowly, subtly, the grass grows, I know.
For all of nature awaits the spring.
Soon her lover will bring the ring,
The Wedding shall burst forth with flowers.
Then its golden minutes will be muted with awe.
When with great delight nature pours forth
her beauty upon all mankind in showers.

    Julita Davis

THE BEGINNING

As the first of its breath touches the earth
   each sigh sparkles on the water.
The tide catches its rays and sends
   beads of shine rippling.
It creeps up the sides of the sky
   struggling to reach around the clouds.
The darkness breaks into small pieces
   of silky gray.
Further it creeps to the peak of its throne
   where it sits to illuminate the world.
And so, it is done, another sunrise.

    Susan Freytag

DEATH'S PERCEPTION

   It lies unattainable to the human senses
not even in the fractions of death.
   One cannot perceive to know when it will
occur or how it shall come.
   Like greased lightning it strikes one's
soul; it's there, then gone.
   There is a perception of death when one
is ill-fated with it; no, there is a fear of it
happening.
   Death's perception lies only in the hands
of God, not in the eyes of man.

    Donna Lynn Utter

A MASTERPIECE CALLED SPECTRUM

Unseen hands trace high above the township steeples.
Up where the imaginary pathway lead is as far as one's eyes
   behold.

Hidden underneath the darkest clouds sketches of skylight
   rainbows are brushed like magic from the master's studio.

The sky as an easel, the sun as a guide, your eyes as the lens;

The prism painting is ready to be hung.

    Susan Anne Mann

Trust in Me and rest in My love;
Be still and know that I am God.
Don't worry about your future plans;
Simply leave them in My hands.
For I made a path right through the sea,
And I surely will do the same for thee.
But don't dwell on what I have done;
Only think of things to come.

There is a place for you to be
Where you can share your thoughts with Me.
I'll show you many open doors
With some of the options that are yours.
Whatever it is you wish to be,
I'll see to it that you succeed.
It may take time before it's done;
First all the battles must be won.

Just trust in My unfailing love,
And set your sights on things above.

Margaret Kelstrup

ODE TO BLUE

'Tis not blue the color
        nor the sign of drear,
For towards blue sky
        do birds raise their heads to sing.
But grey the culprit is.
        Crystal seems a tear,
a pretty shade for such a lie.
        Grey does crying bring.

No birds to hear when blue is gone;
        when sky is dark,
                empty of tomorrow,
                        and grey fills the space.
        Even the clouds are alone.
Grey hears not the beautiful lark
        but brings to many sorrow.
Blue does grant to life its grace
        while grey gives the earth its stones.

Lisa Gerthing

JOHN

When old aunts meet
How they cluck
"Who would have thought"
Indeed, "Who would have thought?"

Have you seen that photo?
A grimy kid with dirty knees
Smiling, proud
Scouse proud
Who would have thought
of the end
Manhattan
Wasn't even an assassin's bullet
Just a madman's delusion
Crushing the flower
With his putrid finger

God bless you John

Adrian Vyner-Brooks

STILL OF THE NIGHT

i heard your voice in the night air,
i gasped for your breath.
But,
By holding you
i suffocated myself.

Elizabeth Durand

JOHN FITZGERALD KENNEDY

I met him in the summer of nineteen hundred and fifty-four;
My Congressman introduced us.
He was the fabled King of Camelot —
A man destined for far greater things than the Senate floor,
Or life confined to a wheelchair.
His smile was warm and friendly.
He held my hand while he talked to me —
Talked with speech so polished and articulate that I envied him.
How could I know what the future held, or how precious those
few moments would become
As I relived them, time and time again, while the years rolled by.
His press conferences — his presentations — his motorcades — I
followed it all,
Rejoicing in his triumphs, sharing the bitterness of his defeats.
I was a part of his New Frontier; I would have followed him anywhere,
Even into the Valley of Death, had he but asked it of me.
All too soon it ended,
In a hail of bullets, near a grassy knoll, in Texas, on a crisp
November day.
Years later, I visited his grave —
Saw the flickering eternal flame, touched the cold, stone slab,
And remembered him with tear-filled eyes —
For Camelot is no more.

Jeanne Larkey Medlin

REMEMBERING

I'll always remember that when I was young, I thought it was easy
to be a parent. I had to grow up to understand that it was not.

I'll always remember that when I was young I appreciated my dad,
but I thought him harsh, and sometimes I felt hurt. I had to grow
up to understand that when the child hurts, the parent hurts too, and
I decided to remember only the good, because it far outweighed the other.

I'll always remember how hard he worked so his family would be
nourished. I had to grow up to understand that his toil was a way
of showing love and caring, and I appreciated him even more.

I'll always remember that when I was young, we celebrated with
root beer floats and stories of years gone by. I remember baseball
games in summer and football in winter, dancing together and
laughing at his jokes. I had to grow up to understand that it was
his way of sharing himself, not an easy task for a man such as he.

Yes, I had to grow up to learn how much love it takes to be a parent.
And he had to grow old before I heard with my ears what his heart
had always said, "I love you, Bobbie." And he heard me say, "I love
you, Dad." Then we smiled, and I'll always remember.

Barbara Rowan

DEAR JESUS

Dear Jesus,
        I'm so sorry for all I've done wrong.
It seems like I'm always going down the wrong road.
But when I get lost and I can't find my way,
I suddenly look up and see your sweet face.

        The times I've been lonely, you've sat by my side.
And the times it got so dark and I've been afraid,
you've always been there to lighten my way.

        There have been so many times I thought I just couldn't go on.
I tripped and I fell, but you picked me back up and helped me along.
The times I thought I just couldn't walk on.

        The road was so empty, with two paths to take.
Then you took my hand and showed me the way.

                        With all my love,

                        Anyone

Jonnie Melia Scott

FAREWELL TO A FRIEND

You were such a part of my existence.
I am a little lost without you now.
I listen for your sounds, a moan, a patter of feet,
A feeling of contentment as you stood and gazed at me.
The deep brown softness of your eyes were eloquence to behold.
Your protectiveness, as you stood near me; bless you for that.

You were ever quick to comprehend.
You knew your importance to me, and that you'd always belong.
Even when I left you behind for a time — you understood.
And adapted to life's changes.
Even to beau that called, often you turned away.
Until Tom came and him you took to your heart, even as I.

None shall take your place; your smartness cannot be found again.
I leave my love for dogs forever with you —
Goodbye, Old Friend . . .

Margaret Renfroe Meyerer

MEYERER, MARGARET RENFROE. Born: Birmingham, Alabama, 3-13-24; Married: 2-14-42 to Albert Meyerer; 12-23-73 to Tom Standfill; Education: L.S.U., B.S., 1965, M.S., 1970; Occupation: Elementary School Teacher; Writings: *Heartbreak* book, Vantage Press, 1985; Comments: *My poems seem to write themselves. When I have an experience that causes some emotional response, words come to me that describe my feelings. The poems I have written have been from these experiences. My book was written as a result of a turbulent ending of my second marriage. The poems I have written since then are more peaceful.*

I CANNOT TELL JUST HOW OR WHY

You ask me how I know I love you:
In truth, I really cannot say.
I only know my heart beats wildly,
At even the thought of you.
My life, itself, depends upon your smile.
Your hair, your eyes, your gentle hands,
Are all a precious part of you;
Your delighted laughter mingling
With my own, and your musical voice.
Yet, I know if all these vanished overnight,
I would still adore you,
And cherish you until the day I die —
Although I cannot tell just how, or why!

Lois Roquemore Carden

I AM A MAN

If I were the sea and you were the soft white shore
    You would know love's caresses o'er and o'er.
By starlight and moonbeam, rapture the more.
The length of my wave would enfold your flanks
    With passion that has no restraint or banks,
A gathering up by the sea of its own,
    Thrilling, possessing, satiety unknown,
'Til close in my arms, deep answers deep,
    My own beloved, my own.

But I am a man and you are a stark white maid
    Afraid . . . Afraid . . . Delicacy is outraged,
Fragile, precise, a Dresden figurine
    To be cherished untouched, but not unseen.
Your smug droning voice and your lukewarm tea
    Are lost in the roar of a held-back sea:
I dream of one who will drown in the moment
    And be lost . . . with me.

Vel Davis Hatch

PERSIMMON

A couple of trees deeply rooted
out in the backyard
look as though they've lost their reasons.

Blossoms are gone and leaves are blown away.
They used to giggle
as the autumn breeze was passing through.

You wouldn't like to picture these trees
wrinkled with failure,
their fatal defects covered with moss,

but they squeeze your hearts with their honest hands
hidden in their wiry body,
and screen-print their facts in your mind.

Remove all the fringes, and what have you got?
A fruit of persimmon,
bitter and sweet, will remain on a branch,

ripened to its core throughout the winter,
until I find it. —
Surely I'll find it in time and in me.

Tamiko Mizushima

MOTHER'S REACH

When just a tiny babe, in my mother's loving arms,
She used to hold me so very tight,
And she'd bring her hand up to my hand,
And I'd squeeze her fingers with all my might.

And as I was growing older,
When off to school I went each day,
She'd take my hand within her hand,
And somehow, I knew it would always be that way.

She shared my joys and my sorrows as well,
She taught me good from bad,
She always was there with her hand on my shoulder,
To guide me and make me glad.

Then one day I married and moved away,
But, not far from within her reach,
Because one's never too old to learn,
What mothers have to teach.

And as I take your hand, once again,
As you sleep so quietly today,
I know deep within my heart,
You'll forever be just a fingertip's reach away.

Karen Hanan

I woke up this morning
    only to realize I had not been to bed.

I got dressed
    only to know I had nothing to wear.

I went to work
    only to find I had no job.

I came home to sleep
    only to remain awake.

I wrote a line
    only to find I had no paper.

I called you
    only to hear you did not want to talk.

I came to see you
    only to discover you were not there.

I looked into your eyes
    only to see they were closed.

I walked away
    only to come back again.

Jennifer L. Setzer

TRIBUTE TO THE FALLEN
February 1985

Where did they all go
    When they went away?
It seems so very long, though,
    Perhaps it was only yesterday.

I remember each so well
    They were young — so strong.
Sent to a land this side of Hell;
    Joined together by War's mournful song.

Who did they leave behind at home;
    A mother — a daughter — a wife?
Who now is left to cry and moan
    Along with them, who lost a life?

What could they have thought and shared
    Given a bright future filled with years?
In the end who really cared?
    Who now is left to shed their tears?

Where did they all go
    When they went away?
What is now left to show
    For such a heavy price to pay?

Stephen H. Stull

ABUSED CHILD

Of their flesh and blood am I,
and they gave me life, but why!
When my parents rile each other,
I'm a football for dad and mother.
Try not to show it hurts a lot,
and remember, they're all I've got.
My face cover from a striking hand,
why I'm treated so, can't understand?
Have been in a hospital, once or twice,
the place was quiet, the nurses nice.
If I had a magic carpet I'd go far away,
and find good pals with whom I'd play.
Sometimes wish, I were an angel in heaven,
Even though I'm six, going on seven.

Cecilia Musumeci

two-forty (corporate ode)

such subtle spirit-deadening
drab outlook bleak design
building of inertia
cesspool of despair
where yr inhabitants
zombie-like frozen large icicles
gaze at me as at some future phantom
flying past their present
changeless reality
like some carrier of death
bubonic plague or cholera
existing in a sealed tomb
vapid eyes of self-neglect
erasing any trace of humanity
creating a cold blank void
poisoned imprisoned mind state
of hollow mouth's voices
without life or feeling
    Brian J. Groth

I love the beauty
of life,
small islands of wonder
surfacing here and there
from under an ocean
of trivia and meanness,
islands creating tears
of soft surprise
within my being,
helping me to touch
an inside reverence
where all living things
feel honored
with respect.

I love the beauty
of life
as it quickens my awareness
and intoxicates my thought,
if only for awhile.
    Mary K. Dockens

ATWOOD'S COLORS

Atwood's colors exploding
luminescent, blazing,
jumping, curling
into the eyeless cavern of mauve.
Stretching sunray long
across the hills
to conjure the temperamental pastiche
of moods born fleetingly
from a shimmering mirage.
Atwood's colors disown the senses
in a raindance frenzy
gently push into the indigo
. . . where the beast of vision
bared free, coils to spring
on the unsuspecting,
groveling, fearing.
Atwood's colors fang and foam
of life the cry
yet what to be . . .
    Mike Repasky

SIBLINGS

Kentucky mist lifts —
two yearlings nuzzle mothers
in white fenced fields.
Sired by a Derby winner,
more nurtured than some children.
    Miriam L. Woolfolk

THRESHOLD

I come here
where tonight thoughts ache
in the darkness of
Minnesota farm lands.

Thoughts strange as whispers
breathe slightly of old misgivings,
living in the shadows
of silent memories.

Between us lay the miles
we have learned to trust,
coming closer as your children
encircle our lives.

And somehow I know
that you will be always
with me;
someone whose voice
will always play in my head.

People change;
and forget to tell each other.

Michelle Scott

SHADOWS IN THE DARK

Shadows of Darkness
Existing in light
Tunnels of visions
Thoughts you must fight

False glory exists
Shattered ego behind
Temptations indulged
Forget Father Time

Drumbeats become habitual
Your head begins to drone
Acceptance is a ritual
You leave the other home

Evil and Purity
Unite hand and heart
Separation is Forgotten
In the Shadows of the Dark

Lori Mankin

LOVERS

Leaning over
Understanding
We resemble
Curious children
In the zoo.

We look and stare,
And gesture
Puckered lips at things
We seem to know
By only looking.

We touch and sense
The sounds we taste
And concentrate
To feel
Each other's presence.

But then again,
Yet altogether well
We seem to know
That what we know
Will in due time be questioned further.

Lorenzo Cuevas-Cumming

COMPUTER MAN

Computers big as houses working up there in the sky
Working for Computer Man who'll judge us by and by
His helpers watching tape machines, the big wheels slowly turning
Keeping track of all the plus and minus points we're earning.

Creation had no Creator! This vast blue firmament
This complex universe we have is all an accident
Yes God is dead, there is no God, false prophets cry with scorn
But on that final day they'll wish that they had not been born.

And how about those clever men of cruel and vicious heart:
Play dirty pool! No Golden Rule! Tear every man apart!
Don't ever stop, get to the top, no matter what the cost,
Win now! Pay later! (Then they'll find out who it was that lost).

And when the wheels stop turning and it's time to search men's souls
Computer Man will gather up the cards with funny holes
He'll pick out all those blessed ones that please him and give joy
Those that offend he'll fold and bend or spindle and destroy.

Computer Man, Computer Man, will we be judged as fools
For counting on your mercy after making our own rules?
Computer Man, Computer Man, ain't it a crying shame
That in the end we'll have nobody but ourselves to blame.

Arpad S. Chontos

ON TO VICTORY

A tiny ad in a local newspaper caught our eyes one day;
Square dance lessons Monday night was about all it had to say;
Except wear casual clothes, bring a partner and come to Eaton Hall,
We would be greeted by a club and a man who knew how to call.

Excited and scared, we showed up at seven,
We were welcomed by those who thought it was Heaven.
We attended the first night — just to watch, you see,
But were soon shown how much fun it could be!

We kept coming back week after week,
More fun to have, more knowledge to seek.
The "angels" or "helpers" were great to show
Just which way to turn — which way to go.

Our first real dance was quite a scene,
We were on our own like King and Queen!
That night we learned we had nothing to dread,
"Your caller has taught you well," they said.

We know that we are not the best,
But we'll keep up with most of the rest;
From eight to a square to thousands on vacation,
We'll be square dancing throughout our Nation.

Gloria C. Higgins

HOPEFUL

A bridge over water flowing through spring
    trees started to bloom, within the heart the same.
Taking tomorrow by the hand, teaching you to sing;
    being helpful in everything you do
    and sharing with everyone your gladness too.

Garden of treasure through a path of flowers blooming within
    the sun, that shines through you and everyone
Catching the wind through thy air, spirit, and soul are in his care
    being together in a storm, always sharing happiness within the fog.

Trees of gold and orange too,
    signs of beauty within the skies of blue.
Dark clouds on high rain by mid-afternoon
    a gust of wind, with spirit free
Climbing with the mist of joy and challenge
    the freedom through the woods just a little gold and a touch of hope.

Karin Kornelson

A PROFESSOR LOVED BY AN UNDERGRADUATE

Enchanted and beguiled and touched,
Embarrassed, flustered by her love —
The middle-aged man asked the girl:
"What is it that you see in me?"

"You are good, kind, compassionate"
Was all that she was moved to say
By her rhapsodic earnestness,
Her innocence of expectation.

She clearly felt such need for love
It seemed to him almost as though
His kindness were in being loved
As much as in conferring love,

Compassion had been substituted
For cries of passion long since muted.

Lawrence Minet

WE COULD MAKE GOD SMILE

Sometimes it seems we're alone
What can a working man do
Don't have time for anything
Seems like days just go by

Success is the key to life
Try hard to get ahead
No time to enjoy life
Or reach out a helping hand

If there were no hope at all
God would have ended the world
Got to be a lot of love
Deep in the heart of the Lord

Someone needs to spread the word
A lot can be done with love
You know we could make God smile
By taking the time to love

William LaSalle

MISSISSIPPI MONDAY

Ruddy skies that tell of summer;
Clouds that brood and make it warmer;
All week long the dawn comes hazy
'Specially Monday when I'm lazy.

Balmy breezes blow o'er beaches . . .
Past the beery, bleary bleaches.
Hear them sigh as they hush on by
Under the surly, sullen sky.

Now and then I hear a rustle
Like a hustle and a bustle . . .
And somewhere in the breaking light,
The fading footfalls of the night.

The dawn is waking with a yawn.
I do too, every single morn.
But do I love to stay in bed . . .
And sleep away this day instead!

Shanton

MY TRIBUTE TO MY SON

My Little Captain is gone.
In him — I could find no wrong
With a salute — he bid farewell.
My Little Captain is gone.

My Little Shepherd will herd
no more.
He left his flock to follow a star.
I loved him then — I love him now.
By faith I can see him afar.

My Little boy Tommy — I love you
mommie.
See the stars and the light.
The smiling moon shining bright.
It will lead any man through
a dark night.

Upon his grave a "Rose" close lay.
Placed on a lonesome October day.
A weeping willow not far away.
The Little Bird with its broken wing.
Now. I can hear the happy song it
did sing.

And the stately "Evergreen" — so lovely —
so strong — so tall.
Will guard all through the winter.
and the spring — summer
and fall . . .

Lillie Seidel Hinton

MAMA MOSES

Mama Moses is her name
Yet, she has no fame.
She works so willingly with her hands,
But never once does she demand.

She loves with her eyes,
And in her heart is the law of kindness.
There is no spiritual blindness,
For she has touched the Master's Hands.

In her tongue is the spirit of gentleness.
With the faith of Moses does she speak;
Not words of doubt and delusion,
But words of love and power.

Her Source is the All Mighty Power.

Why she be named "Mama Moses?"

Because of the many roses she has gathered through the ages.

Roses once wilted by the sands of time,
Roses now touched by the Sublime.
Yes . . . roses . . . lives,
Many, many lives.

Without her touch, there may not be any roses.

So, Mama Moses, keep touching the Roses.

Deborah S. Land

KNOWLEDGE

A small boy, pole in hand
stands patiently erect
from a small rock protruding from the water.
With each cast and plunge
learned fish ignore his bait.

Kathy Morrone

PHOTOGRAPHS

A fragile fragment of the past
    Hearty laughter
    Pink-cheeked babies
    Button busting parents
    Silly party times
    Promising posed commencements
    Rained-on vacations and fond farewells
Held together with the thread of poignant memories
    Photographs!

Margaret A. Fernald

JESUS IS MY MASTER

Jesus is my master, this I know.
He is ever near me, where I go.
When my way seems weary, spirits low
He will light my way, I know.

What He has done for me He will do for you
He will give you strength for your work to do;
He will light the way, from Heaven above
If, within your heart, there is Love.

Marion McIntire

ALPHABET SOUP

When I look upwards towards space,
that vast expanse that appears,
as a mosaic in lace . . .
I wonder what surprises we can't see or feel,
lie beyond our searching, reaching eyes?
Those worlds we dream about, and often fantasize!
Living things above, below and around us; that all
can show and touch the miracles of their universe,
those unknown and known secrets of space.

Richard A. Seversen

A HAT'S HAPPY DAY

I am a hat upon a plump head,
I see all that's done, and hear all that's said.
I'm worn to the bus stop, and then on to work,
And handed right in to the coat-check-in clerk.

Being put on the hat rack is when fun begins,
Where hats can all laugh, giggle, or grin.
But then comes the time when we all must depart,
Each looking forward to tomorrow's same start.

Laura Cook

HOURGLASS

    each grain a moment
      shared or wasted
        no time
          nothing but time
          courageous beginnings trickling
        impetuous present turning to regretted past
    nothing but time
  no time left at all
Time to turn the hourglass again.

Leslie E. Fisher

RAINBOW ARCH.

NOW I LAY ME DOWN MY HEART TO BEAT

To all Mothers of Absalom —
Our human hearts come out from Thee,
And return to Thee,
Our face, its grace, in exile, be.

Hallowed by thy hollow heart,
It stopped — and has refused to start!

My human heart that seeks its own
Was lost — so long ago — its best unknown
To call its Life its very own.

Hallowed be thy one heart-beat,
This Lamb has left its one-to-one heart-bleat.

I'd always bought and sold on Christmas Mart,
And now — I've 'done' gone and lost a human heart,
It was, of course, our birthday part.

I've always known its every beat was just a loan,
I should have known —

Its cross has gone, its even crown,
I can't at all find them around,
Perhaps they're lying hallowed on the ground!

My heart has gone — yes, with its gift,
Lost on rocky shore — could be adrift?
On softly rolling sea —
To seek another wandering Christmas tree.

Hope Divine and I wrote this poem — O Glorious Love Alone!

Georgia Robinson

IF THE WORLD WERE COLORBLIND

If the world were colorblind,
Would it be a better place,

Could we learn to live as brothers,
If there were no such thing as race,

Would the infectious spread of prejudice,
Soon fade and dissipate,

Or would we just replace racism
With some other form of hate,

Would we be forced to see as children do,
Who do not judge by skin,

Who do not distinguish colors,
They only see a friend,

For children are not born to hatred,
They learn it as they grow,

And we much like a farmer,
Can only hope to reap what we sow,

If color were not an issue,
Could we possibly take the time,

To see the wonderful contributions,
In others we could find,

Perhaps we could ask crayola,
To make a contribution to the world of man,

By creating a brand-new color,
And we could call it . . . Human!

Deborah A. Inman

FREEDOMS

On an overcast early morning
I came across
A Japanese fisherman
casting his line
from an empty beach.
His only company
sandpipers skittering down the shoreline
in search of breakfast.
The sea foam wrapped his legs
in chilly socks
he smiled at his own reflection in the tidepool,
content with the life he has made,
simply a man in touch.
I continued down the beach
in search of driftwood.
Looking back at the small silent man
I realized
this is the true pursuit of happiness.

Angela Gail Britton

UNDERSTAND

What, I ask, reflects your attitude on Indians?
To you are they hollow and static, with no glimmer
of their past?

Do you view the white man's past with depth and
perception, full of glory and conquest? While you
hold naught for the red men of history.

Does the Indian spirit beckon from the flowing
waters of a vast unimaginable time, with loneliness
a constant companion? Where wind sun and the blessed
rain are part of a great unknown.

You must pray to their God and worship life as the
Indian standing alone on a distant frontier, or lie
dead in a shallow grave, dug by white men.

Richard Collier

CITY

I watch them every day.
Millions of them scurrying along through
the concrete labyrinth of the city.
As cold as the steel buildings, as impersonal
as the spiteful December wind.
They don't look, they don't talk, just scurry,
scurry, scurry, right along.
But then one of them stops and smiles.
And I realize I am not all alone.

Gino M. Boni

THE VISITOR

O Wind that scratches at my window
    and wakes me in the night,
and shakes the bare tree branches at me
    like a thousand bony fingers.
O Wind that screams just like a banshee
    and often sounds like the most glorious of singers;
and keeps that boy's kite up, high in its flight.
You who are the mighty arm and the malignant scythe,
    that can easily fall the most stable tree.
yes, You about whom the scientists abolish all the myths —
You who are wild and can make one feel free.
it's Your hand that raises the fallen leaf
    from its lowly heap.
to all men You're the one true God that moves them
    in their plight.
it's You who visits me in the night
    and won't let me sleep.

Paul Lennon

FOR A FRIEND

You are my past looking glass . . .

I feel your pain
I hear the rumbling waves from your brain
Crashing and landing on your heart.

I see the wall you build progressively get taller and wider.
I can also see a lonely, fragile person hiding within,
With a yearning too overpowering to hear.

I want to reach out my hand to you in friendship
But I can sense that you'll only touch; not grab my hand
Because you lack trust.

If able, I'd erase your past sorrows and prevent your future ones,
But you are too busy protecting yourself
To allow any outside help.

If only I could clear a pathway from your eyes to your heart,
Maybe then you would realize
That there is no irreparable damage.

I only wonder
When you'll start singing again,
Instead of just listening to the lyrics.

You are my past looking glass . . .

Peggy Ann Spano

STRENGTH

In spite of numbed emotions
I sensed its formation and refused to acknowledge or submit to it.
It grew large and forced its way through the tiny duct
        moved slowly down my face
        lingered for a moment on my cheek
        then plummeted to the pillow upon which I had lain my head.
I closed my eyes tightly
    determined not
        to shed another
           tear.

Naima

THE INTERLUDE

Oh, how I long to leave the greyness of the city and the murky sky
that hovers like a huge umbrella during a summer rain.

I beg to abandon the concrete skeleton of freeways and roads that
seem to weave endless patterns of despair and elements of pain.

How can I escape this jungle of captivity with high rise buildings
that root out and replace all that is dear to me?

The neighborhood grocery, the corner drugstore, the old folk sitting
on the courthouse bench, are things that I no longer see.

My eyes turn to the mountains, or where I think they should be, and
I yearn for the freedom to run through the vastness of trees.

In my mind I can feel the clean, crisp air, with unseen moisture,
caress my face and wet my brow as it passes over my body.

The rushing of a mountain stream passing swiftly over boulders in
its way, echos in my thoughts as I return to reality.

My eyes blink slowly as though to repel the presence of progress
that has destroyed the virginity of my land.

The sky is still grey, the city the same, but for a few fleeting
moments I escaped from the civilization of man.

Barbara S. Smith

dieppe day memorial service

. . . august . . .
far across time . . . the ocean . . .
not in vain the sacrifices . . .
the stolen lives, shrapnelled minds
bodies still litter hospitals

we march up bay street:
in our memories — the battle
— the beach — ripping gunfire
— bleeding, sandbagged bodies — bagpipes
to follow through the din
in search of the lost
prince of peace. where are you?
too much have we suffered

we, who survived, are getting few,
the horror, a bad dream knocking
on our children's doors, steals us away
soon there will be none who remember . . .

Joe Blades

I'VE NEVER SEEN THE SNOW

I've never seen the snow
That latches onto trees,
I've never felt the cold
The cooling, whistling breeze.

I've never touched the snow
That gathers on the ground,
I've never seen a mountain
With snow caps all around.

I've never tasted snow
Or caught it in mid-air,
I guess I'll never know
Until I'm really there.

I want to see the snow
And I don't need a reason
To want to see the beauty of
This coming winter season.

Louella Benson

NO ESCAPE

Passing faces call to me.
Beg me, please, to set them free.
But it's not them I try to hold.
Only age is growing old.

They know not why I am here.
Yet in my eyes they see the fear.
Slowly now, I grow in you.
Each minute I take someone new.

Every person's time will come.
You can't escape, don't try to run.
I'll find you wherever you go.
The fertile seed has started to grow.

I planted it to bring me fame.
The herb is death, my name the same.
The truth is free but you are not.
Life grows short for your soul I've got.

Darleen Lis

THE PUBLIC — TO THE YOUNG POET

Poems, oh poems your scorn
is so sharp
Your laughter too light
for the belly's gone sour
your words are not thoughts
but images in the day
and we'd all rather think
there are other things to say
Enough about clouds
and dark river beds
our measure of patience
is weary and dead
We've heard of your sunsets
your hills and your loves
and silly, how ghastly
the brooks singing wet
We long for the real, the true
the way
that life really is in our dire day
We do not ponder the colors
or dance with the breeze
We turn up our coats
and we snarl and we sneeze
Marianne Moran

A MEAN FARMER

Farmer 'A' was growing wheat
just across the road or street,
while farmer 'B' was growing rye
soon to spray it so it would die;
so he could plant his no-till corn.

And on the day he picked to spray,
blew a mist across farmer 'A'
lighting upon his intended yield,
acres and acres of pure wheat field.
A few weeks past from this event,
and farmer 'B' reaped his intent.

While farmer 'B's' corn grew real well,
farmer 'A's' wheat went to hell,
and all across the U.S. land
you hear similar stories time and again.

I hope you read this poem, my friend,
then you might come to understand,
you need not have something in your hand
to exercise control and command.
George Randall Roberts

BY REQUEST

Silence.
Then suddenly
a sound
a voice
calling me from life
coming to bring me
unto eternal silence.
calling me again
to join him in sheer
desolation.

The voice!
I hear it again.
It's speaking my name
and pleading
pleading.
But, I won't listen.
I don't want to hear the sound
of my own voice
calling and pleading
for a release.
Joan Villa

WINTERBIRTH

1	2
envision	behold
winter's	the
snow	soft
glass	and
with	downy
clear	carpet
and	from
vibrant	heaven's
mystic	flawless
eyes,	skies;

3	4
white	each
embroideries	time
God-created,	we
to	ponder
add	its
some	deep
wonder	hidden
to	magic,
life	we
on	experience
the	the
earth,	mystery
	of
	seasonal birth.

Brian R. Wood

GOD'S FLOWER GARDEN

I saw God's Flower Garden
The other day,
Nestled high in the mountains
Out of the way.

Protected by pines
Tall, stately and grand
A meadow of flowers
Covering the land.

A bright sea of color
Pink, blue, and white,
And yellow and purple —
A beautiful sight.

They lie there so open
Looking up to the skies,
Like innocent children
With trust in their eyes.

Deer live in the Garden
So happy and bright.
And birds sing the song
That things are all right.

I will still see the Flowers,
Each day of the year.
A beautiful picture —
To hang — so dear —
In my memory.
Virginia J. Wing

NEW WORLDS

The cards of the future
change with the sands of time
In a blink of an eye
a new world rises
in a young explorer's mind
Peter U. Loper

THANK YOU GOD

Thanks for the water, God,
Thanks for the fire that heats.
Thanks for the light of day.
Thanks for the many treats

That lavishly You give us,
Each morn and noon and night.
Thanks for the many flowers,
That make the fields so bright.

Thanks for the little aches,
That often come my way,
To make me think of You,
As on the Cross you sway.

Thanks for my beating heart,
To love You more each day,
My fellow men included,
For this one grace I pray.

Alfred M. Natali

GOODBYE

He whispered goodbye to me
in one quiet sigh.
He had a smile on his face,
and I didn't understand why.

I could hear him saying he loved me
as I slowly said goodbye.
I could feel my heart pounding
as I tried not to cry.

Why do I have to be left alone —
someone wanted him more.
Someone could do much more for him —
the man that I adore.

A tear fell off my cheek;
I lost my love today.
I knew I'd never be the same
as they carried his casket away.

Denise Billingsley

ODE TO ANNA MARIE

You are an inspiration to me
To become creative.
To put into words
How I want to live.

You are the possessor of knowledge
Which I seek.
I'm captured by your voice
Each time that you speak.

You are a rarity in life,
Definitely one of a kind.
A person who will always possess
A portion of my mind.

You are my darling, the only one
For whom I'll always wait.
You are the object of my pursuit,
The one I seek, my true soulmate.

John Prokopowicz

Icy fingers
clutch my heart
and freeze all warm emotion.

Lurking shadows
cloud my mind
and darken all devotion.

Dampened eyes
and tear-stained face,
I stand amidst confusion.

I find our love
and happiness
was merely an illusion.

Amy Studer

THREE LIFE STAND

On this shirt a dirty ring;
we and her his love song sing,
then the little playboy plays his thing,
while he spurns his own offspring.

On this floor are dirty socks;
they and she our melody mocks,
so the little playboy plays his rocks,
then goes joshing with the jocks.

On this table places set;
they and me our faces wet,
now the little playboy's off to get,
and we have your places yet.

Helen Pliler

AND SMALL IS THE CLOUD

one cloud hides the sun,
    (one word breaks a heart
    if the word is sharp)
And small is the cloud.

One frown mars the brow,
    (one note soils a song
    if the note is edged)
And deep grooves the frown.

One lone tear escapes,
    (one sad spirit sighs
    if the spirit clings)
And mist is the tear.

Ruth Anne Stibbs

TOGETHER

I hope you know how much I love you
I hope you know how much I care,
I hope you know that when you need me
I will always be there.

Remember this forever, my love
And we will never be apart,
For even when you're far from me
You'll have me in your heart.

So keep my love inside you
Let it guard you from the cold,
And with this love between us
Together we'll grow old.

Kathleen M. Rubino

PUZZLE WORDS

Pink saddle birds
fly out into
the soapy wind

roosting on white shadows
off the houses
flying over the
worn beams

puzzle words move across
the landscape into curbs
running back streets.

John Svehla

SVEHLA, JOHN J. Born: North Platte, Nebraska, 7-4-46; Married: 11-12-76 to Sharon Rubenstein; Occupation: Typist; Awards: California Federation of Chaparral Poets, 2nd Prize, 'Summer,' Published in March Contest Newsletter, 1977; The Pennsylvania Poetry Society's Katherine Lyon's Clark Memorial Award, Third Honorable Mention, 'By White Pottery Windmills,' Published in Prize Poems, 1981; Experimental Poetry Award, 2nd Honorable Mention, 'A Jar World,' Published in Prize Poems, 1977; Poetry: 'Snow Patterns,' Innovative, *Portland Review,* 12-83; 'A Dusty Sunday,' Experimental, *Wind Literary Journal,* 9-84; 'Noon Buckles,' Nature, Fine Arts Press/The American Muse, 9-84; 'A Rusty Wind,' Nature, Cambric Press/Poetry Project 4, 3-85; 'Worm Park,' Nature, *The Poet,* 3-85; Comments: *I am putting forth a new idiom in nature poetry.*

Could each spot but tell its tale
    Of the scenes played on its stage,
Each new dale bringing forth a story
    Never before seen on printed page,
Then the mind of man so enlightened
    Could drink the secrets of the age.

Virgil Carrington Jones

BE STILL AND KNOW THAT I AM GOD

Trees take a sabbatical
from gold and russet;

birds faithfully
divine for seeds;

greyness everywhere
is more afghan than shroud

for God has switched
from colour to sound:
present in windsong, birdflight.

Christ came quietly
but Christmas does not;
transferred from stable to shopping mall.

Jaded, I receive early gift:
chickadee's conviction
of seed in our feeder.

Kathy Fretwell

golfing

we press on —
among some talk of
You and Me —
scuttling over the Greens,
pausing at the Tees,
in and out of the Rough,
avoiding the Traps
like the plague.

the trees lining
the Fairway
secretly sway with laughter
watching our frustration mount from
Hole to Hole
as onward we plod,
our destination —
the Clubhouse —
where We can rest, finally,
and smile,
and figure our
Handicaps.

Patrick Coyle

DOORWAY

Through the doorway
framed by the doorway
in shadow
where manger hay is tangled
like the guts of a radio
Michel sees the sheep heads
staging
a tableau, a kind of symmetry
a pool shark's mad physics
pushing light
across a straw floor
dust shafts dropping
trajectories through perfect lenses
that catch
and raise confusion to an art.
Michel stops
transfixed
but the farmer passes by without a glance
and the hired man
claps his laughing hands and startles God.

John B. Lee

SURVIVING ALABAMA

Born in Alabama, the southern belle state
My inner desire was learning to hate.
I blamed my parents for bringing me here
in a world of desolate despair and fear.

At first I did not understand being in the world,
chances would be slight because I was a girl.
I was determined that I would survive, I was
going to make it: that was no jive.

That was my number one strike, being a girl
I did not like. But on top of that was not
the lack
Of being a girl that was black.

Dark was I, the Ebony, and in the south I could
not see, the profit my blackness would bring
to me,
Only hate, despair and misery.

I grew up wishing that I was white.
Being in the south, white makes you right.
I realize now it is not the color of your skin,
but contents of your mind and soul within.

Rubye C. Miller

VISION

I met one day with a person
Who had eyes that could not see,
God pity her, I whispered softly,
What a dark eternity.

But she recalled the dew mists of autumn,
Low swinging streamers of light,
Cording the meadow like harp strings
Tuned by the fingers of night.

Pictured a sunset's splendor
Outlining a hilltop's spar,
And the lone silhouette of a pine tree —
Tiptoeing to a star.

June dusks that were starred with fireflies
Elfin lights that pierce the gloom,
Like hundreds of tiny torches
Guiding a wanderer home.

God bless you, I said to her softly
In your dark eternity,
You have opened my eyes to new beauty,
Through your eyes that cannot see.

Beatrice Long

THE CHOICE

How do you feel about it? What do you think?
Who do you turn to when you start to sink?
There are so many crutches, you can take your choice
Maybe pray a little or listen for a voice.
But if you listen can you be sure you hear
The voice of wisdom or is it fear.
There is no way of telling, no way to be sure
Is it an answer, or just a false cure?
So if you would like a direction, somewhere to go
Turn to yourself for answers, to the things you know.
For it's there that you'll find a real reason to be
And life will start to get easier and you'll begin to see.
There are so many reasons for living, so much you can do
Pick one that you like, better yet pick two.
Do things that make you happy and in doing them this might
Help others too become strong, help others choose right.
So how do you feel about it? What will you decide?
Will you confront yourself or be taken for a ride?

G. DiFuria

MEMORIES OF YOU

My memories of you are the most beautiful and precious things
in the world to me.
I remember you best as John Wayne with me on your arm,
You stealing every girl's heart and walking on.
You were my knight in shining armor.
Always there to protect and take care of me.
I trusted you more than anyone in the whole world;
You gave me your love and asked for nothing but to be loved back.
That day I came home and you were lying on the bed,
I'll never forget that look in your eyes that day.
When you told me you loved me for the last time,
I knew I couldn't live without you.
As you faded away, I kept telling you I loved you and needed you;
You only smiled and said I'd do okay as long as I knew you were
standing beside me.
Then you were gone and now all I have is
                    Memories of You.

Karen Warren

LIFE WILL BE RICHER

*This poem was written for someone
who had lost a young daughter.*

Your life will be richer because you have known
the joy of a love that was truly your own.
You'll think of her laughter but after a while
you'll only remember her sweet little smile.
She may hang around you and cry if you're sad . . .
don't make her feel guilty as though she were bad
but tell her to go with the angels who wait
to take her to God at the Heavenly Gate.
We know that our sojourn on earth does not last
so think of the future and not of the past.
But while here on earth . . . your duty may be
to help other Mothers and set their hearts free.
Your life will be richer because you have known
the joy of a love that was truly your own.

Carmen Salvadora Ingham

SLEEPING ALONE

Every night — as certain as fire —
She comes into my bedchamber as I retire.
Enticing . . . inviting . . . softly caressing
Holding me . . . freeing me . . . easily possessing.
Until my mind floats between Reality and dreams . . .
Living my life after death . . . sometimes it seems . . .
Trying to prevent all my life's defeats —
I awaken and pretend we struggle in our sleep.
But I know, as always, all victories you own
What fantasies we keep, when we sleep alone.

Derek M. Robbins

IMAGES

I painted a portrait today.
Not an artistic endeavor, neither with brush
    nor oil did I create, but with the center
    of my being my only tool . . . my heart.
I painted not with color or expression as
    would a master, but with gently stirred
    emotion and feeling.
I began with adequate amounts of understanding,
    patience, sensitivity and compassion, blended
    affectionately with equal measures of humility,
    gentleness, strength and warmth.
My creation was an example of beauty yet not
    complete, but by adding softly spoken words
    of encouragement, attentive listening and
    spiritual serenity I found before me a picture
    filled with love . . .
A portrait of you.

Jerelyn L. Woods

AN ODE TO SPRING

At first we see the faintest hint,
The moss and loam reveals a rent,
And deep within a sign of life,
That stirs then moves to warmth and light.

Then sprouts and shoots and buds come forth,
From fatted sap-filled roots of sorts,
In colors fast and tints of green,
A visual symphony, an ode to spring.

Louis C. Russell

A TEAR

A tear hit my cheek today.
It did not stain my face in a romantic way.
It did not burn my eyes.
It did not wet my hair.
It did not fall purposely on a waxed table
so that all would know my plight.
It brushed upon my cheek briefly,
disappeared into the carpet below,
in an uncaring way.

Susan Van Roosenbeek

My Child . . .
    If I could take away your pain
        and never have you hurt again
    If I could make you never feel fear
        or have to cry a single tear
    If I could make you strong from the beginning,
        and make your happiness neverending
    If I could clear the paths ahead,
        on which your tiny feet must tread
    If I could make your heart brand-new
I'm afraid that I'd be cheating you.

Karla Shealy

WORDS FROM THE SQUARE

Under the cold replies the roar of grass,
As lavish dark makes prodigal the way;
Words from the square, how canticled they pass
Over the empty corridors of day.

Long coil the stars, a lanterned sarabande,
After our lives have danced, past aureole;
On will I hold you, candle in my hand,
And reach to touch my taper to your soul.

Susan E. Savercool

sophisticated lady

sophisticated lady
stiffly striding in detached abstraction
eyes — dull and judging
"over thirty" lines fade a once-youthful form
                            since
saddled and ridden to stale separation
where's the goddess within
                        dear
sophisticated lady?

Robert James Kidd

The reflections on the lake become brighter
    as the moon inches across the eastern sky . . .

    The trees begin to dance with the wind
        like small children in the moonlight . . .

        Crickets begin their symphony of sound,
            and ducks silently seek shelter for the night . . .

            Stars begin to twinkle with the innocence
                of a small teary-eyed child . . .

                Night begins to ease its blanket of
                    darkness upon the earth . . .

                    Together they form a oneness that
                        no human can separate . . .

                        Enjoy the peace of the darkness,
                            and the silence that it brings . . .

                            For tomorrow is the dawning
                                of a
                                brand-new day.

Carol Davis

OPENING EYES

I thank you, God, for opening eyes this winter day.
I see my loved ones, home, and pets, all needing care.
I see the snow-encrusted plants, the shining trees,
The rising sun on ice, with dazzling glare.
                I thank you, God!

I thank you, God, for opening eyes, this springtime day.
I see my loved ones, home, and pets, all needing care.
I see the greens and pinks, the yellows, reds,
The April sun on raindrops, glorious glare.
                I thank you, God!

I thank you, God, for opening eyes, this summer day.
I see my loved ones, home, and pets, all needing care.
I see the corn, tomatoes, beans, the velvet greens,
The July sun, with its red blazing glare.
                I thank you, God!

I thank you, God, for opening eyes, this autumn day.
I see my loved ones, home, and pets, all needing care.
I see the oranges, yellows, browns, of changing leaves,
In golden sun, with welcome warmth and weakening glare.
                I thank you, God!

Sadie E. Elliott

MOM

You'll have many loves on this great planet Earth
But none as deep or special as the woman who gave you birth
She loves you whether you're good or even bad
She always listens when you're happy or sad

She fussed when you were little and tugged at her skirt
But she would always give you a hug when it hurt
She knows what to do to make you feel good
And always did it whenever she could

She was there when you were healthy or ill
Always lending you money to pay a bill
When no one else loves you, she always will
She sees only your good, when no others will

Be good and give your Mom a break
Don't give her no reasons for excuses to make
So always respect your Mom and love her with all your heart
Because remember of this great lady you are a part

George P. Blann

ANOTHER GENTLE NOTION

He was a friend, I'd forgot.
He was in my past when I was young,
but not, when I turned into an adult.

Not a kind word could I find,
not in my soul, my heart or mind.
In desperation, I didn't want to go on.
I felt an emptiness that was wrong.

In my despair, not a soul seemed to care.
What could I do? I couldn't think.
My mind swirled, my head ached,
Then he came, silently, gently of course,
my mind eased, it no longer hurt.

God's whisper, hung gently in the air.
As he spoke these words, "Someone does care.
Put your heart in my hands, for I will cradle it gently.
Though you have forgotten me, I was always near.
Though I was pushed out of sight, I stayed close.
For you might have forgotten me,
You, I've never forgot."

Izella Jean Morlan

PARENTS

As we travel through God's Pastures,
Trials and toils at our hand,
God has given us our parents
To guide us through His Chosen Land.

When their job on Earth is over
Then He takes them by the hand,
Leads them on down Greener Pastures,
No more toils, trials, or sorrows,
Love for life is now past plan.

Behind they leave their mark on children,
Love and laughter of past days.
Children question why God's Wisdom
Works in such mysterious ways.

Life is not for us to question,
Trust in God and keep His Plan.
When our days on Earth are over,
God will take us by the hand.
Lead us down the Greener Pastures
To meet our loved ones in the Greater Land.

Helen Rae Wegner

MY FRIEND

My friend I gave you the truth
— as round and whole as the earth —
My friend I gave you my dreams
— as ever-flowing streams —
My friend I gave you my race
— as eloquent as the finest lace —
My friend I gave you my cheers
— and kept within my tears —
My friend I gave you my love
— pure as a snow white dove —
My friend I gave you my mercy
— as deep and full as the sea —
My friend I was to you ever true
— as a relentless sky of blue —
My friend I gave and you took
— as the rain gives to the sounding brook —
My friend I gave and I gave
— and now rush toward the grave —
My friend, My friend, My friend,
        I go very fast
          Hold my hand at last.

P. C. Loftis

SANDS
OF A
SEASHORE

Crying and sighing and wondering why,
Clutching but not grasping your road to the sky.

Living yet lifeless you're tied to a strand,
Leading from your wrist to some master's hand.

People of nations don't seem to see,
That building and breaking won't set them free.

True joy and happiness seem so hard to find,
For out of our living we've grown fetid minds.

Just sands of a seashore blowing away,
Scattered in moments of some yesterday.

Matthew C. Buchholz

MY LITTLE BIRD

As I sit watching the driftwood flow by and
listen to the cries of the birds
My thoughts go to you my own little bird
Flutter your wings my little one
and skim above the ripples
Then soar ever higher and higher onto an oak
where you perch on a branch
where you peck on a caterpillar on a leaf.
Then dive to alight on a branch growing on the banks, nearby
What are you doing, my little friend?
Are you pecking on some bark to gather twigs
to build your nest high on a limb?
while singing on the bough,
stealing seeds from a dandelion
What are you dreaming, my small cherub?
About bees buzzing in clover
as you fly from one dandelion to another
Fly free, then back to your nest
where you rest until the morrow.

Ginny Wilder

I AM

I am what is around you that no one dares speak.
I am the topic of your whispers and stares.
I am the box which I close and conceal myself in,
from the world around me.
I am the key that is bent and cannot open
the door.
I am the darkness that fears the morning's light
because it knows not what that day will bring.
I am the tears that fall so gently but hurt
so much.
I am the pain that reminds me of my "fight."
I am the fear that makes me want to run, but
to whom?
There is only me.
I am the anger that I cannot understand . . .
and the confusion that makes me want to shout,
"why me?"
I am the hope that reminds me that there is a
tomorrow — and I am the victor because I will *win!*

Donna Mittanck

VERNACULAR ARABESQUE FOR A LUNATIC

Ah, a woman has entered the surface transit system. She speaks
of Rocking and Rolling. The blessed cur screams at us to say
that we are dogs, and not just lonesome bus people, afraid of
her hatred.

Thoughts have traveled through her porcelain face and wrapped
it in a paisley arabesque of pain that shoots quietly through
those eyes that shimmer and almost scare. Darkly lit, glass
beady things that move and jerk away from me.

We capture our stares at one another, following the movement
of heads tilting, shoulders hunching, mouths revealing teeth
and smiles, body weight that leans away from the center.

There's something to be said for being a traveling people,
always traveling.

Rounds of applause to the lunatics as they offer a sprawling,
belching kindness to the nightmare where no one speaks. They
are an image of fortune for those whose lives have been revealed
in the lurch.

Carol Goodnow Fox

BRONZED

I am
  A sedentary table,
  With feet entrenched,
  In familiar earth:

Though food
  Is sprinkled on my fist,
  Junco, Robin, Crow,
  Raccoon, Deer and Fawns,
  Mountain Beaver; FEAR:

Wide space
  Does not envelop in coziness
  As home, which comes,
  Gives suck to Hummingbirds.

I leaned,
  An unhappy threat
  To a home I cuddled:

Lumber engineers count my sixty-five rings.

Sister Phoebe Passler

I CAN'T CARRY THEM IN MY HEART ANY LONGER

That for a generation have dragged sin with a cart rope.
That for a generation have lied their way into acceptance.
That for a generation have never ceased to think of
          something else bad to do (to me).
That for a generation have rebuked remorse.
That for a generation have been a thief over funds.
That for a generation have refused to be self-supporting.
That for a generation have adopted an idolatrous
            ideology.
That for a generation have denied help.
That for a generation have begun an amoral behavior.
That for a generation have pulled backwards.

Conclusion:

Multiply these, by many others, who have other burdens
they can't carry in their hearts any longer, from their
families and cities, and one can begin to see an irrevocable
decline in human love, compassion, endurance, and kindness,
coupled with a rigid decline in enlightened civilization.

Estella M. McGhee-Siehoff

COLOR A RAINBOW

Streaks of blue, yellow, pink, violet
Splashed across the universe.
A perfect arch of see-through color
Stretching from earth, beyond space . . .
Curving then fading
Softly out of sight
Across a darkened, balmy background of sky.

Perfect pastels whisper
And my soul rides the colors
Through my eyes . . .
Massaging my insight,
Rousing my spirituality
Making me and my rainbow one.

I no longer look out on the rainbow,
I now look within for its colors.
And the joy of my experience
Makes me unsure
If I saw a rainbow,
Or if I felt a rainbow
But I know . . . I spoke with God.

Judy B. Massey

TIMOTHY SEAN

I've been thinking about you
Each day the feeling grows
Seems forever since you were within my grasp
Thought I was over you at last

But it keeps on growing stronger
Ruining all my plans
Keeps on getting in my way
Guess we all have to pay

You're still a part of me, deep inside
Though it's been so long
Better if I never met you
Now I can't forget you

Still, what you gave remains
a priceless gift
You gave yourself freely
And you gave me

Me

Susan Winton

A SEA SHELL

Am I to be that crooked body, that bent frame,
Propped up by a wooden cane,
Squinting as though it were night,
Seeing but shadows moving in the light?

To smell no more the fragrance of flowers
Swelling in the air?
to touch no more a lock of golden hair?
Better to end my journey than end it a wait
For the rest to come, for all to see.

To feel no more the tides surging through my veins,
Pray would I to spare me such pain
Than a shell to lie, ebbing upon a shore,
Cast out of life, forevermore.

Only to await, lying in the shifting sands,
The touch of a foreign hand,
To lay me onto a warm head,
To listen . . . listen . . . No, echoes not the sound of the sea,
Comes but the silence of me.

R. L. Carpenter

THE SAILOR

Sailing deeper into your night
losing track of what's wrong
and what's right,
guided by the loneliness
of your heart's uncharted sea.
Like a sailor following the stars
at night,
I'll follow your eyes
till they drift out of sight.
Not knowing where
they will lead me,
just hoping
they'll free me

Joseph Gruenwald

A SAFER PLACE

We're all alone — we can't be found
by faithless friends and hangers-on.
The gulls abound on lonely shore
as breakers pound — 'tis nature's roar,
I called to you from near and far
and yet you never found my door.
My thoughts are clear, unclouded now,
'twas once unclean is good somehow.
I spend my time with whom I choose,
is paradise a state refused?
The sun sets on another day,
we never count them
Anyway.

Kay T. Gorczyca

When you and I first met eyes,
I knew that it was meant to be,
    in love with you forever,
Love it comes and love it goes,
And it always reminds me of a rose,
For it has beauty and it has pain,
Though in the end it's all the same,
The beauty is so great it demolishes
            the pain,
Then love turns to you and you know
        you're ready to play the game,
Just remember to always trust,
            never deceive,
Then your love will never leave.

Kathy E. Sakry

RAIN

Rain breathes its own melancholy into Man.
With feline stealth
Its mist enshrouds the soul's repose.

Momentary sadness greets the pain
So poignantly inflicted from without.

And then —
Ensuing ecstasy
As unborn chords are struck;
Whereby that soul cries out,
        Rains its own tears,
            And is renewed.

Lynne A. Arnett

OTHERS' POEMS

Some persons write poetry in homes carefully tended,
In pickles and marmalades and juices and sauce,
Floors scrubbed clean, and blue-jean-knees mended —
Endless endeavor and it's all without union or boss!

Some pen their lines in grasses and silage and huge storage barns,
In toil to provide and maintain and to shelter
Those loved ones given to his care and keeping,
Sometimes in factories where white hot flames are leaping.

If a tree is a poem, and a greensward a-winding,
Then poem it becomes when done is a duty,
In love and in thought and in calm perseverance
For here, too, is verse in the hard-winning beauty.

Thoughts turned to words and then into action,
Move the old oval on its slow-to-move axis.
It has to be thought of before to be said;
Be it "I love you." "I'll not bow to tempting." or
                        "I hate to pay taxes."

Some persons write poetry in thought word and deed.
Some like the feel of the lilting and rhyming.
The thought sires it all; conception takes place,
The message is born in predictable timing.
Each person writes his poem in his own dimension.

Ruth H. Dennison

GUARDIAN ANGEL

I have a guardian angel who watches over me.
Sometimes he's short and fat and sometimes like a tree.
I'm never lonely by myself, he's always by my side.
When things get rough he lifts me up and in his arms I ride.
When I am sad he tells me jokes to help me see it through,
He hopes to show me I'm worthwhile, no matter what I do.
And when I'm smug, or cruel, or cold, he never turns away,
But says "Sleep now my little one, you've had a busy day."
And when I say "What if? when now? I really think I can't."
He says "The choice is yours my love, and if you can't, you shan't."
He doesn't judge, he never nags, he is the dearest friend.
He's only there to help me live from my birth until my end.

Jenny Stamer

TIME'S BENT

Have you ever stood by silence breathing an empty beach
Watching it extend far beyond where the eye could see?

Have you ever stopped to listen to dawn's ordeal
Lamenting the decomposed sighs of reverie?

Its pulse instilling itself in the quiet,
A phantom whisper enveloped in the reclined
Prophecies of yesteryear, to drift away in the resonant
Wishing wells of space, to reflect the jewel pregnancy of time,
Change's mirror vengeance, as it reinstates its grace and dissolves
In the shy faces of shadow waves drowning in succession,
Ever moving among the sand's transparent search to make captive
The tracks of millennial cries.

It is a novel dimension of animation beyond suspicion
Where memories beckon the sky's quilted melancholic gaze
With lapses of desires, to freeze the blue and shudder,
Arresting an eccentric hope to embrace the solace of a rainbow,
The suspended prospect in the ocean sky,
The maddening miles that harvest the pale witness of eternity.

What is left but a celebration of the wind's unfolding,
A raving for dusk's completion, as the gull's flight is ordained
The continuity of a blessed, imperfect creed,
The secret oblivion of tomorrow.

Cyril Christo

PEACE WILL COME

Our sun is there
As bird wings flare
Blithe flowers bestow
A tranquil flow.
People can't be
In life's flurry;
But nature will wait
'Til all hesitate,
For when they stop
   look up with awe
Peace will come
   from what man saw.

Joan Johnson

SOUNDS

I enjoy the music of Strauss
Quietly listening with my spouse
And Beethoven's Symphony
Has a way of soothing me.
I love the soft strains of Brahms
         Lullaby.
Of childhood memories long gone
         By
The beautiful music of Liszt sometimes
         eases my pain,
But the most soothing of them all is
The sound of falling rain.

Theresa F. Pettine

AS I HAVE LOVED THEE

Live my love, be happy!
Love holds more meaning,
For, I have loved Thee;
And felt Thy love —

And found it better,
To have loved — and lost;
(To love in memory)
To pay love's cost,
Than never to have loved
— As I have loved Thee.

J. Tetstone

MS. SPRING

She didn't come in stages this year
I awakened yesterday and She was here!
Seeming the sweeter after such a long wait
Who wouldn't forgive her for being late?
'Tis time to celebrate winter's death
As nature swells 'neath Her warm breath
Who can deny Her gentle mirth?
She's the season of eternal youth!
Singing Her song — dancing Her dance
Dismissing winter with a merry glance
Forgotten is winter's icy sting
Celebrate Her arrival — salute Ms. Spring

Virginia Bond

MULTICOLORED DUST

Multicolored dust,
Scattered with emotion.
Once a composite,
Beloved and smooth.
Now only multicolored dust.
Becomes my heart,
And my dreams.

Monica M. Harmon

YOU'RE LEAVING

I think of your leaving
And tears come to my eyes
We've had so little time
To be together in our lives

You are seeking a future
You need a place to belong
You'll find it I know
And be back before long

I'll await your return
With great hopes and fears
And thoughts of our love
Will wipe away my tears.

Angi K. Badgley

TO KANT WITH LOVE

Long before my first cry
      they'd built the box
      into which I was to grow
Though, I enjoyed play
      that myopic box contained babies
and, prematurely (so they said) I felt;
      "This box is my restraint
      I do not appreciate this being
      I challenge this precision
      Categorical parameters are bullshit"
And, with this rhetorical decision
      I cast the quantifying mind,
      only to find, I had defied reality
      which, came indeed in boxes;
mine was labelled for Treatment

The pain weathers slowly and,
as this world continues building
I long toward the day
my box will rest in final
to begin the last decay

E. U. Mist

STADNEK, JOSEPH STUART. Pen Name: E. U. Mist; Born: Gimli, Manitoba, 12-30-49; Married: 6-29-74 to Charisse Kozub for eight years; August 1982 to Dianne Tchir (poet); Education: Currently in third year of B.A. program at the University of Manitoba, Criminology, Philosophy; Occupations: Ship's Deckhand on the Mackenzie R., Surveyor for twelve years; Memberships: Manitoba Writer's Guild; Society for Crippled Children and Adults of Manitoba; Poetry: 'Bureaucracy,' 'The Field Is Dying,' and 'Seeking Custody,' all rural writings, Summer, 1982; 'Ode to Dirt Roads,' sent to *Bitterroot,* Summer, 1985; Other Writings: *The Man The World Stoned,* novel, unfinished; Themes: *Death, dying, discrimination, time, and space — The Creator; Life, living, socialization, anguish, and logical contradiction — the masters;* Comments: *Man devours the present, excreting it into the past, while destroying the future. Hegemony! The universe began with a Bang, but what went bang? And where did the what which went Bang come from? And who made it go Bang!*

A PLACE IN THE SUN

Baby I am a Rich Man
Baby I am not clutching at the sun
I want a place in it
I'm not shooting at the Moon
The moon shines on me
The stars they sparkle on me
I don't want to Rule the land
God does it for me
There is a place in the sun
For those who seek it
I will find it
The one who puts her trust in me
Won't be let down
And together we will find our place

William E. Woillard

THE ACTIONS OF A LOVER

Love is a special feeling,
For those of us who see.
A certain individual,
Who means a lot to me.

They lend a helping hand,
Whenever you're in need,
And give you some encouragement,
When you feel you can't succeed.

They really show you care,
In everything they do,
For all they really want,
Is for you to love them too.

Jim Huffman

IN SEARCH OF EXCELLENCE

Mastery of our excellence
Is certainly our prevalence.
The only way two perceive
Is to pursue our expertise.
Together we can reflect,
And ponder over what we respect,
Our freedom to live with certainty,
Comes with our solidity.
There are no two ways about it,
Face to face we have to admit,
Stress of life, with all its grief,
Comes before we feel relief.
Unmistaken and genuine,
Meticulously we intertwine.

Susan McInnis

NEPTUNE'S SONG

Feel . . . blue waves cool
rush up feet and legs.
Enveloping your body as you
merge, with the force of element.
The surge of current over rock and vine,
such unbroken direction. Down and
round accumulated at the ocean deep.
And shine into, a body of water, a
school of fish, so quenching and welcome
to plant life beneath. The union:
of stream into lake, to ocean strong,
caressing, encasing the earth as waves
tumble over onto shore chasing
at my feet. Listen to Neptune's song.

Ann Yragui

IF YOU CAN SEE

If you can look at me
    when a smile is on my face
and if your eyes can see
    the quiet, lonely place
that once was filled with heart
    and love for all, so true
and if you see through all my scars
    and say what's deep in you
and if my tears don't scare you;
    if you don't turn away
and if you'll let me say and do
    what I feel every day
and if my eyes go blind
    and my mouth goes silent too
and if you do not really mind
    and you listen when I tell you
and if by chance we part
    and time goes quickly by,
may you always see my heart
    and know why it is I cry.

Tracey Hatton

AMERICA, MY HOME

We flew to Washington the other day,
    And as we gently nestled down,
We viewed the monuments to men
    Of international renown,
Along Potomac's wooded shore
    Our nation prides her hero's lore.

But eons long ahead of man
    Inscribed their earthy artifacts
In hills and vales and watershed:
    Perennial lines for man's review:
With Georgetown spires; Cathedral Hill:
    Remind our soul: "God reigneth still."

O may we see and understand
    The message plain to read:
Eternal purpose strives to be
    While man keeps floundering in greed.
God's work alone, with help of man,
    Can make a nation to succeed.

LeRoy H. Klaus

MUSIC

Music is not song alone,
It is found in every stone,
Every leaf and flower;
It is present in the grass
Where the little field mice pass
To their hidden bower.

It is found in menial things;
In the opalescent wings
Of the butterfly;
In the bright sun's rise and wane,
In the mighty aeroplane,
Skimming through the sky.

There is music everywhere,
On the earth or in the air,
Or the sparkling sea;
But my favorite anthem lies
In the twinkle of your eyes
As you smile at me.

Elbertine Natrillo

REGENERATION

Life viewed through the eye of the potato
Has grown complacent
In the warm dark recesses of itself
This winter.
En la tierra del ciego
El tuerto es rey,
(In the country of the blind
The one-eyed man is king)
So as the earth leans into spring
It casts its wrinkled eye
On fertile ground again.

Nancy M. Ryan

FLACCID

How can that little letter *c*
Alter its sound so rapidly
When trapped within a single word?

To me it seems almost absurd
That one *c* sounds just like a *k*
And then its neighbor — sad to say,
Emerges sounding like a hiss!

A puzzling fact's disclosed in this!

Colette Burns

rite face

your tissue box
                        needs flowers
to camouflage
                        its bogus function
your face
        needs paint
                        and
yes
    a saint
            to perform
                        extreme unction

edward d. beeson

I want to be a whisper,
a glimpse that makes you
happy,
a soft cooling breeze
ever sudden
that comes and goes
before you can fully
smile.

As constant as the ripples
on a lake yet
brief as the falling of one tear.

Lori J. H. Halsey

MOTHER EARTH'S EPITAPH

Estranged and
Unable to live with
The cold political deceit
And the hot
Angry blows of abuse
From her two
Macho Atomic men,
She died of darkness —
No seeds!
No children
In her sterile winds.

Thomas Paul Sledge

LOVERS

Lovers loved each other
One time
Their eyes caught each other's eyes
Came face to face
        Hands to hands
Lovers loved each other
One time

It's sad, when
It's time to say goodbye
It makes you cry, when
It's time to drift apart.

But, remember, lovers
Smile when you remember
For you loved
One time.

Yuann Ling Chang

DESIRE NOT THE NIGHT

Time is a mortal foe.
As she pauses for a moment,
Old lovers' smiles fade;
Life stops in the lonely night.

Love is a quick, happy lie,
Whose pliant hands are soon gone;
Her breath grows cold and fades;
The door opens never far.

To Death is a short journey,
Made certain with eternal promise.
Cold hands quickly bind fast
To place a stone overhead.

War is a circling nightmare.
Trenches scar the once fertile fields;
Bodies fill this, a rotting bog,
Where plowshares are not exchanged.

Night, are you desired?
Your grave's cold mound in the dark?
Silence in the mind's dull voice:
Desire not the night.

Charles T. Eppright

IN THE MIND'S EYE

It seems as though,
I have been away for years.
Yet, I've not been sad,
Nor have I shed any tears.

This place, I am captive,
Seems so foreign to me.
Yet, I've been here before,
Like a lost ship at sea.

Through the minds of millions
I have journeyed for years.
Now my destiny is chosen,
For this my heart cheers.

What once was my fear,
Has now turned into peace.
For the moment of truth,
Is about to release.

All things, now before me,
From the centuries past.
I now must prepare,
To become a child at last.

Paul C. Carpenter

DIFFERENTIATIONS

You are the tongue of flame — reaching to the sky,
I am a Mont Blanc or Everest with the ice headgear . . .
Nice to be flying high — but need to dig deep . . .
This is a life darling — with much eternity.

Suzy Jarady

LASZLO, SUSAN. Pen Name: Suzy Jarady; Born: Hungary, 1945; Education: Agricultural Scientific — Master 1967; "The Waterfall" has 25 verses, will be illustrated with 26 oil paintings (impressionist, naive, primitive) One of these is "Leisure" — the background of my portrait — Another, "The Time Collector," and a hundred more poems and oils; Comments: *It is some order — the only thing that I know "has to be done;"* Ideas: *To brighten up the old pictures with new colours and deeper shine — Create a bigger synopsis in better details from "The Waterfall".*

HARD LUCK

Lying in a freight yard
sipping on a bottle of wine
waiting for a freight train
in the freezing rain to take me on down the line

I want to get back to my little ole shack
across the Mason-Dixon Line
lie on the floor let the warm wind blow
sip on my bottle of wine

Clothes are worn and mighty thin
good Lord knows the shape I'm in
jobs are not easy, and hard to find
haven't worked since last harvest time

Cold and hungry sleeping on the ground
trying to find work so I can settle down
It won't be long before I'm southern bound
I can see the headlights of that train
shining through the freezing rain

I'll get in a box car where it's warm and dry
and trust my soul to the Lord in the sky
when I get back to that little ole shack
I never more will roam
gonna settle down in a country town
and nevermore will roam
I'm headed south where the warm wind blows
Lord I'm going home

Jay Donald Foote

RETURN OF THE LEPER

Ten lepers drew nigh unto Jesus
Shouting, "Master, have mercy we pray!"
With instructions, "Go; show yourselves to the priest,"
He took their affliction away.

And while going as Jesus commanded,
A Samaritan saw he was cleansed.
Turning back he praised God and fell down on his face
As he drew near to Jesus again.

"Thank You, Lord, for your love and compassion!"
But the Master quickly replied,
"Were not ten cleansed? Yea! Who can answer:
Ten were cleansed, so then where are the nine?

Is there no one returned to give thanks now
But this foreigner — Samaritan he?
And what of the nine? Where are they who were cleansed?
Can anyone now answer me?"

I know I am one of the lepers;
God has cleansed me with blood of His Son.
Help me, Lord, to return and give thanks for my life —
Let me not be the nine, but the one.

Gail Christian

PROCESSED LOVE

Even though you are sealed with featherweight headphones
You are still handsome. My God! what a distant look . . .
Doesn't even care for his child's cry.

It seems like yesterday when I spent my time
Caressing the phone with my eyes waiting for your voice to ring.
Our love performed miracles. Now, I'm even questioning our love.
Why, with you I experienced my first love and, again, with you
I've lost it. Help me to get it back, please. Make me cry again.
Are you afraid of my love? I don't ask much, I think.
Just love me and, perhaps, die for me, if need be.

Don't just sit there staring at the video movie. Talk.
I want to be cared for. OK, but don't use my ID numbers.
I feel condensed. Call me by my name. You know,
I might have a metallic smile but I still got a human heart.
I live each day unrehearsed. I want, however, to play it right.

There. Let's sit in front of the fireplace.
Looking at the fire is soothing, like talking.
For goodness' sake, do not use 'Duraflame.'
Put some real mood in the moment.

Why is happiness measured in moments?

Theo N. Vourliotis

LUST AND LOVE

The lights were spinning around me.
I closed my eyes to stop the movement.
When I opened them again, I saw him,
Looking like a great bear,
Standing in a primeval forest.
And I was there, standing with him.
Primeval urges, like the forest,
Consumed us both.
Like two people in the dawn of time,
It was only us, and the passions
That ignited us
Like the spark that ignites a raging fire.
An inferno of lust that could not be dissipated.
An inferno that would carry us forever
Into the red hot explosion of the sun,
That would burn into our souls
And hearts, as love lasts this time,
Forever . . .

Autumn Star Demuth

THE OLD MAN'S FACE

It was a face of many continents,
Mounds fleshed into mounds,
Ages lay across the brows
Like years of gathered moods;

Flecked spots were obvious,
Tributes, perhaps, to endurance,
Or marks implying abuse,
Yet, not one seemed alien to its place;

The face appeared not anxious
Nor did it seem at ease,
It was flushed with an ancient sadness
As if it had never known peace;

A neutral look was in the eyes,
Colored by what was perceived,
Daylight closed the heavy lids
Where once an amber essence glowed;

That face seemed burdened by the world
As friendless as a hermit's wall,
The strain of every indignation showed
Yet, so did the trace of an ancient smile.

J. B. Rake

NO CROSS TO BEAR

If I could take just one short day
And live it only for my Lord
He would take away my dagger
He would set aside my sword
Then I would take one giant step
Upon the Jacob's ladder
My soul would sing out joyfully
My heart would be much gladder.

My God would give me precious gifts
Of beauty, grace, peace, strength & love
And Jesus would smile down on me
From Heaven up above
The snow would be more beautiful,
The rain more precious yet
The snow would be more radiant
The soul, my God would set,
Upon His throne in heaven above
And I'd beam joyously with His love.

If we could come to the old, old cross
And cleanse ourselves in Jesus' blood
He'll reserve a seat in His abode
We'd live forever, in His love.

Judith Roberts Rockwell

STRANGER IN THE NIGHT

When the world is around you
like a fire, flames burn you
up in desire
        You catch the light in his
eyes trying not to despise
Hoping him not to see you
        running like hell into the
night
        running away in fright
Darkened corners wet and damp
        hidden away the nightmare
of a tramp
        caught by the fall from
a cop and a stall
        Behind bars, the man of
the night
        Behind bars, your dreams
and your flight —

Leslie Perlow

A CHILD

Lord, I wish I were a child again
        To start my life anew
For as a child, small and frail
        I was totally dependent on You

I thank You for the dreams I dreamed
        Of seeing You, so real
For the closeness that we shared
        For making it so easy to deal

But as I've gotten older, and
        Supposedly "wiser" too
I see I've focused on myself
        And, unfortunately, not on You

Help me to look in Your eyes
        And see the love that's there
To reach up, and take Your hand
        For You so deeply care

All you want is for us to say "Yes"
        To You and You alone
To take control in our lives
        And make our heart Your home

Please put Your loving arms around me
        And change my adult heart
Do with me as You please
        Make me a beautiful piece of art.

Laura Elizabeth Ludwig

LUDWIG, LAURA ELIZABETH. Born: Arlington, Washington, 8-20-52; Married: 7-7-75 to Brad Ludwig; Education: Everett Community College, Degree of Associate in Technical Arts, 7-2-72; Occupations: Homemaker, Legal Assistant; Comments: *The Lord Jesus Christ is so good! Two days after this poem was written, we were advised I was expecting "a child." (April Joy Ludwig) St. Mark 10:13-16. When I write I obtain a sense of fulfillment and enjoyment. Sometimes it seems easy to express thoughts on paper, rather than verbally.*

TIME

Time comes and time goes
It has its highs and has its lows
But where it goes nobody knows

Dennis D. Sturdevant

DIVINE LOVER

The divine lover
divines and
defines
the beloved's outlines
and disperses eternally
the shape he once declared.

All
for the love of
the moment
matrix
of all possible forms.

We are all created
and die
in the same instant.

We are whole
when together we laugh
and the stars sting back.

We disclose our face
when we define
our world
for the divine.

Lydia Rand

HOSPICE

Momma, dear,
We love you.
This is not your pick.

She told us this was best;
for one like you so sick.

Nurse, dear,
Her dietary ana:
No dairy products?
Vanilla pudding, her desire.

"Sorry. The liver, you know. Dire."

Momma, dear,
What's that you say?
Take you away.
You'll come back another day?

Nursie, dear,
What say you to this?
Come thee here; forth thee hie.

"Here's your morphine, dearie.
You're supposed to die."

Marion A. Sommers

SPRING'S SYMPHONY

Birds chirp their welcoming songs,
Buds sprout upon the trees.
The sun spreads its loving warmth,
Driving winter's blast away.

Blossomed flowers wag in the wind,
Green grasses stretch their blades.
Everything is coming to life,
Each singing its special serenade.

Spring's symphony plays but once a year
Then vanishes with summer's haze.
Only to return after winter's fury,
Its sweet, mellow tunes to play.

Gail Cranford

LOST WITHIN YOUR SOUL

I got lost in your sea-blue eyes.
I fell deeply into them.

I felt myself drifting slowly,
Softly down to your soul.

And when I reached the center of your spirit,
I took hold of your heart.

I felt the sudden strength of your beat,
The rush of your blood.

I knew that your heart was truly mine,
I couldn't afford to leave it behind.

Nina M. Pfriender

LIFE AFTER DEATH

As the days go by,
And the nights come through,

(The days are our lives
And the nights, the dawning of the hereafter),

We feel the pangs of loneliness
For the day's going.

But a welcome too
For the coming of night,

And the dawn of a new life
The spirit of man lives after!

Lillian Kleiser

EPHEMERAL OR ETERNAL?

"Who are you? My theophany? My fate?"
The sightless vision, a wisp of discovery
Flowed like fusion plasma within.
Life's answer in embryo,
Cocooned in spheres beyond grasp,
A hair's breadth from understanding; and,
It called my name. "It called my name!"

"Who are you?" Cried I, again!
The wisp dissipated! Vanished!
Rivers of despair flowed out to the eternities;
Sorrows filled the soul with unquenchables!

A small hand touched my hair. I awoke.
"Dad, I'm afraid! Can I stay here with you?"

G. Layton Galbraith

BOURBON STREET: A REFLECTION

Busy, bustling sights and sounds
On crowded odorous streets,
Under bright, sunny skies
Radiating through white fluffy clouds;
Brightened by the lively actions
Of spirited jugglers and creative painters of
New Orleans.

Street vendors selling their wares
To the mystified curious crowds of tourists,
Raptured by magical antics.
Everyone searching for something different, and
Each seeking a unique experience on a
Truly magnificent, mysterious street,
    BOURBON STREET!

Dr. Maria Valeri Gold

ANOTHER TREE ANEW

From the seedling of an honorable thought
Grows a proud and boisterous juggernaut.
Its evidence then a defiant salute,
Or now, a gnarled righteousness.

In the darkened and demi-dark and dripping caves
Lies a broken visage;
Monument to a nation . . . one citizen less,
A naked soul, clinging to the heel of a jackboot.

And now, conqueror,
What will you please, what will be correct?
. . . to stand atop the world
And brandish the silly skull of a once and future spectre?

Know you that when your ridiculous paw is again raised
It will call forth the mocking
Of a million bloodless faces;
And the cackles will sear through your mind
To the pulpy places;
Exploding hindways,
To pollute history with a sticky shame.

Leon R. Bushara

EXCEPT HAPPINESS

The silhouette scoffed at the exquisite sunset.
The dark outline of a man
(Who was hunched on a fifth-story window sill)
Stared silently at the city street below.

The empty shadow could not reveal
   The achievements of his life.
He had a sports car.
   Its tires were not yet worn.
He showed off his new stereo,
   Though he owned few records.
He watched football games with his companions.
   He claimed to be a Cowboys fan.
His diploma hung on the wall,
   But the realities evaded him.
His trophies were tall and erect . . .
   And dusty.

The silhouette fell.

And the people wondered why.
After all, he had everything.

Vernon Wu

DO YOU . . . ?

   Do you ever think of me? I think a lot of you,
   Even though the days we shared are years away from view.

Do you think of how you held me? I remember your embrace;
I loved the way we hid away in our secret meeting place.

   We shut away the outside world and drew ourselves so near,
   We shared our love in hours and in seconds of the year.

Oh yes, I think a lot of you. I could never forget
The first time that I saw you; the day that we first met.

   I think of days long ago, you filled my hopes and dreams.
   It doesn't feel so far away; just yesterday, it seems.

Do you think of me as close to you, though we're now apart?
Am I still within your thoughts, held close within your heart?

   I wonder if you wonder as much as I still do;
   I wonder if you think of me, as much as I of you.

Donna Bernhardt

THE LOWER FALLS.

MELTING FROZEN PLACES

Today is just a day within a year
But pervasive detail brings eyes to tears.
Discrimination rages in the streets
Slips inside and quietly finds its seat.

Prejudices escape to the surface
When requests are made to leave a safe base.
Behavior amplifies the challenge felt;
Volcano erupts: the disguises melt.

Questions originate from inside walls
And echo wildly through concrete halls.
Then the personal statement finds release,
Shouting mismatch, "My safety will decrease!"

Emphasize the differences as seen.
Have experiences be neat and clean.
So that exposure to others' beauty
Is conduct out of a sense of duty.

Will these stubborn struggles with fear subside?
And leave fertile space to develop pride?
With a surge of hope, no occasion lost
To move relationships despite the cost.

Lana Lea Miller

AUTOPSY REPORT
(Not Written by a Surgeon)

Last night he saw the sky turn gold and red
With sunset color; now he's dead.
This heart that, oh, so recently beat fast
With love and pain,
Has beat its last; the grim terrain
That all must cross he now has passed.
And yesterday, all unaware
Of what today would bring,
These lips parted to sing,
To speak, to kiss;
They've come to this — this dreadful quietness.
This mind, once so alert,
So keen to sense the false or true,
Lies now inert —
A mass of tissue, nothing more.
What lay in store
So soon he knew not.
And these kind hands
That once caressed so tenderly
Are now at rest.
This virile body of a man,
"Well-nourished," as the surgeon said,
Is dead.

Adah Aragon Larisch

TIME

Time passes like sand along the shore
Fleeting moments washed away forevermore
But we know it doesn't stand still
It never did and never will

It inevitably brings about change
Like heavy winter storms and soft summer rains
With change most things grow
Though it be ever so slow

Tiny instants are grains of sand
Throw out the bad and savor what you can
Moving at its own cadence and pace
Each moment a locus in its own space

Time is here for us to use
To do with whatever we choose

Hank Justus

SERVICE WITH A SMILE

"Come in, come in," the clerk did say,
with a smile upon his face,
As he led me into his shop,
Of antiques and old lace.

The London rain and heavy fog,
Made me lose my way,
So the lighted shop and a friendly smile,
Made my fears go away.

"American?" he asked of me.
I said, "On a holiday I've been."
As I slowly walked around the shop,
To a mirror, framed in green.

The price he said was reasonable,
So I bought it on the spot,
But could not leave the shop with it,
As the mirror grew, and got hot.

The mirror did engulf me,
As the clerk just smiled and said,
"Your traveling days are over my dear,
For you're a bride, for the devil instead."

Maxine Elliott

EULOGY

Along the darkened cobblestone pathway
We walk.
Cloaked in bloodied memories,
Agonized by festering pain and malignant guilt.
Knowing and aching, I am tormented each waking hour.
Dodging, grasping, stumbling,
I flee from my lifelong captor.
But the masked martyr clings to my side,
His lips curled in a disgusted sneer.
"Fool," he drawls.
He is my distorted reflection,
My grotesquely disfigured self-image.
Sobbing, crimson tears
I fall to my knees before my juror.
I plead to be set free of my shackles,
The chains of yesterday which bond my spirit.
"You are forever the prisoner of fate," he croons,
"entombed within the wrath of past mistakes."

Debbie McTavish

IN AUTUMN WITH NARCISSA

The little squirrel
In pigtails with primped dress
Of fall leaves' colors
Preened her chestnut hair

The day the north wind's comb caressed our locks;
And apples nearby shone their crimson glare

Back to us from forked brown hand mirror limbs.
"Are we those gnarled, hard knot crabby whims?
Or are we cherry circles in blue ribbon air?"

I pondered as cobalt-eyed creature dared
Me to swim like the snow geese in lake at our feet.
I took off my cordovan shoes. The creak
Of branches of oak by tanned soft leather stream,
That flowed into that millpond, was millrace dream,
Driving wheel of my grist mind as trance had before,
When I'd shaken my slippers' knit soles on grained floor
Of my bedroom, as if those toe mittens were salt.

Beside a last-rose sealed ledge, shore's cryptic vault,
The bushy girl's image reflected in water
With gumdrop pomes' red over head of my daughter.

Ted Yund, M.D.

ALTER EGO

She whispers, "I am the LIGHT, the WAY,"
And gently guides me through my day
With Her, my consciousness takes flight:
Her gossamer wings carry me through my night . . .

She comes to me with essence, deep
She suckles me, that I may sleep,
She nurtures me with juice of TIME
She instills in me a joy sublime.

She cradles me from deep within
Sets me apart from other wo-man.
She cuddles, murmurs, gently croons
Together, we discover ancient RUNES.

I blindly follow her every lead
E'en though it means I sometimes bleed.
For the joy of be-ung is in the BEING
With thanks to HER, I am now seeing

She is my well from which rapture springs
She's the BEGINNING — the END of all things!
Without HER, I could never be,
For I am SHE, and she is ME.

Elsie Ruble

AS IT IS

It was from cosmic dust that I came;
To where I will return, but with no shame.
However, insignificant that it would be
That I should ever make you believe in me.

By the Gods! — that I should ever dispense
With any and all disgusting incompetence —
With sincere heart, and to be quite frank,
Respectfully, I would have you to thank.

It doesn't matter what I should say;
Yet it does matter to this very day!
That my spirit would be shattered anew,
When and if I should disappoint you.

Does it matter that I admire a deity so kind,
And continually make immortal in my mind?
That upon any paper I'll ever write —
In your mind's eye will it ever shine bright?

When to cosmic dust I will return,
Will the spirit be so eager to learn?
Should fate allow us to meet anew,
Will the soul remember those sessions with you?

Elizabeth A. Ruhland

I was somewhere deep inside your eyes
when I first knew I loved you.
Standing before you, wanting to kneel
with silent words I said, "I love you,"
and heard an echo inside my head — "I love you."

The night I held your hand
and turned your face to meet my kiss
my heart's longing spread throughout my soul,
with my eyes I said, "I love you,"
and heard only an echo
in a frightened heart — "I love you."

Side by side we shared the darkness
and a passion new to us.
Courage put sounds to my feelings
with nervous words I said, "I love you."
From the darkness close beside me
came an answer — "I love you, too."

Kim Turner

SPIDER

Spider, I love the way you created your airy mold.
The ornateness of your silvery case,
it looks like Phoebus' tress.
A fold of eternity
your lace
in age-worn space . . .

Marge Hallum

ICE

Ice is nice,
On wintry morns,
When nature paints its mountainlands,
And the sun pops out
To melt the snow,
As droplets from each heavy bow go,
Glistening on their way,
To statues
Formed by God's own hand,
And placed in nature's wonderland,
Where
Ice is nice.

John Bates

VICTORY OR REVENGE

Burning, if only to dust
These keys to hell, God's trust
Weeping in torment and pain
I see the doomed consumed in the flame
Souls shackled eternally in the fiery pit
Begging for mercy in hell where they sit
I walk on and pity the ones with no hope
For them no peace, not even at the end of a rope
Only visiting am I, for I can get out
Upon my leaving profanity they shout
I turned the key, now freely I float
Is victory or revenge the name of my boat?

Mike Palmieri

PHILOSOPHY

Sometimes we tend to underestimate ourselves. We set our
sights on things well within our reach, instead of projecting
them just outside our grasp. We are merely content to settle
for what we can attain, when we should, in fact, strive for
the unattainable. To suffice ourselves to living without our
dreams, is the same as having the sun without ever seeing it
set. To be content with what we have gained, yet still be
able to have the projection of our hopes is, perhaps, the very
key to one's happiness. To never be satisfied is, of course,
the key to one's demise. To realize what we have, how far we
have come and to understand how much further we have to go is,
in my philosophy, the very essence of life.

Lynne A. Chapman

MOTHER

Now you are gone, what am I to do?
It seems life is not worth living without you,
There are memories that I have and will always hold dear,
I will cling to them and remember year after year
Among Mothers you were the best,
Always ready to help and often without rest,
I know you are in heaven with God up above,
Still watching over us with all of your love,
As time goes by my heart will heal,
But the love I have for you I will always feel,
My greatest wish is for you to be happy and free,
Hoping we'll someday be together in eternity.

Judith Guerrero

THE VISION ABOVE THE RUBBLE

I know the laboring love
in the vision above the rubble:
the imagination carves words of validation
while the brain systems surge in the sensory bubbling rage,
but time tests the feel of an age
as the universe stretches, beckons, and waves.

As the full moon howls at the face of a man,
I command these words to stand on this page.
These words that stretch, and beckon, and even wave,
shine while they're wired throughout for sound.

I nourish this heart, this babble, this art
to break up the parable type
of the authorized everyday version
of this inextricably human me
and put to print a new text
as I and the universe beckon and wave.

Earl S. Hardin, Jr.

THE FINE LINE

Here I am walking the fine line, the thin line
    the lose or win line
My mind is not my own, a semblance of reality
    as I dangle on my rope
    being jostled around
As I am not me, I have gone out to play.
    way out beyond the normal boundary of real
    as I feel my way and find my life line, yet
    my world has changed
    been rearranged by realities, disguises of.
Reason
The game has changed all the rules for my
    foolish mental endeavors into the realm
    of the unreal
As I feel my way back to my life line,
    my routine of life that keeps me balanced
    upon the thin line.
    Fine line.
The lose or win line.

Robert Tanner

FLIGHT

Flight
    Daedalus, build not the wings for Icarus,
    For he enjoys the warmth of the sun
    And he shall be undone.

Flight
    Icarus's wings of wax melt,
    Yet he flies on.
    His joy, his pride to be where none could go
        drive him on.
    Falling, he had known what it was to fly.

Flight
    Fly Along!
    Soar to New Heights!
    Damn Waxen Wings and Go Onward!
    To Fly is worth the fall . . .
    Fly On!

Kenneth D. Thomas

I NEED

I need to look back at the victories I've won.
I need to be proud of the things I have done.
I need to show others the lessons I've learned.
I need to be loved and to love in return.

Martha J. Grable

I saw the old North Star burning tonight,
shiny and gleamy, big and bright.
It was a blazing, never hazing
and guiding some men through the distant night.

I lay there looking up in the sky,
other stars not visible to the naked eye.
But your beauty astounds me, you never change
during your nights trekking through the sky.

And who have you guided through these nights?
Those who were going on precarious plights?
You watch over everyone as they trek for their homes;
the lowly, the richly, the weakly, the might.

Your job's been the same for many years,
you are God's watchman, his eyes, his ears.
The most ancient of mariners and adventurers know
your guidance of lost ones brought many cheers.

And as dawn's light in the east starts to grow
you'll move and guide men in lands I don't know.
But you'll be back to help me as soon as it's night
and I'll welcome your guidance, your power and might.

Peter J. Laucks

WE ARE NOT ALONE

Smoking, drinking, and "pill popping."
Surges through our bodies and minds
Euphoric is the feeling
        We are alone
In the far corners of our minds,
Outside existence fades away.
Unwelcome prisoners of our needs
        We are alone
Hoping against hope, that tomorrow will come,
Holding onto our beings, "that's where it's at."
Living life becomes so hard.
        We are alone
Talk to us, can we hear you?
Today we'll try to hold our hearts high,
The feeling someone does care.
        We are alone
Today, we'll try, please walk with us,
Please don't push us aside.
You're caring, we'll strive to go on.

        We are not alone

Barbara J. Myron

I HAVEN'T LOST IT

I haven't lost it,
that feeling for a friend,
it remains, and grows,
like a fountain that gives water,
like a tree that bends.

Friendship is sharing, and caring in deeper ways,
than we may be able to say.

But it is still there, and in respect
to friendship, nothing, little, has changed:
you are still as important as I am important to you,
I still want you to be happy,
I want you to have something useful to do.

I haven't lost it,
it blossoms in the Spring
and heats up the Summer
like the waves beat the shore until we are no more:

they beat eternally, never relenting,
trying to tell us things will be O.K.

Robert S. Cassidy

MY FIRST PET

My very first pet was a little black cat
　　I named her Miss Blackie Bow.
　　　　For she had a white spot
　　　　Right under her chin
Where a bow could be tied — just so.

I picked her myself from a litter of cats
　　That were born on my Grandpapa's farm.
　　　　She was my very own
　　　　From that moment on
My kitten so soft and so warm.

She had oodles of patience with my clumsy attempts
　　As I learned to care for her needs.
　　　　To feed and to brush
　　　　To love and caress
But never, but never to squeeze.

Can anything equal or even come close
To the very first time in our lives
When we give of ourselves
And receive in return
The love which makes all life worthwhile.

　　　　Inez H. Synan

LIVING IN ECSTASY

I watched with a sigh, as you walked on by;
　　Swaying so gracefully.
I closed my eyes, to try and visualize;
　　That you belong to me.
I would make-believe, we married Christmas eve;
　　A gift for my eyes only.
You would be dressed in gold, for me to behold;
　　And never, never, be lonely.
Your hair would be brown, complete with a crown;
　　With a strong smell of cologne.
You would have such finesse, when you were full dress;
　　You would need — a chaperone.
And with eyes of green, a shade of aquamarine;
　　That adds brightness to your smile.
With a dimple on your chin, causing beauty within;
　　You'd look like the queen of the Nile.
Now! When you walk by, my mind can't deny;
　　You're mine for all eternity.
I could see at a glance, I want a romance;
　　and hold you with dignity.
I cannot help but find that peace of mind;
　　Happens, when I'm near you.
Now I'm feeling hot, as I haven't forgot;
　　How you walked the avenue.

　　　　Angelo Del Orfano

THE VELVET BOND

There is a bond between the two
The likes of which are given to only a few.
A bond, velvet soft, but strong as steel
Giving no quarter to what they feel.

Reaching from day one across the years
Binding together, good and bad, joy and tears.
Springing from a source that has no ending
Withstanding great pain and separation, but ever enduring.

Their lives are separate, but the bond is ever strong
Pulling them together despite the years so long.
A change must be made, but by which of the two?
One step forward, two steps back, what should they do?

So much struggling to gain control, but alas, to no avail
As the bond quietly binds and their struggles ever fail.
What should they do, how will they respond?
What knowledge is yet to come from the velvet bond?

　　　　Carolyn Burke

WORDS

I was taught to never swear,
Try to be nice and always care.
I learned what to say, and when to say it,
What to pray, and when to pray it.

When speaking to a friend, let it all hang out.
When we are far apart, I learned to shout.
Words always seem easy to say,
But what can be said when you have to go away?

"Goodbyes" are too difficult, "Later" seems too cold,
"So Long" is too carefree, "Till we meet again" is too bold.
I never want you to leave, but what more can I do?
All words have been said, does this mean we're through?

　　　　Susan H. Washabaugh

IN THE PARK

The lazy stirring leaves by breezes kissed
The warmth of sun released from mist
The tang of piney resin damp with dew
And I am filled with thoughts of you.

When Winter's harshness blows against the bough
There are no longer leaves for kissing now
And though piney needles' scent still fills the air
There is no time for thinking of you there.

Will Spring awaken all the memories sweet?
I wonder, as I hurry on the street
And will I walk again with stirring heart
When we have been so very long apart?

　　　　Flo Salo

ILLUSIONS

Like candleshine against the fog, you blazed no comet's trail
Across the heavens and hells of my settled life. Instead,
In a vagabond mist you slowly wrapped yourself around me
And drifted delicately into the recesses of my too lonely soul.
I didn't mean to care for you or to lie in another's bed
And imagine your touch. That's only for the young, for those
Less seasoned than we. By now our illusions have been rubbed low,
Our hearts skinned from too many scrapes on reality's concrete.
These days romance is consigned to poetry, and hurt-earned wisdom
Prevails over the heat of infatuation that first blushes betray.
Yet I bleed in the quiet of the night beside someone else,
Hiding the hemorrhage with hands that will never touch you.
And, as I rise over the other for consolation once again,
Your face becomes the one I hold beneath my body's pain.

　　　　H. Henrietta Stockel

YOU

You said you loved me, I believed.
You said you cared, you deceived.
You said it was forever, I thought it was true.
You said we'd hold together, but you always knew.
You made me promises you knew you couldn't keep.
You made the pain burn within me deep.
You took my trust, I had no fears.
My life is drowned in bitter tears.
You reached inside me and brought out from;
the happiness,
the life,
the glowing sun.
But for no reason all this came,
you played a silly child's game.

　　　　Heather Stevenson

LOVE'S INVITATION

Oh sweet love, how enticing is the banquet
you've prepared. How grand a table with
its delicacies spread just for my delight.
Love, you are a gracious host . . . I'm glad I came.

Now the flavor of that night is but a memory.
The dance of merriment has ended. The clock
of time has struck twelve and you are gone;
leaving a gnawing hunger in me for another summons.

Once more to have a dish of laughter; to drink
from your cup of savoring smiles. To feel your
breath evict the coldness I now feel in my heart.
Pity . . . the rarity with which your invitations are sent.

None can dine at your gracious table forever,
nor can one boast of being your only guest.
None will depart with appetite completely appeased;
but of all invitations . . . yours is the loveliest.

Janie Rood

TAKE ME NOW
The comfort is flowing from my body,
And into my mind,
To overcome the insecurities time has shown me,
If only for the second of your touch.

Security now felt as our bodies lie adjacent,
Lying in the warmth of emotion,
Exploring as if this journey was the first,
Secure, if only for the moment of our passion.

Hold today in the depths of your memory,
For it is all we ever really have,
Love can never conquer the fate of time,
Only fulfill what is needed in ourselves
   for the moment we hold each other.

Take me now . . .
For this moment is all that matters,
Our bodies living the fantasies we feel,
Our love giving reason to surpass all else.

Deborah Donaldson Mallino

IN THE BACK YARD

Why was that baby all alone,
in the back yard in the mowed grass,
naked to the day's sunny tone,
bared to the sky of tinted glass?

I don't suppose we'll ever know why,
But we do know why the bird came —
an iron-clawed hawk from the sky —
to claim its dinner and eat the same.

With a pair of claws two feet in length
with nails much longer than a Papermate,
it snapped his ribs, it had such strength
and carried him off, where it picked and ate.

Why was that baby all alone,
out in the open, where all could see?
Now he remains a cluster of bone,
in a cave, on a cliff, overlooking the sea.

John Minder

I like to watch it lick the edges of
its bed, lap the castles up with foamy tongue.
Its white fingers moving rhythmically
up   and   down with the moon.
Its rolling hips sliding   in   and   out.
Its body pressing against the sand.
Its gentle sucking at the pier.

Then I watch it withdraw, recoil.
It pulls in its tongue, leaves sand flat
no trace of moats. The piling dries and
barnacles grieve, sing for the battering waves.
Each time it should come stronger, louder.
The thirsty wood begs to be shattered, cast adrift,
rather than stand with a taste of salt
drying in the red sun. But it has moved to lap
a cold, coral cave and it wets only the
surface of the lips of stone.

gina scanlan

EVER FOREVER

I can see the light at the end of the tunnel
The tunnel is a funnel.
I look through the wide end,
Discerning life, tapering to a blend
Where all things must come out
And the ending is filled with doubt.
The neverending particles drifting asea,
Visualizing a single particle as me.
Searching, seeking life's mysteries to unravel,
Relentlessly in my eternal travel
I do not know but I suppose
Infinity is the Cosmos.

Eloid Williams

FAVORITE ROOM

My favorite place is my room at home,
Where I have my TV, stereo, phone,
I can talk until late at night,
Watch MTV at the same time and write,
My room's a disaster,
With all the posters and pins in the plaster,
My home's my palace,
Just as JR's is Dallas,
Every day my mom yells "clean your room,"
But I know it's destined to doom,
I promise to change my ways,
In the next twenty days,
I promise never to be rude,
But don't interrupt Duran Duran on the tube,
This poem is ending soon,
Because I'm back in my room.

Maxine Loffredo

AT DAY'S END

How tranquil the water at the end of the day,
Seems to soothe the soul as if to say,
"Ease your mind; let your worries subside,
As does the water with its evening tide."
Do not dwell on pain and sorrow
For the sun is brighter with each new tomorrow.
Live each day as if your last,
Enjoy the present, not future or past.
Relinquish your tensions to the calm of the night,
With dreams of joy, not struggle or fright.
Have faith in the Father, for He will show
You how to cope; to live; to grow.
Fear not the darkness that the evening brings,
For day will dawn and birds will sing.
Happiness will appear at your front door,
With peace of mind and much, much more.

Donna Mae Mueller

COMFORT AT THE CROSS

When you start feeling lonely and getting depressed,
just get on your knees and begin to confess
all of your sins and all of your cares,
just call out to Jesus he'll hear your prayers.
He fills you with comfort and peace within,
for there isn't another that could even begin
to lessen your heartaches and wash away your tears,
than our loving Jesus that we've known all these years.
You can go to a friend or an in-law or boss,
but there's no one as helpful as our Lord on the Cross.
Amen & amen

Carol Ann Guglielmoni

(FROM WITHIN ME)

Something different has happened to me.
I can't explain it with mere words.
It's a feeling that wants to spring forth
from every part of my being.
Is this the Living Water Jesus spoke of?
How can I contain such a feeling?
It's as if my whole body, soul, and spirit
could burst forth as a mighty dam.
I can no longer suppress this feeling inside.
Too much too wonderful to keep concealed
in this vessel.

Linda Gail Hernandez

TEARS AND MEMORIES

There are no tears left to cry.
There are no longer memories of you in my mind.
The tears washed away all traces of you from my memory.
The memories of you were not really the kind of memories
you like to remember.
The tears were not sad tears, they were happy tears.
At one time the tears were sad and the memories were
memorable, but I guess when two people use each other
the memories can no longer be happy.
The tears turn happy when the pain and guilt subside,
at the same time they erase your memories from my mind.

JoAnn Callazzo

MEMORIES

A lonely old woman rocks in her chair
With no one to talk to and no one to care.
The house that she lives in is shabby and old,
It has little heat, its dim rooms are cold.
She stares at the pictures on the mantle above —
At the memories of people she once, long ago, loved.
They left her at home to lead their own lives.
Her daughters found husbands; her sons took on wives.
She stares out the window through the misty night air,
This lonely old woman who rocks in her chair.

Martine E. Germain

CONFUSION

Confusion runs rampant in our hearts —
dwelling larger than our minds could hope to roam,
growing fungus in the words we long to mouth,
making spoilage of the dreams we hope to grow.

Insanity lurks not far behind
on the path of this mean destruction.
To be lost in life is all that it asks.
With knowledge comes understanding of a deeper world to ponder —
with minds tied in thought Confusion may enter the soul.

Bridgett McKinney

ANCIENT HOUSES

I live in an ancient house.

If I were in India
my house would be a baby

lacking ghosts that
ramble the walls
and fill damp spaces
of the marble halls
that Alex of Macedon tainted with blood.

or Paris

the ancient streets
having seen the young whore
so beautiful
grow haggard
and lie quiet as Mr. Darrell
listens to the ghosts of Alex draw him home.

But my house
sits alone in a desert
no demons to haunt me
no soul to rage on

There are no revolutionaries in America

only empty walls.

Leigh Allen

WATCHING YOU

I keep watching you, when you don't see me
On ordinary days, when you don't know,
When you drive, or across the room, as you sit
I try to hold every detail of you
In my memories as long as I live
I want to reflect in old age
Of our simple life of todays.
You know, I love you,
I wanted to tell you many ways
But never said a word about it,
I'll hope, you feel it, and know
As we live in harmony, in togetherness
I want to capture this feeling
Of our life, growing with you, old.
I watch your breathing, as you sleep
Beside me, afraid to touch
Just sleep, sleep, I want to have
This feeling, this peace, forever to last.

Eva Sylvia Puskas-Balogh

PUSKAS-BALOGH, EVA SYLVIA. Born: Budapest, Hungary; Occupations: Poetess, Writer; Comments: *It's an honor to be born as a Hungarian. My best works are in my mother tongue.*

WINTER

Every year winter knocks at our door
We pile up the wood and go to the store
Stock up on food to keep from going out
When the snow drifts start blowing about

The old folks sit by the fireside and chatter
While children play with lots of laughter
The time passes by so very fast
We wonder how long the snow will last?

Snowmen to make snowballs to throw
We skate and ski to put on a show
The children like to sleigh ride down a hill
Snow and ice can give us a thrill.

When the wind blows with all of its might
The snow piles up covering everything in sight
We cough and sneeze and shiver too
And wonder when winter will be through

The trees are covered with snow and ice
Icicles hang making winter look nice
There is nothing so pretty as sparkling snow
When the sun comes out putting on a show

We cover our eyes and talk about the mess
That people make and we must confess
Snow is pretty when left all alone
And nothing can beat eating a snowcone

Eva Cook

JUST BEFORE WINTER

Around about October time
Some little boy will always find
That one first minute crystal joy of whiteness
Crowding softly down in secret greeting
To stir his dreams;

But, you and I mature, we know
October is much too soon for snow.

Harry R. Park

ONE SOLITARY REIGNED

Like some red Samurai,
Under the squalid eye of storm,
Repose he gained,
Where morning mists were formed.

The moments had fallen as leaves on a tree,
Led along the uttermost branch,
He felt bereft of his destiny.

Watching her, he mused,
"Truth, they go where they will,
But how could I detain them?"
Remaining alone, pensive and still.

And yet they held a single flowered branch,
Leaves unchanging in that quiet mind,
Given as token of strange innocence,
Staunching fate, turning the blade of time.

Of a course he would yet fain,
And heard it whispered in the ear of some angel,
How she fell, giving birth to earth's light, heaven's pain,
The end of endless light, the start of hell.

Trees moving slowly did not see,
In that sheltered green arbor's leafy arms,
One resting there, perchance to sleep,
Enfolded the well-met traveler from all harms.

James Davis

MARY AND DARBY

Mary had a little pup, Darby was his name,
With coaxing he would sit right up
And jump through a ring of flame.

He'd carry the paper to his owner, and proudly did he walk,
Until one day he pulled a boner,
Which caused the neighbours to talk.

Darby took good care of Mary, walked with her to school,
Watched for cars and, happy? Very.
In any emergency was quite cool.

Then came a day when Darby chose to change his way of life.
He met a Peke with upturned nose
Who caused him nothing but woe and strife.

Mary, such a little girl, needed Darby for protection.
Mummy's brain was in a whirl,
While Peke and Darby escaped detection.

Darby ran to look for Mary, saw her by the school gate,
Frightened by a big, fat bully.
Darby's body shook with hate.

Lightning quick he reached her side, snapped and barked
Until the bully ran off. "Help; Help!" he cried.
Darby's joy knew no bounds as Mary held him tight.

Darby said, "I'll never roam from those I love the best.
I'm a lucky dog to have a home."
Now don't you think he passed the test?

Milly McIlroy

GARDEN SPLENDOR

The cool rain drizzled much throughout the day
But by four it stopped a bit and I was on my way

I grabbed my coat and camera before it was too late
I had a special close-up lens to help accomodate

My purpose was to capture what only rain could bring
That special kind of splendor that comes in early spring

I saw so many wonders as I stood alone out there
And was amazed at how much I saw by being more aware

I noticed how the colors when wet are deep and true
And I noticed how the little vine along the bricks it grew

I saw the raindrops sparkle like jewels upon the tree
And leaned to snap a picture to aid my memory

The tiny little flowers were covered with the dew
They made a pretty picture for me to take for you

I had the most marvelous feeling deep within my heart
And it made me feel so special just to have a part

If we just look for little things to make our heart feel glad
Then many are the blessings just waiting to be had

Then before I knew it the light had begun to fade
And I smiled in satisfaction because memories had been made

Connie Bailey

FRACTURED FOLK LOVE

Once upon a pond,
Not a time,
But a pond,
Lived a rebellious toad named Willie.

Why Willie you ask?
Well, you see it's like this,
Willie's parents were christened
Billy and Tillie.

Now Willie one day,
Found the love of his life,
A gorgeous Siamese cat named
None other than Millie.

Willie's parents didn't approve,
They were of the old school,
Where mixed marriages
Were slanderous and silly.

But Willie defied all,
Unfortunately to find,
The ravenous appetite
Of his beloved Millie.

Lynne Armstrong

TIME

When I look
On the
clock

I can't see

Time goin' on
without
thee.

You're the hands
that, once
removed,

Take the time
'way from
me.

Cheryl Lieteau

HARMONY

How nice it would be
to feel on my face
the gentle soft breeze
and a warm embrace.

The fresh morning dew
and dawn in the air
the sincerity of love
a feeling of care.

A chill on my brow
from a brisk mountain spring
the one that I love
these dreams he can bring.

He can fill up my heart
with an abundance of love
jewels from the earth
joys from above.

The music he sings
is surely to please
a harmony of promises
a symphony of trees.

Connie S. Danford

THE SUNDAY HUSBAND

I see you sitting there
In your dirty underwear.
A two-day beard upon your face,
A perfect sample of disgrace.

Empty bottles by your side,
The smell of beer you cannot hide,
Cigarette ashes on your chest.
I surely didn't get the best.

You've watched the ball game all day long.
Life with you is not a song.
Empty plates upon the floor,
Now you'll close your eyes and snore.

Dirty dishes I must do,
And I'm cooking up a stew
To feed the kids, they gotta eat
And keep them from playing at your feet.

Eventually you'll come to bed,
With dreams of romance in your head
Well baby, I've got this to say
There'll be no romance here today.

Bob Graf

GOD MAKES EVERYTHING BRAND-NEW

God don't have to patch you up.
God makes everything brand-new.
In times of tribulations, I know
God will see you through.

You may be out there in the world.
Your body may be filled with sin.
You just open up your heart today.
Then let the Master dwell within.

God will change your heart, fix your mind,
and heal your Spirit too.
Just in case you did not know.
That's not all that God will do.

God will guide you on your journey.
God will be a friend indeed.
God will direct your footsteps.
God's love is all you need.

God don't have to patch you up.
Every word I say is true.
My God has the power.
TO MAKE EVERYTHING BRAND-NEW.

Peggie Hall

HERITAGE HOUSE

He took me a time ago.
To another world I did not know.
To a private world beside the sea.
A world made perfect just for me.
The wind blew crisply on my face,
In that other world, that other place.
The ocean roared with its mighty sound.
The waves came swiftly, they were bound,
To have the rocks, the earth, and I.
To know their power beneath the sky.
The beauty of this other place,
Was made more perfect by another's face.
A face that's patient, kind, and dear.
One that's comfortable to be near.
My private world beside the sea,
That world made perfect just for me.
Will always live in memory clear.
As will the face that I hold dear.

Bonnie J. Allen

SEA LIFE

Ride the sea of happiness,
Drift the sea of joy,
Climb the mountain of success,
Find beauty God's only toy.

See the beauty of a flower,
Feel the summer breeze.
Don't waste one single hour,
Do anything you please.

See the beauty in a tree,
Taste sweetness of new love.
Hear the whispers of the wind,
Set your spirit free.

Explore new found fresh feelings,
Reach out and touch its hand.
Taste, smell, see, and feel,
Enjoy life while you can.

Richele Larsen

LARSEN, RICHELE DENISE. Born: Oakland, California, 1-20-63; Education: Heald Business College, Career Clerical Degree, 7-6-82; Occupations: Receptionist, General Office Clerk, Engineering Aide; Award: Literature Award, 1977; Poetry: 'Sea Life,' 1982; 'See, Smell, Taste & Feel Life,' 1982; 'Beauty,' 1984; 'Special Love,' 1981; 'The Warmth of a Fall Day,' 1983; Themes: *Positive life thoughts, love, friendship, senses.*

I fell in love with you, but
you didn't seem to care.
  You wanted someone to have fun
with, just to enjoy a time of life.
  You had no idea that I would
fall in love with you.
  And now that I have, I want
to hold you in my arms.
  I know it could never happen,
although it happens in my dreams.
  Maybe one day my dreams
will come true.
  But until then I'll have to
suffer and learn how to live
without you.

Michele Childress

HOME

When the orange and yellow sunset
presents its golden hue,
In the blaze of the sun's sweet setting,
I am thinking then of you.

Where the trees in splendor, blossom
And the birds sing their same old sweet song
There the fragrance soft, still lingers;
That is home, where I belong.

In meadows the grass still is growing;
The memories, now seeped through and through.
There, my heart lives forever,
As night shades the sun's golden hue.

Shirley Wilber Frank

ENOUGH

It should have been a brunch
Instead of a potluck lunch.
We women are patient, heaven only knows
But when it comes to eating
We become impatient listening
To the preacher going on and on
Particularly when our stomachs growl
And we would like to howl
Enough! Enough!
The time was wrong and the speaker too long
But what could we do, only smile and do what we should
Not what we would.
Partaking of spiritual food is fine
But not at the wrong time.

Florence M. Ditzel

HERITAGE

Take root in your heritage
drawing life from those
that came before you.
Let each generation branch forth,
adding strength to the vine;
nurtured by wisdom, fortitude, and foresight.
In fulfillment, let the excellence
of the fruit bear witness
to the labors of the vine.
As none of us are separate
but a part of the whole,
as the sap flows to give life,
let love be the entity that binds us,
the root to the grape.

Kathleen Conradson

MY MOTHER WITH ROSES AT SUNSET

In her garden of a hundred roses,
She admired now Camelot, now Double Delight.
While sun dipped low, she felt how soon day closes,
Enfolded in bloom of sunset intensely bright.
More fiercely independent than most mothers,
She lived on acres of lawn with tall trees set.
At eighty-eight, she still reached through to others,
Making friends with anyone she met.
Her last week she called everyone she knew,
Making talk like cheerful roses unfurled,
To her premonition never giving a clue,
As she said her goodbyes to the world.
Swift, like an internal rose, her heart bloomed her
Into the unseen, a gallant voyager.

Charline Hayes Brown

GOD SO LOVED THE WORLD

God so loved the world, He sent us His Son.
He bestowed Him with love to show us the way.
Christ came as a small babe, was born in a stall.
Came to show the way, to teach one and all.
Came on that still night to brighten world with light!
God so loved the world.

God sent His Son down in image of God.
Christ walked and talked with men, He taught them to love.
He speaks to us now, we must just hear.
Open up our hearts, let Him be near.
If we just believe, then we shall have always . . .
Everlasting Life.

God so loved the world, He sent us His Son.
He bestowed Him with love to show us the way.
Came as a babe, born in a stall.
Suffered of man, servant of all.
God so loved the world, sent us His Son.
Gave us His All!

Sharon Albury Fry

MAGIC LOVE

If I were a great magician
who knew the alchemy of this life reborn anew
I would mix you a magical brew
in my cauldron of true love and emotion
and bring you back to my love . . . magic love
back to the complete memory of what is happenin' brother
back to this macho flexin' world that is still plannin' to die
If I were a great magician
I would make you whole, brand-new and ready for love again
Then give you a new love to love only you, sanctified and true
With no more agony and sweet pain from a one-way love
to deceive you and leave you feelin' empty and blue
I would play you a new tune just to see you git down agin'
just to hear you rock me, rock me, rock me after midnight baby
If I were a great magician
who knew the alchemy of this life reborn anew
on the night of a new and magnificent moon
I would mix you a magical brew
and bring you back to my love . . . magic love
right back to these inner city blues you left too soon

Ernestine Williams

NIGHT WINDS

She has desires yet unknown
as she stands in the night winds.
Not knowing what the mystery is,
she's puzzled by thoughts unclear.
Knowing that she must travel on
but pausing here, to ponder on direction.
No matter which, the destination is the same,
and she must cross the mountains.
Destiny will have its way.
But in the coolness of night she travels . . .
for comfort and safety.
There are less distractions in the quiet night,
except for the night winds . . .
They call to her, whispering words unknown,
bringing hidden thoughts into the openness of her mind.
She doesn't want to leave this place
or the soft touch of the whispering wind.
She is thankful for such a peaceful feeling,
the time alone, and for the soft caress . . .
of the Night Winds.

Penny Toscano

309

GOOD OLD DAYS

'Twas quite a different world back then,
And folks who wore the pants were men!
My Mom used dresses, as did I
But not a garment with a fly!

Our meals were always cooked from 'scratch,'
Anyone was hard put to match
Mom's fried potatoes browned just right,
And tempting biscuits feather light!

I've learned the bane of motherhood
Is her home, empty of its brood;
She no more sheds her lonely tears
For Mom's been gone these many years.

Now I have known motherhood, too,
I understand how 'twas with you;
Our world is full of mothers, old
Just yearning for a child to hold!

There should be places both could meet
To hug and laugh, life could be sweet,
Our time is short, but seems so long
It's like a bird, without a song!

Sarah M. Boring

MEDUSA SLAYER

In a petrified forest of creatures and men
He stalked with mirrored shield and sharpened sickle thin
Perseus sought with great foreboding
To gain the head without beholding
The face of the Medusa Gorgon
With cautious eyes fixated upon
The mirrored shield face
He swiftly moved with grace
With hand guided by Athene
He slew the serpent-haired queen
Her homely head touched the floor
And the Gorgon Medusa was no more
He placed the grotesque head within a sack of gray
And he went to Seriphos to save his mother Danae
He came before the wicked king
Who got to see what Perseus did bring
The Gorgon's head turned him to stone
And Perseus took Polydectes' throne

Robert Hill

SAND

I am the soil the breakers boil
and scrub to Ivory white,
brought from some heap in water deep
where it is ever night.

I paint the Earth where the wind gives birth
to the dunes you see in me,
and boggle the mind with heat-rilled signs
as far as the eye can see.

I show the touch of an Ermine brush
in the moon's artistic light,
but create dread with a muffled tread
in the chasm of the night.

I ride with mirth in the whirlwind's girth
yet gently bury the dead,
where throughout time on this timeless Earth
I am their eternal bed.

For I was thrown in the eons gone
when the mountains pierced the plain,
and shall abide till there is no tide
and Sand be the mountain's name.

Carl Don Warriner

TAKE MY HEART

Take my heart, gently hold it in your hands
and no matter where you go, just remember that
a touch away is where I'll stand.

If you get sad and start to put on a frown,
Just remember that a touch upon my heart
will bring a smile around.

Never let the tough times get you down
because you may grow weak,
And drop my heart upon the ground.

The bad times should make us strong,
So that when the good times come along it
will enable us to sing love's song.

What we have is a sure thing, that with time,
A life full of happiness it will bring.

So my sweet love I ask you to,
Take my heart, gently hold it in your hands
And remember that someday soon we will be
together, as we have planned.

Linda Lee Riesdorph

FACING THE WIND

I turn to the wind and begin my journey;
    Rising high into a dream of glory.
With the ability to go wherever I please;
    It is a freedom untold in story.

Racing with unimaginable speed;
    The world revolves below me.
My feet in the air, my head upside down;
    There is the sky, the earth, the sea.

Maneuvering about through space and time;
    A freedom like no other feeling.
Commanding at will to do as I may;
    A control and power worth dealing.

I am received once more by the likes of a stamp;
    Many may think I'm insane.
But I wait for the wind to face once more;
    To enter my world of freedom again.

Kim G. Farral

ROAD TO DESTINY

At times we've all been down that dusty road
And we are looking for a hand to hold.
You shake my hand and say goodbye.
You've got somewhere to go and so do I.
We often wonder when we'll see
A clear road to our destiny.

A handshake from you is just not enough.
We need some hope and a little more trust.
Some caring from you and a little love, too
You know, I'm walkin' down the same road as you.

There will be another time
When your path will be crossing mine.
Remember in life, what you do
Will get back to you.

So, when we meet again,
If you shake my hand and say hello,
And walk with me where I go.

Your reward someday might be . . .
A clear road to *your* destiny!

Laura L. Azzue

THE WONDERS

Have you ever sat by the ocean
And listened to its roar,
And watched the churning water
Rushing to the shore?

Have you ever looked at a mountain
With its beautiful towering peaks,
And talked to a mountain climber
And shared the power he seeks?

Have you ever gazed at a forest
And the beautiful stately trees,
And marveled at a power,
Much greater, than you and me?

I have seen all these things
And the wonders that they be,
But, the greatest wonder of all,
Is, this baby on my knee.

M. Jane Austin

FRIENDS

Friends you and me.
    Different in many ways.
    Different views.
    Different means.

Friends you and me.
    Seem so and the same.
    Sharing thoughts.
    Experiencing everything new.

Friends you and me.
    One day blue.
    One day bright.
    One day sad.
    One day mad.

Friends you and me
    Together — Apart
    Sharing — Giving
    Wanting — Needing

Remaining Forever Friends,
    you and me.

Becky Sue Zimmerman

KASHA

Her tiny young face
So sunny and bright
With a shy little smile
Such an innocent sight

Big button eyes
And curly black hair
She passes her days
Without any cares

From sunup to sundown
She's a mischievous elf
A loveable clown

Oh, she's special
Of that, there's no doubt
You can tell as she plays
Amid laughter and shouts

Out in the backyard
She runs and she whirls
A joy to my heart
That little girl

Dolores Saldano

VIGIL

In movements,
after the risen day,
it was the angle & color

of light that released
a sadness (new light to us,
coming from the darkened

patterns of sleep)
that rose to the edge
of tears at the sheer

beauty of the incoming day,
the light on the trackless,
white road: the windless morning

awaiting in perfection,
that first imperfect thought
we usually seem capable of.

Bruce Lloyd

A BEGGAR

Eclipse
In the eye of a beggar
Walking full with hope
How hurt and sad he is
When there's no hello received.

Where does his future lie
His stomach is empty
Yet whose fault is it
For he didn't collect enough
        food for the day.

In the morning
He'll be stiff and cold
By the pavement
At the edge of the road

We who see him
Can only feel sorry
For there is nothing more we can do.

Jasmin Mazlina Bt. Abdul Manap

CITY LIGHTS

City lights through the window
    Prior to the sparkling iridescence
The trees reign in darkness
    Twinkle, continuous, no evil can
you perform
    Forming slowly, lastingly, impressions
on my mind
    I look out to see the answers
But in the darkness of the yard
    I see only a reflection of myself
Hollow, transparent in its image
    I greatly wonder which is me
The brief light cast from above me
    Is small compared to your glow
Lighting the city until dawn comes
    To protect us from the harm of night
There are no individuals
    Just the city as a whole
I stop my wishing and my dreaming
    And look out to see my soul

Craig Anderson

COSMIC DANCE

Oh, I have thoughts of you each night,
And when are yours of me?
If they should blend in misty light,
Exciting that would be.

So when you see the stars tonight
And just one dominates the sky;
Beyond the pale of lunar light
Awaiting you am I.

Then let your thoughts run free and wild.
Your heart to pound with glee,
And come just like a playful child,
And dance among the stars with me.

And every night ere you retire,
Just cast a skyward glance;
And if that star is still afire,
Join me in cosmic dance.

Joseph V. Money

SURREAL

Ghoststeps in the leaves . . .
Night sifted through the rain . . .
Green eyes, lamps of memory,
Glow with the flame of pain.

You have gone into that night,
A sad drenched night, uncertain,
And left that night of tears and rain
Between us like a curtain.

Ghoststeps in the leaves . . .
Coming back upon my dreams . . .
Memories of moon-lustered hair
Above a face of white moonbeams.

A kiss of seeking doubtful lips
A sudden smile, a bosom heaves . . .
Rain washed away, now only
Ghoststeps in the leaves.

Elsie C. Wood

SHE SAILS NO MORE

Tied to the dock, tall stands she,
Her sails wrapped tight, harnessed energy.
Her spars and masts, so straight, so high,
Shear the wind and touch the sky.

Brown and weathered, touched with gold,
Her timbers creak and moan and scold.
Eager to be off, to sail so free,
Living by wind, by sun, by sea.

But evening's come, her day is gone,
Remembered just in poem and song.
Her lovely grace, her ancient line,
Destined now to age — like wine.

Replaced by ships of cold hard steel,
Gigantic, swift and yet I feel,
For her grace and beauty from days before,
'Cause she only sits, she sails no more.

Vicki May

PEACE AND UNDERSTANDING
(The true American Way)

Somewhere out there a person lives
    With thoughts a lot like mine,
Someone with love and warmth to give
    Whose heart can break and pine.

I've never wished to curse or fight
    A neighbor who deeply feels
His border pride and country rights
    Nor jar his peace with steel.

I want to know and understand
    The knowledge he's stored in life,
To see the beauty in his land
    And never cause him strife.

Knowing each — country's beauty
    And the person's need to strive,
Feeling his idea of duty, and
    How he feels to be alive.

Seeing for myself the beginning of his day
    Ending the experience watching him pray.
I know *Peace and Understanding* is:
    The true American Way.

Shirley Rae Harvey Torres

FOR A FRIEND

How sweet the warmth of friendship
That takes the time to share
The joy and sorrow, laughter and pain,
That takes the time to care.

A truer love can never be known
Than that of a Christian friend
Who stands beside you in bad times or good,
Who stays faithful to the end.

None other can know the sweetness
Of the friendship that is true;
So, I count my many blessings,
For I've found this friend in you!

Andrea G. Hajducko

1969

Love is their world
And wading in streams
And building sand castles
And eating ice cream.

What happens to love as they grow older?
What happens to racing through fields of clover?
Will they learn to hate, riot, and kill?
Whose land will they live in?
Whose ranks will they fill?

Will they wander a garden midst shouts of glee?
Will the girls enjoy the puppets while the boys climb the trees?

Or

Will they hobble on one leg, eyes brimmed with pain,
While crawling through trenches or hurling from planes?

Will they feel the greed harbored in man's heart?
Will they sense the hatred of the dark for the light?
Will they know children starve while the economy grows?

Will they care if their children enter a world where love is
Replaced by greed and guns, poverty and pain?

Barbara E. Lai

THE CITY

The city goes on!
The young people grow old in it
But — the city goes on!
Love's dimmed by the evening tide
Hope slowly shrinks out of sight
But the city goes on!

The city goes on
In endless repetitious fact,
Only the players change — in —
Each new act — but the city goes on!
The city goes on
Though all worldly deeds end —

Why then do we so much
On the transitory depend?
When the only uncertain — certainty is —
The beyond in which is reserved our place
Why all this effort then?
In — this passing chase?

The city goes on!
Unmoved — unfeeling — offending!
Each day it buries a million endings!
And one day — one day — it will be my turn,
And what will have been the reason
For my sojourn?

A. S. Christina

MOMENT

Gray dawned the day after Christmas and cold;
Snow sheeted the highlands,
Plows plied the roads from Wytheville to Bristol.
Frosty was Tennessee; the
Sky was breaking up in lights and darks;
Late sun poured into Sevierville.
    Suddenly,
Dwarfing the tawdry traffic of Pigeon Forge,
Rising from purple clouds,
Le Comte's white mass loomed ghostly on the sky —
Spirit-mountain, not quite there.

Anne Wilson Frye

PATH OF DREAMS

I wasn't sure about blind ambition,
    following a dream I'd kept hidden deep inside.

Afraid of what someone else thought,
    I kept it bottled up in my heart.

Then I heard a voice telling me;

    "It's worth taking a chance on what you believe in
        because you're nothing without dreams."

With that it was decided for me.
    I had to take a chance just to see what happened.

That voice came back to me saying;

    "Your life is what you make it! If you're
        willing to try, nothing will get in your way."

Now here I stand before you,
    Living out my fantasy.

Thinking back,
    that voice was right;

        "You're nothing without dreams!"

Pam Kurelo

ONE OF THE GREAT MYSTERIES OF LIFE, "WHY!"

Do men serve without question,
Trust in the promise,
Believe in the utmost,
Purely on word?

Labor for lost souls,
Give for their comfort —
Stilling the cries,
That have never been heard?

It's the indwelling Spirit
That rules the believer,
To bring into focus,
That in which we believe.

It's that very same Spirit
That gives men the vision,
To reach out and conquer
The blessings recieve!

Elsie B. Webster

WEBSTER, ELSIE BERYLE. Pen Name: Island Savannah; Born: Hope, Bartholomew County, Indiana, 3-18-18; Married: to Howard Price Webster; Education: Indiana Business College, two years; Occupations: Bookkeeping, Accounting, Part-time Literary Work; Memberships: Former member of National Association of Accountants; Awards: *Remember to Love Me,* Christian novel, Carlton Press, 1971; Writings: 'The Diligent One,' 4-4-85; 'Beyond Crucifixion,' 4-83; 'Afterglow,' 4-84; 'He Arose,' 4-80; 'Homage,' 1982; all published in *Republic,* local paper, Free Methodist Publication, *Wabash Courier;* Comments: *Much is written and inspired by the love I have for Christ — dealing much with the crucifixion, the resurrection, the hope we have in Him. Many articles, non-poetry have been written on diversified subjects and published in our Wabash Christian Courier. Often inspired by occasion, the need to write, and personal feelings. I have been writing seriously since 1966 . . . with many publications. I am a prolific writer . . . with many types, and titles of poetry accumulated.*

IN MEMORY OF —

You're gone — Yet
with us still.
these words (seemingly
inadequate and incomplete)
express our loss.

You left behind
some treasured gifts
and your picture
in a park,
but mostly —
memories.

Neil Farney

MY HORSE

If I had a horse,
    You know what I'd do?
I'd name it first
    And so would you.

It's been a week now
    What should I name it?
If it was mad
    I wouldn't blame it.

Hilbert, or James,
    Or even Stan
I don't know — but —
    Maybe 'Big Man.'

It's been a long time
    And no name of course
So now he thinks
    his name is HORSE.

Lynn Underwood

SOMEWHERE AGAIN, SOMEPLACE IN TIME

I've been here before,
same place, different time.
I knew you before,
same person, different life.

We were friends here before,
same meaning, different type.
I loved you before,
same feeling, different kind.

We fought here before,
same action, different lie.
I lost you before,
same ending, different "why."

I'll meet you again,
different place, different time.
somewhere again,
someplace in time.

Karen Hixon

WHISKEY WONT

Sweet golden drops,
Smooth liquid fire
Ignites the walls,
Fuels men's desires.

Escape is near . . .
Unraveling will.
The searing taste
Bites deeper still.

The demon's brew
Releases reins
On fettered souls
And fetid pains.

But freedom soon
Numbs dry iced veins . . .
'Twas but a dream
Bound tight in chains.

Iris U. Paschedag

AS IF TO CLAIM THE SKY

Pages of sky
lie unread
a bookmark cloud
floats by
in unchartered lines
of mist
and rings of light.

The author's name
is not known
the cover
never found.

Sunlight brightens the sky
an unwritten world
lies open to the eye.

A traveler's hand
can touch the breeze
but cannot change the light
nor claim
the stranger's view.

Elizabeth Anne Burke

THE PHYSICAL BEAUTY OF LOVE

The physical beauty of love is something
that you can't describe

A shaky feeling deep down inside

A feeling so different you can't hide

The physical beauty of love

Like a sore that never heals

That bleed and bleed at will when your
heart is weak and you cannot speak

It is something compared to a love

That physical beauty of love you can try
and wonder what it's about

But when that feeling hit you there's no
doubt it's the physical beauty of love

Geraldine Arhin

GENTLE LITTLE FLOWER

Gentle little flower
resting in a summer breeze
showing off your colors
glistening in the day
waiting for the chance
to send your seeds afar
gentle little flower
how beautiful you are
Standing tall in a field of grass
your eyes watch all that has passed
displaying colors of yesterday
for tomorrow may not come
gentle little flower
resting in the noonday's sun
now summer showers coming down
they moisten your petals
before they hit the ground
your seeds fall to
in the field of grass
gentle little flower
can't wait for you to come back

Gregg Jones

she was a little girl
so unsure so all alone

so taken unawares

both in her spirit
and in mine

I felt the tragedy
inherent in a life
gone by

I wouldn't know what
else to say

except to say

I saw her die

but even that
even that

would never say
could never say

what I alone
what I alone

have seen within
her eyes

Richard M. Macht

GROWTH

He gave me the support to grow
  a limb, my vine to grow against
    reaching ever to the sun.

Yet, in my fear of growth
  my vine became entwined
    in his branches, twigs
      too entwined, snarling
        limb
          vine
            growth.

Gently, then even harshly
  he pushed my vine away
    so he could breathe
      so I could grow.

Unentwined, I sought a new vine
  to lean against, to grow
    it was myself
      alone.
        I moved away . . .

My vine is now a limb
  for other vines to lean against
    to grow
And I am now strong
  a limb
    a tree
I am me.

Marilynn Stanard

SPRING TINGLE!

The roses bloom in the spring.
Some are red,
  Some make you tingle with a ding!
The grass greens, and it looks so nice.
  That is what spring is about.

Stephanie Kochevar

THE OATH

This child of mine will never cry,
will never have to say, I am sorry . . .
This child of mine will never see,
if I can help, the misery in life of mine.

An oath I took when He was born,
that I will guide Him
and if I must alone.
To the best of life. To happiness,
And if it means my emptiness.

Yes, I must say. The road has been,
the worst of all that I have seen.
The thorns have torn the skin of mine,
clouds became rocks of dying.

But He will be the only one
that knows what it is to die for one.
He is part of mine and He will know,
because part of him must also go.

Yana Wilson

WILSON, JANE (YANA) PALAMARA. Born: Athens, Greece, 11-9-44; Married: 10-3-65 to Stanley Wayne Wilson; Education: Accounting School, Athens; Dental Assistant for Red Cross; continuing for Art degree; Occupation: Civil Service Housing Referral Officer; Memberships: Hairdressers Association, AWOG of Athens; Poetry: 'I Am a Proud American,' 'Why Me,' (in Greek); many more; Themes: *Romantic, patriotic.* Comments: *I am trying to express my internal world, depending on the strength of the feeling. At times of sadness or happiness, I find it easier to write or paint.*

GRIEF

At first
It was bottomless.
I was afraid
I would drown.
Now I can touch
                    bottom.
And I do.
Often.

Susan Hagen

WOE UNTO THE LITTLE ONES

Woe unto the Little Ones
for they will feel the suns

of bright, hot, burning flames
caused by needless war games.

They will know what fear is
as they go into hot darkness.

knowing not when life becomes death,
or when time gives its last breath.

Kimberlee E. Coker

Ribbons, Ribbons wrapped up in braids,
Colorful things from childhood days.
Chocolate noses, smiles of marmalades.
Ribbons, Ribbons wrapped up in braids.

Precious memories that lightly fades,
Wrapped in magical mysterious haze.
Ribbons, Ribbons wrapped up in braids,
Colorful things from childhood days.

Angela Polk

WHY?

Banners wave
  and bullets fly.
Around the world
  women cry,
    for sons and lovers
      who pay the costs,
        of battles won
          and battles lost.
But men on high
  the tears heed not
    and weep for battles
      never fought.

Donald C. McNabb, Sr.

45 REMEMBERED

In the half-shadowed light
of the world before dawn
the memories shift
and cease to move on.
In the patterns revealed
from the dreams of the dead
my futility cries
but is left yet unsaid.
For the passions of guilt
etched deep in my skin
say the body may die
still the soul lies within.

Georgina Ferenz

THE MAGIC OF WORDS

They give me comfort
They tell me a story,
that puts me in my glory.
They take me to a faraway place;
They put a smile on my face.
I can go to the beach,
or to some resort out of my reach.
They take me to the highest mountain;
They take me to the lowest valley,
even right down my own alley.
Does that sound absurd?
No, that's the magic of words.

L. T. Hordges

FALLS OF MONTMORENCY.

WAITING ROOM

Morning light shines through curtains
His baseball cap aglow
Bookcases give poetry prose photography and dreams
Collecting studies of human conditions
His typewriter surrounded by mail advertisements
Hides opened letters with pictures from the family back East
Dishes overdue clothes for the laundry
A box of pennies near the refrigerator
His calendar marks future plans
The woman goes to church in a Van Gogh print

Friends and relatives travel far
Quiet and sincere
Imagining from letters and calls of yesterdays
Powerfully alive their love for him
Not expressed and felt this strongly
Until now
They will sort and decide the use of his treasures
Spending a long time
Learning
Who he was

Jeff Petrill

THE TRAIT

Is my life existent upon the pen
    I fear, not;
Yet my life is as a sonnet
continuing on into eternity;

Yet it is a dim flickering beacon
continuing so others can follow;

Yet I have followed others
and fell into their fate;
    I fear, not;

For in every man there is a guide to follow
because he was there before;

For his works were there to form me
because I was to carry the trait;

For I was predestined to give
and to pass others their fate.

R. Scott

GRANDCHILDREN!

When people have reached that adult stage,
   Where there are grandchildren, life is a rage!

It has happened to us, in our home and life,
   There are thirteen to share in the joys and strife.

Each in their own, individuals, yes,
   Each in their own, they are the best.

The girls are Lisa, Sarah, Jessie and Jill,
   Anna, Amanda, all pretty, healthy and well.

The boys are Joshua, Samuel, Jeffrie and Shane,
   Lance, Anthony, and Austen — all — everything but plain.

It is a great joy, when they visit and play,
   Always, they like to eat, and for the night — stay.

Then, when they go home, we are tired but happy,
   'Cause we're proud of each one, both Grandma and Pappy.

Wayne E. Flory

COURAGE

As shadows danced to the rhythm of the flame,
infant shadows grew in fame.
Regal stature, satin fur so fair,
baby felines eyes a glare.

Armored with the courage of ten
crouching low,
upon his lips a licking grin.
A sudden sharp explosive sound!
Within his heart fear abounds.

With ears cocked and courage coward,
a great leap across the room,
Super Power!
A clumsy trip, three rolls in defeat.
With one mighty pounce, he was back upon his feet.

With royal courage firmly restored,
echoing whisperings of the ages,
Victor! Victor! Victor!
With regal pride, he turned toward me
as if to say, "another night, another day,
i will reign King, over my prey."

Yvonne Smith

WINTER FOG

The might of memory is its easy presence.
This fog cannot hide
The bare branches of unseasonal neglect,
The slippery routes and reroutes
Of premature lust, and farther,
The hungry winter birds of regret
Gathering at the brittle edge
Of the frozen river, Loneliness.
Love, unlike Evil, is less unseen.

This fog is a flimsy veil.
Suddenly, it thins and lifts
And your errant face appears
To mercilessly renew an unshareable penitence.
Still not knowing when,
It thickens and descends
But your face, truly tenured, exacts, and remains
Unblurred even as fresh snow
Powders long fallen snow.

Lestrino C. Baquiran

SMALL TOWN OLD MAN

He's a piece of machinery
Tractor talk and coggy memories
To sit and listen is sometimes like
Getting pelted with nuts and bolts to sleep

"Back in '51 we laid the sewage lines
Usta work for Kittery Printers
I was foreman at the shoe factory in Exeter
Yep. Want some ginger ale?"

Old dog   old man
His dachsund is sixteen and doesn't walk
Two years ago this man was climbing gutters
But since last summer he feels so rusty
He's talking to me about throwing his ashes
    behind the garage

I can leave his house, go down by the pond
Saucy green with algae and dip my toes
In the clear sunlight I begin to see deeper
the bottom
the wheelless bicycle
the broken carriage

Joseph Richey

MEETING OF THE STONES

There are certain places
on the bottom of the sea
resembling landfill on Long Island
abandoned by the mackerel
and the blue-tailed bass
as we have left the stem of Manhattan
to the youngest architects
who have no money no blueprints
only dreams. I wonder
if the quiet coral seems
as unimaginative to energetic sea-urchins
or rippling eels as Manhasset
is to commuters ground away
by railway stones.
The ocean mimics every outcry
of the land building layers
building sandstone quarries
underneath our cities.
Look around the corners of buildings
At night you'll touch the pebbles of the sea.

Anita Brysman

ANGER

The day was cold, the wind so bleak
It called from man all that was weak.
I was handed the devil on a tarnished platter;
That I welcomed him not, seemed not to matter.
From the dear lips came curses and words so foul
They tumbled, they jumbled, came out as a howl.
Such an ugly flay on that special day.
The curses and words chipped, chipped away
At respect and love along the way.
My soul was seared, my bones were chilled;
With such abuse love can be stilled.
A pain so deep, it did choke my throat;
Over despair and shame the devil did gloat.
Cold, sad and gray passed the special day.
The rage was long spent; again all was calm;
Repentance, kindnesss and love were the balm.
For many a day the tears flowed and dried;
Forgiveness came not easy, though it tried.
Dear Father in Heaven, please tell me, I pray
Why are we sometimes in the devil's pay?

Clare Weiss

BEING WITHOUT YOU

If one day I should wake to place
a world without your familiar face
I'd feel as though there's nothing more
holding the meaningful thoughts you tore
a time to sit beside the phone
Waiting to realize I'm all alone
It seems without you my heart lost its place
For no one else's love could fill your space
Longing to sit, to share through your eyes
After shedding the tears of forgotten goodbyes
Feeling the need to hold you tight
And dream of you on endless nights
Pouring my feelings to an open mind
Telling myself, another I'll find
But deep down inside I hang on tight
Not loosing grip, the feelings are right
For even if my mind broke free
From the memories of you and me
My heart would still be locked away
Until your love came back to stay.

Toni Dybala

THE DELICATE ONE

When I was just a litle girl,
    I lived within a constant whirl
    of friends and neighbors thus concerned
    and sisters and brothers
They lifted me, they sat me, and they
    brought me fruit and flowers, because
    I was diff'rent from the others.
My mother's love was something that I
    really can't explain, just endless and
    enduring, and she never did complain;
A cheerful smile, a friendly word, a
    sympathetic nod, and her one reply
    to questions, always ended with
    "Thank God."
Apparently she endowed me, with ideals
    very high, for my life has been
    as shining as the stars
        up in the sky.

Shona Lamond

SCHIRP, GRACE STEWART. Pen Name: Shona Lamond(Seonag, pronounced Shona, is Gaelic for Grace; Lamond is my mother's maiden name, also the name of her Scottish Clan); Born: Glasgow, Scotland; Married; now Widowed; Education: Cape Cod Community College, Fisher Junior College, Writer's Digest School; Occupations: Accounting for 35 years; Owner/Manager of Motels; Memberships: NAFE, Inc., NWC, USSC, also the local Women's Clubs, Garden, etc.; Awards: *American Poetry Anthology Vol. 1, Nos. 3-4,* Fall/Winter, 1982; *Vol. 3, Nos. 3-4,* Fall/Winter, 1984; *Vol IV, Nos. 3-4,* Fall/Winter, 1985; Poetry: 'The Delicate One,' 'Signs and Songs of Spring,' 'Nature's Colors,' 'Nite Sky,' 'Contemplation,' nauture, Spring, 1985; Comments: *Right now I am trying to write fiction, and hope to write a book or short story worth publishing eventually.*

KEEP FLYING

Sing little bird, sing your song in the trees,
Flutter your wings in the springtime breeze;
New season coming make haste my dear friend,
Hold on to life for someday it shall end,
Stretch your wings and reach for the sky,
The view is all yours so Fly my friend, FLY . . .

Robert J. Darrigan

GO TELL IT

Go tell it to the people.
Let them know.
Tell them of the wonders
Beyond the rainbow.
Tell them of the treasures;
The mighty stone wall.
Tell them of the story
But don't tell them all.

Rachael Flora

NIGHTLY JOURNEY

welcome back to
your youth
your friends
your education
your nightmares
welcome back to

"VIETNAM"

Donald Paul Angotta

IN PRAISE OF VON NEUMANN

There was once a mathematician named
Von Neumann,
Some thought him definitely not human,
Infinite series he'd find
So simple in mind
'Twas nothing for his mental acumen!!

Felix Meyer

WASTE

You run from
You run to
You run in search of
You seek answers
You shut out truths
You chase rainbows and sunshine
So busy trying to catch tomorrow
That today goes by untouched.

Barbara Schore

WALK WITH ME AWHILE

Take my hand
As we stroll,
Share with me
Your thoughts,
Feel the concern
Touch the warmth
Hold tight the embrace
Treasure the experience.

Judy T. Ciccarelli

FAIRY TALES

She's a child in a fairy tale.
With wishes, dreams and boats with sails.
Boats will soon all sail away.
Dreams are for those who sleep, they say.
Wishes brought by stars far away,
fade as night turns into day.
The fairy tales will never come true.
The child cries. She never knew.

Debera Urschel

WHY DO POETS?

Why are there poets? And why do they write?
What gives them that special ability to have such insight?
The ones predicting doom, being so bold.
Are these modern day prophets, just like the ones of old?
Or of them who write of nothing but happiness and bliss.
Is the world really so black and white and all the grays amiss?

Maybe it's a special something for the rest of us to share.
To be our painter of words, to show people that they care.
To come so close to reality when the world is so blind.
To be our forerunner of truth when we lag so far behind.
So don't be so hypocritical always asking of poets why.
Just enjoy what is given to you and understanding may come by and by.

Alan L. Rizzonelli

CHRISTMAS LOVE

Christmas love is loving cards decked with real life caring,
joy, filling wishes like old Santa's childrens' stockings.

Happy gifts of happiness to wipe away the snow and wrinkles on
grandpa's face, looking to see if he remembered today.

Christmas love is like the snow gently falling on a sleepy town
warmed by goodness and kindness that comes at Christmas time, like
Christmas candy.

Christmas love everyone is reminded by the bell chimes that come
each passing year.
Always hoping those that are dear will always be near.

Mary Meadows

ACKNOWLEDGMENT OF THE ETERNAL

At times I yearn to be a Browning or a Thoreau
To pen the mighty sword of knowledge
To strike down the mundane drudgery of today
To put in simple words the complex solution of the world's great problems
To flower in the brilliant light of an easy wit
Or ease through the solemn bonds with disguised and subtle humor
Oh the power, the might of words, actors on a stage of paper
Flourishing, changing, blowing soft at first, finishing the crescendo with a
mighty roar so the power will be remembered
From the smallest but mighty "if" to the majestic "amen"
Would that I could fit the pieces together to form the intricate but complete
patterns of the creative
At times I yearn

C. Elaine Simpson

LAW

Deep into my eyes, deeper. That's it, now don't blink.
Catch the color — brown, you say? Huh, that's what you think.
Round, you say? It may be. Pentagonal, the last I looked.
I shut and reopened them? No, the earth just shook.
Tears? What are they? Oh, you're speaking of the flow.
That's just my heart — it's bleeding now. My blood is clear, you know.
Yes, I bleed upside-down. Strange? No, don't you?
I've heard them call you "blue eyes," but to me they don't look blue.
Round? Oh, no they're not. They've five sides, just like mine.
Crying? Oh, no. Your blood's clear too. Then, we'll work out
    just fine.
Round and blue eyes crying? If you say so, I say myself.
Everything is what it is, but also something else.

Tina M. Ryon

THE CALL

The scent was heavy in the air
Carried on the wings of the wind
With the coming of a winter storm
It filled me, overpowered me
Urged me to go
To become one, one with the land

In the stillness of the morning after
The crystal clear stillness
That covered the land like the snow
The dazzling, purifying, hypnotizing snow
Through the stillness I heard the call
The unmistakable, unceasing call, the call of the land

Then came the sun
Massaging with her warm rays
Penetrating the cold, turning the snow to water
The earth opened to receive the gift of life
And from deep inside the earth I felt the pulse
The pulse of the heart of the earth
And we were one

James P. Glasco

THE HOLY PARROT

As dews turn my hair gray each morning
Early morning hymns won't stop me each day
From giving righteous respect to memories
As the holy parrot gives my favorite version
Of the mornings' designed sessions and versions.

By the holy relic, and by the pew
Where the pastor purified me with holy water,
The holy parrot sings my favorite version
Reminding me of old forgotten versions
At dawn, each day, and by the holy relic.

Uduma Igwe Kalu

KALU, UDUMA IGWE. Born: Calabar, Eastern Nigeria, W. Africa, 11-16-59; Single; Education: Presently a student at Suffolk University, Boston, Massachusetts, U.S.A.; Occupation: Student; Poetry: *Modern Poems,* Poetry Book, Tod & Honeywell, New York, 1985; Other Writings: "The Penitent Child," Short Story, IBS Radio Station, Nigeria, 1979; Comments: *'The Holy Parrot' is a religious poem. It tells about a parrot that sings versions in the church hymnary every morning, which remind me of the days of my childhood in church, when I was baptized. Familiar sessions and versions were sung; the parrot reminds me of them all.*

GOLDEN MEMORIES

She was lonely when I met her.
I saw passion in her eyes
    and revenge in her heart.

I knew she was hurting from a loss so great
    she dared not tell a soul.

She kept inside her a box of jewels.
Riches of golden memories gathering dust from years of torment
    that could never be healed.

Those jewels she held under guard
    from pain, loss, and the greed of a past lover.

The only key to the lock was in her heart
    which could only be opened by that one special man.

That man who fled when he couldn't give to her
    what her heart poured out to him — love.

Now the riches are covered with many cobwebs of loneliness
    and heartache,
And no one is able to reach her.

Will the webs be cleared by the midnight stars
    awaiting her lover to sweep her away?

Or will she be sealed forever in her golden memories.

Justine Gillespie

LOVE WILL SEE US THROUGH

Remembering how to smile,
Oh how hard; but so worthwhile!
Loving and sharing love,
And remembering how,
And to share with all those around you,
Yesterday, tomorrow, and NOW!

This season could be sad and blue;
But Momma and Daddy wouldn't say that would do.
Bless their happiness, peace, and love,
And remember, they're watching us from up above.

My heart is heavy
And not so bright;
But your love, support, and caring,
Will help to make it right.

Share goodwill, friendship, and love,
To make this holiday
One we will cherish with love.

To those who feel somewhat dark and lost,
Remember the smiles and love as I do.
Maybe they'll lighten your load
And see you through.

Tonight, I light a candle
And pray that we will all be together soon,
Maybe on one Christmas day.

Mrs. David M. Smith

Youth does not always mean immaturity.
For you are not as old as I
And yet in some ways you surpass all others.
I think of you often — and also I look.
My thoughts are of seeing you
And the physical contact we share.
How fun it is to be with you.
My values — they seem so shallow when I am with you
And I sometimes question them as to their validity.

Laurie A. Pace

319

CALIFORNIA CHRISTMAS

Poinsettia blooms in whites and reds,
Mountaintops with snowy heads,
Orange trees with navel fruit,
Lemons yellow, bright but mute.
Liquid amber in many hues.
Scarlet, gold, but no blues.

Emerald hills, in summer brown,
Cattle graze each grassy crown.
Among the shrubs and cacti plants
Spotted hides shine and dance.
Baby calves, and mothers, too,
Amble by and loudly moo.

Houses trimmed with colored lights
Making brightness through the nights.
Firs and pines with sparkling limbs,
People singing Christmas hymns,
To celebrate the Christ child's birth
With their gifts of song and mirth.

Beatrice M. McCaig

QUESTIONS SONT REPONDU

What has the minds covet lost?
    undying love, prevail
    cease all harmful treasures cost
    price to bear, for sale.
What have I done to permit
        this buying?
Answer, "unknown," to me.
Should I be right in want
        for dying?
These questions bother me.
What have your feelings
        done to me
that I feel for shame.
Fearing for life, what is to be —
Shall I gain wisdom? or fame?
Has yet that tempest storm
        to be?
Pallid fear, regain.
Soul set fire, then set free.
the questions still remain.

Lisa Muturspaw

WHEN LOVE'S WIND BLOWS

The tides of change
        Who knows what comes
Listen to the world
        The way it hums
Our love is so new
        No promises broken
Guarantees are only
        Words that are spoken
Imagination wanders
        Excitement grows
There's no protection
        When love's wind blows
Flicker to flame
        Flame to fire
Soon we're consumed
        With shared desire
Flirting with romance
        In a dangerous sea
When love's wind blows
        Together we'll be

Jamie Haydock

DEAD BIRD DIRGE

the silent scream of the bird
Will never be heard
Again,
It sounded so sweet,
but now it will meet
Death
In bird heaven.

Once it flew
Like a cuckoo,
but now it's dead,
And its head
Is a memory,
Impressed by a car
As it went too far.

Alfred Elkins

holler

coolness, wet, in the shadows of
bare rock-faced bluffs, overhanging,
green creepers jump from tree to tree,
budding ferns and dank moss cover
greasy, black rocks, dwarfed by
Longleaf Pine, echoing with
chirps, twitters, caws and the
constant hum of tiny insects

Under these bluffs Cherokees squatted
around cooking fires, with children,
hunters and warriors.
All that remains are a few arrowheads
lost in closets, some dusty bones and
their spirit in the family blood.

David Cook

FOOL'S PRIDE

Your face is always
in my mind,
slightly out of reach,
but, nonetheless, you
are still there.
Very much a part of me,
of what was and could
have been.
Had we listened to
our hearts,
not giving into pride.
Allowing it to rob us
of what we held
most precious —
EACH OTHER.

Deborah Wireman

MIRAGE

Autism quivering amid basking skies.
Temptation has imprisoned this soul
In a universe of abstraction —
A painted reality, by the artist illusion.

A fevered fascination
Bewitching mine every perception,
Dancing to the tears of a
Wanting heart.

Blistering passion, ever increasing
With passing time. Condemned to chase
This apparition — which, by but one
Forbidden touch, vanishes —
Forever lost.

Alex Aretakis

HAIKU

Red. red, spinning white
captured crystal heart shattered
Cupid's arrow scored.

Mary S. Johnston

SMILEY'S PROVERB

Somewhere between
the calm and the storm,
life is a breeze!

Kristin A. Smiley

HEAVEN

If each individual could find himself,
Within himself,
Could the soul rest?

Ruby Pauline Cherry

HAIKU

No camouflage, still
the cardinal in the snow
does not wish to hide.

L. Ann Black

COMPANION

In the slanting rays
Of the setting sun,
The jogger was teaching
Her shadow to run.

Helen Lee, Ph.D.

OCEAN

Boundless seasoned sea,
Tepid rays piercing through waves,
White frothy seaside.

Becky Korb

THE TV REPAIRMAN

"No ma'am, your TV set's OK,
    There's nothing wrong at all;
Just take this little AC cord
    And plug it in the wall."

Jack R. Lewis

She marries him to her
when she folds his clothes;
the soft clothes
that only she folds
and he never folds.

Pamela Rymer O'Dwyer

SONS OF REFUGEES

There's a story of a young man from a country across the sea.
With a longing in his bosom; how he wanted to be free.
All his life he had been in bondage, in a cruel tyrant land.
Tearfully he left his parents, hoping they would understand.

After many nights of travel, he came to the dreaded wall.
Many young men came before him; it was here death met them all.
Fear within him said, "Let's turn back." Freedom whispered, "I am nigh."
In his heart his courage building, "I'll be free, or I will die."

In a moment he was running, pole in hand to vault the wall.
From behind him guns were firing; any moment he could fall.
As he rolled across the summit, he felt burning in his side.
But he lived to tell his story to his children filled with pride.

This is not just one man's story, but of many refugees.
How they left their friends and loved ones for this home of liberties.
Glorious freedom! Let's preserve it. For there's no place whence to flee.
If we must we'll fight to keep it; we the sons of refugees.

Ernest T. Presnell, Jr.

PRESNELL, ERNEST T. JR. Born: Native Tarheel from Haywood County; Married: to Peggy Fleming from Madison County, North Carolina; Occupations: Developed "Pretty Pops" popcorn. Its natural colors range the entire spectrum and is very tender and delicious . . . pops out snow white; Memberships: Haywood Writers; Poetry: 'Taraxacum,' Easter poem, *Sunburst #6,* August 1984; 'Little Mama the Rose of My Heart, *Sunburst #6,* August 1984; 'Haywood,' *Sunburst #7,* August 1985; 'That Song of "Love Me Tender",' memorial poem to Elvis, *Sunburst #7,* August 1985; 'Spring, Spring, Spring, *Sunburst #7,* August 1985; Themes: *People, places, things, faith, hope, love, heaven, justice, mercy, temperance, etc.;* Comments: *I write of anything and everything that has been meaningful in my life. Poetry is the woven fabric of life. I write primarily what I feel; to be myself; I thoroughly enjoy other people's work, but I never try to be like others though.*

THANKS, MY FRIEND

Thanks, My Friend
I'd like to say
Because through to the end
Your help saved my Wedding Day.

With all the love and kindness you share
You show
How much you care
And you are someone I'm proud to know

You are one who is truly blessed
In every way
You are someone who is greatly missed
I'm glad you were part of my Wedding Day.

Thanks, My Friend
I'll never forget
Until our lives end
You are the best friend yet.

Laura A. Chicon

SMOKE DETECTOR MOCKING

Grief-prolonged end.
Day dogged by night
no silvery dawn
no bird in flight.

The sun extinguished
as the earth for moon
unless abysm of ash
glows above lost noon.

A rabble crowd: only
the unlucky undead;
the leaden heart past
comprehending dread.

Arson claiming all
with man-made fire,
tourbillions of flame
etch a funeral pyre.

H. W. N. Hall

CHEATING HEARTS

Your cheating heart did tell
on you —
I know you must be feeling blue —
Just like ole Hank said you'd do —

Once you did go —
And once you were caught —
That's all it took to show me,
Dear —
Just how much you really cared!

Now, it's plain to see —
So, it's time to say —
No one treats me the way you do —
And, then goes and brags about it, too —
NO, Love! not even you —

Because, now my love is all gone —
And only GOD knows for how long!

Sandilyne Chamblee

MY LOVE

Words cannot describe
what I feel for you inside,
But I swear my love is there
and nothing can compare.

I love you with my entire being
my heart and soul is yours to command,
I love you with my life
for you hold it in your hand.

I love you with each breath I take
with each beating of my heart,
I love you with my smiles
and my tears when we're apart.

You're the warming sunlight
the birds singing in the sky,
You're the flowers that grow in the springtime
and I'll love you till I die.

Susan L. Milanez

ALL OF MY LIFE . . . (YOU NEVER MOVED!)

All of my life I've been a music man, singing songs,
some I knew and some I didn't.
Sometimes I could only hum along,
but always my heart was singing!

All of my life I've been a dancing man,
tapping my foot in time.
Sometimes I couldn't remember the steps,
but always my soul was dancing.

I lived a life of song and dance,
thinking everyone knew the tune.
But many times when the music began,
I started and ended alone.

And sometimes when I looked at you,
I saw your heart singing, too,
and your soul dancing.
But, yet, you never moved!

Franco Ray

TO THE PRIESTS OF THE COLLEGE OF SYMBOLS

in the wet braille pages of night illumined
by the violet tongues of wax dripping tallows,
immobile, the ancient ciphers wither
like antiphonal flowers wired to whiteness.

ink-stained druids of the gnomic heart
sculpting abstract sonnets with wounded palms,
bleeding incoherently, to ache is to be silenced
o priests of the college of symbols, your faith

clicking ominously in gaveled hands. o you
who have eschewed solemnly and rescinded
the fermented wheat of famished years. o you
with your aesthetics of supply and demand,

how many souls have you let sink quietly
with scarlet quill and spattering click in the night?
what of x's novels, y's stories, z's poems?
they are all dead now, which one is lazarus?

Hale V. Mason

BLUE GLASS

Why hadn't I seen it before?
It's plain as the reflection in the mirror.
Plain as the blue uniform I wear — we both wear.
Plain as the blue in your eyes.
Eyes like fine blue glass.
I see myself mirrored in your eyes.
I see my image reflected in your image.
        Look at us . . .
        We look like twins.
        You in blue.
        Me in blue.
        I wear a badge.
        We perform the same God-forsaken job.
        You understand it.
        You understand me.
Gazing again at the reflection in the mirror.
        Blue melded with shimmering silver.
        Black patent shines.
        Once proud.
        Now disillusioned.
        What's beneath these uniforms of the law?
        These glinting badges?
        Two people . . .
        Just two people.
        Karen Sontag-Holthof

WHEN WE LOVE

Why is it
        that when
my feet run toward their destination five
minutes becomes eternity,
but When We Love an hour is a second?

Why is it
        that
the Moon rises from His shadow in the night
and
the Sun does Her backbend,
becoming a rainbow in the morning
when
we enter their presence?

Why is it
        that When
We Love
beauty can stand still like a posed
painting from
Leonardo da Vinci and
yet our time can pass as quickly as
scenery does from a train?
        Audrey Najor

ISOLATION

Tumbleweed is kicking up the dust inside my mind.
Someone spurred a horse inside.
It's running blind. So far to ride.
When the dust settles it covers the hoof marks left behind.

I try to follow aimlessly but can't see the track.
I run a little, stop, and stare.
Where'd they go? Over there?
Nothing is in front of me. No way to go back.

The empty, lonely desert can stop a person cold.
No image of man.
Just rocks in the sand.
There's no one here to talk to me. No one near to hold.

The echoes of my desperate cries softly drift away.
Empty tears, I start to cry,
Fade to nothing from my eye.
Why should I be seen or heard? There's no one here today.
        Leila A. Brazo

SLOW DANCING

I watch the rain,
It's slowly fading away
In to the gloom of a weary afternoon.

An empty feeling surrounds my life
And I slowly think over, last night

My body is numb
My brain is fogged
I'm looking for an answer
With every drop of rain that falls
With the hope of clearing skies
There will be a clear path.

I feel the pounding of my heart
It's slow and uneasy
With a sinking feeling
I enter another room
And see a dream fade away
With just one Slow Dance

Vicki Lynne Rolfes

ASK

Shall I sell you a day
By a silent sea
When the waves widen their span,
Or a night that is right
For a future star bright,
And the water catches the sand?

Shall I give you an hour
Of cool breeze and sky
That captures the grin of night,
Or a moment with flowers
That climb to their tower
At noon, when God's sun is bright?

Shall I show you a road
That leads to the lake
Where lilies and lilac bloom,
Or steal you away
For a day in May —
Come, tell me, soon!

Elizabeth McDonald Pickens

THE WAYS OF WAR

Mortars pop!
In the still of night.
People's faces,
Are plastered with fright.
Bombs screaming,
Out of planes,
People running for shelter,
In the acid rain.
Fighter-jets speeding,
Past the speed of sound.
Ground-to-air missiles,
Bring them to the ground.
Radiation perverts
The fabric of life.
Destroying the promised future,
The young were to lead.
Chaos, the tool of war,
Rears its hideous brow.
It wins the war,
And inherits the Earth.

Stefano Noto

LOVE TO HATE

The height of my ideal
(If you really need compare)
Can be seen by how I feel
In the depths of my despair.

The longing of my senses,
And emotions I deny,
Are defeated by defenses
As I turn a cynic's eye.

The power of my caring,
And the glory I perceived,
Are revealed in my sharing
Of the hopes I once conceived.

The love I held for living —
Unrequited, uncontrolled —
Was best seen within my giving
Of my heart, and all that told.

The strength of my emotions
Is diverted from above;
And my downcast new devotions
Now seek hate, but once sought love.

Carlos Kame

ENCOUNTER WITH A SQUIRREL
For Jessie

There's a squirrel
  in the branch
of a hickory tree
  and he sits
on the limb
  and looks down
at me.

His almond eyes
  flicker as he
cautiously stands
  and contemplates
the peanut
  in my outstretched
hand.

For a moment
  there's stillness,
as he sniffs
  with his nose.
Then, quickly
  grabbing the peanut,
off he goes.

Steve K. Bertrand

OUT HERE, AWAY FROM THE CITY

In this small part of the country,
the anxieties of the contemporary
are lines in the paper which
we choose not to read.
Like we choose not to go
to the city which is only
two hours away.

We stay with the land
and it stays with us,
feeding the cattle and
running with the horses.

The cries of the doomsayers
and those who feed their anxieties
are far away, characters in a play
that we don't go to see.
Mika Applebaum

WINTER HUNT

While sitting here all alone
On this big piece of stone
The wind has chilled me to the bone
While sitting here all alone

There he is like a flash
Across the field with a dash
And when I turn around to see
The one and only looking back at me

Then I lift and slowly squeeze
The piece of lead progressed with ease
I found my mark upon the shoulder
When he fell like a boulder

Daniel Pierce

PIERCE, ROBERT DANIEL III. Born: Huntsville, Texas, 1-25-64; Education: Currently attending Sam Houston State University majoring in Psychology and English; Occupation: Floral Designer at Heartfield Florist in Huntsville; Poetry: 'Nature's Imbalance,' November, 1983; Other Writings: "My Most Frightening Moment," short story, March, 1983; Comments: *A theme of subliminal parodies and natural phenomenon, are more prevalent than other thesis topics, in my poems. The pleasure and satisfaction received from the ability to express inner feelings with the use of symbolism and paradoxal expressions, is a powerful motivation.*

He swallowed my life
My heart broke in two.
Blood spilled freely as his
mouth twisted words into my awaiting ears.
Ivory speckles bonded our happiness.

Water falls down my chest
Into my empty nothing.
The blood has clotted
no more to be shown.
    That saying has no meaning
For in the sea
    He is the only   fish for me

Alicia Grey

323

shoot the arrow straight

pierce life, oh poet of emotions
uplift the flesh to fate's
stretched and wrinkled marks, yet
tramp not upon the bliss of age
nor tread the wisdom of angelic souls . . .
poets lighten your heart's burden
clothing nakedness in nature's softness.
crown life's brow with morning-glories
entwined with daisies and daffodils,
touch the heart with gentle nobleness . . .
pierce life, oh poet of fate
become the priestly slave, emotionally
toiling to replace hate and tears by fruitful promise,
be quenched in happiness and cherish breath
gathering life upon your solitude
in the spent of the pilgrim shepherd,
who shelters all from desolate waste and tempest.
pierce life, oh poet of emotions
string the bow, take aim and shoot straight . . .

Edward Robert Lang

A HOSPITAL ROOM — CLEAN AND SERENE

A hospital room, clean and serene.
Yet in another is heard a groan and a moan,
Down the hall is heard the ringing of a phone.
Doctors and nurses hurrying to make their rounds,
Their wealth of medical knowledge: hopeful abounds.
The screech of an ambulance siren is heard outside,
A team runs to meet — silence! A person has died.
Still my room so clean and serene,
To others it may seem.
The pain in my head —
There seems no relief,
For years I have suffered this grief.
Doctor after doctor after doctor,
What new medications can they offer?
My life it seems with pain is doomed . . .
To suffer beyond belief.
Perhaps sleep — if it would only come
Will help me dream
That my life too could be serene.

Rozie Seltzer

ON HIGHWAY 50

Windshield wipers slap grey rain
Onto glazed highway and dirty
Swollen rivers drown the
Soggy trash and empty
Beer bottles that mate
in the ditch. OUT
of COn
      trol   SCREAming metal grating tan-
             gled STEEL shat-
                  tered pieces sprayING through
                 the air and empty
            windows — Spinning to a
        Stop.

A twisted wad of
Japanese steel like
just more
crumpled paper and broken
beer bottles
in the ditch.

Karen DeWitt

REMEMBERING

I look around my world and see,
All the little parts of me;
Old pictures, letters, books and more,
A "Hush, baby sleeping," that once donned a door;
My trunk overflows with so much to say,
Like a ride on a Harley, on a warm summer's day;
My first Valentine, from the boy next door,
My best friend and I, playing jacks on the kitchen floor;
Old school days that came and went,
Words of love that were never sent;
A wedding promising endless bliss,
Love like ours could not possibly miss;
Then one warm midsummer's morn,
Came the pride of my life, my son was born;
The bond between us day one did grow,
His playful laughter, I treasured so;
Now he's grown, he's now a man,
He works hard doing all he can;
If I could turn time back in some way,
Small words unsaid more often I would say
I love you son, and the time we've had,
And of my past, I'm so very glad!
        Lynda Needham Willis

TUG OF WAR

Gray fog covers, like a blanket,
Houses and trees on the hill.
Half of the Golden Gate Bridge
Is concealed by the misty haze.
It is shifting
From one tower of the bridge
               to the other.

Gray fog clouds travel fast;
They cover the bridge completely.
Warnings of a foghorn sound.
Who will win today?
The pale sun that manifests itself behind the clouds
Or the dense fog which rushes to cover everything?

Spots of blue appear between the clouds.
Red gleam the tower tips of the bridge
Above the dark-gray fog bank.
The misty haze is dissipating —
Struggling with the sun — changing —
Into clouds like cotton balls that encircle
The blue, sunny sky above the city and the bay.
      Elena Shaw

MASTERS OF THE UNIVERSE

"Look into my eyes." I am staring back at you.
  Words would only demean the moment . . .
  Like a faithful and powerful hero,
    your body approaches mine,
  Somewhat like a Greek god; Neptune!
"I am your goddess, Venus!
  Shhh! mythology rules us now."
The power absorbs us, and your once lustful touch is now
      Hungry; we are starving.
      Taste; it is not enough.
      Eat; my flesh is your food.
You are consumed into my senses
  as we become one in an explosion
    of pouring, hot, lava,
  bursting into chills,
  running back into each other,
    the substance that forms the core of life,
            of us,
          Man and Woman.

  We are perfectly whole;
    perfectly us.
Amy L. Horne

I SEE HIM LAUGHING

I came to shop.
I saw a psychic instead.
"I see him laughing"
the psychic said.

My heart felt like paper,
bloodless and flat.
She described my future husband —
why react like that?

She could see him and I couldn't!
Should I press for details?
No, I decided I shouldn't.

I wanted to know more
about this wondrous man
I would someday adore —
but I felt it grew late,
said my thanks,
and left the floor.

Anne Keough

INCIDENTAL

Where is land of the just?
Did she fly to sit?
Where is land of the lust?
Did she sink to pit?
That small home on poor land,
Kept strong in one piece
That small home on beach sand,
Kept free from all lease.
She lived in, but no joy,
It brought her to tear.
She lived in, as one toy,
It caused her to fear.
I look past a fogged glass,
To see night clear sky.
I look past a drowned mass
To hear Dodge truck die.
Wish I could move to past,
And change the real now.
Wish I could run too fast,
And change the know-how.

Gerard Klusak

I SAW A STAR

I saw a star
The other night,
A big, beautiful, bright star.
It sat up there in heaven
And showered the earth
With its soft, peaceful light.
I saw that star
And it filled my heart
Full of an inner peace,
A peace only I felt
And only then.
I've sought that star
Every night since,
But it seems to have disappeared,
Left the heaven
To hide its beautiful light.
I saw a star,
Awhile ago,
I saw a star,
A special star.

Candy Whitesel

WHY MUST I?

Why must I march
to the thrum
of the drum
of another man's whim
when the lights are dim?

Why must I march
to the beat
of the feet
of another man's pace
when the cards down face?

Why must I march
to the call
of the fall
of another man's tone
when his heart turns stone?

Why must I march
to the toll
of the roll
of another man's stick
when his feet aim kick?

Mary Hrenchuk Pankiw

PANKIW, MARY. Pen Name: Mary Hrenchuk Pankiw; Born: Winnipeg, Manitoba, Canada, 6-1-23; Married: 6-3-50 to Alexander Pankiw (died 12-24-68); Mother of five children; two daughters and three sons; Education: University of Manitoba, B.A., 1965; B.Ed., 1969; M.Ed., 1972; Ukranian Free University, Munich, West Germany, Ph.D., 1978; Occupation: Teacher; Memberships: Canadian Authors' Association; Manitoba Modern Language Association, President; Canadian College of Teachers, Manitoba Chapter, Treasurer; Chairperson of Manitoba Multicultural Anthology Committee; Poetry: 'Unborn Loser,' Winnipeg Free Press, 9-1-79; 'Jealousy,' Winnipeg Free Press, 9-22-79; 'Form in Space,' Pierian Spring, Spring 1979; 'What Does Santa Do All Year?' *The Stonewall Argus*, 12-19-84; 'No Time for Mother,' *Progress*, 5-12-85; Themes: *Life around me, life's experiences, reverence for life;* Comments: *Why I write: as an outlet for my emotions; very therapeutic; What I try to express: my feelings, experiences, personal philosophy of life. I feel compelled to write about what is bottled up inside of me. I can become very absorbed in writing poetry, my hobby.*

Sitting here daydreaming
     With nothing to do
I thought I'd write a line or two
          for you
     As I began to think,
  it seems I'm out of ink
So I'm still sitting here with
       nothing to do
     but think of you.

Valerie Collins

INNER JOURNEY

I would not follow those
Long and distant roads leading
Off to the horizon
For there are roads I
Have not yet explored
That lead within,
And something tells me —
Is it that secret self I hear —
That there is greater treasure
Hidden in the secret recesses
Of my being
Than I could ever hope to find
In other lands.

Donna Miesbach

HOKKAIDO FOX

The young fox, blind from birth,
sat down in the sand
on the edge of the breakers
he could only hear.
Washed toward the sea,
graced by sun and wind,
he turned his sweet face
to the East, and walked
to the shore with no fear.
Once, he looked back toward home;
blank eyes searched the open field,
but he was
alone.

Margaret Ann Jacquin

AN IRISH LOVE PRAYER

I met you by a wayside cross
   On the emerald isle of Ireland.
      The shamrocks were growing
         And God's blessing flowing.

I meant to say a prayer for you
   But my tears fell,
      And where they fell
         More shamrocks grew.

For the tears were my love
   And my prayer for you
      And my joy in you.

Helen M. Williams

Velvet, butter-colored notes
attached to glistening chrome.
We were here. We have passed —
Our living bodies reduced again
to basic elements by a mechanical
Predator.
See the remnants of our beauty —
the symbols of our force.

As the passing poet leaves behind
scrawled symbols of her visions,
so the butterfly leaves her emblem —
Her gift to us — a wordless epitaph
at the point of her departure.
She leaves her wings.

Sharon Lynn

ALIVE

Birds soaring the sky,
Ants crawling over hills,

Trees growing along lanes,
Flowers springing from pots,

Babies playing in playpens,
Grandfathers spinning tall tales,

Books of history from the past,
Pages of prophecy for the future,

These all seem quite alive!

Ruth Lowery

LITTLE ORPHAN CHILD

Weep no more my lonely child
Close your eyes and dream for a while
Think of a place you can belong
Of loving arms and caring hands

Do not regret the breath of life
Your reason for being or need to be
So great in number but one in time
Abandoned in many ways too soon forgotten

Love knows not who you are
One of another not one of my own
Fear not my Little Orphan Child
Take my hand come live with me

Juanita B. Johnson

A RAINY DAY

The clouds are billowed in the sky,
The Wind's fierce voice is calling;
And through the misty skies above
Rain's silver spears are falling.

Sometimes torrents, often showers
Mighty grey downpour;
Showers clearing, then darkening
Ever less and ever more.

Overcast still is the sky
The Wind's fierce voice is stilled;
And now the brightened skies above
Are with birdsong filled.

S. Vahni Capildeo

DAYS WITHOUT YOU

With every thought
I am trying to bring you back.
I display your portraits
everywhere:
    The Sun,
    The Sea,
    Blue Sky,
    White Sand,
    Hands of Labor,
    The Touch of Yesterday,
    The Evening Dream,
and the most favored one,
    the Smile,
I hang it a hundred times over.

Helga Maria Volk

ROOTS

The roots of the tree that blew down this spring
are still recumbent where they reached

                                    when the tree was leafing out.

Wherever I dig in the grass
                        to shape a foundation, they wriggle
and bend toward my shovel
                        like a family of snakes
                                            going everywhere
under the lawn.

Euclid is no help, his right angles and straight lines
having nothing to do
                        with where roots want to go.
                            They go where they have to go
while I
            keep making corners
                                    and straight lines :
        they have to nourish and grow;
I have to follow these lines drawn ages ago.

Robert DeYoung

TRANSCENDENCE

Cast; in roles that reach beyond our shadows, bigger than both of us
We follow the sun relentlessly, swearing
At the scarce light passing through our lives
As it determines our refracted images.
Then thanking darkness when it comes
For not letting us see the light for what it really is: a revelation that sheds the truth.

Condensed; are the years into a "last mile" walk
Through death row and beyond.
It is dark but we can see
Nothing is there anymore.
Our combined silence is deafening
Revealing what misguided, sometimes well-intentioned words never could.

Reaching; to find we are not there, for each other.
One-for-one and consequently, all-for-none; which is a dubious, thankless existence.
While only meaning to manage our lives, we managed to live beyond our means.
Seeking redemption, we continue following the sun grudgingly
Groping, blinded; by a light that should be guiding.
Destined instead, as moth to a flame.

John Gardner

A TREASURE

Wisdom lies before me as I grow older still,
Memories of my yesteryear are treasures I hold dear.
Thinking of my childhood days are the kindest thoughts I know,
Deeply woven lessons are embedded in my soul.
As days roll by and turn into years, it's over for my childhood life,
And soon my deepest thoughts and dreams are centered on being a wife.
This job itself was short but sweet, for soon I found it was not complete.
Another dream had come to mind, a baby I thought would be divine,
And so God granted us the joy of giving birth to a baby boy,
But eight weeks later to the amazement of us both,
We found we were back on the very same boat.
Another baby to bring us joy, and I felt in my heart it would be a boy.
Eleven months apart is all they were, they would have a special closeness,
We knew that for sure.
A few years have passed now and I can plainly see,
I have the most beautiful family that there ever could be.
I hope that all the treasures I have had in the past,
Will remind me that all my new ones can forever last.

A thankful wife and mother

Cindy Lee

A SPECIAL MOTHER

Mothers are so very special!
True wisdom they display.
Showing love and affection,
To their children every day.
Their smiles are like the sunshine,
Their tears, like drops of rain,
Their honesty and compassion,
Are like rainbows, bringing brightness once again.
A mother is the best friend,
A son or a daughter could ever find.
She's there whenever needed,
Bringing happiness and peace of mind.
She's there when you are happy,
She's there when you are blue,
She's there when you're in trouble,
Sharing love the whole year through.
We're thankful to our mothers,
Every day the whole year through,
We're glad God gave us mothers,
Who are as dear and sweet as you.

Elaine Teasdale

DIABOLICAL FORCE

Diabolical Force, I spit in your eye!
If only I had the power
To vanish all your tomorrows.
Go home to that bottomless pit
Filled with snakes and crawling things,
Where you can all consume each other!

Diabolical Force, I spit in your eye!
Why don't you satisfy your blood thirst
With the Manson's, the O'Hara's . . . your kind.
Why don't you leave the rest of us alone?
Why don't you just go home?
You grotesque and hateful malignant sore!

Diabolical Force, I spit in your eye!
If someday we should meet — you and I,
I'll deny you the pleasure of tasting my fear.
I'll lie down and die without even a tear.
My soul will rise — immune to your poisonous slime.
And someday it will witness your final demise.

Daisy Russell

INTO THY HANDS

The doctor said, "Your daughter has cancer."
And his words kept ringing in my ears
As my world crumbled all around me
Breaking my heart and bringing out my tears.
How could this have happened to her life?
Lord, is she being punished or am I?
I've got many unanswered questions Lord,
As I turn my prayers to You up high.
I'm putting her life into Your hands Lord
As I'm trying to cope with this devastating news
That has her life perched on the edge of a cliff
Like a hangman at the end of a noose.
Lord, give me the strength to carry on
And believe that tomorrow stretches on forever
As I put her life into Thy hands
And try to accept the news of her cancer.
This is the hardest thing I've ever had to do
Accept the news that my child is terminally ill.
But with Your help Lord, I'll make it through
And be able to accept that this is Your will.

Shirley B. O'Keefe

MISSING YOU

Here, I sit all alone again missing you so.
I can't manage a grin.
My thoughts are so strong,
that I'm convinced you have never been wrong.

I'm a very difficult person to understand.
but my reason for living is our tiny wedding band.
I have always worked to the best of my ability.
trying my best to meet my responsibility.
As the sun warmed the earth today,
my love for you grew like foliage in May.
I love you more than I can explain.
I miss you so much I can feel the lonely pain.

I sometimes fear the strength of my love for you.
may at times be so strong. it makes you blue.
I'm jealous of course.
But, I feel that if I wasn't things could be worse.
Another lonely day has come and gone.
with all my thoughts of only one.
As the time slowly comes for me to retire,
I wish you here, rather than where you are.

Sue E. Armstrong

THE COWBOY

Long and lean, his arms are mean, his face tanned from the sun
From dusty boots to fiery eyes he's streamlined like a gun
Shiny hair waved darkly 'neath his faded cowboy hat
His strong arms showed that he could fight —
His eyes showed more than that.

A silver-bullet gray were eyes that glanced about the place
He quickly sized up fighters, no expression on his face
His style was typed a legend that no western could enhance
I had to make him notice me — I had to take the chance.

I made my way up to him and I handed him a glass
He saw me through the smoke and grabbed my arm as I walked past
For a while I loved and held a man no one could ever hold
And though I dreamed I'd be the one — I never let him know.

The nights went by — I looked for him to saunter back again
But since that night no sign of him has come to ease the pain
He's gone away back riding — alone he'll always be
On the endless plains of wind and stars
Where there's no room for me.

Colleen Corrigan

MY MOTHER

Mother's Day comes once a year.
We should remember the ones so dear.

Mother was with me in my peace and fear.
She was there to help me dry my tear.

When she told me something to do.
It was best for me I knew.

How I loved my mother
I didn't need love for another.

She loved me from the time she gave me birth.
She loved me until the time she left this earth.

She is now in a heavenly place.
When my life on earth is over I will see
    her sweet face.

Love your mother here on earth.
Remember her after she leaves this earth.

Ella H. Hollander

FIDDLER CRABS

Fiddler Crabs in the middle of
    a tomato field
Red circles contrast green fields
The colors of the crabs contrast
    the scene . . .
A bizarre ritual,
    Almost a dance
  Up, then down
  Up, then down
So many colors, so many hands
    The sun beats down 'til
    the flies seek shade
    The dance of the crabs
    goes on
    The beat's never lost
        Up, then down
        Up, then down
'Til the red disappears
    from the green

Jo Hendijani

HENDIJANI, MARY JOANNE. Pen Name: Jo Hendijani; born: Ft. Lauderdale, Florida, 10-11-51; Married: to Jahanriz Hendijani; Education: one year away from B.S. in Psychology, last enrolled at Nova University, plan to attend F.A.U. in September; Occupation: Bookkeeper; Memberships: Former Member of Florida Freelance Writer's Association; Current Member, City News Service (also enrolled in NIA courses); Awards: 'Thorns,' and 'Some Seek Silence,' Ursus Press, two selected poems; Poetry: 'Freely,' 2-85; *Window Pictures,* collection of poetry, 1-85; Other Writings: "White Chick Growing Up Black," short story, 12-84; "The Sayids of Iran," article (psychic), 2-84; "Grandma's Escape," short story, 12-84; Comments: *I have traveled a lot (Iran, England, the Islands), and I try very hard to present the unusual beauty I sense in everyday things. I am also enchanted with children's eyes — how they see things so clearly. I am an incurable romantic.*

LEARNING TO LOVE

When I can put my arms
Around the whole world
Making no difference —
Of Color or Creed
Realizing, under the skin
All blood is just as red

Helping all, with their every need
Plus all living things
In the air, on land
And in the sea
Feeling their grief and pain
Hunger and their strain

Always putting "God" first
And others before myself
My giving up a little —
Only a few earthly things
To help my brother
In his time of need
And help him be a better man you see

Then, I feel very strong
The "God" within me
And "His" arms about me
I know then —
I have learned to love

Lamorah S. Spivey

SERPENT

Snakes in the grass and leaves,
Looking for food, smelling the air,
Listening for movement.
A coiled tube wiggling in the sun,
He's ready to strike when danger calls.
Moving silently with no arms or legs.
As he looks for a warm rock to sleep on —
Hiding from noises.
Slowly, silently, slithering —
Waiting for its next victim,
Basking in the warmth of the sun.

Kevin Biekert

THE FAIRY

In pure delight
I watched one night
A fairy glide on gossamer wings
So sheer and frail
O'er moonlit dale.
Persistently that memory clings.

The elves came out
And stood about.
They laughed to see the fairy play.
An ugly troll
Out for a stroll
Sat down and watched the dancing fey.

And, but a child,
My heart went wild.
I felt the magic in the air.
The night unfurled
A fairy world.
I blinked, and there was nothing there.

The memory burned,
So I returned
To live once more that magic spell.
I looked again,
As I had then.
There was no fairy in the dell.

Helen Gloria Fiske

I AM THE BLACK WOMAN

I am the Black Woman
Born out of darkness
Into a world of light.
I have borne the pain of slavery
Which I can't undo.
My black people
Equal
Black and beautiful.
I am the Black Woman
Who was born out of darkness.
I will not be put down
for being black.
I will always stand up
for my people.
Being the Black Woman
I am.
I am a Black Woman
Born in darkness.
I have been abased and degraded
for what I am.
I have scars
printed on my memory
to last a million years.

Angela A. Scott

A PORTRAIT

A golden frame.
A pretty face.
A silken gown, all trimmed in lace.
The sweetest thing I have ever seen.
An answer to a lover's dream.

I glanced again, as I walked by.
Her tiny ankles, silk-clad thigh.
Inscription, that was etched upon.
With all my love,
I give to John.

Where is John? Wonder, where?
Did he know? Or really care?
This portrait of a lovely queen,
Among these cast-offs, could be seen.

I walked another swap meet aisle.
My conscience, I couldn't reconcile.
I hurried back, just one more time.
I bought her portrait
For a dime.

Haydn Dustman

The cottonwood explodes
its strength
into tiny tendril-lined seeds
floating at the whim of wind
bouncing on delicate spokes
off window sill and pane
on to other places, spaces
— mostly lost.

One came in to visit me —
danced off the toy bear
and on to the rug
stopped for a moment
before it tiptoed
out the door.
I warned it
silently
that there was no better fare
out there,
but it kept to its business
rounded the corner
and continued
on its way.

Janet E. M. Andersen

DISTANT HEARTS

It seems I watched a million mornings
From your shoulders in the dawn,
I'd smile to say "I love you," but turn to find you gone.
I reached to take your hand
To hold forevermore,
But it slipped and dreams went flying, falling scattered on the floor.
I touch you with my words
To bring you close to me,
But words can't fill the emptiness, that's deep inside you see.
I cry in hopes your heart will hear
My tears, my last reserve,
To reach you now would mean the end, to a pain I can't deserve.
Time has made us memories
And kept us far apart,
For the road is rarely traveled between two distant hearts.

Reashea Hodges

NOT TOGETHER NOW

And here I stand, my heart in my heart in my trembling hand.
Free to the touch, loving you both so much.
From time to time I wonder who I am.

Having such an abundance of love, yet so little to give.
Today it's so hard to live.
So many wants and needs being fulfilled by two and just one of me.

It's unfair I know, but tonight my empty heart longs to be loved
and I know if I call, you'll be here loving me.

You know, I never meant to hurt either of you.
From time to time I wonder who I am and live forever   not together,
now.

Judie Sinclair

MY CHILDREN

I bore two children, both I adore. First a girl and then a boy. The
girl — she grew up, got married, she lives with me no more. Though we see
each other often, we talk, we shop, we sew. Things are not like they once
were. There comes the time she says, "I must go," for he will soon be in for
dinner and she must be on her way. She has other things to do before it grows
late.

The boy — he finished High School and when only seventeen he joined the
U.S. Navy. Now he sails the troubled seas. He bought for me a present. Lovely
Japanese Chimes. Tucked them away lovingly, thinking everything was fine.
Until they hit a typhoon in their hiding place they lay. Then all at once every-
thing was all over the place. Now our little Japanese Chimes had a terrible
wreck for they came crashing down on that destroyer deck. They had a Navy
burial. They were buried at sea and that took care of the present, the one my
son bought for me.

Pat Griffin

I never have, nor ever shall,
    possess any right to own another person.
It is only my privelege to love and understand,
    to care for with empathy, to edify with patience and tenderness,
to genuinely and intimately desire another person's good,
    and to fight for well-being and meaning.
It is my duty, yes, I ought do no other,
    than to pursue justice in the face of wrong-doing,
to heal though others wound, to trust, to listen, to provoke no anger,
    to give, even in the presence of those who know only how to take.
It is my self whom I give away, knowing full well,
    in giving I receive.
It is I who die daily, knowing full well,
    it is dying that I live.
For only as I do these things am I a person;
    and, in being a person, I no longer own myself, but,
Behold! I am yours.

Ron Snyder

THE POTOMAC, FROM MARYLAND HEIGHTS.

LOST LOVE

Once you were my guy, always by my side
Through thick or thin, whether near or far
I always knew I was in your heart

We parted though I know not why
Years have passed without you by my side
I wonder about you, you crossed my mind
I always thought you would be mine

I only wish I could be so strong
To forget the love we once shared
All of the good times, and all of the bad

When I look at your picture, or just have a thought
I get a pang in my heart, I can't even talk
If I could ever see you again, I know just the feeling I would experience
My knees would go weak, my heart skip a beat
My mouth would not open, and tears start to fall
Knowing the love we once shared, and know there's no love at all

The years have gone by, my feelings are still the same
I love you as I always did, and I can still feel the pain.

June Drao

DRAO, JUNE KAY. Born: Brooklyn, New York, 7-10-48; Memberships: Credit Women International; Comments: *This is the very first poem I am having published. It is very exciting for me. I write how I feel about people and situations in my life and those around me. If I feel something strongly I sit down and write about it. I try to make people feel the same things that I do, and bring a situation to light.*

THROUGH THE YEARS!

Through the years, we've shared a lot,
Most memories could never be bought;
We were right and sometimes we were wrong,
But we learned by our mistakes and made it right along;

During the years we may have lost friends,
But for some — their friendships will never end;
There wasn't all happiness involved — there was sadness too,
Illness, growing pains, friends fighting etc. we did pull through;

Our class of '85 deserves the best,
Because we were different from all the rest;
Of course at first together we fought,
But along the way we were taught;

To treat others the way you would have them treat you,
Really it's not that hard to do;
Because now when we look back,
We were the best of friends that's a fact.

Dina Dilucente

MY FRIEND

Life was made for dreamers.
    Dreamers we must always be.

Through thoughts and silent prayers,
    we'll build the world we see.

Our world will not be for scoffers,
    or people who lag behind.

But rather for those who are cheerful,
    and lovingly considerate and kind.

When fate slips in for a moment,
    and closes the door on your heart.

Stand fast to your dreams of tomorrow.
    Stand fast to your need of self.

While today we must bend for others,
    our souls must never be still.

For our dreams are of things much greater
    than make up our day to day.

Hold fast my friend as your courage
    has helped to soothe my way.

Hold fast my friend as tomorrow,
    is but a moment away.

Mary M. Hicks

LOST

What have you done to my golden field
where memories of youth and joy did yield?

Where once I ran through grasses tall
with carefree speed to nature's call

In warmth of sun and cushioning green
my cares were small and life serene

On golden days my path did glow
with sun and sky and me below

I loved that field and all its ground
A perfect place that I had found

I gave it thought, I gave it song
My field and I were firm and strong

I only left it for a while
to learn life's stage and its new style

When I came back the other day
machines had cut my field away

And in its place were structures tall
fading out my nature's call

Blocks and steel of great design
can ne'er replace that field of mine.

Betty J. Wilson

PLEA

Lord, send another planet
Quick, quick, quick
Because we've made this one
Sick, sick, sick.

Margaret G. Denton

JUST A COUNTRY GIRL

I was born to a country life,
Mostly good, but with some toil and strife.
Living on the farm was never a bore —
There always seemed to be a chore.
To a one-room country school we did go
To learn our ABC's just so,
With a pot-bellied stove in the middle of the floor
And a water jug over by the door.
The water was pumped by hand
From a well sunk deep in the sand.
Two prairie fires we did fight,
Each of us with all our might,
To save our school house on the hill.
To think of that still gives me quite a chill.
We went to a little country church, too,
To listen to a sermon, sitting on a hard wooden pew.
I'm sad to say, though I remember them still,
Gone are the church and the school on the hill.
But the farm is still in family hands,
And that, I think is just GRAND!

Sharon L. Kreutzer

MUSE ON PAPA

This man, whose face and wit and charm
Known by legions, barroom elite and like
Whose word could move the mighty
And quell the beast more oft than not.

His quest, like yours and mine
Though spent not in hunger, pain and kind
Would sometime stop to rest and quench his thirst
(Harry was good for this and that).

This man, whose pen spent in beauty, joy and flight
Journeyed 'cross the mountains, seas and lofty heights
Soared with eagles more powerful than the storm
Did seek to route the demon from his soul.

The old man of the sea, the roar of a lion
Mountains bolder than a man's whisper
Mere mutants of this mighty giant
Fashioned dreams for us mortals to see
And thus, did make us free.

Patricia Elmore

ENGLISH LIT. 101

Innocently lying beneath the pines
Upon a bed of needles with intricate lines
Beyond my feet there lies the shore
Whispering echoes of "Nevermore"

With Shakespeare seething into my mind
And Poe's philosophy of mankind

Finding myself far from the place I used to know
No pines towering above me
No waters to and fro

Only a space inbetween time
Not a reason, nor a rhyme
Everything there just had to be mine

Though the echo still ringing inside my head
It wasn't the "Raven" nor was I dead . . .
Just inbetween lines of books that I've read.

Barbara DeVandre

TIME

Looking at your baby in the crib,
Time is standing still.
Tick, tick, tick, tick.
Graduation day, remembering your own,
Where are all my friends?
Tick, tick, tick.
His marriage day comes and goes,
Old memories rekindled.
Twenty years in a day.
Tick, tick.
Grandchildren! Tears, more tears,
Yesterday Grandpa Bill bought me a toy.
Tick.
Great Grandchildren! Again more tears.
Joy, happiness, contentment, silence, peace.
Tock.

Reg Gabriel, Jr.

PAY DAY

It's pay day again and I'm feeling down
There's just not enough money to go around.
My take-home is never as much as I'm worth —
I guess there's no good job anywhere on this earth.
After taxes and bills there's just nothing left
I'm a hard-working pauper; I'm a victim of theft.
But today I start over, a new pay week begins.
I hope for more hours before this one ends.
No matter how much or how little I make
I'll keep on a-grinding until my back breaks.
There is little pleasure when pay day comes,
But there'd be even less, if I didn't have one.

Theodore R. Munsch

What's the ball without the bounce?
What's a cat without the pounce?
What's a heart without the pain?
What's the sky without the rain?
What's the ladder without the height?
What's the bulb without the light?
What's the land without the sea?
Without a doubt, what would I be?
What's the life without a clue?
And what am I when I'm not with you?
What's the earth without the space?
What's the body without the face?
What's the arm without the hand?
What's the beach without the sand?
What's the pencil without a pen?
What's the army without the men?
The answer is without a doubt,
that something is nothing when with a without.

Julie Derouin

LIVING IN A FANTASY WORLD

1: Living in a fantasy world. Where none of my dreams
   will ever come true. Although, I've been living with
   you; I'm still dreaming.

2: In a fantasy world things will never change.
   How can I gain the strength to resolve my fantasy?

Bridge: The strength to face up to reality with all
        its pain. The heartaches of life and things
        which plague my heart with fear. Someday things
        will turn out right or remain the same.

        Living in a fantasy world. Where none of my
        dreams will ever come true. Although, I've
        been living with you I'm still dreaming.

Brenda Gordon

THE PASSER-BY

Understand.
Preserve the land.
It's in our hands —
    until we die.
Does time see us
    "The Passer-by?"

Joseph F. Hauch

STILL

Listen . . .
            To the sounds of dawn . . .
Early morning quiet,
Mankind new awakening,
And as the hours spend,
            Silence becomes noise.

Kibbie Thomas

ideas are like walls
        hemming me in
            chaining me to my desk
                to my pens and paper
when i'd rather be running
        through a meadow green and gold
            with the sun shining all around
                and lazy golden butterflies

Cyndi Crow

NEW LOVE

Your touch so new,
        yet old in many ways.
Remains on my skin,
        warm for days.

Joan McCoy

WINTER'S JUST AROUND
THE BEND

A gentle breeze plays with my hair,
squirrel scatters for food of its share,
Leaves drifting in the wind,
Winter's just around the bend.

Jeffery Gauvin

REVERSION

The touch of a soft withered hand
Memories of castles in the sand
A thought of things that might have been
The meeting of an old friend.

Marie Jenkins

LOST IN THOUGHT

Quiet and peaceful I sit alone
Thinking about a time that passed
Wondering if my mind can clone
A happy thought I hope will last

Carl A. Sernoskie

NOON
To My Wife

Midday stretches out over moss-grown slates!
Midday-mother-of-pearl amidst bronzed roofs and stupas' feathers!
Midday-dew-drenched, snoozing in the arbored silence!
Light-showered-tree, sifted sunshine!
And, coming to life: a tree tainted by the horizon. Barely blue. Barely light.
And I rouse myself, strolling on the sands under shady bowers barely peppered
with shadow, lonesome and sole, walking towards the beach, at high noon.
Sea-breeze-breath brushing the leaves!
Arbored sweat, kissing my neck!
A ray of sunlight quivers in the nook of a branch, and balmy sweet,
a tree smiles at the praise of a bird.

Thus, I shall wait until dusk, until night sinks in.
And when, in turn, the day sleeps in slumbers, and when o so softly,
the sky will starspangle the frill of the waves, I shall know to come to you

    For Your love burns the oil of my lamp.

Nicobar

THE KEY

I sat thinking one afternoon wondering were there any answers to
        the questions about life I had.
Wanting for nothing and being at peace with others, I still felt
        incomplete.
Something from my life was missing and I could not rest until I
        found the key, the key to unlock all that was missing from
        my life.
I set out on my holy quest to find the elusive key, to unlock the
        doors of my soul so that I would be whole.
The search took me far and wide, meeting people and seeing places
        that were new to me.
But because of the intensity and savagery of my search, I left an
        ugly mark on all who came in contact with me.
After years of searching and inner and outer turmoil, I thought I
        had found the key to the problems of my life, the key that
        would unlock my soul and make me whole and at peace.
As I place the key into my soul I found that my values and outlook
        on life had been twisted by desire and obsession.
And all too late I realized that the lock had been changed.

Frank Brevard

IF I COULD FLY

If I could fly with wings that would take me high into the sky;
I'd see the land below, God's own kingdom far below.
I could soar high into heaven's open door,
beyond the stars to the land where I'd be free from pain,
free from worry.
If only I could fly,
Birds can fly,
Bees can fly, there are planes that take you high into the sky,
yet no wings have I.
Rockets go far into space way beyond tomorrow, there may be a place,
Out there for me, but today I am here, I must make do until
I find the wings that will set my soul free, to climb,
to the top of God's blue sky.
Touch the moon and stars above.
Oh why can't I fly?
No wings have I!
Birds have wings,
Planes have wings.
Why? Oh why can't I?

Helena Metcalf

QUIET WINTER

Winter, quiet winter.
No voices break the stillness
only the soft creak of the
woodstove fighting winter,
cold winter.
Snow blankets all
vague and quiet.
I slumber,
my clock has stopped,
winter is one long night
I sleep in its dark womb,
waiting.
I see reflections in the ice;
past, future and a globe sun
moving north.
The ice shatters.
I pick up the pieces
slowly assembling;
silent winter continues
and the stark silence
of the mind waiting,
patiently waiting, for
the clamor of spring
the crescendo of summer
far away from quiet winter.

Suzanne Murray

BLUE DAWN

Let me lead you,
    let me warn you —
Before you enter,
    just peek through.

Cover up your mouth,
    or they'll hear you yell —
You cannot enter Heaven,
    unless you've lived through Hell.

You'll never know what awaits you,
    in the aftermath of life —
The clergy seek the answers,
    but their ignorance is rife.

I have seen in all scurry,
    only to seek the red —
The Divine Gates will close,
    when Lucifer strikes you dead.

The message is quite lucid,
    from beginning to end —
The children cry in anguish,
    for Lucina has failed again.

Anthony Rutella

I'M YOUNG — ONLY SEVENTY-FIVE

Oh, now that I'm — seventy-five,
Most say — "Be happy — you are alive!
Take it easy — that's real pleasure,"
I've lived a lifetime — to be sure,
A new chapter, I will now do —
Something I want for me — not you!
I'll write about all those long years,
Of work, laughter, pleasure and tears.
I'll do well for seventy-five,
Yes — going to try to stay alive
Doing many different things a day,
No pressure, problems in the way.
Now — each twenty-four hours are mine —
Travel, music, new, new, friend and dine,
Can't sit and rock as you all say,
Going to try to do things my way,
For a much longer life I'll strive,
'Cause I'm young just seventy-five!

Helen Meyer

THE EXECUTION

As I walk in feeling dirty
And overwrought with guilt;
Alone she sits, crying silently,
Clinging to the tiny quilt.

As I pay the man his money,
And prepare for the execution;
Across town she stays alone,
In her new found destitution.
For what she has lost,
I'm about to kill,
For when hers was born,
It was born still.

You see how funny life is,
And how different
Things turn out.
So if you're smart
You'll never think,
You have anything planned out.

There is a way
Without any doubt,
To avoid the execution,
For somewhere there is
A loving soul,
Willing to take over,
Without any retribution.

For what you may not want,
They may always pray for.

Kathy McGowen

THE WALL

At first, the woman objected
When He showed her blueprints
Of the wall he planned.
She wanted illumination, windows
Or a simple skylight.
        A wall will give breadth,
        He said,
        Digging the foundation.

When she found herself in shadows,
She beat fists on granite and slate
Asserting with anvils.
Fear made her shrewish
Her chisel of gall
Ignored.

In time, conflict compressed
And the Wall took shape.
Aloof.
Obscuring openness
Defending differences.

With years, a pillar arose
Firmly mortared
Darkly silent.

Tears dried to apathy
As Woman quietly,
Privately,
Added
Bricks.

Margarete Miller

DISAPPOINTED

When you think the door of love is closed
    and you have lost your way; —
Don't forget you've broken a heart
    "Just to pass another day."

Callie Louise Drewry

THE VIKING

The Viking with long limbs and flowing
blonde hair.
The cool smile, the blue eyes which
masked true feelings, was that fear?
They pulled away as I clutched at
her — a fast moving cloud out of reach
we turned and walked away looking
back at each other — was that a tear?
"let's keep in touch, call me"
I smile now as I will when my
hair is white
A long limbed form laughing with blonde
hair blowing freely in the wind running
wildly through the meadow
The mink which stared at us aloof
and beautiful
We will shed tears separately because
The time wasn't right.

Daniel L. Casias

CASIAS, DANIEL L. Born: Dawson, New
Mexico; Single; Education: Washington State
University, Ph.D., Counseling, Psychology,
1978; University of New Mexico, M.A., Coun-
seling 1978; University of New Mexico, B.A.,
Secondary Education, 1970; Occupation: Clini-
cal Psychologist; Memberships: American Psy-
chological Association; Other writings: "The
Journey of Christy Lynn," fiction, young adult,
unpublished, 1984; Comments: *I strive for truth
and emotion into the inner psyche — of what
one feels when he/she is by themselves, of how
we perceive physical beauty and how relation-
ships shape us — as we are what we have and
will experience.*

LIFE

Not to snuff the candle
Or bushel the light

Short the grieving
Long the night

Helen M. Dawson

SITTING ON TOP OF THE WORLD

Where may I find a moment's peace
From the humdrum of the crowd,
The schemings of the office,
The telephone's ringing loud?
In a Boeing 737,
Guyana Airways brand,
3100 miles above the Atlantic,
Captain Hall controls in hand!

Now drifting into peaceful sleep
When nothing's there to see;
And radar guides our airship,
Artificial as could be;
Now rocking, swaying gaily
In the ocean current's hold;
Now gliding most serenely
As panoramas unfold!

Where can I find a moment's peace
From the humdrum of the crowd?
In the humdrum of a Boeing
Way high among the clouds!

Norma Evans-Barber

PASSION

As I await you,
my body shivers with rising passion.
My blood running hot,
as my hunger for you starves.

Your body,
so warm to the touch,
As the fire inside you burns.
Your hands so tender,
and so soft,
as they caress my body.

The excitement in me
runs wild,
as you hold me tight
and kiss my tender mercies.

And then at last
my love,
we come face to face
in passion.

Kattie Danzeisen

RISKY ROMANCE

It's like a delicate spring flower
That needs special, gentle care.
To keep the beautiful bloom alive,
Must be nurtured in Valentine's Day air.
Yes, reaping romance is risky business,
Can't let it wilt in the harsh heat,
Must be fed in order to survive,
But it never counts the cost
'Cause what's given in love
Is emotional progress gained,
Never financial time lost.

And no, it hasn't been easy
Keepin' the romantic flame burnin' bright,
Almost blown away by callous chill
Gripping the wintry night.
Like a sensational, scandal sheet story,
No one ever believes what you say.
Laughed at, scorned and ignored,
I don't like it, but I don't care.
'Cause the pain all melts away,
When I get to match your lovin' stare.

Keith Higgins

A LADY I ONCE KNEW

She came to me in the spring
Like a blossoming flower
Planted in my midst
Her presence enhanced me
Her laughter was my joy
Her smile made me her friend
Her swan-like poise
Told me that she
Was a lady
But like all flowers of spring
I knew that I could not keep her
That winter would take her away
I am grateful for the few moments
That I had her with me
Though short was her stay
Her smile, her beauty
And her laughter
Have remained with me
Though she has long since
Gone away

Garey D. Frierson

FRIERSON, GAREY DARNELL. Born: Bronx, New York; Married: 7-21-73 to Clarice; Education: Queensboro Community College, Associate Degree in Lab. Tech., 1976; Occupations: United Postal Service; Memberships: Fredrick Douglass Center For Creative Arts; Poetry: 'Rains of Monsoon,' Vietnam poem, Blind Beggar Press, 1983; 'Fadding Notes,' jazz poem, Blind Beggar Press, 1982; 'Got A Job For You,' inflation, *Presstime*, 1981; 'No One Ever Said He'd Last Forever,' sports, *Presstime*, 1980; Comments: *I do not limit my themes to any one area. My subjects range from love poems, music poems, political poems to nature poems. I write as a means of expressing my personal feelings about a given subject, person or event that has stirred my emotions.*

PIGS, AN AWARENESS

I remember when Blondie, the runt
My grandfather gave me,
Had nine.
A child's mind can accept
Nine miracles.
I examined each one
Carefully;
They were pink
And squeally
And wonderful.
The old man died.
The bicycle I bought
With pig profits is gone.
Blondie became a sausage
And only the moment remains.

Vess Quinlan

QUINLAND, L. VESS. Born: Eagle, Colorado, 11-23-40; Married: 9-6-59 to Arla Quinlan; Education: High School Graduate; Occupations: Cowboy, Logger, Truck Driver, Farmer; Memberships: U.S. Committee on Irrigation and Drainage for International Conference on Irrigation and Drainage; Poetry: 'Spring,' 1984; 'Calvine,' 1984; 'On Dreams,' 1983; 'Reaching the Colt,' 1985; 'Selling Out,' ballad, 1963; Comments: *I started writing cowboy poetry many years ago. I attended the Cowboy Poetry Convention at Echo, Nevada in 1985. I write mostly about little things that really matter, but tend to get lost in our rush to become rich or famous or loved.*

WHATEVER MAKES ME

Whatever makes me is all inside,
It's not my face,
It's not my eyes,
It's not the pretty clothes I wear,
It's not the color of my hair,
It's not my clean white teeth,
It's all under far beneath,
All in my heart, snug and warm,
Ringing like a little gold charm.

Angie Atkins

I'M NOT ALONE

Way down here, far from home,
I sit in my room, but I'm not alone.
I've a friend I did not know I had.
He talks to me, when I'm feeling sad.
He is company to me, when I stay in my room a lot.
The only sound he makes is tic toc, tic toc, tic toc.
I stand looking out my window feeling all alone,
My thoughts become of you, in memories I have known.
I get so sad, when I think of that a lot,
But then I hear him, tic toc, tic toc, tic toc.
There is no one here to talk to, or hold me tight,
To kiss me in the morning, or hug me at night,
To greet me, when I come home at five o'clock.
Until I hear him, tic toc, tic toc, tic toc.
I pick him up, and hold him with a gentle love,
As I wind him up, and put him on the shelf above.
I hope he never loses his tic-er or pops his toc,
For way down here, far from home, he is all I got,
And he talks to me, tic toc, tic toc, tic toc.

William Edward Blacklin

BLACKLIN, WILLIAM EDWARD. Born: Cumberland, Maryland, 12-18-51; Married: 6-5-71 to a beautiful lady Mary Ann (Wright) Blacklin. She gives me much support — thank you! Education: Fort Hill High School, Cumberland, Maryland (enjoyed English, Poetry, Writing, and Art — majored in Auto Mechanics); Lincoln Technical Institute (furthering my education in mechanics); Occupation: Diesel Mechanic; Poetry: 'Visit to a Grave,' 'A Special Gift,' mother's day poem; Other writings: *Numps, Grumps & Dandelions,* children's story book in rhyme; *The Rainbow Maker,* children's story book in rhyme; *Watch Out! Here Comes Dale,* children's story book in rhyme; Comments: *I write because I enjoy it. Poetry is a way I can express myself in what I am feeling. When you read poems, they give you that unique moment when you can become the writer's mind or heart, and touch inner feelings, and see things you never have before. Those special feelings are what I try to express. I like writing fantasy stories for children, with a little realism between the lines, something they can dream about, but then think: maybe it could be!*

LUNAR TRYST

(Moonrise over Lake Ontario during August)

The moon slips silently over lapping waves,
    and brushes against the hot, summer-soft night.
She mimics fall's sunrise, as she boldly shaves
    a sliver off evening, and takes a small bite
        of the horizon . . .

Climbing the water's verge, that round, brilliant mass
    trades her sanguine splendor for warm, yolk yellow.
She sheds this for silver, to clothe her slow pass
    over star-dappled lake, keeping her mellow,
        lofty liaison . . .

Stephanie A. Kalicki

RIVER STYX: DA CAPO

The seat of my baggy trousers shines
As I grow old now before my time
No more dimes for coffee can I find

The boat fills with sad, sullen faces
Etched by streams of countless moon chases
For the stars in far-flung dream places

Ripless, still waters circle our core
As silent Charon smiles evermore
Waiting for us to enter death's door

I puncture the universe with pen
And discover that men never win
But just envision what could have been

And what will be of tomorrow's child
If she is seized by Erebus' wild
Dance of nothingness — endless and pre-styled

Erskine D. Henderson

HENDERSON, ERSKINE D. Born: Aurora, Colorado; Education: Wesleyan University, B.A., 1971; Columbia University School of Law, J.D., 1976; Occupation: Attorney.

MATRIX

            determined
Right here and
Nowhere else.

On a plane in space, defined by clearly, distinctly
Demarcated lines,
Of exact length and breadth and depth.

It is like a science; there
Are alphas and omegas and variables;
Yet, it is more exacting:

For even its constants vacillate and vary, shrink
And grow, concretize and evanesce,
Transfix and transform,
With the most subtle ionic punctuation.

On this landscape, whose geography is built
Upon the topography of the mind:
The trees are drawn, the rocks sculpted,
The water brushed, the characters animated,
Inspired and infused,
The air is hung
With care and precision.

I wonder how and how long it took the Almighty Above
To decide the shape and flavor of the strawberry
And on which He first decided.

Todd Young

Written and dedicated to Ed Kaske,
3-13-53 — 10-15-84

You carried a rough image with your leather and your chains,
but few of your friends knew you were as gentle as they came.

When you rode your Harley bike to work, others would whisper as they
stared . . .
"hey, do you believe that biker is a nurse in critical care?"

Just to be with other bikers you'd travel to Sturgis once a year.
Your favorite food was steak and you'd drink — Budweiser beer.

All these things meant the world to you with them you'd never part —
and when it came to caring for patients Ed Kaske — you were all heart!!!

You always took pride in your nursing because you loved your occupation —
and it was just part of your nature to give patients comfort, care and
dedication.

Your lifestyle was unique, your personality was magic.
One can only wonder why it had to end so tragic.

You were riding your pride and joy just before your death,
and where you once saved peoples' lives you fought for your last breath.

Yes, you were very special what more could be said
Except that we all love you and we're gonna miss you Ed.

                              forever with you, your fiance — I am

        Lou Ann Mellinger

WEAR DO I GO FROM HERE?

The fact is . . . I've put on a few pounds.
You want to talk denial? You want to hear irrationality? Try these:
    — my exercise makes my muscles more dense. It's O.K.
    — my scale is not that accurate; forget it.
    — my proportions are appropriate for my age and build. Never mind.
    — I need my nutrition. Don't get foolish about dieting. And others.
Then, I tried on last year's pants.

They

                looked

                        like

                                hell.

Considering the options available to me now, I ponder . . .

Should I starve myself and strain myself and
get back into the damned pants . . .
(which are practically worn out anyway)???
                or
should I give in, at long last, and buy
some pants in a larger size???

Let me think . . .

When is the next class reunion?

        Marilee S. Niehoff

SYMPATHY

Birds sound so sweetly near;
Flutter of wings go past me;
Pecking on my window . . . the beggars!
My heart goes out to them.

Swiftly they glide this way and that;
I wonder if they will come back.
Remember me, remember me, they cry . . .
When winter's back.

I give them feed in a house of glass,
They watch as I fill it full.
Swooping down until all is gone . . .
Waiting, waiting for more.

The winter is so cruel to them;
Their tiny legs like twigs,
Huddled in the tree for warmth,
My heart goes out to them.

        Nikki Scott

SCHEHEREZADE

Not the Arabian tale
Told to a Sultan to save the bride
Too much the touch of now
To be the kingdom, phantasy —

Plethora of the richest
Rarest of all
None but a few to have the joy
A few hours to indulge —

Difficult to catch the phrase
It may not be
Grant the power
To put it justly —

Most not to know
The glory
To have seen and had
Scheherezade, orchid

        Rebecca I. Christ-Janer

MY REFLECTION

Waving blues speak with me
with actions — for knowing no
other. Vibrant rays
release opinions of gratitude.

As I look upon the water
what I see is abnormal —
untrue. Standing upon river
bank, I see someone. Long and
unknown, thin and disguised,
transparent and unreal.

I stare into this picture,
studying its every clue.
Difficult to figure, yet
obvious as fact. The someone
in the sea, staring —
eye to eye . . . approving of its
observation; the other me.

        Lori Galloway

A RACE WITHOUT WINNERS

I once ran a race, a simply useless race
at quite a fast pace.
        Notice the strain on my face. The result
of the race?
                A head like leather
                A heart like lace.
                Hard to penetrate, easy to break.
Now my heart seems hard
  I seem to have lost
                        The feelings I once had
                                And the consequences are sad

At times I can't cry,
  Even when "to tear" would show no weakness
at all
Don't try to understand, just cushion my fall
I once was here,
  but that was long ago
Now there seems to be a stranger in my place
The eyes are still blue
  but the smile's a bit strange
and something's missing in the face.

John Wesley Seale II

TO PARENTS OF CHILDREN NOT YET GROWN

Don't confront me with my failures —
I'm still looking for myself,
And I'm sure to make mistakes.
But I don't ask, either, for complete submission
  to all my whims and my will.
To give in to me because you love me
Could be just as bad as
Opposing me completely without reason.

What I need is not an extreme —
Just someone who believes in moderation.
Someone who's been through these things before,
And can lend some advice ever so often;
Someone who can take my emotions
And untangle them carefully,
Like countless wires in fine machinery that
  must be put together just so . . .

So, please, don't be too harsh with me,
Because I'm not finished yet.
Give me some room to learn and to grow,
And just be there when I need you.

Pamela Ann Pipkin

I SAW A MAN

I saw a man walking down the road
  worn out shoes, tattered clothes.

In his hand a little bag, I wonder
  is that all he had.

His face was weathered from wind and sun,
  I thought of a family, did he have one.

He had a beard with hair of gray, I wonder,
  Had he chosen to live that way.

An old man like he was, I wonder,
  Had his family shut out their love.

I wonder if he knew of God above,
  And of His everlasting love, had
  he ever prayed for help from above.

GOD loves all young and old,
  Even worn-out shoes and tattered clothes.

E. J. English

UNIVERSAL JUGGLERS

The problems, balls, and clubs are circling
And I have more in the air than my hands.
In shapeless circles that are orbiting,
But let one fall, and no one understands.
I try to keep all objects in the air;
To strive for grand perfection can be hard.
Accepting cheers and boos and countless stares
I practice daily, hoping to be starred.
Supplying satisfaction, giving pride.
My timeless revolutions bring much life.
But floating in the air are pain and 'cides
and unresolved dilemma drops the knife.
        A limitless potential freely flows
        Producing life and death and endless shows.

Gideon Oswitch

THE FLASH OF THE HATTERAS LIGHT

        Adrift on the stormy sea one night, a mariner
looked to the sky,
        but the guiding stars could not be seen, and
the swells were running high.

        Then upon the horizon, he saw a glow, which
brightened, becoming a flash,
        and caused him to turn, barely in time, to
avoid a disastrous crash.

        It is but a chapter in history, that the
mariner was saved that night,
        just one of many whose lives have been saved,
by the flash of the Hatteras Light.

Bernard N. Dapron

FIRST TOOTH

Why do you want my thumb in your mouth?
Why do you chortle and chew?
Ouch! I have found the reason
You have a tooth that is new!

An ATTACK baby we have at our house.
Nothing is safe from you now.
You bite on Mommy and blankets and rattles.
That tooth must be useful somehow.

Soon you'll have a mouth full of teeth.
You'll show them again and again.
We'll admire your many accomplishments,
But I'll still love your toothless grin.

Edith C. Kair

FUTURA

Where, oh, where is my life on its way to?
I am put here but to wait,
I have my God to pray to.
Don't bother me while I serve my time,
Let me hold my breath in peace,
While I make this arduous climb.
One day it will all happen, and I'll see & know
The purpose of my venture,
And I'll know where to go.
Nothing goes right, but then again, who cares?
Caffeine and nicotine —
The keep me going stress in my life . . .
— Can I go now?
        This has gotten away from me.

Gloria Korby

FOR EVERYONE CONTEMPLATING SUICIDE

For everyone contemplating suicide
Remember Mr. Hemingway,
No one said life was a very fun ride
Just an experience of days.

The best you can do is meet each demand
Or try with what skill you possess;
To willingly confront each reprimand,
Be determined not to regress.

But life and love readily leave their mark
And the more you live the more you must refrain;
From choosing easier paths of the dark,
It is easy to put a bullet through the brain.

Grant Todd Sparks

HOW TIME STANDS STILL

We found each other and started out our life.
Together with our trust.
We worked in the rain, we played in the sun.
We watched new life begin that grew into a boy.

Then time stood still a little while.
For us to be together I traveled across the sea.
We listened to the rain, we watched the ocean calm.
We learned about the world, we felt the baby move,
A part of you and me that died beside the sea.

Then time stood still a little while.

Together we saw big city lights near the hustling crowd.
We found a house to make a home.
We planted trees, you bought a car.
She found you thus, I guess.
Faded became our trust.

Then time stood still a little while.

We came together to another place.
Each one of us alone.
Faded was our trust, sadness to the end.
Wasted was our time.

Esther Chapman Mullis

UNTITLED

This is a poem to
my son,
Michael
    beautiful-eyed child
alive, running, fragile, vulnerable.
Your health and wholeness is
a vital statement of
hope and goodness in
this world.
"Beautiful body, mama," you say to
me, patting my bare belly with
your tiny, luscious hand and
"Hugs, hugs," as
you try to fill the void of
my weaning breasts with
another closeness.
Running, laughing, bicycle, scooter,
sniffing, singing with
unbridled joy-burst movements,
you make the world whole.
My sorrow oozes out as I
see your newly-born openness, so vulnerable
and my fear cuts through me as I witness
your fragility. I weep and
I want all the world to be as
you, my child, my hope, my Michael.

Regina M. Falsetto

REFLECTIONS

*And ye shall know the truth, and the
truth shall make you free.* John 8:32

As I look back over the years
I remember Momma popping pills
and Daddy drinking all those beers

My older brother was caught with drugs and put away
And while I tried to understand
My younger brother was busted for GTA

At our house there was no joy, just fear
No time for Church or talk of God
Because Daddy had to have his beer

I now manage my home and pay the bills
My children see no beer
And occasional asprins are the only pills

Each time they see their Grandparents, I only pray
As they come to me with their questions
God will supply the words for me to say

Frank Randant

FOREVER

I see the wind race across the sand
Like so many spirits sailing to another land
Their voices blend with the roar of the wind
The waves they say never will be again
Forever is here

The sea is alive her heart pounding against the shore
Like a lover wrapping around me wanting more
I am afraid I do not understand what I am going through
Here I stand in the palm of God's hand and I am not with you
Forever is here

I see yesterday, being blown away by tomorrow
And today had nothing to say it was lost in sorrow
All of the people I have ever known
In one brief moment to my eyes are shown
Forever is here

Forever is here and it may set with the sun
And forever tonight will be forever done
I cannot believe what I have seen — what I have been shown
Forever is here and I am alone

William McWethy, Jr.

A NEW BEGINNING FOR MOTHER'S DAY

There is a time for all things to change.
To make things better or rearranged.
Like the love of a daughter to her mother.
That only they can share together, like no other.
That sometimes gets lost and nowhere to be found
But you know it is there somewhere around.
So if we take the time again to begin,
And with the help of God we will always win.
For God helps the flowers that bloom in the spring.
And God taught the birds the songs that they sing.
So let us take the time for a fresh new start
With our arms wide open and love in our hearts.
And we will grow closer than ever before.
And we will thank God, whom we love even more.
Because He has brought us back together.
And with His love we will last forever.
I will always remember this special day
Because my love for my mother is here to stay.
And I thank God again, for He has taught us in His
    own special way.
So this is for you mom . . . Happy Mother's Day.

Winifred C. Morris

339

GOD

How can I describe a being
as wonderful as You?
So patient, kind, encouraging
and filled with love so true.
You never cease to be there,
to shine Your guiding light,
No place too dark for You to dare
You fill with joy the darkest night.
The weak You make both strong and bold,
With You the hurt will laugh once more.
Young again shall be the old,
The watchful ones You never bore.
Your love for us is so complete.
It has no how or when or why
So just it is, I can't compete
Without You Lord, I'd surely die.

Connie Christianson

GOD'S DREAM

He once had a dream,
a wonderful one,
of earth and His children
living together in love.
As time goes by,
we children stray,
and His dream and reality
are miles away.
We kill each other needlessly,
destroying His dream.
We hurt God, whose love shines upon us —
a radiant beam.
His dream turns to nightmare,
there is nothing but fear.
God tries to warn us,
but we turn a deaf ear.

Kristen Morry

Give your body
to the light of the day
Willingly
and you will become part
of the omnipresent
rainbows
and radiant sunbursts
give yourself also
to the glows of the moon
in all its splendor
a diamond on black velvet
sparkling endlessly
in bursts of
joyful color

Lisa A. Malinowski

CAMERA

Human-made Technology
Extension of the eye with a
Telescopic view of the world
filtered and changed as we Wish
Only seeing what we please
filtering and Molding Reality
Extension of the Modern mind
nothing stays the Same
As in previous lives
Camera on the Universe
Artificial Eyeball
Clear but not
Necessarily true
The shutter clicks
False smile falls
The camera

Josh Baker

IN SEARCH OF SELF

To search for yourself
May not seem sincere.
For isn't your 'self'
The one in the mirror?

Your physical form?
Well, that's a start.
But your search should lead
Down into your heart.

You may be surprised
When you see what is there.
Beneath all your worries
And everyday cares.

It's there where your dreams
Are nurtured and grown.
It's there where the seeds
Of your talents are sown.

In your quest for self
Is where you begin
Not so much to look out
As to look deep within.

Rhonda Sisbower

THE MOODS OF THE MOON

The melancholy moon moved across
the darkened sky,
And with a sigh
I watched it.

For its melancholy came not from
within itself but
From the depths of my own soul,
And a tear silently ran its course
Within the turmoil there.

While in another soul, joy
was derived
From the passage of the moon
through the night.
And a smile passed across the face
Of that soul so different from mine.

Lynna B. Cox

I AM A BLACK WOMAN

I am a black woman,
God made me with his hands;
He made me well and turned me black,
Thus became a sculpture grand.

I am a black woman,
And black is my life;
To live the life of a black woman,
You go through toils and strife.

I am a black woman,
Blacker than eyes can foresee;
I am a black woman,
Because God made me!

I am a black woman,
And black I'll always be;
For to be that black woman,
Brings great joy and pride to me.

I am a black woman,
And black I shall always proclaim;
I am a black woman,
But a woman, just the same.

Kathy L. Floyd

Color me in warm colors
When a cool night is
My lover . . .

Color me if night is so clear
Embraces you near, then

I will color Thee for
Thousands of Eternal Years!

M. Nelly Zamora Jones

JONES, M. NELLY ZAMORA. Pen Name: Nelly Zamora Jones; Born: Cuba, 2-15-52; Married: 1979 to W. Martin Jones; Education: Miami-Dade Junior College, Florida, A.A., 1972; University of South Florida, Tampa, Florida, B.A., Art Education, 1974, and M.A., Fine Arts and Education; Occupations: Artist; Teacher, Halifax County Senior High School; Art Department Chairperson; Memberships: National Educational Association, Virginia Education Association, Halifax Education Association, National Art Education Association, Piedmont Literary Society, Parson-Bruce Art Association, Virginia Museum; Awards: Cintas Foundation Fellowship in the Arts area of Painting; Readings to the Women's Baptist Association, *The Collected Poems of Nelly Zamora Jones;* Other Writings: *Words from the Heart,* series of poems and ink drawings, 1985-86 by artist, this work is in its final stage. Comments: *As an artist who also writes poetry, I express my experiences and ideas through both media. Painting is non-verbal poetry, and poetry is a journal of the silent images in my mind. If in my poetry others can see the images and hear the silent words, then I have accomplished my purpose; to communicate in a universal language as understood through emotions and feelings. I express my innermost feelings of my relationship to nature and God.*

WHO AM I?

I don't know that I'm dreaming
either I don't know if I'm awake
I don't know if it is the truth
I would like that somebody would bite me
I want to feel the pain
The pain that I have inside
inside me very deep
in my soul in my body
is hard to endure
To bear it anymore
I know that I came to the world nude
But, there are blows in our lives
that make us feel angry
To be human, to be Christian
To give everything that we have
To the wretched who whine and weep
Spilling their venom that devours oneself.

Prince William

When I was young and carefree
O'er the mountains I did roam
Without a care or worry on my mind

But now the scene has changed
And I find my home sweet home
On the sagebrush-covered prairies of the plains

Oh! My hands they are tied to the prairie
That my loved ones may have daily bread
But at the close of each day
My heart says "Come away
Come away to the mountains beyond."

Dorothy Povey

LOVE GONE BY

Since you've gone I often think of how it used to be.
I never gave much thought back then of what you meant to me.

I simply took for granted that you'd always be around,
and never realized just how great the love was that I'd found.

Then came the time when you decided to just walk away.
You had enough of my assuming that you'd always stay.

So now I'm left with memories of blissful love gone by,
and all the guilt that burdens me because I let it die.

Karen Yori

THE GLAD EASTERTIDE

Church congregations, hymns are chanting,
People their spring flower gardens are planting,
The Easter lily blooms,
Young men are wooing, in hopes of being bridegrooms;
When Easter Sunday comes, the Easter Rabbit;
Will come to all children, who obey their parents;
Which is a very good habit.
Pansies, narcissus, hyacinths, and jonquils are in their
Full beauty.
Let us all go to church to worship the Lord,
That we might be free from sin;
Which on Easter Sunday is every true Christian's duty.

Mary Catherine Peterson

GOD'S NATURE — WORLD OF BEAUTY

The birds' sweet melodies flow through the trees
        As a gentle breeze whispers along.
Above, the sun shines big and so bright
        While the trees sing their own kind of song.
My world seems so calm, so full of beauty —
        I treasure GOD'S nature . . . a world of beauty.

Amy Nicole Miller

LEAVES

Branches swinging, catching showers of spring water
From a sky, green with uncollected clouds

A single ray that guides creatures into separate,
Unique worlds in their struggle for survival
They harness endless rivulets of commonality

Summon these streams and witness the music of their beauty

Branches swinging, nourished by beads of spring water
A single ray that warms the blood of God's creatures

Manuel Nanez Rodriguez

FORGOTTEN MAGIC

I see the sparkling patterns, of the city lights;
    From the window of the plane
As if some careless god
    Had placed a lady's necklace
On the ground below.

The city streets and cars
    Surround the lady's jewels.

Forgotten magic haunts my memories,
    As the plane moves silently
Toward another city
— In the cloudless night.

Diane Michaels

DISTANCE

Our miles of separation,
    don't dampen my thoughts of you
Though a picture is all I have

The emptiness is something that cannot remain
So a temporary filler replaces you,
    but it's never the same

The nights are lonely; the days are bleak
The distance between us has made me weak

These feelings I have, are ones hard to hide,
For without you, something inside me has died

Bari J. Perlman

INTRA-ARROW

is the mind alone, just as solo,
reason being that of agreement,
for sharing information seems redundant,
similarity being few and far between,
better off seeming to be silent,
for every word, just as spoken,
creates opposition, by concept itself.
that is, that two do not equal one,
while at the same time, only one is one,
an existence of intellectual disgust,
to duplicate, as one and reflection in mirror,
except not to view self this time,
instead, one opposition to every other

william robert

NURSE

Five o'clock one morning, four the next. Today it
is three a.m. and once again I arise under the guise
of needing drugs.
Medication is a band-aid covering a severed artery
of self-esteem.
My aspiration is to reach out and communicate,
to have a friend who will listen and not judge.
It is pleasing to be able to open my soul and express
what therein lies without being parodized.
Please forgive me if I burden you, that is not my intention.
I am profoundly grateful that you are willing to extend
your hand
as I reach for you.

K. Scott

TO MY WIFE

I remember our wedding and the church that day,
    When we were just starting our matrimonial way,
With a love so very strong and hearts extra bold,
    Together we head out, our whole lives to mold.

The lean years — the hard years, they went by in a flash,
    Then came our three boys, and they added a dash,
of fun and excitement, we would never have known,
    like the joy and laughter, that they brought to our home.

They added two daughters, the girls we never had,
    Two wonderful daughters, and they make our hearts glad,
Two granddaughters too, and our spirits are now high,
    For they are two angels, plucked right from the sky.

We both have now aged — that is as it must be,
    The health we have enjoyed is starting to flee,
But with our lives so very good over the years,
    And a family so great, I can shed no tears.

Were I to do it over, I would change not a thing,
    For my best days started, when I bought her that ring,
I now thank you, dear Lord, for answering my prayer,
    That joined us together in life as a pair.

    Elbert R. McPherson

Amid the human refuse floating in the street
and cluttering the gutters
lives a little girl.

Well-acquainted she is with life.
Watching those around her kill each other,
fast and easy with knives and guns
or slow and hard with empty words and emptier feelings.

A part of this world is our girl, and her shell is tough
But she observes strangers around her and feels alien,
she watches friends she loves and feels different.

Her lovers come and go.
Nameless, some of them;
faceless, most of them;
yet innocence shines bright in her eyes.

The steady flow of booze, drugs, and sex
has swept past her leaving her untouched.

Of all her lovers, not one has ever
gotten through to touch her soul.

And innocence shines on in her eyes.
    Victoria Anne Wofford

I stood agaze.
Eyes fixed.
watching
studying
captivated
Starbeams radiated the night sky.
wondering
wandering
worrying
A ray of phosphorescence illuminated the heavens; then:
dissipation
desolation
degradation
Pleading desperately I cried —
"LISTEN TO ME!"
I waited
hesitated
disconsolated
I turned away
    lifeless . . .
      B. D. Roth

MY EMILY OF TODAY

You walk with grace and elegance.
You hold your head with style.
You have a lovely self-respect.
You have a pleasing smile.

You listen well with patience.
You speak so sweetly and so well.
You conduct yourself in a comely way.
You are quaint and charming like a dell.

You are a lovely lady
Whom I shall not forget.
You treated me with kind respect;
This meant so much to me — and I shall not forget.

How could I soon forget
Your peaceful eyes and lovely shape?
I know you are a friend forever —
My Emily of today.

    Carl E. Bowen

TRANSITION

It's a cold and rainy Thursday —
A chill is in the air,
And Death has settled close to me,
I feel its morbid stare.

My tears were wasted long ago
The dull ache still remains —
Now nature duplicates my tears,
My sorrow's in the rains.

        The first snow of the winter
        Is blanketing the streets.
        The frosty air is whispering —
        "Be calm, he only sleeps."

        The midnight sky shines bright and white —
        With snowflakes swirling 'round
        As if to say, "Be happy now!
        His soul is Homeward bound."

    Dawn Ringling

THE DRAGONFLY

I saw a dragonfly
Struggling
To loose himself from the snapping grip of the fish's bite
As with shivered wings
He flailed and beat against the air
Like some frail and faulty craft from man's early days of
Flight.

Another Exodus.

And Moses-like, the bamboo rod I held
Became a staff of life
And reached the staggered breath into the haven of a certain
Tree
From whence it fell from grace
As
  Man
    With
      God.

    Léonie Nielsen Longshore

SPARE TIME?!

Time so ominously long and lonely
on one's way back to mental health:
Friends say good-bye in their hellos,
Coffee tries to stretch minutes to hours,
Rudimentary living gets lost in medication
        regimes
Wherein physical dictates bleed restlessness.

Keep busy, some advise as they do it
But we can't reach the "how"
When "spare" is all that's there
aggravated by worries and stress of
what to eat
where to live
and that empties into echos that
        working on work has no where.

Beryl M.A.-Khabeer

CRAVE

            flying like a tucked pelican

                        I reach

        we rendezvous without manners taught

            GRASP oh *HURRY!*
        flow river flow,

WE arouse mysteries drenched with our lust

            Quench *ME*

    Fright we declare is essence of our vibrations
collapse in blissful sheep cries

    Clocks burn our limiting fragrance of liFE!

    Auwah   we cower   into   silence

    whyyyyYYAAH   eMOtions.

            i wake

    Anton Kazandjian

GONE ASTRAY

I stumbled and wandered astray; into the pleasures of sin
for a day

O Lord, I know not why I left your peaceful path, only to
deserve your anger and wrath

The agony of failing and letting you down, after you so
faithfully lifted me up when life couldn't be found

Still, you show your love and grace as you so mercifully
wash the shame from my face.

Even now, before these words are humbly done, mysteriously
renewing this broken spirit of repentance, through sacrificial
cleansing from your precious son

Left only with the trace of an aching heart, as it silently
prays for all weary souls who have still to know your royal
path is a haven's nest waiting with its forgiveness and rest

While I go on praising you for lifting me up, to once again
drink from your heavenly cup.

With joy

Jeanette Moody

REFLECTIONS IN THE PORCELAIN THRONE

We ponder, we think
We wonder, we sink
Reflections in the porcelain throne
Matter of Man?
Groping fingers probe the mists of illusion
What is amiss?
Shards of reality, but a delusion
Wallow in false bliss
Truth? Honor? Anal exubrience of the finest kind
Lies? Deceit? Façades of beauty for the blind
To laugh and cry, to love and lie, to live and die
To live and die
And we ponder, Matter of Man?
Some actually believe they are alone
As they ponder their reflections in the porcelain throne.
    S. N. Couture

STACKING HAY IN MISSOURI

A biblical reading ritual — a stupid father's game
To restrict my cousins with guilt and blame
They begin to rebel against Mom and Stepfather
Away from ill rules and carnal lovers
Petronila runs to her lover's arms — to his bed — a babe
A crying youngster sobbing for her dad to be
A lonely blue-eyed girl wishing to be married

Stacking hay in Missouri — the "Show Me" State
Show me how to preserve life to constrain my fate
Show me state
Show me how to love without blame
Show me state
Show me love without disdain
And I'll show you love with pain
    Hermelinda Gonzales

WHITECAPS

(A Sonnet)

Beyond the crash of surf against the shore
The whitecaps dance upon the wind-swept sea,
Harking not to bearded Triton's roar
Nor yet the warning voice of destiny.
That they are borne by some relentless tide
To unknown shores is held without belief.
In ignorance they merrily abide
Until they're dashed to foam upon a reef.
And then they meet irrevocable fate
And moan as they are driven to the strand.
They see where they have come, too late, too late,
And leave their lives in lace upon the sand.
But Man is wiser than the heedless seas —
He *plans* his death in calculable degrees.
    Rima Corder Magee

THE NIGHT

The night looms ever on, over hill and over grave.
It puts the daytime, shining bright, to shame.
The air is calm and peaceful, as the crickets play their tune.
The dark and all things in it are dominated by the moon.
It rules above the sky and land
With an unyielding father-like hand.
From lighted street corners, where children gather in sin
To dim shadowed alleys that beckon you, "Come in."

To most it seems quite silent
But to a few 'tis not.
Just close your ears and eyes and open up your senses wide.
Your mind will be so surprised for you will see and hear a lot.
Come join us who know the night,
Who live there long and feel no fright.
    Daniel J. Moore II

MY MAN'S WOMAN

She was a short fat lady who took my man,
But I sent him packing with his suitcase in his hand.
I couldn't take his drinkin' he got a D.U.I.,
She paid his Attorney's fee, he called her his pumpkin pie.
He gave her such a sweet name, with thyme — nutmeg and allspice,
and bit off mor'n he could chew, an alcoholic person is not
always nice.

I never want a pumpkin pie on my table, with sweets and allspice,
I will think of my man's woman, things that are not so nice.
She had money, so I was *told:* A Condo, swimming pool and yacht.
He told me — I was too wrinkled and old.
He walked out on this woman when he learned she couldn't pay
her rent — she was a broke alcoholic, without a red cent.
She sang with the T.V. he said, and sang loud with the radio,
2 or 3 o'clock in the morning she was yelling out —
"Where the hell did everybody go — ?"

Mabel Dow Green

GREEN, MABEL DOW. Born: Greensville County, Emporia, Virginia, 7-12-26; Occupation: Bar
Maid (Owner); Awards: Plaques for years in Bar Business, 32 years; Comments: *I write my feelings
— what is on my mind — usually sad — I am usually depressed in love, scared, hurt, jealous, etc.
Only then do I feel better.*

THE BEES

We are but the denizens of our own human hive,
So we bustle, we covet, we compete and we thrive.

At the top, the royalty, the "ever-be's,"
served by their consorts, the "new-to-be's."

While at the bottom, barely buzzing, the drones we find,
with lethargy, with dross, with barely a mind.

There dwell the "never-could-be's" and the "used-to-be's;"
there also the "don't-care-to-be's," deigning to please.

But between these two strata the buzz ever increases.
Movement there is electric, and it never ceases.

Thus between hope the "may-be's" buzz the "want-to-be's;"
dream the "someday-will-be's," stir the "try-to-be's."

While these are largely innocuous, only a tease,
here also lurks danger — the "guaranteed-to-be's."

Yes, most surely we are as our busy-bee cousins;
likenesses abound, we are there by the dozens.

Alas, the only real difference is where we deliver our sting.
While our cousins protect, death to each other our venom doth bring!

John A. Short

SNOW

When I was young and full of life,
A measured snowfall meant delight.
I played the scene with nature's gift
and felt the sting of winter's bite.

I swung at life in spite of snow
and challenged days of ten below.
No snowfall claimed my outing day,
I surged ahead and went my way.

In age, my clock of life unwinds.
My bones request more summertime.
Although the sun can warm like wine,
my heart is pinned by winter's sign.

A blanket snow can tease my mind,
paint picture thoughts of Christmas time.
Amazed and awed at nature's show,
I've spent a lifetime loving snow.

Hazel L. Cottington, BMI

AND I HAD TO THANK HIM
FOR HIS THOUGHTFULNESS

The half-wild bitch
felt the call of the flame.
Fanged firefighters
with hardened hose
fought the fickle flame.
My neighbor vowed it improper
for children to view it —
this canine copulation,
so he fought fire with fire
wielding his twelve-gauge
fury-flinger
to deposit double aughts
in her proud pink flesh
driving the fever aground.
He left her lifeless there
for the fly-blown worms
as a rueful reminder
for all sinning species.

Royce Ray

Reflecting back on good times past,
A sort of melancholy mood swept over me.
It comes very seldom,
so I catch the chance,
to get to know myself.
My thoughts, my dreams,
my ambitions, all seem,
to have,
drifted with the tide,
and floated away.
New waves are splashing in,
with each turning moment.

When those moments arise,
in God's endless horizon of eternity,
capture and crystallize,
those thoughts.
Let your ideas flow,
just as an artist,
strokes his brush,
sketching a sunset.

Ruby Louise Sealy

SCENES IN DRUID HILL PARK.

JUST A FLOWER

I am merely a flower, nurtured by love,
I was planted here by One up above,
In violent winds, to the ground I bow,
And softly whisper, Lord is it Thou?
Soon after the storm the sun will appear,
Again I know my dear Lord is near.
One day He will come to pick this flower,
Don't know what day or what hour,
Taken beyond the stars and the sky,
Forever to bloom, never again to die.

Genevieve Wawarofsky

WAWAROFSKY, GENEVIEVE ANN. Born: Praha, Texas (a little Czech settlement where my grandmother had settled when she came from Czechoslovakia), 1-29-40; Married: Dan Wawarofsky; Education: Little country school in Praha, Texas; Two years at Flatonia High; clerical courses until married; Occupations: Live-In Housekeeper, Store Manager, Raised five children, ages 18, 19, 22, 23, 24; Poetry: 'Happy Memories,' 1985; 'Brother's Gift to Me,' Hempstead Printers, 1984; 'Love Is Rewarding,' Hempstead Printers, 1984; 'I Hear Your Cry,' 1985; 'A Message from Jesus,' 1985; *Feelings,* booklet; Have written few songs, not yet published; In the past year, have written about 30 poems; Comments: *I came from a small family, only one brother (5 years younger) and I. In 1983, he was killed in a motorcycle accident. He and I were very close and the pain was about unbearable. Then I wrote a poem about him and realized I can express my feelings from deep within. Most of my poems are peaceful, death, love, and God's beautiful creation.*

EUROPEAN BRIDGE AT SAINT LAZARE*

A geometric structure
upholds the bridge,
and yesterday's godspeeds.
A steam locomotive
puffs cobalt blue
where arrivals, departures,
ungeometric,
gather melancholy.

Below the Bridge,
Monet focused
on the Paris of the past,
where background buildings
loom iridescent
as if through veils,
and distant tunnels
shadow old intrigues.

Within Saint-Lazare's smoky vault,
we solve axioms of all travel.
The fading tracks
wind through our isolation.

*Impressionist Exhibit,
Los Angeles County Museum

Virginia E. Smith

THE DISGUISED WORLD

The world around me that I see
Is different from the world it could be,
Cries . . .
Spies . . .
And untold lies,
With tears,
Fears,
And shadowed years.

My world I would trade
For a minute or two,
To help fade
Unhappiness for a mere few.

Natalie Poulton

MY LADY

Tired eyes —
holding my lady,
touching the air of her scent
between my finger tips,
holding her thoughts
through the space of miles,
knowing something is wrong,
with my eyes wide open,
so early in time.
Not seeing you,
out, touching, holding, caressing
the love for you,
my lady.

Richard E. Horton

UNTITLED

No other can
Possess my soul
Eyes, lips, hands, touch
Tremble I
As the void opens
Beneath me
A leaf in the wind
I fall
Under your spell
Seduced
Your power absolute
In the temple of desire
I dance for you alone

Nancy J. Davies

THE LAST HAWK

Soaring lazily on coils
    Of air,
Watching;
Gazing down onto
    A patchwork of concrete and steel.
Chestnut back shines brightly
    In the cool autumn sun;
Yellow eye darting from
    Rooftop to rooftop;
No more tree top!
Empty talons grasp
    The empty future.
No future for the last hawk.

Wade Rogers

AT FORTY

Forty weary paces from the cradle
In the scorcher and the rain-storm
Groping in the dark for the success path
To chase the faint footprints of Fortune;
Trudging and fumbling without forty winks
Have sapped the aroma and the nectar
Leaving me no charm, force or lustre
Near the brink of the bottomless abyss.

Kwasi Asante

ASANTE, KWASI. Born: Nkawkaw, Ghana, 9-24-44; Married: 8-11-68 to Cecilia Asante; Education: Osei Tutu Tr. College, Certificate 'A', 1964; Specialist Tr. College, Specialist Certificate in English, 1968; University of Ghana, B.A. Honors 2nd Upper English, 1973; Instituto Rio Branco, Brasilia, Diploma in International Relations 1978; Occupation: Diplomat; Poetry: 'Gem of Life,' 'Growing Old,' 'The Poor Do Not Belong,' 'This Is Not My Home,' 'The Betrayal,' all published in the *American Poetry Anthology;* Themes: *My poems generally deal with death, the transitoriness of life, injustice, poverty, and what I see as the vile nature of man. Most of my themes are derived from my own experiences of life. My first child died in 1969, my uncle in 1973, my mother in 1981 and my father in 1982.*

NIGHTMARE

The street is dark
gloomy and empty
I stand alone, amid debris
No houses to be seen
No sign of life
Frantically, blindly, I search
for a sign of living
All I find is my shadow
and hear the echo of my voice
In the still of the night

Bena Ferencz

LOVE OF LAW

God's nature; finally revealed;
Would bring a consistently just and
    Merciful guideline. The very rod
Of the almighty; This is far from the
    "Mere" law of nature which is
So highly prized, by the carnal mind; Rather
    It is supreme, far above our earthly
Understanding of confused doctrinal beliefs.
    Oh the price one must pay to look to a
Higher law yet what a challenge to render our
    Worldly laws into the very rod of God;
A control, despite ourselves; Here we have
    The very drift of the enlightenment;
Handed down by Gaius; What a prize! And
    What a shame we rejected it for
Aristotle; Is it too late? Or is there
    Actually time to recognize the "supreme."
'Tis the law that promotes peace, justice,
    Mercy, equity; These are the things I love;
For "God Almighty" is the lawgiver; I am
but a mouthpiece.

Joseph A. Stewart

THE POWER OF LOVE
(To Roy)

We said "good-bye" beneath the moonbeams,
And all the stars hid inside the skies,
And a lingering cold took charge within me,
And reached for the twinkle in my eyes.

In each new morning's golden sunshine,
Ghostly shadows fell along my way,
And there came blowing such a wild wind
Chasing dreams of love far, far away.

Only dark and lonely held my hand,
As love seemed trapped in drying streams,
But then one day I dared to search,
And found you, love, amidst new dreams.

You captured my heart when we first met,
And heaven's stars danced across the skies,
And in the glow of lovelier moonbeams,
You restored the twinkle back to my eyes.

Ruth Shelton Turner

JESSE STUART

Father, I lift to your throne this moment
Jesse Stuart, your son. Naomi, his beloved,
faithful, true wife. Jane, his daughter,
of whom he was justly proud and a teacher,
writer, too. The grandsons who loved him
greatly and loved Kentucky hills.
Jesse's heart, mind and soul roamed the world
loved its beauty, history, culture, too,
But most of all he loved his students great
and small and opened wide their hearts
to write and create for others
a thing never dreamed before. His heart
was great and he expanded many minds
to sing joyously of the simple things
kin to all. To richly share
was his fatherly dare to everyone.
He loved Greece, Scotland, many lands.
But his heart belonged to His Kentucky hills
and his mind-heart shared fully with everyone.
Thank you, Jesse Stuart, teacher, friend,
one of America's truly great.

Mary Agnes White

HUMAN RAINBOWS

There's a rainbow all around the world
No beginning and no end
Its colors are constantly changing
With the blowing wind

And that rainbow is my Father's work of art
The Earth a canvas for His paint
It's an abstract mosaic of color and culture
It's a smile from the heart of God

It's a human rainbow
Splashed across the world by the Master Artist's hand
So many rainbow colors in this painted world of ours
A brand-new world in every thread of humanity

Every place on Earth has its own
Rainbow personality
Every place, every race of man
Another heaven dream

Humanity is filled with diversity
In total rhythm with the rainbow world
It's a patchwork quilt of colors and shapes
Stitched together by the thread of love

Travis M. Whitehead

POETRY

Poetry is a song
    Running through the mind,
And it teases all day long
    Until you pause to find

A catch-phrase here with full intent
    To start you on a merry way.
The words come clear and truly bent
    They come and go, you wish they'd stay.

Messages to tell the lonely.
    Thoughts react to ancient days.
Deeds to spur and not you only,
    Many are the poets' ways.

Good intentions, tell a story?
    Place a fact, submit degrees?
Old and modern, happy, gory?
    All on earth want to be pleased.

Now I sleep and wager, ponder,
    Some more words to pass on free,
Until in Heaven I'm sleeping yonder,
    Poet's life, we do thank thee.

Anne Mary Davis

THANKS MOM

The time is well past due to express my thanks to you,
For being my wonderful mother
who loves me like no other.
The times of pain no doctor could cure
I found relief through your open door.
You gave me hope for a brighter day
and greater knowledge of a better way.
Those times of sorrow through wear and tear
you helped me along by being there.
Mom, if at times I do neglect to give you time
and true respect,
remember, these emotions that I hide
are true devotions deep inside.
When I begin to wonder what I'd do without
a mother who loves me beyond any doubt,
these thoughts are frightening to me
for there is no replacement . . .
nor CAN there ever be.

Qui

MIDNIGHT PRAYER

Thank You, Lord, for this new day.
Make me a blessing, whatever comes my way.
Thank You for the day I've just been through.
Thank You for making me more like You.
Forgive me, Lord, for the wrongs I've done
And not always trying to be like your Son.
Help me change what You don't approve of.
Give me a heart all full of Your new love,
In Jesus' name, amen.

Donita Rae Jenkins

JENKINS, DONITA RAE. Born: Kansas City, Kansas, 2-22-66; Awards: Honorable Mention for poem, 'When Enemies Become Friends,' 1984; Comments: *I write to give glory to Jesus Christ, to express my love for Him and His love for people. Everything I write glorifies God in some way, whether directly or indirectly. Jesus is number one in my life.*

MY FAVORITE PLACE

Oops! There I go up on my cloud,
higher than you can see
I am only sitting and thinking,
of you and me.

No I don't want to come down to misery,
pain and all the rest.
I'd rather stay up here,
dreaming and looking —
from my cloud's nest.

Why did you cast that spell on me,
which makes me tremble inside.
Surely I am fearing your embrace,
which binds me,
oh, where can I hide.

When I come down there and see you face-to-face,
sensations spread throughout me,
leaving me helpless in your embrace.

Oh let me go back to my cloud's nest,
where it's peaceful and I can hide from you,
feeling safe and at rest.

For I am afraid you will hurt my gentle heart,
leaving me wounded —
like the rest.

Afraid, Afraid, I have to escape.
Oh let me go back to my cloud's nest,
so far above this place.

Bernadette M. Gonville

THE RAINBOW'S END

Beneath the candy-colored ribbons,
    within the rainbow's hue, I
lay in silent wonder, my thoughts
    revolving you.

So fleeting is the rainbow's stay, one
    moment here, then gone. It's almost
like our love affair, a short but sweet
    love song.

Your voice, it was the music that brought
    new life to me. While in your eyes
romance was born, you made me feel
    so free.

With your smile reflecting like the rainbow's
    haze, you captured my affection,
by sprinkling colored sunshine throughout
    my rainy days.

From your touch there came a spark, that
    lit the torch thereof, and with
your flaming passion, you taught me how
    to love.

Even though we've parted ways, this life
    has been so kind, to have let
me see "the rainbow's end," and spend
    a little time.

Robert A. Moore

MOORE, ROBERT A. Born: Milwaukee, Wisconsin, 8-26-53; Single; Education: 2 years UWGB, Green Bay, Wisconsin, 1980-81, Gateway, Racine, Wisconsin, 1984-85; Occupation: Student; Poetry: 'Patience,' Inspirational, January, 1983, *Racine* Journal, 'Fading,' Prison experience, March, 83, *Racine Journal;* Comments: *I write about various experiences. But my main themes are on loves won and lost, prison experiences, people who've suffered in life, and some on the magnificence of God. I write to bring across my deepest feelings and thoughts to others, because I'm often inspired by other people, and because I someday want to publish my own volumes and write songs.*

LEVEE STONES:

Dionysius waits for us.
I drink from the silver bowl
and white powder lifts my head
up to the bottom of the green sea.
We are weird, nude stars
fallen from sanity.
Other minds could take us over
sounds of voices drowning near
and they can't be anywhere else
but here.

Chris Devine

1985 PRISONER

Heartless time upon us,
Endless searching for love

Like a child lost in the wood,
Without hope

My restless soul searches
For that one love that
Will release me from the
Pain.

Like a prisoner, unduly
Charged and held for a
Crime — innocent

I need only be released

Joseph Pitkat

CAFE

Walking alone, the streets of the city.
Cool breeze, tired feet, I stop in a cafe.
An Italian waiter serves me cappuccino
and sits down at a table nearby.
He lights a cigarette and
asks me if I'm Danish.
I smile at him and shake my head.
He is an actor out of work,
I am a student of philosophy.
Sipping my coffee, I watch him get up.
His brown eyes and soft black hair,
turning away to play his part,
while I play mine, studying him.
Both of us too lost to know
the desires of a stranger.
For I am not Danish and he waits tables.
So I return to the street alone.

Victoria Fann

WOOLLY BEARS

Going down the highways
Fightin' WOOLLY BEARS
Everywhere my feet touch
I was stepping on their hair.
Just the plain and simple life,
Makes a guy a millionaire,
There's no beginning to the roads
And there's no end to woolly bears.

Now the season is the fall.
And the harvest is in its peak
And the trees have got a glow.
That makes them very distinct.
There's a smell of burning leaves
The aroma fills the air.
And the highway's overgrown
With mammoth WOOLLY BEARS.

Clara C. Purtee

UTTERANCE OF LOVE

You're sweet as you can be,
And do have lots of class.
I hope that you'll remember me,
And let our love life last.

Sometimes you make me happy.
Sometimes you make me cry,
But when I'm with you Sweetie Pie,
Oh, how the time goes by.

I hope you like my poem.
I wrote it just for you.
I hope that when you read it,
It'll brighten your whole day through.

These words are sweet and mushy.
I know that you'll agree.
I wrote them 'cause I love you,
And hope that you love me.

Sylvia Elaine Stephens

STEPHENS, SYLVIA ELAINE. Pen Name: Sylaine Conquer; Born: Dallas, Texas, 10-11-58; Single; Education: Senior at University of Texas at Arlington, Major: Pre-med, Psychology, Minor in Biology; Occupations: Supervisor of the Nursing/Math Library at University of Texas at Arlington; Memberships: Alpha Beta Kappa, National Honor Society in the Medical Profession, Associate of the Smithsonian Institute, Association of Female Executives of America; Awards: published in *New Voices in American Poetry,* 1985; published in *Our Western World's Most Beautiful Poems,* 1985; Poetry: 'The Lonely One's Friend,' Vantage Press, Inc., November, 1985 and World of Poetry Press, April, 1985; 'Utterance of Love,' American Poetry Association, April, 1985; Comments: *I have no common themes and ideas when I write poetry. I like to write poetry with different themes and ideas, and I write poetry because I feel that it is one of the most beautiful ways that I can express myself.*

HALLOWEEN PARADE

Witches and goblins
Witches and cats
Witches and monsters
Witches and bats.

Witches and ghouls
Witches and brooms
Witches and ghost
Witches and tombs.

Witches and pirates
Witches and brew
Which is me?
Which is you?

Beatrice M. McLaughlin

AURORA

Aurora, I beseech you,
Wake the fields.
Remove the tender coverlets
That smother
Babes of green.
Bring the dew that settles
On every leaf and blade.
Illuminate the amber buds
Left clinging to the skeletal tree
Make every cloud
a pink-gold sheathe
of glittering moiré.
Ignite the stilled darkness,
Explode it into day!

Candice S. Thomas

A MARBLE TOMB

Her dress is a violet perfume,
Blue roses are her eyes,
She kneels beside a marble tomb
As a wind from phantom skies

Accosts the ribbons in her hair
And slips them from her dress,
Sprinkles a soft dust on her stare —
It is a light caress.

The wind then shivers as she laughs
In fear and pale delight,
Shading the painful epitaphs
Against the edge of night.

Hugo Walter

raindrops

rain taps softly on my windowpane
my problems gently fall
lying outside in a puddle
can I sort them out?

many times i have sat by the window
listening for answers in raindrops
but they fall to the ground
too swift for me to answer

perhaps the solution i seek
as i reflect upon life's storms
cannot be formed in raindrops
until i look within myself

Rita M. Light

CONSIDER A FOREST

Consider a forest
and its many trees
some have fallen down
in the shadow of taller trees

i'm sad for the fallen ones
they were young
they missed their chance
to laugh in the sun

i'm glad for the taller ones
they are old
they teach me to reach
for all i can hold

consider a tree
how it adds a leaf
and root as time flies by
consider a tree
how it must grow tall
or slowly die

consider me
so must i

Larry B. Lee

MILEAGE

It's forty kilometers through hell
   by bus or plane
or blue-stained tennis shoes.
Forty kilometers
   from border to border
shoulder to shoulder
   weeping and gnashing of teeth
over memories of nights in heaven
   and fires that did not scorch
but only burned.
   Repentance is a cardboard box
ninety-three and a half inches square
   taped shut by choices
made or not
   and hands that held in darkness
desire.
   Heaven is a heartbeat from here,
forty kilometers plus one.

M. I. Hopffgarten

LET ME IN

I want to become a part of you
   in each and every way.
I want to tell you how much I love you,
   but the words are not there to say.

Sometimes it's difficult to tell the other
   exactly what you feel,
But don't be afraid to let me in,
   your thoughts, too, are real.

Let me just encourage you
   to be just who you are.
And I don't expect perfection,
   from that we all stand far.

I want to share your every joy,
   and your every sorrow as well.
I want to know your happy times,
   or the anger that may dwell.

I do respect your private thoughts,
   and with that, I'll not interfere,
But anytime you need to talk,
   I'm listening, my love, I'm here.

Barbara J. Glyda

LIFE

Life is like the stars,
A neverending mystery.
It glitters in all its splendor,
And is ever-changing.

Life is also like a river,
Rushing wildly and constant.
The sweetness of its water
Creates yet more life.

Elizabeth Matta

THE PROBLEM

Is it them?
Is it us?
Is it we?
Or is it me?

Where do I turn?
Whom do I see?
What do I do?
The Answer is ME!

David McLaughlin

A POEM FOR MY MOTHER

You were tortured
By destruction
How you suffered at my door.
Waiting, watching, barely breathing
Hoping life could be reborn.
Now, at last, a moment's sorrow
Life thereafter will spring forth
Love will flow in gentle rivers
Bringing peace upon your shore.

Nancy Jane Safeblade

ARE WE DOOMED?

Acid rain,
Smoke in the air.
How much more
Can this planet bear?

MX missiles,
Leaders in error.
How much longer
Must we live in terror?

Kathy-Lynne Hunt

SPRINGTIME

Sitting out on a bench
Deep in thought, entrenched.
Mind involved in little things,
Summer, autumn, now it's spring

Birds a-flying all about
Green grass growing, flowers sprout.
The wind doing silly things
Thank God it's spring

Dr. Ralph Rogers

GODLY WOMAN

A Godly Woman is to be blessed!
For her there is little rest!

Daily she feeds and clothes the needy,
Her work on earth is always speedy!

She trusts the Lord, for all her needs,
She goes daily to plant His seeds!

All of her neighbors know her to be,
In her life, Jesus they see!

She always has a smile to warm the day,
She never grows tired of kind words to say!

The love she shows is not hers, I know!
She allows the Holy Spirit to flow!

Our Father in Heaven is filled with love,
For this blessed woman, who'll reign above!

Donna Jones

WHEN LOVE WAS LOW

Indian glances purge the room with
illusion.
On the state of New York with confusion
and fat lips, seeking you in the fragile heart of
betrayal.
Fashion covers the mental pasion motioning
an entrance for strange belief.
Dressed in a fast suit for the liberation
that goes to pieces on a sad official beauty
stuttering a submission in a city dream returning
to the handsome air.
Alone, sweating styled emotion and you
blame.
I sweep the crowds from my heart.
I'm with summer in its disappearance.
Legend covers flesh with its blame as
desire stumbles with its weakness and we embrace
our silent demands.
The heart's memorial is covered by aggression
as you attack.
The bride throws her bouquet to the refusing
hand. You hate her and become the other
man.

Sidney Stein

NEVER KNOWING

written for my daughter Cheri
with love & appreciation

I don't know how
        Your heart takes the pain
            Of never knowing.
Inside your heart —
            Seems the war would never end.
How can you stand the thoughts being tossed
            Not knowing,
The dreams you wish to see
            Vanish in the wind — ?
I see the unshed tears, trembling of a child
Yet — I see you standing proud
            Not knowing.
Never knowing —
            Of what will or will not be,
Hopes built within you and a smile.
I see the strength it takes to win
Let your mind be open —
Be humble — it's needed to grow —
Then you too — will know
                Love of life.

Jeri Jo Wade

CURBSTONE LOVE

After the hard cold work day's done
When the moon is high and the night's begun
That's when I need to have the fun
Dancing in the arms of someone in
        Curbstone Love

We never know when we will meet
Or why we suddenly feel the heat
And take it carelessly to the street
Into the room where we perform the feat of
        Curbstone Love

And the next day when the sun is high
And I wake up and look you in the eye
I wonder how I can be so shy
When the night before I was witty and sly
        Curbstone Love

So I chance the exposure and throw out an attack
I'll want you to stay but understand if you pack
My hopes are with you for the love that I lack
Maybe I'll be lucky and change all this black for
        Curbstone Love

Joan Anglin

A BABY TO SEE

A tiny baby was born today.
A baby boy, he is beautiful they say.
Very few knew, it was going to be;
This unborn was hidden — so not to see.

It was a secret not to be seen.
You see, the mother was only sixteen.
A few close friends did stay by her side.
The father? Well, he had little pride.

The first and only; she is not.
For this is a story, one hears a lot.
Happiness, Sadness, Blame and Despair
Was held in her heart like a jumbled prayer.

Other answers could have found their way
But it was up to her to have that say;
And now, happy and proud as can be
A mother and new son for all to see.

Cecilia Marcum

ON OBSERVING CATS

Cats, curious critters are they.
Theirs is the game of imaginary prey.
It's "Hide and Seek" and "Tag, you're it."
With a ball of yarn, they seldom quit.
Gracefully bounding, bursts of great speed,
Luxurious lounging, pausing only to feed,
Purring from petting, nipping for fun,
Make a fast move, see how they run.
Mischievous frolic is on their minds.
Preening and cleaning suit their kind.
They're silly to some, sacred to a few
And nearly all have some kind of mew.
Slithering sometimes, creeping real slow,
Cats are like actors, putting on a show.
Elusive and wily, garish at best;
Kittens are lively, cats have got zest.
Sometimes they'll sleep for most of the day,
But nightfall draws them out to play.
Rolling and tumbling, stretching to yawn,
Kittens can keep you up until dawn.
The cat, a pet unlike others,
Would, having its druthers,
Curl up right in your lap,
For a most lengthy nap.

Michael E. Dante

VESSEL OF DREAMS

A Vessel of dreams
Hidden in the soul
A Vessel of dreams
To make the spirit whole.

A Vessel containing
Answers for mankind
A key hidden in the Vessel
That will release the mind.

Vessel of hope
Comfort and peace
To soothe the insolvent spirit
And set the heart at ease.

A Vessel of dreams
In the ocean of my mind
I'm sailing through the waves
Where answers I will find.

Vessel of dreams
Where wishes come true
A fool's paradise
Let it happen to you.

Ann Moutray

GROWING UP IN THE CITY

Growing up in the city
where children play
growing up in the city
there's no better place

Hear the laughter of the children
look at the smiles on their faces
there is love all around them
God has blessed them with another day

A runny nose kid has fallen
goes home with a frown
meets mama in the doorway
comes back making a happy sound

Food on the table
as daddy goes to work
mama's in the kitchen
and I'm playing in the dirt

Life seems so simple
in the city when you're young
there are friends all over
everyone's having fun

Reginald Eugene Hoyle

LADIES OF THE NIGHT

Physical Friendship
turn your back
and I will spit
into the face of those
who carry themselves that way
Alone, at night I'll always pray
never to be like them
girls of night
girls of sin
painted faces
dark traces
of lovers of the night
who lay men down
just for spite
and leave them crying in the sun
while into the darkness
they will run
until night dawns a new day.

Carol Marasa

PAST, PRESENT, FUTURE

Like a string of dreams,
The past
Lives in my mind vividly.
Those passed away,
May be met
Somewhere.

Like a series of electricity,
The present
Races ahead unawares,
Days, months, years,
Footsteps and shadows remain
Everywhere.

Like a group of floating clouds,
Floating, floating, floating,
Here and there.
The future
Remains unseen,
Fumbles along with a beam of hope,
and goes
Nowhere.

Christina Ching Tsao

TSAO, CHRISTINA CHING. Pen name: Chris Ching; Born: Shanghai, China, 11-12-19; Married 12-20-69 to T. C. Tsao; Education: London School of Accountancy, MBA (Correspondence); Occupations: Accountant and Investor; Memberships: The Insititue of Chartered Secretaries, ACIS, London, England; Awards: 'Snowball, Snowball, I Mourn for You!' World of Poetry Press, 2-14-84; Poetry: 'Life,' 1981; 'To Think and To Forget,' 1982; 'Tribute to John,' 1983; 'Snowball, Snowball, I Mourn for You!' 1984; all published by World of Poetry Press; Comments: *While in school, I always enjoyed reading the works of William Shakespeare. However, because of earning a living in the past, I never had the opportunity to learn how to write poetry. Sometimes, when my feelings disturbed me and urged me to express my thoughts, I would jot down a few lines on paper even in the dead of the night. I would read over and read over until I found them smooth and pleasant to my ears. Then, I felt very much relieved. Poetry is the song of the soul. The arms race of nuclear weapons between the super powers inspired me to write 'Present, Past, Future.' The future looks bleak: End of the world?*

I have long not believed
Love and poetry were intertwined and
Kindreds of the same spirit
Yet you are returning
And when I learned
It seemed as if I turned the corner
And now I cannot move fast enough
To satisfy my feelings about loving you
Again

Gregory E. Evans

SILENCE

The gentle hush from drops of gold
Upon a sky of blue
Another moment's silence slides
The everchanging hue
For silence reigns o'er beauty
As it tortures in despair
And silence is to wings of soul
As birds climb through the air
Behold the simple infinite
In quiet mind is bound
And listen to the voice of life
That speaks without a sound.

Kevin A. Shuey

MY BEST FRIEND

I have a friend that's true and dear;
We cherish each other's caring.
It's her love and strength and cheer
That keeps me from despairing.
She knows me well and thoroughly,
And deep into my eyes she sees.
For an excellent confidante is she,
And even still, she likes me!
This friend I know and love so much
Whose name can match no other,
Because the name of someone such
Can only be my mother!

Lynora McWhorter

THERE ISN'T TIME

There isn't time, there isn't time
To do the things I want to do,
With all the mountaintops to climb
And all the woods to wander through,
And all the seas to sail upon
And everywhere there is to go,
And all the people, everyone
Who lives upon the earth, to know.
There's only time, there's only time
To know a few and do a few —
And then sit down and make a rhyme
About the rest I want to do.

Jerrold A. Johnson

IMPRINT

Bottle of ink
    Spilling your life
        On the pages of time

Will you go down
    Fine and smooth
        To encyclopedic length

Or will you thicken
    And dry up
        After one paragraph?

Connie Frieburg

and in the morning embers
wind scours   the canyon raises
city lights   the dawning forest glows
some moon glory stallion white captures

the result of ages

a vessel chosen for the task triumphant
and history proves   my words true

Andrew Karvelis

LOVE'S GOODBYE

To hold the daylight in our hands
To touch
To see
To love,
We open up our hearts
And then,
As if too late
The darkness falls again.

Sharon Lee Fernberg

WOMAN

Born stronger, live longer,
Cry louder, work harder,
Touch deeper, love better,
Child blessed, no rest,
Self-elation,
Master creation.

Lynette Stevens

TOO LONG

She came smiling;
Hips swaying wild confusion.

We stayed too long
With LOVE'S sweet song.

Now she is gone;
Less than half of us is left.

L. Elcan Walker, M.D.

Have you ever heard a painting?
It sings to me
With its vivid colors, its brief glimpse
Of a moment of life.
It captures a feeling, a mood,
A state of being as a song does.
An isolated moment of life
To be lived
Or over and done with
Yet definitely remembered.

Jane Coker

BREEZE

The gentle nudging,
Cooly pushing,
Drifting winds
Surround
And go by.
They move a little,
Touch everything,
And drift away.

Billy Isbell

Pressure, Pressure everywhere!
Light a match I don't care.
There's a time bomb in my space.
See its reflection in my face.
Yelling, screaming, screaming, shouting.
Never certainty, always doubting.
Take a trip on the guilt express.
See me smile all the less.
I am a robot without a soul.
I am a human, out of control.

Angie Miller

GROWING OLDER

There seems, no longer, to be any humor, excitement or amazement;
Lacking, are the visions I once crusaded for . . . lived for . . . and pressed-on for;
The greed of the world, having taken them *all*, not seeing their invaluable ends, . . .
Like shoppers at the "bargain rack," having fifteen dollar expense accounts, driven
By "two hundred dollar tastes," then discovering the "bargain rack," genuinely
Held *only* "twelve dollar items," left . . . leaving behind a disarrayed, and strewn
"Bargain Rack" . . . the excitement of discovery now lost, somewhere between the "nine
and the twelve dollar pullovers" . . .

My visions, and what *now* seem to have become my "delusions," of a "New
Way," have been somehow, left on the "bargain rack of life"; Left for a younger,
Stronger, visionary, or dreamer than *I* have come to my vision as . . . "hope", no
Longer feeds my spirit daily, but comes now, moreover, as the result of end results
And experiences . . . and "inspiration," only *seems* to visit, to remind me "it" still
Is a "word," though nowadays "it" happens by *only* after the rain has fallen for
Several hours, during one of life's storms; then "it" comes under guise of a
Milestone or omen, in the sign of the sun's rays parting through storm-darkened
Skies and clouds . . . There seems no longer any humor left, nor personal touch . . . nor
Even a "*silvered* glimmer of hope" . . . maybe at death! — perhaps — ?

James Lee Bolding

THERE'S ALWAYS A BEGINNING

My life was twisted like the wild whirlwinds,
And full of wild and forever unending sins.
I wondered if anyone really cared,
For I never could stand and be a man, for I was scared,
And then that day came, at the age of thirty,
Lying there slowly dying, in a gutter, drunk and dirty.

Then a young boy walked up to me, while lying in the gutter.
As he got closer I could see he was crying, then he began to stutter,
"Why do you lie there in the gutter like a dirty hog,
And whimper and whine like a mangy old dog."
Then he knelt down and held my hand and looked up at the sky.
He then walked away, turned, and said, "Stand up and be a man and try."

But can a man really change his ways?
Believe so, for a week has seven days.
Yes, this was the ending and a beginning of a new man.
For I stood up and I cried and really wanted to be a man.

Now another thirty years have past,
But I still can feel the warmth of that young boy's prayer.
And for that boy's understanding, I still do care,
For I now live my life without a drunken stare.

Mike Giedd

REBORN

Yesterday I looked at a mountain, looked at the sea;
I looked at the eagle and looked at me . . .
But saw nothing.
Today I looked at a mountain and saw strength, saw courage in the sea;
I saw wonder in the eagle, uniqueness in me . . .
And saw life.

Yesterday I heard the wind, heard the rain;
I heard the children and heard a train . . .
But listened to nothing.
Today I heard the wind and listened to its story, listened to the music of rain;
I listened to the innocent wisdom of children, the sorrow of a train . . .
And listened to life.

Yesterday I touched a tree, touched the sand;
I touched a flower and touched the land . . .
But felt nothing.
Today I touched a tree and felt leadership, felt brotherhood in sand;
I felt sharing in the flower, love within the land . . .
And felt life.

Yesterday I looked, I heard, I touched.
Today I see, I listen, I feel . . . I live!

Dawn P. Bergstresser

THE SQUARES

To smell
the light of the fireflies,
to feel
the essence of evergreen,
to touch the sun
at the top of the sky . . .
things I vaguely recall
from a time long ago;
a time I never realized
was only a time,
and the world that came to me in circles
was doomed to fall away —
fall away in squares —
squares like building blocks
                    tumbling down

from the top of my eyes
to the dust upon the ground.
Sure enough it comes around
— again and again —
but only to fall away, to evaporate,
leaving me filled with vapors,
and wishing that I were still a child.

James D. Jordan

BLESS THE WIND

She said girl be strong
It's not like you think it to be
The wind will be in front of you
Listen to me girl
This is reality

She died and I was strong
And the wind did push me
It kicked and I trembled
Life and the wind went wrong

But fell in love with a man
And so love made me strong
Reality came and dependence won
My love was too strong and he left me
With independence and a son

Push over mighty old wind
Still young am I and strong
It's now how I thought it to be
Was nature's way, nature's wind
In making strength for reality

Maureen Reardon

FOREVER MY LOVE

A long ago love
cast adrift on a sea of time,
comes edging its way through
    the reefs of the years.
    It bears the scars
of long battles to stay afloat,
yet sails in with the confidence
    of belonging.
    Covered with barnacles
of pain and strife, it clings
to the shoreline of memory
    for comfort.
    Refusing to lose way
in the dense fog of dreams,
it has sounded warnings and
    kept its course true.
    Safely nestled in
the harbor it sailed from the
weary traveler drops anchor.
No more to be tossed on seas
    of strange tears.

Mary L. Stoffel

AGNES

She was thin.
Touching her face while
walking to the door,
suspiciously, she looked
at the white telephone
with her green eyes.

She lifted her hand, and
touching her long nose,
she thought about
Barbra Streisand.

She extended her hand
and grabbed the knob
of the door, pulling it.

Seeing a man with
ragged clothes, mud on
his face, and mud in his hands,
she pushed the door forward.

Jose H. Soto Matos

SOTO MATOS, JOSE H. Pen Name: Pepito; Born: Puerto Rico, 10-3-38; Single; Education: Studying writing right now in Mercer County Community College in New Jersey, to write novels; Occupation: Going to school only; Memberships: Book of the Month Club; Writings: I am writing a novel now hopefully to be published next year; Comments: *I write poems putting specific details about what is going on. I can write an outline and bring a specific feeling in my poems. In fiction I try to bring the drama of life and more.*

MEMOIRS

When I am as my grandmother,
I too will ponder of days forgotten.
Of the times I danced,
Sang the song of love,
And of the man I married.
I will reminisce of picnics,
Late night conversations of the future,
And of the children far from home.
These are the rewards of age that
Life bestows upon us all.

Angela Stransky

STRANGERS IN THE BAR

Strangers in the bar
rub elbows on high stools
furtive glances darting here and there
in the hope of making contact
with someone
anyone

Phony laughter superficial small talk
loud music and stale smoky air
and the pain of loneliness

Glasses clink and liquor flows
    and flows
        and flows

For one fleeting moment
lost hope and despair are forgotten
the mind is numbed
the heart susceptible
there's comfort in companionship
friends
or strangers rubbing elbows on high stools
in the bar.

Marion Wolff

WOLFF, MARION. Born: Germany, 1930; Married: 11-20-60 to Paul M. Wolff; Education: University of Manchester, England, B.A., 1952; California Polytechnic State University, M.A. Ed/Counseling and Guidance, 1977; Occupation: Community Prison Representative at California Men's Colony, San Luis Obispo, California; Memberships: National Association of Volunteers in Criminal Justice (NAVCJ), Friends Outside, National Wildlife Association; Comments: *I try to express deep personal feelings about the human condition, world events and my own experiences as they relate to my childhood (as a refugee from Nazi Germany) my role within the family, and my work within the prison system. I find self-expression through writing very therapeutic and exciting. This is my first formal submission for publication.*

MY KING

I waited for a man to bring me friendship,
I waited for a man to bring me love,
I waited for a man I had often dreamed of;
a man who could make me feel whole.

For this man I began my search traveling land and sea,
knowing this man was like me in ways most cannot see.
As the cat moved toward its victim, it was apparent from the start,
the cat within him was clever; and it was he who had stalked me.

Giving to one another, in ways only a man and woman can, the gift of love
and sharing,
touching, feeling and caring; giving each other strength, the strength of a
spiritual warrior.
This man is a gift, a gift of love, a gift of joy, a gift of life.
The gift that exceeds all other gifts; the gift, that indeed, brought us
back to life.

This gift of man I'll cherish, cherish forever and a day;
a gift so wonderful, so precious, I love him more each day.
This Man, my King, my Lover can only be heaven sent,
a gift, for me from the big house, from the hand of God himself!
With all my love,
Missy

Deborra Harris Kintana

A DAUGHTER'S DAD

Why is it I'm afraid to think of how it's going to be,
    When my daughter meets another man she'll love as much as me?

Why is it that this little fear keeps spinning in my brain?
    Am I afraid that when she leaves, my life won't be the same?

Why can't I just accept the fact my little girl has grown,
    And someday she will meet a man whom I have never known?

She'll fall in love in a different way than she's been in love with me,
    And I will have to let her go and finally set her free.

I want her to be happy in whatever life she leads.
    I want her to meet someone who will take care of her needs.

And yet I fear that day will come too quickly and too sure,
    And in my heart will be a place that's dark forevermore.

There's nothing anyone can say that can dispel this fear.
    Although she's young I feel as though I've always had her near.

It may be hard to understand the reason that I'm sad,
    Unless of course you are a man who is a daughter's Dad.

    G. Thomas Perry

OLD AGE

I married a man much older than I,
Knowing that someday, ahead of me, he might die.
We lived in good health for thirty-five years,
Until past eighty was he,
And I knew the time was close at hand when he would be leaving me.
I loved him still as I always had;
The thought of his passing made me incredibly sad.
But the man I'd loved had already gone;
He'd drifted off like a faint faraway song.
So I tucked away memories of what he had been,
And sent what was left to a home fairly near,
Where I could visit and bring him constant good cheer.
And he would be happy in the fog of old age,
And not miss me too much,
As he now thought only of pills and eye drops and such.
While I wept like a baby for I knew the real truth.
God takes some too soon and others too late,
And my husband was one to suffer that fate.

    Mary Orr Denham

The wood burns away
Ashes spill down
Black smoke billowing up the chimney
The fire a blaze
Yellow and blue flames
Red coals beneath
Sparks float upward
Light soot covers the brick face
Heat circulates about the room

With a glass of red wine and cheese
A silk blanket with a feather pillow
And a thick love novel
The comfort, the fireplace
    Pamela J. Baron

ONE STAR

One star can fill the night with hope
With wishes for tomorrow.
For one small light helps lead the way
To pass away the sorrow.
We must have a beginning —
Some way to show us how —
To love and share our lives in joy
With others, for us now.
For many eyes will see this light,
And know they're not alone,
In wishing for a better world
O'er which the star has shone.
And soon the sky is filled with stars,
Who've come to join the one,
That gave us a beginning
In hoping for the sun.
    Marlene Paoletti

TROUBLED SLUMBER

Let the dreams take me away
And float me to another time
Another space
And if my nightmares follow
Let me learn to live with them
For remaining awake the rest of my life
Just to avoid the fears
Of my nightmares entering my dreams
Is impossible
And futile
My nightmares haunt my waking thoughts
And flash non-stop before my eyes
Open and wide-awake
So, I may as well sleep
Because if my nightmares enter my dreams
At least I will sleep.
    Marian Paula Freidin

AS I RECALL

It was a lovely sunny afternoon
On my way home from school
That I met an aged white-haired man
Who at first seemed quite a fool
His feet were bare as he hobbled up
And soon he started to talk
Good morning he said coming up to me
As we began to walk
He told me of wars that he had known
And of ships that he had sailed
Places and people of olden days
Parades and presidents hailed
It was time too short and too soon gone
As the tales went on till home
I'll never forget that white-haired man
This boy recalls in his poem
    Robyn M. Rogers

TOMBSTONES TO THE SKY

If each man's sapience of mind, heart, soul
Vastly metamorphosed;
Every thought, feeling, dream, aspiration
Magnified toward infinite perfection;
Memory imprinted, engraved, infused in DNA —
All upon paper written and pages stacked —
Were made each man's tombstone;
Then, the spiral helix, monolithic monument
Would tower high above the concrete metropolis;
Far beyond the floating, mystic precepts
Of earthly imagination
To embrace in ecstasy
The very eye of God!

But most men die, their tombstones
Cold, gray granite graveyards of rock,
Not one foot high.

Tal Lynch

PEBBLES

As the waves crashed against the shore
Hundreds of tiny pebbles washed in,
then away again
Moving in perfect harmony
with the ice-blue water
They must be special friends, I thought
To move so swiftly together
Occasionally one pebble cast aside,
as if in anger
Others still united and peaceful
I am aware of the feelings of being
united with that wave
So calm, moving with such grace
Yet I too have been occasionally cast aside,
left alone
To fend for one pebble
Myself.

Susan E. Sheppard

A FEELING FOR WORDS

A soft compassionate feeling reveled me
For innovative strings of words
To the complex division of semantics
As my heart trampled with ambivalent feeling
Colorful strings of words appeared in many shades
As emotion raced through my veins
My nerves began to tremble
And my blood began to boil
As if those same string of words felt compassion for my body
And I felt a feeling for words.

Mark Shuster

TO MY DEPARTED PARTNER

You once asked to write a poem "at" you;
Has the statute of limitations expired?
That *nudum pactum* was binding on me,
So that my hopes and its terms have required
That, though this is clearly *ex post facto*
and probably bunk or junk,
I submit it to you notwithstanding,
Nunc pro tunc.

You say there has been such irreparable harm
To the love we once had we can't fix it.
I can only plead the contrary to
Such a groundless bald-faced *ipse dixit.*
the issue this suit presents on appeal
Concerns my heart and whatever you broke it for.
Please find reversible error below
Release this *res* that *ipsa loquitur.*

James Thurman Kahn

It is a white day in winter.
There is no snow.
It's that hazy look that makes the sky and water
turn into one blending piece of dull silver
having been neglected for other duties.
A monochromatic world that stirs no feeling.
The fowl fly like dark silhouettes
against the dull sheen of the water,
bumping their wings on the icy, mirrored face of the lake.
Reflections on the water are fuzzy;
as if they've been drugged,
and they stagger onto the water's surface
setting off a frenzied vibration.
The consistency of clouds upon clouds
leads the mind to the tiny crack
where the sun may show itself — weak as it is.
The sun does not fit on this wintery canvas and it knows
and; therefore, chooses to paint itself
into sunny settings far away from the reach
of this white and gray winter day.

Sharon Gossett Hudson

SOMEWHERE

Somewhere, sometime, somehow we'll meet again,
Somewhere the lark will chant its lay as then,
A gypsy's rhapsody will haunt the trees
In fantasy's soft call with every breeze.

Somewhere, someday on wings of lost refrain,
Love's sweet incense will flame to life again,
Somewhere again life's springtime will unfold,
Carpeting the earth with green and gold.

Somewhere a trail of roses kissed with dew
Will bless again the love that once we knew,
Somewhere again timeless time will reign,
And bless our love beyond predestined pain.

Somewhere the moon will spill its silvery glow
On each enchanted pathway that we go
Impassioned violins will fill the air,
And trembling on each star will hang a prayer.

Somewhere again when day and darkness meet,
Two hearts will sing with one ecstatic beat,
Somewhere when tearful clouds have drifted by —
We will re-live a love that cannot die.

Nellie De Loach Gowens

SOIXANTE-DIX

I am sixty and ten today as Frenchmen say.
Three score and ten among my fellow men
The mileposts passed so fast and blurred away.
I reflect and introspect, at sixty and ten:

More than a chance shadow passing by,
More than computer input am I.
A speck on a dot in the shoreless sea
But somehow I can always spot me.

Too busy with life to ask who, why, where,
On this short trip with a one-way fare.
I feel the world's heartbeat; I'm in sync.
Then it's a toast to life . . . our glasses clink.

Waving, I hold my credit card high
As I try to catch Father Time's eye
Wondering — with no little apprehension —
Will the old guy grant an extension?

I am sixty and ten today as Frenchmen say.
Three score and ten among my fellow men.
Was it worth it so far: joy and laughter, grief and strife?
Yes! I'll wager my all — I'll even bet you my life!

Samuel Pavlovic

SPRING

Ah, Spring!
You are most beautiful before you have quite begun . . .
When your swollen buds smile with hidden promise
and the gentle breezes and sun-kissed skies tease me out of hibernation.
When birds sing and dance,
     yes, party on my rooftop,
And lovers touch again . . . as if for the first time.
Oh my sweet Spring,
     You are as if with child . . .
       mysterious and lovely,
       offering hope and new paths to the winter-weary!

    Jean M. Wenzel

MY BEST FRIEND AND LOVER

    I once had a best friend — who listened patiently to all my troubles
    She even listened when I told her lots of wonderful and secret things about my new lover
    My best friend was always willing to give me plenty advice on how to make my lovers and my love affair twice as nice
    Because I spoke so much of him she couldn't wait to meet him — and soon after they met, my lover became her best friend too
    I no longer have that friendship — nor do I desire that lover
    What I have now is a better best friend — who also happens to be my new lover

    Lisa Smith

Do you know what a day is like without you?
I'm not jealous that you're with her,
I'm lonely, you're not with me.
And what's worse is you are with me.
Maybe we should be in two separate countries;
Separated by more than the distance you created when you married her.
You've never broken a promise to me.
No, you only broke my heart and shattered my dreams.
Some people have never loved;
Some have loved and lost;
I love and forever keep loving you.
Please come back, someday, to me.

    Gail E. Cantor

if i were the sun

i wish that i could be the sun.
to warm you,
    to light your way throughout the day . . .
to make your eyes squint in appreciation when you see me . . .
to be there when you awaken . . .
to make your body bask ever so beautifully in a rich, vibrant tan . . .
i really wish that i were the sun,
    so that i could forever keep my promise to be with you
       every single day for the rest of your life . . .

    Baron John Gushiken

I wish for no more in my life than to hold you gently in my arms,
    to gaze into your precious eyes, and adore you.

My heart beats stronger, my hands tremble and my body quivers,
    my voice cannot utter a word, and my soul fills with great joy
    as your heavenly beauty captivates me like no other ever shall.

If only you would grant me my cherished dream, and swear your love
    for me as I have mine for you, so long ago,
    would I know that God truly cares for me.

    Bill Schaffner

FOR LOVE OF A STRANGER

Little Miss Sally, such a pretty little girl,
Jump into my car, and I'll show you the world.
Weeks went by, no one had seen Sally,
That sweet child lay dead in an alley.
Looking at her body, all mangled and distorted,
How could anyone do this to my only daughter.
I walk away with pain, fear, and anger.
All because my child loved a stranger.

Valerie A. Collins

DEW

the tiny drops of rain
are caught by silver threads
of patient spider webs

Carmen Elston

She is gone
there's an empty room
deep within my heart
no she did not die
she was married yesterday.

Elizabeth J. Potter

SUNSET ON THE GULF

Flood-tide surf, splashing
crimson red on white sand beach,
carried shrimp boats home.

Edna D. Drake

PNEUMA

Oh sweet breezy air,
how I cherish thy life gift
which nourishes me.

Ronald Weiss

LITTLE MUSIC BOX

Black wood, oblong,
Gold flowers
Design on top,
Your little song
I could play for hours
And not stop.
Its pathos
A passing mention
In musical
Holographic dimension
Moves through my gloom
Like perfume.
Pure xylophone tone
Sings
On butterfly wings.
Just the ticking, clicking of clocks
And me and
Little music box.

Alberta Anna Hannaman

HANNAMAN, ALBERTA ANNA.

GLORIOUS CHERISHED CHILDREN

O Holiest, Heavenly Father of all glorious cherished children
let us highly adore their sublime sacredness. Remember their
virtues of awesome innocence, their charity-filled hugs which
shine with glorious splendor, and their abundant joy.

The little one's play is endowed with the great childhood
treasures of knowledge, creativity, and the atoned for little ones
are partakers of salvation.

Let thy children spiritually sprout into a happy, holy,
Heavenly Daddy as glorious as thee.

The power of thy Spirit has increased thy charity between me
and my beloved little ones.

The Mighty Father maketh the barren woman to be a joyful
mother, and grants enthusiasm, perfect patience, and the promise
to live eternally with the beloved ones in our Spiritual Father's
Mansions above.

Heed the mighty cry of righteously raising thy beloved,
cherished children in light and truth.

The Inspired Child has said: O Most Noble Heavenly Daddy let
me be cuddled in thy Divine Spirit and live worthy to return to
thy Sacred Bosom in thy Holy Kingdom.

Paul Milford Hill

HILL, PAUL MILFORD. Born: Fontana, California, 10-3-64; Education: High School Graduate; Occupation: Child Care; Memberships: Church of Jesus Christ of Latter-Day Saints; Poetry: 'Glorious Cherished Children,' American Poetry Association, 1985; Other Writings: "O Holiest Heavenly Father of All Glorious Cherished Children," hymn, 1985; "The Eerie Black Dog," short short semi-comical horror, 1983; *Ending the Nuclear Threat,* letter to editor, 1984; Comments: *Some of my works were published in a school district's anthology and received praise from teachers and students. What sets my writing apart is its rich appropriate description of every action. I desire to write that which has never been written which has a large audience. I am enthusiastic about writing children's stories, poetry, religious fillers, and letters to editors.*

CASTELLATED ROCK

T

ADDENDUM